THE
12-YEAR
REICH

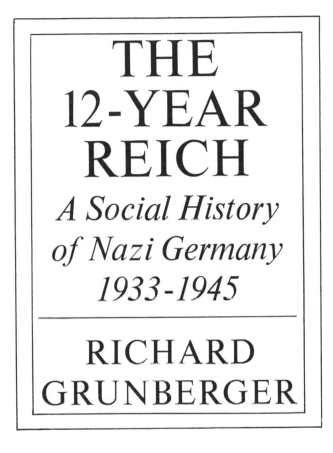

THE
12-YEAR
REICH

*A Social History
of Nazi Germany
1933-1945*

RICHARD
GRUNBERGER

HOLT, RINEHART AND WINSTON
New York   Chicago   San Francisco

To the memory of
Bernard Weber (1923–1955)

————————————

Published simultaneously in Canada by
Holt, Rinehart and Winston of Canada, Limited.

Published previously in England under the
title of *A Social History of the Third Reich*.

Library of Congress Catalog Card
Number: 69-16189

First Edition

SBN: 03-076435-1

Printed in the United States of America

CONTENTS

Photographs Follow Pages 184 and 344.

THE
12-YEAR
REICH

WEIMAR

A quarter of a century after the end of the Second World War the 'German question' which caused that war still dominates world affairs – though in a vastly different form.

Today the German question is a function of East–West relations and its solution depends more on the world than on the Germans themselves – but when it first arose it had little to do with the state of the world and a great deal with that of German society.

The root causes of the German question were – very broadly speaking – retarded unification (and therefore nationhood), capitalism maturing in a late-feudal setting, and a national preference for *konfliktlose* synthesis (synthesis without conflict).

Germany's belated emergence as a great power, which led her to a preoccupation with foreign policy and a neglect of home policy and reforms, marked and distorted all her subsequent development. This distortion was compounded by another. In 1871 industry had brought German military triumph, statehood and great-power status, but the agents of that victory – the middle classes – failed to gain their own political victory, or even a commensurate share of power. (An outward symbol of their failure was the situation of the universities where middle-class students formed associations aping the mores – e.g. duelling – of the military-agrarian élite when that élite was in economic decline.)

This cumulative imbalance of power had dire consequences: the middle class grew used to trading their political rights for economic advantages; a constitution was evolved that married authoritarian substance to the shadow of universal manhood suffrage. Political opposition to the government became confused with opposition to the country – treason. Bismarck described the Social Democrats as 'vagabonds without a Fatherland'.

Scarifying propagandist devices for preventing the alternation of government and opposition, fostered by Bismarck's constitutional gerrymandering, helped to develop the German penchant for *Konfliktlosigkeit* – for sweeping conflict-inducing issues under the carpet – and 1918 produced a great trauma precisely because defeat brought in its train a reversal of all these tendencies.

Foreign policy ceased to be Germany's main concern when she became an object rather than a subject in world affairs. The collapse of the Empire put an end to pseudo-constitutionalism and to the exclusion of commoners from political power. The chimera of *Konfliktlosigkeit* faded further as the Weimar Republic articulated – and tried to institutionalize – the interplay of contending social and political forces.

One of the most poignant aspects of 1918–19 was that it was the first, and therefore the seminal, instance in Germany of alternating political parties in office – the essence of the democratic process. The Social Democrats, Left Liberals and Catholic Centre, which under the Empire had been permanently relegated to the opposition benches, now became the government – but their assumption of office owed less, in the last analysis, to the ballot-box (and to the barricades put up in November 1918) than to Allied arms.

In 1918–19 most Germans became democrats. Even the 'national classes' took up democracy – as a means of obtaining easier peace terms from the West and of fending off Bolshevism in the East. Versailles and the failure of revolution to take root outside Russia soon ended their aberration; democracy once again became an alien device, a creed whose victory had resulted from German defeat, and bitterness at losing the war threw into lurid relief the gain of power by an inexperienced minority.

Weimar's office-holders were indeed a new, and – thanks to the Imperial constitution – a somewhat *parvenu* élite. The Social Democrat, Ebert, who replaced the Kaiser as head of state was a master-saddler. Similarly suspect (in Conservative eyes) were figures whom the November 1918 upheaval had catapulted into the centre of the political stage: journalists such as Theodor Wolff, editor of the *Berliner Tageblatt* and co-founder of the *Demokratische Partei*, as well as Leftist writers such as Ernst Toller, a participant in the short-lived Bavarian Soviet Republic of 1919. Politically Toller was at the opposite end of the left-wing spectrum to Ebert, who – 'hating social revolution like sin' – approved of the suppression of the Munich Soviet, though the Right persisted in lumping together Social Democrats and revolutionary socialists as Marxist scum.

Dour pedlars of the conspiracy-theory of history alleged that Germany had not been beaten in battle but 'stabbed in the back' by traitorous politicians (such as Ebert); the fact that Wolff, Toller, the outstanding woman Socialist Rosa Luxemburg and the architect of the Weimar Constitution

Preuss were Jewish served as a pretext for dubbing the whole Weimar state a 'Jew-Republic'.

A climate envenomed by character assassination bred physical assassins. Rosa Luxemburg was murdered by officers 'collaborating' with the Ebert government, and *Fehme* gunmen killed the Catholic Centre leader Erzberger who had signed the Versailles Treaty, and the 'Judeo-Democrat' Foreign Minister Rathenau who strove to implement it. The courts treated right-wing terrorism with a leniency best exemplified by Hitler's one-year jail term after the bloodily abortive Munich putsch of November 1923. The whole tenor of political court decisions highlighted a crucial flaw of the new state: though its law-making was democratic the application of the law had remained in the hands of anti-democrats.

The death of the Republic which this division foreshadowed – and ultimately precipitated – occurred in two stages. While the majority of the people actively deserted democracy only during the Depression, the majority of the élite (the civil service, the judiciary, the officer corps, the academics and even the clergy) had rejected it virtually at birth.

It was precisely in order to propitiate these forces that the Republic's leadership retained the name *Deutsches Reich* (German Empire), with its Imperial and authoritarian undertones, and that Ebert – though himself a target of 'stab-in-the-back' accusations – contributed to the nation's self-delusion by describing the returning German army as 'undefeated on the field of battle'.

The Republican idea had been so drained of vitality by 1925 that a man like ex-Field Marshal Hindenburg was elected President of the Reich. Both terms are actually misnomers: Hindenburg was seen less as a man than as a national monument; the word election, which implies electioneering (i.e. exertions to win the voters' approval), cannot convey how the ex-GOC, once the immediate post-war swing to the Left had abated, simply re-emerged as the father-figure remembered from the war.

Looking upon Germany as a fief entrusted to him during the Emperor's absence he had actually sought the ex-Kaiser's leave before accepting the Presidency from the people. The new President's appeal to Conservatives was axiomatic – whereas Republicans felt sharply divided about him. While the radical academic Theodor Lessing, with uncanny prescience, called Hindenburg 'a Zero paving the way for Nero', moderates looked to the rather incongruous new head of state to wean the 'national classes' from their hostility to the Republic. Developments during the first half of Hindenburg's presidential term seemed to confirm these hopes, although in

3

narrowly political terms the 1928 elections merely brought the Republican bloc a derisory gain of four seats in the Reichstag. None the less, 1925–9, the middle years of the Weimar Republic, were also its best. After the end of the French occupation of the Ruhr and the period of runaway inflation, Germany experienced internal stability and an economic revival for the first time in over a decade. With the currency restored and the Dawes plan facilitating foreign investment, industry embarked on schemes for rationalization and expansion that result in the 1927 production index exceeding the highest pre-war total.[1] By 1929, a smaller Germany was producing 10 per cent more coal, 100 per cent more lignite, and 30 per cent more steel, than in the pre-war period, and in 1930 Germany ranked second after the United States among the world's exporting countries and indeed first as an exporter of finished products.[2]

Yet for most of this time German industry was in fact operating at only 50 to 80 per cent of her full productive capacity.[3] The effect of rationalization had been double-edged: during 1929, when the absolute number of gainfully employed reached the all-time high of $20\frac{1}{2}$ million,[4] industry threw $1\frac{1}{2}$ million men on the scrap-heap because it was unable to utilize its own full potential owing to insufficient home demand or export scope.[5]

Germany's export difficulties stemmed from foreign discrimination against her, but the low home demand was an internal matter and the remedy lay well within her own power. The crux of this problem was the divergence between wage and price levels: prices of industrial goods were kept high through the operation of cartel agreements, while aggregate purchasing power was depressed by the wage policy of industry, and by unnecessarily dear food. The latter was a direct result of the government's solicitude for the grain-producing aristocrats within German agriculture.

The excessive concentration of ownership in industry – in 1925 less than 2 per cent of all enterprises employed 55 per cent of all wage earners[6] – was not unrelated to the relative scarcity of capital. The war and its aftermath had destroyed large capital reserves and bequeathed a heavy tax burden to the post-war economy. This tended to push up the interest rate on loans – with the result that large economic units obtained access to capital more easily than small ones.

The extensive rationalization of industry in the mid-twenties, financed by high-interest loans, was based on the assumption of infinitely expanding markets – an assumption that was called in question at the outset by foreign limitations on German exports and the low level of home demand and was finally negated by the Great Depression. Even so, during the intervening world-wide upsurge of economic activity, German industry could claim some notable achievements. The number of patents taken out annually doubled compared with before the war; in the sphere of transport and communication Germany progressed faster than the powers that had defeated her; the production of electricity, for instance, rose by over 50 per cent[7] between 1925 and 1930.

The annual number of bankruptcies, which, in 1925-6, still exceeded the pre-war number, dropped to half the 1913 level within a year or two.[8] The relatively prosperous years at the end of the twenties also accelerated the change in occupational distribution that had been taking place ever since full-scale industrialization in the eighteen-seventies. This restructuring of the total work-force involved a steady reduction of the agricultural sector of the population (which declined from 42 per cent in 1882, to 29 per cent in 1933). Figures concerning the redistribution of ownership and economic status are equally significant: the number of independents fell from 38 to 20 per cent, while that of employed dependents increased from 4 to 11 per cent. The proportion of workers went up only very slightly (50 to 52 per cent); that of white-collar workers and civil servants increased markedly, from 8 to 18 per cent.[9]

(In other words total number of workers remained constant, but rural emigrants were joining the working class at the same rate at which white-collar workers were leaving it.)[10]

The white-collar group, over two-thirds of whom were skilled,[11] increased especially fast during the period of rationalization, and the proportion of women within it grew at an even faster rate. The qualifications required for desk jobs also changed more rapidly than those for industrial work. In addition, white-collar workers were at an advantage because they enjoyed greater job security, had a separate status in wage contracts, and had their own insurance funds. Another difference between the two groups was in their conception of the social structure. To industrial workers, society appeared to be a straightforward dichotomy, divided into 'bosses' at the top and themselves at the bottom, whereas the *Angestellten*, or desk-workers, saw it as a graded hierarchy, with employers above them, themselves in the middle, and the proletariat below them.

This feeling of occupying a precariously elevated middle position was, of course, not peculiar to white-collar workers, but pervaded all intermediate social groups during the Weimar period with an intensity bordering on neurosis. It strongly affected the great mass of retail traders, whose number had gone up by a quarter since before the war,[12] though there was no sound economic justification for this increase. Many shopkeepers, independent artisans, small farmers and others aspired to a middle-class identity which was contradicted by their economic circumstances. During the mid-twenties boom, when, if judged purely on job and social criteria, twenty-five million Germans belonged to the proletariat, as many as forty-five million Germans (almost three-quarters of the entire population) were actually living on proletarian incomes.[13]

With the placing of workers' unemployment insurance on the statute book in 1927, organized labour achieved the implementation of its basic programme. Insurance against accidents, sickness and old age had been in force since the days of Bismarck, and to these pioneering social measures the Weimar Republic had added wage contracts underwritten by the state, paid holidays, and the right of association for collective bargaining. (Twelve to fourteen million employees were working under collective agreements.)[14]

Capital took a jaundiced view of these gains by labour. Entrepreneurial complaints about the heavy burden of social contributions placed on industry abounded. These were – in a limited sense – justified, since Weimar's social security schemes afforded less protection to small employers than to their employees. However, even though labour might appear as the Republic's particular beneficiary, its sphere of effective action was somewhat circumscribed. Thus, the 'closed shop' idea was entirely absent from the industrial thinking of the period; explicitly precluded by the Weimar constitution, it hardly crossed the minds of labour leaders. Trade-union moderation can be statistically demonstrated: during the years 1927–30, a period of relative prosperity and increasing employment, the number of working days lost through industrial disputes annually was – at 3·7 million – only half the comparable pre-war total.[15] The subsidence of industrial warfare resulted partly from Weimar's labour legislation, which drew the government into all wage agreements as a participant and stipulated an elaborate conciliation procedure before strikes could legally be called. Not one offensive strike, i.e. a strike to advance workers' claims as against warding off employers' encroachments, occurred from 1930 onwards, yet already two years earlier the Ruhr steel industrialists had imposed a lockout on 250,000 workers.[16] Although unable to defeat the unions at the time, the employers' associations succeeded in blunting the government's power to make collective agreements mandatory on all firms within an industry. Industry was opposed to state participation in the collective-bargaining process, because it considered that the government was unduly biased in favour of the workers. This situation changed rather drastically in 1931–2, when the Brüning Cabinet showed itself prepared to enforce wage cuts as part of its general deflationary programme.

By this time, Weimar had entered its third and final stage, and although the government was still ostensibly republican, it had ceased to be democratic in the sense of enjoying majority support in the Reichstag. In fact, the demise of the Weimar Republic was presided over by governments that were authoritarian in terms of both constitutional procedure and political complexion. This drastic shift of the political power constellations was a concomitant of economic disaster. The Wall Street crash of October 1929 had spread to the rest of the world within a very short time, and hit Germany harder than most other countries. Unemployment figures started climbing to astronomic heights* from their already disturbing pre-Depression level; even so they followed a gentler gradient than Hitler's electoral appeal: in the traumatic election of September 1930 Nazi representation in the Reichstag shot up overnight from twelve deputies to 107!† Before this cumulative landslide had hamstrung the government, industrial and agrarian interests had displayed completely divergent attitudes to the state. Industry had managed to prise the economy from the tripartite Weimar pattern so that it might confront labour head-on without the government holding the ring or propping up the weaker contestant. Agriculture, on the other hand, continued to hold an attitude that dated back to Bismarck's abandonment of free trade in 1879, and leaned heavily on the government for support and subsidies. Before the slump these differing attitudes of industry and agriculture towards the state had not taken on an overt political form – though, as an approximation, one could say that the (absurdly named) German People's Party represented industrial interests, while Hugenberg's National Party constituted the agrarian lobby of the Reichstag.

Repeating parrot-like arguments of authoritarian conservatism which increasingly lacked relevance to events, the National Party had remained obdurately opposed to the Republic. The People's Party displayed greater agility: following the behaviour pattern of capitalist interest groups in the

* Between September 1929 and September 1932 the number of registered jobless rose from 1·3 million to 5·1 million. cf. Richard Grunberger, *Germany 1918–1945*, London, 1964, p. 81.

† Between the 1928 and July 1932 elections the Nazi vote increased from 800,000 to 13,750,000, i.e. from 2·16 per cent to 37·3 per cent of the national poll. cf. Karl D. Bracher, *Die Auflösung der Weimarer Republik*, Stuttgart, 1954, pp. 86–106.

period of rising Fascism, it initially supported the Republic, but deserted it by 1931 to advocate the transfer of power from Parliament to a quasi-dictatorial president.[17] Up to the slump the industrialists themselves had distributed money freely among all respectable anti-Marxist forces, but from 1931 onwards they directed their largesse increasingly towards the mushrooming Nazi movement.[18]

Industry, which thus showed itself intent on burying the Republic, had in fact not been hit as hard by the Depression as other branches of the economy, such as agriculture. The fortunes of German agriculture after 1918 had been mixed. It had benefited from an indiscriminate post-war demand for foodstuffs, and later from the inflation which wiped out all agrarian debts – but unusually bad harvests had followed and by the end of 1925 farmers were selling their crops at any price to raise cash. Prices fell below world-market levels and long-term credit became unobtainable.

The economic revival that followed the restoration of the currency interposed a price-lag between manufactured and agricultural goods, and in the late twenties the gap widened between high industrial prices dictated by cartels and dropping agricultural prices, (a phenomenon known as the 'price-scissors'). An estimated 60 per cent of German farmers were already living on proletarian incomes[19] when the Depression exacerbated an already critical situation; unlike the cartel-protected industrialists, the farmers responded to the decline in public purchasing power by increasing their output, which lowered prices even further and started a continuous downward spiral. As early as 1926 the forced sale of farmers' holdings had exceeded the pre-war average,[20] and between 1927 and 1932 nearly 25,000 farms came under the hammer.[21]

Within the country's agriculture as a whole, the Junker-owned lands east of the Elbe had long loomed disproportionately large, and this state of affairs continued during the Republic. The economic viability of the estates east of the Elbe had been a problem even before the war, and the Polish Corridor created by the Treaty of Versailles had cut a swathe through the Junkers' compact grainlands and severed East Prussia from the Reich. This aggravated an already difficult situation (which was further compounded by the post-war slump in the world price of rye).

The Republic adopted a policy of protecting agriculture – primarily the estates east of the Elbe, which were threatened economically as well as strategically – out of the tax contributions from the remaining three-quarters of the German population. The high Imperial tariffs designed to safeguard German grain producers against cheap foreign competition were continued, and the German consumer was obliged to pay both higher food prices and heavier taxes for the benefit of '13,000 big landowners'.[22]

The tariff and subsidy system militated against the rationalization of the dairy and vegetable industries in the other agricultural regions; by stimulating fodder production the government could have given considerable assistance to the dairy farmers, but 'instead it retained grain tariffs and thus protected the most costly and the most capitalistic sector of agricultural production'.[23]

Despite state support of rural credit institutions, estate-owners obtained loans on more favourable terms than middle-sized or small farmers. Overall, interest rates in the twenties were double those before the war,[24] and in the process of increasing output, German agriculture trebled its pre-war labour costs. Notwithstanding a fair amount of government-subsidized land improvement, agriculture as a whole did not carry out a rationalization programme that would have both increased output and reduced expenditure, largely because the cost of machinery and chemicals was fixed by industry.[25]

At the height of the Depression, food prices in Germany were about twice as high as those obtaining abroad[26] – while, paradoxically, German farmers were pricing themselves out of the market through productivity increases that yielded ever-diminishing returns. By this time, the specific East Elbian crisis had grown so acute that the Brüning administration initiated the 'Eastern Aid' (*Osthilfe*) programme,* a vast publicly financed blood transfusion to the moribund Junker economy.

In his attempts at tackling the broader aspects of the Depression, Brüning embarked on a course of severe deflation. Civil service salaries, which had been appreciably increased as recently as 1927, were reduced by up to 15 per cent during the winter of 1930–1.[27] In 1931, too, the government decreed a 10 per cent reduction in rents, as well as prices,[28] and wages, which had continued to rise beyond the onset of the slump in 1929, were depressed to their 1927 level by emergency decree.[29]

The authorities also tried – at this late date – to tackle the problem of cartelization, but to no avail.† The opportunity for effective action in this sphere, i.e. for forcing German prices down to world-market level, had

* The Eastern Aid Act of 31 March 1931, ostensibly brought in by Brüning to relieve the suffering of the population of the eastern provinces, actually became a device to preserve the socio-economic status of the Junkers. Franz Neumann, *Behemoth*, New York, 1942, p. 392.

† The presidential emergency decree empowering the Cabinet to nullify the existing cartel agreements led only to the dissolution of the lignite cartel. Franz Neumann, *op. cit.*, p. 261.

existed up to the September 1930 elections, when the government lost majority support in the Reichstag. A minority administration, depending on the constitutional reserve powers of the President, was no match for heavy industry – even though the latter, too, was affected by the crisis. (The slump had caused overall industrial productivity to drop by 42 per cent; in certain branches, such as the manufacture of producer goods, output had been halved.)[30] By 1932 this had resulted in 6 million unemployed, of whom less than 2 million received unemployment insurance; another 1½ million were catered for by the emergency unemployment administration, and nearly 1¾ million received poor relief from their municipalities. In addition, there were 850,000 people[31] who received no kind of public support whatever.*

The seismic waves of the Depression spread outward all the faster because inflation had wiped out the savings which might have cushioned the urban middle classes against the shock. (A phenomenon specifically affecting the lower middle class was the invasion of the retail trade by jobless white-collar workers desperately bringing their savings and book-keeping expertise into an already overcrowded profession.) But ranging far beyond economic effects, the slump transmitted its destructive impact into every area of public life, for the Germans, more than people in other Western countries, had come to judge institutions by their effectiveness, rather than by their intrinsic merits.

By any purely pragmatic yardstick, the slump-ridden Republic and the structure of democratic beliefs and practices on which it rested had forfeited the right to exist. On men for whom industry and technology had become substitute deities in a secularized, amoral universe, the paralysis of the industrial machine had an effect comparable to Nietzsche's 'God is dead' bombshell of fifty years earlier. The moral and political disorientation that had affected Germany since the war made the Depression assume a significance far beyond the purely economic one it had elsewhere;† there was a mood of living in an '*Endsituation*' (final situation), which presaged either chaos or an 'ineluctable transformation'.

* The financing of the unemployment fund set up in 1927 had been based on the figure of 1·2 million people out of work. C. W. Guillebaud, *The Social Policy of Nazi Germany*, London, 1941, p. 13.

† 'Germany was the only industrial country that underwent a political transformation during the Depression – yet the United States were actually hit harder by the crisis. The question as to why the economic crisis ended in dictatorship in Germany cannot be answered within the context of economic causality.' Karl Erich Born, *Moderne Deutsche Wirtschaftsgeschichte*, Cologne, 1966, p. 22.

At a comparable turning-point fourteen years earlier, the Left had been the driving-force of Utopia, but now the Right imparted the momentum. In their view, the crisis was the climax to a chain of events linking together the patriotic upsurge of 1914, the transfiguring experience of the trenches, the soul-searchings of the pre-war *Jugendbewegung* (Youth Movement) and the earlier quest for the Holy Grail of German-ness pursued by Wagner, Langbehn and Lagarde. To the disciples of those *völkische* (ethnic) prophets, to Nazis and Hugenberg nationalists, the slump was the head on the Weimar abscess, suppurating with corruption and betrayal – and it had to be lanced with brutal surgery before it burst into a Red revolution.

Germany has been aptly described as a 'belated nation',* and the Republic's liberalizing innovations – occurring, as they did, over half a century after their due time – lent a hothouse aspect to the Weimar days. Though this was a far from happy augury for the stability of governmental institutions, it prompted remarkable developments elsewhere.†

The year 1918 saw the end of authoritarianism in spheres other than the purely political – in family life, education, and sexual mores. The removal of constraints and taboos released creative impulses – especially in the arts – which focused outside attention on Germany to an extent unknown since the heyday of the aristocratic patronage that had sustained a Goethe or a Beethoven. But, unlike that earlier flowering of culture, which had been based on a small leisured class, phenomena such as Expressionism, the Bauhaus or twelve-tone music flourished in the context of a precarious experiment in democracy.

The decade and a half between the democratic apotheosis of the Reichstag and its burning down witnessed a creative explosion – and for the first time in history Berlin vied with Paris as a Mecca for devotees of new styles in art, as well as living.

Yet at the same time the very vogue for the experimental and modern aroused reactions that turned the arts into an area of intermittent warfare. As early as 1920 Arthur Schnitzler's play *Der Reigen* (familiar to filmgoers as *La Ronde*) was the object of organized disruption and legal proceedings on grounds of alleged immorality.‡

Franz Werfel's novel *Not the Murderer but the Murdered is Guilty* attracted

* cf. Henrich Plessner's *Die Verspätete Nation*, Kohlhammer Verlag, 1959.

† For some years during the nineteen-twenties Germany published more new books than England, France and the United States combined. Robert A. Brady, *The Spirit and Structure of German Fascism*, New York, 1937, p. 13.

‡ For a detailed treatment of this *cause célèbre*, see the relevant chapter in Ludwig Marcuse's *Obszön*, Munich, 1962.

such epithets as 'a prescription for moral anarchy'. Einstein's Theory of Relativity became – at the hands of the same conservative critics – a nihilist denial of absolute values. Walter Hasenclever faced court proceedings for 'undermining Christian values' in his play *Marriages are Made in Heaven*[32] and the artist Georg Grosz was convicted of blasphemy for portraying Jesus wearing a gas mask in one of his pacifist *Ecce Homo* sketches.[33]

But it was Erwin Piscator's presentation of *The Good Soldier Schweik* by the Czech Jaroslav Hasek that constituted the most outrageous affront to propriety and patriotism.*

The situation in the theatre as a whole was highly ambivalent: while the discerning minority of theatregoers felt the imminent arrival of a golden age under the aegis of Reinhardt, Piscator and Leopold Jessner, growing sections of the public saw the stage – dubbed 'a moral institution' by Schiller – as a privileged platform from which deracinated playwrights enjoying Jewish critical acclaim (and financial support from the state) launched an assault on the national heritage and conventional morality. There were riots at performances of Ernst Toller's *Hinkemann* (1923), Carl Zuckmayer's *Happy Vineyard* (1926), Bert Brecht's and Kurt Weill's *Mahagonny* (1931) and many other plays.† *Danton's Death* by Georg Büchner had to be taken out of the repertoire in 1924 because audiences threatened to wreck the theatre when the orchestra intoned the *Marseillaise* as part of the play's incidental music.

As time went on, even some of the *avant-garde* succumbed to the prevailing mood. Piscator was called a 'Stahlhelm pacifist' for interpolating quite extraneous military 'business' as box-office bait in the anti-war play *The Rivals* (1928) and the Berlin production of Arnold Zweig's pacifist *Case of Sergeant Grischa* in 1930 showed similar incongruous touches.

Stage and screen showed a simultaneous preoccupation with the seminal Prussian hero figure of Frederick the Great. The 'Fredericus Rex' cult even spilled over into the work of liberal authors: Bruno Frank's

* Cf. the Hugenberg Press Trust's columnist, Friedrich Hussong, who wrote: 'Women wearing *décolletage* down to their navels and diamonds on their shoes screeched their delight at the worst obscenities. When Schweik-Pallenberg disappeared into a privy to deliver his *causeries* and *weltanschauliche* disquisitions from the cesspool, they kept their costly opera-glasses trained on the lavatory door lest they miss the rapturous moment of his return in some state of indecent *déshabillement*.' Friedrich Hussong, *Kurfürstendamm*, Berlin, 1933, p. 62.

† For this and subsequent information, see Alfred Kerr's mimeographed booklet, *The Influence on Theatre and Film of German Nationalism during the Weimar Republic*, Fight for Freedom Publications, London, 1945.

The Twelve Thousand depicted him as frustrating the designs of princes prepared to sell their feudal subjects as cannon-fodder for George III's American war. (Hans Rehberg quite gratuitously made Cecil Rhodes – in a play of the same name – visit Frederick's palace at Sans-Souci for inspiration before taking the crucial decisions of his career.)

The late twenties had seen a decline from the heroic age of the German film, which was characterized by *The Cabinet of Dr Caligari* and *Metropolis*. A few artistic masterpieces such as *The Blue Angel* were exceptions among a morass of tendentious historical and military epics and barrack-square drolleries. This situation arose partly because the leader of the Nationalist Party, Hugenberg, controlled the UFA film company, and partly because of a change in public mood and taste. 'Fredericus' films played to full houses for months on end, but when the American screen version of Erich Maria Remarque's *All Quiet on the Western Front* (a best-selling novel in Germany as well as abroad) reached German cinemas, disturbances provoked by the Nazis led to a ban in the interests of public safety.

The universities were the traditional nurseries of a chauvinism which had survived defeat.* In 1919, the theologian and Rector of Berlin University, Reinhold Seeberg, began the official memorial service for students who had died in the war with the words: '*Invictis victi victorii*' (To the undefeated, the defeated who shall be victorious).[34] In 1924 another eminent academic theologian, Otto Procksch, began his inaugural address as Rector of Greifswald University with: 'All we brought back from Versailles was a dunce's cap. We are *heerlos, wehrlos, ehrlos* (deprived of our army, our defence and our honour).'[35]

Though, as a body, Weimar's academics inclined more towards authoritarianism than democracy, a fair number of them were simply locked up in their ivory towers – but in a state that was deeply unsure of its citizens' allegiance, indifference was itself a form of hostility.

Yet not even lack of civic spirit and revanchism was the most ominous response that the crisis provoked among the academics.

New philosophies sprang into being fully armed. The metaphysical inquiry into Good and Evil was replaced by historicism, so that the only knowable good became that of the present moment; a perverted existentialism attempted to transcend the crisis by leaping into a passionately felt certainty that needed no rational justification. Through the desperate

---

* In 1915, a statement by ninety-three eminent scholars had exonerated Germany from guilt in the invasion of Belgium. The academic world had endorsed the undiluted expansionist war aims of the Pan-Germans by a four to one majority.

commitment of 'the whole person', irresponsibility was legitimized as the rule of life.[36] This mode of thinking, which was in itself a denial of thought, elicited a ready response among undergraduates.

In 1927, 77 per cent of all Prussian students voted for a charter of academic self-government which excluded non-Aryans from membership of student corporations.[37] Prussia's Democrat Education Minister, Becker, had the melancholy duty of denying the students the rights of autonomy they were bent upon utilizing for anti-democratic purposes. By 1931 support for Nazism at the universities was proportionately twice as great as among the general population. An incipient pogrom atmosphere spread through the colleges, and the few academic historians who drew analogies between Versailles and the German-dictated treaties of Brest-Litovsk and Bucharest were beaten up.* To counteract mounting undergraduate vandalism, the 1932 university teachers' conference was urged to issue an unequivocal statement of condemnation. This move was thwarted by the eminent educationist Eduard Spranger – not a Nazi sympathizer. 'I considered the national movement among the students genuine in essence and undisciplined only in form. It would also have damaged the University if it had only expressed itself in a schoolmarmish manner about the national wave, which at the time still carried much that was healthy along with it, and aroused the most hopeful anticipation.'[38]

In the country at large this 'national wave' led to the collapse of moderate politics: the Democratic Party went into liquidation and the German People's Party changed from a wary toleration of the Republic to unambiguous opposition.

The national wave derived a great deal of its thrust from the anti-capitalist yearning of the petit bourgeois masses (to paraphrase Gregor Strasser). This mood owed little to Marxism and has aptly been defined as shopkeepers' socialism:† slump-ridden retail traders, artisans, small farmers and others stridently demanded both the rights of private enterprise and Government protection from its attendant risks. Their guild-socialist *Mittelstandsprogramm* (middle-class programme) demanded a trading monopoly for independents, the denial of retail outlets to industrial firms, the closure of artisan workshops attached to large plants,[39] tax relief for shopkeepers, a moratorium on loans to small debtors,[40] a curtailment of

* Munich University was temporarily closed in June 1930 after a riotous mob had battered down the doors of a lecture room used by Professor Nawiasky, the reader in international law. Professor Gumbel, a prominent pacifist at Heidelberg, was the object of similar demonstrations. cf. Helmut Kuhn, op. cit., p. 37.

† By David Schoenbaum in his excellent study, *Hitler's Social Revolution*, London, 1967.

the scope of one-price shops, department stores and co-operatives, and general control of the market in the interests of the 'little man'.[41]

Among the mass of shopkeepers, craftsmen and farmers crippled by lack of credit, the Nazis' attacks on 'interest slavery' touched a deep chord. 'Interest slavery' evoked a host of hateful allusions: to banks and money-lenders, to the Republic's 'Manchester system' of liberal economics, and to Jewry as the personification of usury (the Jews were alleged to be the puppetmasters of the Weimar marionettes).

Deep-rooted social and economic anxieties did not find their outlet in abstractions – such as the social system or market mechanism – but in the Jews.[42]

The Jews became the embodiment, on a scale unprecedented in history, of every ill besetting state and society in the final stage of the Weimar Republic. A few prominent Jews had helped to found the Republic, or been active in the Press, in literature and the theatre – the arenas in which battle had been joined between order and freedom, between archaic and permissive attitudes. Jews had espoused internationalism – the majority as partisans of the League of Nations and a few as Marxists or pacifists. Some of them were practitioners of psycho-analysis, others pioneered new ways of tackling problems such as abortion, homosexuality, criminality or penology.

If the relaxation of censorship in the Weimar era led to the publication of lesbian and homosexual magazines, and discussion and literature on all aspects of sex and the human psyche proliferated; if there was an economic-ally conditioned increase in the incidence of abortion and the number of juvenile prostitutes (male as well as female); if some advanced schools included sex-education in their curriculum and had pupil committees claiming shop-steward status,[43] it was tempting to echo Treitschke's phrase 'The Jews are our misfortune'. The Judeo-democracy was blamed for the twenties cult of the new, the meretricious and the sensational that saddled Germany with twice its pre-war cosmetics bill,[44] fostered the smoking habit among women,[45] riveted public attention on six-day bicycle races, and pruriently reported murder trials. Yet the main charge against the Jews was that they dominated such spheres as banking, business, real estate, brokerage, moneylending and cattle-trading.

Ringed round with hostility (or at best indifference), the Jews looked in vain for defenders among Republican politicians and in the mass media. The once influential bourgeois Press had discounted Jew-baiting as an anachronism early on in the Weimar era, and subsequently confined itself to reporting anti-Semitic incidents without comment;[46] it now favoured discretion in place of forthrightness – and argued that newspapers whose readers overlapped party boundaries had to avoid partisanship.

The provincial Press was no different: local editors tended to balance the propriety of denouncing pogroms against the likely effects of this on advertising revenue.[47]

Republican politicians also shied away from a head-on confrontation with those who kept on raising the 'Jewish Question'; the German democrats of Weimar bore little resemblance to the *Dreyfusards* at a not dissimilar juncture in the history of the French Republic.[48]

The great crisis found the partisans of the Republic on the defensive. Fear of provoking a clash that might flare up into civil war prompted the Social Democrat leaders to acquiesce in Chancellor Papen's illegal suppression of the Prussian Social Democrat *Land* government in the summer of 1932.* Their timidity seemed to derive substance from the state of emergency that existed in many rural areas, where foreclosure and unemployment had precipitated bomb attacks on town halls and the burning down of tax offices. Elsewhere, during seven weeks in the summer of 1932, pitched battles between contending political factions claimed 500 dead or severely injured.[49] And yet, beneath the fractured surface of political order, an infra-structure of stability endured, and the underlying facts of the situation did not really bear out alarmist premonitions of chaos.

In spite of endemic violence, in many towns, there was no single instance of local party headquarters being attacked and burnt down by opponents. At an inter-departmental conference in 1932 the Minister of Defence, General Gröner, stated categorically: 'There will be no civil war. Whoever makes the attempt will be smashed down with the utmost brutality,'[50] and a few months later he imposed a (temporary) ban on political uniforms, which the Storm Troopers and the SS obeyed without demur.[51]

Visions of a Red revolution emanated partly from the imaginings and slogans of its own advocates – although the slump had in fact only raised the Communist share of the total vote from 10·6 per cent (in 1928) to 14·3 per cent (in July 1932).[52] KPD membership at no point exceeded 300,000 – but this was sufficient for men who wanted to frighten the

* 'One lieutenant and ten men sufficed to send the people's tribunes packing' was the derisory comment of the *éminence grise* of the Junkers, von Oldenburg-Janoschau, on the bloodless coup by which Hitler's subsequent Vice-Chancellor removed the Braun-Severing government (cf. Ferdinand Friedensburg, *Die Weimarer Republik*, Hanover/in Frankfurt, 1957, p. 153).

middle classes and heavy industry into supporting them against peril from Moscow. The spectre of Karl Marx was effectively raised to haunt Germany: when in 1932 Werner Best, who was later to be Gestapo commissar, was charged with preparing the violent overthrow of the Republic, he adroitly persuaded the court (and public opinion) that the incriminating Boxheim documents merely set out Nazi counter-measures to an anticipated pre-emptive Communist strike.[53]

In August 1932 Hitler used his position as leader of the largest single party to achieve the judicial acquittal of five Storm Troopers who had sadistically murdered a Communist in the Silesian town of Potempa. Despite this unprecedented identification of a contender for the Chancellorship with the most heinous offence in the legal code, every third German (33·1 per cent of all voters)[54] voted Nazi ten weeks later, in November 1932.

Though the coming of the Third Reich may have lacked the quality of inevitability sometimes attributed to it, it is difficult not to consider the Weimar Republic's fate as inescapable. The political immaturity of the German people (especially of the élite), a deformed social system and a malfunctioning economy all interacted to bring about its collapse. But the particular form this collapse took was by no means predetermined. In Germany (where, incidentally, public executioners exercised their office in top-hat and frock-coat) the hangmen of democracy might as easily have worn gold braid as brown shirts, since the perverted minority Republican governments of 1932 faced the choice of either instituting a narrow, army-backed, Presidential dictatorship or of surrendering to the broadly-based Nazi movement.

The alternative adopted on 30 January 1933 (the day of the so-called 'seizure of power') was in fact the more democratic one – absurd though this may sound. Although Hitler failed to give Germany the proffered Millennium, he did drag her, half-heartedly kicking and screaming, into the century of the common man.

2

THE THIRD REICH:
A GENERAL SURVEY

The Nazis never tired of invoking 'the law according to which they had first formed ranks' – and since it could more truly be said of their regime than of any other that in its beginning was also its end, this prime law invites examination.

It was a hybrid of popular will and authoritative *fiat*: populist by virtue of Hitler's mass following, and authoritarian because his investiture had been at the hands of Hindenburg.

Thus the Third Reich came into being with mutually exclusive attributes: it belonged simultaneously to Prusso-German history and to the Century of the Common Man. (This paradox was resolved by semantics: in German the word *Volk* denoted both 'the people' in the radical-democratic sense and 'the folk' in the racial sense.)

A characteristically high-flown Nazi epithet for the events of 1933 was '*Volkwerdung*', a linguistic monstrosity which meant 'a people becoming itself'. Half a century earlier the 'pure German' (*völkische*) philosopher Lagarde had written: 'Voters no more constitute a people than canvas and colour molecules constitute a painting by Raphael' – and now, ironically, Germany had found her super-Raphael in a failed art student capable of structuring 65 million atoms into a nation. Another metaphor applied to the Nazi revolution was that of the 'national wave', betokening the return to the patriotic high tide of August 1914. Nineteen years afterwards the Nazis put into practice the Kaiser's fervent 'Henceforth I no longer acknowledge different parties – I only acknowledge Germans' by smashing all political parties, refought the world war between Germans and non-Germans as a civil war between Germans and un-Germans, and reincarnated the mystic all-rank communion of the trenches in their projected 'folk community'.

'Folk community', a constantly used slogan promising a society no longer split into haves and have-nots, accorded ill with the unchanged class structure of the Third Reich – the extent of whose anti-capitalism was marked by a 6 per cent ceiling on distributed profits.

This contradiction generally escaped notice thanks to Nazi propaganda and the impact of the Depression on the collective consciousness: people were too busy hoping the national cake would not disappear to scrutinize the apportionment of its slices.

Armed with business backing and fortuitously benefiting from the first post-Depression upswing of the trade-cycle, the regime embarked on a massive job-procurement programme – public works projects, subsidized house repairs and so on – which cut the peak unemployment figure of 6 million by over 40 per cent within a year.[1]

Nazi measures for creating jobs had twofold repercussions: apart from providing material benefits for the workers they transformed the psychological climate of an industrial society that, more than any other, had equated economic crisis with existential catastrophe.

Another three years – and the arms drive – saw more Germans at work than 1928, the best year of the pre-Depression boom.

By that time, however, the overall psychological improvement was outpacing the material advantage accruing to a labour force denied the freedom to take full advantage of the transformed situation.

In the spring of 1933 the trade unions – in an attempt to swim with the tide – had voluntarily offered the regime their co-operation (as of course had the churches, the non-Marxist political parties, the academic senates, the professional associations and other would-be riders on the 'national wave').

The unions' offer was flagrantly spurned – the regime smashed their whole movement on the morrow of 1933's mammoth May Day celebrations at which, sped on their way by priestly benedictions and lachrymose middle-class enthusiasm, employees marched alongside their employers – but this did not necessarily contradict the process of *Volkwerdung*.

After all, the nation as now defined did not automatically comprise all Germans, only those who genuinely *felt* German. As accessories after the crime of class-warfare, trade unionists were by definition excluded from the folk – and, at first, the Nazi seizure of power could be almost as readily interpreted in terms of the victory of one half of the country over the other (at the elections on 5 March 1933 the Nazis and their nationalist allies had gained 51 per cent of the votes cast) as in terms of national re-integration.

From 6 March onwards a wave of conversions cumulatively transformed the almost one-to-one balance at the polls into a crushing majority-minority ratio. Life-long Democrat voters assured each other – and themselves – that National Socialism was the faith they had sought all their lives. Whole professions (the civil service and teaching for instance) felt an overwhelming compulsion to join the Party.*

Husbands returning from work found that wives had on their own initiative gone out and bought uniforms for them – expecting this investment to yield rich dividends in the future. Opportunism was rampant – but not exclusively so. Professional men with a social conscience went into the SA to rub shoulders with people living on the wrong side of the tracks. Brass-band enthusiasts followed cronies who had turned themselves as a body into storm-troop regimental bands. Some joined the Party to 'prevent the worst' – a few even to subvert it from within.

Even so, a sufficient number of enemies of the regime – men either compromised by the past or lukewarm about the present – remained as potential targets of attack and denunciation.

The situation in 1933, of unification and, simultaneously, civil war, proved a most potent emotional stimulant. Alexis de Tocqueville had written a century earlier, 'There are no revolutions in Germany, because the police would not permit it,' and now the root-and-branch transformation of the Weimar Republic into the Third Reich afforded unique opportunities for enjoying the liberating *frisson* of a revolution and the reassurance of police protection at one and the same time. Throughout its subsequent existence the Third Reich continued to exert this initial appeal to the law-breaker (not to say the criminal) and the policeman who slumbered inside many a citizen's breast.

The antithesis of policeman and criminal is capable of resolution on a higher plane: in the persona of the soldier, who prestigiously combines upholding the law at home with breaking it abroad. This, of course, was not the only reason for the potency of the military ideal in Nazi Germany: there was, too, the prevalent mood of revanchism for the Great War and – consciously or otherwise – obeisance to the law according to which the country had first formed ranks. While in the eighteen-sixties Italian unification was accompanied by popular insurrection, war had been the sole effective begetter of the Reich. That seminal circumstance contributed to the public's lack of concern at seeing the rule of law superseded by

* For further details see chapters on the Party (p. 56), the civil service (p. 127) and education (p. 287).

20

martial law, and for its view of the Führer as a Commander entitled to take arbitrary, pre-emptive, warlike measures in the midst of peace.

Because of its orientation towards war, the regime was initially circumspect in its treatment of the nation's sole bearer of arms, the *Reichswehr*. As was the case with other institutions already in existence when the Nazis came to power, the *Reichswehr* was absorbed into the Nazi state in an outwardly unchanged form, and within eighteen months of the seizure of power the regime twice demonstrated its desire not to ruffle military susceptibilities – once in the form of farce and once in that of tragedy.

On 23 March 1933, at the Potsdam garrison church, a frock-coated, top-hatted Hitler made theatrical obeisance to Hindenburg in front of Frederick the Great's coffin and the serried ranks of the Prussian nobility; on 30 June 1934 he decimated the storm-troop leadership (which had made a ham-fisted attempt to seize control of the army) as an earnest of his intention to respect the *Reichswehr*'s autonomy. Subsequently, the Nazis employed three methods to change the none too resistant *Reichswehr* into an adjunct of the regime: dilution, decapitation and corruption. Conscription produced a massive influx of progressively more Nazi-indoctrinated new recruits into the hitherto homogeneously reactionary *Reichswehr*; in consequence, support of Hitler spread upwards from the ranks to non-commissioned personnel and to the junior officer corps, and beyond. Having infiltrated the base of the military pyramid, the regime truncated it by dismissing War Minister Blomberg and Army Chief of Staff Fritsch on faked charges. At the same time, most senior officers allowed themselves to be corrupted by promotion (and some by outright money bribes) into serving the regime as gold-braided automata. During this complex process the army's outward image changed only imperceptibly, and the public – accustomed to looking upon the military as a pillar of the state – was given a strong impression of continuity with the past.

This sense of continuity was reinforced by the outward permanence of the civil service, the judiciary and the universities – tradition-encrusted institutions which the regime similarly forebore to transform, but managed to adapt to its own purposes with an astonishing economy of means.*
The aura of apparent continuity clung not only to the limbs of the body politic but hovered round its very head.

Photographs of the Reich Cabinet in 1933–4 showed Brownshirts

---

* See also the chapters on the civil service (p. 127), justice (p. 116) and the universities p. 305).

scattered sparsely among a frock-coated phalanx of Hugenberg's Nationalists and 'non-Party' bureaucrats – and even among the Nazis there was one who sported impeccable antecedents: Hermann Goering, the highly decorated air ace, was the son of a former Governor of German South-West Africa.

The Foreign Service doggedly continued to limit its recruitment to the same charmed circle as before – the 0·74 per cent of the population whom the noble prefix '*von*' set apart from the remaining ninety-nine and a bit per cent. Judges on the bench, priests in the pulpit, teachers upon the *Cathedra*, idols on the screen and athletes in the arena remained substantially the same as before. Even bourgeois newspapers like the *Frankfurter Zeitung* continued to appear – refracting the new and raw realities of Nazi life through the traditional filter of their Mandarin style.

Continuity with the past was not merely maintained but positively intensified in the military sphere – with the regime creating an ambience of martial glitter recalling the Empire manœuvres, those nostalgically remembered red-letter days of the Hohenzollerns' *belle époque*. The reintroduction of conscription in 1935 forged another link with tradition: military service had been part of the German way of life as far back as men could remember. Conscription was not merely welcomed as begetting triumphs in foreign policy (such as the remilitarization of the Rhineland) and as a step towards reversing the Treaty of Versailles – it was part of popular folklore that no man's education was complete without the discipline of the barrack-square.

This – plus a repugnance for the juvenile street-corner idleness which had been such a familiar sight during the Depression – also determined public reaction to the six-months' Labour Service which was obligatory for eighteen-year-olds. (At the same time, though, the spade-wielding drill-obsessed *Reichsarbeitsdienst* – national labour service – with its coarse, anti-religious atmosphere and ill-trained instructors promoted parental misgivings – as did the SA and the Hitler Youth – and the Wehrmacht was widely looked to to provide a corrective.)

There were other reasons for the country's affirmative response to the Nazis' remilitarization measures, however. The concept of a supranational order underlying the League of Nations Covenant lacked all credibility in German eyes – and not only because the Covenant was seen as an afterbirth of the Versailles system. On the philosophical level the notion of supranational law clashed with Ranke's view that the state was 'not a subdivision of something more general – but a living, individual, unique self.'[2]

The dogma of sacred state egotism fused with the *Deutsche Michel* syndrome, i.e. the Germans' self-image as artlessly homespun butts of foreign guile. Taken to its ultimate conclusion, this implied that Germany could only overcome her unfitness for the machinations of diplomacy by recourse to the 'honest' use of arms.

The Germans saw themselves as a nation wronged by history and they now meant to redress that wrong. Having entered the immoral arena of politics they would not let 'moral' objections deflect them from single-mindedly pursuing their advantage. The notion of morality as a component of international life struck most citizens of the Third Reich as pharisaical, or at best otherworldly.

If we turn to attitudes to German home policy, we can take a Goethe dictum as our text: 'I would rather commit an injustice than endure disorder.' One would be hard put to devise an apter gloss on the mood of the millions who had voted for Hitler after his avowal of solidarity with the Potempa murderers in August 1932. In that year five elections – on a national or provincial scale – had forced a plethora of decision-making on voters, whose bewilderment was articulated in Gerhart Hauptmann's plaintive 'If only life would demand no more solutions from us!'[3]

This 'fear of freedom' was speedily assuaged. The destruction of the political parties, the trade unions and the Press was presented as ushering in an era of *Konfliktslosigkeit* in which further upheavals were inconceivable. Such assurances – plus Hitler's bland description of the seizure of power as 'bloodless' – created a mood of surface calm which even such drastic innovations as the setting up of concentration camps failed to shatter. Indifference to the camps was not merely due to the public's fear and partial ignorance; Press polemics going back to the early twenties[4] about 're-education camps' (to which the state could rightfully relegate 'alien nuisances') had long prepared the ground for Dachau and Buchenwald.

Many Germans, persuaded of the state's pre-emptive claim on citizens' lives,[5] absolved the head of state of culpability for its crimes. Moving within the most tightly structured governmental system in Western history, they nevertheless managed to dissociate centrally directed atrocities from the man at the centre – an attitude of mind that found expression in such cant-phrases as 'It's all the fault of the little Hitlers' or 'If only Adolf knew about this'.[6]

Every so often the regime obliged its subjects who wanted sand thrown in their eyes, even going so far as to stage mock trials at which a handful of the thousands of participants in the Crystal Night – the countrywide anti-Jewish orgy of pillage and arson in November 1938 – were charged with breaking and entering and given derisory sentences.

The November pogrom, incidentally, also illustrated how the Nazis contrived to invest parts of German speech – in this case the word 'order' – with new meaning. The crowds watching the atavistic spectacle of synagogues on fire could not but be impressed by the efficiency of the public services (police and fire brigades) in preventing the spread of the flames from Jewish to adjacent Aryan property.* Order came increasingly to mean minute regulation of the dosage of violence deemed appropriate to the regime's purpose in any given situation.

The restructuring of words reflected a restructuring of consciousness. Gerhart Hauptmann, whose initial reaction to the Nazi take-over had been: 'Ah, those few Polish Jews! Good God, it's not all that important – every revolution starts off by bringing the dregs to the top',[7] told a friend in 1938: 'This wretched Austrian decorator's mate has ruined Germany – but tomorrow it's the turn of the rest of the world . . . This dog's muck will cover the world with war; this miserable brown ham actor, this Nazi hangman is pushing us into a world conflagration, into catastrophe.' Asked why he stayed on in Germany if he felt like that, Hauptmann burst out piercingly, 'Because I'm a coward, do you understand? I'm a coward, a coward!'[8]

This kind of disintegration of the personality resulted from the entanglement of all dissenters in a cat's-cradle of tripwires. Above them was Authority – its arsenal of deterrents ranging from deprivation of livelihood to deprivation of life itself.† All around them its reinforcing agency: Public Opinion. (To quote one example: on the high holy days of the Nazi calendar when all house-fronts were expected to be swathed in swastika bunting, local Party functionaries had no need to go round and chivvy backsliders; the rare flat-dweller who omitted to put out flags was invariably scolded by his fellow-tenants for giving 'their house' a bad name.) The majority's meddlesome conformity ensured that those of

* In 1943 the inhabitants of Warsaw living near the ghetto were similarly impressed when German soldiers told them to keep their windows open lest the blast from the dynamiting of the Jewish quarter should shatter the panes.

† At Dachau the regime's method of reducing prisoners to mere numbers in the guards' eyes was to warn them against shooting prisoners because each bullet cost three pfennigs. The guards were overawed by the power of the state that so easily disposed of human lives. cf. Bruno Bettelheim, *The Informed Heart*, London, 1961, p. 241.

24

doubtful allegiance to the regime lived in a state of unceasing fear of anonymous informers, sometimes with an element of auto-suggestion.

Auto-suggestion was crucial to the process of totalitarian conditioning. Adjustment to requisite forms of conduct often occurred in anticipation of, rather than in response to, official orders. The regime's punishment of offences not yet defined as such in law made people do the state's bidding ostensibly of their own volition, since it was an individual's sense of anxiety rather than a published *ukase* that immediately governed his conduct. This steady curtailment of autonomous behaviour could proceed with remarkable ease in a society in which an individual's self-esteem derived less from a sense of autonomy than from his professional function or role within the family; this was strongly linked with the national preference for good (i.e. efficient) government rather than self-govern-ment. There was also a lack of antibodies capable of resisting the con-tagion of Nazi ideology. Dissent required a viable counter-faith, going beyond mere non-acceptance of the currently ordained creed: but mem-ories of the Republican débâcle lay like an incubus on all political beliefs; not even the now illegal Social Democrats thought in terms of a return to the practices of Weimar after Hitler had been removed.

Though the Germans had by all reasonable criteria been infinitely freer in the days of the Republic, Nazi invocations of freedom did not ring ....ow in their ears: the term no longer meant freedom *per se* – but their freedom to be Germans at the expense of the interest of all non-Germans.

'In Thy service is perfect freedom' (for God read State) turned the abdi-cation of autonomy by 65 million individuals into an act of collective self-sacrifice for the national good.

The 'nobility of sacrifice' theme was to recur constantly, as the Third Reich, reversing the Enlightenment's secularization of the State and of public life, re-spiritualized them. A resident of Eichkamp (a Berlin suburb) recalled the mid-thirties thus: 'It was only Adolf Hitler who had brought it to Eichkamp – the knowledge that such things as providence, eternal justice, and the Lord Almighty exist. There was a lot of talk about these invisible powers at the time. An age of piety had dawned.'[9]

These spiritual changes had their counterpart in the world of aesthetics. Beethoven's music framed the radio addresses of Nazi leaders, and Hitler's annual pilgrimages to the Wagner shrine of Bayreuth became as much part of the public scene as the Royal Opening of Parliament in Britain. The Reich Chancellery recalled a classical temple; new post offices were adorned with statues of naked youths clasping burning torches: a Hellenic dawn suffused the landscape of the Third Reich.

The spirit of 'classicism' was all-pervading. Goethe's favourite oak-tree some miles outside Weimar served as the central point round which Buchenwald concentration camp was constructed. Influenced by the classical concept of ineluctable destiny, the man in the street came to believe that events had been decreed by fate. Since human events were held to emanate from the womb of nature and not from that of society, the Third Reich was transmuted into a manifestation of nature – like a tidal wave or a lunar eclipse.

And, like such cataclysms, the Third Reich was above all dramatic. The fall in the crime-rate after 1933,* though partly due to economic resurgence and the diversion of aggression into approved channels, had one other root cause: vicarious participation in the vast drama unfolding on the political stage engaged energies which would normally have found anti-social outlets. At the same time, the public's social conscience was bombarded with charitable appeals.

'Public before private good' became a pervasive theme in public life. This manipulation of the 'Samaritan syndrome' benefited almost everybody: the recipients, the Nazis, whose mesmeric grip on the populace relied on stimulating aggressive or lachrymose emotions alternately, and the donors, who wallowed in socially approved self-denial as in a steam bath.

At Eichkamp preparations for the first 'one-pot meal' – the officially prescribed monthly Lenten fare, the saving from which accrued to Winter Relief – did not fail to engender inward emotion: lumpy barley broth brought lumps to diners' throats, transmitting (via the taste-buds) evocations of folk community, greatness and conviviality.[10] These periodic semi-fast days exemplified the regime's invasion of personal privacy, though their relative infrequency (there were only six one-pot meal days per year, occurring between September and March), made this relatively unimportant. Up to the outbreak of war most people retained the impression that within their own four walls life remained appreciably unchanged – though outside them, above all at work, few could avoid compulsory involvement in the activities – processions, meetings,

---

* 691,921 offenders had been sentenced by German courts in 1932; there was a decrease of 100,000 in 1933, and by 1937 (the only year in which an amnesty for minor offenders did not distort the statistical picture) the number stood at 504,093. cf. *Statistisches Handbuch für Deutschland 1928–1944*, Franz Ehrenwirth, Munich, 1949, p. 633.

training courses – of the mammoth German Labour Front or other Nazi
Party affiliates.

Most Germans never knew the constant fear of the early-morning knock
on the door, and found such encroachments on their privacy as the monotonous appearance of Winter Relief and N S People's Welfare collectors on
their doorstep merely irritating. Other official – and officious – callers,
were block leaders, addicted to *Suppentopfschnüffelei* (prying into cooking-
pots), and air-raid wardens exercising their right of entry into people's
homes in quest of inflammable materials stored in lumber-rooms. As the
political situation grew tenser, so these snoopers became more active.

There was, of course, a not inconsiderable minority for whom the
regime's permeation of all spheres of life was intolerable. The fear they
felt of revealing their true feelings took many forms. Some forwent skiing holidays for fear of talking in their sleep in the communal huts; others
avoided operations for fear of giving themselves away under the anaes-
thetic.[11] The German Labour Front leader, Robert Ley, stated com-
placently – 'The only person still leading a private life in Germany today is
someone who sleeps'; but even sleep reflected the pressures of life under
the regime. An office employee dreamt that he had finally decided to
lodge a complaint about prevailing conditions. In his dream, he inserted
a blank sheet of paper into an envelope and felt proud to have made his
complaint – and deeply ashamed at the same time. One housewife dreamt
that a Storm Trooper was searching her flat for subversive material; as he
opened the door of the tiled stove, it started repeating in a jarring voice
every 'disloyal' conversation the family had ever had.[12] Sometimes the
subconscious prefigured future submission: there were dissenters whose
dreams already projected the outstretched right arm, the clicked heels and
the alliterative parrot-cry even before they had taken the conscious decision to knuckle under and join in the collective hailing of Hitler.

The 'German greeting' was a powerful conditioning device. Having
once decided to intone it as as an outward token of conformity, many
experienced schizophrenic discomfort at the contradiction between their
words and their feelings. Prevented from saying what they believed they
tried to establish their psychic equilibrium by consciously making themselves believe what they said.

For the public at large, on the other hand, the blessing of the leader, far
from serving as protective mimicry, expressed a collective emotion felt
with religious intensity. The leader as a being elevated above the common
ruck of mankind belongs to universal folklore, but in Germany the

leadership cult has always been uniquely stamped with atavism – as exemplified by the transformation of the Kaiser in 1918 from a semi-divine figure into a scapegoat bearing the guilt of defeat into exile with him. This predilection towards atavism inclined the Germans to remove the figure of the leader from the rational sphere to that of the myth. In the brief space of time between the seizure of power and the 'Roehm Putsch' Hitler grew to mythical stature and achieved apotheosis as the Fredericus-*cum*-Bismarck of the twentieth century.

But if leadership was to fulfil the diffuse emotional requirements of the led in the century of the common man, it also needed to provide opportunities for self-identification. This was a role for which Hitler – clothed as he was in superhuman attributes – naturally proved rather unfitted (other than through sharing the handicap of the masses in such matters as background, education and wealth). The opposite applied to the fat, corrupt Goering. When, pausing during a Nuremberg open-air address, he removed his Storm Trooper's cap to mop his dripping brow, the onlookers went into transports of joyous identification with that perspiring mound of corseted flesh.

Similarly, gales of enthusiasm used to rock factory canteens at Robert Ley's announcement, 'I am a worker just like you' as he sat down to a helping of sausages and sauerkraut. Once a leader had established himself in popular affection, disreputable revelations about his way of life – such as Ley's dipsomania or Goering's gargantuan greed – enhanced rather than undermined his standing. Even so, newsreels featuring Goebbels in a grand seigneurial setting had to be withdrawn because of the hostile reactions of cinema audiences, and there were occasions when the Gauleiter of Berlin had to order the capital's Storm Troopers to line his route in civilian disguise and to cheer 'spontaneously'.

Basically, of course, the Nazi leaders, like the state they represented, evoked anything but public hostility or indifference. The war so intensified the general sense of dependence on leaders like Hitler and Goering that entire social groups felt pained if their own contribution to the war effort failed to gain an honourable mention in their speeches. Thus, Hitler's Reichstag address of August 1940, according to SD (Internal Intelligence) reports, gratified armament workers, while farmers felt slighted because it made no mention of the Reich Food Estate. Two years later, Goering gladdened their hearts by his Harvest Thanksgiving speech, while industrial workers felt neglected.[13]

Public trust in the leadership, in fact, received striking confirmation throughout most of the Nazi period. Even though the overwhelmingly affirmative plebiscite returns – invariably announced by Goebbels – were undoubtedly doctored, they misrepresented the true state of popular feeling only by degree and not in kind. As an index of the regime's popularity, maternity wards ranked immediately behind polling stations: within a year of 1933 the birth rate shot up by 22 per cent (to 18 per 1,000 of the population) and in the pre-war crisis year 1938 this rose to 20·4 per 1,000 – an all-time high. This was almost maintained in 1940, though 1941 saw a slight decline to 18·6, but the 1942 drop to 14·9 was followed by a rise to 16 in the year after Stalingrad.* [14]

Another indication of confidence in the regime was the response to the People's Car (Volkswagen) project launched in 1938. The plant's foundation stone was laid two months after the *Anschluss*, and the first show models – no others were ever built during the Third Reich – were exhibited at Munich and the Vienna autumn fair at the height of the Sudeten crisis. The scheme, which, in contrast to universal hire-purchase practice, provided for delivery only after payment of the last instalment, had attracted three hundred thousand purchasers by November 1940. [15]

The Volkswagen phenomenon was also a pointer to two major trends operating in all modern societies: technocracy and consumer orientation. Nazi commitment to the technocratic ideal was exemplified by the rise of Albert Speer from Nazi court architect to overlord of the industrial war effort and by the inclusion of the motorway builder Todt and the car designer Porsche in Hitler's entourage.

Todt and Porsche paved the way to cheaper motoring, which traditional high-unit cost car manufacturers had not catered for sufficiently. Even so Goering's 'Guns before Butter' slogan quite unmistakably spelt out the regime's scale of precedence. Optimists and cynics alike chuckled at the story of the Volkswagen employee who, having sedulously filched all the car's components from the factory assembled them at home and wound up with a Bren gun carrier.

But the available evidence did not wholly belie the public's more sanguine assumptions – even while the juggernaut took shape on the production line. The spectacular decrease of unemployment (January 1933, 6,013,600: January 1938, 1,051,500) [16] produced a gradual but unmistakable improvement in the standard of living, and within five years of

---

* The 1943 increase was largely accounted for, however, by the introduction of labour conscription for women without small children.

the seizure of power – rather less in the strategic industries – there were more jobs than jobless.

One visible symptom of rising standards of living was alcohol consumption. During the Third Reich's peacetime years beer consumption went up by a quarter, wine consumption almost doubled and champagne consumption increased five-fold.[17] The champagne statistics strongly suggest an expansion of the affluent stratum of society in terms both of total size and individual wealth. Increased overall alcohol consumption *per se* can of course also be an indication of lower resistance to tension and pressure.* Another set of statistics – of suicides – shows a slight rise during almost every peacetime year during the regime (from 18,723 in 1933 to 22,273 in 1939).[18] In 1936 the incidence of suicides per every 100,000 deaths was 28·6, compared to 12·4 in Britain and 14·2 in the United States; the assumption that Jewish suicides might have distorted the German statistics is refuted by a steep wartime decline: 1942, the climactic year of the holocaust, saw only 7,647 suicides – a third of the immediately pre-war total.

The war, in other words, prompted a significant improvement in Germany's social health – an impression reinforced by other statistical evidence. Thus male criminality decreased by half as much again during 1940 than 1939 – a phenomenon only partly attributable to the call-up.[19]

While war universally tones up the national psyche and integrates the individual more fully within the collective, the Third Reich's transition from peace to war involved something more. In Sebastian Haffner's perceptive analysis, the population of Nazi Germany divided into two groups – Nazis and loyal Germans – both of whom supported the regime: the former because they were happy and the latter although they were unhappy.[20] The cumulative Nazi triumphs of 1938–9 – the annexation of Austria (the century-old cynosure of the Pan-German vision), of the Sudeten and the rump of Czechoslovakia – had heightened the dilemma of loyal Germans to a level of schizophrenia. Their misgivings grew as they witnessed such phenomena as the *Kristallnacht* pogrom, the shortages of food and consumer goods, the increased industrial and military conscription, the feverish construction of the *Westwall*. But there were also the tangible, gratifying fruits of the regime's policy. September 1939 radically

* 'We know that many of our countrymen spend on beer and whisky the money which should go to the purchase of bread and clothes, the payment of rent and school fees – we know from frequent experience that alcoholism is more often produced by impoverishment than by prosperity.' Dr Fleig, '*Von Steigen und Stand des Alkool – und Nikotinverbrauchs*', *Die medizinische Wochenschrift*, 65th series, No. 9, 1939, p. 347.

altered the stance of loyal Germans – catapulting them from a grudging recognition of Hitler's pursuit of the national interest to an identification of him with the national interest. In war the nation – notwithstanding the resistance activities of individuals and even groups – became the '*verschworene Gemeinschaft*' (oath-bound band of brothers) linked together '*auf Gedeih oder Verderb*' (to prosper or to perish).

The bewilderment of early September 1939 – so different from the euphoria of August 1914 – speedily yielded to a resolve to see it through. War, the law according to which Germany had first drawn up ranks, an ever-present memory compounding the belief in certain victory in 1914 with the trauma of defeat in 1918, evoked a response from the deepest layers of the collective psyche. Morale was high because of the lightning victories in East and West, and because the civilian population was kept amply provisioned. The ration scale in 1939 was higher than the average calorie consumption, and during the first war years food supplies were almost up to peacetime level. The consumer who before the war had been living far from luxuriously remained quite impervious to the impact of the war for some considerable time.

The soldiers' reactions varied. One ex-student, comparing his fellow-countrymen and the peaceable – though occupied – Dutch, wrote: 'We Germans have already progressed further; we are in possession of chaos ... the precondition for our bringing forth out of the depths what is new.' Another spoke of a struggle 'whose value lay in its devaluation of the human spirit – whose sense consisted of its senselessness'.[21]

Those with less of a bent for philosophy accepted the war at worst as pre-destined; or at best as serving the nation's self-interest. Personal self-interest also influenced the national mood; for a long time the war seemed to be a great source of material benefit. Thus the working wives of serving soldiers not infrequently gave up work because they could live on their dependants' allowances – supplemented by the National Socialist People's Welfare. As for their menfolk, most of the continent rapidly became a buyers' market in which the power of the purse spoke out of the mouth of a gun. After the fall of France so much perfume found its way into Berlin that the German capital 'smelt like a gigantic hairdresser's'.[22] Similarly Norwegian furs, Dutch dairy produce, Belgian coffee, French silks, and other wares found their way to Germany. It became a reflex action for German civilians to offset reduced rations by appeals to soldier relatives stationed abroad.

The realization of what war and occupation meant to the occupied dawned on only a few Germans, and – unlike the euthanasia killings of German incurables and mental defectives – never agitated public opinion. One reason for this atrophy of the sympathetic faculty may be that occupation practice varied in different areas – razing villages to the ground, normal practice in Russia, was exceptional in France; the round-up of Jews, which was absolute in Party-controlled Holland, was not so thorough in Wehrmacht-administered Belgium.

Of greater relevance was the acceptance of the war as a justifiable assertion of German claims on a hostile world, which meant that the regime's aims were approved of; and if one approved of the ends one could not reject the means.

At times public opinion was even 'ahead' of the authorities; when the Reich government's Black Book on the German-Polish conflict glossed over the mass-executions of Poles, German eyewitnesses criticized official mealymouthedness – and argued that earlier Polish misdeeds had amply justified the executions.[23]

The Poles were of course the Germans' particular *bêtes noires*, and Hitler's denial of human status to the Slavs corresponded to deeply ingrained folk beliefs.* The metaphor *Polnische Wirtschaft* ('Polish business') popularly signified chaos, and the 'bleeding frontiers of the East' – i.e. the amputation of East Prussia by means of the Polish Corridor – had prompted violent revanchism ever since 1919.

The Poles were considered to be racial anti-types of the Germans; the Danes, the Norwegians and the Dutch, on the other hand, were fellow-Nordics perversely siding with the Reich's enemies under a guise of neutrality.

Belgium's guilt lay in her satellite position *vis-à-vis* France; the French aroused vengeful loathing and were seen as hereditary enemies ever since the Westphalian and Versailles treaties, breeders of decadence and revolution.

Britain was seen as hypocritical and a worshipper of Mammon: residual awareness of British fairness (for instance in the treatment of prisoners during the Great War) did not survive the beginning of the bombing.

The United States had faults similar to Britain's – though without the

* In the days of the Second Empire, when the liberal Heinrich von Gerlach had criticized the Prussian authorities' anti-Polish measures in the province of Pozen as an infringement of human rights, he elicited a rejoinder from the eminent sociologist Max Weber which could serve as a classic exposition of a national syndrome: 'It is only thanks to us that the Poles are human beings!' cf. Hans Kohn, *The Mind of Germany*, Macmillan and Co., London, 1961, p. 269.

latter's saving grace of tradition. America's entry into the war (although, in fact, Germany had declared war on her) was seen as prompted by cupidity and *hubris*. Hitler's 'one Beethoven symphony contains more culture than America has produced in her whole history'[24] expressed a widely held view; the German image of America was that of a Philistine, polyglot, mongrelized community descended from convicts and the unwanted dregs of other societies.

Propagandist cliché and popular stereotype thus largely converged, (although the German image of Italy was a contradictory amalgam of official respect and boundless popular derision). The prevalent image of Russia was similar. On the Third Reich's calibrated scale of subhumanity, the Russians ranked lowest but one, i.e. just above the Jews, and the German public's encounters with Russians were arranged accordingly. Prisoners from the eastern front arrived in the Reich in such a state of emaciation (after endless forced marches or suffocating cattle-truck journeys) that their appearance corroborated the stereotypes of Goebbels's propaganda. At the front itself, the savagery of the fighting often left Russian civilians living at the subhuman level which allegedly obtained in the 'Judeo-Bolshevik paradise'. Accordingly, Russian prisoners were housed and made to work under appalling conditions. The regime's success in making East-European reality appear to conform to its own clichés could, however, be counterproductive – the public found it difficult, for instance, to reconcile received truths about the nightmarishness of life in Russia with Hitler's project for settling a German feudal yeomanry in that infernal land after it had been conquered. But this caused no more than a few random apprehensions, unrelated to immediate concerns, and other colonization ventures were by no means unpopular. Many German farmers coveted land in the Warthegau (a depopulated, formerly Polish province). Rhinelanders who reached Styria, their reception area in southeast Austria, under the overall evacuation scheme from bombed areas, were sorely aggrieved to discover that – contrary to rumours of wholesale Styrian resettlement in the Ukraine – the local population was very much in possession of its farmsteads and had no intention of yielding them to the newcomers.[25] Since transfers to factories and mines in occupied Europe invariably involved increases in pay and status, there was no dearth of industrial colonizers either. Career-minded white-collar workers crowded evening courses in Polish, Ukrainian and Russian, and early on in the war the study of Swahili, Yoruba and other African languages engaged the interest of would-be planters and administrators.

The vogue for African languages declined after the Battle of Britain. The post-Dunkirk euphoria, illustrated by such popular predictions as 'We're going to sweep up the British Isles with a vacuum cleaner', was already evaporating while the inconclusive Blitz prompted *cris de cœur* like 'Why don't we smoke the swine out with gas, and have done with them once and for all?'[26] The subsequent RAF 'terror raids' triggered off powerful mass emotions of solidarity in hatred. Thus Hitler's declaration that he intended to raze the towns of Britain to the ground in hundred-fold retaliation for every Royal Air Force bomb dropped on the Reich was stopped in mid-sentence by frenetic applause from a largely female audience.[27] Allied bombing in the West agitated the collective consciousness in good times – such as the 1941 triumphs over the Russians – and bad alike. It undermined morale and yet cemented it. Those living in areas vulnerable to aerial attack so craved the arrival of the regime's much-vaunted *Vergeltungswaffen* (vengeance weapons) that Cardinal Galen's denunciation of vengeance as un-Christian lost that venerated prelate a great deal of esteem. When Professor Popitz, a leading participant in the Officers' Plot, asked a resistance-minded Westphalian industrialist about the effects of air-raids on his workers, he derived little encouragement from the reply. 'I admit that I am honestly impressed by the way they maintain the will to work, and by their discipline on the job.'[28]

A major consequence of the air war was the evacuation of millions of women and children (as well as of male employees of transferable enterprises) to the country. The efficiency of the evacuation programme, which amounted to an inter-continental exodus, was undoubtedly due to the efficiency of the state and Party agencies involved – though certain instances of class discrimination did not go unnoticed. Berliners complained about disproportionate official concern for the safety of the middle classes (offices had evacuation priority over factories), and about the transfer of children from the bourgeois western districts of Berlin being more thorough than that of its proletarian northern ones.* In South Westphalia, the unauthorized drift back from the reception areas assumed such proportions that the authorities cancelled the returnees' ration cards, thereby precipitating riots outside food offices.[29] There was a widespread return movement from the Warthegau, which most evacuees found unendurably primitive. The preferential allocation of food and scarce

* Between July 1943 and October 1944 the child population in the West was reduced to 33·1 per cent, in the North to 59·6 per cent. cf. Kurt Pritzkoleit, *Berlin*, Karl Rauch, Düsseldorf, 1962, p. 55.

consumer goods to the inhabitants of danger zones also contributed to population movements in the wrong direction.

Though the spirit of folk community was tirelessly evoked, it hovered only fitfully above the encounter between evacuees and the 'natives' of the reception areas. The popular South-German epithet for women evacuated from Rhineland towns was 'bomb wenches' (sometimes expanded into 'bomb or trouser wenches with Indian war paint'), and the story of the woman from Essen who made a dress for herself out of the curtains in her rooms was circulated in as many variations among the natives as the one about the farmer's wife who stopped a mother billeted on her washing nappies was among the evacuees.[30]

The fact that farmers – who were designated 'self-suppliers' – were excluded from the rationing scheme did not help matters, either; evacuees who shared their hosts' cooking facilities tetchily contrasted their own meagre rations with the abundance in which self-suppliers seemed to wallow.[31] 'They eat like kings but live like pigs'.[32] The villagers, in turn, said the townees were lazy and claimed that, while they themselves put in endless hours of back-breaking toil in the fields, the evacuees whiled away their time with gossip, pram-pushing and raids on the meagrely stocked local shops. Regional antipathies also played a part. Inhabitants of the Allgäu resented their region serving as a reception centre for the distant Ruhr instead of for Munich, where the villagers had many relatives.[33]

Evacuation also had certain politically undesirable side-effects. The Rhinelanders, for instance, encountered a form of undiluted Catholic piety in the Alpine villages which, under conditions of wartime strain and separation, acted as a powerful antidote to the neo-paganism ever more openly espoused by the Party. Religion also affected parental attitudes to the official scheme for evacuating entire schools *en bloc*. The policy known as *Kinderlandesverschickung* ('sending children to the country', KLV for short) served a dual purpose. It both complemented the overall evacuation scheme and removed the child from the ambit of family life and religion. Parents who withheld their consent to a child's evacuation were officially accused of gambling away his future – in the educational sense as well, since schools in bombed towns closed during 1942–3. The authorities discouraged parents from visiting the KLV camps, so as not to provoke homesickness and strain the transport system; teachers who tried to dilute the totally irreligious atmosphere in the camps were speedily inducted by the Wehrmacht as replacements for the eastern front.

Yet even at the height of the war, military manpower requirements could still be partly met by volunteers. Entire classes of the secondary-school population (eventually the age limit for armed service was reduced to sixteen – and below) continued to volunteer for selected branches of the service, until early in 1945. Far beyond the ranks of youth, the war had produced a craving for military awards and promotions; the soldier decorated with the coveted Knight's Cross – an award open to all ranks, news of which was broadcast over the Reich radio – became the cynosure of all eyes.

For thousands of status-seeking lower civil servants, teachers, white-collar employees and others, a Wehrmacht commission held out the prospect of self-advancement and vast social prestige. (This syndrome prompted the Delphic prediction that the war would not end before the last elementary schoolmaster had received his 'pips'.)

Reverses on the eastern front and in North Africa terminated the halcyon days of the early war, which had been characterized by peacetime levels of consumption and by certain high-ranking state officials indulging in the sporting practice* of exchanging dull office routine for short bursts of freelance soldiering. The popular *aperçu*, 'Enjoy the war, peace is going to be terrible' began to acquire a new urgency. Piece-work pay schemes and generous dependants' allowances interacted with a shortage of consumer goods to produce a situation where too much money was chasing too few goods. Officials concerned with 'population policy' discovered that newly-weds could not set up homes because inflation and devaluation rumours turned household furniture into items of investment. Only a fifth of all wage- and salary-earners participated in the government-sponsored Iron Saving scheme under which savings were exempt from taxation but could not be withdrawn before the end of the war.[34] People preferred to spend surplus money on black-market goods in short supply and on various forms of gambling. The distorted wartime economy produced a unique class of *nouveaux riches*, such as a Berlin wine-waiter who purchased a small country estate out of the lavish tips with which certain clients bought preferential treatment. A bombed-out charwoman, sporting the priority-clothing voucher – which was given to all air-raid victims – asked her employer to recommend a *couturier* where she could have herself fitted out.

These anecdotes reveal something about the period, though rather little about the conditions of industrial work. In industry, 'effort wages' had

* Such as Gestapo chief Heydrich, Dr Mansfeld of the Ministry of Labour or the Bavarian Trustee of Labour.

superseded the customary pay structure; this meant that productivity increases resulted in disproportionate rewards, while static output was penalized by pay reductions.

Germany's impressive wartime productivity can be attributed to three factors: rationalization of the labour process, patriotism, and incentive – partly represented by the black-market cost of goods in short supply. Productivity increases were all the more remarkable considering the circumstances under which they occurred: air-raid and blackout dislocation, a heavily diluted labour force (comprising 13 million German men and 14·5 million women, alongside 7·5 million foreigners, by 1944)[35] and an increasingly overstrained transport service. Trams and railways carried far heavier loads than they had been designed to cope with. The overcrowding of public transport reached ludicrous proportions. 'On the train there was indescribable confusion. I had my dress half torn off me, my shoes spoilt, I was kissed by the soldier nearest to me and could not resist because I had my arms pinned to my side,' read the diary entry of one traveller.[36] Another wrote: 'Passengers on the Munich–Berlin express alighted by climbing through the windows. Standing on the platform, I opened the carriage door, but someone immediately pulls it shut from inside. I get on nevertheless – the person next to the door thrashes about and throws punches as if demented.'[37] This Hobbesian struggle of all against all spilled over into most spheres of life. Soldiers on leave from the rigours of front-line existence were 'puzzled and shocked by the bad manners of the civilian population'.* Noting that 'in the streets and in public transport, in restaurants and theatres, a tone has developed which jangles one's nerves and recalls a herd of pigs',[38] Goebbels launched a 'public politeness' campaign – but publicity drives could do little about such indications of deterioration of morale as an increased rate in divorce and defamation-of-character cases before the courts.†

The courts were also kept busy administering savage wartime laws against looters and other would-be beneficiaries of the dislocation resulting from the blackout, air raids and shortages. Looting after air raids carried such severe penalties that passers-by made wide detours round

---

* This is an actual quotation from a broadcast by a soldier on leave, on 7 May 1942. cf. W. W. Schütz, *The German Home Front*, Gollancz, London, 1943, p. 101.

† Not to be overlooked is the increase of defamation-of-character cases which must be attributed to the growing nervousness of the population. Divorce proceedings increased continuously, although the greater proportion of them related to wartime marriages. cf. *Stimmungsbericht des Oberlandesgerichtspräsidenten von Bamberg an des Reichsjustizministerium* of 27 November 1943, Institut für Zeitgeschichte, Munich, File MA 430,1.

bomb sites. (In Berlin they told the macabre tale of a family who had used the 'break' between two consecutive raids to roll up their dead grandfather in a carpet for transport to the mortuary – only to discover during the 'all-clear' that the 'winding-sheet' had been pilfered, together with its contents.) Towards the end of the war the judicial extermination of so-called *Volksschädlinge* (enemies of the people) was expedited by summary S S action. Thus, in October 1944, seventeen Viennese post-office employees – who were found in a spot check to have filched bars of chocolate or soap from badly-wrapped Wehrmacht gift parcels – were marched from the Southern railway station to a near-by square and publicly executed.[39]

The legal category *Volksschädling* also comprised *Feindhörer* – people who listened to enemy radio broadcasts. Though the authorities failed to eradicate illegal listening, they were given a great deal of public support. There were instances not only of adolescents denouncing their own parents but even of mothers with missing soldier sons reporting *Feindhörer* who had given them news of their children's survival.*

The suppression of news and increasing tension encouraged superstitious rumours: Theresa Neumann of Konnersreuth (a peasant girl famed in the twenties for displaying the stigmata of Christ) was rumoured to have died prophesying an end to the war within three months.[40] This rumour was strengthened by reports that the spring in the grotto at Lourdes had overflowed. Dresdeners, demoralized by rumours that their city would be incorporated into Czechoslovakia after the war, took new heart upon seeing a cloud formation resembling Frederick the Great's profile appear above a church steeple one Sunday morning.[41] Other superstitions – borrowing from science rather than religion – attended the often postponed launching of Hitler's V-weapons. Rumours suggested that these weapons included aircraft so fast that they had to fire backwards to avoid colliding with their own missiles,[42] and gigantic compressed air pumps capable of scattering entire divisions like chaff on the threshing-floor.[43]

When the actual V-weapons did eventually materialize the Reich radio had to repeat its broadcast of a V-2 launching by insistent public demand, but subsequently the 'vengeance weapons' to which such vengeful and sanguine imaginings had been attached turned into objects of resigned humour: the V-1 was dubbed *Versager Eins* (Dud number one) the V-2 *Versager Zwei*, and so on.

* See chapter on denunciation (p. 114).

Such treasonable witticisms were not so much expressions of anti-regime feeling as safety valves for frustration and tension. But, whatever the mainsprings of political humour, the approaching end concentrated jokesters' minds wonderfully. The heavy raids on the capital, for instance, prompted a new definition of cowardice: 'A Berliner volunteering for front-line service.' The threat of Russian advance inspired this item of comfort: 'Not to worry – they'll never get across the Pyrenees.' Tribute was similarly paid to the Wehrmacht's unique *esprit de corps*: 'Whenever a soldier returned from home leave, the whole regiment came to meet him half-way.'

Spine-chilling official forecasts of whole new generations of miracle weapons occasioned the quip, 'The ultimate V-weapon will become operational at the precise moment that "closed because of call-up" notices appear outside old people's homes all over the Reich.' When men up to sixty-five were pressed into the *Volkssturm* (the last-ditch defence force set up in the winter of 1944) it was said that anyone called up for the *Volkssturm* could gain exemption if he could prove that he had a father serving at the front.

Yet it would be wrong to infer widespread disaffection – for indeed anything beyond fatalistic resignation before the inevitable – from the country-wide diffusion of defeatist jokes. The dramatic events of 20 July 1944 struck many as merely an irrelevant interruption of the main sequence of developments in the war. The reaction to Stauffenberg's deed was largely negative: the man who faced his drum-head firing-squad shouting 'Long live free Germany' was seen as a potential destroyer and not a would-be saviour of the fatherland.

This was partly because of the hermetic isolation within which the conspiracy had taken shape through necessity, and also by design and partly because the death of all anti-Nazis in the Third Reich took on a religious rather than a political aspect: their martyrdom served as vicarious atonement for German crimes rather than as a call to action by their fellow-Germans. Even the Social Democrats involved in the Officers' Plot – Leber, Reichwein, Mierendorff – acted as individuals rather than as spokesmen for the working masses they had once represented in the Reichstag.

The workers' attitude to the regime was – contrary to Gestapo expectations – overwhelmingly loyal. Even during the last winter of the war Albert Speer interpreted the 'Everything is shit – but we've still got the Führer' voiced by some fortification worker as an expression of the

General Will, and discarded an idea for assassinating Hitler by pumping gas into the Chancellery bunker.[44]*

The last phase of the war saw Germany – with isolated exceptions – still in thrall to a regime pursuing chimerical objectives at ever heavier cost to German lives and property. A tangle of short-term and long-term fears (of Nazi reprisals, for instance, or the vengeance of foreign workers in the Reich, or Allied retribution under the 'Morgenthau Plan') helped to anaesthetize the collective instinct for self-preservation.

But this automaton stance in the face of destruction cannot be explained simply in terms of fear – in spite of the fact that the Wehrmacht and SS were now summarily executing would-be deserters and civilian capitulators. Majority attitudes to the regime had never been primarily motivated by terror. The average Nazi citizen did not so much live in a state of terror as in a state of delusion tinged with delirium – and hallucinatory reflex action had almost become second nature to him.

Though the national consensus on the certainty of victory had not survived Stalingrad, subsequent reverses in the East were widely rationalized as stratagems for luring the Red Army to its doom in the centre of the continent. After D-day many people exorcized the spectre of a two-front war by viewing it as a necessary prerequisite for the East-West clash which would finally splinter the Allied Coalition. Roosevelt's death was also expected to bring this about; Hitler's last birthday a few days later was similarly expected to produce a turn of the tide.

Even anticipations of defeat were accompanied by fanciful ideas: rumours circulated about a mild gas that the Führer was keeping in reserve, and which he would use to put the Germans out of their misery rather than have them fall into the hands of Allied torturers.† At Arnheim a captured German soldier dismissed the sight of the Allied air armada crossing the Rhine with a yell of 'Propaganda!'[45] A Hamburg headmaster thought that it exceeded the bounds of possibility that German 'culture and idealism should succumb to the united materialism of the world'.[46] Defeat was similarly inconceivable to men returning from the East, who chilled their compatriots' spines with phrases full of warning

* Sitting unrecognized in a dug-out near the front (in February 1945) Speer came to the conclusion that 'they believed in Hitler as in no one else, believed that he and only he both understood the working class from which he had risen and the mystery of politics which had been concealed from the German race – only he could work the miracle of their salvation'. cf. H. Trevor-Roper, *The Last Days of Hitler*, London, 1950, p. 90.

† Such rumours were current in areas hundreds of miles apart; see chapter on ritual and Führer worship, p. 88.

innuendo: 'If you had seen what we saw you'd know we mustn't lose the war.'

A widespread awareness of atrocities among Germans was deduced by one British officer from the type of photographs found in the wallets of hundreds of captured German soldiers. These came in three sets, as it were: snapshots of *Mutti* (Mummay) and Inge, obscene postcards – and photos of floggings and executions.[47]

Similarly, civilians managed to compartmentalize their feelings. In February 1942 – months after the Yellow Star had become part of the street-scene, as broken shop-windows, burning synagogues and 'Dogs and Jews Not Admitted' notices had earlier on – an irate radio subscriber took exception to a front-line soldier's use of the phrase 'Lick my arse' (actually a quotation from Goethe's *Götz von Berlichingen*) on the air and asked what amends the broadcasting authorities intended to make to listeners who had been exposed to this obscenity.[48] A landlady at a Baltic Sea resort on whom SS had been billeted was horrified to discover Himmler's 'Procreation Order' (addressed to all front-bound SS men – single as well as married) among papers left behind; she had known all along of the existence of concentration camps.[49]

To the irate radio subscriber and the horrified landlady concentration camps and Yellow Stars were part of the natural order of things: camp inmates were anti-social elements being 'banged to rights' and preliminaries to genocide helped remove an alien presence. When shown photographs of Belsen (by a British officer) a German farmer commented 'Terrible – the things war makes happen!' as if talking of a thunderstorm which had flattened his barley.[50]

War made other things happen, too; it might have interested the aforementioned radio-subscriber to know that the gratuitous destruction of enemy and German homes by retreating Wehrmacht soldiers included the prominent deposition of excrement. Yet essentially Wehrmacht morale cracked only on the eve of surrender. The tenacious fighting spirit of the German soldier astounded the world; unlike its American counterpart, the Wehrmacht never lacked firing-squad volunteers for the execution of court-martialled soldiers.[51]*

In the east morale was cemented by fear of the 'Red Genghis Khan'; though soldiers in the west displayed a marginally greater readiness to surrender, three out of every five prisoners interrogated by the Americans in January 1945[52] still expressed confidence in Hitler, and inmates of

* See chapter on the army, p. 146.

Canadian P.o.W. camps largely doubted the truth of Allied communiqués right up to VE day.[53]

The fact that the Wehrmacht machine continued functioning in the midst of massive withdrawals induced an '*Alles klappt*' (everything is ticking over) mood which made soldiers consider the war virtually as an end in itself – quite irrespective of whether it could still be won. Loyalty to primary groups also played its part: as the realities underlying vast nebulous concepts like the Reich or the Wehrmacht disintegrated, individuals kept fighting just for the sake of their own particular company or even platoon. The primary groups into which town-dwellers broke down were shelter communities. In the words of one Berlin shelterer: 'Our cellar population are convinced their cave is one of the safest. Nothing is more alien than an air-raid shelter of strangers. Each one has its own tricks and its own taboos . . .'*

It was in the shelters that the Third Reich expired. Hitler prepared his quietus in the bunker; having taken leave of him, Goering – who six years earlier had told the Germans he would change his name to Meyer if they ever got bombed – was forced to descend into a public air-raid shelter. He jovially introduced himself as 'Herr Meyer' to the assembled shelterers, and they had sufficient equanimity to see the joke[54] – despite the fact that 600,000 of their number had been killed during the Second World War. (Total German casualties were about ten times that figure. In Berlin, 47 per cent of all dwellings were rendered uninhabitable, in the Reich 32 per cent – a proportion that also applied to destroyed or damaged industrial plant.)[55]

Soon afterwards Red Army soldiers were plundering suburban Berlin villas, and hard on their heels followed Germans intent on removing everything that could still be moved.[56] The spirit of folk community drained away like blood from a haemophiliac. Privation may have motivated looting of German property by Germany – but what of the subsequent wave of mutual denunciation? In Breughel's painting 'Two Blind Vagabonds' the one who has stumbled into the ditch still smiles – in bruised

* The account went on: 'In our old one they had a mania about water; everywhere you went, you bumped into cans, pails, pots and barrels full of dirty liquid. Frau W. tells me that in her shelter practically everybody has a thing about the lungs. As soon as the first bomb drops, they all lean forward and practise shallow breathing, pressing their sides with their hands. In the shelter where I am now they have a wall mania – they all sit with their backs against the wall, with only a gap under the ventilation shaft. When the bombs drop, there's cloth mania too – everybody covers their mouth and nose with a cloth and ties it behind their heads.' cf. Erich Kuby, *Die Russen in Berlin, 1945*, Munich, 1965, p. 179.

anticipation of the other's fall. Denunciation procured the same sort of perverse satisfaction for individuals as the Russian occupation of the eastern provinces (whose complacent peacetime existence had so jarred on West German nerves during the Allied bombing) provided collectively. It was a means of redressing the inequality of fate – particularly for informers who were persuaded that their victims had benefited more or suffered less in the course of the war than they had themselves.

A hundred and fifty years earlier Heine had thus described the reaction of the citizens of Düsseldorf to French occupation: 'They put on new faces and their Sunday clothes, looked at each other in French and said "*Bonjour*".' Now, a woman in a Berlin cellar, who resisted a Russian soldier's attempt at rape, was admonished by an irate male fellow-shelterer, 'Why don't you go along with them? Don't you see you're endangering all of us?'[57]

In Germany's Year Zero, when it was almost as unbearable to look into the future as into the past, one prediction could safely be ventured: the repeal of the law according to which the Third Reich had first formed ranks would require the most painstaking knowledge of parliamentary procedure.

3

FOLK COMMUNITY

On the threshold of statehood the Germans had voiced two great demands – for unity and for freedom. Unable to realize either during the Year of Revolutions, they purchased the former at the expense of the latter in 1870–1. But political unification – however rapturously received – was somehow not enough: there has always been a German search for a social parallel to the atavistic myths of 'Androgyne' (i.e. the creature pre-dating the division of humankind into male and female). Hence the preoccupation of such *Denker* or 'thinkers' as Hegel and Marx with thesis and antithesis and of *Dichter* or 'poets' such as Rilke, Hesse or Mann with one-ness and duality.

Moreover, in the eyes of many nineteenth-century Germans industrialization did not so much tap the hoard of the Nibelungs as open a Pandora's Box of uprooting and disorientation.

The euphoria of August 1914 resulted from the confluence of two powerful currents of feeling: the expectance of victory and relief that at one fell swoop all social and political divisions could be solved in the great national equation. After 1918, a pervasive aversion to democracy because it seemed to destroy national unity – through party warfare at the polls, in parliament and even inside the coalition governments – helped to prevent the Weimar state from putting down roots in Germany. Out of the social disorientation of the Depression (Gregor Strasser's 'anti-capitalist yearning of the masses') arose a craving for a return to the womb of community; this collective infantile regression would obliterate all conflicts – between employers and employees, town and countryside, producers and consumers, industry and craft – requiring continuous and infinitely complex regulations.

The Nazis exploited this craving for 'folk community' and evolved their own synthesis of quasi-socialist promise and quasi-capitalist fulfilment. They used the slogan of revolution to divert attention from the realities of political continuity and slaked anti-capitalist yearnings with a diet of pseudo-social change: Jews were attacked as the embodiments of cap-

italism, and department stores were boycotted. Even so, tricks of this type –
reinforced by the imposition of a 6 per cent ceiling on dividends – enabled
the Nazis to claim implementation of the key clause in their Programme,
demanding the 'abolition of the thraldom of interest'.

But, in fact, the regime's policy of effecting social change which was
purely symbolic accorded with the basic wishes and aspirations of many
Germans. Not merely the huge petit-bourgeois segment of the anti-
capitalist masses, but many workers, too, equated radical alterations in the
social structure with levelling down, and looked instead to an improvement of their own position. Pre-capitalist yearnings, i.e. the desire for the
certainties of a static traditional order, created an undertow within the
general anti-capitalist current of the period. It was of more than purely
semantic significance that, in Germany, miners' lodges bore the medieval
appellation *Knappschaften* (colliers' corporations), and that factory fore-
men, those NCO's of the industrial army, were known by the antiquated
guild term of *Meister* (Master).

The notion that the work situation was one of underlying social conflict
had never quite superseded the guild ethos of social harmony and pride in
craftsmanship. But although the survival of pre-industrial terms and
concepts in an industrialized context damped down revolutionary pressures, such pressures obviously existed – and furthermore found muted
expression after the seizure of power.

Till mid-1934 the seemingly irresistible force of under-privileged expectations lent some credibility to the revolutionary posturing of the SA
leadership – only to come up against the immovable object of Hitler's *fiat*
in the bloody dénouement of the Roehm Putsch.

Hitler's decision conformed to widely held views on social gradation;
in petit-bourgeois eyes workers or domestics often rated as 'canaille' while
figures of authority inspired deference from afar.[1]

To defuse the encounter between the 'irresistible force' and the 'immovable object', the Nazi upholders of the economic *status quo* shifted the
ground on which it took place. As a sham substitute for curtailing the
socio-economic power of the *Besitzbürgertum* (the property-owning bourgeoisie) the educated middle classes were denigrated as 'acrobats of the
intellect',[2] 'intelligence-beasts with paralysis of the spine – hothouse plants
incapable of genuine achievement – turning the ground they stand on into
a morass'.[3]

Hitler dubbed them 'rejects of nature',[4] Goebbels (the Nazis' very own
intelligence-beast) called them 'a pack of prating parasites'.[5] The SS paper

Schwarzes Korps correlated IQ inversely with male fertility: 'Intellectuals validate their claim to existence within the community by a paucity of children';[6] and the country's leading medical journal ascribed the decline in the population to the mania for educational self-improvement and social climbing.[7]

Since, in a technological society, wholesale denigration of brain-work would have ultimately proved self-defeating, a fine distinction was drawn between intelligence and intellectualism – the former denoting a healthy, the latter a treasonably depraved form of mental activity. Similar ambiguities abounded. Hitler, for instance, turned down the offer of an honorary doctorate, while Goebbels was reverentially referred to as *Herr Doktor* on every possible occasion.

Nor was verbal violence the Nazis' only device for modifying the relationship of the educationally privileged to the rest of the community. The student fraternities, in whom social and educational privilege were glaringly combined, were officially suppressed after the Heidelberg asparagus incident.* Although the grammar-school master who in 1933 encouraged his pupils to call him 'Uncle' instead of *Herr Studienrat* in token of the spirit of the folk community failed to set a trend, the new quip 'Teacher's wife is washing kiddies' bums', indicated the Nazi Women League's success in pressuring teachers' wives and other middle-class ladies into social work among large families. At the same time, classes in girls' grammar and boarding-schools were adopting some deprived child as their particular 'form baby'.[8] One of the earliest manifestations of folk community at school were the bonfires which grammar-school boys made of their own distinctive coloured caps to demonstrate the abolition of class distinction. Within the Hitler Youth leadership corps, children from grammar-schools were initially discriminated against, until the passage of time put an end both to ceremonial bonfires and to populist selection methods.† Towards the end of the thirties, most Hitler Youth officials were recruited from middle-class and academic families, and at many grammar schools matriculation candidates could once again be seen wearing their coloured sashes.[9]

Ceremonial bonfires were not the only trick the regime deployed to conjure up the folk community spirit. Hitler – the first German head of state to do so – used to walk about among the lathes and share the podium with shipyard workers during launchings. He would also personally

* See chapter on the universities, p. 320.
† See chapter on youth, p. 276.

order the release of a number of 'anti-social' concentration-camp inmates every Christmas; Streicher did the same for a handful of Communists from his Gau – the district of which he was Gauleiter – ceremoniously welcoming them back at Nuremberg as 'salvaged' members of the folk community.[10]

The Day of National Labour in 1933 saw the rector of Heidelberg University sharing a festively decorated brewer's dray with a labourer – in token of the solidarity of workers of brain and hand.[11] Similarly, Hitler's dictum 'I only acknowledge one nobility – that of labour' prompted the newspaper *Völkische Beobachter* to publish a full-length interview with a municipal dustman.[12] When some workers died in an accident on a construction site on the Berlin Underground they received a state funeral attended by the Führer himself, and the contractors and engineers involved were arraigned at a show trial.[13]

Judicial proceedings with folk-community overtones were the trial and execution in 1935 – on charges of espionage on behalf of Poland – of two titled ladies. The fact that not even gentlewomen were spared the executioner's axe created the impression of a law serenely indifferent to the finer points of pedigree.[14]

Obligatory training-camps for entrants into the learned professions were instituted, with a similar end in view. Press photographs of junior barristers scrubbing the floor on such a course at one of these camps and captioned 'Labour is an indispensable method of education'[15] carried the implication that, however well-tutored, these *Herren Referendare* were not acquainted with work as the man-in-the street was and were now being forcibly familiarized with it for their own good. A newspaper report about members of the legal profession from the surrounding districts entering a train at Cologne station for the All-German Lawyers' Congress in Leipzig read: 'The man-in-the-street was amazed at the unaccustomed sight. The high and mighty gentlemen before whom he has to stand up in the courts and who can dish out sentences to him – now they have to obey the commands of a much younger man in a brown shirt and must march in formation, so that each individual's rank and name becomes quite unimportant.'[16]

In contradiction to the 'cutting-privileged-groups-down-to-size' campaign the Nazi Party itself provided many opportunities for vested interests among its members. In a bid to obscure this contradiction the Party imposed certain self-denying ordinances upon full-time members of its organization, such as making them put in spells of unpaid factory labour (which provided extra holidays with pay for the workers they displaced).[17]

The sight of Party officials – or (as they were derisively known) *Bonzen* – relinquishing the levers of power for those of humble machinery prompted appreciative and cynical reactions. Opinions among the population as a whole depended less on what the regime actually did than on what it projected itself as doing. In this situation, semantics played a crucial role. The term 'worker', for instance, was given lofty associations of unprecedented flexibility. When Hitler addressed the Reichstag in 1938, he claimed grandiloquently, 'During the last five years, I too have been a worker.'[18] When the new Chancellery was completed early in 1939, he made a point of receiving the building workers before the diplomatic corps, and stressed the representative function of the building to his proletarian audience to mitigate the grandeur of his own quarters.[19] The sometime Nazi Minister of Agriculture, Backe, a wealthy leasehold farmer, insisted on being called a worker on every public occasion – on the grounds that during his student days he had done a few weeks' vacation work in a factory.

Some callings were apparently so lacking in social esteem that an even more prestigious term than worker was required to give them status: the spirit of folk community elevated *Dienstmädchen* (housemaids) into *Hausangestellte* (domestic employees) instead of simply into *Hausarbeiterinnen* (domestic workers).

Paradox was, in fact, an essential part of the ethos of folk community. The S A had made the appellation *Kamerad* obligatory among its members and Prince August Wilhelm of Prussia (the ex-Kaiser's younger son)was accordingly addressed as 'Kamerad Auwi' – whereas Magda Goebbels invariably called her husband's adjutant, Party Comrade Prince Schaumburg Lippe, 'My dear Prince'.[20] Despite official disparagement of the traditional term *gnädige Frau* (gracious lady) and of the associated practice of kissing a lady's hand, press photographs of Hitler showed him, year in, year out, kissing Frau Winifred Wagner's hand upon arrival at Bayreuth. The vast German Labour Front of Robert Ley, who fulminated against bourgeois customs more than most Party leaders, financed the construction of *Ordensburgen*, the training establishments of the future Nazi élite, at which hand-kissing was taught as an integral part of deportment.

While the Party and its affiliated formations spawned ever new hierarchies of rank and title, the Lord Mayor of Nuremberg circulated a memorandum to all city officials demanding that their wives should stop calling themselves '*Frau Vizebürgermeister*' (Madam Vice-Mayor) or '*Frau Stadtdirektor*' (Madam town clerk).[21] On a state visit to Dresden, Goebbels was incensed to see no one at the opera – not even the occupants of the boxes – wearing evening dress. When Gauleiter Mutschmann quoted Party statements deriding bourgeois forms of dress, Goebbels brusquely called him a vulgar Marxist.[22] Goebbels also espoused the cause of elegance in the controversy provoked by the predilection of the Nazi leadership for discarding plebeian first wives in favour of socially – and physically – more accomplished ones. An elegant woman, he argued, could absolutely transform a proletarian Gauleiter and thus make an essential contribution to the public good.[23]

What exactly constituted a contribution to the common good remained a moot point. Thus, the Honour Court for Trade and Commerce (set up to deal with unfair business practice) was asked to adjudicate on a commercial traveller's submission that a businessman who had not placed an order with him had shown himself malevolently unappreciative of his efforts and had thereby contravened the spirit of folk community.[24]

This spirit was notoriously difficult to attain in the strictly Darwinian sphere of commerce, where allegations – launched anonymously if possible – that a particular competitor had 'dodged the column' during the Great War or was advancing bogus claims to party veteran status became a common device for securing business.[25]

Elsewhere the drive towards fuller folk community bordered on the macabre. Thus, in preparing to meet their Maker the burghers of Tübingen had to forgo the props of social distinction from 1939 onwards: the municipal undertakers offered only a standard-type funeral instead of the expensive, medium and cheap varieties previously provided.[26]

Yet beneath this penumbra of social demagoguery edged with farce, the Third Reich did partly instigate and partly accelerate developments towards greater social equality, or at least upward mobility. The chief force promoting change along these lines was the Party, within which promotion depended far less on family background, wealth or education than on fanatical political commitment. Although the Party did not supersede the state machine, it spawned various parallel establishments of a fairly classless composition. The *SS Verfügungstruppe* (reserves), for instance, was both socially and educationally more plebeian than the army: while every other Wehrmacht subaltern came from officer stock, only 5 per cent of SS Junker could boast a military pedigree. Two out of every five SS subalterns just before the war had no *Abitur*, the matriculation certificate which was obligatory for army officer cadets.[27] Would-be candidates who were debarred from the foreign service by their humble origins could hope to embark on diplomatic careers via the Party's foreign political department, created by von Ribbentrop. Similarly, young hopefuls who failed to enter university could still fix their sights on glittering Party and state positions if they secured a place at an *Ordensburg* through the sheer intensity of their political commitment.

But the Third Reich provided opportunities for advancement to segments of the population far broader than the circle of would-be leaders, officers and diplomats. After some years, even non-elementary teaching careers no longer involved university attendance, and entry into the higher branches of the civil service ceased to depend on the *Abitur*. The civil service and local government service became avenues for advancement in which political qualifications could make up for the lack of academic ones; the whole of the Third Reich's proliferating bureaucracy – such as civil and local government services, the Party apparatus, industrial, agricultural, trade and craft organizations – absorbed over a million people of working-class origin.[28] During the six peace-time years of the Nazi regime, overall social upward mobility was double that of the last six years of Weimar.* However, working-class people applying for posts which would previously have gone to middle-class candidates needed to produce proof of stronger political commitment to compensate for their social inferiority.

In industry itself the scope for advancement from shopfloor to boardroom remained as small as ever; on the other hand the *Reichsberufwettkampf* (Professional Competition) – the winners of which gained vocational scholarships or promotion in their particular work spheres – attracted nearly 4 million contestants in 1939.

Some workers were susceptible to other kinds of Nazi fringe benefits. An old master craftsman reacted to a concert given by the Reich symphony orchestra at his factory in Württemberg with emotion: 'Who would have dared think that the Kaiser would send his orchestra to us here in the plant,' he said with tears in his eyes. 'Now the Führer himself has sent us his orchestra; we can never thank him enough.'[29]

Even the less gullible workers approved of the idea of folk community when they saw such symbols of lower-middle-class status as wireless sets

* Twenty-nine per cent in West Germany and 20 per cent in East Germany between 1934 and 1939, compared with 12 per cent overall between 1927 and 1934. (cf. Karl Martin Boltern, *Sozialer Aufstieg und Abstieg*, Stuttgart, 1959, p. 139).

and even motor-cars* gradually coming within their reach. And, of course, another symbol of social advancement in which growing numbers of workers invested during the Nazi period was a uniform. Dr Ley – who defined socialism as 'the relationship of men in the trenches' – decreed that the same simple blue uniform had to be worn by everyone in the German Labour Front; as a result, employers and employees could not be told apart on public occasions. In 1934, in the ranks of the 'Court of Criminal Justice' section of Berlin's May Day procession, a solitary figure in mufti – the court president – was flanked by shorthand-typists and court ushers in martial array.[30] A familiar figure on the industrial scene of the Third Reich was *Geheimrat* (Privy Councillor) Kirdorff, the octogenarian pro-Nazi coal magnate, who made a fetish of walking about in a black *Knappschaft* (collier's) uniform adorned with double rows of buttons and crossed-hammer lapel badges.

The army, too, was told to breathe fresh life into the dry bones of military folk community. In 1934 the War Office instructed Wehrmacht commanding officers to select guests for mess evenings from a much broader spectrum of local society than had hitherto been the practice.[31] However, it still took a war – specifically the casualty rate on the eastern front – to make the officers' corps broaden the social base of its recruitment.†

With magnates, judges and generals exemplifying the spirit of folk community, those at the opposite end of the social scale were not found wanting either. When the Lord Mayor of Dresden visited some of the worst slums in his city, he encountered the following scene:

Here, where the step-children of fortune live, one-and-a-half rooms and a kitchen have to suffice for a family with six children. The window looks down into a narrow dark courtyard. The air is sticky with children's nappies hung up to dry. The Winter Relief has already supplied this family with coal and potatoes. On the door panel are displayed the three last monthly plaques of the Winter Relief. Here, among the poorest of the poor, they still think of folk comrades perhaps even worse off than themselves.[32]

Despite the lack of logic in the last sentence, it would be a misrepresentation of the popular mood under Nazism to discount the reserves of idealism tapped by the propagation of the idea of the folk community.

* Although the Volkswagen did not come off the drawing-board during the Third Reich, some relatively inexpensive cars were available: the cheapest model produced by Opel or DKW cost between 1400 and 1600 marks.

† This development is dealt with in the chapter on the army, p. 139.

When the middle-class mother of a dedicated leader of the *Bund deutscher Mädchen* (or BdM, the German Girls' League) complained of the body odour exuded by her daughter's proletarian subordinates her daughter retorted: 'Do you think people like us smell any better?'[33]

Proof of folk community was provided by the miners donating a half shift per month for the benefit of colleagues who were still unemployed, by pupils of girls' secondary schools 'adopting' deprived children, and by students replacing workers so as to give them additional paid holidays.

Such acts, when suitably embroidered and magnified, gave the impression that the whole nation was finding itself through mutual aid. Even anti-Nazis proved to be impressionable: the resistance leader Carl Goerdeler (who was subsequently executed) credited Nazism with having 'taught Germany the lesson that people have to help one another'.[34]

In the religious sphere the regime even managed to pose as an agent of ecumenical enlightenment, as when it pressurized Bavarian parents into 'supporting' the desegregation of certain church schools.* The *Schwarze Korps* could claim similar intent in its report on an old people's home on the outskirts of Munich, where minor panic had broken out as a result of a fire at a nearby factory. When the sister in charge had calmed the inmates, she inquired whether the burning factory was owned by Catholics – in which case, it would be everybody's duty to pray for them.[35]

The paradox whereby the Nazis could pose as champions of tolerance in inter-denominational matters also operated in the social sphere, where political disaffection occasionally manifested itself as snob-prejudice, as, for example, in this wartime diary entry by an anti-Nazi conservative: 'It augurs well for the spirit of opposition among the respectable classes that a wealthy lady with a large domestic staff, overhearing her Bulgarian maid call the German washerwoman *"Dame"* (Lady) instead of *"Frau"* (Woman), rebuked her thus: *"She* is the *Frau, I* am the *Dame!"'*[36]

In fact, the lady of the house was right – the essential distinction between *Frauen* and *Damen*, however much obscured by social demagoguery, remained operative throughout the Nazi era.† The only changes in the basic relationship between the haves and have-nots were political inversions of the social pyramid, exemplified by janitors in apartment houses

* See chapter on religion, p. 442.

† The *Frau/Dame* dichotomy, incidentally, also reflected the persistent distinction between blue-collar and white-collar workers in industry. Clerical staff continued to be differentiated from blue-collar workers by their mode of dress (the *Stehkragen* or winged collar), by their receipt of monthly salaries instead of weekly wages, and by the type of insurance scheme to which they subscribed.

who, in their role as Party block wardens, inspired fear among their socially superior tenants. At calculated intervals the authorities took dramatic steps with the same end in view. On one occasion Goebbels even stage-managed the arrest of a director of the *Reichsbank* who had made use of a perfectly valid interpretation of the law to evict a difficult tenant from a house he owned. While the arrest of this 'plutocrat' was given maximum publicity, his subsequent release remained a non-event as far as the public was concerned.[37] Thrusts at privilege involved the spilling of printer's ink in inverse proportion to the amount of blood drawn. The *Schwarzes Korps*, for instance, indulged in a weekly ritual display of outrage at assorted trivia vaguely connected with class-differentiation: they tilted furiously at a Berlin newspaper for advising a bachelor reader against marrying someone untutored in etiquette,[38] and at a landowner for insisting that mail addressed to him should bear the inscription *Rittergutsbesitzer* (owner of a knight's estate) instead of *Herr Landwirt* (farmer).[39]

The folk-community concept was not only questionable in its social aspects; even as a national rallying cry – as in 'One folk, one Reich, one Führer' – it papered over rather than filled in deep fissures.

The supremacy of Prussian Berlin – resented ever since unification – was made even worse by Nazi over-centralization. Business and professional men in the provinces felt themselves at a disadvantage compared to their Berlin competitors, who had close access to the corridors of power. (Among businessmen the anti-metropolitan feeling was not confined to those tendering for government contracts: the 'siege economy' reduced all firms to some dependence on the state machine.) Munich, the 'capital of the movement' and the headquarters of the NSDAP – one section of which, the *Reichszeugmeisterei* (Reich inspectorate of ordnance) alone, provided employment for thousands of uniform-makers – attracted similar resentment. When Austria was incorporated, its century-old name 'Österreich' was erased from the public consciousness and replaced by the archaic term *Ostmark* (Eastern March); the creation of Greater Germany, however ecstatically welcomed, did not reduce the currency of derisory epithets – '*Piefke*' for North Germans and '*Schlawiener*' for Austrians – on either side of the abolished frontier. After the outbreak of war, Saarlanders evacuated from the military zone were pained to hear people in the reception areas call them Frenchmen from the Saar or gipsies;[40] the *Volksdeutsche* ('ethnic Germans') brought back to the Reich from various Balkan countries, whose dialects differed noticeably from current German speech, had similar doubt thrown on their ethnic authenticity.

The bombing, with its large-scale evacuations, naturally added to these regional animosities; in addition, it created a clear-cut differentiation of feeling between the vulnerable safe parts of the Reich and those which were safe for the moment. 'Most people here are Bavarians,' an Englishwoman married to a German officer wrote in her diary in 1942. 'As long as only West Germany was raided, their detachment was truly Olympian, but after last week's raid on Munich, the telephone lines from this HQ were tied up for a full ten hours.'[41] Towards the end of the war, when the hitherto unaffected hinterland was overrun by evacuees from the east, another Englishwoman married to a German noted: 'Provisions for their welfare depended entirely on measures taken by the authorities. Well-situated Germans, who still had their homes, showed little civic spirit towards the unfortunate refugees. In the country districts, soup kitchens, even if only for potato soup, could have been set up and barns set aside to shelter passers-by for the night. Something could have been done to alleviate their distress, but nothing was done.'[42]

It is difficult to gauge how much this indifference was due to regional antipathies, and how much resulted from an atrophy of civic spirit after twelve years of complete regimentation, but regional divisiveness went even further than that. As the war approached its inevitable end, the inhabitants of various regions tried to slough off their German-ness like so much reptilian skin-tissue. 'Ethnic Germans' procured the colours of their Balkan countries of origin, Alsatians called themselves Frenchmen, Bavarians drew up plans for a Catholic Free State, and the inhabitants of the Ostmark, who in 1938 had hysterically welcomed incorporation into the German Reich, rediscovered their Austrian-ness. 'When you get back to Vienna,' wrote an embittered Austrian SS man, 'you can only be ashamed that the much-vaunted golden Viennese heart has turned into something so nasty and egocentric. They threw a Sudeten woman out of the tram with the words, "First the Viennese, then the Bohemians."'[43]

The final epitaph on the folk community was written not so much by 'local patriotism', nor by the widespread German looting of German property, but by the post-war epidemic of mutual denunciation, which was more bothersome to the Allied occupation authorities than the threat of the Werwolf operations.

4

THE PARTY

Before the seizure of power, 850,000 Germans out of 66 million (i.e. one in every seventy-seven) were card-carrying Nazis; at the height of the Third Reich, Party membership stood at 8 million (out of 80 million 'Greater Germans'), thus conforming to Hitler's one-in-ten requirement for the élite of German folkdom. In other words at least every fourth German adult was a member of the National Socialist Party. But this quantitative fact, though far from insignificant, matters rather less than the qualitative aspect of the Party's overlap and interaction with other élites comprising the power structure of the Third Reich.

Partaking in equal measure of revolution and restoration, the seizure of power had obliterated certain élite groups – e.g. the Republican establishment – while elevating others. Its chief beneficiaries were industrialists, generals and top civil servants on whom a Zeus-like Führer showered a golden rain – of money or medals – as reward for their complaisance. In exchange for powers of decision-making, bosses could earn ever greater profits, and brass hats (or bureaucrats) ever higher advancement.

Their eager acceptance of this situation stemmed from misconceived notions of corporate self-interest, chauvinistic delusion and – certainly among civil servants – subservience tinged with masochism.

Such abject subservience, however, did not preclude continuous friction at the ill-defined boundary where Party and civil service prerogatives overlapped. This long-drawn-out war of attrition reflected Hitler's deliberate vagueness concerning the inter-relationship of Party and state, the competing priorities of ideology and expertise within the Nazi scheme of things, and the rivalry of two huge hierarchies with quite distinct mores and traditions.

Thus, while preferment in the civil service depended on social background and educational attainment – the precondition for entry into the administrative branch, for instance, was a doctorate, or for the executive branch, the *Abitur* – the Party's sole criterion was seniority (i.e. the length of membership). Although particularly pushing individuals with high membership numbers did occasionally claw their way to the top, basically it was only those who had joined before September 1930 – the date of the Nazis' electoral breakthrough – who ranked as Party aristocrats. Recruits of the 1930–2 vintage comprised the Party's middle stratum, while the derisively nicknamed 'March violets' (the gigantic entry of March 1933 and after) constituted the broad bottom layer.

Party and civil service were two organisms existing in a complex state of symbiosis, so that it was not always easy to ascertain which one fed parasitically upon the other. Superficially, the Party appeared to be the primary parasite, deploying over 100,000 civil servants as honorary political leaders[1] who brought a wealth of administrative expertise to the running of the Party apparatus. In addition, under the Party's job-procurement programme for old fighters (i.e. pre-March 1933 members), a large number of ill-qualified Party veterans were inserted into posts in the government service. In 1935, for instance, Hitler specifically decreed that 10 per cent of all vacancies at the lower and middle levels of the civil service should be filled by Party members who had joined before September 1930.[2]

Nazi job-procurement did not, however, benefit the Party's unemployed alone. After the seizure of power, a practice grew up whereby Nazi ward and district officials took over communal and administrative posts corresponding to their Party functions – *Ortsgruppenleiter* (local branch leaders) doubled as town mayors, *Kreisleiter* (district leaders) as *Landräte* (executive directors of rural counties) – but from 1935 onwards, these combined functions were increasingly dissolved.[3]

By 1935 it was estimated that Party members were occupying three-fifths of over 52,000 executive posts in state and communal agencies, but that only one-fifth of these officials had been Party members before 1933. In other words, the 'March violets' heavily outnumbered tried old Nazis in the administrative services.[4] This development prompted a *Schwarzes Korps* staff-writer of a particularly maudlin turn of phrase to pen an indictment of the power relationship between veterans and March violets:

'The man in the official chair tries to make it plain to you that the criterion of achievement has to apply in the first instance. You look up to the picture of the Führer hanging above his desk in its gilt frame. Your soul weeps. In self-defence, you press the small snapshot of Adolf Hitler in Landsberg prison, the treasure of your old frayed wallet, close to your heart.'[5]

The same theme also inspired the SS paper to a flight of humour:

'A: We veterans have been completely by-passed. Look at the March violets, they've pulled it off. B: How right you are! If the Führer had joined the Party later, he would also have got further.'[6]

Not only were the March violets inconsiderately blocking the access of some of the unqualified Party comrades to the feeding-troughs, the self-image of quite a few Nazis who had obtained administrative posts in local government also underwent a characteristically German transformation: they tended to look upon themselves increasingly as state officials rather than Party functionaries, so that by 1935 nearly 40 per cent of Nazi-appointed mayors and more than half the *Landräte* had become inactive in the Party.[7]

The Minister of the Interior, Frick, a bureaucrat to his finger-tips, totally dedicated to Nazism, backed the civil service in its holding action against Party encroachment. He issued memoranda – such as one to the heads of the Reichsbank and the German Railways in 1935[8] – affirming the administrative principle that the appointment and promotion of officials was the sole prerogative of the department concerned. The conflicting claims of ideology and expertise were only resolved when the Third Reich, gorged on wartime conquest, expanded its power structure enough to accommodate all job-seekers. Even so, every stage of the expansion process triggered off a new fracas. Thus, after the *Anschluss* with Austria Gauleiter Bürckel of Vienna had to apply rhetorical balm to the bruised egos of Austria's veterans. 'I know that many of you are angry because former enemies of the movement are proposing to lord it over you with increased authority here and there. This state of affairs needs to be changed, but you must also appreciate that I cannot paralyse the machinery of state.'[9] (What inflamed the Viennese Party stalwarts, incidentally, was not only the sight of better-qualified men in jobs they coveted, but also the non-Austrian Bürckel's predilection for an alien Gau clique made up of functionaries he had imported from his home province, the Saar-Palatinate.)

The erratic handling of Party state relations by many Gauleiters resulted from their holding the posts of Gauleiter and *Oberpräsident* (i.e. administrative director of the region) simultaneously; this duality of function frequently producing symptoms of schizophrenia. As long as Gauleiter Lauterbacher of Hanover, for instance, had been merely provincial Party boss, he had incited his *Kreisleiter* to make life as difficult as possible for the *Landräte* as a matter of policy. But on assuming the office of *Oberpräsident* he began to look down on his own Party apparatus as a sort of counter-administration which he could not allow to exceed its subsidiary function.[10]

Next to status, finance was a bone of contention which made the less fortunately placed Gauleiter resent their more resourceful colleagues. Party salaries were not very high, and although a Gauleiter's perquisites ranged from expropriating Jewish property to the misappropriation of Party funds (which was less widespread because it involved greater hazards), there was hardly a provincial Nazi official who did not envy Julius Streicher his considerable private income from the half-million weekly circulation of *Der Stürmer*.

Among the *Reichsleiter* (departmental heads of the Party) Robert Ley occupied a similarly envied position as leader of the German Labour Front – an organization surpassing in size and scope anything in Western history: it operated in such spheres as mass-tourism, building societies or publishing.

Julius Streicher and Ley, the most enterprising among their respective colleagues, were also the most pathologically uncouth, thus confirming the findings of a sociological study, which revealed that the highest officers of the Nazi Party had less education than middling ones and still less than ordinary members.[11] This inverse relationship of education to power within the Nazi hierarchy is related to another conclusion that emerged from the same study: the Nazi movement was dominated by plebeians who, having joined the Party early on, rose to control its administrative apparatus and retained this control throughout.[12]

There were three mutually exclusive groups among the Nazi cadres: administrators, propagandists and coercers, each of which exhibited its own social and educational traits. This, while every other propagandist was a graduate, only one out of every four administrators had a degree – a corollary of the fact that propagandists tended to be of bourgeois background and administrators of small-town or rural origin. The coercers (Storm Troopers and S S men, for instance) were the least educated and the most plebeian in origin. In the upper and middle echelons of the Party apparatus administrators who were socially and educationally inferior outnumbered the propagandists by two to one. A case in point was the Gauleiter themselves. Out of thirty Gauleiter, twenty-seven were of small-town origin, and twenty-three had received only elementary schooling. Five had been to a university, but only three had taken degrees. Among old-time Nazis with university backgrounds, every other one was in fact a drop-out; similarly, their non-academic confrères never held a job for long.[13]

Almost half the Nazi leadership came from the rural districts of southern Germany, and from a lower-middle-class background: their parents were customs officials, shop-keepers, farmers, artisans and elementary-school teachers.

Of the thirty Gauleiter, six were elementary-school teachers, ten were white-collar workers and three were manual workers (including one agricultural labourer). The social composition of the Party as a whole showed interesting similarities with that of its élite. Thus in 1935, when Party membership stood at 2½ million, its distribution was as follows: workers, 30 per cent; white-collar workers, slightly under 20 per cent; self-employed independents, the same; civil servants, 12·5 per cent; and farmers, 10 per cent. Compared to the national distribution of these groups, the farmers were 100 per cent, and the industrial workers 30 per cent under-represented, while white-collar workers were 65 per cent, self-employed independents 100 per cent, and civil servants 160 per cent over-represented.[14]

The over-representation of civil servants (and teachers) within the Party was further accentuated by their above-average participation in the corps of political leadership. The political leaders and Party functionaries made up about 20 per cent of total Party membership. In 1937 there were 700,000 political leaders, of whom well over a third came over from the teaching profession (160,000) or the civil service.[15]

Teachers and civil servants in Germany were members of socially esteemed professions; their massive presence within the Party both improved its organization and softened its plebeian image at the grass-roots level. At a more exalted level, the identification of substantial sections of the aristocracy with the Party was at least equally beneficial to its image: the Hohenzollern prince, August Wilhelm, the Dutch Queen's brother-in-law (the Duke of Mecklenburgh), the Italian King's son-in-law (the Prince of Hesse), the Duke of Coburg and the Duke of Brunswick – who was to have a daughter in the leadership of the German Girls' League and a son in the Gestapo prison – all espoused National Socialism; Prince Auwi especially set a trend which resulted in the *Almanac de Gotha* and the Party membership register overlapping quite extensively.

This mass-conversion of the aristocracy was prompted in part by failing family fortunes. The House of Lippe, for instance, sent its scions into the Party *en bloc*, and one of them, Prince Schaumburg-Lippe, actually became Goebbels's ADC. Prince Waldeck-Pyrmont – who in 1944 was to dispatch the Crown Princess of Bavaria to Buchenwald concentration camp – achieved the rank of an SS *Obergruppenführer* (i.e. General); the nobility, who formed 0·7 per cent of the total population, provided almost one in ten – 58 out of 648 – of the SS leaders, from the rank of *Standartenführer* (Regimental Commander) upwards, as well as seven out of nineteen Storm Troop *Obergruppenführer* and *Gruppenführer* (section leaders).[16] (After the Roehm purge had reduced the importance of the SA, however, these seven blue-blooded Storm Troop generals found their niche elsewhere in the Nazi power structure: for instance, Count Helldorf became police chief of Berlin, and von Killinger became ambassador to Rumania.) Even so, the aristocracy suffered some corporate disappointment in the Third Reich. Whereas aristocrats made up 16 per cent of Germany's bureaucratic and economic élite in 1925, by 1940 their proportion had been reduced to 12 per cent.[17] Hitler unequivocally ruled out the possibility of monarchical restoration, excluded members of princely houses from military commands, and set his face against the appointment of von Jagow as SA leader after the wartime death of Roehm's successor, Victor Lutze.

But this was a long-term, gradual development; beneath the trappings of social demagoguery, the basic attitudes of Nazi leaders towards the aristocracy oscillated constantly between resentment of social 'superiors' – and one must remember the small-town petit-bourgeois origins of the leadership – an inclination towards *parvenu* attitudes of deference and emulation *vis-à-vis* hierarchical figures.

At official receptions, Hitler, newly-installed as Chancellor, was visibly affected by the proximity of blue-blooded personages[18] and he addressed Party Comrade Prince Philip von Hesse with the lavish phrase 'Your Royal Highness' (an appellation ludicrously inappropriate to the quasi-revolutionary National Socialist German Workers' Party, in which the Prince was, moreover, Hitler's subordinate). As we have seen, at Goebbels's sumptuous residence, where well-bred adjutants provided tone as well as advice of the Emily Post type (on seating arrangements at dinner-parties, choice of wines, and so on), Frau Goebbels's way of addressing her husband's ADC – 'Prince Schaumburg, be so good as to pass the cigarettes' – similarly showed how overawed she was at having a sprig of the nobility dance attendance upon her.[19]

Early on in his career, Goebbels had belonged to the leftist Strasser wing of the Party, which also spawned the *'radikalinski'* Gauleiter of the east such as Koch of East Prussia, Hildebrandt of Mecklenburgh or Hanke of Silesia, all agrarian areas in which a rural proletariat subsisted in a state of semi-feudal tutelage to the landed aristocracy. Both Koch and Hildebrandt exuded a spurious mood of *les aristos à la lanterne*. The reputation of Hildebrandt, who was once a farm-labourer, rested on the murder of two estate owners – but these were acts of vendetta and not signals for a peasant rising. Indeed, it would have been difficult to find a more vivid illustration of the social situation after 1933 than the shooting-parties organized by the ex-poacher Hildebrandt, at which District Forestry Superintendent von Bulow acted as Master of Foxhounds and the gentry of Mecklenburgh was conspicuous by its presence.[20] The poacher-turned-rider-to-hounds had, in addition, been a ranker in the First World War and now craved vicarious identification with his military superiors: Countess von Schulenburg, whom he summoned to his office after the failure of the Officers' Plot to inform her of her husband's arrest by the Gestapo (which meant certain death), wryly noted that the Gauleiter's desk was dominated by a bust of her husband's father, General von Schulenburg, the Great War army commander and adjutant to the Crown Prince.[21]

Gauleiter Koch outdid Hildebrandt both as a murderer* and as a *parvenu*. High-ranking officers' wives and landed gentlewomen fawned on the '*Frau Gauleiter*' – to have black-uniformed, white-gloved SS men pour the tea and pass the cake – but criticized the drab décor and furnishings of the Koch villa in Koenigsberg, so he built himself a wartime palace with Polish slave labour. At Schloss Krasna, 'everything was just one degree too elegant, too aristocratic and too dignified. Servants shuffled silently and full of gravity through spacious rooms. Everyone disported themselves in a manner modelled on cinema counterfeits of life among the *haut monde*.'[22]

Alone among the *radikalinski*, Gauleiter Hanke of Silesia actually made an exalted marriage: an engine-driver's son, he married into an aristocratic land-owning family.[23] Though this was a unique case, its counterpart – divorce – assumed considerable prominence in the lives of Nazi cadres after the seizure of power. To the *condottieri* whom the twenty-eight short months between the electoral breakthrough in 1930 and Hitler's investiture had catapulted from obscurity to virtual omnipotence, women represented the spoils of victory quite as much as power and wealth. Some indulged their libido by flagrant promiscuity, others merely discarded their first wives in favour of sexually (and socially) more desirable substitutes.

* During the war Erich Koch was Gauleiter of the Ukraine and committed atrocities on an indescribable scale, for which he was eventually tried and hanged.

From the point of view of the Party's public relations, neither alternative had much to recommend it. Although Goebbels – himself arch-adulterer of the Third Reich – approved of the drift of low-born Nazi leaders into re-marriage, because he felt it would be conducive to social refinement, Hitler considered it politically damaging. When War Minister von Blomberg made an unwise marriage – Frau Blomberg turned out to have been a streetwalker – the Führer exploited this so as to discredit him in the eyes of his fellow-generals and to get him sacked.* He tried to stop marital instability among his paladins from becoming too obviously public; since divorce proceedings would have had that very result, he adamantly vetoed Goebbels's and Hans Frank's plans in this direction; in other words, the sexual mores prescribed for top Nazis were clandestine promiscuity balanced by the maintenance of a family façade. Himmler, on the other hand, left his wife marooned on their Bavarian smallholding and lived with his secretary in Berlin – an arrangement that was motivated by eugenic considerations rather than sexual desire, since Frau Himmler had presented the SS chief with only one child, and a female one at that.

Robert Ley was the most prominent of the many second-level Nazi leaders who acquired younger wives. He took such proprietary pride in the second Frau Ley's physical charms that house-parties at their residence invariably ended by the host drawing back curtains to regale visitors with a life-sized oil painting of his wife in the nude.[24] As time went on, the faith of the Labour Front leader in the capacity of art to mirror nature declined; to convey his wife's charms adequately to occasional callers he literally tried tearing the clothes off her back in their presence.[25]

The Third Reich was such a male-centred society that the wives of its most representative figures appeared only peripherally in the public eye. Mesdames Goering, Goebbels, Hess or Ribbentrop discharged few of the social, charitable and decorative functions incumbent upon leaders' wives in other political systems – they never visited schools, hospitals, orphanages or old people's homes. The woman who could have been described, for want of a better term, as Nazi Germany's first lady was Emmy Goering, the statuesque actress wife of Hitler's heir apparent. In the Führer's shadow, Goering combined the greatest power and popularity of any Nazi leader – the latter partly on account of his appearance (although the ravages of time and corrupt living soon turned this erstwhile over-ripe Siegfried into a malignant Gargantua). Largely because of the bizarre

* At about the same time Hitler axed his Chief of Staff, General von Fritsch, against whom Heydrich had concocted a fake charge of homosexuality.

malformation of public life, and partly because of her considerable limitations, Emmy Goering never quite lived up to her role of first lady. The only two occasions on which she fulfilled expectations being at the quasi-royal Goering wedding in 1935 and the birth of her daughter Edda two years later.

Goering, son of a colonial administrator, ex-officer and huntsman, cultivated the company of aristocrats, industrialists and military top brass, while the low-born ex-journalist Goebbels struck a new and socially revolutionary note by patronizing artists and film stars. The Führer's two closest henchmen vied with each other in the sumptuousness of their own homes and the displays and receptions arranged under their auspices. Goering's Opera Ball in 1936, for instance, at which guests of honour were drawn impartially from throne-rooms and boardrooms (the ex-Czar Ferdinand of Bulgaria and Krupp von Bohlen, the ex-German Crown Prince and Werner von Siemens), was an ornate junket costing no less than a million marks. Within weeks, Goebbels arranged a nocturnal festival at Peacock Island on the outskirts of Berlin, access to which was afforded by temporary Wehrmacht pontoon bridges. The paths of Peacock Island were lined with torch-bearing page boys in tight-fitting white breeches, white satin blouses with lace cuffs and powdered rococo wigs – drawn from the *corps de ballet* of the state theatres, as well as from the chorus lines of less august establishments in Berlin.

Since Goebbels's social contacts were less exclusive than Goering's, he had leavened the festive crowd with Nazi stalwarts, but these burly veterans of street fights and tavern brawls were so affected by the rococo setting that they hurled themselves upon the bewigged page boys and pulled them into the bushes. Tables collapsed, torches were dimmed, and in the ensuing fracas a number of Party old fighters and their comely victims had to be rescued from drowning.[26]

The Propaganda Minister's personal social circle was, of course, rather more hand-picked. Among his boon companions Goebbels numbered the author John Knittel, the portrait-painter Professor Hommel, the stage-designer Benno von Arent and the boxer Max Schmeling plus his wife (the film actress Anny Ondra). One of their favourite haunts was the *Kamerad-schaftsklub* (Fellowship Club) of German artists in Skagerrak Square, Berlin; within the intimate ambience of the club, Benno von Arent acted as procurer and the Minister charged with cleansing Germany's cultural life of all decadent phenomena sat surrounded by daringly *décolletée* starlets listening to the band playing highly suspect Broadway jazz tunes.[27]

By contrast, certain members of the Nazi élite – admittedly not figures that fired the imagination – managed to exude an ambience that was in better taste than either Goering's ornate flamboyance or Goebbels's raffish opulence. The Minister of the Interior, Frick, presided over receptions at which his wife, an impassioned amateur *Lieder* singer, entertained members of the ministerial bureaucracy and the *Bildungsbürgertum* (the cultured middle classes) who, incidentally, purchased admission to these private concerts by contributing to Nazi charities. Frau von Neurath, the wife of Hitler's first – and genuinely aristocratic – Foreign Minister,* organized knitting circles for the Winter Relief which were attended by other titled ladies. The Winter Relief was, of course, the Third Reich's top O.K. charity. Werner von Siemens, the electrical tycoon, installed six hundred gilt chairs in the vast music room of his private residence to accommodate audiences who paid handsomely to hear their host conduct the Philharmonic Orchestra at benefit concerts for the Winter Relief campaign.[28]

Despite these attempts to set out rituals of a bygone age, the tone of social life in the Third Reich showed unmistakable signs of deterioration. At the Crown Princess's Meissner Ball, Fräulein Kerrl, the daughter of the Minister for Church Affairs, could be overheard loudly discussing the forty-eight 'positions of love' with her two SS escorts.[29] On one occasion the Hohenzollern Prince Carolus took his mistress, a shop-assistant, along to the Turkish Embassy ball. When this led to a polite remonstrance, he flared up, 'After all, society's full of important Nazis who quite legally drag along ex-cooks, seamstresses and shopgirls to functions such as these.'[30] His Highness knew whereof he spoke. When the second Frau Ley was asked by the assistant serving her in an exclusive antique dealer's shop what type of tapestry she would like to buy, she answered: 'It doesn't matter which, as long as it's genuine.' At a diplomatic *soirée*, 'Frau' Himmler rushed up to Frau von Mackensen, the wife of the German ambassador in Rome, felt her dress material and exclaimed, 'What! You still have real silk?'[31]

This social inadequacy was not confined to the wives of Nazi leaders. When Storm Troop Chief Victor Lutze (Roehm's successor) sported white gloves at an Italian Embassy reception, Edda Ciano – Mussolini's daughter – inquired of Prince Philip of Hesse, 'Since when do waiters wear SA uniform?'[32] Lutze's death in a car crash during the war was popularly

---

* The noble prefix '*von*', which Ribbentrop, Neurath's successor, adopted, was highly dubious.

accredited to driving under the influence, and alcoholism, of course, constituted an almost congenital form of Nazi self-indulgence. The early
morning sight of Christian Weber – an ex-cab driver transmogrified into
the owner of a fleet of buses, a filling-station syndicate and one of Germany's finest racing stables, as well as the District President and Forestry
Superintendent of Upper Bavaria – lying prostrate in the gutter became a
regular feature of Munich life during the Third Reich.[33] The citizens of
Munich probably took this calmly because they had become accustomed
to dipsomaniacs among the top Nazis, such as their Gauleiter (who was
removed in 1942, partly for that reason) and Hitler's photographer and
art expert, 'Professor' Heinrich Hoffmann, who was known as the
'National Drunkard-in-Chief' (Reichstrunkenbold). The Party foundation
celebrations held by the old guard at Munich's Hofbräuhaus became annual high points of collective inebriation in peace and war alike.[34]

When veteran Storm Troop leaders commemorated the earliest Party
rally in Coburg at the height of the war, one paralytically drunk participant fell to his death from a second-floor hotel window. The permeation
of the state apparatus with Party protégés – and mores – had similar
results. At least one member of the Reich Cabinet, Economics Minister
Funk, was a habitual drunkard; convivial evenings attended by civil
servants could end with light bulbs and paintings being used as targets for
small-bore rifle practice.[35]

It was against this background that Robert Ley initiated in 1939 a 'keep-
healthy-through-abstinence' campaign. The campaign slogan he proclaimed at the first meeting ('Moderation is not enough') aroused doubts
in the audience as to the speaker's control over his subconscious, but Ley
showed sufficient grasp of the agenda to continue with 'We must also be
radical in abstinence!'[36]

This unusual form of radicalism did not – despite high-powered advocacy – recommend itself to the 'old fighters'; Goebbels noted in a late
wartime entry: 'During the preceding twelve years of easy living, most
Party stalwarts had completely drunk away the modicum of grey matter
which had originally brought them into the movement.'[37]

If one applies conventional criteria, even the term 'modicum of intelligence' would appear to have been a misnomer in the case of some of the
Nazi leaders. For instance, Hans Schemm, head of the Nazi Teachers'
Association and Bavarian Minister of Education, produced this proof of
learning: 'In my youth I read Praxiteles and Sanskrit, the holy book of
the Indians.'[38] The egregious Robert Ley was wont to make the most

ludicrous statements both in public and in private. He once told a factory meeting – presumably to dispel lurking feelings of intellectual inferiority among manual workers: 'A scientist considers himself fortunate if he comes across one germ in the whole of his life, while a dustman uproots thousands of them with each sweep of his broom.' Having summoned a prominent Berlin physician to his ostentatious residence in the Grünewald, Labour Front leader Ley greeted him with 'How good of you to help a simple working man!'[39]*

Julius Streicher liked to regale visitors with a tale about an old Nuremberg Jew nailing his gentile housekeeper to the cross – and would repeat this story word for word at two-hourly intervals.[40]

A similar form of mindlessness abounded in the lower ranks of the Nazi hierarchy. In 1934, when the campaign to liquidate unemployment was at its height, the mayor of Giessen announced a change of programme at a municipal concert with these words: 'Instead of the soloist Edmund Fischer, we shall now hear the Frankfurt Symphony Orchestra – another example of the regime providing work for many where previously just one man was employed.'[41]

But it would be wrong to think that Nazi officials generally lacked intelligence. A modicum of intelligence, however indistinguishable from animal cunning, was a prerequisite for holding on to any post within the power structure of the Third Reich, which was slit by the rivalry of self-aggrandizing institutions (Party, Labour Front, Food Estate, S A, S S) and headed by ruthless political operators.

Though the S S ultimately proved to be the most successful of these predatory institutions, the up- or downward shifts within the power structure were too complex for any generalization. Thus in regions where the Gauleiter was at cross-purposes with the regional S S leader, it was politically inadvisable to cultivate the friendship of Himmler's man.

On the other hand, not every Gauleiter enjoyed the reputation and backing from on high of men such as Terboyen (the Coordinator [Gleichschalter] of the Rhineland and wartime governor of Norway), or Sauckel (Gauleiter of Thüringia and Reich Commissioner for labour mobilization).

One who manifestly did not was Gauleiter Wahl of Augsburg. After

* This temperance-preaching alcoholic and horny-handed villa-owner, who, as we have seen, defined socialism as the relationship of men in the trenches, similarly showed little sign of soldierly disposition: his arrival in occupied parts of Russia, where he inspected the slave labour force, was invariably signalled by Air Force orderlies trundling a sedan-chair type of portable commode on to the airstrip just before Ley's plane touched down. (Interview with Herr Gustav Zerres, Cologne, April 1967.)

National Organization Leader (*Reichsorganisationsleiter*) Ley had declared Wahl redundant in connection with an administrative reform of the Reich, the latter immediately hared off to Berlin to remonstrate with Hitler. Having been left to cool his heels for ten hours in an ante-chamber of the Chancellery, he had to take a train back to Augsburg. But he still refused to accept Ley's dismissal notice, which, incidentally, was counter-signed by the Führer, and obstinately carried on governing his Gau. Some months later, a visit by the Führer to Augsburg was rounded off by a gala performance at the municipal theatre. After the final curtain, Hitler expressed himself highly satisfied with the standard of acting and, *inter alia*, confirmed Wahl's retention of office.[42]

In general, of course, the Gauleiter were virtually omnipotent in their region. Posts at Gau (regional) level could therefore have been expected to offer maximum opportunities for the exercise of power, but in fact the Party apparatus was such that more actual power resided with the nominally subordinate *Kreis* (district) level – a circumstance which caused many a veteran for whom seniority had procured a niche in the Gau administration to envy the March violets who, with the instinct of true time-servers, had ensconced themselves in the *Kreis* administration.[43]

Ranked lowest in the Party hierarchy were the block wardens, function-aries whose job it was to keep all the residents of a particular tenement block under the closest surveillance and to thrust the Party's collecting tins under their noses on every occasion. Because of this, the block war-dens were classed as importunate snoopers, and even within the Party apparatus the more elevated functionaries tended to give them a wide berth. Even so, the functions and local importance of the block warden increased with the passage of time. Upon orders from the Ministry of the Interior, local agencies of the central government – tax offices, for instance – granted block wardens access to confidential files, so that they could thereby supplement their own information about every one of their 'charges'. In all houses divided into flats or rooms, block wardens were in charge of Party notice boards, which featured, as well as propagandist exhortations, announcements on a whole range of topics: the address of the nearest advice bureau, details of forthcoming collections, black-out exercises, changes in the social insurance scheme or the rationing system.

Aware of the equivocal feelings with which the public regarded the Nazi cadres, the Party ordered its regional and district functionaries to set aside six hours a week for citizens' surgeries – Gauleiter Wahl claimed to have personally attended to 30,000 petitioners during his twelve-year term of office.

A great deal of popular resentment against the Party had apolitical roots and arose out of the privileges enjoyed by Party members. Since the Party had its own internal law-courts, mere folk comrades found themselves at a disadvantage when it came to initiating legal proceedings against Party members. A dentist from Gelsenkirchen, for instance, wanted to sue a Nazi dental surgeon who was accredited to the Hitler Youth, because the latter had instructed the youngsters under his care not to have treatment by anyone other than a dental surgeon. The plaintiff soon discovered his total impotence: the court ruled that, since the statement complained of had been made by the dental surgeon in his official Party capacity, the only aspect of the case which came within its jurisdiction was the investigation of whether he was, in fact, a Party official and whether he was entitled to give such advice.[44]

The privileged status of Party members was complemented by negative sanctions: expulsion from the Party frequently involved dismissal from one's job. For lapsed Party members in the civil service or the teaching profession, dismissal was automatic; attempts were made to extend this practice into all spheres of employment; but in a remarkable judgement the Kottbus Labour Court ruled that dismissal was warranted only when the work of the expelled Party member encompassed specific obligations to the National Socialist state, and found that this did not apply to the plaintiff before them, who was a gardener in a cemetery.[45]

Another judicial problem connected with Party membership was the contentious issue of whether Party comrades ought to be judged more rigorously than folk comrades. When a veteran Storm Trooper received a severe sentence for non-payment of the car registration tax, the local court added the rider, 'More can be demanded of veterans', but the Court of Appeal quashed the sentence and ordered a re-trial, stating that 'services rendered to the movement ought to bring about a reduction rather than an increase of punishment'.[46] An old Party stalwart who had been passed over in the allocation of spoils felt sufficiently assured of his facts to state quite openly in a petition to Hitler, 'I must be the only veteran of the movement not to have gained any advantage through the revolution of 30 January 1933.'[47]

As far as its public relations were concerned, the Party did, of course, try to create the impression that its members were expected to have higher standards than other people. A court case in which two greengrocers who had exceeded price regulations were respectively fined forty and twenty marks – the heavier fine being imposed on the Party member – elicited full approval of the *Schwarze Korps*. 'The public reacted positively to the sentence, which provides clear refutation of rumours about nepotism.'[48]

During the war, when it was widely alleged that, in contrast to the 60 per cent communist party membership among Russians serving with the Red Army, only 35 per cent of NSDAP members were on active service in the German forces, the Party retaliated by publishing casualty statistics showing that the percentage of Storm Troopers and SS men killed was proportionately higher than in the population as a whole.[49]

The NSDAP now asked its members to perform boy-scout type good deeds to endear the Party to the people. Party comrades were expected to volunteer for work on fortifications, to help clear air-raid damage, to do welfare duties among refugees, to volunteer for the *Waffen SS*, etc. It was also during the war that the Party produced two notable additions to the fauna populating the bestiary of the Third Reich: 'birds of death' and 'golden pheasants'.* 'Birds of death' was the popular term for Local Branch leaders who had the onerous duty of informing soldiers' families of the death of their next-of-kin, and sometimes arranging the subsequent ceremonies (an innovation which helped the Party's ambition to supplant the Church as the prime dispenser of spiritual solace in wartime). 'Golden pheasants' was a term applied to the gaudily uniformed functionaries staffing the higher Party administration, especially in the occupied territories; it implied self-importance, ostentation and inordinate cupidity.

Lastly, what of the Gauleiter? Their image of themselves as territorial princelings obliged them to dispense parochial patronage – as when, after 1939, they would procure exemption from the armed forces for local athletes, so that they could compete in war championships for the greater glory of their particular region.[50]

Von Schirach, Gauleiter of *Kulturzentrum* Vienna, did not let the pressures of war deter him from arranging special birthday celebrations for the doyens of German drama and music – Gerhart Hauptmann and Richard Strauss. He installed Hauptmann in the baroque Palavicini Palace and presented Strauss with a specially designed diamond-tipped baton.[51] Hitler, who in the course of his visit to Rome in 1938 had contravened Italian court ceremonial by shaking the hand of Beniamino Gigli at the end of a

---

* The fact that the German eagle was one of the most notable features of the Party uniform inspired a crop of ornithological nicknames for Party officials.

palace concert, ordered Wieland Wagner's exemption from military service,[52] and instructed Goebbels to do the same for a whole range of prominent artistic personalities.[53] Goering, who considered that the artists at the Prussian state theatres were his personal court jesters, indulged his pretensions to the role of *grand seigneur* by arranging Easter garden parties at which he personally concealed the coloured eggs which actors such as Gustav Grundgens or Käthe Dorsch had to search for.[54] Even Julius Streicher posed on occasion as a patron of the arts; he assisted in the production of the film epic *Das ewige Herz* by enlisting the aid of Nuremberg's entire Party membership and Storm Troopers as medievally attired extras, and ordered the removal of all tram-wires, electricity cables and so on from the city centre to lend verisimilitude to location shots.[55]

No episode in Party history exuded a stronger Renaissance flavour than the wedding in June 1934 of Gauleiter Terboven at Essen. The capital of the Ruhr became one vast backdrop to processions and speechifying, while fireworks, floodlighting and 20,000 torches (borne aloft in military formation) lit the night sky. The Lord Mayor of Essen toasted the bride as 'a tender flower sprung from forebears of hardest steel',[56] and Hitler lent mythic significance to the nuptials by his presence. Next morning, he flew south to direct the massacre of the SA leadership (the 'Roehm Putsch'), the plans for which had been drawn up actually during the wedding celebrations.

During the war the Gauleiter's Renaissance aspirations found their most marked expression in a trend towards territorial particularism. Backed by Bormann, they resisted Speer's centralizing measures in an effort to keep the economies of their regions intact, hindered the transfer of skilled workers elsewhere, and delayed the closing down of consumer-goods industries.[57] In an attempt to court popularity they circumvented directives concerning the intensification of work and the reduction of living standards, which the central authorities deemed to be essential to the successful continuance of the war. Rationalizing this subtle form of sabotage, they claimed that by helping to keep up morale they were furthering rather than impeding the war effort. Nor should another aspect of the wartime record of some Party cadres be overlooked: in situations which overtaxed the resources of civil servants – accustomed as they were to working through the usual channels – Party officials usurped the local functions of the government machine by directing the re-allocation of labour, the distribution of food, the evacuation of refugees and the building of fortifications. Even though Party officials were more corrupt in discharging these tasks than civil servants, some of them still displayed the energy and skill that had enabled them a dozen years earlier to provide the driving-force for the transformation of German society from democratic torpor to totalitarian mobilization.

5

RITUAL AND FÜHRER
WORSHIP

In the winter of 1937 the following news item appeared in the Press: 'New housing estate in Braunschweig-Lehndorf, which has been in the course of construction since 1933, includes a Protestant church without a tower. The entire settlement will be dominated by the tower of the *Aufbauhaus* which is going to be the local Party headquarters and the hub of public life.'[1]

This announcement illustrated what is probably the pithiest description of National Socialism ever formulated: 'Catholicism without Christianity.' The central organizing principle of the pseudo-religion of Nazism was to obscure a total lack of transcendence by means of ever-larger infusions of ritual. (Nazi pseudo-religion in this context does not signify the German Faith Movement which – whatever Hitler's post-war intention – was not strenuously promoted during the Third Reich, but the officially fostered attitude of reverence towards the Party, its personnel, history, practices and aims.)

A key device for inculcating this mood of reverence was the institution of a cycle of high holy days, which leavened the mundane routine of the year with uplifting occasions. In this way, a sequence of Nazi red-letter days – 30 January (Day of the Seizure of Power), 24 February (commemmorating the Nazi Party's foundation), the National Day of Mourning in March, Hitler's birthday on 20 April, May Day (rechristened the National Day of Labour), Mothering Sunday, the Day of the Summer Solstice, the annual Reich Party Rally at Nuremberg, Harvest Thanksgiving Day, 9 November (Anniversary of the 1923 Munich Putsch) and the Day of the Winter Solstice – was evolved, which bade fair to supplant the Christian festivals, with the obvious exceptions of Christmas and Easter. Actually, the Nazis parodied the Easter celebration of death and resurrection in two of their festivals: the National Day of Mourning and the Anniversary of the Munich Putsch. Before 1933, the National Day of Mourning had been closely linked with the work of the association for the care of German war cemeteries and celebrated in a manner implied in its name. The Nazis rechristened it 'Heroes' Remembrance Day'* and gradually drained it of its original mournful associations – annually scoring (whether by accident or design) a bloodless military triumph on or near that date with clockwork regularity: the reintroduction of conscription in 1935, the remilitarization of the Rhineland in 1936, the incorporation of Austria in 1938, and the annexation of the rump of Czechoslovakia in 1939. In 1939 they also lifted the restrictions on public entertainments, hitherto in force on that day, permanently fixed it for 16 March (instead of on Reminiscere – the fifth Sunday before Easter – as previously), renamed it the 'Day of the Restoration of Military Sovereignty', and gave it the motto, 'They have not died in vain'.[2]

Thus, within a short time, past grief was overlaid by exultation, seemingly meaningless bereavement was made meaningful by subsequent triumphs, and death was robbed of its sting.†

The next important festival was 20 April, Hitler's birthday – heralded by the ubiquitous twig and flower garlanded photos of the Führer in gilt frames displayed in shop windows, and the drenching of house fronts in a sea of red bunting dotted with white circles offsetting black swastikas. The focal ceremony of the day was the induction of new entrants into the Party political leadership corps at the Königsplatz in Munich – a nocturnal mass-initiation rite, which used searchlights, pylons, flaring torches, flags, drumbeats, fanfares, massed choruses and the sternly classical backdrop of the Party's administrative buildings to spectacular theatrical effect.

All the (German) world was the stage of the subsequent festive occasion, the Day of National Labour, which overshadowed every other event in the Nazi calendar in terms of sheer mass participation. The Nazi May Day ritual combined two disparate traditions – the industrial one of banner-waving, marching columns; and the Arcadian one of garlanded junketings on the village green.

Rural eve-of-May-Day celebrations comprised felling maypoles, lighting bonfires and the proclamation of the May King and Queen.[3]

---

* Similarly the Hamburg war memorial was changed from a sculpture of a weeping mother holding a child to that of a rampant eagle. *Manchester Guardian*, 16 November 1938.

† On the occasion of Heroes' Remembrance Day in 1939, the *Berliner Illustrierte Zeitung* published a cartoon showing a wizened old mother with a steel helmet on her lap and a photograph of her son on the sideboard, with fir-twigs round it. The caption was: 'By living with them in thought, one can bring the dead back to life.' *Berliner Illustrierte Zeitung*, 10 March 1938. For a related example of Nazi techniques designed to turn death into a non-event, see the chapter on cinema, p. 388.

Next day the May Queen rode in procession, flanked by 'honour formations' of the Party and the armed forces, with folksong and dance groups in regional costume and garlanded carts symbolizing crafts, farming or trade. The procession passed beneath triumphal arches adorned with the Party symbol of sovereignty (the stylized eagle clutching a wreathed swastika). In the industrial urban centres, employees assembled at their work-places, whence they marched – alongside their factory leaders – to central May Day rallies, which were followed by Bank Holiday diversions in the afternoon and evening.*

On Mothering Sunday, the second Sunday in May, crosses of honour were awarded to prolific mothers at public ceremonies: a number of regions also evolved the practice of decorating houses where children had been born during the preceding year with wreaths or the so-called Rune of Life.[4]

The summer solstice was celebrated with nocturnal bonfires into which commemorative wreaths (dedicated to the memory of war heroes or Party martyrs) were tossed. After the chanting of *Feuersprüche* (literally: incendiary incantations) pairs of participants leapt across the flames to the accompaniment of gongs; later they lit torches from the waning fire and formed ranks for the homeward procession.

The centre-piece of the larger solstice ceremonies were known as 'fire speeches'; in Berlin's Olympic Stadium, Goebbels annually addressed a crowd of a hundred thousand.[5]

The whole ritual year came to a climax with the rally at Nuremberg where (to quote the official phraseology) the marriage between Party and people was consummated anew year after year. What set the Party Rally apart from other Nazi festivals was not only its duration, but also the vast number of rehearsed actors rather than manipulated extras (as on May Day) participating in it. Thus, at a nocturnal consecration ceremony on 10 September 1937, 100,000 members of the political leadership corps of the Nazi Party marched past Hitler, bearing 32,000 flags and banners. The whole of this vast spectacle was enacted under a 'light dome' 800,000 metres high formed by vertical searchlight beams stabbing into a black sky.

At Nuremberg, parodies of Christian worship alternated with atavistic

* All this created an atmosphere in marked contrast to Weimar May Days, with their ambience of class struggle and agitation, or of resigned, listless masses performing an annual ritual in which they had long ceased to believe. Karl Heinz Schmeer, *Die Regie des öffentlichen Lebens im Dritten Reich*, Paul and Co., Munich, 1956, p. 85.

rites: when Hitler annually consecrated new Party colours by touching them with one hand while his other hand clasped the cloth of the bullet-riddled *Blutfahne* (the 'blood banner' allegedly drenched in the gore of Nazi martyrs killed during the abortive Putsch of November 1923), he acted as a priestly medium transmitting the magical *fluidum* of the old sacred symbol through his body to the new ones.[6] Within weeks of the September Party Rally, Hitler again played a central role at the Bückeberg Harvest Thanksgiving ceremony, where he arrived after driving through a hundred decorated 'harvest gates' in various villages *en route*. He ascended the slope of the Bückeberg amidst a great concourse of farmers and their families to officiate at the award of the harvest crown before a harvest altar laden with fruits of the soil;[7] the ceremony ended spectacularly, if incongruously, with motorized Wehrmacht units fighting mock battles across the terrain at the foot of the hill. This celebration of the Reich Food Estate was paralleled in parochial ceremonies all over the countryside, during which farm workers with long periods of service received awards, while the Nazi village bigwigs became inebriated with their own verbosity and alcohol.

The 9 November, by contrast, was a uniquely holy occasion on which the venerated cadre of the survivors of the Munich Putsch silently re-enacted their march through the crowd-lined streets of the Bavarian capital in a bombastic travesty of the Passion Play.[8] Their march route to the *Feldherrnhalle* was an evocation of the Stations of the Cross – with one signal difference: the Saviour marched upright, grim-visaged and jackbooted, in the front rank of his disciples; Calvary and Resurrection had blended into one sombre, soul-stirring event.

Soul-stirring is an apt term – connoting both the hallucinatory response and the restless emotionalism elicited by Nazi ritual. If the first casualty of war is usually truth, then the very first casualty of the Third Reich was calm and equanimity. (See Friedrich Georg Jünger's underground poem 'Burst with cannons the air/I cannot tolerate laxness. Silence borders on treason./Evermore shall your brow drip with sweat of applause.') The regime's immense thrust stemmed from its capacity to make increasing numbers of Germans regard themselves as anonymous combatants with leave-passes revocable at a moment's notice, rather than as individuals rooted in their civilian existence. Turned outwards upon the world, the Nazi dynamic produced cumulative aggression: turned inwards upon the Germans, a permanent 'stand-by' syndrome. All complex social organisms involve their members in diverse but simultaneous roles – within the family, the work situation, the local community, etc.; the Third Reich, in contrast, conditioned its subjects to act out on command a single role to the exclusion of all others.

To prise the individual loose from his roots and habits, the regime made the intervals between ritual occasions and foreign-policy triumphs vibrate with urgency. Martial music established the pulse-beat, and parading columns – a riveting sight in German eyes both during the days of Imperial surfeit and in the time of Republican dearth – gave a dimension of excitement to the daily street scene. The American journalist Shirer recorded in his 1934 diary that he had to keep ducking into stores to avoid having to salute the standards of passing S A or S S battalions – or risk getting beaten up for not doing so.[9] (In a court case arising out of an onlooker's failure to salute the flag, the public prosecutor stated: 'Although there is no law enjoining a compulsory salute, the custom of this greeting has nevertheless established itself and non-adherence to it is therefore an obvious act of provocation.)'[10]

Most Germans did as they were told – partly from fear of reprisals, but also because onlookers reacted to the martially disciplined sight[11] of goose-stepping S A columns with a mixture of fascinated revulsion and vicarious identification. Such identification grew steadily less vicarious as more and more Germans – to paraphrase Lenin – 'voted with their feet'; their cumulative subjection to the thump of march-rhythms and songs resembled brain-washing. The song 'as a montage of slogans gradually transforms reality in favour of the expressed idea, provided it is sung often enough and gradually assimilated by the psyche. The associations set up by the rhythm of the march are transmitted to the whole of the body and defection from the marching column appears tantamount to the loss of content of one's previous existence.'[12]

As a Party owing its success to the spoken rather than the printed word, the Nazis deployed all available resources of aural and visual décor in orchestrating* the ritual of their meetings[13] – and frequently achieved an effect aptly summarized by Goebbels in 1932: 'The *Sportspalast* roared and raved for a whole hour in a delirium of unconsciousness.'[14]

The mood of such meetings was widely disseminated by radio, and procedures were devised whereby listeners could join the direct participants in

* Orchestration was indeed the operative term. The stage managers of the Nazi Party had their own decibel scale for the volume of applause to be achieved on ritual occasions: when the U-boat hero Gunther Prien and his crew were fêted, the Berlin political Party leadership was ordered to produce '*NS-Jubel dritter Stufe*' (peak volume National Socialist jubilation). cf. Walther Hagemann, *Publizistik im Dritten Reich*, Hansische Gilden, Hamburg, 1948, p. 75.

these orgies of self-intoxication. Communal listening was obligatory in factories and offices: in restaurants and cafés all noise had to be kept to a minimum,* waiters stopped serving, and individual diners felt embarrassed to continue chewing their food in this reverential atmosphere. If this atmosphere could not be created, then (according to a Ministry of Propaganda directive to the catering trade),[15] the onus was upon the *restaurateur* to switch off the radio, lest the ceremoniousness of the occasion be marred by the clatter of cutlery and plates.

The ritual of public meetings was invested with additional elevation by the nomenclature employed. They were often called *Appelle*, a word with a double connotation: militaristic (cf. *Morgenappell* – roll-call) – and spiritual (e.g. *Appell an das Gewissen* – an appeal to one's conscience).

The *Lager* – straightforward training camps for the Party formations or 'educational' camps for members of the professions – played a key role in inculcating ritualistic responses. Camp ritual depersonalized participants by weakening their links with family life; prised loose from the context of their civilian existence, people became more susceptible to indoctrination. The entire conditioning process was geared to producing what we have termed the 'stand-by' syndrome: the notion that private life was no more than an indeterminate period of leave from which the individual could be recalled to active service at short notice.

Another instrument in the process of depersonalization was the uniform. Pressed into a semi-military tunic, the wearer shed his civilian status, and frequently had to take orders from men socially and professionally beneath him – this, too, undermined the foundations of the ego, and cut the individual off from his social bearings.

In another context, uniforms were a vital part of the Third Reich's visual backcloth. Their very ubiquity and variety created an awareness of the vastness of power residing in the Reich. Every Nazi functionary with executive responsibility was termed a 'bearer of sovereignty' (*Hoheitsträger*); the thicker the bearers of sovereignty were on the ground, the higher the sum total of the power they represented seemed to loom up to the sky.

Uniforms are not much fun without medals. A new medal for soldiers

* A citizen of the Third Reich visiting Italy remarked on the absence of German 'bestial seriousness' with which similar ceremonies were performed there. At the Opera, although the entire audience stood and raised their right arms during the obligatory playing of the *Giovenezza* (the Fascist anthem), private conversations continued, sweets were offered round, doors banged and children made a noise. cf. Erich Ebermayer, *Denn heute gehört uns Deutschland*, Vienna, 1959, p. 261.

injured in the Great War, minted twenty years after the event, was applied for by nearly half a million veterans,[16] ten per cent of whom had their hopes dashed, since they could only prove illness and not injury. Medallists formed nation-wide associations with their own ritual. Thus, 1,200 members of the National League of Wearers of the Life-saving Medal – aged from eight to eighty-six – celebrated their *Reichstunde* (the 'national hour' set aside for them) by marching through the Lustgarten in Berlin.[17]

The authorities devoted a great deal of care to the medal ritual: wearers of the Cross of Honour of the German Mother, for instance, were provided with miniature replicas of their decoration for everyday use (the original was reserved for ceremonial occasions), but the authorities did not always gauge correctly the number of would-be medallists. At the award of 'western rampart' badges of honour the Party and SA functionaries in charge received priority, with the result that the actual construction workers had to go short.[18] Private enterprise, however, rose to the occasion: cheap stores hurriedly procured 'western rampart jewellery' (commemorative rings, brooches or tie-pins), which satisfied a real demand among fortification workers and their families.[19]

This brings us to the application of ritual to industrial life in the Third Reich – an endeavour producing great diversity as well as some bizarre innovations. A Württemberg factory arranged for two employees to entertain the work-force every morning with a song or a tune on the mouth-organ as a regular overture to the day's labours.[20] A Magdeburg firm substituted fanfares for the customary siren blasts at the beginning of the mid-morning and lunch breaks. Morning and evening roll-calls took the place of clocking-in and clocking-out.[21] (This was an innovation particularly dear to the heart of Labour Front Leader Dr Ley.) A Leipzig model plant* instituted a peal of bells to signal the beginning and end of the day's work – a pseudo-religious ritual which the local German Labour Front boss justified by stating that creative work was the highest blessing known to Germans.[22]

The notion of blessing, in the sense of 'it is more blessed to give than to receive',† also dominated what was to become the Third Reich's gratuitous ritual *par excellence*: the Winter Relief. From 1937 onwards, when Germany overcame the effects of the Depression and there were more

* Awarded by the German Labour Front to firms who improved safety and hygiene arrangements and provided special amenities such as washrooms or canteens for their staff.

† This quotation from the Bible was actually used by Goering when he rattled a collecting-tin in person during Berlin's 1934 Winter Relief campaign. cf. Willi Frischauer, *Goering*, London, 1950, p. 119.

vacancies than job-seekers, the Winter Relief campaign was a form of activity purely for its own sake, and as such exactly served the regime's aim of permanent emotional mobilization. Thus a vast collecting and publicity machine kept moving into top gear afresh each winter under manifestly false pretences; even wartime collections of comforts for the troops served less as antidotes to what, in some instances, amounted to genuine deprivation, than as levers for manipulating popular feeling and eliciting a self-sacrificing response. (Goebbels himself had the candour to call the winter 1941 textile collection for the Eastern Front 'a retroactive plebiscite'.)[23]

Considerable ingenuity went into devising the Winter Relief campaigns. As we have seen, one of the chief ritual innovations was the monthly 'one-pot meal', which meant that the bill of fare in every German household was reduced to just one course; all the money thus saved was to be donated to the Winter Relief. At times this essentially private ceremony was celebrated publicly: in 1937 the Mainz carnival procession included thirty mobile field kitchens escorted by chefs and guards dressed in white. At the procession's terminal point, large tables were set out in the open, where the public could partake in a simple meal of pease pudding and bacon to the accompaniment of military music.[24]*

One Winter Relief ritual was so widely practised that it became part of the public scene; this was the collection drive. Every winter, from October to March, special monthly plaques were sold and purchasers displayed them on their front doors. This gave them temporary immunity from the avid collectors who indefatigably pounded the staircases of apartment houses in the large towns, rooting out the last possible donor.

This type of collecting was the prerogative of the dedicated rank and file, whereas more highly publicized public collections were occasionally undertaken by film stars, athletes, and leaders of Party and state.

At this point, His Excellency Foreign Minister von Ribbentrop manned a collecting pitch. Laughing, the Minister expressed satisfaction at the way Berliners were making their sacrifices. The crowd engaged in hearty banter and exchanged friendly greetings, coins rattled, a band played, two workmen danced and others joined in the singing. A man who had managed by luck to push his way through the crowd handed a rose to the lady with the collecting tin, Magda

---

* Communal feeding with pease pudding was, according to the *Westdeutscher Beobachter* of 9 October 1935, a commemorative ritual, since pease pudding exuded the aroma of the barrack square. 'It is out of the hail of shells from the enemy's cannon and out of the steaming cauldrons of the field-kitchens that the generation from which Germany's present leadership is drawn was moulded.'

Goebbels, the wife of the Minister of Propaganda. When the police asked the crowd to move on, a female voice was heard, 'But I must look her in the eyes'.[25]

The interaction between rulers and ruled which expresses itself in democracies in ritual inversion of the power structure at elections (when the ordinary citizen fleetingly exercises the casting vote over those who normally have the casting vote over him) was travestied here by leaders who, cap – or rather collecting-tin – in hand, pleaded with the led for gifts.

The pressures brought to bear on those who resisted supplication varied. Berlin was toured by an open *Schwarzes Korps* van, from which SS men chanted the jocularly spine-chilling chorus, 'Quickly pull your pennies out or you'll appear in the *Schwarzes Korps*' at bystanders.[26] At times, the Winter Relief organization itself put ominous notices in the Press. 'The retired *Rechnungsrat* (finance counsellor) Amberger has not donated one pfennig since the beginning of the 1934–5 campaign, although he draws a monthly pension of four hundred marks.'[27] Small rural communities erected what were known as Boards of Shame, listing those who 'despite financial ability, refuse to make donations'.[28]

Not infrequently, 'selfish elements' were victims of organized physical violence: 'Widow B. of Volksdorf, who had only contributed riding-boots to a Winter Relief collection of clothing, had to ask the police to take her into protective custody after a threatening crowd gathered outside her house and started to smash her greenhouses.'[29] 'Hereditary farmer Bernard Sommer of Krempdorf, who had told the collectors that if they wanted any fruit from him they were at liberty to pick it off the trees themselves, had to be taken into protective custody when a crowd of hundreds gathered round his farm chanting demands for his imprisonment.'[30] The denigration of helpless individuals took many forms: the District Party Headquarters in Duderstadt announced cryptically that 'hereditary farmer' Josef Bohme of Weissenborn, who had donated three pounds of mouldy fruit, was now 'exposing himself to the scorn of the entire National Socialist orientated population'.[31] In a different context, the caption beneath a photograph (published in the *Schwarzes Korps*) [32] of a village group giving the Hitler salute, ominously identified one person in the background – Pastor Erich Gans of the confessing church, incumbent at Niederbieber – who had failed to raise his right arm. After the plebiscite of spring 1936 a banner stretched across the main street of a hamlet near Neustrelitz bore the inscription:[33] 'Take note. In this village reside thirty-three traitors to their country. Anyone interested in their names need only inquire at the local Party Office.'

New ceremonies that served to engender sadistic *frissons* (or frozen indifference) in the onlooker were evolving continuously. One March morning in 1933 an Englishwoman resident in Saxony was amazed to see political prisoners under SA guard scouring the road surface with Bath brick and scrubbing brushes (to expunge the anti-Nazi slogans they had whitewashed in a few days earlier), while postmen, bakers' roundsmen and others continued on their lawful business – circumspectly picking their way past the prostrate figures without a flicker of surprise.[34] Local signposts pointing to Dachau (the site of the infamous concentration camp) assumed the form of woodcarvings on which mirthful SS men beckoned to Jewish and criminal-looking characters humping bundles of swag.[35]

During the autumn of 1935 Sunday afternoons in Berlin's fashionable Kurfürstendamm were hideously enlivened by Storm Troop squads positioning themselves on the pavements, whence they bellowed renderings of 'When Jewish blood spurts from the knife, things go twice as well' or 'SA comrades, string the Jews up, put the jobbing politicians against the wall' at 'captive' audiences in crowded open-air cafés.[36]

At Nuremberg a jeering crowd of 2,000 people formed up in procession behind the cart on which Storm Troopers trundled a girl through the streets in the manner of a medieval penitent being taken to the stocks: her hair had been shaved off and she bore a placard with the inscription, 'I have given myself to a Jew.'*

Allegations of race pollution in the Nazi Press instantly brought lynch-mobs upon the scene. At Königsberg, where, according to the *Schwarzes Korps*,[37] a Jew had enticed a seventeen-year-old girl employee into midnight bathing in the nude, and only an SS patrol's timely arrival had prevented the girl from committing suicide, a mob a thousand strong besieged the Jew's house and forced the police to take him into protective custody.

---

* The Nazi authorities also saw a socially prophylactic value in the placard method of pillorying recalcitrants. At Hoyerswerda notorious drunkards were made to walk through the streets with placards stating: 'I have drunk away the whole of my wages' (cf. *Frankfurter Zeitung*, 8 December 1934), and, according to *The Times* of 17 August 1938, Austrian children sent to stay with foster-parents in the Reich during the summer of 1938 had to wear placards proclaiming, 'I stole from the foster-parents who befriended me', round their necks upon their return to Vienna.

Occasions like those proliferated, reaching a climax in the November pogrom of 1938, when literally millions of Germans witnessed nation-wide ceremonies of arson, vandalism, pillage, battery and homicide. When the war came, visible sadistic rituals (inside Germany, at least) were partly toned down – although all over Thüringia a mobile three-branched gallows was used for the public execution of Polish land-workers charged with race pollution. Just as the Germans had become conditioned to earlier forms of ritual in peacetime, so they now readily adapted to a visual environment in which no street scene was complete without clearly marked stigmata: Poles with the large letter P on their jackets, Ukrainians with blue-and-white shields and the word *Ost* (East), Jews wearing yellow stars and so on.

The most frequent and widespread adaptation to Nazi ritual in the Third Reich was of course connected with the Nazi salute. The obligation incumbent upon all citizens to use the 'Heil Hitler!' greeting on every occasion was one of the most potent forms of totalitarian conditioning conceivable.*

There were some who employed all sorts of stratagems, ranging from feigning not to recognize acquaintances in the street to an infinitesimal movement of the right arm accompanied by an inarticulate mumble, so as to avoid having to make the hated gesture; but most people grew completely used to this unusual form of greeting within months of the seizure of power.

In the autumn of 1933 a Dresden woman was observed telling her little daughter, 'Go over to the auntie on the other side of the road, *und mach hübsch dein Hitlerchen!*' (and perform your 'Heil Hitler-kins' like a good little girl).[38] Even so, the prescribed ritual created problems of its own – as exemplified by these guidelines to punctilious conduct proffered by a Nazi counterpart of Dale Carnegie:[39]

If people belong to the same social group, it is customary to raise the right arm at an angle so that the palm of the hand becomes visible. The appropriate phrase that goes with it is 'Heil Hitler' or at least 'Heil'. If one espies an acquaintance in the distance, it suffices merely to raise the right hand in the manner described. If one encounters a person socially – or through any other circumstances – inferior to oneself, then the right arm is to be fully stretched out, raised to eye-level; at the same time, one is to say 'Heil Hitler'.

And, as a rider:

* See chapter on the Third Reich, p. 27, and, for a more detailed analysis, Bruno Bettelheim, *The Informed Heart*, London, 1961.

The greeting should always be carried out with the left arm if one's right arm is engaged by a lady.

Similarly, when the Minister of Postal Communication enjoined the Nazi salute upon the entire personnel under his jurisdiction (which included a proportion of wartime cripples and other disabled people) he added that any who were impeded in the use of the right arm should, as far as possible, raise the left one. There were other Gordian knots that required official cutting; for instance, the Minister of Justice was asked whether bailiffs carrying out sequestrations of property should omit the German form of greeting in the course of their duties. He decided that to deny them the right to tender the German form of greeting would involve a disparagement of the status of bailiffs as receiving officers.[40] On the other hand, the German Labour Front announced in 1933 that dismissal notices issued by firms, especially at Christmas time, were not to end with the phrase 'Heil Hitler'.[41]

Consideration of the problems involved in tendering the Hitler salute either orally or in writing brings us to Hitler himself, the deity who gave meaning to the whole elaborate structure of Nazi ritual. The relationship between the German people and its leaders was quite different from the situation which generally existed in other countries in the West, whose leaders tended to be little more than their compatriots writ large.

In Germany, especially since Bismarck, leadership had been popularly conceived as existing in some extra-terrestrial dimension of its own. Typical of this was the glory-besotted Kaiser, who, at a time when horse-power had long superseded the horse as a status symbol, signed his state papers balanced on a saddle-mounted chair.

Hindenburg, the totem President – aptly dubbed 'the wooden Titan' – presented a similarly larger-than-life image.

In between the Emperor and the Field Marshal the chief magistracy had devolved upon the ex-master-craftsman Ebert, a leader who proved to be sufficiently unmindful of the susceptibilities of the led to let a Press photographer snap him in his bathing trunks on a Baltic beach in August 1919.[42] Seeing their supreme executive's paunch dismayed the German psyche; a man who thus revealed his all too common humanity before the world's gaze was congenitally unfit to be a leader.*

* It is hardly surprising that during his remaining five years in presidential office Ebert had to bring 173 court actions against members of the public for defamation of character. cf. *Der Spiegel*, 20 June 1966.

From Bismarck until well into the Adenauer era, Ebert's countrymen despised leaders who were no more than magnifications of themselves. In fact they craved not statesmen, but idols endowed* with superhuman qualities. Nor did it matter much if the attributes of those outsize figures were other than purely positive ones; a leader's positive qualities provided vicarious identification in prosperity, his negative ones exculpation in adversity (as happened with the Kaiser after 1918).

In Hitler, the prime German condition of leadership, of being quite unlike the led, found unique fulfilment. Immune to what life meant to the average man, he was teetotal, vegetarian, a non-smoker, asexual, a man without family, without human ties of love or friendship. And yet, despite these differences, his personality reproduced aspects of the more diseased side of the German psyche, above all its unappeasable capacity for resentment, drawing on limitless reserves of self-pity and auto-suggestive feelings of paranoia and persecution. According to popular legend he also exemplified his compatriots' capacity for hard work; but Hitler's prodigies of effort – three speeches in the course of one evening, maintaining a rigid saluting stance during a four-hour military parade† – were on a different plane from the average German's steady, methodical application. The legends conveniently ignored the Bohemian mainspring of Hitler's nature; a case in point was an incident that allegedly occurred during a pilgrimage to the Berghof by some Upper Austrians (i.e. Hitler's close compatriots), who craved a glimpse of the all-highest presence. They found themselves debarred from the sanctum by Hitler's sister (and housekeeper), who curtly informed them that Adolf was asleep and she could not possibly disturb him. At that precise moment, a voice boomed out 'I never sleep' – it was Hitler's.[43]

Within a short time of his accession, a whole cluster of similar myths formed round Hitler's name. The sun shining out of a cloudless sky on to the gabled roofs of Nuremberg during the week of the annual Party rally was popularly described as 'Führer weather'[44] – an adaptation of the phrase 'Kaiser weather' current in pre-war days. In 1936 quite rational spectators agreed that whenever Hitler appeared at the Olympic stadium the German team gained a victory.‡

Hitler's selflessness (he forwent his official salary, of which – as Germany's

* I am indebted for these ideas to Sebastian Haffner, specifically to his *Germany: Jekyll and Hyde*, London, 1940.

† As he did in Berlin on the occasion of his fiftieth birthday on 20 April 1939.

‡ The *Sunday Times* correspondent wrote on 9 August 1936, 'It is uncanny how often Adolf Hitler's entrance coincides with a German Olympic win.'

best-selling author – he had little need anyway) and his apparently tireless dedication to public duties* created an image designed to engender a guilt-feeling in many German minds. The abstemious half-monk, half-soldier who denied himself in the service of his country what even the humblest subject took for granted – a private life – acted as a huge superego, an institutionalized conscience (or agency of moral blackmail), upon the collective German psyche. Hitler's *persona* as a soldier had quasi-mystical connotations. The anonymous World War corporal who allegedly lost his eyesight in a gas attack (some experts in fact attribute this temporary blindness to psychosomatic hysteria) conveyed the image of the 'Unknown Soldier', simultaneously belonging to the dead as well as to the living. Public awareness of his temporary blindness lent even greater hypnotic force to Hitler's transfixing gaze, which, when disseminated via photos, displayed everywhere, established a psychic compulsion towards loyalty among onlookers, especially among the younger and more impressionable ones.

Hitler's monkish *persona* engendered a great deal of sexual hysteria among women in the Third Reich, not least among spinsters, who trans-muted their repressed yearnings into lachrymose adoration. A little episode characterizes this situation: a Jewish woman[45] who had been robbed of most of her possessions during the 'Crystal Night' soon afterwards went to buy replacements for the cutlery she had lost. When she told the shop assistant the reason for her purchase that elderly female burst into tears and shouted, 'How can you tell me a thing like that? I shall never believe it, I shall always love my Führer and adore him, and if all the Jews try to drag him into the mud, he is still my Führer, the greatest man of all time.'

A Press photograph of Hitler bent over Olga Tschechowa's hand (at a reception during a state visit by Mussolini) brought the actress a huge – female – fan-mail: 'It is good to know that you will marry Adolf Hitler', 'At last he has found the right partner!'; 'May God save and bless you!'; 'Make him happy – he has deserved it!'[46]

Hitler constantly received basketfuls of letters from female admirers, many of them married, imploring him to father their children; some preg-nant women cried out his name as an analgetic reflex during labour pains.[47] The extraordinary dissociation of consciousness that Hitler-worship induced in the female mind was exemplified by the reaction of the mother of a Hitler Youth who had been killed by Storm Troopers in an inter-Party squabble. Hitler had sent her a wreath with a message, 'I weep with

---

* In 1933 alone he spoke fifty times on the radio.

you for this young martyr to Germany.' She proudly showed everybody this letter.[48]

In addition to the role he played in the fantasy life of women, Hitler was also, of course, all things to all men. There was no major section of German society that could not in some way identify with him. Farmers saw him as sprung from peasant stock,* workers as a horny-handed son of toil endowed with unique insight into their situation, soldiers as a classless military man – part-corporal, part-Supreme Commander, and members of the professions as a self-taught man who, by-passing academic routine, had graduated *summa cum laude* in the school of life. And with all this he was also *musisch* (receptive to the Muse) – for was he not a watercolourist and an architect, with a predilection for Wagner?

Widely regarded as a medium, an intermediary between the German people and providence, he was even credited with the powers of a faith-healer who mingled with the bereaved at the funeral of some Berlin Underground construction workers in a manner evocative of a medieval monarch's laying on of hands.†

Hitler was a man so manifold that he also encompassed the role of a St Francis. At a course arranged by the Nazi Party of Jena in the summer of 1935[49] the lady lecturer recounted an experience with a talking dog of which she had been told at the house of Baroness Freytag-Loringhoven a few days earlier. 'The Baroness prompted my husband to put a difficult question to the dog. My husband asked, "Who is Adolf Hitler?" We were deeply moved to hear the answer, "My Führer", out of the mouth of this creature.' At this point, the lecturer was interrupted by an old Party comrade in the audience who shouted, 'This is in abominably bad taste. You are misusing the Führer's name,' to which the lecturer – on the verge of tears – replied, 'This clever animal knows that Adolf Hitler has caused laws to be passed against vivisection and the Jews' ritual slaughter of animals, and out of gratitude his small canine brain recognizes Adolf Hitler as his Führer.'

Sublime or ridiculous, there was no limit to Hitler's imagined protean capacity. Sports officials solemnly announced to members of cycling clubs,[50] 'The Führer demands the unity of the whole German

* At the Berlin exhibition, 'German People, German Labour' Hitler's family tree was displayed in the Hall of Honour. According to the *Berliner Illustrierte Zeitung* of 6 May 1934, Hitler's forebears back to the fourth generation had all been farmers with the exception of his father, a craftsman turned customs-official, and his grandfather, a craftsman.

† The *Berliner Illustrierte Zeitung* reported this episode under the headline, 'The Führer was among them' on 27 June 1935.

cyclists' movement', and bowls players were informed that they owed it to the Führer that their sport had now received the recognition due to it. At the other end of the intellectual spectrum writers, scholars and even prelates were expressing similar thoughts in suitably orotund phrases. The abject obeisance made by many intellectuals to Hitler can be explained only in terms of the capitulation of bankrupt rationalists before the principle of irrationality incarnate. Ina Seidel (see p. 344) provides a good example:

We products of a bygone generation, conceived in German blood, had long been parents of today's youth ere we were vouchsafed the premonition that among our multitude there was one above whose head the cosmic confluence of fate was mysteriously gathering into a swelling force inexorably to resume its rotation within a new order.[51]

In contrast to this effusion, the homage of her colleague, Agnes Miegel,[52] 'It is not with the gushing gratitude of youth that I witness the miracle of your approach. I am overwhelmed with humble gratitude that I experience this, that I may still serve you, and join with all others in blessing you' bore traces of what passed for understatement in the Third Reich.

Dr Arthur Dix, a literary critic, drew an ophthalmic analogy between Hitler and the archetypal figure of Faust:[53] 'Goethe let Faust become mentally clairvoyant through the loss of physical vision. Hitler, too, has, after temporary loss of his physical sight, been graced with a vision that is all the sharper.' Cardinal Faulhaber saw him as possessing greater diplomatic finesse and social grace than a true-born king:

Unlike governments in the days of parliamentary controversy, he doesn't let matters drift, but steers their course. Withal, he can be solemn and almost soft, as when he says, 'The individual is nothing; he will die. Cardinal Faulhaber will die; Adolf Hitler will die. This makes one inward and humble before the Lord.' The Chancellor, there is no doubt, lives in a state of belief in God.*

While leaders of the Church praised Hitler's secular attributes, leaders of the state extolled his spiritual ones.

Hitler loves every member of the German nation, and forgives each one of them everything that is humanly fallible in them. He loves you and me. He

* Fritz Richard, *Die Nationale Welle*, Siebald, 1966, p. 106. The quotation is an excerpt from a confidential report which Cardinal Faulhaber circulated to the German bishops and the Vatican for their information after a visit to Hitler at Berchtesgaden on 4 November 1936.

loves the whole German people, and it is this love that forces them all towards him. He knows no hell and no purgatory through which he would have them pass in order to be made worthy of him

said Robert Ley.[54] Rudolf Hess described Hitler as pure reason in human form. The Bavarian Gauleiter Wagner extolled him as the greatest artist; Goebbels as the greatest general; and Himmler as, quite simply, the greatest man of all time.

The elevation of Hitler into the spiritual realm provoked a surge of piety – especially among women.* Churchgoers who grieved at Hitler's refusal to attend divine service prayed for the remission of his sins and that illumination would reach his erring soul. People who regularly attended church may have been a minority among the population, but most Germans showed themselves susceptible to pseudo-spiritual concepts such as destiny and providence, and to the notion that Hitler was the medium-like instrument[55] of immanent forces. When Goebbels, at the height of the war, exhorted all Germans to pray for Hitler, those who responded by lighting candles in the 'Hitler corners' of their homes[56] included many who had never bought a votive candle for any other 'saint'.

War added a new dimension of intensity to Führer-worship, of course. Hitler's voice on the radio boosted the morale of SS soldiers on the Eastern Front more than letters from home.[57] In towns subject to air attacks it was widely rumoured – and believed – that when a bomb demolished a house it spared the wall with the portrait of Hitler on it. In Berlin, heavily-laden mothers pushing their way into the crowded Underground appealed, 'I have given the Führer a child; help me with my pram.'[58] When news of Hitler's alleged death on 20 July 1944 reached the Paris headquarters of the Wehrmacht, scores of panic-stricken girl telephonists dissolved into tears.[59] The subsequent nation-wide reaction to the news of Hitler's survival showed the enduring potency of Goebbels's slogan, '*Hitler ist der Sieg*' (Hitler is Victory itself).

Even when the war was visibly and irretrievably lost, Hitler's charisma persisted. Speer was deflected from his assassination plans when he eavesdropped on workers on the western rampart expressing their faith in Hitler,[60] and in places as far apart as East Prussia and Bavaria it was rumoured that the Führer was keeping a mild gas in reserve to put his

* In his diary Shirer noted that the faces of women outside Hitler's Nuremberg hotel reminded him of the Holy Rollers about to hit the Louisiana trail. William L. Shirer, *Berlin Diary*, London, 1941, p. 24.

people out of their misery, should the occasion warrant it.* Thus in the spring of 1945, in the minds of many Germans, Hitler still ranked as lord over life and death. There was little evidence that the German people felt any hatred for him, even in the midst of destruction. This may have had less to do with a persistent sense of identification with him, than with the impression that he was a supernatural phenomenon, eerie rather than hateful. The eventual news of Hitler's death was accompanied by a wave of suicides, and less sacrificially inclined devotees of the Führer exhibited two characterististic reactions: a refusal to accept the evidence of Hitler's misdeeds,† and a denial of the finality of his death. Recurring post-war rumours of Hitler's survival point to the intensity and persistence of the phoenix-image he offered. Absorbing traces of the Frederick Barbarossa myth, the unknown warrior soldiered on in 1945, and the demi-god resisted human burial.

* See Count Lehnsdorff's *East Prussian Diary*, London, 1963, p. 10, and Friedrich Percival von Reck-Malleczewen, *Tagebuch eines Verzweifelten, Zeugnis einer inneren Emigration*, Stuttgart, 1966.

† Professor Victor Klemperer met one such specimen weeks after the end of the war, who said to him, 'I concede the crimes of the regime. The others have misunderstood him, have betrayed him, but I still believe in him. In him I still believe.' See Victor Klemperer, *Lingua Tertii Imperii*, Aufbau, Berlin, 1949, p. 127.

6

CORRUPTION

As we have seen, the Party Rally in 1936 reached its visual climax with the march past of the political leadership corps under a *Lichterdom*, a cupola of vertical searchlight beams. The idea had occurred to Hitler's court architect, Speer, when wondering how to direct attention from the weight of flesh that the 'old fighters' had put on during their few years of enjoyment of the fruits of office. The sight of brown cloth and leather taking the strain of their heaving bulk afforded a near-caricature of military ceremonies.[1]* Speer's dome of light provided a neat allegory of corruption in the Third Reich: a dazzling optical contrivance obscuring the public's view of gross flesh protruding through every chink in the regime's armour.

It was a paradoxical situation. Having dinned it into the collective consciousness that democracy and corruption were synonymous, the Nazis set about constructing a governmental system beside which the scandals of the Weimar regime seemed small blemishes on the body politic. Corruption was in fact the central organizing principle of the Third Reich – and yet a great many citizens not only overlooked this fact, but actually regarded the men of the new regime as austerely dedicated to moral probity.

Deception was meshed with self-deception in a unique structure of social engineering. After the seizure of power the regime made many flesh-creeping 'revelations' about corruption among the Weimar parties, the trade unions, financial bodies with Jewish or political links (such as the Co-ops) and even the Catholic Church. It projected an image of itself as a new broom scouring every nook and cranny in the structure of national life and exacted unprecedentedly stringent penalties for routine offences ranging from vagrancy to tax evasion. The impression of an ever-vigilant

* In a speech to the Prussian Upper House a year earlier, Hitler had commented on the obesity of Party functionaries and ordered the transfer of the most unsightly to back-room positions, where their distended appearance would occasion less public comment (cf. Friedrich Prinz zu Schaumburg-Lippe, *Dr Goebbels*, Limes, Wiesbaden, 1964, p. 142).

state keeping its entire citizenship under surveillance – an impression sustained by the public's vague but pervasive awareness of the terror unleashed against political deviants and Jews – helped clothe the regime in an aura of censorious omnipotence. Deference before the state and fear of the Party bullies created taboos in the collective conscience that people were reluctant to violate.

Thanks to the 'Führer principle', the Party's mechanism for internal control operated in such a way that the penalties for corruption varied in inverse proportion to its extent. Small-scale derelictions by petty officials committed within the sight of the man in the street frequently earned exemplary retribution, while crime at the top regional or national level largely went unpunished.

In addition, various circumstances helped to blunt the public's sensitivity to Nazi malpractices. Ordinary people reacted rather tepidly to evidence of corrupt enrichment when they themselves enjoyed an improvement in living standards. This *laissez-faire* attitude was also influenced by the fact that the bigwigs were not so much battening on them as on groups with whom the public felt no kinship, such as the Weimar establishment, the Jews, or the nationals of occupied countries. Since the majority of Germans themselves derived emotional satisfaction from the discomfiture of these enemies of the Third Reich, their resentment of compatriots deriving more obviously material satisfactions was frequently prompted by envy – a corroboration of the thesis that corruption was the Third Reich's central organizing principle. Nazism was in fact corruption writ large – if for no other reason than that it vouchsafed ruling-class status to all Germans under the feudal New Order being imposed on Europe. Here, however, we are less concerned with ideological corruption than with those phenomena that might have been commonly recognized as corrupt, had the regime allowed them to be consciously understood as such during the Third Reich.

The example *par excellence* was Hermann Goering, who carved out fiefs and sinecures for himself on a scale commensurate with his own Gargantuan bulk: Prime Minister of Prussia, Economic Overlord of the Reich, i.e. Commissioner for the Four-Year-Plan, Minister of the Air, Speaker of the Reichstag, Marshal of the Air Force, National Hunt Master.

In addition to half a dozen salaries – plus generous 'representation' allowances – Goering had directorships and shares in many enterprises: the *Essener Nationalzeitung* and other newspapers, for instance, and the

Reichswerke Hermann Goering, the Benz and BMW (*Bayrische Motoren-werk*) companies, and aircraft firms. All this, plus his book royalties, added up to an annual income of 1,250,000 marks.[2] Over and above this he managed to tap yet vaster sources of wealth by a system of graft so much greater than anything Germany had known before that many who saw it in operation experienced a block about accepting the evidence of their own senses.

This Falstaff-like predator, exuding *bonhomie*, marked true north in the magnetic field of Nazi corruption. As Prussian Prime Minister he stayed tax-evasion proceedings against a large tobacco firm – a kindness reciprocated to the tune of 3 million marks.[3] As the Reich's Economic Overlord he set in motion a conveyer belt traffic in bribes; in his ante-chamber palm-greasing contact men trod each other underfoot soliciting contracts and licences for big-business clients.

The most manifest instances of Goering's cupidity were his wedding in 1935 and his wartime continent-wide plundering of the art galleries, museums and private collections of Europe. This historically unique seizure of artistic loot is too widely known to require amplification, but the circumstances surrounding Goering's wedding deserve some detailed mention. The ceremony and the mood of the public recalled the days of the royal Hohenzollerns. Tribute was exacted from rich and poor alike – the latter making up in numbers for what they lacked in means. Thus all Goering's ministerial employees – and their numbers ran into many thousands – had a small percentage deducted from their salaries to purchase a staff present; while at the other end of the scale the National Industrial Group (who had been requested to donate either a painting, a porcelain dinner-service or a country-house) plumped for the last-named, which, at 30,000 marks, was the cheapest choice available.[4]

As Prime Minister of Prussia Goering administered what were known as the 'Prussian domain lands'; he converted some estates into personal property (e.g. the sumptuous country seat of Karin Hall, on which he employed state foresters and huntsmen at public expense),[5] and turned others into clover pastures where deserving warhorses hitched to the Nazi chariot, such as President Hindenburg and ex-Field Marshal Mackensen, could kick up their venerable hooves.

The readiness with which these exemplars of the imperial past accepted castles and estates from the Nazis showed how much the much-vaunted Prussian virtues had atrophied – and foreshadowed the susceptibility of a younger generation of Wehrmacht generals and ministerial bureaucrats to Hitler's largesse. Out of a special fund put at his disposal by the Finance Ministry, Hitler, *inter alia*, paid Field Marshal von Brauchitsch's divorce costs, awarded 250,000 marks to Field Marshal von Kluge, and over 500,000 marks each to Dr Meissner and Dr Lammers, the heads of the President's Office and the Reich Chancellery.[6]

Hitler, the multi-millionaire pandering to the cupidity and vanity of the brasshats and the top bureaucrats, basked in the reputation of being the selfless first servant of the Third Reich. Ostensibly ascetic, he had renounced all emoluments accruing to the Chancellor – a self-denying gesture which the Reich's best-selling author and newspaper co-proprietor could make with ease (in fact much of Hitler's income came out of the taxpayer's pocket since the municipalities had to pay for the free copies of *Mein Kampf* which were given to all newly-weds). The Führer's reputation was also quite untarnished by the aura of corruption – financial or sexual – that persistently clung to his underlings.

Popularly known as the 'he-goat of Babelsberg' (the German Hollywood), Goebbels was the front runner in the Nazi élite's promiscuity stakes, but failed to keep up with his peers in financial self-aggrandizement, though he procured palatial residences by dispossessing Jews and exacting dues from the municipality of Berlin – his own Gau – as well as from the film industry. Goebbels lacked the calibre of a Croesus because he enjoyed neither the confidence of big business (as Goering or Economics Minister Walter Funk did) nor personal control over such mammoth empires as the German Labour Front or the Reich Food Estate.

The czars of these mammoth empires, such as Robert Ley and Walter Darré, had measureless opportunities for self-enrichment, since the Labour Front and the Food Estate were not subject to public audits of accounts. The institutionalized blurring of the distinction between, for instance, Ley's personal fortune and Labour Front funds* and between salaries and perquisites of office shrouded the financial affairs of these mammoth organizations in an impenetrable mist. That the Labour Front existed in a legal twilight was borne out by the fact that Ley could not persuade Hitler to invest it with a clearly defined status.[7]

But even Nazi leaders without vast personal estates had unique opportunities for self-aggrandizement. Konstantin von Neurath, the frock-coated aristocrat who headed the Nazi Foreign Ministry until 1938, simply aryanized a luxury villa in Dahlem, a leafy, lake-lapped suburb of

---

* Thus it was said that Robert Ley simply pocketed 100 million marks' worth of deposits for Volkswagens when the war broke out. (cf. Fritz Thyssen, *op. cit.*, p. 211.)

Berlin.[8] Von Ribbentrop went one better than his 'conservative' predecessor: he had the estate owner Herr von Remnitz (a nephew of the multimillionaire Fritz Thyssen) committed to Dachau concentration camp and killed – and then took possession of his splendid castle and grounds at Fuschl in Austria.[9]

The German civil service had been traditionally immune to corruption, but the gradual influx of Party members eroded this immunity. This change was most marked when newly spawned Nazi institutions were grafted on to existing structures. Goebbels's Propaganda Ministry was a case in point. A Nazi innovation, it outwardly conformed to civil service usage, even though appointments, promotions and seniority were subject to far less rigorous qualifications than elsewhere. How far this typically Nazi ministry departed from the conventional civil service ethos was revealed in an intra-ministerial inquiry: within the first year of its existence, Propaganda Ministry staff had found jobs for 192 of their relatives in the Reich Radio alone.[10]

It was a typical feature of the Third Reich that investigation of corruption could actually lead to its proliferation. This happened when Joseph Reusch, deputy leader of the German Civil Servants' Association, with a membership of 1,200,000 and an annual income of 32 million marks, was investigated for malpractices. Reusch, who had acquired a villa valued at 100,000 marks out of Association funds, had bribed the investigating judge, Assessor Crotogino, to destroy incriminating documents. Crotogino had done so, had resigned his judicial post and had been given a position on the staff of the Association.[11] In this particular case the very nakedness of the ruse doomed it to failure, but elsewhere the frustration of investigations into corruption was more often attended by success than failure.

Two editors of the Nazi paper the *Westdeutscher Beobachter* acquired in 1933 the building of the defunct *Rheinische Zeitung* in Cologne, with a 600,000-mark mortgage advanced by the Cologne municipal savings bank. Using uncovered savings-bank cheques, they ran up debts amounting to a million marks. Schacht initiated proceedings against them, but on the advice of a highly placed administrative official these proceedings were quashed, whereupon the official concerned was appointed City Treasurer of Cologne.[12] The manner in which the town's finances were managed under his aegis received apt illustration when the Lord Mayor of Cologne, who owed his post to the patronage of Gauleiter Grohe, gave tangible proof of his gratitude by presenting Grohe with a thirty-room mansion purchased out of municipal funds.[13]

In each region it was, of course, the Gauleiter who was most advantageously placed for conceiving as well as for concealing racketeering schemes. Erich Koch, who had originally made his way to his East Prussian satrapy by cycling from the Rhineland – a margarine carton contained all his movable assets – within a decade controlled a 'foundation' with assets totalling 300 million marks. The acorn from which the oak-tree of this Foundation had grown was the Gauleiter's share in the Nazi publishing house *Sturmverlag Koenigsberg*, which became a valuable asset after the seizure of power; during the Third Reich the Gauleiter-cum-Lord Lieutenant, who left the distracting task of running the East Prussian Party and State Administration to his deputy Grossherr, branched out into mechanized lumbering, papermaking, fish-canning and high finance; Koch's syndicate made a real killing during the annexation of neighbouring Memel in 1939, when the exchange rate was fixed to the disadvantage of holders of Lithuanian currency.

In this relentless pursuit of profit the Gauleiters spared no one; even Party members who owned businesses were coerced into handing them over at prices dictated by Koch. Though he had grounds for claiming that his commercial empire-building had also incidentally benefited East Prussia by bringing new industries to an area of rural depopulation, the aura of depredation and terror* which he spread across the province grew so noisome that at one point Berlin cracked down on him† and deprived him of his post as Lord Lieutenant for six weeks.[14]

Other Gauleiters were on occasion dealt with more harshly. Kube of Kurmark, who in 1933 had commercially exploited information which an aristocratic female confidante had gleaned from conversations with the Führer,[15] was dismissed in 1936 on a charge of having attributed Jewish ancestry to Major Buch, the supreme Party judge, but he eventually re-emerged as wartime governor of White Russia.

Globocnik of Vienna was dismissed for vast illegal foreign-exchange

* When the head of the East Prussian Labour Front killed an airfield mechanic by drunken driving, Koch ordered the Gestapo to pressurize the mechanic's widow into not taking legal action. He also arranged the murder of the chief witness in order to suppress an anti-corruption trial to look into allegations of graft in respect of special workshops for the war-disabled.

† Ex-railway employee Koch's consciousness of his own worth was attested by a statement concerning Schloss Krasna, his palatial residence, built with slave labour, in the part of occupied Poland incorporated into Germany. 'I have purchased the ground quite legally from the Reich, I am not letting the Reich make any gifts to the Erich Koch Foundation. I only used the best materials which I procured in Warsaw.' (cf. Count Fritz Schulenberg in a letter to his wife during the winter of 1940.)

speculations in January 1939 – to be rehabilitated by Himmler in November of that year and appointed SS and police leader to Lublin[16] (we shall encounter this ghoul of the Holocaust Kingdom again later on in this chapter).

Streicher of Franconia was dismissed in 1940; one of the charges that weighed most heavily against him was his allegation that Goering was impotent. His contemporaries all found him so loathsome – except Hitler, who was an avid *Der Stürmer* reader – that even the defendants at the Nuremberg War Crimes Trial (each a multi-murderer in his own right) were at pains to deny their friendship with him. Streicher was like something from the pages of de Sade and Krafft-Ebing. He derived sexual gratification from horsewhipping political prisoners, a practice he admitted in his public speeches;*[17] he visited Dachau concentration camp to extract confessions from the inmates concerning their sexual fantasies, and toured police stations to submit juvenile delinquents on remand to detailed cross-examination about their masturbatory practices.[18] Obsessively occupied with his own potency, the omnipotent governor of Franconia ascribed sexual inadequacy to other Nazi potentates, as we have seen, and proudly bade his chauffeur scrutinize the gubernatorial bed sheets for evidence of nocturnal emissions.[19]

A bevy of young actresses satisfied the more orthodox side of Streicher's libido, and he in turn catered for their material needs. The newspaper *Fränkische Tageszeitung* was ordered to provide retainers for them and jobs for their fathers (the ex-soup-vendor called Seitz, for instance, was put on the newspaper's payroll at 300 marks plus 120 marks expenses per month), besides having to finance the construction of a country house with a special love chamber for the Gauleiter and Anni Seitz, his favourite mistress. A jewel-case which Streicher gave to Fräulein Seitz was fashioned out of melted-down wedding rings he had confiscated from officers of the district administration. He rationalized the confiscation by deriding men who wore wedding rings as effeminate, and sequestered the ring of the head of the district organization, a man called Enzberger, on the fictitious ground that the latter had committed adultery.

Streicher was equally capable of ordering a subordinate to commit

---

* After Streicher had come out of Professor Steinrück's prison cell carrying his rhinoceros-hide whip, he unwound in convivial company at the 'Deutsche Hof', stating contentedly '*Jetzt bin ich erlöst*' (I feel a great sense of release). At a public meeting in the Herkulessaal in Nuremberg, he subsequently described how he had whipped Professor Steinrück. (cf. Document PS 1757 IMT *Trial of Major War Criminals*, Nuremberg, Volume XXVIII, p. 154.)

suicide: with impeccable timing his adjutant, S A Oberführer König, took his own life during the short interval that elapsed between the much-talked-about abortion of Fräulein Balster, an actress, and the arrival of a commission dispatched by Goering to Nuremberg to investigate aryanizations undertaken in Franconia during and after the Crystal Night pogrom.[20] The commission found that Streicher's closest collaborators in the district administration received huge commissions and bribes for permitting the sale of valuable assets for a pittance. In thirty-three investigated enterprises the difference between the sale price and their actual value amounted to 14·5 million marks.[21]

Two years later Streicher was at last dismissed from his position as Gauleiter, while retaining his seat in the Reichstag, the rank of an S A General, and the ownership of the *Stürmer*. This former elementary-school teacher lived out the war on one of his superbly appointed country seats near Lake Constance where, according to rumour, 'the pigsty alone cost more than a one-family house'.[22]

Corruption in the Third Reich did not merely result from the venality of individual Nazi functionaries; it arose out of the specific nature of the new power constellation. The Nazi power structure was a forcing-house of endlessly proliferating rival interests – state institutions, economic chambers and guilds, the Party, the S S, the Labour Front, the Food Estate – and bribery became a condition of survival for firms and individuals whose livelihood involved them with this array of authorities.

This complex and opaque situation placed outsiders unfamiliar with the rivalry and mutual cannibalization of Nazi institutions at a serious disadvantage, but it also created golden opportunities for middlemen who were sufficiently well connected to facilitate intercourse between powerholders and their supplicants. One such man was Wilhelm Reper, who rose to affluence as a bearer of gifts from industry to Goering, though he suffered a temporary setback when his unorthodox fund-raising practices among industrialists for the Winter Relief campaign attracted unfavourable attention. Although charged with negligence in differentiating between his own commission and the remainder, he managed to exculpate himself by hinting at evidence that might incriminate top Nazi personalities.[23]

The darkness enveloping Nazi institutions was at its most dense in the realm of finance. In the early months of 1935 the German Press reported over one hundred cases of misappropriation of funds involving officials of the Winter Relief, the National Socialist People's Welfare, the Labour Front, and the Strength-through-Joy (*Kraft durch Freude*) Organizations –

and cases coming before the courts presumably constituted no more than the tip of an iceberg. This led to so many rumours and speculations that the German Labour Front decided to discontinue door-to-door collection of subscriptions in favour of deductions from wages. As for the Third Reich's chief charity, it became a verbal reflex action for passers-by to exclaim 'There goes the Winter Relief' whenever a party official drove past in his new motor-car. This popular witticism, however, could not be applied universally; venal though the Nazis were, they did not allow corruption to permeate their entire apparatus, but confined it to the top level by keeping the Party's NCOs under lynx-eyed scrutiny, while permitting its officers to commit every sort of transgression.

War, of course, always provides other ranks with a golden opportunity for achieving officer status. A *Wehrmacht* report on the staffing of the administration in the reincorporated Danzig area read: 'All posts of Mayor (*Bürgermeister*) and District Magistrate (*Landrat*), except for two, are occupied by officials from the Danzig Party organization of whom some lack all training, others are totally uneducated, and a third group have criminal records. Most trustees administering agricultural and industrial enterprises are unequal to their tasks and try to feather their own nests.'[24]

In a macabre pastiche of the British nineteenth-century practice among middle-class families of shipping their black sheep to the colonies as remittance men, the Party disgorged its most corrupt officials (whose continued employment in German-inhabited areas would have harmed morale) into occupied Europe. Since corruption apparently caused less offence as distance increased, the inhabitants of Alsace, like the 'ethnic Germans' of Danzig, though theoretically Germans who had 'returned to the Reich', found themselves governed by kith and kin, selected according to their degree of moral gangrene. The case of Herr Lemke, administrative director of the Bürger Hospital in Strasbourg, was typical. Aided and abetted by a small coterie of beneficiaries, Lemke, who had recently arrived from Freiburg in Germany, subjected the entire hospital staff to chicanery, humiliation and a blatant display of naked corruption. He diverted the hospital's food supplies to the black market, used service cars for amorous joy rides, and regularly dined and wined his mistress (the wife of a soldier serving at the front) in a hospital sick-room converted into a *chambre separée*. Protests about his conduct were shrugged off with the rejoinder that Lemke was a meritorious Party comrade whose return to Freiburg – demanded by the petitioners – was ruled out because it would be tantamount to a demotion. After a year of acrimony involving senior consultants, doctors and others, Lemke precipitated his dismissal by an action designed to undermine the very foundations of Nazi social order: one Sunday afternoon at the end of the customary concert given by the Labour Front's district orchestra in the hospital grounds he got his mistress to hand the conductor a bouquet of flowers on behalf of the hospital retinue – to which she only belonged in her capacity as a consumer. The administrator celebrated his departure from the hospital with a party after which regurgitated food from the hospital larder and wine cellars covered the furniture, the carpets and the walls of his service flat. (Fear of being sent to the security camp at Schirmeck prevented his housekeeper from reporting this at the time.) Some months later Lemke returned to Strasbourg to read a paper at a conference of hospital administrators – its title: 'The Rational Utilization of Food in Hospitals'![25]

Of course, seen in perspective, Lemke, however big a pike in the pond of the *Bürgerspital*, was no more than a minnow beside the big fish. Just as in nature sharks cannot normally outgrow whales, so the growth potential of the Lemkes within the Third Reich was limited by their membership of a particular species within the Nazi animal kingdom. The leviathans of corruption were *Reichsminister*, *Reichsleiter*, *Gauleiter*, *Reichskommissarè* (governors of an occupied territory), higher SS and police leaders – and possibly *Stadtdirektor* – (Town Clerks).

In 1933, when he was barely thirty, Herr Esch, the leader of the Nazi group on the Düsseldorf municipal council, rose meteorically from inland revenue clerk to chief tax inspector for the whole city. Within four years (assisted by fifteen accomplices in the civil service and the municipality) he had misappropriated 1,350,000 marks, some of it extorted from the Mannesmann Company (the industrial giant which had provoked the pre-war Moroccan crisis). Esch's depredations came to light only as the result of a Catholic municipal official daring to alert non-Nazi officials at the Ministry of Justice and leaking information to German *émigré* journalists. Esch was brought to trial and given fifteen years' imprisonment.[26]

Hermann Esser was Bavarian Minister of Economics after the seizure of power, and as such acted as forwarding agent for large donations made by industry to Nazi Party funds. Of the 700,000 marks donated, no more than 170,000 actually reached the Party coffers. One summer's evening in 1935, revellers at a Munich tavern were startled to see an enraged female slap the bibulous Minister's face. This dramatic incident had equally dramatic repercussions: the assailant – the daughter of a brewery owner whom Esser had made pregnant and subsequently tried to pressurize into having an abortion – was sent to a concentration camp, and the Economics Minister lost his portfolio.

One of the safest forms of corruption was the takeover in 1933 of the property and facilities of trade unions, co-operative societies, financial institutions and newspapers. Max Amann, head of the Eher publishing house and publisher of the newspaper the *Völkische Beobachter*, derived such advantage from this form of sequestration that he was a multi-millionaire by 1945. (As we have seen, ownership of newspapers was the primary source of the fortunes of many Nazi leaders, such as Gauleiter Koch and Julius Streicher; in addition, the *Schwarzes Korps* and other Nazi newspapers made it a regular practice to threaten business firms with blackmail unless they appointed 'editorially' nominated Party comrades to lucrative directorships.)[27]

The war added a new dimension to corrupt practices with its plethora of regulations and its growing dearth of the essentials of life. Soon after the outbreak of hostilities a special commission for investigating corruption in awarding defence contracts was set up in Berlin, because firms tendering for huge – and hugely profitable – orders bombarded officials of the War Ministry with vast bribes (such as motor-cars or suites of furniture). The commission obviously failed to root out the evil. Four years later Armaments Minister Speer expressly forbade his subordinates in a confidential directive to accept expensive electrical appliances such as cameras, radios or refrigerators from firms tendering for contracts. In a significant rider to his directive, Speer stated: 'I cannot protect any of my collaborators who contravene this order, however great their services have been.'[28]

Occasionally the very pervasiveness of corruption drew guarded admissions from the Nazi Press. Thus the *Kölnische Zeitung* wrote during the first winter of the war: 'A decision on the supply of certain goods cannot be obtained until the matter has gone through five provincial centres to headquarters at Berlin. Very important people, however, are directly in touch with the capital and advance their own interests without caring one jot how the folk community suffers.'[29]

As always, conditions in Germany still compared favourably with those in Occupied Europe. The restrictions on the export and import of currency and divergences in supply and rationing between the Reich and Europe presented a positive incentive to black-market practices involving every institution of the Third Reich, including the armed forces. Until 1942, occupation officials in Paris conducted a brisk trade in illegal export licences and permits for transfers of funds across the zonal frontier into unoccupied France.[30] In the summer of 1944 some German tanks in Normandy had to be abandoned for lack of fuel while army petrol was on sale on the Paris black market for £1 per gallon.[31]

A highly prized – and highly priced – wartime commodity was exemption from military service, for which certain privileged groups (e.g. full-time party officials and film stars) qualified as a body.* It was outside these groups, i.e. in areas of selected exemption, such as agriculture, that corruption flourished: Nazi officials of the Nazi Farmers' Organization (*Bauernschaft*), who could pronounce individual farmers indispensable to the war effort, were showered with bribes. Regional army commands in Germany were known as 'contractors' headquarters' (*Lieferantenzentralen*); persistent rumour had it that they provided home postings for the sons of businessmen supplying the armed forces.[32]

Wartime scarcity of labour, on the other hand, worked to the advantage of officials in the labour-directing agencies. 'Employers give the labour-exchange officials certain things. Now I, too, shall offer them money so I can change my job,' wrote a Croat volunteer worker to his family in 1943, and a compatriot of his reported to his family: 'I wanted to go home and somebody offered to help me in this for 100 marks, but then he changed his mind and said, "I shall only do it for three kilogrammes of bacon." Those that have bacon leave one after the other – the rest are disgruntled.'[33]

As the war progressed administrators of camps for conscripted foreign workers hired them out privately on a strict barter basis. One such camp leader received one packet of cigarettes for each male foreign worker, and half a packet for each female he made available to a publican whose premises had been bombed and who required labour to rebuild them quickly.[34]

That bacon or tobacco replaced money as the currency of corruption demonstrates the wartime rarity value of food. Rumours of racketeering in foodstuffs surrounded Party functionaries. In Hesse a large number of people were sent to prison for alleging that Gauleiter Sprenger was the chief beneficiary of a vegetable ramp.[35] It became public knowledge that the death of SA leader Lutze in a car crash during the war had occurred while he was engaged on a food-foraging expedition into the countryside.

* When *Jud Süss* – the German cinema's contribution to genocide – was being cast, Werner Kraus contracted to play half a dozen supporting roles, while Ferdinand Marian hesitated to accept the lead part. Goebbels, however, resolved Marian's doubts by threatening to revoke his exemption from military service. Remorse at his acquiescence – or fear of punishment – led Marian to take his own life at the end of the war.

Less well known was the discovery by the Berlin police of evidence linking three Ministers – Frick, Rust and Darré – and two commanders-in-chief – Brauchitsch of the army, and Raeder of the navy – with the black market in foodstuffs. By sheer coincidence, Berlin's Chief of Police, Count Helldorf, happened to be a happy racketeer himself. For some time before the war, when Jews began to realize that speedy flight was their only chance of survival, Helldorf operated the simple device of confiscating the passports of wealthy Jews, for resale at prices averaging 250,000 marks.[36]

The most concentrated opportunity for capitalizing on the Jewish catastrophe was provided by the Crystal Night pogrom. In Nuremberg all male Jews were – before being dispatched to concentration camps – herded into the German Labour Front offices, where notaries were on tap, and coerced into signing powers of attorney in favour of Deputy Gauleiter Karl Holz, who then tranferred their property to persons of his choice at 10 per cent of the value assessed for tax purposes.[37] In Vienna Jews were forced to make over real estate and businesses to Party members for a nominal sales price of 10 marks.[38] At a Berlin jeweller's which had been ransacked by the Hitler Youth, a ten-year-old mite crouched in a corner of the shop window, put rings on his fingers, stuffed watches and bracelets into his pockets, spat into the shopkeeper's face, and dashed off.[39]

Aryanization, which ideally married profitability to ideology, was the Nazi's favourite form of pillage; corruption progresses geometrically, however, and the authorities were put out of countenance by the mushrooming of 'private-enterprise' aryanizers locked in fierce competition and impeding the smooth progress of the operation.

A report on the economic situation of the Berlin municipality spoke censoriously of 'tenants of former Jewish property being presented with rent demands by competing individuals and organizations . . . For every Jewish retail shop there were usually three or four applicants – various trade organizations split into factions to back up individual applicants and canvassed support from the authorities by denigrating their rivals as pro-Jewish'.[40]

To curb the epidemic of 'wild Aryanization'* a month after the Crystal Night Goering announced that spoliation of Jewish property was the sole prerogative of the State, to be undertaken only under the aegis of the Economics Ministry.[41] Spot-checks showed that the profit margin at some

* The *Völkische Beobachter* disingenuously complained of barbers becoming textile merchants overnight, suspender salesmen turning into sawmill owners, and men without any skill whatever running cinemas. (cf. *Völkischer Beobachter*, Viennese edition, 6 March 1939.)

aryanized shops in Vienna ranged from 80 to 380 per cent,[42] and Gauleiter Bürkel felt obliged to dispatch a dozen Aryanization Commissars, whom he had personally appointed, to Dachau concentration camp (where they temporarily joined the men they had expropriated).[43]

With a monstrous rapidity the war reversed the century-long emergence of the Jews from pariah status and ghetto living; the steeper the descent of Europe's Jewry into the pit of the holocaust, the wider the scope for German (and non-German) self-enrichment. The Final Solution saw a wide cross-section of German society – ranging from employers of forced labour through State, Party and police functionaries to apartment-house janitors – batten on the carcass of a martyred race. Officials with access to deportation lists procured the equivalent of a lifetime salary with one stroke of the pen by substituting the name of one Jew for that of another; similar prizes were within the reach of civil-service clerks concerned with the distribution of identity cards, ration books and labour permits – provided always they had the nerve to hazard imprisonment for such high stakes. Jews were rounded up in their homes amidst scenes of ghoulish rapacity – their escorts often forcing them to take off and hand over on the spot the good travelling clothes they had put on for their last journey.[44]

The official procedure for the disposal of Jewish property was this: after deportation Jewish flats were to be sealed off until their contents could be publicly auctioned, and the proceeds of the sale transferred to the Exchequer in Berlin; but this procedure was honoured more in the breach than in the observance.

Within minutes of his mother's and sister's deportation, a Jewish doctor in Berlin (who had been reprieved because of his privileged – i.e. mixed – marriage) had to show a Nazi official over their flat. As the functionary moved from room to room, his excitement mounted visibly. At the end he burst out 'All my life I have always dreamt of furniture like this!' Early next morning, some time before the hour fixed for the auction, removal men arrived and proceeded to strip the flat of its contents.[45]

Nazi officials often took their wives into the vacated flats to sample all the clothes in the wardrobes and other belongings left behind, an activity conducted in fierce competition with janitors equipped with duplicate keys. (In Amsterdam Baldur von Schirach's wife was invited to visit a school: 'In one of the class-rooms the yellow school benches were covered with heaps of well-worn wedding rings and in little chamois leather sacks precious stones of all descriptions, divided by colour.' Her guide, an SS officer, asked: 'Do you want any diamonds? They go at a ridiculous price.')[46]

The SS were, of course, the Nazi agency simultaneously charged with carrying out the Final Solution and cleansing Germany of corruption. Himmler, who combined the command of a historically unparalleled assemblage of thugs and depredators with notions of personal austerity, prided himself on the spirit of comradeship that imbued his death's-head order: there were no locks on wardrobe doors in SS barracks. In reality this élite formation, around whose atrocities Nazi mystagogues wove a puritanical veil, was riddled with corruption. We shall limit ourselves to some illustrations of the SS – the Third Reich's very own 'vice squad' – combating corruption within its own ranks.

As previously stated, after his dismissal for massive financial swindles, Gauleiter Globocnig of Vienna had been appointed higher SS and police leader for Lublin, where he pioneered and directed the systematic extermination of hundreds of thousands of Jews. He remained so addicted to vast self-aggrandizement – pocketing *inter alia* half the super-profits that the contractor Walter Toebbens had wrung out of ghetto slave labour – that an unsatisfactory audit of accounts led to a second dismissal and subsequent posting to Trieste. While Dr Morgen, a lawyer with a roving commission from Himmler to investigate SS corruption, followed up allegations of widespread looting in the Lublin area, he came across irrefutable evidence incriminating SS Colonel Dirlewanger (whose regiment was recruited from the scum of Germany's prison population and whose own personal taste favoured injecting Jewish girls with strychnine and watching their death agonies in the regimental officers' mess). Morgen's application for Dirlewanger's arrest was frustrated; the convicts' commando, not being subject to the local SS hierarchy but directly to the SS staff office in Berlin, was moved to White Russia and promoted to the rank of Lieutenant-General.[47]

Dr Morgen's one-man anti-corruption crusade inside the SS was attended by greater success in a case involving Koch, Commandant of Buchenwald, whose wife – Ilse – has become a universal byword for horror. Koch's rise to millionaire status began with the influx after the Crystal Night of thousands of Jews, whose personal belongings he seized for himself and for some of his accomplices. Additional sources of self-aggrandizement involving hiring out concentration-camp labour to civilian employers, racketeering in food supplies earmarked for prisoners (and even for the SS guards), diversion of the camp workshops' production for private use, and so on. The life of the Kochs and their entourage of SS officers was a phantasmagoria of promiscuity and self-indulgence; thus the nymphomaniac Ilse Koch (an accomplished horsewoman) had a riding hall – costing 250,000 marks and thirty human lives – built for her own use, where she performed *haute école* exercises to the accompaniment of the Buchenwald SS band.[48] Koch, a wealthier man – understandably – than some of his superiors, had purchased their silence by regular bribes of 10,000 marks, but in 1941 the SS Inspector of concentration camps, Theodor Eicke, was posted to the front, and this left his flank exposed.[49] The Thüringian Ministry of Finance started insistent inquiries into the non-payment of taxes: with its workshops, quarries and vegetable gardens, Buchenwald camp was a considerable source of fiscal revenue. A speedy transfer to the Lublin area seemed to give Koch a new lease of life, but Prince von Waldeck-Pyrmont, the Thüringian higher SS leader and police leader, and long a personal enemy of Koch's, picked up the scent. In 1943 Dr Morgen's painstaking compilation of evidence bore fruit in the arraignment of Koch and his accomplices on a large number of capital charges. The preliminaries to the trial were notable for the virtual identity of methods employed by prosecution and defence. When Dr Morgen was about to investigate allegations of corruption in the Lublin camp, the camp command reacted with such alacrity and thoroughness to the danger that all its 40,000 Jewish inmates (any one of whom might have been a potential prosecution witness) were massacred within a single day. At Buchenwald a camp doctor called Hoven,[50]* one of Koch's accomplices, poisoned an SS NCO, a potential key witness for the prosecution, with alkali. To establish the exact composition of the poison the investigating team had different alkali solutions put into the food of selected Russian prisoners – and when none of this proved conclusive, the human guinea pigs were throttled.[51]

At the trial, Koch (whose profit-orientated rule at Lublin had facilitated a mass escape of prisoners) was duly sentenced to death, but was given a temporary reprieve; Prince von Waldeck Pyrmont ultimately had the satisfaction of ordering his enemy's execution shortly before the end of the war. Not surprisingly, the SS prince's corrupt practices differed in degree,

* Dr Hoven exemplified a rather bizarre aspect of SS corruption. He got two camp inmates to write his doctoral dissertation, learned the contents off by heart, and was duly awarded his degree – with distinction – at the University of Freiburg. Hoven's colleague, Dr Ding-Schuler, contributed half a dozen learned articles written by prisoners in Block 50 of the concentration camp to medical journals, and thus built up a considerable reputation in the world of contemporary German medical science.

but not in kind, from those of his 'victim'. During the last year of the war he ordered – via the Waffen SS Institute of Hygiene – a refrigerating plant ostensibly for the production of vaccines for front-line casualties; in reality he used it for preserving game that he had killed hunting. Waldeck Pyrmont also arranged for the establishment of a dozen fictitious SS agencies (such as building inspectorates for Russia, or bureaux for the Germanization of eastern races), which served no purpose other than keeping a number of his intimates from being transferred to the front.[52]

Such breaches of the military code – an 'ethnic German' SS man at Buchenwald owed two years of uninterrupted leave to an unceasing stream of food parcels from home[53] – coexisted within the SS alongside the martial fanaticism of the Waffen SS, the military branch of the order. The Wehrmacht, too, was capable of dispatching munition trains on their homeward journey crammed with officers' booty while visiting capital punishment upon occasional looters. And inside the Nazi Party sybaritism and austerity rode in harness. Gauleiter Eigruber of Upper Austria got his wife to cook his meals for him,[54] but at the height of wartime exigence Weimar's 'Hotel Elephant', the 'Fürst Von Stollberg' in the Harz Mountains, and Horcher's restaurant in Berlin, were oases of peacetime gourmandizing because their respective patrons were Gauleiter Sauckel of Thüringia, Gauleiter Jordan of Magdeburg, and Field Marshal Goering.

A German prisoner of war in Normandy, asked why there were pictures of Hermann Goering, but none of Adolf Hitler, on the walls of army billets, replied: 'Adolf Hitler is high above us. He tells us what to do, and we do it, but Goering is one of us. He likes his food, his women, and his graft – especially his graft.'[55] The soldier's reply goes some way towards explaining public acceptance of corruption as a concomitant of life in the Third Reich. After 1939 there was a widespread, disingenuous expectation of a victorious peace bringing normalization – the armed forces and the 'sincere Nazis' between them would flush out the corrupt 'golden pheasants' from their sinecures. Then, of course, the regime also staged regular anti-corruption drives and the public could only divine that such piecemeal cleaning up of the Augean Stables as did occur was largely prompted by power struggles within the Nazi hierarchy, such as Waldeck Pyrmont's feud with Koch, or the hugely ramified Lasch affair (Dr Lasch, the governor of Radom, was involved in a continent-wide racketeering enterprise – which 'broke' as the result of an SS vendetta against Hans Frank, the Nazi Governor of Poland).[56]

Lastly, and most crucially: Nazi corruption occurred during a period of expansion after four long years of contraction and economic crisis; since most Germans derived benefits from the regime, they were annoyed but not excessively incensed that some counted their bounty in marks, while they counted theirs in pfennigs – and anyway the bulk of those marks had in the main been taken away not from them but from others. There was, of course, a great deal of gossip and grumbling about illegally procured wealth. This was motivated less by its existence than by its mal-distribution. In 1943 the following report on the state of public morale reached the Ministry of Justice from a provincial judge:

Since air-raid victims often arrive here poorly dressed and without their possessions, people ask 'What happened to the property of the Jews? Their belongings would suffice to meet the need of all evacuated air-raid victims.' It is wrong that people who in those days acquired the property of the Jews for little money or without compelling reason should now remain in undisturbed possession of their loot.[57]

7

DENUNCIATION

Though the citizens of the Third Reich showed an almost automatic readiness to conform to new patterns of behaviour laid down for them, they also displayed zest and inventiveness in mocking these patterns. Thus the authorities' designation of the '*Heil Hitler*' salute as the 'German greeting' soon inspired a popular counterpart: the 'German look', a furtive rotation of the head and eyes by which people reassured themselves of the absence of eavesdroppers before broaching a confidential topic of conversation.

In the *Leviathan* Hobbes describes man's natural state as one of war of all against all. What made the situation in the Third Reich approximate to a cold war of all against all was the ever-present possibility of denunciation, from which a whole range of advantages accrued to the regime; it created mutual distrust, paralysed opposition, and 'strengthened the bonds' of folk community: no matter how humbly stationed in life, every man enjoyed equality of opportunity for laying information against his social superiors. This harnessed a vast reservoir of personal resentment and spite to the purposes of the state.

It is difficult to measure the extent of the effects of denunciation, though there are some useful pointers, one being the official statement[1] that the total of unproven accusations before the courts in 1934 was double that of 1933 (itself a year in which old scores had been settled on a massive scale). Two inferences can be safely drawn from these somewhat imprecise statistics: while the regime had good grounds for satisfaction at the widespread readiness of Germans to exercise unpaid (and even retrospective) surveillance over their neighbours and workmates, the volume of information received and its partly unverifiable nature made the job of evaluation exceedingly strenuous.

In inviting members of the public to lay information against their fellow-citizens, the regime tacked an unsteady course between the Scylla of anonymity and the Charybdis of proof.

Hitler's deputy, Rudolf Hess, announced in April 1934: 'Every Party and folk comrade impelled by honest concern for the movement and the nation shall have access to the Führer or me without the risk of being taken to task,'[2] and thereby loosed such an avalanche of denunciations that within a few months he had to ask informants to shed their anonymity.[3]

Similarly, paragraph 42 of the 1937 Civil Service Law placed the onus of reporting anti-state activities on civil servants, yet in one of the subsequent issues of the *Deutsche Verwaltungsbeamte* the head of the service, Reichsminister Lammers, appealed for an end to the flood of correspondence that had ensued.[4]

Party and state agencies seesawed continuously between a preference for quantity or for quality of poison-pen information (for quantity read anonymous bulk). On the one hand the Cologne Labour Office refused to investigate unsigned allegations about 'black work' and double earnings,[5] the Gauleiter of Hesse put anonymous complainants on a par with belly-achers and grumblers, and some government offices in Berlin even displayed posters proclaiming 'Informers receive a cuff on the ear';[6] on the other hand, the Gauleiter of Vienna said: 'Those who aid the work of the police and the Party by correct depositions about abuses have nothing at all in common with informers. Whosoever neglects this duty cannot claim to be a decent German.'[7] His chief of police, when asking the public to offer information against price-stop infringers, expressed interest not in the names of informers but in those of shopkeepers.[8]

Denunciations were often the result of appeals to public-spiritedness. In 1933 travellers on Berlin's public transport system were prompted by the prominently displayed slogan, 'The fare-dodger's profit is the Berliner's loss' to report fellow-passengers for not paying fares of 10 or 20 pfennigs.[9] When the incidence of road deaths in the mid-thirties alarmed officialdom, Himmler (as head of all German police forces) asked the public to report every instance of careless driving to the nearest policeman without delay;[10] at the same time the police department at Essen warned anonymous letter-writers that modern criminological techniques rendered detection inescapable.[11]

What the regime was pleased to term 'wrongful accusations' eventually imposed such a strain on manpower (and morale) that rewards of up to 100 marks – the monthly income of an unskilled worker – were offered to anyone able to lay correct information against false informers.[12]

Inconsistencies in the official attitude to the question of denunciation manifested themselves in various ways. In November 1934 the newspaper the *Mannheim Hakenkreuzbanner*, in a banner headline, announced that it was in possession of an 'erotic diary' belonging to the Jew Erlanger, in which twenty-five 'playthings of oriental lust' were alphabetically listed. The paper published the names, addresses, ages and occupations of four of them as a first instalment. After describing in its next issue how 'crowds had spontaneously gathered outside Erlanger's house to vent their sense of outrage', it then, however, went on to renege on its earlier promise: 'Hella Lang has meanwhile managed to prove she had no dealings with Erlanger in the sense of our article, which loosed a flood of suspicion and vilification. Names were bandied about and all sorts of coarse conjectures expressed – but we have no intention of publishing the full list of females in the Jew Erlanger's diary.'[13]

Such turnabouts on the part of the new establishment had their counterpart in the disorientation among private citizens. When a pork-butcher and a farmer were haggling over a pig, the butcher had offered to pay above the official rate, but when the farmer held out for more he reported him for usury; in court the accused revealed the plaintiff's initial offer – and both were given jail sentences.[14]

Within the complexities of the overall situation a lop-sided equilibrium existed between the bosses of the Third Reich and the politically powerless. Though newspapers, official bodies (such as municipalities which placed the names of allegedly tardy donors to Winter Relief on 'boards of shame') and Party officials enjoyed wide latitude in calumnifying victims, the little man could occasionally turn the tables on Party bigwigs.

A whispering campaign imputing gross corruption to the governor of Braunschweig-Anhalt assumed such proportions that he felt compelled to 'place his honour in the hands of the old guard', who were to apprehend all rumour-mongers and slanderers.[15] Similarly, the Munich police asked the public to report anyone commenting on the financial affairs and marital conduct of Lord Mayor Fichter.[16]

To the victims of denunciation, the possibility of denouncing their denouncers sometimes offered a fragile chance for extricating themselves from their predicament. In the privacy of his home a combat-weary veteran on leave from the eastern front had called Hitler a murderer, whereupon his own uncle had denounced him to the Gestapo. The soldier's only hope of survival lay in undermining the credibility of his accuser, a Party member with a teenage son. This son was almost of military age and his father had told neighbours he wanted him to join the Wehrmacht in preference to the Waffen SS. The defence adroitly made this expression of fastidiousness appear relevant to the case, suggesting that a Party member disinclined to send his son into the Party's very own military élite corps had made his loyalty too suspect for any reliance to be placed on his evidence.[17]

A situation where one family member handed another over to the hangman (of which this incident was not a unique example) reflected less on a weak family structure within German society than on a weakness or malaise in German society itself. There was little solidarity with the victims of denunciation. In consequence, few informers – even notorious stool pigeons – suffered the ostracism of their neighbours. Germans incline towards a form of unsociability thinly masked by garrulousness, and quite a few of them derived gratification from seeing others overtaken by tragedy. On the other hand the fact that the Party's tentacles reached into the social sub-soil of every community compelled local Nazi officials to live with the reputation they had made for themselves. An SD report from Westphalia in the mid-thirties bears this out: 'Grumbling in factories and shops no longer leads to as many denunciations as formerly. It can be assumed that reliable Party comrades are loath to report these matters for fear of thereby incurring disadvantages.'[18] Similarly, when a court in Wesermünde jailed a man for making remarks criticizing the regime, it felt compelled to add the rider that the man's neighbour, a Party official, could not help overhearing those remarks since the wall separating their flats only had the thickness of half a brick.[19]

Denunciation took place at all levels of society, ranging from recipients of charity to élite groups such as writers, academics and officers. According to an official report 'many applicants for relief being denied assistance from the Winter Relief complained that allegations of their having patronized Jewish shops emanated from envious or hostile neighbours'.[20] At the opposite end of the social spectrum, the poet Börries von Münchhausen publicly imputed Jewish ancestry to Gottfried Benn, a *Rektor* (or vice-chancellor) of Heidelberg University submitted names of suspect colleagues to the Gestapo, and officers denounced brothers-in-arms sympathizing with Stauffenberg.

Establishing a rival's guilt by referring to Jewish association in the past was often motivated by material considerations. Unsuccessful contenders for the post of president of the Reich Film Chamber, for instance, bombarded Goebbels's assistant, Hinkel, with information about the current incumbent, Scheuermann, who had allegedly displayed cowardice at the front twenty years earlier and was rumoured to be the offspring of an aristocrat's liaison with a mysterious – i.e. probably Jewish – woman.

Scheuermann defended himself adroitly by pointing out that his chief accuser had, long after joining the Party, continued to share his law practice with a Jewish solicitor.[21] The president of the Reich Theatre Chamber, Körner, whom rivals tried to topple by revealing his one-time association with Barnowsky, a Jewish theatre director, also counter-attacked in the same manner: 'And who has been working under Rein-hart, Jessner, Saltenburg and Klein?'[22] The assistant conductor of the Frankfurt radio orchestra tried to supplant his superior by stigmatizing him as a typical Jew who had sponsored Hindemith and Stravinsky to the last; but he lost even his subordinate post when the chief conductor managed to produce a flawless pedigree, as well as expert opinion attesting the plaintiff's professional deficiencies before the Labour Court.[23]

The tendency for denouncers to 'inherit' the denounced person's post caused the Party hierarchy some disquiet; thus, a departmental head of Goebbels's Propaganda Ministry felt moved to question the equity of appointing as head of the Königsberg radio station the very man who had instigated the previous director's dismissal.[24]

Denunciation could also be turned to profitable account lower down the social scale by freelances endowed with the requisite degree of enter-prise. Early in the war two strangers happened to start drinking together in a Bavarian village pub. One rapidly grew intoxicated, and when he sobered up the other informed him that he had talked treason while under the influence, and that a Party member who had been sitting at the next table, would, moreover, probably report him. Within forty-eight hours the apprehensive tippler received a letter from a Party official demanding payment of a 60 mark fine for the benefit of the Red Cross. He complied, but further 'charitable demands' arrived. Eventually he went into the Wehrmacht – and the letters still kept coming. At long last his near-bank-rupt wife reported the matter in desperation to the authorities, and the blackmailer – who had netted 350 marks – was traced, tried and executed.[25]

Wartime separation of families naturally enlarged the scope of writers of poison-pen letters, who hastened to inform serving soldiers of their wives' or fiancées' infidelity. This practice, with its potentially lowering effect on fighting morale, prompted Draconian deterrents, not excluding the death penalty. One man so punished was a railway worker who, chagrined at his sister-in-law's rejection of his amorous advances, had accused her of marital misconduct in letters to her soldier husband.[26]

The permutations of sexually motivated denunciation were endless: wives often acted as instigators. Thus a Mannheim wife laid false information against her husband just to have him out of the way while she enter-tained a nineteen-year-old soldier at the conjugal home;[27] another arranged for two policemen to listen outside the open window while her husband unsuspectingly expressed sentiments against the regime (thus talking himself into a four-year jail term as well as a divorce);[28] a third denounced her teacher husband (in a letter to Hess) for listening to Radio Moscow and for his unwillingness to father any more children – where-upon the teacher lost his wife, his job and his liberty.[29]

A variation on this theme was provided by cases where Jews had been caught up in triangle situations. In Frankfurt a wife reported her hus-band's help to 'Jewish U-boats' (i.e. Jews who had gone into hiding) after discovering his liaison with a girl.[30] At Königsberg a cashier who was in love with her boss denounced the boss's wife for surreptitiously giving a few slices of sausage to a starving Jewish acquaintance.[31]

Though cases of intra-family denunciation involving Jews automatically produced the desired result, at other times the outcome was not always predictable. A barber in a provincial town, who spread a rumour that his brother – the owner of a rival hairdressing establishment – was the product of their mother's 'sidestep' with a Jewish lover, received five months' jail.[32] On the other hand a twenty-one-year-old Party member who accused his mother and brother of Communist subversion managed to get them jailed for two and six years respectively.[33]

This brings us to the topic of denunciation as a weapon in the conflict between the generations. Youth officers circulated questionnaires among secondary-school pupils and apprentices, in which they had to list obstacles that parents, teachers or employers put in the way of their discharge of Hitler Youth duties.[34] This sort of encouragement naturally produced results in other spheres, too. A leading Viennese ballet dancer received a three-year sentence for being a radio criminal (listening to foreign broadcasts in wartime) at the instigation of his teenage daughter. A nine-teen-year-old lad from Berlin whose stepfather had hit him for drinking away his wages tried to achieve a similar result – but the stern pater-familias cleared himself of the charge in court by demonstrating that his wireless set was not built to receive foreign broadcasts.[35] At times a child's denunciation of its parents could be entirely innocent. In 1934 a Berlin schoolboy brought about his father's temporary incarceration – and scar-ring for life – by interrupting a teacher's anti-Semitic diatribe with the remark 'My daddy says Jews are not damnably vile'.[36]

The fear of denunciation gripped all those who had any sympathy for

Jews: a Berlin woman who periodically visited her Jewish friends found the door of their flat sealed one day. When she inquired what had happened, the porter's wife (whom her friends had described as humane) described the dreadful deportation scene in two short sentences, then implored, 'Go quickly, otherwise someone hearing us talk will tell the Gestapo.'[37] The denunciation of Jews – and of those who helped them – was prompted either by straightforward anti-Semitism or by an active form of bloody-mindedness, the passive variant of which is known by the German term *Schadenfreude*, meaning 'malicious gloating'. The motive behind denunciation was often 'socialistic' in the perverted sense of the word in which it was constantly misused by Party propaganda. The electrician re-wiring a manse who, by reporting an anti-Hitler joke that the pastor had told, instigated the latter's execution[38] was probably motivated as much by the resentment of the horny-handed son of toil for an educated bourgeois as by 'patriotism'.

The emotional tension brought about by war naturally intensified the mood of suspicion and increased the flow of denunciations. Women tended to take the lead both because there were more of them about and because many thought that prying into their neighbours' affairs constituted a female contribution to the war effort while their menfolk were at the front. Women were capable of informing the Gestapo about someone giving a crust of bread to a starving Russian prisoner,[39] and of threatening to report lodgers who preferred not to sleep in air-raid shelters, so that in the event of their death no compensation would be paid to next-of-kin.[40] A half-Jewish 'U-boat' who had gone to ground in a reception area, describes a village as 'full of evacuated Berlin women incessantly spying on one another: did X obtain potatoes on the black market, was Y listening to the B B C, and did Z pass food-scraps to French P.o.Ws?'[41] A Nazi newspaper openly acknowledged this situation and provided a partial explanation for it: 'Who brings the most accusations of felony and high treason? Women whose husbands are at the front, or have been killed in action.'[42]

Possibly the most bizarre instance of patriotic denunciation by women was the case we have already noted, where a mother in a South-German village, who had been informed by a neighbour that the name of her missing soldier son had been read out on a Russian P.o.W. list – and who thereupon denounced her for listening to Radio Moscow.[43] (Fear of punishment for 'radio crimes' also produced the absurd situation of a family going through a proxy funeral ceremony for their son, serving on a submarine, who was posted missing, presumed dead, although they knew via the BBC that he was alive in a British prison camp.)

A confidential report on the state of morale towards the end of the war reads, 'An obnoxious concomitant feature of the totalization measures is the increase of anonymous letters to every conceivable authority, in which individuals affected by a particular measure try to denigrate their fellows from low motives of hatred or envy.'[44]

A major category of wartime denunciations was concerned with infringement of the rationing regulations. The atmosphere of mutual suspicion that resulted was vividly evoked by a South-German local paper:

If a rural self-supplier sends a food-parcel to his godson in town, there is no reason to talk about the black market and hoarding and drag a fellow-citizen's honour through the mud. . . . A self-supplier sending his child to school with provocatively buttered sandwiches while the boy at the next desk unwraps bread and jam has no inkling of the harm he is doing.[45]

Not quite as widespread – but literally lethal in their consequences – were denunciations of 'defeatists'. Thus a Viennese who expressed scepticism about the much-vaunted *Endsieg* (final victory) for Germany in a letter to a former workmate, was denounced, put on trial and executed.[46] By the end of the war the process of denunciation had almost become a conditioned reflex. In late April 1945 the inhabitants of Konstanz, on the shores of Lake Constance, were still laying information against each other, despite the fact that the advance of the Allied forces had already made the local Gestapo staff beat a precipitate retreat into the 'Alpine redoubt'.[47]

8

JUSTICE

A hybrid of revolution and restoration, the seizure of power left many Germans deeply confused – a confusion that the Nazis adroitly deepened by presenting aspects of their rule as revolutionary or restorative, not in accordance with the facts, but with the predilections of the public.

While admitting their destruction of freedom (in the western sense), they ostensibly shored up order; but in fact under the Third Reich the institutions of order expired as surely as those of freedom – and by only superficially different means: the court of parliament immediately and by a symbolic fire; the courts of law lingeringly, by coercion, arbitrariness, and finally by total nihilism. During the early days of the regime many of its subjects could be deceived – or could deceive themselves – into believing that they still lived in a *Rechtsstaat* (a state based on the rule of law). The wheels of justice ground on through well-worn grooves, and legal rituals were enacted with little change in either continuity or personnel; indeed some lawyers considered that the Third Reich was more fully a *Rechtsstaat* than the Weimar Republic had been.

Today's identity of law-giver and government ensures the authoritarian guidance of judges. It gives them a firm frame in which to exercise their discretion. . . . It guarantees that every act of the leader's will is expressed in the form of a law and satisfies the widespread desire for a sense of legal security among the people.[1]

The martyred winner of the Nobel Peace Prize, Carl von Ossietsky, had earlier described such delusions when he wrote apropos of the Weimar judges trying him for pacifist 'machinations' under the Republic:

They are men disoriented by fate, placing them in a time that is out of joint. Property, family, name, everything has become questionable. The world is dancing to a jazz band but there must be an authority somewhere. . . Upon a film strip, showing all things upside-down and back to front, a huge spurred officer's jackboot is superimposed – and this is the ultimate authority in which they believe.[2]

However, the legal profession had been worried about its status even before the coming of the Republic. Under the Kaiser the judiciary had already had to yield influence and standing to the army and the civil service, while characteristically blaming the rise of parliament for its own social displacement. This relative displacement notwithstanding, a very close link existed between the legal profession and the state machine, so close that on average one jurist in two became a state official, and over half of all senior civil servants were law graduates.[3] These jurists had made their way into modern German society as jurists of monopoly, as functionaries of the empire's monopolistic power élite. The monopoly disintegrated in 1918, but the jurists remained, and continued to orientate themselves by it. Accustomed for generations to administer the law in the name of the king and not of the people, they were congenitally biased against the people's representatives. During the first two years of the Weimar Republic, German courts imposed eight death sentences plus 177 years of imprisonment on left-wingers implicated in thirteen political murders; and no death sentence, one life term plus thirty-one years of imprisonment on right-wing nationalists implicated in 314 murders.[4] In the winter of 1931-2, the Chemnitz assize court allowed a complaint of incompetence against two judges who were Democratic party members on the grounds that such membership constituted a threat to their impartiality.[5]

However, the majority of the legal profession did not hold clearly formulated Nazi beliefs, and nor did they necessarily adopt them after the seizure of power. (The basic faith of older jurists – as of academics, officers or civil servants, – was authoritarian rather than totalitarian). But although authoritarianism and totalitarianism diverged, they also shaded into one another, and it was temptingly easy to cross the boundary while pretending not to notice it. A striking example of 'bringing oneself into line' (*Selbstgleichschaltung*) among the judiciary was afforded by Herr Bumcke, the president of the Supreme Court of Justice at Leipzig, who had never displayed any Nazi sympathies. Shortly after the seizure of power, when a guest at a reception at the Supreme Court committed a breach of etiquette by appearing in SS uniform instead of tails, Frau Bumcke commented acidly, 'I see you, too, are wearing the murderers' uniform.' But at the end of Herr Bumcke's first audience with Hitler, when the latter gripped his hand, gazed deeply into his eyes and said intensely, 'Bumcke, you must help me', the plea made an instant convert.[6] Elsewhere *Gleichschaltung* was effected partly by coercing those in practice and partly by conditioning those still at law school. All practising lawyers were grouped together in the Nazi Lawyers' Association, (*N.S. Rechtswahrerbund*), the 'honour courts' of which were armed with formidable disciplinary powers: members failing to 'Heil Hitler' faced severe reprimands; those who failed to vote in Reichstag elections and plebiscites were excluded from the bar.[7] Students reading law were subjected to a rather more intense degree of indoctrination and supervision, both in the course of their academic studies and at extra-mural training camps, where Nazi ideology and PT drill crowded out forensic studies.

There were unending innovations in the sphere of court procedure. Judicial self-government was abolished; whereas previously the President of the Court and the members had distributed various offices among themselves, now the Ministry of Justice not only appointed judges (as it had always done) but also allocated each office. Under the Civil Service Act, judges could be compulsorily retired if there was any doubt whether they always 'acted in the interests of the national socialist state'.[8] ('Old fighters' replacing officials thus purged could be extraordinarily young: Wilhelm Stuckart, for instance, became president of the Supreme Regional Court of Hesse, an area with a population of 5 million, at the age of thirty-one.)[9]

The application of criminal law was gradually reduced to a technique of administrative bureaucracy. Hitler sponsored the legislation of endless decrees, which often applied to specific cases. The triangular interrelationship between judge, prosecutor and counsel for the defence was profoundly modified, with the defence counsel's role diminished and that of the prosecutor enhanced. Defence counsel could only be appointed with the approval of the chairman of the court; their moral duties were converted into legal ones: if they did not prevent their clients from lying under oath they could themselves incur prosecution for perjury.[10]

There was a continuous increase in the scope of the prosecutor's activity and power; this process reached its logical culmination in the view of the law expressed in a statement by an official in the Ministry of Justice in 1944: '. . . since National Socialism and justice cannot be separated, there should be no distinction between judge and state prosecutor'.[11] The prosecutor usurped many of the judge's functions: the censorship of letters of the accused (even to his defence counsel), the authorization of visits – and, most importantly, the right to deal with petitions for clemency.[12]

In 1939 a special division of the Supreme Court of Justice was set up, before which the chief public prosecutor could bring cases directly, thus by-passing the lower courts. He could also request this special division to re-open any case (unless it had been tried before the specially created 'People's Court') within a year of a decision becoming final.[13] Such a request was mandatory upon the court. It was therefore the prosecutor who actually determined the final sentence, usually capital punishment (which was extended to cover forty-six categories of crime between 1933 and 1943, instead of just three, as previously). The decree setting out the increased functions of the public prosecutor expressly stated that these initiatives were granted him by order of the Führer.[14]

Judicial proceedings in the Third Reich also reflected the will of the sub-Führers – Gauleiter and provincial governors (*Reichsstatthalters*) – and of the *Schwarzes Korps*.[15] By criticisms of judicial proceedings and backstairs pressure, this mouthpiece of the SS gradually assumed a supervisory function over the administration of justice, a situation which was recognized by the Ministry of Justice in 1939 when it officially published its own exchanges with the *Schwarzes Korps* on contentious court decisions.[16]

Time and again the sentences pronounced by the bench were savaged on the editorial desk. When, adjudicating on a collision between a car and a train, the courts had found against the motorist involved, the *Schwarze Korps* objected: '. . . according to the Führer-principle every man is accountable for his deeds as well as his omissions – the crossing keeper is responsible for his actions and the Reich railways are responsible for the competence of the crossing keeper.'[17]

Sometimes the *Schwarzes Korps* impugned even the law itself, as when it declared Paragraph 51 of the penal code (under which drunkenness counted as a mitigating factor in shooting affrays) to be untenable because the National Traffic Regulations (a sort of highway code) contained no such provisions for motoring offences committed under the influence of alcohol.[18]

The chief point of the paper's charges against the administration of justice, however, concerned its alleged lack of severity. When the Supreme Fiscal Court sentenced a floor-polish manufacturer for marketing worthless wartime substitutes to forfeiting the bulk of his profits, the *Schwarzes Korps* commented: 'It would have constituted a greater deterrent to other would-be profiteers if the wood that has been transformed into the closely written files of this case had been used to erect a solid gallows.'[19]

Draconian punishment was indeed the chief aim of Nazi justice. Its proponents were fond of adducing Nietzsche's dictum 'Penal law consists of war measures employed to rid oneself of the enemy', a definition Alfred

Rosenberg had 'refined' into 'Punishment is . . . simply the separating out of alien types and deviant nature'.[20]

A few examples will show how this definition of punishment and the desire for severity usually, but not always, worked out in practice. The first is a sentence pronounced by the Court for Hereditary Health in Kiel (under the act for the prevention of hereditarily diseased offspring). 'Sterilization cannot be eschewed either because the hereditarily diseased has stated he will take his life after the operation . . . or because he himself is fifty-nine years of age and his wife fifty-six.'[21] This pronouncement was delivered in 1934, the same year in which a Berlin court sentenced various Communists arraigned on an unsubstantiated charge of political murder to jail terms totalling 133 years. It stung the *Völkische Beobachter*, the Party newspaper, into shrill complaints about the 'anaemic, lifeless *rigor mortis* of legalism . . . The court has shown as little understanding as in the case of the Reichstag fire trial!'[22]

However, Dimitrov's acquittal by the Supreme Court of Justice did illustrate the fitful survival of judicial nonconformity in the first years of the Third Reich. Similarly, when the regime tried to remove Karl Barth, a professor of theology and its most outspoken opponent in the Church camp, it was thwarted by the Supreme Administrative Court. It required a ukase by the Ministry of Education to purge Germany of this turbulent priest.[23]

Another interesting example can be found in the ruling of a labour-court on the dismissal of a lady's companion by her employer, whose politically suspect conversation she had reported to the police. The court upheld the dismissal (without notice!) on the grounds that the lady's companion had committed a breach of confidence and loyalty.[24]

But in 1937 the Supreme Court ruled that criticism of the regime was actionable even if made within the family circle or to a person pledged to secrecy. Only if a citizen expressed such sentiments to himself in the belief that he was not being overheard, or if he committed them to a diary nobody else was expected to see, did they not constitute grounds for prosecution.[25] (Even this qualification lapsed in wartime, when a Luftwaffe captain was arraigned on a capital charge of 'military subversion of his own person' (*Wehrkraftzersetzung*) – after the diary to which he had committed his doubts on Germany's capacity to win the war had fallen into the wrong hands during an air raid.)[26] 'Subverting one's own person' typified the regime's relentless and illogical encroachment on the citizen's autonomous behaviour. Ordinances and regulations came off the legal assembly line so thick and fast that the public was hard put to it to keep up with them, and the authorities were forced to offer repeated amnesties for minor offenders. (In 1933, 1934, 1936, 1938 and 1939 they conferred blanket acquittals on law-breakers incurring sentences of up to six months' imprisonment. These amnesties produced entirely fortuitous legal categories, since the classification of an accused person into a first offender or a recidivist hinged on how far proceedings against him had progressed at the time of the amnesty. If they had reached the sentence stage, his record was transferred to the criminal files.)

The high percentage of offences pardoned by amnesty can be deduced from the criminal statistics: 504,093 in 1937, a year without amnesty, compared with 381,817 in 1938, a year with one. Although the amnesties blurred the overall picture, the graph of criminality showed a definite downward trend throughout the Third Reich, moving from 590,165 in 1933 to 335,162 in 1939.[27] (The decline between the two amnesty-free years of 1932 and 1937 – 691,921 to 504,093 – is not all that impressive, but it is certain that, as widely noted by the German public at the time, the incidence of crime declined during the Third Reich. This reduction was a function of the regime's ability both to intimidate* criminal energy and to manipulate it for its own purposes. Thus murder, but also such crimes as robbery, theft, embezzlement or petty larceny all declined to a significant degree; yet there was a number of important exceptions to this general downward trend, all of which in their various ways provided a commentary on the prevailing climate. Prosecutions for wrongful accusation and libel increased markedly – actually doubling between 1933 and 1934[28] – and between 1934 and 1938 cases of homicide through negligence went up by half, and of injury through negligence by one third.[29] The increase in prosecutions for sex crimes – an area in which it is difficult to distinguish between heavier incidence and more intensive surveillance – was even steeper: by 50 per cent for rape and abortion and by 900 per cent for homosexuality (where the number of prosecutions rose from 3,261 for the years 1931-4 to 29,771 between 1936 and 1939).[30]

In the latter instance prosecution was of course indistinguishable from persecution. Homosexuals were predestined concentration-camp 'fodder' – one court brought in a verdict of guilty under the 1935 intensified anti-homosexuality legislation against a voyeur who, when apprehended for watching a copulating couple in the park, confessed to having

* The proportion of long sentences trebled between 1930 and 1939 (cf. Franz Exner, *Kriminologie*, Springer, 1949, p. 106).

watched only the male![31] The savage Nazi persecution of homosexuals began during the Roehm Putsch of 30 June 1934, the wide-ranging massacre which was retroactively legitimized by law concerning emergency defence of the state promulgated some days afterwards on 3 July 1934.[32] Indeed, retrospective legislation became an integral feature of Nazi legal practice. In 1938 holding up motorists on lonely country roads was made a capital offence with application to all crimes committed since the beginning of 1936. Similar retroactive laws were promulgated concerning kidnapping, as well as for certain wartime offences.

Two other characteristic Nazi innovations were the adoption of phenomenological criteria in evaluating crime and the introduction of the 'sound feeling of the people' as a normative legal concept. An idea of the phenomenological approach can be gained from Dr Freisler (president of the 'People's Court') in his declaration that 'criminal intent' was the 'main target of the authorities' offensive action'. Another Nazi legal dictum declared that 'A person taking an object not belonging to him is not therefore necessarily a burglar – only the nature of his personality can make him such'.[33] Legal philosophy thus centred on the punishment of the criminal rather than of the crime. Instead of defining criminal actions, the phenomenological school described criminal archetypes, such as the war profiteer, the '*Volksschädling*' (someone who harmed the nation) or the brutal criminal. It followed that courts showed an ever greater preoccupation with the 'pictorial impression' of the accused and his family history, rather than with the actual *corpus delicti* of the case.

Thus a superior court granted a husband a divorce on the grounds that his wife came from a family of bad repute (one of her sisters had a criminal record). 'In cases of doubt,' the court summed up, 'it is becoming legal practice also to take the outstanding characteristics of the accused's clan into account'.[34]

The advent of war produced an increase in legislation, and since some of the new misdemeanours were rather loosely defined, the courts fell back more and more on phenomenological interpretations. A petty criminal who had attacked a victim with his fists and stolen 65 marks, appeared before the Special Court in Stuttgart. On the strength of his previous history – two punishments for minor offences – and the method of attack employed, the court adjudged him to be a professional gangster and imposed the death sentence, despite the fact that the relevant law prescribed capital punishment only where a dangerous weapon had been used.[35]

A marriage swindler arraigned before a Berlin court was similarly punished because a previous two-year sentence indicated 'an inclination towards criminality so deep-rooted that it precluded his ever becoming a useful member of the folk community'.[36]

'The sound feeling of the people,' a rather amorphous concept which could be defined only by meticulous search through the pronouncements of Nazi leaders, was invoked in connection with a whole range of offences, both trivial and grave. A Cologne court held the threat 'You'll come crawling to me on your knees yet!' to be actionable and libellous because no German man ever crawled on his knees under any circumstances: 'Whosoever addresses a remark of this type to another person is imputing something un-German to him, and thus injures him in his manly honour.'[37]

During the war it was felt that pedantic distinctions between juvenile and adult criminality affronted 'the sound feelings of the people'. Youngsters from sixteen upwards could now be sentenced to death 'if their mental and moral development corresponds to that of adult criminals'; and this age limit was even further reduced subsequently: by 1944 death sentences were imposed on fourteen- to sixteen-year-olds.[38]

Closely related to the concept of 'the sound feeling of the people' was that of the folk community. A Berlin court ruled that a tenant's attempt to commit suicide in his flat had rendered his tenancy agreement null and void. 'His turning on of the gas taps denoted such a lack of conscience *vis-à-vis* fellow tenants that the landlord could not be expected to continue the tenancy agreement.'[39] For having contravened the 'unwritten law of the folk community', a Lüneburg court sentenced a man charged with failure in helping to put out a fire to six months, double the jail term demanded by the prosecution. Exceeding the norm in meting out punishment became a legal fashion. The Supreme Court even extended the death sentence to cases where the defendant's unsound mind clearly indicated diminished responsibility.[40]

In cases of 'race defilement' (sexual intercourse between Germans and Jews) courts passed sentence even where coitus was not proven, but where substitute actions, such as petting, could be adduced.[41] Where coitus was established, the death sentence sometimes replaced the prescribed ten-year prison term.[42] But this made little practical difference, since the Gestapo invariably transferred Jewish 'race defilers' to concentration camps on completion of their prison sentence.

The practice of not actually releasing prisoners on the expiry of their sentence had begun in the early thirties. In 1936 the customary police surveillance of discharged criminals was replaced by protective custody.

Political prisoners, wartime offenders against the *Heimtücke* (a special treason) Law, for instance, were frequently transferred to institutions such as lunatic asylums after their release.[43] The Gestapo also intermittently replenished the concentration-camp population with batches of 'social undesirables' against whom no charges had been preferred (for instance, in 1937 Himmler ordered 2,000 professional, habitual and sex criminals to be rounded up).[44]

The outbreak of hostilities increasingly put an end to the discharge of convicts on completion of their jail term, because, in the words of a Ministry of Justice statement, 'congenital criminal inclinations are easily aroused in wartime ... and the release of prisoners constitutes a danger to the folk community'.[45] Himmler and Justice Minister Thierack arranged in 1942 for the automatic removal to concentration camps of prisoners completing sentences of six years and over.[46]*

The coming of war had in any case engendered the relentless intensification of penalties. The Draconian measures customary in political cases, such as the execution of a Berlin pastor for telling an anti-Nazi joke,[47] were given far wider application, with the result that the annual total of executions quintupled between 1940 (926) and 1943 (5,336).[48]

Volksschädlinge thus executed included a married couple who advised their only son to cultivate his bladder complaint to secure exemption from front-line service,[49] two teenage lads who broke into the home of a soldier,[50] an unskilled woman worker who pilfered five towels, one sheet, and one pillow from an air-raid storage depot,[51] a man who filed a bogus claim for war-damage compensation,[52] and a pensioner who took a pair of trousers (contents of pockets: 3 marks and some cigarettes) lying outside a bombed house during an air raid.[53]†

The impact of the war on overall criminality was ambiguous. Homicidal offences continued their peacetime decline, and sexual offences – in marked contrast to the pre-war periods – also diminished (the incidence of both being 50 per cent lower in 1943 than in 1937),[54] while burglaries (especially of food shops) as well as pilfering of mail and rail freight increased steeply (despite twice the number of railway guards, the 1943 incidence of the latter was sixteen times as great as before the war).[55]‡

* Some sympathetic judges deliberately handed down long sentences to give the accused a chance of surviving the war.

† 'Black-out crimes' were particularly heavily punished: the newspaper *Stockholms Tidningen* reported eleven executions on one single day (19 February 1942).

‡ Another significant wartime development in this sphere was a marked increase of criminality among women and young people.

The war naturally also produced further streamlining of legal procedures. Possibly the most drastic instance of wartime 'judicial co-ordination' was the 1941 conference at Berlin's House of Aviators, where presidents of upper courts and regional attorneys were told to explain the operation of the euthanasia programme verbally to their local subordinates with the instruction that all petitions, protests and subpoenas concerning the mercy killing of inmates in institutions were to be forwarded to the Ministry of Justice unanswered.[56]

In 1943 the confrontation between accused and witnesses was dispensed with because of transport difficulties; instead, depositions made by witnesses before the police were read out in court. A mounting backlog of cases was adduced as a reason for putting back certain divorce hearings until after the war. This was done on a selective basis, i.e. cases involving older couples were not heard, while younger litigants – who were still capable of begetting children with other partners – received priority.[57]

The rationality (from the regime's point of view) of measures such as these coexisted with widespread inconsistency in court decisions pronounced for identical offences. Some of the most glaring disparities arose from contraventions of the regime's racial taboos on sexual intercourse. Thus in 1941 courts at Speyer and Leitmeritz sentenced German women to four months and five years respectively for identical 'sex offences' with French prisoners of war.* A woman from Königsberg received a ten-year jail term for coitus with a Polish prisoner in 1939; eighteen months later the identical offence earned a woman at Radolfzell a twentieth of that sentence.† The SD also noted the public's barbed puzzlement when courts imposed identical three-month prison sentences on a motorist who killed a pedestrian by negligence and on a woman worker who played truant from work for a few days.[58]

The judiciary received a far sharper – in fact a traumatic – censure in April 1942, when Hitler, in the course of an address in the Reichstag, scolded them for 'patently ignoring the laws of the present time'. This thunderbolt from on high, which a minority interpreted as a back-handed tribute to their integrity, left the majority of the profession nurturing a

---

* Public opinion, incidentally, largely concurred with the regime's ban on sexual relations with Serbs, Poles and Russians, but it saw little wrong in affairs with French prisoners and in addition found the official distinction between French workers and prisoners-of-war illogical.

† The treatment of the Poles concerned was even more dramatically variable. Unless medical ethnic experts classified them as racially suitable material for Germanization, they faced the harshest punishments, including execution.

deep and impotent sense of grievance for the rest of the war. What had ostensibly aroused Hitler's ire against the legal profession (cf. his private outburst: 'I'll see to it that no one will want to become a lawyer!') was a five-year sentence by a provincial court on a man whose ill-treatment of his wife had unhinged her mind and caused her eventual death.[59] The underlying reason, however, was that, despite an infinite readiness to serve the regime, the judges' grounding in the ethos of legalism – however hidebound and blinkered – prevented them from completely fulfilling its nihilistic demands. Hitler's vituperative comments in the Reichstag released a flood of appeals for retrial issued by previously unsuccessful litigants who buttressed their (insulting or blackmailing) 'petitions' with incontrovertible quotes from his speech.[60]

A more important result was the gradual erosion of the last vestiges of judicial independence. It became standard practice for judges and public prosecutors to confer together in advance of each trial, with a view to pre-determining its outcome. Undoubtedly as far as a large section of the judiciary was concerned, this was a welcome development: it absolved them from the burden of sole responsibility for court decisions.[61]

At times the pressure of business on the officials concerned resulted in these 'pre-trial conferences' not taking place until the actual hearing, with the result that during breaks in the judicial proceedings the accused, defending counsel and others present in the court room could hear heated – and often comprehensible – discussion coming from adjacent rooms.[62]

The president of one Supreme Court felt moved to protest against this procedure, not because he considered 'judicial engineering' wrong per se, but because it reflected adversely on the court if its members could be publicly observed conferring with the prosecutor before or during the trial.[63]

But legalism was not entirely bereft of achievement in the Third Reich. In the mid-thirties Justice Minister Gürtner complained about confessions obtained under Gestapo torture,* and some courts objected to their use on those grounds. When the matter was referred to Hitler, he upheld the Gestapo practice, but stipulated that confessions which had not been made voluntarily should be marked 'obtained under pressure'.[64]

* It should not be inferred from this, however, that the judicial authorities were averse to 'physical intervention'. In 1937 a conference at the Ministry of Justice determined that for the purpose of 'intensive interrogation' beating was permissible, as long as it was restricted to the posterior and did not exceed twenty-five blows. In addition, a doctor had to be present from the tenth blow onwards, and a nationally standardized cane was decided upon which would rule out 'arbitrary application' (cf. Ilse Staff, *Justiz im Dritten Reich*, Fischer, 1964, p. 119).

9

THE CIVIL SERVICE

German attitudes to government could almost be described in terms derived from theology. One such term is *'Staatsfrömmigkeit'* (a quasi-religious reverence towards the state); another is 'Manicheanism' (a view of the world as split into opposing kingdoms of darkness and light). In the German view of government, *Politik*, which Goethe had already dubbed as *garstig* (nasty), was concerned in the kingdom of darkness and administration in the kingdom of light.

It followed that government officials (the term 'civil servant' is inadequate to convey the flavour of *Staatsbeamter*) enjoyed an esteem almost on a par with that accorded to soldiers, and that conversely they were nearly as strongly affected by the débâcle of 1918. In 1933 the service avidly volunteered its co-operation to the regime, partly because of nostalgia for Hohenzollern authoritarianism, partly because it craved identification with a powerful state, and partly because of a wishful confusion of the Third Reich with a *Beamtenstaat* (a state run by apolitical expert administrators).

This confusion resulted from a superficial equation of the abolition of political parties with the abolition of political patronage. Not all civil servants, however, were deceived; joining the Party at the rate of thousands per week, they led 'old fighters' everywhere to take up the warning cry, 'The lawyers are diluting the Party!'* (A contemporary joke spoke of civil servants replacing weather-vanes on church steeples since they always knew quickest which way the wind was blowing.)

Soon afterwards the Party stopped admitting new applicants, but with the lifting of the embargo on membership in 1937 the process of bureaucratic mass-conversion continued, so that by the end of that year only one in every five Prussian civil servants was still not a member; in 1939 Party membership actually became a condition of entry into the service.[1]

A comb-out of political undesirables affected one civil servant in five in

* Higher civil servants were invariably law graduates. For the reaction of the pre-1933 membership to the influx of the so-called 'March violets' see chapter on the Party , p. 56.

(formerly Social Democrat) Prussia, and one in ten throughout the rest of the Reich.[2] Non-Party members were purged in considerable numbers. This purge of so many officials who had seemed irremovable up to then both served *pour encourager les autres* and to persuade a public which envied civil servants their job security and pensionable status that the new regime recognized no privileged castes. The Nazis further earned public approval by making the service subsist on Depression salaries (resulting from Chancellor Brüning's cuts of between 11 and 19 per cent in 1930–31) throughout the whole of the thirties, while all other incomes gradually climbed back towards their pre-slump levels. (The Brüning cuts were eventually restored in 1940, but this was never made public.)[3]

As immediate employees of the state, civil servants – like teachers – were more directly exposed to the whole gamut of Party pressures than members of any other profession. They were subjected to telephone tapping, to their acquaintances being shadowed, to inquiries into their past political allegiance, to checks on their matrimonial conduct and even on their eugenic performance. The following exchange exemplifies the manner in which Party officials dealt with the demographic situation among state employees, in this case a postman who had been married for some years:

'Why have you no children?' 'My wife is in poor health, my salary small and we are quite happy without children.' '*Mein Herr*, you receive state money and therefore have to serve the state's interest. I give you one year in which either to beget a child of your own or to adopt one.'[4]

A Ministry of Interior memorandum in 1937 stated:

All single applicants for promotion in the civil service must make a written deposition setting out why they are not married and when they intend to marry. Each childless married civil servant of at least two years' duration of marriage must set out the grounds for his childlessness prior to receiving his permanent establishment (such depositions to be incorporated in his personal file).[5]

In a number of regions Party high-ups even went further. In 1937 Gauleiter Schwede-Coburg issued a ukase with a time-limit stating: 'By this date every civil servant and state employee in my Gau above the age of twenty-five must be married.'[6]

But eugenics were only one of many extra-mural duties enjoined upon officialdom. The Ministry of the Interior repeatedly stressed the civil servant's obligation not merely to subscribe to Party newspapers but also to canvass new readers for them.[7] Prussia's Supreme Administrative Court upheld a civil servant's dismissal on the grounds that as a non-newspaper reader he knew about the 'restoration of defence sovereignty' and the National Socialist state's attitude to the Jewish question only by hearsay.[8] All civil servants had to take an oath of allegiance to the Führer and use the *Heil Hitler* greeting; customs and excise officials working on the railways, where Hitler salutes had been mistaken for signals and caused accidents, were ordered to employ military forms of greeting instead.[9]

A civil servant could be dismissed if he did not contribute to the National Socialist People's Welfare, if his wife conducted herself in a manner unbecoming to the wife of a state official[10] and if his children attended private schools, associated with denominational youth groups, or did not belong to the Hitler Youth.[11]

Civil servants themselves were not explicitly forced to give up Church membership, but because they were debarred from religious associations and exposed to official pressure, they were, alongside teachers and full-time Party functionaries, the profession most heavily represented in the neo-pagan German Faith Movement.*

A law of 1937 obliged them to report all anti-state activities that came to their notice. This, plus the scramble for Party membership, led to what the Nazi lawyers' leader, Dr Frank, described as the civil servants' 'Party psychosis', which produced either a withdrawal syndrome or the compulsion to be a '150-per-center'.[12]

They were compulsorily enrolled in the *Reichsbund Deutscher Beamten* (the 1·2-million-strong association of Nazi civil servants), which entailed payment of a substantial contribution, attendance at meetings after office hours, small-arms practice at rifle ranges, and observance of the boycott of department stores decreed by the Association.

Civil-service pay scales at the lower level – though not only there – were abysmally low. The bottom-grade starting salary was 150 marks per month, and the maximum (reached sixteen years later) was 210 marks. This compared with an average monthly industrial wage in 1936 of about 130 marks (while in the metal-working and building segment of the industrial labour force the average was probably two or three times that amount). Full-time Party officials were also better remunerated than some civil servants, since the Party paid thirteen monthly salaries per year.[13]

The sliding salary-scale for middle-grade civil servants ranged through

* See details in chapter on religion, p. 444.

twenty annual increments from 320 to 420 marks, that for the administrative grade from 400 to 640 marks per month.

This salary structure not only made civil-service recruitment difficult – one of the reasons for the huge turnover of jobs in industry in the late thirties, which endangered the government's priorities for manpower mobilization, was the understaffing of labour exchanges – but also discouraged young civil servants from raising families.

Ever vigilant in the eugenic cause, the *Schwarzes Korps* proposed the introduction of higher pay-scales for civil servants at the beginning of their careers, i.e. at the peak of their procreative life-curve, and corresponding reductions later on,[14] but this suggestion was never acted on.

Yet the formidable list of disadvantages – from surveillance to frozen salaries – under which the Third Reich's civil servants laboured was only a part of their problem. For the quintessential state official the crucial question was the nature of the state in whose service the *raison d'être* of his existence resided. Judged under that aspect, Nazi Germany's civil servants were, if not as happy as under the Kaiser, at any rate much happier than they had been in the Weimar shadow state. The regime was successful in both its home and foreign policies, parliamentary controls had been removed – as had the political parties and the patronage they had commanded.

The contradiction that the NSDAP singly exercised more patronage than the Weimar parties had done severally did not concern them, for the Party was co-terminous with the state, and the civil service existed to serve that state.

One more fact was vitally important: the service, far from being broken up and devoured by the Party apparatus, as some had feared it would be, was integrated into the ramified Nazi state machine with its structure essentially intact. The purge of Social Democrats, liberals and Jews in 1933 had struck the bulk of the service – and of the public – as a cosmetic rather than a surgical operation; nor had there been widespread appointment of Nazis to key positions. In the diplomatic service no single head of a foreign mission was replaced[15] and all departmental chiefs of the Ministry of Justice similarly remained, though one political, i.e. Nazi, Secretary of State was grafted on to the existing structure.[16]

This surface impression of continuity, however, masked crucial shifts in the distribution of power within the government machine. Thus the Foreign Ministry was soon merely discharging ornamental or switchboard functions (none of its top officials – except possibly Secretary of State von

Weizsäcker – had any inkling of political aims), while the Party's rival Foreign Office, the *Büro Ribbentrop* (endowed with 20 million Rm. by the Adolf Hitler Foundation) actually initiated policy.[17] (Characteristically, Ribbentrop's elevation to the post of Foreign Minister in 1938, in place of the aristocratic von Neurath, signified not an increase but a diminution of his influence, a fact so little understood by his new subordinates that some of them developed the reflex of rising to their feet whenever the *Herr Minister* spoke to them on the telephone).[18]

The ministries created after the seizure of power – Goebbels's Ministry of Propaganda and Goering's Air Ministry – were hybrids of civil-service convention and Nazi innovation. This mixture accounted for the prevalence of irregular – not to say corrupt – practices at both institutions. At the Air Ministry the statutory waiting period for promotion from the third to the fourth grade of the service (*Oberregierungsrat* to *Ministerialrat*) occasionally shrank from four years to as many months;[19] the Propaganda Ministry, too, observed existing rules of civil-service seniority mainly in the breach, because the Party propaganda services were staffed by extremely young men, whereas seniority rules required officials to serve many years before qualifying for promotion. In the broadcasting section of the same Ministry some officials managed to draw two salaries by simultaneously doing work for the Reich radio.[20]

Career-minded entrants into the service could not but welcome the Nazi expansion of the bureaucratic apparatus which doubled career opportunities in the government administration within the space of eight years.[21] Between 1934 and 1939 budgetary allocations to military ministries increased tenfold, to the Ministry of the Interior twenty times and to the Ministry of Justice thirty-six times.[22] This bureaucratic hypertrophy was something of a mixed blessing, however: though benefiting some civil servants, it interacted with the general labour shortage to impose a heavier workload on others still receiving Depression-level salaries.

The regime's manner of tackling the pay-incentive problem was typical: instead of raising salaries it engineered an inflation of titles, – for instance, it made the head of the service a *Reichsminister* – and adjusted the retiring age upwards so that officials could draw their maximum pay for longer than previously.[23]

In 1938–9 the rules governing the civil-service establishment were modified. The initial probationary period for the middle service was reduced from four to two years (or even one year for applicants with the requisite Party qualifications) and winners of the National Vocational Competition became eligible for posts in the middle and higher service without the educational attainments previously deemed essential (i.e. the *Matura* [school-leaving examination] and a university degree respectively.)[24]

Despite such dilutions, which were excellent propaganda because they seemed to implement the promise of a folk community, the service continued to attract bright young men, especially university graduates; fears that Party careers would divert young talent proved as unfounded as fears of the Party making unendurable inroads upon the service's powers.*

By and large the Party and the civil service remained distinct. The overlap between the two institutions occurred either at the local level – 4,000 Local Branch Leaders (*Ortsgruppenleiter*) doubled as rural mayors and 60 per cent of District Leaders (*Kreisleiter*) as town or city mayors (*Bürgermeister*)[25] – or at the exalted level of Secretary of State in such heavily Nazified ministries as those of the Interior, Agriculture and Propaganda. The whole intermediate range of officialdom (except for cases where a Gauleiter was also a Government President (*Regierungspräsident*)† preserved relative immunity from Party encroachment.

The reasons behind this were entirely pragmatic. The civil service could draw on traditions of expertise and *esprit de corps* which the haphazardly developed Party apparatus lacked. Besides, the regime had no need to permeate and re-structure an institution which was abundantly prepared to do its bidding. The bureaucracy provided signal proof of this by its painstaking preparatory work for the genocide programme, in which the ministries of Foreign Affairs, Eastern Territories, the Interior, Economics and Transport all played essential subsidiary roles. (Eleven Secretaries or Under-Secretaries of State participated in the 1942 Wannsee conference at which an 'interdepartmental blueprint' for the extermination of European Jewry was drawn up.) This type of co-operation was dutifully extended,

---

* In the face of specially irksome Party interference, some civil servants were capable of employing the most absurd rationalizations. 'I only hope,' said one high-ranking official in October 1939, a month after war had irrevocably blocked the escape route of emigration for European Jewry, 'that the last Jew will soon emigrate; then we shall return to more orderly conditions. At the moment the Party constantly interferes in civil-service matters by way of reference to the Jewish question.' (c.f. Dr Wanda von Bayer-Kaethe, *Autoritarismus und Nationalismus, ein deutsches Problem*, vol. II, Europäische Verlags-Anstalt, Stuttgart, p. 41.

† Yet these very pluralists provided instances of the state encroaching upon the Party, as it were; about 40 per cent of the mayors appointed by the Party and over half of the district magistrates were inactive by 1935, a trend recognized by the municipal code of that year, which did not allow one man to combine Party and civic functions (D. Schoenbaum, *Hitler's Social Revolution*, Weidenfeld & Nicolson, London, 1967, p. 236). For details see chapter on the Party, p. 57.

despite the fact that a substantial number of civil servants disapproved of the means, though not necessarily the overall ends, of the Nazis' Jewish policy.*

The war made the situation of the civil service even more contradictory in a number of ways. Not only did civil servants have to do a great deal of additional work that the Party failed to procure from its own honorary officials, but it also became an institutionalized whipping-boy for a public frustrated by wartime shortages and delays.

Traditionally politics had been equated with the bad, administration with the good, but now politicians were sacrosanct, which meant that the guilt had to be heaped on to administrators in expiation of the government's shortcomings. Party spokesmen loosed a whole arsenal of epithets at the service: 'pedantic jacks-in-office hidebound by routine', 'arteriosclerotics with ink in their veins', 'pen-pushers divorced from the pulsating reality of the National-Socialist struggle'.

Hitler's vilification of the legal profession in April 1942 also rubbed off on to the service, whose higher echelons were entirely staffed by law graduates. All this was bound to affect civil-service morale adversely, although it did not markedly impair efficiency. This report from a district judge to the Ministry of Justice sets the scene a year after Hitler's speech:

The attitude of our officials remains beyond criticism. They are, in the main, older people of impaired health who are already heavily burdened by their civil-service duties. Yet, in addition, they are called upon to carry out extensive honorary functions within the Party, the National Socialist People's Welfare, the Air Raid Precaution Service, etc., duties the performance of which many Party comrades in the free professions frequently refuse. In fact, one can almost say that the civil servants discharge the administrative duties of the lower and medium Party agencies, and in spite of this, the attitude of political circles towards officialdom has hardly changed.[26]

During the peacetime years of the Third Reich underpaid civil servants discharged their duties mindful of the old adage about Prussia starving her way to greatness; in war they sustained themselves against drudgery and

---

* Nor did this preclude some civil servants from bringing norms of civilized conduct which were utterly anachronistic in the Nazi context, to their official dealings with Jews. Thus a Jewish ex-civil servant who had emigrated to Belgium had his pension restored to him after occupation had transformed him into a *Deviseninländer* (non-foreigner for currency purposes) and kept receiving it regularly up to his deportation to Auschwitz (cf. Kurt Jacob Ball-Kaduri, *Das Leben der Juden in Deutschland*, Europäische Verlags-Anstalt, Frankfurt, 1963, p. 199).

denigration, recalling how Minister of the Interior Frick acclaimed the service as the 'second pillar of state beside the army'[27] and how Goering (Hitler's putative successor) was descended from a colonial civil servant. Many indulged in the fashionable dream that after victory the Wehrmacht would restore normality and cut the Party's wild men down to size.

Garnishing the categorical imperative of duty with chimeras like these, the civil service deployed its expertise and energies to the end, on behalf of a regime that not only used it simultaneously as a maid-of-all-work and a whipping-boy, but that denied the very precondition of its existence: the conformity of administration with law.

THE ARMY

The Treaty of Versailles had lent a new topicality to Count Mirabeau's *bon mot* about other states possessing armies whereas in Prussia the army possessed the state: the Weimar army's minuscule size (100,000 men) made many Germans call the Weimar Republic a 'shadow state'. Pacifism enjoyed a brief vogue immediately after the war, but throughout the subsequent years public opinion increasingly echoed the assonant revanchist catch-phrase *'heerlos, wehrlos, ehrlos'* (disarmed, defenceless, dishonoured').

President Ebert had acclaimed the German forces in the Great War as undefeated (and thereby suicidally authenticated the 'stab-in-the-back' myth); other Social Democrats were privy to schemes for circumventing Allied limitations on German armament. General Beck's highly descriptive phrase for his countrymen was *Militärfromm*, i.e. filled with a sense of awe before things military,[1] and the existence, under the Republic, of five separate unofficial armies – the secret Black *Reichswehr*, the Communist *Rote Frontkämpferbund*, the Social Democrat Ex-Service Men's Association (*Reichsbanner*), the Nationalist Association of Ex-Service Men (*Stahlhelm*), and the Nazi *Sturmabteilung* (*SA*) – was motivated by more than purely political passion.

The clause in the Versailles Treaty prohibiting universal military service appeared to some observers as the germ cell of Nazism. 'Prohibition of the army was like prohibition of religion, of specific and sacrosanct practices without which life could not be imagined – and this resulted in unlimited recruitment to the Nazis from within the nation.'[2] Two petty, though preposterous, incidents in the early thirties illustrate the validity of General Beck's above statement. At a film studio where shooting of a wartime farce* with a large cast of extras had just begun, the extras' canteen presented the following sight at the end of the first morning's shooting: officers and NCOs at the head of each table, with other ranks below the

---

* This occurred in late Weimar times. In Nazi eyes the combination of humour and the army constituted sacrilege, and military farces – a stock-in-trade of the cinema in the twenties – were banned.

salt. In March 1933 the police, searching the flat of a young anti-Nazi actor, came across a still of him playing the part of a general. They asked, taken aback, 'Is this your father?' and when he – equally startled – nodded, they hurriedly left.[3]

Every vacancy that arose in Weimar's armed forces with their 100,000 men had, on average, attracted seven applications.[4] When Hitler re-introduced conscription in March 1935 the popular response was overwhelming. Thus in Catholic Westphalia, which had previously shown itself less enamoured of the new regime than other parts of the Reich, the 'restoration of defence sovereignty' and the subsequent remilitarization of the Rhineland wrought a change of mood. From then onwards (according to SD reports) Party demonstrations and torchlight processions attracted far larger attendances.[5] The first concerts by regimental bands since the war occasioned emotional scenes in towns like Aachen,[6] and eighteen-year-old lads passed as fit for army service donned floral buttonholes and coloured sashes as they returned from their induction centres.[7]

Paradoxically, though, one motive contributing to this mood was apprehension at the ceaseless growth of Nazi influence. Catholics and moderate conservatives welcomed the expansion of the military machine, because it offered, among other things, the possibility of creating a counterweight to the Party within the state.

Until 1936 the Wehrmacht maintained the rule that every soldier had to belong to one of the two official Christian denominations, and its full complement of regimental chaplains made parents who were alarmed by the Nazis' paganizing tendencies glad to see their sons inducted into it. More crucially, conservative opinion as a whole looked upon the army as a repository of German tradition; in a distorted mirror-image of the pre-1933 situation, self-deluding traditionalists saw War Minister Blomberg as playing a prophylactic role in the plebeian Nazi state, analogous to Hindenburg's anti-democratic one under Weimar.

There can be little doubt that Hitler's gamble in savagely crushing the Storm Troop leaders' desultory takeover bid for the army paid huge dividends. Appropriated by the million strong SA the *Reichswehr* would have become a husk drained of its formidable expertise and age-old *esprit de corps* and conservative opinion would have been outraged by the plebeian erosion of a sacrosanct pillar of state.

In the eyes of others besides the conservative 'national classes' the presence of the steel-helmeted aristocratic figure of von Blomberg at Nazi ceremonies invested them with an aura akin to consecration – for the first five years, at any rate; by the spring of 1938 the Wehrmacht was so indissolubly wedded to the regime that Blomberg's replacement by General Keitel – nicknamed *Lakeitel* (lackey) – did not disturb either the public or the officers' corps unduly. Despite changes in top military personnel the relations between Party and Wehrmacht still seemed to conform to Blomberg's scheme, under which neither institution was to infiltrate into the other, and their co-existence was to be regulated by liaison at the highest level only.[8] No War Ministry official or employee was allowed to join any of the Party's auxiliary formations, and Party membership lapsed during periods of active service.[9] The Ministry's prerogatives were so sacrosanct that on one notable occasion the bureaucrats of the Army Weapons Department even over-ruled the Führer when they insisted that the guns made by Krupp for the Wehrmacht should be made of poorer material than those for export, on the principle that German arms should be made only of such materials as the Reich would possess in the worst case, i.e. if cut off from all foreign sources of supply.[10]

Nor was the social composition of the army subjected to revolutionary innovations, although the vast post-1933 expansion – a fourteen-fold increase in four years – inflated the previously existing structure to the point where the increase in numbers began to affect quality. By the spring of 1939 the original 100,000 men had been increased to 1,400,000; by the autumn of 1944, the rate of expansion compared to March 1935 was 130:1.[11]* The officer corps underwent a six-fold expansion, from 4,000 in 1935 to 24,000 in 1939.[12]

Even in imperial days the officer corps had been open to gradual bourgeois penetration, a fact illustrated by Ludendorff occupying the key post of Quartermaster-General in the First World War. Though Junker monopoly of the highest military positions was no longer axiomatic, bourgeois top-brass were nevertheless very thin on the ground. During the Great War they contributed one out of seven field-marshals, four out of fifteen colonel-generals and nine out of twenty-nine infantry generals.[13] In the Republican *Reichswehr*, three out of every five generals were still aristocrats: of 4,000 officers, 35–50 per cent came from military families and another 35–40 per cent were the sons of clergymen, higher civil servants, academics, doctors and lawyers.[14] On average, 20 per cent of all *Reichswehr* commissions were held by the aristocracy; there was even a

---

* This does not, however, mean that the Wehrmacht actually had at its disposal 13 million men during the last year of the war, since casualty figures – probably amounting to about 3 million – have to be deducted from the total.

regressive tendency during the Weimar era. The proportions of aristo-crats among newly commissioned lieutenants rose from 21 per cent in 1922 to 36 per cent ten years later.[15]* Lieutenants had, incidentally, con-stituted the most heavily Nazified stratum of the officer corps before the seizure of power. Between 1933 and the outbreak of war, promotion, proselytization and new recruitment motivated by the policy of expansion interacted to make the rank of major the mean high-water mark of out-and-out Party penetration, but during the war the Nazi tide engulfed the highest levels of the military hierarchy. The reorganization of the Wehrmacht in 1935 had involved the break-up of the old Guard and cavalry units who had often recruited officers by an old-boy network. The follow-ing year, record numbers of men who had taken the *Abitur* enlisted as officer candidates; during the Second World War, however, only seven of the Reich's eighteen field marshals were of bourgeois origin; seven of the eleven aristocratic marshals even stemmed from the old nobility (Brauchitsch, Kleist, Manstein, Reichenau, Rundstedt, Weichs and Witzleben). Possession of ancient patents of nobility did not, however, necessarily imply a similarity in outlook. While von Reichenau was Hitler's gold-braided stirrup-holder *par excellence*, von Witzleben expired on a meathook for his part in the Officers' Plot against Hitler. (Among the non-aristocratic field marshals, there was an analogous contrast between Rommel, one of the 20 July conspirators whom the Gestapo coerced into killing himself, and the 'last-ditch warrior' Schörner, whose flying commandos were still executing deserters after the cease fire had come into effect on all other fronts.)

Immediately below the rank of field marshal, however, the Wehrmacht was dominated by commoners. The aristocratic segment among the generals – 61 per cent in 1920 – had shrunk to just over one in four by 1936. During the Second World War twenty-one out of twenty-six colonel-generals and 140 out of 166 infantry generals were middle class.[16]

The precipitate expansion of the Wehrmacht caused widespread appre-hension about its technical efficiency no less than about its social cohesion. 'Dilution' (*Verwässerung*) was the term current among the senior officers of the old *Reichswehr*, who now saw themselves submerged by an inflow-ing tide of reactivated ex-officers, reserve officers, transferred police officers, and S A leaders. (S A leaders underwent only a few months' training

* Two events contributed signally to this restoration of Junker influence in the Republican officer corps: the election of Hindenburg to the presidency in 1925, and the departure of the Allied Control Commission from Berlin two years later.

and dispensed with the customary two years' War School, since they were largely First World War officers made redundant through the drastic post-war reduction of the military establishment. Similarly, many police officers had held commissions during the Great War and had been subsequently shunted off into another branch of government service.) It was feared that some of the men now promoted to the rank of general would have been overtaxed by being given command of a battalion or even a company;[17] writing to von Brauchitsch, in 1939, General von Leeb called the Wehrmacht 'a blunt sword',[18] and fears of this sort were intensified during the war, when officer recruitment was expanded by such devices as the pegging of the failure rate for officer cadets at 20 per cent, irrespective of the standard reached, by the promotion of non-commissioned officers, and by the dropping of the *Abitur* as a precondition of selection. This lowering of educational, and thereby of social, qualifications resulted in the emergence of the novel category of 'people's officer' (*Volksoffizier*), who was simultaneously a symbol of the implementation of the folk community and a source of acute dismay to his caste-conscious seniors. Although, by and large, the new entrants readily adjusted to the mores of the charmed circle into which they had infiltrated, solecisms like 'May I introduce my wife to you?' and similar *faux pas* began to mar receptions in the officers' mess and inspired the derisory acronym 'VOMAG' (*Volksoffizier mit Arbeitergesicht* or People's Officer with proletarian face).[19]

In certain regiments the proportion of former NCOs given a commission during the Second World War was as high as 75 per cent.[20] Officers of the old establishment found their new colleagues socially insecure and given to courting popularity by taking part in drinking bouts with the other ranks; subordinates of the new officers, on the other hand, feared their predilection for death-and-glory situations, which were prompted more by considerations of self-advertising than strategy.

But the social and political* dilution of the officer corps also led to an improvement in the relationship between officers and men. Newly commissioned lieutenants practised the community ethos inculcated by the *Bündische Jugend* (Confederate Youth) and the Hitler Youth; drill-ground procedures became more rational than the ossified rituals of the old *Reichswehr*. Barrack-square routine was none the less still observed with

---

* The Wehrmacht personnel department was headed by '150 per-cent' Nazified generals, and candidates for officership with low Party membership numbers received preference over others.

fanatical punctiliousness, and *Schleiferei* (literally 'grinding', i.e. the excessive and gratuitous drilling of recruits) remained a constant source of grievance; but graduates of the Hitler Youth and, above all, the National Labour Service had been broken in previously, in addition to which the aura surrounding the wearer of field-grey was a powerful compensating factor – not least in female eyes.

In matters of provisioning, the Wehrmacht private not only enjoyed priority over the civilian population,* but, when in action, parity with his officers. Even at the front, of course, the officers had greater scope for 'organizing supplementaries', although the ordinary private, despite strict Wehrmacht regulations and company orders, was not exactly deprived of opportunities for looting either.

Among the social factors making Wehrmacht service attractive to many was the relatively equitable officer/men relationship (in contrast to which Russian officers enjoyed much wider differences in pay and provisioning, and Hungarian or Rumanian ones were allowed to cane their subordinates) and the feeling that the ordinary German soldier – unlike his First World War predecessor – was the object of unsparing official solicitude. The authorities' concern and foresight† extended from rations and equipment (the soldiers in the East, for instance, were issued with special lice-proof silk underwear) to the organized satisfaction of their leisure time needs, whether sexual, cultural or even vocational. The army's network of medically supervised brothels segregated according to rank was organized on a continent-wide scale; in Warsaw, for instance, the men had to hand over their paybooks and arms on entering, received army-issue condoms – popularly known as 'close-combat socks' – and before leaving had to report to the medical orderly room for an injection. The Wehrmacht's provision of entertainment for the troops was just as minutely regulated, and even more massive and lavish: by the summer of 1944, concert parties, theatrical troupes, operatic ensembles and orchestras had performed before audiences totalling 275,000,000.[21] Leisure-time vocational training in handicrafts was also provided on a continent-wide scale; participants in

* The average peacetime calorie intake of German civilians per day was 3,159. The soldiers received 3,880 calories normally, but when engaged in manoeuvres they received a field ration of 4,258. During the war, when normal consumers received 2,334 and the privileged 'heavy workers' 3,429, soldiers in what was known as the 'field army' received 3,720 and those in the reserve army 3,520 (cf. Army Superintendent Piescheck in *Die deutsche Verwaltung*, quoted by the *Frankfurter Zeitung*, 26 February 1938).

† One glaring example of lack of foresight was belatedly remedied by the huge collection of winter clothing for troops on the eastern front; the home front was regularly and effectively asked to provide comforts, clothes and books for the army.

such training schemes stationed in occupied territory even complained that masters' examinations could not be taken outside the Reich.[22]

Field-grey totally transformed the lives of millions; farm-lads, for whom abroad had started beyond the local market town, visited more capital cities than they would have nearby villages, in the normal course of events. In joining the Wehrmacht, Germans launched themselves on a journey into two disparate spheres: outwards to the rim of Europe and inwards to the womb, with the womb signifying the individual's submergence in the group and insulation from responsibility and decision-making.

The steel helmet served as a cap of invisibility, which (unlike Siegfried's) shielded the wearer not from detection by others but from his own conscience. Donning uniform was tantamount to shedding the restraints of civilian – and civilized – existence; and so the Second World War truly became Germany's 'war of liberation'.

This unleashing of the collective libido at the expense of non-Germans did not preclude displays of martial valour and self-sacrificing comradeship. By early 1944 over half a million Iron Crosses, First Class, and more than 3 million Second Class ones had been awarded: i.e. almost every third member of the Wehrmacht had been decorated for bravery.[23] Eligibility for the highest award of all, the Knight's Cross, was not – again in contradistinction to First World War practice – confined to officers but extended to NCOs and occasionally even to privates; the recipients' names were ceremoniously announced over the Reich radio. Another illustration of the Wehrmacht's trend towards egalitarianism was the fact that eighty of its generals died in action during the Second World War.[24] In essence, of course, the notion of a military folk community remained strictly subordinate to old hierarchic principles.

The prizes of victory which Hitler vouchsafed his warriors in the conquered east were hierarchically graded too: manorial estates for officers, farmsteads for other ranks. Even before final victory, the rewards for success awarded to high-ranking officers could be astronomic. Field Marshal von Kluge, for instance, received a cheque for 250,000 marks on which Hitler had scribbled, 'Half to be spent on building on your estate; Speer has received the necessary instructions.'[25]

Bribery with money, real estate, promotion and declarations (e.g. award of the highly prized golden Party badge) was as instrumental in weakening the cohesion of the military caste as were Hitler's successes and his deification by the populace. The havering of the military opposition to

Hitler is sufficiently well known to preclude explanation. Truly symptomatic of the army's retreat from previously sacrosanct positions was its effeteness in the face of Nazi anti-monarchism. The same Kaiser whose consent Hindenburg had sought before accepting the presidency was presented to millions of cinema-goers – in Hans Steinhoff's *Die Entlassung* (*The Dismissal*) – as a homosexual more interested in a piano-tinkling 'friend' than in the ruin of Bismarck. In 1938 leading generals protested in vain against Streicher's denigration of the nobility;[26] after the death of a Hohenzollern prince during the French Campaign, Hitler, fearful that royal deaths might stimulate monarchical sentiment in the country, could unhesitatingly order that all scions of former ruling houses be dismissed from the service. The purge of the princes from the entire German officer corps was carried to its conclusion after the overthrow of Mussolini, which the House of Savoy had helped to engineer.[27]

Yet fully a year after the seizure of power it had still been possible for a regimental commander in Silesia to regale his subalterns with this cryptic utterance: 'There has been a lot of talk about a certain Herr Hitler recently. I have been to Berlin. Herr Hitler is no *Herr* (gentleman) and that is that.'[28] Similar instances of the army's mainly symbolic autonomy could be quoted *ad infinitum*. When Goering's order was read out banning the formal address in the third person singular for other ranks it was followed everywhere by the warning, 'Woe betide any soldier who dares address an officer in the second person!' The War Ministry rejected the 1939 decree requiring Party membership of all civil service applicants,[29] and Baldur von Schirach, who joined up after the reorganization of the army in 1935, was not only refused a commission but threatened with detention for complaining about it to Party headquarters. Early in the war he joined up again and was again slighted, though he rationalized his frustration with characteristic bombast: 'Now no one, however highly placed in the state he may be, can claim that it is beneath his dignity to serve the Wehrmacht as an ordinary soldier.'[30] Even after the failure of Colonel Stauffenberg's bomb, when an order from the Führer replaced the military salute by the '*Heil Hitler*' greeting, many officers concluded the announcement of this very order with an extra-smart military salute.

The day of the bomb plot, 20 July 1944, was a turning-point in German history when – in A. J. P. Taylor's phrase apropos of the 1848 Revolution – German history refused to turn. The plotters' military background gave them a degree of camouflage but not, apparently, the wherewithal for effective rebellion, a circumstance which makes one suspect a deeper malfunction behind Stauffenberg's half-functioning briefcase bomb.

Although German history records many tyrants it has – but for Wilhelm Tell's longbow shot (and Tell was a Swiss) – known no acts of tyrannicide. A society thus hereditarily endowed produced officers who after 1933, when they were the only body in the country capable of autonomous action, still lacked autonomy of thought; the 'inner-directed' few among them susceptible to Jefferson's thought that the tree of liberty needs watering with the blood of tyrants shrank back from actions liable to redound to Germany's military disadvantage or to involve German casualties. (What deserves mention too is the strange moral myopia of some subsequent military resistance heroes after the seizure of power: Stauffenberg had called the Night of the Long Knives – the abattoir-style liquidation of the SA leadership in June 1934 – the 'lancing of an abscess', while Field Marshal von Witzleben actually regretted that he had not taken part in the hunting down and execution of fugitive Storm Troop leaders skulking in the forests of Silesia.)[31]

Strange collation of dates: 30 June 1934 and 20 July 1944 were the only two occasions when the regime which floated on oceans of anonymous, largely non-German blood shed the blood of well-known Germans. The Night of the Long Knives and the day of the Officers' Plot stand in symmetrical relation to each other: the former concluded the pseudo-revolutionary overture of National Socialism and the latter inaugurated its pseudo-revolutionary finale. A tangle of social conflicts was resolved after 20 July, among them the rivalry between the traditional élites and the petit-bourgeois upstarts of the Party apparatus. During the wave of persecution that followed the Officers' Plot, an Evangelical deaconess was executed for describing Himmler, the newly appointed C-in-C of the reserve army, as 'a man of simple background not sprung from the soldierly estate'.[32] Since the nobility and the officer corps were inextricably linked the ferocious anti-aristocratic slogans with which Nazi leaders abreacted the plot perforce sounded rather theoretical during the concluding stages of the war. In keeping with his leadership of the German Labour Front Robert Ley spoke of 'blue-blooded swine whose entire families must be wiped out'[33] while Goebbels, who was more prudent – as well as more methodical – simply issued directives for the post-war liquidation of the aristocracy.[34]

Outside the political sphere the connection between the aristocracy and the army found its echo in the 'tone' of the officer corps. As late as autumn

1939 an inspecting general could allow his chagrin at a bungled field exercise along the West Wall to be dissipated by a rendering of *O du holder Abendstern*, (the tenor aria from *Tannhäuser*) by a conscript[35] and express the conviction that 'as long as our soldiers can sing like this, we need have no worry for the future'. Songs could likewise serve as a device for bridging socially embarrassing situations. Thus when the screen idol Olga Tschechowa, after baptizing a Stuka aircraft by flying in it, alighted green-gilled and close to vomiting, the squadron leader barked at the assembled airmen: 'Squad, about turn – a song: one – two – three . . .'[36]

The civic-spirited Olga Tschechowa was also honorary colonel of an artillery regiment which she visited at Christmas 1939, when it was positioned opposite the Maginot Line. 'An icy wind blew over the trenches as I crept up to the outposts, bringing each soldier a candle, a fir-twig, a packet of cigarettes and greetings and kisses from his loved ones. Fear nearly made me die a thousand deaths at first, but later the sentry's eyes brimming over with tears made me forget everything.'[37] The actress's appeal to the military heart was so total as to transcend all distinctions of rank. Even Field Marshal von Brauchitsch, commander-in-chief of the army, yielded to entreaties to release the conscripted actor Karl Ludwig Diehl for a film: 'How could I refuse your wish, Frau Tschechowa? You know that I married a woman who resembles you as one twin does another.'[38]

So 'heart' was not a scarce commodity in the Wehrmacht. Humour, too – with the appropriate gallows touch – was rarely in short supply. Officers coveting decoration, especially if their ambition focused on the Knight's Cross (which was worn round the neck), were commonly described as 'suffering from sore throats'. In barrack-room parlance, the *Ostmedaille* (the Eastern Medal) was variously called the 'Frost Medal' or the 'Order of Chilled Beef' (*Gefrierfleischorden*). Since there was slightly more scope for licensed criticism in the Wehrmacht than elsewhere, the portals of military establishments were even occasionally graced with such *bon mots* as 'The Führer knows it, God has an inkling of it, and it's none of your bloody business.'[39]

The military's relative immunity to all-pervasive political control also led to people with an incriminating dossier, or compromised personalities such as the humorist Werner Finck or the writers Gottfried Benn and Ernst Jünger, going to ground in the army, in the hope that field grey would provide an effective camouflage against Party zealots. The Wehrmacht's mitigating effect on the worst rigours of Nazi rule did not manifest itself only within its ranks; externally, too, the military were marginally less inhuman than the Party or the SS. Military control over Belgium, for instance, led to a smaller proportion of its Jewish population being done to death than in neighbouring Party-administered Holland. The rivalry between the Wehrmacht and the SS had many facets. Army officers showed a disdain for their SS colleagues which was sometimes based on genuine social, educational and military superiority.* The army, traditionally the 'sole arms-bearers of the nation', looked askance at their upstart rivals, who not only claimed that their special formations were the real élite, but were in fact better equipped and provisioned. Front-line soldiers had ambivalent feelings about fighting alongside Waffen-SS units. Though they appreciated their neighbours' bravery, they had every reason to fear the greatly increased guerrilla activity that often followed SS excesses against the civilian population. Finally, the very existence of the SS served the army as a self-exculpating device, since all responsibility for atrocities could easily be laid at its door. But in fact the Wehrmacht – at least the greater part of it that saw service in the east – cannot be said to have been imbued with an ethos radically different from that of Himmler's troops.

When he addressed the Prussian army corps under his command on the eve of the 1813 War of Liberation, the famed Count Yorck defined courage, endurance and discipline as the soldier's chief virtues, adding, 'But the fatherland expects something more sublime from us who are going into battle for the sacred cause: noble, humane conduct even towards the enemy.' In bleak contrast, Kaiser Wilhelm II exhorted his expeditionary force sailing for China (and the Boxer rebellion) in 1900: 'No mercy will be shown, no prisoners taken.' And one generation later, the head of the armed forces, Blomberg, said: 'The duty of the Prussian officer was correctness – that of the German officer is cunning.'[40]

The rot of the German army's moral fibre found its pre-ordained culmination during the Third Reich. Among the officers those avid for promotion denounced their colleagues for political dissent, while in the ranks there grew up a system of surveillance so fool-proof that a defeatist letter by an old peasant woman to her son, found in the ambulance that was taking him to a military hospital behind the Russian front, resulted in her arraignment before the People's Court on a charge of treason.[41] Like their

* Although the Order of the Death's Head had attracted a relatively large aristocratic leadership segment, which served as a top dressing, SS overall officer recruitment was more egalitarian than that of the Wehrmacht before its wartime dilution.

civilian counterparts, the army's judicial authorities worked with the same remorseless application and were fired by the same commitment to deterrence as the solitary *raison d'être* of punishment. There were well over 10,000 executions following court martial during the Second World War. Military judges would apply the letter of the law with stupefying pedantry. In Russia, for instance, two soldiers sent foraging to a remote collective farm were executed because, having been delayed by engine trouble, and with their travel rations gone, they had helped themselves to some of the *kolkhoz* produce without authorization.[42]

As characteristic of Wehrmacht court martials as the judicial officers' inclemency was the readiness of ordinary soldiers to man the firing squads. By contrast with the US army – where the heaviest possible pressure including threats of court martial, was required before the death sentence on Private Slovik (the only American deserter thus punished during the Second World War) could be carried out, Wehrmacht companies ordered to execute one of their own men invariably produced more volunteers than were needed.[43]

However, there were instances of deviant behaviour here and there. Non-Nazi officers denounced by their colleagues were occasionally saved by regimental commanders who failed to transmit the accusations through the appropriate channels.

The officer who had instigated the court martial of the soldiers who had helped themselves to *kolkhoz* supplies without permission (see above) was transferred to another unit because all his brother officers cut him in the mess.[44] But, in the army, social ostracism as a reaction to heinous behaviour was the exception rather than the rule. Thus, when an inmate of an officers' convalescent home regaled fellow-diners one evening with a first-hand account of a massacre of Ukrainian village children, and one of the five convalescents at his table got up and walked out, the others stolidly remained seated; the doctor in charge of the home filed a report on the incident in which he – successfully, as it turned out – ascribed the isolated officer's gesture to an unsound state of mind resulting from his recent illness.[45]

Behaviour also depended on geographical location; in the west, the occupation forces' conduct was rather better than in areas inhabited by Slavs, but even in the east the military code of correct behaviour could operate fitfully in the midst of excesses. The official and private plundering of Russian resources proceeded alongside 'normal' transactions, in which German soldiers dutifully paid farmers the stipulated price for chickens and pints of milk. Similarly, soldiers were court martialled on rape charges (though the death penalty prescribed for this offence was invariably commuted, sometimes to transfer to a punitive battalion) at the same time as Nazi-organized famine conditions compelled women to trade their bodies for a loaf of bread[46] and some Wehrmacht brothels were staffed with female slave workers and Jewesses.

It was the west – especially France between her capitulation and D-Day – which represented the German soldier's favourite stamping ground. Looting was relatively restrained – below the official and officer level – though an artificially fixed rate of exchange enabled the occupying troops 'to go through French shops like an army of locusts'.[47] It was not unusual for German soldiers with rural backgrounds to spend their off-duty hours helping local villagers with their farm-work. Paris, with its museums and brothels, its Wehrmacht theatre agency, its obscene sideshows and black market opportunities, was the Sybaris of the occupation forces – in addition to being a source of illicit champagne for officers' messes across the whole of Europe. As regards looting and generally corrupt practices, front-line troops were highly conscious – though not always justifiably so – of a sharp dividing line between themselves and the military base-wallahs and Party 'golden pheasants' of the occupation administration. At base and front alike, officers naturally enjoyed greater opportunities for self-aggrandizement than their men. A case in point was the ruling that luggage and furniture belonging to Jewish *émigrés* stranded at the Channel ports should be 'democratically' distributed among the naval units stationed there, despite which the officers restricted the share-out entirely to themselves.[48]

It was usual for munition wagons and the long-distance lorries of Organization Todt to make their return journeys crammed with unofficial booty. One group of officers enjoying particular opportunities for self-enrichment were those posted to Transport Command. Others stationed west of the Rhine frequently sent their batmen home on leave to convey valuable paintings from France and the Low Countries into the Reich. In addition, workshops which were ostensibly producing army requirements in these countries in fact turned out furniture, metal-ware and fripperies according to officers' private specifications. In the area round Paris, 100,000 troops enjoyed the Wehrmacht's softest posting, and many officers were almost exclusively occupied in pursuing the pleasures of the hunt and the table. Administrative services teemed with young ladies of aristocratic background, who owed their postings to sponsors ensconced in the Wehrmacht's High Command. The euphoria characteristic of the early occupation period expressed itself graphically in Luftwaffe personnel using champagne as shaving-water. This sort of military behaviour was often laced with coarse humour. Soldiers derived great amusement from heating the franc pieces that performers in Parisian 'establishments' picked up with their private parts, from using pliers to shave bearded Jews or from receipting food taken at gun-point from Italian farmhouses with chits signed 'Reichsmarschal Arsehole'.[49] When the German rear headquarters were withdrawn from Kharkov, evacuated 'essential war material' included carpets, paintings, furniture – and Ukrainian typists (who, however, fared better than the Russian women elsewhere on the eastern front, for whom no space was available among the military baggage, so that they were mown down by the departing troops).[50]

As the war drew to its close, retreating Wehrmacht units reacted with an ever greater propensity for gratuitous destruction and looting, a reflex that continued even on their native soil; soldiers would selectively plunder the property of fellow-Germans in response to letters from their own families asking for commodities in short supply at home.[51] It was in the east that the Wehrmacht's conduct approximated most closely to that of the SS. Field-Marshal von Manstein instructed the troops under his command that 'in enemy towns, a large part of the population will have to starve. Despite this, misconceived notions of humanity must not lead to the distribution of goods among prisoners and the local population – those are goods the home front goes without for our sake.[52]

Army directives resulted in the razing of villages and the massacre of their inhabitants in 'anti-guerrilla reprisals', in the forced marching of Russian prisoners back into the Reich along a thousand-mile Road to Calvary, or their transport by rail under conditions which resulted in an estimated 10 to 20 per cent survival rate. Of well over five million Red Army prisoners, a bare million survived the war.[53] Inside the PoW camps the Wehrmacht propaganda company filmed scenes of Russian prisoners regressing to cannibalism as a result of being systematically starved. The Wehrmacht guards of PoW camps accepted the Nazi scale of racial evaluation, which ranged the Russians even below the Poles, at a level hardly above that of beasts. They rationalized the barbarous treatment meted out to the Russians by their own apprehension of being stampeded by a huge, brutish mass, unless it was kept in an abject state of emaciation and fear.[54]

Lastly, what of the Wehrmacht's role *vis-à-vis* the Jews? In 1942 a court martial at Piatigorsk in occupied Russia actually imposed a year's imprisonment on a warrant officer charged (*inter alia*) with the murder of seventy-five Jews, stating:

Under Paragraph 211 of the penal code, he who intentionally kills a man and carries out this deed with deliberation is a murderer. The accused has done just that, since he himself stated that he reflected minutely upon the execution of seventy-five Jews. The large number killed aggravates the offence, but since there are extenuating circumstances – his concern for the security of his men, the danger of a link-up between the Jews and the partisans, etc. – the court considers one year's imprisonment sufficient.[55]

Though ludicrously irrelevant to the fate of the seventy-five – or of the 6 million – this sentence deserves to be recorded, indicative as it was of the faint stirrings of a moral sense among the officer corps in the tenth year of Nazi rule.

Equally deserving of record, however, and of infinitely greater consequence, were Field-Marshal von Manstein's description of Jewry as the 'spiritual carrier of the Bolshevik terror', and an order of the day signed by him, by Field-Marshal von Reichenau and by Generals von Küchler and Hoth, which stated, 'The soldier in the east is not merely a fighter according to the rules of war, but also a protagonist of a merciless racial idea, who must fully understand the necessity for hard but just punishment of Jewish sub-humanity.'[56] Major-General Eberhardt, the town commandant of Kiev, arranged complete Wehrmacht liaison with Blobel's commando task force* during the mammoth murder of Jewish civilians at Babi Yar,[57] a massacre which caused the commander-in-chief of Army Group South, Field-Marshal von Rundstedt, to issue an order forbidding soldiers to watch or photograph command task force actions.[58] In the Field-Marshal's mind, stewarding mass carnage was less reprehensible than voyeurism and amateur photography. A month later an SD dispatch from the Ukraine reporting 55,432 executions described the majority of victims as Jewish prisoners-of-war handed over by the Wehrmacht.[59]

Elsewhere along the eastern front, the headquarters of Army Group North were actually situated at Kovno while the massacre of the town's Jews – carried out by lunatics whom the SS had released and armed with iron bars – was proceeding in the streets.[60]

* These Einsatzkommando were highly mobile killer units ('slaughter-houses on wheels') charged with wiping out Communists, partisans, saboteurs and Jews. A number of Wehrmacht generals told Chief-of-Staff Halder (at Orscha in December 1941): '*Einsatztrupen* are worth their weight in gold; they preserve our rear communications and save us the use of troops' (cf. *Der Spiegel* 26 December 1966, p. 58).

It is no exaggeration to say that Pontius Pilate achieved multiple reincarnation in gold braid and field-grey. An officer conducting visiting industrialists through a chemical plant attached to Auschwitz camp made this comment: 'Nasty things are conceivably happening here, we don't want to know anything about them and are glad to have nothing to do with them in the line of duty.'[61] Less equivocal was the reaction of Field-Marshal Ernst Busch, an army group commander on the Eastern front, to his ashen-faced adjutant's announcement that men and women were being shot outside the headquarters building. Busch rapped out a brief, military order: 'Draw the curtains!'[62]

THE LAND

After the Great War land continued to affect the political power nexus and the social delineation of Germany – where it had ceased to be the mainstay of the economy for at least two generations – more profoundly than in other advanced countries. In inter-war Britain only one out of every twenty gainfully employed persons was in agriculture; America, whose rural population segment – a quarter of the total – roughly equalled Germany's,[1] had neither a Junker-type agrarian-military establishment nor a president unable to distinguish between the needs of the nation and the landed interest.

Before the seizure of power the Nazis had preached a gospel of urban unscrambling; on the land where German folkdom had its inviolate being, they intended to rear a new, hardy nobility of blood and soil. Schemes of rural resettlement, however, accorded ill with the Nazis' overriding aim, which was to revise the Versailles Treaty, since rearmament necessitated industrialization and urbanization; they also ran counter to the natural trend of economic development which was emptying the countryside for the benefit of the towns in all advanced countries.

Of course, many small farmers – themselves only a sub-group of a much wider social stratum including artisans and shopkeepers, whose bourgeois image of themselves conflicted with their proletarian incomes – also tried to ignore the trend of economic development; their defiance of the laws of economic logic both provided Nazism with a huge voting reservoir and exacerbated the problems of German agriculture, which were, in any event, quite formidable. Although inflation had wiped out the farmers' post-war burden of debt, a number of factors – outlay necessitated by changes in the consumption pattern, taxes imposed by Weimar,* wage and social insurance increases, high interest rates and the operation of the price scissors – all interacted to push agriculture into debt again.

* On the eve of the Depression, the tax burden on agriculture had increased $2\frac{1}{2}$–3 times above its pre-war total. (cf. Frieda Wunderlich, *Farm Labour in Germany 1810–1945*, Princeton University Press, 1961, p. 41).

When the Depression intervened to cut farm-sale proceeds from 10 billion marks (1928) to 6·5 billion (1932), total agrarian debts – notwithstanding the Brüning government's reduction of interest rates – rose to 10·6 billion, and the repayment of interest alone consumed 15 per cent of all agrarian income in 1932.[2] The effect of the Depression on the various sectors of agriculture differed; large estates tended to be hard hit, but the sizeable subsidies they received under the 'Eastern Aid' programme featherbedding agriculture east of the Elbe, cushioned them to some extent. At the other end of the scale, day labourers and farm hands, who had previously been lured away by higher wages in industry, drifted back to the land, where they were more sure of getting at least a bare minimum than in the towns.* On the whole, small farmers weathered the Depression better than large ones, since they were less dependent on the market, paid out little in wages and could adjust to hard times by living more frugally.

Even so, impoverishment and indebtedness engendered a mood of militant desperation among sections of the normally quiescent agrarian community, and in 1932 peasant discontent, flaring into violence, spread from Schleswig-Holstein across the whole of Northern Germany; court officials involved in foreclosures and evictions were manhandled, and tax offices and town halls blown up or set on fire. As if to symbolize the central position of the agrarian problem within the overall political pattern, Hitler's appointment as Chancellor occurred just one day before his predecessor Schleicher was to publish the report of an official inquiry into the 'Eastern Aid Scandal' (so called because of a misappropriation of public money earmarked for salvaging large non-viable eastern estates).

The area east of the Elbe comprised the bulk of the large estates of 250 acres upwards, which amounted to over a sixth of Germany's total arable area, and was owned by 17,070 Junkers and middle-class land owners (representing 0·5 per cent of all cultivators). Two thirds of all arable land consisted of medium-sized farms of between twelve and 250 acres, worked by two-fifths of all agrarian entrepreneurs, while smallholdings of up to twelve acres totalled well under a sixth of the cultivable area and served three-fifths of all farmers. Dwarf holdings predominated in the cottage-industry areas of Thüringia, the wine-growing regions of the Rhineland, and such pockets of rural backwardness as the Rhön, the Eiffel, the Taunus and the Westerwald.

In the context of German agriculture, backwardness was a highly relative term. Two-thirds of all farms lacked a piped water supply, a factor which, combined with the widespread fragmentation of holdings in scattered strips, added up to twenty kilometres' walking to the daily work-load[3]. More often than not, ploughs were drawn by oxen and grain tied into bundles manually. The lack of mechanical aids was most graphically represented by comparative statistics concerning tractors. Though, by 1939, Nazi Germany had almost trebled the country's total of 24,000 tractors during the Depression, the overall requirement was still estimated at somewhere in the region of half a million.[4] Whereas British farmers deployed one tractor for every 310 acres of land, the German ratio was one for every 810 acres,[5] and the daily area ploughed by one German ranged from a fifth to a quarter of the American average.[6] Fertilizers were not used to optimum advantage, so that increased investment in them did not produce commensurately higher crop yields, and bookkeeping was a rarely practised skill.

Relative technical backwardness was accompanied by social backwardness which assumed medieval proportions in places. A Berlin illustrated paper likened Worpswede Moor – a rather untypical area of extreme backwardness – to Bethlehem in Biblical times, with humans and animals sharing the same dwelling.[7] In the Rhön region, peasants unable to afford straw were entitled to gather leaves in the forest as a substitute.[8] Villagers in the Nuremberg area still followed the ancient custom of visiting the barber twice annually to be bled.[9] Not only did country people follow old customs, in economically mixed areas, at least, farmers also tended to be older than non-farmers. In a part of Württemberg which was statistically investigated, men over fifty constituted two-thirds of the agrarian work-force, while in industry and handicrafts they constituted only one-third of the total.[10]

Whereas on average every eighth German owned a wireless set, only one in twenty-five did so in the countryside.[11] Similarly, the rural population, especially in the more thinly peopled east, had little access to cinemas, a situation that the Nazis remedied by arranging regular visits by mobile cinemas to remote villages.

In looking at German agriculture after 1933, one has to separate the realities of the Third Reich from the constructs of Nazi ideology. It was a basic premise of Nazism that farmers constituted the incorruptible nucleus of the *Volk*, and that the asphalt of cities spelt degeneration and racial decay; but when Gottfried Feder* tried to reverse the population imbal-

* Feder was one of the leading ideologues during the early history of the Party, but his influence declined drastically after the seizure of power.

ance between town and country (70/30 per cent) by settling labourers in semi-peasant villages round decentralized factories, his plan was thwarted by a powerful lobby of brass-hats and Junkers. Rural settlement was anathema to the generals because it inhibited rearmament, while the Junkers regarded it as inimical to the prospect of turning their estates into grain factories for the urban market. Schemes of internal colonization, which the Weimar Republic had pursued quite successfully, also lapsed into relative insignificance after 1933. The regime's solicitude for the landed interest went even further. Once in office, the erstwhile sniffers-out of Weimar corruption swept the findings of the Eastern Aid inquiry under the carpet and continued to pay subsidies.*

The Third Reich's rearmament drive not only restored the army – and with it the Junker officer corps – to its prestigious pre-war position in society, but simultaneously brought the owners of large estates tangible economic benefits. Land values rose as a result of heavy government spending on the construction of roads, airfields and barracks; in addition, the Wehrmacht itself provided the horse-breeding Junker estates with a profitable and steadily expanding market. The regime promulgated a law limiting the mortgage interest rate to $4\frac{1}{2}$ per cent in June 1933, and itself advanced generous credits for improving silos, drainage and labourers' dwellings on large estates.[12] The re-absorption by industry of millions of unemployed, increased urban purchasing power, and prompted an expansion of the market from which the large food-producing units with sufficient liquid assets to make the requisite investments benefited disproportionately.

But financial security notwithstanding, the Junkers were neither politically nor socially entirely at ease in the Third Reich. Though on the surface the Nazi displayed a scrupulous regard for title deeds, and Feder-type resettlement plans rarely got beyond the drawing-board, many Junkers were uncomfortably aware that their heightened affluence masked a decline in status, in that they were gradually becoming administrators rather than owners of their estates.

To harness agriculture to the requirements of the state the Nazis had set up the Reich Food Estate, a mammoth corporation comprising Germany's total of more than 3,000,000 farms, nearly 500,000 food and drink retail stores, and 300,000 food-processing enterprises.[13]

The programme of the Food Estate was a rag-bag of anti-urbanism,

* On 13 September 1933 the German Press reported the adjournment *sine die* of the trial of General Regional Director Dr Heppel, the central figure of the *Osthilfe-Skandal*.

blood-and-soil racism and pseudo-socialism: Food Estate leader Walter Darré spoke of replacing the market mechanism by an organic exchange of commodities.[14]

More mundanely, the Food Estate, with its formidable apparatus of 20,000 full-time and 113,000 honorary officials, fixed all agricultural prices and wages, set production quotas, determined what crops were to be sown, and allocated scarce resources (the latter signifying, in plain German, that political recalcitrants were starved of spare parts for farm machinery until they came to heel). Although there was an aristocratic segment among the leadership of the Nazi Farmers' Association – there were a dozen names with the aristocratic prefix 'von' among forty-five national and regional leaders in 1933[15] – power was basically in the hands of large-scale farmers; this subtle change in the power structure of the countryside was symbolized by the appointment of Walter Darré, the lower middle-class pig-breeder, as Nazi Minister of Agriculture in place of the customary Junker incumbents of that portfolio.

Despite an extensive convergence of Nazi and Junker interests, the landed aristocracy's position within the Third Reich power structure can best be described as tangential. The Gauleiters of the eastern regions (Koch of East Prussia, Hildebrandt of Mecklenburgh, Karpenstein of Pomerania, Kube of Westmarck and Bruckner of Silesia) in which the bulk of the large estates were situated, were *Radikalinskis* (radical or leftist members of the Nazi hierarchy); one of them, Hildebrandt of Mecklenburgh, even earned notoriety as the instigator of the murder of two estate owners. Yet, by and large, these plebeian bigwigs tried to ape the mores of the Junkers, who were at the same time socially superior and politically subordinate to them. Early in 1939 that erratic mouthpiece of pseudo-revolutionary Nazism, the *Schwarzes Korps*, raised a dreaded spectre as far as the Junkers were concerned. 'To have as many people as possible work the land independently, it is necessary to carve up the mammoth estates.'[16] Yet before the year was out Junker estates were actually being enlarged by the inclusion of former Polish territory.

Similarly, while local Party and Food Estate officials could exercise considerable pressure upon estate owners to make them provide better amenities – above all housing – for their labourers, the latter were still subjected to all manner of semi-feudal obligations, such as the performance of socage service as beaters during hunts.[17]

Hunting remained the land-owning aristocrats' pastime *par excellence*, a factor the regime exploited by refusing a hunting licence to non-members of the Nazi Hunters' Association.[18] And yet the Nazi pseudo-revolution affected the time-honoured routine of hunt meetings only marginally. After hunt dinners all the participants – women in evening dress, men in tails – still went out into the nocturnal forest to 'bring in the quarry', having their paths lit by foresters and beaters with burning torches, while the rest of the estate's retinue and their families stood about deferentially in the shadows and the mort was sounded over the carcase of each noble stag.[19] Some aristocrats, however, dispensed with hunt dinners when the 'spirit of folk community' required extending dinner invitations to bailiffs, foresters and other '*Portugiesen*' (a snobbish term for the small fry of rural society), who were frequently not merely card-carrying but fanatical members of the Party.[20] On the other hand, Nazi officials usurped many functions traditionally discharged by the lord of the manor. In the patriarchal context of agrarian society, it was the Party that now arranged the annual harvest festival, at which villagers were treated to beer, sausages, dancing and political harangues, and it was the local leader of the *Frauenschaft* (the women's subsidiary of the Party) instead of the lady of the manor who went visiting farmers' and labourers' wives who had fallen ill or were pregnant.[21]

Alongside this subtle social displacement of the aristocracy the regime also engineered a high-decibel rhetorical revolution: it labelled some 600,000 medium-sized farms (averaging thirty acres in 1933) as *Erbhöfe*, i.e. hereditarily entailed holdings which were not to be mortgaged nor wholly or partly disposed of, and inflated their owners into a 'new nobility of blood and soil'.[22]

Erbhöfe passed intact from father to eldest son, a practice which involved disinheriting younger sons, who, in parts of south-west Germany, had previously been entitled to co-inheritance. The Nazi regime favoured the young: under the legislation for the hereditary estates the 'senior portion' (*Altenteil*) which old farmers had previously received in the form of money upon retiring was converted into maintenance and kind, an arrangement which exposed the old to the chicanery of the young and made not a few of them put off their retirement as long as they possibly could. By 1939 the *Erbhof* farmers had nearly doubled their average acreage (fifty-five compared to thirty acres six years earlier), thus illustrating that, in the economic sphere at least, and the *kulaks* of the Third Reich had little to complain of; but in the non-material sphere, too, the regime did them proud: they were the only farmers to be known as *Bauern* (farmer/peasant, a term whose normally neutral – not to say pejorative – connotation the Nazis did their utmost to refurbish), while large estate owners, as well as 'small' smallholders, all came under the blanket heading of *Landwirte* ('farmer').

Another – and several times larger – rural section which benefited markedly under the new dispensation were ordinary farm workers. The gross wages of agricultural labourers, which, in common with everyone else's, had been cut by about a fifth during the Depression, were restored to their 1929 level as early as 1937.[23] In addition to being virtually untaxed, they were exempt from unemployment and health-insurance payments* while their obligatory Food Estate 'subscriptions' and Winter Relief contributions were fixed at the unusually low rate of 0·5 per cent of their income and 25 pfennigs per month respectively. But in spite of such improvements, farm workers' pay remained abysmally low. The absolute maximum a skilled farm worker in East Prussia received for a working year of 2,950 hours was 1,176 marks, whereas the semi-skilled industrial wage for four-fifths of those work-hours averaged 1,560 marks per annum (in addition, farm workers' wives were obliged to do unpaid chores while many industrial workers' wives brought in a second wage-packet).[24] An interesting feature of the German agrarian pay-structure was the survival of payment in kind. The East Prussian farm worker's annual wage amounted to a mere 240 marks, the remaining 79 per cent of his income being made up of 'perquisites', i.e. grain, animals, a small tract of land, free housing, lighting and fuel. In more westerly rural areas the proportion of wages tended to go up, while advanced areas like the Rhineland had abandoned payment in kind completely. (Actually the high proportion of 'perquisites' comprising the wages of farm workers east of the Elbe was a fairly useful buffer against the effect of price rises.)

The regime's chief financial tokens of solicitude for the rural proletariat were connected with the battle of births and the battle of harvests. Married partners who had both spent five years in agriculture, and who undertook to continue therein, were eligible for 1,800 marks (in other words, eighteen months' top wages) in the shape of grants, as well as marriage and furnishing loans convertible into free gifts.

Since agricultural workers' families tended to be above average size, they also benefited from the regime's schemes for family allowances – both the basic children's allowance, a lump sum of 100 marks per child for families with four or more children under sixteen, and the continuous

---

* Exemption from health-insurance contributions applied only to farm workers with large families; this stipulation, however, made the majority eligible.

allowance of 10 marks per month for the third child, 20 marks per month for the fourth, and so on.*

One of the most deplorable aspects of the farm labourer's existence was housing, a sphere in which the regime attempted two forms of improvement. Estate owners were induced to construct new dwellings by means of tax incentives, and workers themselves were offered government credits for long-term house purchase.†

Estate owners who did not fulfil their social obligations were subjected to strong official pressures, and every so often backsliding 'plant leaders' were arraigned before the regime's Courts of Social Honour. One particular estate-owner, for instance, was divested of his right to be plant leader for six months, for forcing one of his labourers to make eight children sleep in four beds in a room 11·5 sq. m. in area, although he had additional accommodation at his disposal.[25]

A further means of helping the agricultural worker to improve his lot were the occasional polemics launched by the radical wing of the Nazi Party against 'reactionary' estate owners. In the course of one such polemic, the *Schwarzes Korps* highlighted the semi-feudal conditions obtaining on a 'Knight's estate' fully three years after the seizure of power.

Herr von Wedemayer pays his labourers eleven pfennigs per hour, i.e. 315 marks per year, plus 465 marks' worth of *Deputat* ['perquisites'] (consisting of rye, potatoes, timber, accommodation, an area of garden land and the right to stable a cow). The labourer in question was obliged to provide a *Hofgänger* (additional labourer), and since his eldest son was too young, it had been demanded of him that his wife, the mother of nine children, should perform seven hundred hours' work per annum.[26]

Feudal survivals, though, mattered less than the dearth of basic amenities. In 1937 the total of agricultural workers' dwellings in the Reich was 350,000 short of the actual number required, a backlog which explains the excessively low marriage rate (one in three) among eligible farm labourers.[27] In the same year 2,500 married farm workers were out of work in Silesia

* These applied to everybody from 1941 onwards, having previously been restricted to families with a monthly income of under 185 marks, a category which had included all farm workers anyway. Additional Nazi social innovations benefiting farm workers were payments for working days lost owing to illness, a death in the family or the birth of a child (cf. Frieda Wunderlich, *op. cit.*, p. 352).

† Houses valued at 5,000 to 6,000 marks elicited government loans of up to 75 per cent at 4 per cent interest payable over sixty-five years. The rent therefore worked out at 12 to 16 marks monthly. In addition, the government offered short-term loans at 3 per cent for the initial down-payment of one quarter.

because prospective employers were unable or unwilling to provide family accommodation for them.

The juxtaposition of rural deprivation and urban amenities (such as shops, cinemas or cafés), as well as opportunities – a Hamburg docker earned half as much again as a Pomeranian farmhand – engendered a massive exodus from the land. In West Prussia, for instance, where the rate of rural depopulation for the last ten years of the Weimar Republic had been 1·5 per cent per annum, it rose to 2·5 per cent during the Third Reich.[28]

This meant that a regime which had pledged itself to staunch the draining of the countryside's vital human substance by the 'Moloch megalopolis' – *der Moloch-Grosstadt* was a favourite term of Nazi demonology – far from redeeming its pledge, was actually precipitating rural debility.

One method of preventing the flight from the land would have been to establish parity of industrial and agricultural wages by reducing the one and raising the other; alarmed by the attraction of better-paid jobs on military and motorway construction projects, the Ministry of Labour actually proposed such a scheme in 1935, only to be over-ruled on the grounds that it would be politically impossible to enforce industrial wage-cuts.[29]

Another antidote to the flight from the land was legislation prohibiting farm workers to leave their jobs; a standstill order was imposed in 1934, but within two years their frustration, together with manpower requirements of the construction industry, necessitated a change in official policy. The freedom of movement that resulted from this lasted only till the outbreak of war, but by that date an estimated 1,000,000 to 1,500,000 farm workers and their dependants had forsaken the land for the flesh-pots of Megalopolis (though not all the exodus was, in fact, towards the towns: construction sites, quarries, brick-works, i.e. places of industrial employment in the countryside, all attracted their quota of rural emigrants).[30]

Although the flight from the land eased the manpower bottle-necks, the road-building and rearmament programmes, it confronted the regime with a need to mobilize new labour reserves for agriculture, a need to which Nazi officialdom superficially proved quite equal. Cheap adolescent labour, in the form of an agrarian ninth year for poor schoolchildren, the girls' land service year, Hitler Youth and student harvest camps, a Reich Labour Service, was, in fact, mobilized on a massive scale. But most of these replacements, though often idealistically willing, were neither very able nor permanent. Other stop-gap measures included organizing harvest commandos in factories, and directing job-seekers into agriculture on pain of forfeiture of unemployment benefits.[31] To attract young people to the land, a new type of apprenticeship for farmworkers was created. However, of 41,000 apprenticeships offered in 1937, no more than 7,000 were actually taken up.[32] As always, the regime invoked ritual and semantics to redress the situation. The passing-out ceremony of apprentices in Hesse took place in a medieval castle courtyard; having received certificates entitling them – and them alone – to be called 'land workers' in future, the assembled lads intoned strophe and antistrophe of choric speech, ending in the refrain 'The Lord gives life and we give bread. That's why we farmers are closest to God.'[32a]

The Hitler Youth land service placed 18,000 boys and girls from urban environments on the land in 1938, and at the end of their term of service one-fifth decided to stay on and take up an agricultural career. Similar results were obtained by the Reich Labour Service, although there were Service camps where the whole complement of recruits refused *en bloc* to take up permanent residence on the land. In 1938 more than 100,000 Italian and Hungarian seasonal workers helped bring in the German harvest, and this – rather than any back-to-the-land schemes for German youth – prefigured the Nazis' ultimate method for solving problems of agricultural manpower; in other words, they conscripted millions of European war prisoners and slave workers for labour on German farms.

With the war gradually draining the countryside of male Germans, farmers' wives increasingly shouldered the burden of responsibility for keeping Nazi agriculture going. Even in peacetime women's share of the agricultural work-burden had been prodigious. Women constituted nearly 50 per cent of the rural labour force (a proportion exceeded only in the catering and clothing industries; the overall female segment of the urban labour force was 30 per cent); but three-quarters of them were members of farmers' or labourers' families, and were therefore unpaid.[33] Their working hours, which tended to be up to a tenth longer than those of men, were on average seventy-five per week (eighty-two during the war),[34] over and above which a hundred-hour working week was the norm at harvest time. The feminine age-group doing the greatest share of work was that of the over sixty-fives. On small farms, women did three-quarters of the work, on medium-sized ones half, and on large ones a quarter.[35] In 1939, Secretary of State Pfundtner of the Ministry of the Interior noted the conspicuous increase of miscarriages among farmers' wives as a result of overwork attributable to the shortage of female rural labour.[36] It was hardly surprising that women were widely held to be the moving force behind the rural exodus. Party propagandists regularly – but ineffectively – berated them for their susceptibility to the glitter of city life. Such charges were corroborated by a study of matrimonial preferences carried out among village girls in the Tübingen area after the outbreak of war. This study established that, while it was the ambition of well-dowered farmers' daughters to marry such local notables as pastors or village schoolmasters, the most eligible spouses in the eyes of unportioned village girls were soldiers on active service or industrial workers. What made marriage to farmers a highly unattractive prospect was the shortage of agrarian labour and the additional wartime burden imposed on farmers' wives. In one particular hamlet, only eight out of thirty-seven marriages between 1932 and 1937 were to farmers.[37] The report concluded: 'The single men hardest hit by this trend are the younger brothers of farmers [those most adversely affected by the hereditary estate legislation]; the only possible way out of their dilemma is a planned settlement of German farmers in Eastern Europe.'

The hardship suffered by deprived co-heirs through the Nazi enforcement of primogeniture was not only matrimonial. In south-western Germany their expectations had traditionally centred on inheriting a small patch of their father's land, which, together with their wives' marriage portion, might conceivably amount to a viable smallholding. Deprived co-heirs who did join the rural exodus were given the choice of taking up apprenticeships in rural artisan workshops or applying for *Neubauernscheine* (licences to cultivate newly created farmsteads).[38] Some new farmsteads were created by government amortization of the debts owed by heavily encumbered estate owners in exchange for the latter's surrendering a portion of their land. This land could then be acquired freehold by small farmers, who in many instances had previously been mere lessees, provided they could raise the cash required for a deposit.

Other fiscal measures beneficial to agriculture have already been mentioned. The reduction in the rate of mortgage interest payment amounted to the equivalent of £280 million between 1934 and 1938. During the same period the tax burden on agriculture was reduced by £60 million.[39] In the last peacetime year the annual tax burden on agriculture (£569 million, equivalent to about 10 per cent of agrarian income) was £50 million less than ten years earlier, although the overall incidence of taxation had been increased in the interim.[40]

To some extent the regime thus appeared to be discriminating in favour of agriculture at the expense of other sectors of the community – an impression reinforced by a 34 per-cent increase in farm income (accruing largely from higher prices charged to the urban consumer) between 1933 and 1935.[41] Thereafter, however, farm income stagnated, and from 1937 onwards the price scissors once again operated against agriculture: in that year the farmers secured only a sixth share of the national income (17 per cent) compared to their quarter share (24 per cent) of national work.[42]*

The blessings conferred upon agriculture by the Nazi autarchy programme were similarly mixed. The drive for self-sufficiency necessarily promoted an intensification of agriculture, but it also put into operation the law of diminishing returns. The limitation of fodder imports limited livestock production, which in turn reduced the supply of natural fertilizers, thus increasing the dependence of agriculture (as well as its outlay) on chemical fertilizers.[43]

The increased expenditure on chemicals and machinery necessitated by the high production targets set by the Food Estate, as well as the rural labour shortage, resulted in the agricultural debt burden once again equalling the total value of farm production by 1937–8. Even before this date the degree of indebtedness had actually increased on the smaller farms, while for medium-sized and large farms the trend had been the other way. The incidence of rural depopulation showed analogous divergences. Whereas large estates only lost one out of every ten workers between 1935 and 1937, small farms lost more than one out of every three.[44]

Rigorously enforced production quotas, punitive prohibitions on the use of food grains as animal fodder and the illicit slaughter of livestock were all part of the Third Reich's straitjacketing of agriculture; even so, some farmers doubtless preferred the warmth of a straitjacket to exposure to the keen blasts of the free-market mechanism. The market went into limbo as the Food Estate stood ready to take all his produce off the farmer, though it only paid him after the unconscionable time lag that is endemic in all mammoth bureaucracies.

This, at any rate, was the tip of the iceberg; the contours below the surface were more formidable and more complex. The Food Estate regulated and enforced both prices and delivery quotas most minutely;

* While farm income had increased 34 per cent by 1937, wages and salaries had gone up by nearly 50 per cent, and profits of trade and industry by 88 per cent.

for instance, each hen had to lay sixty-five eggs per year. There were monthly visits to farms, when Food Estate controllers milked the cows and determined the prescribed milk yield (milk, incidentally, had to be sold to creameries, from which the farmer bought back skim milk). The price of milk was tied to its fat content. This, however, depended upon cattle fodder (in short supply owing to the autarchy programme), a dilemma which rather taxed the resourcefulness as well as the resources of most dairy farmers.

The Food Estate maintained a dossier on each farm, in which it entered monthly reports on the state of crops and livestock, labour force and wages, delivery obligations and actual delivery data. Intent on its self-sufficiency drive, the regime also partly coerced and partly coaxed farmers into reducing the area under such crops as wheat, rye and – temporarily – hops in favour of beet, flax, rape and sunflowers.

Occasionally, when dirigism came into too harsh a conflict with the realities of the economic situation, the authorities gave way; for example, 10 per cent of all farmers on entailed estates were juridically exempted from prohibitions on the sale, division, mortgaging or renting of their land, all of which were enshrined in the hereditary estate legislation.[45] At other times, farmers adroitly managed to transfer the burden of financial hardship imposed on them on to the shoulders of others. Thus in 1935, when many stock-breeders were prepared to let their animals perish rather than fatten them for sale at the officially fixed price, they forced cattle dealers and butchers to pay illegal prices which almost wiped out their profit margin, but the latter were prepared to do this rather than report offending farmers and cut themselves off from their future sources of supply. (The butchers, of course, tried to pass on the increase to their customers in the towns, but here they ran very grave risks, since the police were lynx-eyed in their surveillance of retail shop prices, a highly sensitive area as far as the penny-pinching public was concerned.)

In fact, peasant cunning drove more than one coach and four through the tight network of Food Estate regulations. To circumvent fixed prices, for instance, they diluted quality flour with inferior grades, or made the sale of one regulated – and therefore unprofitable – item dependent on the buyer's purchase of an uncontrolled, profitable one. 'Linked' and other illegal transactions carried severe penalties in peacetime. During the war the deterrents invoked against such malpractices as barter, black marketeering, illegally retaining produce or the illicit slaughter of livestock included the death penalty.* In German, the last-mentioned offence was called *Schwarzschlachten* (black slaughtering) and there can be little doubt that the discrepancy between the black and white statistics for this form of crime – its total incidence compared to the number of prosecutions – was quite staggering. The wartime diversion of manpower naturally reduced the degree of supervision that the authorities were able to enforce, and in addition to which the urban population was both prepared and able to pay more for scarce food than ever before. The war also improved the farmers' situation in a number of other respects. They could no longer be pressurized into investing money in machinery; expenditure on repairs and maintenance declined, owing to the shortage of raw materials and tools; and the foreign workers 'attached' to many farms were cheaper than German labour.

Offsetting these advantages was the further movement of the price scissors against agriculture (in 1941, industrial goods cost the farmer a fifth more than before the war),[46] the pre-emption of scarce luxury consumer goods and medical supplies by the towns, and an even heavier work-load arising from the dearth of men of military age.

While the urban population envied country folk their undisturbed peace and well-stocked larders, the latter coveted the town-dwellers' greater resistance to disease and work-strain, and their better provision with non-edible items of daily consumption.

The duties incumbent on the (mainly elderly) farmers multiplied. They were enrolled in a rural Home Guard (the *Wachdienst*, not to be confused with the military *Volkssturm*), had to do duty in village fire brigades, and man search parties on the lookout for colorado beetle. Even in wartime, when food production assumed greater importance than ever before, one-fifth of all agricultural enterprises (the majority of them dwarf holdings) failed to provide their cultivators with an adequate livelihood,[47] and as late as the spring of 1944, farmers, in letters to the Press, protested against the evacuation of factories to the countryside, because of the unsettling effect of industrial wage levels on their labour force.[48]

With the countryside's resources stretched to the maximum, the government alternately offered farmers positive and negative incentives to maintain and diversify agricultural productivity. It handed out premium

* One issue of the Viennese edition of the *Völkische Beobachter* (16 February 1944) reported four executions of farmers who had illicitly slaughtered pigs. A dairy farmer was sentenced to twenty-one months' imprisonment for not delivering milk. Sentences of over one year disqualified the farmer from ever owning a farm again.

payments to hold price levels, gave sugar to farmers producing turnips and boot leather to owners of forests who collected tanning bark; but in 1944 it also forced farmers to make deliveries in excess of their quotas.[49]

By this time, 2½ million workers from the east, plus hundreds of thousands of Frenchmen (prisoners and others), as well as free Italian, Slovak and Hungarian free workers were deployed on the land, and farmers had come to depend on their foreign labour to such an extent that the transfer of Poles from agriculture to industry and mining occasioned widespread complaints.[50]

German farmers were commanded – on pain of dire punishment – to integrate eastern workers economically at the same time as segregating them socially. Their accommodation was to be kept well apart from the other living quarters, and under no circumstances were they to eat at the same table as the farmer's family. The latter prohibition was often honoured only in the breach, since its observance, which was difficult to supervise anyway, would have entailed additional domestic chores. But labour-saving motives were not the only ones behind the evasion of race-hygienic quarantine measures on the farmstead. It seemed illogical to some farmers, whose eastern workers were pulling their weight, not to consider them as part of the farm family.

In addition to work, religion could be a factor militating against acceptance of Nazi race taboos. Some Catholic farmers looked upon their French and Polish workers more as co-religionists than as non-Germans (although the relatively 'liberal' official treatment of French PoWs was also the burden of many a rustic complaint).* Taking a cynical, though partly justifiable view of the phenomenon, Nazi officialdom explained the kindly way in which some farmers treated their foreign workers as a bribe to ensure the secrecy of black-market deals and illicit slaughtering.[51]

Sexual needs also had a bearing on the situation. Despite drastic deterrents – 'racially defiled' females incurred both ostracism and long jail terms (their defilers, if Polish, generally suffered execution) – farm women deprived of husbands and fiancés were driven to share more than their tables with eastern workers and prisoners-of-war.

Nazism had thus defaulted on its agrarian Utopia twice over; in peacetime, by partly depopulating the countryside it had meant to restore to the centre of national life, and in wartime, by exposing rustic German

---

* Cf. the grievance of farmers in the Regensburg region of Catholic Bavaria: 'While we begin our work at five in the morning, the French prisoners only arrive at 6.30 to start theirs.'

womanhood – the much-vaunted repository of the nation's eugenic substance – to the importunities of lower breeds.

The many foreigners around them filled country folk with a sense of unease. The villagers' apprehensions about the tendency of Poles to congregate in large crowds on their work-free Sundays were all the greater because they knew that the police force was spread rather thinly in the countryside during the war. This odd ambiguity of relationship between serfs and masters led a district leader of the Nazi Farmers' Association to advise his members:

Foreign workers are pigs, dogs, they are creatures who are the counterfeits of human beings. We have to treat them with the utmost severity, smash their faces in and kill them if they dare so much as to open their mouths to remonstrate. No judge will find against a German farmer who has done such a deed.[52]

It was not a judge but a civil servant – the head of the District Labour Office – who, in a letter to the leadership of the Nazi Farmers' Association, adjudicated on the content of this speech by pointing out that it ran completely counter to the directive on the treatment of foreign workers issued by the Reich Commissioner for Labour Organization, Gauleiter Sauckel.

The divergence between the racist phantasmagorias and the rational calculation of exploitation thus diversified still further the pattern of relationships between native yeomen and their alien serfs. The deterioration of the military situation inclined a growing number of farmers to take out insurance policies, as it were, with the slaves who might turn into their masters overnight. During the collapse of the Third Reich many foreign workers helped their former taskmasters escape westwards, accompanying them on long-drawn-out treks through the snow. But there were far more instances of pillage and vandalism as thousands of uprooted men, long denied human stature, wreaked vengeance on their exploiters.

Even so, though the use to which German farmers put foreign labour fell only marginally short of naked exploitation, the rural eastern worker was still an object of envy to those of his compatriots who were put into German factories or mines. The top strata of agrarian society – from whatever motives – here too proved more aloof from the regime than their counterparts in industry. *Mutatis mutandis* the 20 July plot prompted Nazi reprisals approximating to a minor social revolution even before Junker society east of the Elbe passed out of history at the same time as East Elbia passed out of German control.

12

BUSINESS

Of all of Germany's socio-economic groups the business community, especially if we take it to include the electorally crucial economic 'middle class' of independents (*Mittelstand*) such as shopkeepers or master craftsmen, assisted the Nazis most in seizing power. While it is true that a circumspect section among big business only subsidized Hitler once the electoral tide had started flowing in his direction, there can be no gainsaying industry's role as chief grave-digger of the Weimar Republic. 'Fascism,' as Franz Neumann has rightly observed, 'arose out of the need of economic power holders . . . not to react to the Communist threat but to suppress the democratic movement which aimed at utilizing political power for the rational and social structuring of the economy.'[1]

The lure that irresistibly drew the mass of independents into the Nazi camp was the Party's 'middle-class ideology', a panacea for all their economic ills. This envisaged state aid to small business and artisan enterprises, state action against trade unions, and state curbs on big firms, department stores and co-operatives.

The need to balance electoral and power-political considerations, i.e. to retain the support of this central section of the community despite the way heavy industry was favoured in the army drive, made management of the Nazi economy a function of the complex interplay of three forces: big business, small business and the state. To enumerate those disparate interest groups is to touch on a key question about the inter-relationship between politics and economics in the Third Reich, a question some Marxists have answered by depicting Hitler as the puppet of the Ruhr barons; postwar apologists for big business have represented industry as the helpless accessory after the fact of the all-powerful Nazi state. Both theories are highly contentious; where there can be no disagreement is on the way the *Mittelstand* fared in this tripartite contest: it came off worst.

Early on in the Third Reich there was little indication of this, however. In settlement of their debt to a social group to which they owed a good deal, the Nazis passed a series of measures forming major planks in the

Mittelstand platform. The trade unions were smashed; co-operatives and particularly department stores, though surviving, suffered such curtailment that at one time they seemed to be heading for extinction. The law for the protection of the retail trade froze all chain stores at their existing size, forbade the establishment of new ones, and prohibited them from providing such services as shoe-repairing, barbering, baking and catering.[2] Public agencies were forbidden to let department stores and co-operatives tender for contracts.

The law of November 1933 limiting price rebates to 3 per cent was a direct blow against co-operative dividend policy. But the mammoth German Labour Front which had fed the co-operatives into its capacious maw paradoxically kept them alive in an attenuated form, partly because some of its 'old fighters' had obtained sinecures in the co-op administration. (Within three years the number of co-operative outlets declined by over a quarter, and membership by just over a half; but the considerable contraction of a ubiquitous competitor did not benefit the *Mittelstand* proportionately, since only 1,000 out of 3,000 co-operative outlets that were closed down passed into the hands of the retail trade.)[3]

The authorities combated illicit cut-rate competition (*Schwarzarbeiten*) which posed a real threat to craft enterprises, by police raids on workshops. Unemployed 'black workers' caught in this way were debarred.[4] The establishment of all new shops and artisan enterprises required official permission, which was made dependent on local need and the applicant's professional, personal and political suitability. From 1935 onwards it became compulsory for everyone wanting to open a new artisan enterprise to pass the Master's Examination in his craft. This exam had previously been optional. In 1931 less than a third of all practising artisans held master's certificates – but after 1935 all younger, non-qualified owners of craft enterprises were obliged to qualify for a certificate of employment.

The certificate-awarding bodies concerned were the various trades guilds, membership of which was made compulsory. In addition to controlling the entire apprentice and vocational-training programmes within their trade, the guilds operated honour courts for adjudicating disputes among members, and could regulate the size of their branch of artisan production by closing of inefficient units.[5] Despite this accretion of guild power, however, such key proposals in the guild programme as the substitution of artisan production for the factory system, and the enforcement of de-mechanization as a cure for unemployment, were rejected out of hand; such Luddite prescriptions could hardly find favour with a regime bent on industrial preparation for war.

In token discharge of its debt to the petit-bourgeois masses the regime implemented the *Mittelstandsideologie* no further than was compatible with the requirements of industrial mobilization. Within those limitations, retailing fared better than artisan production – the only sector of the latter not ultimately deemed expendable was that of village-based crafts catering for the needs of countryfolk.

This did not, however, signify a conscious official intention to harm the small producer. Crafts were given a fairly assured place in the Nazi economy with the important proviso that they remained subordinate to the interests of industry. Nor did the regime's refusal to promote qualitative change in its status preclude various quantitative improvements. The grant of a 500 million-mark subsidy to house-owners in 1933 (for renovations, the installation of indoor lavatories and bathrooms, the conversion of large apartments into smaller units, and so on) was a boon for the construction trades, giving work to nearly a third of the total artisan labour force. An additional, minor, building boom was triggered off by the proliferating Nazi institutions and their need for administrative and ornamental buildings: contracts for this type of work were invariably awarded to artisan builders.

Similarly, Party formations were instructed to order uniforms and jackboots only from craft workshops and retail traders, and the NSV had to purchase its supplies for charitable distribution from the same source.[6]

But the rising tide of orders could not set the wheels of handicraft production turning without the lubricant of credit. Although the regime established special institutions advancing loans bearing an interest of 8 per cent, of the three purposes for which craftsmen with insufficient collateral required credit – re-equipment, settlement of debts, or the discharge of pending orders – only the last merited official consideration. In 1934 no more than a fifth of all credit applications – the average sum applied for was 3,000 Rm. – were granted.[7] In addition to this officially promoted pump-priming, the general upswing in the country naturally also benefited small business, but as the *Frankfurter Zeitung* pointed out, large-scale enterprises participated to an above-average extent in the overall increase in turnover, while the share of the smaller ones was less than proportionate to their numbers.[8] This statement appeared at the end of 1936, a year which constituted something of a turning-point in the development of economic life in Nazi Germany. The launching of the Four-Year Plan of precipitate industrial mobilization for war logically spelt the end to all hopes of reconstructing the economy on an artisan basis. By the same token, the mid-thirties were years of maximum expansion for small businesses. Retailing and crafts had been overmanned sectors of the economy for a long time, with the slump accentuating the imbalance, and the Third Reich raising expectations in excess of fulfilment. The number of artisan enterprises had increased by nearly a fifth between 1931 and 1936 to 1,650,000, but the last pre-war years were to see a decrease of 11 per cent.[9]

This official shake-out of economically non-viable units to supply fresh reserves for a tightening labour market met with an ambiguous response from the guilds. They welcomed it because it would make the available cake divisible into fewer and therefore larger slices, and yet were uncomfortably aware that it simultaneously reduced the overall size and importance of their organization and provided a precedent for further shake-out measures. These considerations, coupled with the fact that the guilds were empowered to carry out the streamlining of their own trades, made the winnowing-out process proceed at a slower pace than was officially considered desirable. Central to this process was the imposition, in 1935, of a universal obligation to keep accounts. Ledgers for incoming and outgoing goods ('supplies books' and 'customers' books') now enabled officialdom to subject all enterprises to searching tax control and to investigations of economic viability. This process was intensified by the ruthlessness of the fiscal authorities in collecting tax debts and refusal of the licensing authorities to grant new concessions to small shops wishing to diversify their selling lines. In addition the regime promoted compulsory cartelization in trades which were previously open: the number of radio retailers, for instance (60,000 in 1933), was more than halved by 1939, and wholesalers declined by a third under a new requirement that they must possess an unmortgaged capital of 30,000 marks.[10]

There were times when shopkeepers and food-trade middlemen found themselves caught helplessly between the upper millstone of the Food Estate's pricing policy and the lower one of the mandatory price freeze enforced in the shops. This situation, in which Food Estate, farmers and consumers benefited at the expense of grocers and butchers, provoked crises of conscience among officials of the guilds directly affected. In the presence of his local member the plenipotentiary for the food trade in the Rhineland challenged the authorities to send him to a concentration camp,

'I have myself long contravened price regulations and cannot report any colleague for the same offence.'[11]

As a rule, however, guild officials championed members' interests only if they coincided with their own, and the multiform economic bodies spawned by the Third Reich provided a happy hunting-ground for empire builders. 'Old fighters' who carved out niches for themselves in the guild structure tended to be both tyrannical – for instance they would rigorously fine members absent from meetings without the alibi of a medical certificate[12] – and notoriously venal: between 1932 and 1935 one particular sub-organization of the retail trade increased its personnel budget from 40,000 to 220,000 marks, while membership had only risen from 20,000 to 54,000.[13]

A typical case of venality came to light in East Prussia in 1938, where a district guild master of the tailoring trade who, in addition to running his own enterprise, was also the business manager of a consortium of tailoring workshops supplying the Wehrmacht, defrauded the Dresdner Bank of 200,000 marks by falsifying production quotas for uniforms to cover the deficit of his own firm.[14]

It was symptomatic of the nepotism prevalent within the guild organization that nine key officials of the East Prussian economic apparatus were members of the bakers' guild: the provincial craft master for the whole of East Prussia was a master baker.

The proliferation of guild officialdom reached remarkable proportions. A special trade association comprised the 12,000 itinerant fairground exhibitors throughout the country,[15] and another controlled the activities of nearly 100,000 hawkers and street-traders. (One of the manifestations of this control was an ordinance jointly promulgated by the municipality and the guild in Berlin, whereby fruit-vending vans had to be coloured ivory and light red, cigarette vending vans dark yellow, and so on.)[16]

The slaters' guild demanded guild membership (annual subscription 25 marks, insurance 48 marks) of farmers who supplemented their income 'to the extent of 7 marks a day for six weeks annually' by thatching roofs during the agricultural off-season. The art section of the Chamber for Arts and Culture (see p. 423) levied a contribution of 200 marks on the masters of the stone and monumental masons' guild.[17]

Just as in the Middle Ages every man owed allegiance to his lord, so in the Third Reich every individual owed allegiance – plus subscription fees – to his 'association'. Another medieval parallel that suggests itself was the importance of ritual in the life of the guilds. Annual craft days were celebrated at Frankfurt where, before a medieval backdrop and vast audiences – 250,000 in 1935 – the members of the cutlers' guild performed sword dances; choruses of bakers' apprentices recited declamations about work with corn, flour and bread (*Brot*) bringing them closest to God (*Gott*); journeymen's names were ceremoniously entered on guild rolls, and so on.[18]

However, neither archaic junketings, demarcation disputes about subscriptions, nor even sinecure hunting were central to the main concern of artisans and shopkeepers, which was economic. The *Mittelstand* saw itself in the midst of a resurgent economy, but such factors as tight credit, big business influence, the regime's scale of priorities, and the elephantine slowness of the official agencies in paying for work done perversely conspired to deprive it of a commensurate slice of the national cake. The extension of cartelization to the printing industry, for instance, resulted in many restrictive innovations: obligatory bookkeeping and the control of inventories; prohibition of price reductions which impaired the ability to meet tax obligations; freezing of investments at present levels; and restrictions on the sale of printing presses to limit further competition.[19]

Some food traders, caught in the cross winds of autarchy and the Food Estate monopoly, took evasive action. They circumvented the price freeze by offering lower-quality goods at the prescribed charge, or coupled the non-profitable sale of essentials with the advantageous one of non-essential items – and thus fell foul of the law. A fruit wholesaler was fined 10,000 marks for coupling transactions, with the *Schwarzes Korps* clamorously demanding that he be 'shortened by a head' if the offence should recur.[20] As for retailers, they sometimes circumvented price regulation quite involuntarily since they were hard put to it to orientate themselves amidst a welter of complicated directives and constant variations in the quality of the goods supplied to them. Police fines on shopkeepers who contravened the price legislation became an appreciable source of income. Such fines, moreover, constituted a potential reason for closing enterprises as part of the shake-out process. The threat of closure was not an empty one. By 1939 the 350,000 supernumerary enterprises – as estimated in 1936 – had been reduced by roughly one half.[21]

In addition, the economic *Mittelstand* evinced a pattern of growing senescence. In 1933 one out of every five owners of artisan enterprises was under the age of thirty, and only one out of seven above the age of sixty. By 1939 the proportion of under-thirties had halved and that of over-sixties gone up by a third.[22] In Berlin the total number of independents had declined by nearly a quarter within that period, and the number of – largely white-collar – employees had increased by 16 per cent.[23]

Yet concurrent with a decline of many craft occupations, there was an expansion of others. Such craftsmen as shoemakers, tailors, potters, weavers or smiths were all vulnerable in various degrees to the competition of large units, while artisans connected with the modern service industries – electricians, radio mechanics, garage hands – both increased in number and improved their lot.[24]

It should not be assumed that the retail trade as such – as distinct from certain branches of it – fared badly under the Third Reich. For one thing the regime showed itself more inclined to enact discriminatory measures against large-scale units in trade than in industry, thereby removing some of the retailers' chief grounds for grievance. These related specifically to the department stores which, because of their ambience (Jews had both pioneered and owned a large sector of this business) and because attacks on stores were expedient substitutes for anti-capitalist measures in industry, seemed almost predestined for extinction. They were subjected to a two-pronged method of attack: governmental prohibitions on their economic activities (as outlined on p. 168) and boycotts promoted by the Party and such affiliated formations as the League of Civil Servants. In 1935 a local official of the Labour Front could confidently threaten, 'If Frau W. is seen shopping at Karstadt's store once again I shall have her husband deprived of his military pension.'[25]

Despite harassment and boycott, however, the department stores eventually weathered the crises, and from 1936 onwards right up to the war their turnover increased annually by 10 per cent.[26] One of the factors ensuring their survival was that the ruin of the department stores would involve 90,000 employees at a period when unemployment was still a major problem, and the German Labour Front took up cudgels on behalf of these employees, who were already aggrieved as being stigmatized as second-class citizens on account of their work.[27]

Partly overlapping with the question of the department stores – though exceeding it in scope – was the issue of Aryanization. The idea of eliminating Jewish competitors by sharing their businesses held irresistible attractions for many artisans and retailers. In the early heady days of the Nazi revolution the regime still paid lip-service to this *Mittelstand* vision. Thus in 1934 the deputy Gauleiter of Franconia announced the take-over of a formerly Jewish department store at Nuremberg by the city's business community, with each trader staking a 500 Rm. share in the enterprise.[28]

But in the long run Aryanization decisively redounded to the advantage of big business, in addition to expediting the shake-out of the economy. The elimination of Jewish ownership halved the number of enterprises in certain branches of the textile and clothing industries, while Aryanizers active in machine building, flour milling, and the shoe and leather trade were actually the first pioneers of larger than middle-sized enterprises in the history of these industries.[29]

In retailing, too, streamlining took precedence over *Mittelstand* aspirations – of 3,750 Berlin shops still owned by Jews at the time of the Crystal Night, only 700 passed into other hands;[30] 'Aryanization would have had still better results in relieving pressure on the retail trade,' wrote a Nazi periodical in 1939, 'if chain stores had not used the opportunity to rent evacuated shop space in the business areas and thus moved their affiliates from unfavourable to better locations.'[31] Overall, thousands – instead of tens of thousands – of members of the class *Mittelstand* profited from the economic elimination of the Jews in a 'small' way; but, as the *Frankfurter Zeitung* stated in 1935, 'the main beneficiaries of Aryanization are a few big industrial concerns'[32] such as Mannesmann, Flick, Otto Wolff or the Hermann Goering works.[33]*

In the wider sense, Aryanization was typical of the changes wrought by the Nazi revolution at two separate levels:

(a) confiscation of Jewish property was substituted for the levelling-out of property as such (commercial, financial, landed and – above all – industrial) on a *Mittelstand* scale.
(b) Jewish expropriation typified the working of the Nazi economy: the larger the unit concerned, the greater its percentage share of the profits.

Some of the non-material benefits anticipated by industry had already been spelt out at the time of the Nazi take-over. 'The elections of 5 March will only be of use,' stated an editorial in *Stahl und Eisen* (the journal of the Ruhr industry) in 1933, 'if they are to last for a long time . . . Only if no

---

* The profits of these were so exorbitant that a special decree was issued for the taxation of profits made through Aryanization. When this still proved ineffective, a special ruling of the Ministry of Finance instituted retroactive taxation in cases of a specially aggravating kind. Aryanization also helped to change the structure of economic life. Industry gained a larger control over retailers by taking over Jewish enterprises with their own retail outlets. It infiltrated into the banking sphere, where the number of private banks was drastically reduced from 1,350 to 520 between 1932 and 1938 (cf. Franz Neumann, *Behemoth*, p. 275, and *Der Deutsche Volkswirt*, No. 41, 1938).

heed needs be paid to votes can the outstanding great changes in constitutional, administrative, fiscal and social matters be carried out.'[34]

These anticipations were overwhelmingly fulfilled. From March 1933 onwards industry no longer had to pay the slightest heed to voters, to parliament or to the trade unions. At the same time it signified its own readiness to participate in the outstanding changes by dismissing the director of its National Federation *Geheimrat*, privy councillor Ludwig Kastel, as well as the secretary of the powerful Langnam Verein Schlenker, because they were Jews.[35] (Incidentally, another group of industrialists – the *Ruhrlade* – broke up in 1938 because Krupp von Bohlen objected to criticism of Nazi corruption voiced by the – unrepresentative – anti-Nazi magnate Karl Bosch.)[36]

While certain forms of entrepreneurial organization declined, others grew more important. The '*Freundeskreis Heinrich Himmler*', a quorum drawn from the top echelons of industry, banking and insurance, formed a powerful connecting link between the holders of political power and the holders of economic power in the Third Reich. Through support ranging from financing the crucial 1932–3 election campaigns to supplying additional Waffen SS divisions with arms and uniforms ten years later,[37] they had built up a huge stock of credit with the regime, part payment of which consisted of their being made privy to the most closely guarded secrets of Nazi rule. In 1937 Himmler in person conducted members of the *Freundeskreis* on a guided tour of Dachau concentration camp, and five years later the SS intelligence chief Ohlendorff lectured them on aspects of the SD's work – especially the operations of the four commando task forces responsible for killing over a million Jews in Eastern Europe. (Ohlendorff was himself head of the Crimean commando task force for a time.)

Although symbolically the *Freundeskreis* represented rather more than its own membership, its experiences and the functions assigned to it were not necessarily the same as those of industry as a whole. All economic life was organized in what were known as National Groups (*Reichsgruppen*) (of which the Industrial Group was the most important) with each in turn sub-divided into Specialist Groups (*Fachgruppen*) according to particular trades. Based on a system of internal self-government, the Specialist Groups were an extended arm of the government civil service, with the important difference that economic officialdom consisted of representatives of the businesses involved. As an ever-larger segment of the economy came to depend on arms and other state orders, government and Wehrmacht nominees were increasingly appointed to their boards of directors.

Moreover, many firms considered it politic to give directorships to the 'golden pheasants' who could smooth their path in dealings with state or party authorities. Apart from being advisable when tendering for contracts, this exercise in protective camouflage could be essential in helping firms to by-pass government restrictions on foreign currency, and to secure allocations of raw material and labour supplies. The obligation to appoint such officials as *Mob-Beauftragte* (anti-sabotage and anti-industrial espionage directors) caused larger enterprises to place additional functionaries, from the Labour Front or the Gestapo for instance, on their boards. The entwining of the business structure with the state and Party machines was a complex process, the direction of which varied considerably at different times. As long as Schacht remained the key figure in the Nazi economy (he was Minister of Economics until 1937 and president of the Reichsbank until 1939), he used his remarkable ingenuity to secure entrepreneurs considerable room for manœuvre. He eased big business out of the direct form of Party control that had been envisaged by the Nazi populists and *Mittelstand* ideologists, helped it maintain corporate profit margins, and in fact reinforced the structure of private enterprise.[38] But thereafter the ever-growing importance of the Four-Year Plan initiated in 1936, the escalating arms drive, and the precedence of autarchy requirements over economic considerations all helped to reduce industry to a subordinate position *vis-à-vis* the state.

These modulations of the business/state relationship proceeded alongside changes in the very structure of economic life, though not independently of them. One aspect of these changes was the growth of industrial concentration. The number of joint stock corporations declined from 9,634 in 1932 to 5,418 in 1941, but their nominal capital increased by 2,000 million marks. From 1933 onwards government statutes enormously strengthened the organizational power of cartels. Armed with unlimited arbitrary powers of cartelization, the Ministry of Economics bestowed official sanctions on what had previously been private organizations, for restricting capacity and subordinating whole industries to the wishes of monopolists.[39]

A Frankfurt financial journal could well speak in terms of a rapidly increasing process of concentration charged with the greatest dynamic: in 1933, 40 per cent of Germany's industrial production was monopolistic, and this had increased to 70 per cent by 1937.[40] The huge steel trust formed by Kierdorf, Thyssen and Vögler dominated over a third of heavy industrial capacity, with Kloeckner, Krupp, Haniel, Mannesmann, Flick, Otto

Wolff and the Goering works forming additional centres of industrial agglomeration.

A somewhat similar process was transforming the structure of the joint stock corporations – a process which the newspaper *Deutscher Volkswirt* described as the starving-out of shareholders by the application of the Führer principle.

Under the 1937 corporation law the assembly of stockholders lost the power of deciding on questions of corporation policy. Stockholders could not question the balance sheet as it was presented, but they could abstain from the distribution of all profits that the board of directors had declared distributable; in other words, all the shareholders could do was to reduce their own share of the profits.[41] Managers who were appointed by the supervisory board – elected every five years by the general meeting – continued to serve on the boards and were permitted to receive bonuses. These bonuses were to be proportionate to the profits and to the social contributions for the benefit of employees. (The latter provision gave the German Labour Front an indirect share in corporate dividends.) The major changes in the working of capitalism to be engineered by the Nazis were: a rapid increase in undistributed profits; the precedence of managerial over stockholder interest; the diminished influence of banking and commercial capital; the permeation of the distributive apparatus by industrial monopolists; and a partial reduction of the dominance of heavy industry by the emergent chemical industry and certain of the metallurgical industries.[42]

The last-named process was typified by the rise of I. G. Farben. Unlike the 'conservative' steel industry, which had to be coerced into operating the officially prescribed breakneck expansion schemes, this dye trust made the regime's dizzy economic goals its own (partly because the production of synthetic materials necessitates a dynamic infrastructure by its very nature). The labour force of this chemical giant expanded 50 per cent to 330,000 between 1938 and 1943, while its profits increased 150 per cent to 822 million Rm.[43] Not only did it completely concur in the ends of Nazi policy (in addition to running large enterprises at Auschwitz, I. G. Farben contracted for the delivery of toxic gases to the gas chambers), but it also provided the means. One of its directors held a key post in the administration of the Four-Year Plan, and two thirds of the staff of the Reich Office for Economic Expansion were I. G. Farben men.[44]

While the chemical industry thus straddled the dividing line between private enterprise and the state, the steel industry had to countenance an invasion of its own domain by the state. The reluctance of the steel bosses to commit additional resources to the development of plant for processing low-quality domestic ores while their own available capacity was not fully utilized, led to the setting up of the National Hermann Goering Works under conditions of bizarre duress. Such firms as United Steel Works (*Vereinigte Stahlwerke*), Mannesmann, Flick, Krupp and others were made to invest 130 million marks (at a $4\frac{1}{2}$ per cent preferred-dividend rate, to be held at least five years) in the 400-million project★ – in other words, the steel industry had to pay protection money to the state by financing its own competitor. This competition took various forms: when the industry wanted to expand at the end of 1938 it was told that the National Works had pre-empted all available labour and materials,[45] and in addition the works' director, Pleiger, flagrantly exceeded the original limitations on the scope of their operations by smelting Swedish ores and producing finished articles.[46]

But that was not all. From its impressive base at Salzgitter in Brunswick† the Hermann Goering Works expanded successively into the Ruhr, Austria, Poland, and France, until rivalry between Pleiger's mammoth and the giant United Steel Works over the sharing out of the rich ore deposits in Lorraine aroused acute misgivings throughout the steel industry about a lack of balance between its public and private sectors. (Pleiger, a small-town ironmonger, who had clawed his way to the top via a succession of party offices, aroused quite different feelings in Hitler, who said in 1941, 'If I had six generals like Pleiger the war would have been won long ago.)[47] The Hermann Goering Works constituted only one, though undoubtedly the most dramatic, example of the way in which the regime exacted heavy tribute from industrialists to finance schemes harmful – or at least not advantageous – to themselves. In the pursuit of the autarchy programme, the Four-Year Plan Office forced Krupp to finance the Buna synthetic rubber project; compelled I. G. Farben and other soft-coal mine owners to invest 100 million Rm. in the Brabag company (set up to extract petrol from lignite); and made the textile industry capitalize synthetic fibre plants.[48]

★ The state lightened the load of its own investment of 70 per cent in the *Reichswerke* by making such corporate bodies as the *Reichsgruppe Handwerk* (National Craft Group) take up blocks of shares (cf. David Schoenbaum, *op. cit.*, p. 135.).

† The original blueprint had envisaged the siting of the Hermann Goering Works at Hanover, but Brunswick was chosen, although this involved an additional 40 million Rm. to cover the cost of constructing a canal. Director Pleiger was a close associate of the prime minister of Brunswick, Klagges, who carried out the confiscations required to make the site and its access routes available.

A more widespread form of tribute levied on the economy was taxation. In 1931 Brüning had instituted public accountants, and the Nazis developed this device to plug loopholes offering opportunities for tax-evasion even further. The writing-off of depreciation, formerly a way of concealing profits, was reformed, so that the state could go back ten years when making assessments, and could thus add to taxation the written-off values which subsequently turned into boom profits.[49]

In 1937 taxes constituted a net burden of between 60 and 70 per cent of the net profits of industrial undertakings.[50] The proportion of public investment in the national income quadrupled within five years (military spending, for instance, went up by 2,000 per cent), so that by 1938 public spending accounted for 35 per cent of Germany's national income, compared with 23·8 per cent in the UK and 10·7 per cent in the United States.[51]*

Yet, in spite of heavy taxes and the gentler slope of the upward curve, the net profits of large corporations quadrupled within the first four years of Nazi rule, and managerial and entrepreneurial income rose by nearly 50 per cent (from an average of 3,700 marks in 1934 to 5,420 marks in 1938).[52] Things were to get even better: in the three years between 1939 and 1942 German industry expanded as much as it had during the preceding fifty years.[53]

An episode related in the course of the Nuremberg trials† provides an illustration of the euphoric atmosphere in which this expansion proceeded. On 18 May 1940 Krupp, a partner in Henkel, the detergent manufacturers, and two other industrialists spent hours listening to the radio while seated round a table covered with a map of north-western Europe. As news flashes of the Wehrmacht's advances into the Low Countries came in, they grew increasingly agitated and started waving their hands about to jab at the map. 'This one here is yours, that one there is yours, we shall have that man arrested, he has two factories . . .' In the midst of the hubbub one of the four industrialists got up to telephone his office staff and ordered them immediately to request Wehrmacht permission for two of their number to proceed to Holland the following day.[54]

Further phone calls over the next few months and years procured for

---

* 1938, incidentally, was the year when Germany's national income had once again reached its pre-slump total of 76 million million marks; by contrast, by 1937 Britain had already achieved an excess of 20 per cent over her 1929 figure. (cf. Gustav Stolper, *The German Economy 1970–1940*, London, 1940, p. 63.).

† Although the defence denied the veracity of this eyewitness account submitted by Arthur Rühmann in the course of the hearing against Alfried Krupp, the American presiding judge accepted it.

Krupp's Dutch shipyards, Belgian metalworks, a large slice of the French machine-tool industry, Yugoslav chromium deposits, Greek nickel mines, iron and steel plants in the Ukraine, and so on.[55]

The war, which caused this prodigious rate of expansion in industry, did not visit commensurate benefits upon the *Mittelstand*. Some months before the war a government edict declared that the trades of baker, barber, butcher, shoemaker and tailor were overcrowded, raised the criteria of competence in these trades and decreed the closure of shops which were inefficiently financed, or did not perform economically justified tasks. The actual outbreak of hostilities inspired spokesmen for the crafts to some ingenious special pleading to the effect that artisan enterprises (being small-scale and scattered throughout the countryside) were more immune to air attack than large-scale industry and should be awarded commensurately bigger state contracts.[56]

Suggestions like these, needless to say, went unheeded, but the outbreak of war did not signal a decisive switch-over of the economy to a war footing. This was one of the reasons why the initial wartime comb-out of craft and retail enterprises affected only 100,000 at the most, and it was left to the post-Stalingrad totalization drive to eliminate an additional 250,000 or so.[57]

Those who were allowed to stay in business did not fare too badly. Under an imaginative scheme adumbrated by the Labour Front, crafts in the countryside were to be co-ordinated and made more efficient by means of village pools of artisan resources, which were known as *Dorfgewerke*. Although successful in certain areas, the project did not really get off the ground. Things were different in the towns: urban artisan workshops combined to form delivery co-operatives (*Lieferungsgenossenschaften*); orders were placed with those, instead of with individual enterprises, and each member invested 5 per cent of his working capital in them. Though these co-operatives were run by local guild officials – almost invariably 'golden pheasants' – who tended to manipulate them in their own interests, they did enable craft units to compete with middle-sized industries by helping to obviate the wartime vagaries of shortages, dislocations and excessive red tape.

Although there were recurring complaints from the crafts, mostly not entirely unjustified, about industry being favoured at their expense, the authorities showed sufficient solicitude for *Mittelstand* needs to channel a proportion of PoWs and conscript labour into artisan workshops. (The craft masters who did best out of the war were those who ran ghetto workshops, such as the ones in Warsaw, where for some years labour could be literally worked to death without this in any way affecting its availability.)

Nor did those retailers who escaped the shake-out do too badly during the war, though those in the food trade tended to be overworked by a combination of longer shop hours (in 1943 bakers' shops and dairies, for instance, had to keep open from 6 a.m. till 7 or 8 p.m.)[58] and insistence by the authorities on a meticulous and time-consuming check on ration coupons. On the other hand, retailers had readier access to goods in short supply than anyone else, and could exploit this advantage by mutual barter or black-market deals. In addition, neither retailers nor owners of artisan enterprises were subject to labour conscription, which meant that they could move their businesses into areas safe from air-raids.

While in wartime the mere discussion of the *Mittelstandideologie* would have been an antiquarian pastime – the subordination of small enterprises to big business had become irreversible by 1936 – the tug-of-war between industry and the state continued spasmodically throughout the war. The fact that the interplay of those two huge forces had still not reached the point of equilibrium had precious little to do with reservations about the regime and the war; the involvement of industry in the 20 July plot was minimal* compared with that of the aristocracy and the officer corps. Top industrialists were in fact cognizant of the conspiracy, but their instinctive calculation of the unprofitability factor in any enterprise – in this case the expectation that the plot would fail – plus a Neanderthal unawareness of moral issues – precluded their doing anything beyond providing occasional alibis for Goerdeler and Popitz.

In so far as industry disagreed in matters of political policy, it did so constitutionally by submitting memoranda, though even this form of opposition was eschewed in cases involving undue hazard. Thus when Goerdeler and General Thomas of the Wehrmacht's economic office drew up a memorandum designed to convince Hitler that the economic situation made an early termination of the war essential, leading industrialists refused to put their signatures to the document.[59]

Other industrial memoranda did, however, get beyond the drafting

---

* One industrial plotter was the Krupp director, Ewald Löser, tipped as a possible Finance Minister in the Goerdeler cabinet; he survived Gestapo arrest, but received a seven-year sentence at Nuremberg on charges of spoliating occupied countries and exploiting slave labour (cf. Norbert Mühlen, *Die Krupps*, Frankfurt, 1960, p. 177).

stage. One in the hand of Dr Roland of the United Steelworks (the deputy leader of the steel industry under the regime's scheme of industrial self-government), stated the case against the utilization of foreign conscript labour. 'Panzer' Roland* developed his argument by reference to the increase of 1·9 million in the number of German officials between 1935 and 1939.[60] This was a refutation of the need for forced labour by foreign workers to counteract the Reich's alleged basic labour deficiency, as well as a protest by a spokesman for private enterprise against increasing bureaucratization.

The anti-bureaucratic tenor of Roland's memorandum influenced the powers that be more than his reservations about conscript labour. Although there were a few exceptions – the Upper Silesian coal industry managed to keep its intake of concentration-camp labour to a minimum by adroitly arguing that work alongside unstable elements would reflect adversely upon an honourable profession[61] – most large German industrial enterprises employed prisoner and slave labour during the war. Although employers were to some extent forced into this situation by the call-up of German workers and the pressure of tight delivery dates, the fact that the Nazi slave-labour boss, Gauleiter Sauckel, had to warn employers against 'neglecting the most primitive measures for maintaining the will to work' and against 'the mass deployment of eastern workers arousing primeval capitalist instincts'[62] speaks volumes.

In 1944 Krupp housed 70,000 non-German 'employees' in fifty-seven prison camps within the Essen area, 2,000 of them Hungarian Jews hired out by Pfister, commander of Buchenwald, at 4 marks per day. In addition to meeting the extra cost of barbed wire, watchtowers and searchlights, the firm also spent a daily 70 pfennigs on feeding each Jew.

At times quite bizarre items swelled the overheads of enterprises employing foreign labour. Solicitude for the sexual needs of 'free' foreign male workers prompted the authorities to make firms finance the construction of B (for brothel) Barracks, on pain of denying them future supplies of labour.[63] A statement by the Nuremberg chamber of industry and trade provides a characteristic gloss on this aspect of state–business

* A form of nomenclature analogous to such Welsh appositions as 'Evans the post'. Another wartime industrial example of this usage was 'Cannon' Müller; Erich Müller, chief designer in the artillery department of Krupps, owed his fame to Fat Gustav, the Second World War's successor to Big Bertha, which devastated Sebastopol; he was made a professor *honoris causa* and personally collaborated with Hitler in the design of a simplified anti-aircraft gun, eventually exceeding the head of the firm in importance (cf. Norbert Mühlen, *Die Krupps*, Frankfurt, 1960, p. 162).

collaboration: 'Although the firms concerned in no way underrate the biological importance of the matter and are prepared to undertake the necessary tasks, they refuse to be brought into direct contact with the venture.'

The state was not always able to get business compliance in financial matters in such a short space of time. A case in point was the switch-over from the cost-plus method – the greater the cost calculated the greater the 3–6 per cent plus – to price-fixed payments for government contract work; this switch-over took longer to accomplish in totalitarian Germany than in the democratic United States.[64] Originally firms could choose between the two systems. Those who accepted fixed prices received exemption from profits-tax and preferential allocations of raw material and labour. As the *Frankfurter Zeitung* pointed out, the overall enforcement of price fixing in 1942 resulted in 'large concerns whose costs were below those of average-sized plants automatically making additional profits'.[65] It was also in 1942 that on the initiative of Minister Speer the state and army agencies, which had previously administered the arms programme, were replaced by a network of committees, representing every branch of the manufacturers involved. Speer's cadre of 6,000 honorary administrators, drawn from the entrepreneurial and managerial classes, was responsible for a staggering increase in arms output. Its creator has subsequently and convincingly claimed that, but for this productive spurt, Germany could not have continued the war after 1943.[66] The war effort did not, however, engage the attention and interest of the whole of industry. While Speer's 6,000 presided over a wartime 'economic miracle', some employers threw off their frustrations at controls, restrictions and interference by expatiating on the theme of entrepreneurial initiative in trade journals and at business conferences.[67] At the same time, the more sanguine among the entrepreneurs looked forward to an undreamt-of prosperity after the war, when the pent-up demand for consumer goods, reinforced by the tremendous accession of wealth plundered from the occupied countries, would produce an unprecedented boom.

The war eventually reached a point at which even Krupp's, until then undeviatingly loyal to the regime, divined that the interests of the firm and the fatherland diverged. Their opposition to the moribund regime took the form of divesting themselves of government loans, pressing demands for compensation for war-damage and for the recovery of debts from the Reich, and keeping their assets as liquid as possible, instead of immediately re-investing capital in new plant for war production.[68]

An even more notable instance of industrial disloyalty to Hitler occurred right at the end of the war, when Speer, abetted by 'Panzer' Roland and other executives, persuaded Paul Pleiger to sabotage the Führer's last-ditch orders to destroy Germany's industrial resources.[69] Their success in this terminal act of defiance does not, however, invalidate the force of the simile which likens German business during the Third Reich to the conductor of a runaway bus who has no control over the actions of the driver but keeps collecting the passengers' fares right up to the final crash.

Within a few weeks of taking power, on 1 April 1933, the Nazis organized an anti-Jewish boycott. The poster reads 'The Jews have till 10 A.M. on Saturday to reflect. Then the struggle commences. The Jews of the world want to destroy Germany. German People—resist! Don't buy from Jews!' (SÜDDEUTSCHER VERLAG, MUNICH)

A race-education lesson. Using an ideally Aryan-looking pupil a teacher instructs the class in how to measure the length and width of the skull as a means of compiling a 'cranial index'. (SÜDDEUTSCHER VERLAG)

Goering's wedding at the Berlin Dom in 1935—probably the greatest social occasion in the history of the Third Reich. The trumpeters in the foreground belonged to the premier band of the Wehrmacht.

Procession at the opening of the 'House of German Art' at Munich in 1937. (INSTITUTE
OF CONTEMPORARY HISTORY AND WIENER LIBRARY, LONDON)

From September to March one Sunday in each month was designated 'one-pot Sunday'—an occasion for belt-tightening in aid of the needy. Flag-day techniques were employed to pressure the public into having frugal 'one-pot' meals and donating the resultant savings to Winter Relief. (INSTITUTE OF CONTEMPORARY HISTORY AND WIENER LIBRARY)

A Winter Relief 'sacrificial column' erected outside Hamburg's Town Hall. At night a flame lit atop the column illuminated the townhall square. (INSTITUTE OF CONTEMPORARY HISTORY AND WIENER LIBRARY)

Judges of the Berlin Criminal Court display the emblem of the Nazi state on their robes for the first time at a ceremony in 1936.

The Reich Labour Service 'presents arms' at the 1934 Nuremburg Party Rally. Such drill served the two-fold purpose of pre-military training and investing labour service with an aura of dash and glamour. (ULLSTEIN BIL-DERDIENST, BERLIN)

Mealtime in the Reich La-bour Service. A 'hut leader' dishes out rations to his eighteen-year-old fellow con-scripts. (INSTITUTE OF CON-TEMPORARY HISTORY AND WIENER LIBRARY)

Navy gymnasts at the 1938 Breslau Sports Festival. The Nazis wanted youth—in Hit-er's words—to be 'tough as eather, swift as whippets and ard as Krupp steel', and laced heavy emphasis on hysical fitness. (INSTITUTE F CONTEMPORARY HISTORY ND WIENER LIBRARY)

Reinforcing the ban on Jewish visits to swimming pools, theatres and cinemas, 'unofficial' JEWS KEEP OUT signs proliferated everywhere. The one shown here was put up in allotments on the outskirts of Berlin. (Most restaurants displayed the notice 'Dogs and Jews not admitted'. (ULLSTEIN BILDERDIENST)

German street-scene 1933. Escorted by armed guards, a Jew stripped of his shoes and trousers carries a sandwich board with the 'humorous' legend 'I am a Jew but I have no complaints about the Nazis'. (ARCHIV GERSTENBERG, FRANKFURT AM MAIN)

Arrival at Auschwitz, the huge death camp and industrial complex in south-west Poland. At its railway sidings SS men decided who was to be gassed immediately and who was to be spared for 'extermination through work'. The people here are wearing the yellow star which every Jew was forced to display. (SÜDDEUTSCHER VERLAG)

The dining-hall in the barracks of the *Leibstandarte*, Hitler's SS bodyguard. The legend on either side of the SS runes (beneath the eagle) reads 'The will of the Fuehrer remains our faith'. (SÜDDEUTSCHER VERLAG)

'Squire' Goering among the villagers of Mauterndorf. (INSTITUTE OF CONTEMPORARY HISTORY AND WIENER LIBRARY)

An 'honour diploma' awarded to a farmer whose holding had remained in the possession of his family for two hundred years. (INSTITUTE OF CONTEMPORARY HISTORY AND WIENER LIBRARY)

13

THE WORKERS

Emblazoned on the camp gates at Auschwitz, the adage *Arbeit macht frei* (Labour liberates) was history's sickest joke, but as a sampler motto on the walls of German workers' dwellings (trailing an aura of the Protestant Ethic and of Samuel Smiles) it had nothing incongruous about it.

The workers – numerically the largest class and politically the richest breeding-ground of anti-authoritarianism in German society – constituted a key social group without whose co-operation (or even acquiescence) the Third Reich could not have functioned as it did.

The key to labour's attitude towards the regime lay in the single word 'work', though the positive incentive of the folk community and, to a lesser extent, the negative one of terror, must not be left out of account. Restoration of the right to work seduced the workers into accepting the loss of trade-union rights of association and collective bargaining; to gain the ends of liberation through labour they accepted the means of servitude to the Labour Front.

Though long alienated from the imperial regime, the workers had enthusiastically joined in the patriotic consensus of 1914, only to withdraw from it before the end of the war. Having helped to establish the Republic, they subsequently turned out to be the last social group to desert the middle ground in politics; during the terminal phase of Weimar, the Social Democrats retained their hard-core electoral support (as well as their identity), while the middle-class Democratic Party had to go into voluntary liquidation and the People's Party veered violently to the right.

Revolution had made Russia's proletariat the bearers of Soviet patriotism; by an opposite process of restructuring consciousness the Nazi revolution integrated the Reich's workers into the 'proletarian nation' to which the Germans saw themselves as belonging, in contrast with the Western plutocratic powers. Inside this 'proletarian' nation class-realities, of course, continued to operate, but the material attractions of work and the emotional ones of folk community turned the workers into an undifferentiated segment of Nazi society.

Nothing helped the new power holders as much as the circumstances under which they seized power. Since 1930, 6 million workers (a third of the labour force) had been thrown on to the scrap-heap, and the average weekly earnings of the rest had dropped by 33 per cent.[1] In actual fact, the peak of mass unemployment had already been passed in the autumn of 1932, and the incipient revival of the economy was reflected in the November elections of that year, when the Nazi vote declined by 2 million. The Third Reich was thus established at a moment when the public consciousness was still dominated by the general fear of crisis, but also when the Depression was already beginning to recede, and the first upward swing of the trade-cycle was making itself felt. After the seizure of power, this improvement, together with the Nazis' energy-charged measures to procure public work and to resuscitate industry (in themselves proof of business confidence in the new regime) persuaded the workers that things were better now than they had been and made them accept the promise of deferred rewards as a substitute for current gratification.

They compared the conditions of life in the Third Reich with the abnormally low standard of living obtaining in 1932 and not the more representative one of 1929. By raising living standards a few points above subsistence level the Nazis thus appeared to have improved things drastically, even though the standard of living was well below what had been taken for granted during the late 'twenties, which now seemed so remote. So modest had the workers' expectations become that older men who continued drawing unemployment benefit after 1933 were envious of the younger ones employed in public work schemes for pay that only marginally exceeded their own dole money.

The public works, autarchy and rearmament programmes started biting within a fairly short time; early in 1934 the unemployment figures of 1932 were halved, and by 1936 the employment level approximated once again to that of the boom year, 1928. By 1937–8 workers – for so long a drug on the market (even the 'economic near-miracle' of 1924–9 had not produced full employment) – became a scarce commodity, and by 1939 the effective demand for labour exceeded supply by half a million.

The overall labour situation was characterized by two contrary developments. On the one hand there was ever greater regimentation, beginning on May Day 1933, when millions of workers were shepherded into stadia while SA assault groups throughout the country seized trade union offices and assets on behalf of the Labour Front.*

Henceforth workers ('plant followers' in Nazi parlance) were subjected to a double regimen designed to get maximum effort from them: the plant leaders, actuated, as ever, by the profit motive, and the Labour Front leaders, motivated by their hunger for political power.

But the counteracting force to these pressures built up during the mid-thirties was the growing shortage of labour. Skilled workers enjoyed the conditions of a seller's market, particularly in the metal and building industries, where permission for job changes had to be obtained from the labour exchange from 1935 and 1937 onwards respectively.[2]

These mutually contradictory tendencies were reflected in the wage situation. The chief instrument of Nazi economic policy was a legislative freezing of wages at their Depression level, and this was complemented by a price freeze. Neither form of standstill could be enforced very thoroughly. Although rents remained stable and the cost of light and fuel even dropped slightly, food prices and especially clothing prices went up, not least because of the deterioration in quality and the reduced availability resulting from the autarchy programme. The operation of the freeze on wages was ostensibly more effective. Thus between 1934 and 1937, the year preceding the saturation of the labour market, weekly earnings increased by 15 per cent, but this average masks wide differentials. While key industries, such as building construction and materials, optical and fine mechanical instruments, and certain types of machine building, showed rises of up to 30 per cent, the pay of workers in the consumer goods industries stagnated. Wages in textiles, food-processing and printing increased by no more than 2 or 3 per cent, and those in the leather and garment industries even decreased.[3]

By the beginning of the war between a quarter and a third of the labour-force still drew pay based on the hourly wage levels current in 1932, though their weekly earnings were of course higher.

The relative success of the Nazi wage freeze is attested by the fact that by 1943, after years of growing scarcity of labour and wartime difficulties, the average hourly earnings of German workers had increased by 25 per cent and their weekly ones by 41 per cent; if we offset this against the steady rise in prices, we find that real income per week had in fact increased

---

* This blow dispatched a semi-consenting victim. Between the seizure of power and May Day Herr Leipart and some other trade-union leaders had offered the regime their collaboration in the vain hope of purchasing the unions' right to survive on Nazi sufferance.

by only 23 per cent and the hourly rate by 9 per cent; in other words, hourly wages increased by less than 1 per cent during each year of Nazi rule. (Between 1914 and 1918 workers' wages actually doubled.)

Real wage levels were also depressed by the compulsory exacting of membership dues for the German Labour Front and NSV contributions, in addition to insurance and tax deductions. In all, deductions from industrial pay packets in the Third Reich totalled about 18 per cent* – i.e. workers had 3 to 4 per cent more lopped off their gross income than before.[4]

However, certain priority industries constituted significant exceptions within a far from dynamic wages situation. Between the summer of 1933 and 1937 the labour-force in the building industry more than trebled, and in the metal industry it increased two and half times.[5] By 1937, when the average weekly industrial wage was 27 marks, it was possible for skilled metal and building workers to gross as much as 100 marks per week with overtime and output bonuses. Conversely, though, the work-load imposed on the building industry was such that 1938 witnessed a drop of almost 20 per cent in productivity, which was due to a dilution of the labour-force, to work being speeded up and stretched out, and a resultant lowering of working morale.[6]

In mining, average shift productivity dropped 12 per cent between 1936 and 1938;[7] the Gelsenkirchen Mining Company – down by 10,000 tons of coal per day – attributed falling output to the miners' practice of hawking themselves from pit to pit in search of higher wages, as well as to the attraction of more lucrative and less strenuous jobs in the nearby motor industry.

Workers in some technologically advanced industries displayed an absolutely euphoric mood. Thus the IG–Farben film factory at Wolfen, with 600 unfilled vacancies early in 1938, had workers taking afternoons off to go to the cinema and returning drunk from their tea-break. The management cut the Gordian knot by recruiting Polish labour and handing over undisciplined employees to the Gestapo.[8] In tackling the problems of the mining industry, the regime used the stick and the carrot alternately. In 1938 lead- and zinc-ore miners had their jobs frozen and their work hours increased from six to seven and a half per day.[9] Soon after, the daily

* Unemployment insurance 4·5 per cent; health and pension insurance 5–5½ per cent; wage and poll tax 3½ per cent; Winter Relief contributions were fixed at 10 per cent of the wages tax per month from October to March. (cf. Wallace R. Deuel, *People under Hitler*, New York, 1942, p. 310).

eight-hour shift in coal mining was extended by forty-five minutes, beyond which colliers were given time-and-a-quarter overtime pay, plus additional double-time premiums for productivity increases. Output was further boosted by switching over from flat rates to piece-work rates wherever possible, though this could be counterproductive because it put qualified men at a relative disadvantage.*

Metal and construction workers – and to a lesser extent miners – belonged to the Third Reich's aristocracy of labour. To round off the industrial scene, we must also look at such comparatively underprivileged groups as women workers, workers in consumer goods, labourers, and workers in cottage industries (Heimarbeiter).

Women workers received a third less than men of equivalent skill (the 1937 average rate for male skilled workers was 78½ pfennigs per hour and for females 51½ pfennigs),[10] – and thus formed a pool of cheap labour, especially in the countryside. Thus the official rates for women workers in the toy industry in Thüringia were 30 pfennigs, in the metal industry 38 pfennigs, and in uniform factories 45 pfennigs per hour, although thanks to piece-work they could average 40, 45 and 60 pfennigs respectively.

Reference has already been made to the fact that certain branches of the clothing trade actually reduced wages during the Third Reich. In 1937 young unmarried textile workers on short time were, moreover, debarred from unemployment relief and forced to enter other occupations.[11]

As for lower-paid labourers and unskilled workers (average hourly rate: 50 pfennigs), their purchasing power actually dropped by 15 per cent during the early years of the Third Reich, but later on things improved. In order to utilize the available labour-force more fully the regime stepped up industrial training programmes, from which some unskilled workers benefited, while others took advantage of piece-work opportunities.

The undisputed bottom segment of the peacetime labour force were the half-million or so 'home workers'. The men known as 'trustees of labour' (regional plenipotentiaries of the Ministry of Labour) were hard put to it to enforce protective legislation, since cottage industries were by definition located in the areas that were most backward economically and least amenable to thorough surveillance. The thirty female outdoor workers in

---

* A wartime radio talk, 'The Problem of Performance Wages in Mining', instanced a skilled collier earning 86 pfennigs per hour who badly wanted to do semi-skilled work at which he could have earned up to 1.30 marks.

the metal-working craft who only earned 20 pfennigs per hour in Silesia one year before the war,[12] and were forced to supplement this by part-time prostitution, may not have been typical, but they demonstrated the vulnerability of outdoor workers to exploitation.

Such exploitation was not necessarily deliberate; during the aftermath of the Depression many small employers beyond the confines of the putting-out system felt compelled to keep overheads low in defiance of the law, a practice connived at by the Labour Front, which realized that insistence on official wage-rates might undermine the viability of smaller firms.

It was only from 1937 onwards that the Labour Front enforced really stringent supervision of wage regulations, a factor which, taken in conjunction with the wage freeze, explains why under conditions almost approaching full employment over 10 million people – 16 per cent of the population – were still receiving Winter Relief parcels or subsidies in that year.[13]

With labour a scarce commodity from then onwards, small and medium-sized firms were once again at a disadvantage compared to larger competitors who could offer more fringe benefits and also had a 'pull' with labour exchanges; but in this situation the employees of the former stood to gain from their plant leaders' discomfiture. Competition for workers led to firms making wage offers which ran counter to basic Nazi economic policy. To remedy this, Goering empowered trustees of labour in the summer of 1938 to fix maximum – rather than minimum as before – wages in certain specific industries, and the Ministry of Labour issued this characteristic directive in 1939:

Firms can pay thirteen months' salaries per year, if this was their practice before the summer of 1938. They can also give plant followers financial subsidies for such major expenses as are incurred in the bulk purchase of coal and potatoes. They can furthermore subsidize their employees in connection with house purchases, purchase of a People's Car (Volkswagen), holiday expenses and give them loyalty bonuses if they have been employed for five years and over, but they must not offer permanent children's allowances or marriage allowances. If staff are provided with hot meals, the employees should pay at least one third of the cost.[14]

Despite these detailed instructions the problem kept on recurring. In 1941 the Ministry of Labour instructed trustees of labour to countermand wage increases resulting from improved techniques rather than from greater effort on the workers' part, to investigate 'dirt-pay', bogus promotions, gifts of insurance policies and health premiums, rent bonuses, and so on.*

But from 1941 onwards, such gains as the workers continued to make – that is those still in civvies – by exploiting their own scarcity value were increasingly cancelled out by the drop in the value of real wages. Consumer goods as well as certain foodstuffs were in ever shorter supply, so that wage increases were largely siphoned off by supplementary black-market purchases. In addition, long working hours, stretched out even further by journeys in the blackout and with air-raid disruptions, left workers relatively little leisure time.

Average working hours did not in fact lengthen appreciably for some years after the seizure of power. During the economy's reabsorption of huge numbers of unemployed short-time working was not infrequently decreed by the government: in the summer of 1934 fibre firms were instructed to limit the working week to thirty-six hours, and only workers employed for less than two-thirds of that time qualified for social-insurance benefits. 1936 saw the end of official reductions of working time, but the flow of production often depended on the fluctuating allocation of raw materials affected by the autarchy programme.[15] Since the work schedules of firms on military contract hinged on procurement by the Wehrmacht of raw materials, and official delivery dates were invariably short, such firms had alternate bouts of hectic overtime working and periods of short-time and rest days.

There were of course considerable differences between the consumer-goods and production-goods industries. During the last pre-war year a section of the labour-force in the textile industry was still doing less than forty hours per week,[16] while the metal, coal and building industries were operating a twelve-hour or even fourteen-hour working day.[17] Within the various branches of industry work hours in 1939 were anything up to 10 per cent longer than they had been before the slump;[18] (it should be remembered that during the thirties working hours had been reduced by President Roosevelt in the United States, by the Popular Front government in France, and even the Mussolini regime in Italy). In the course of the war the average working week for men increased slowly at first –

* A plant leader in Westphalia was fined 30,000 Rm. for raising the wages of seventy-three of his followers, paying their fares to and from work, and converting piece-rates for the benefit of maintenance workers. Enterprising firms which granted newlyweds higher pay to enable them to raise a family faced trustees with a real poser. It is not known how they resolved this dilemma without flouting either the eugenic or the economic directives of the regime.

from forty-nine in 1939 to fifty-two in 1943, after which it rose to sixty hours (seventy-two in key industries such as aircraft production). This belated totalization of the war effort involved women in industry working fifty-six hours; even bank employees worked fifty-three.[19]

The inescapable corollary of longer working hours was a deterioration of workers' health. While the peacetime industrial labour-force expanded by approximately 50 per cent (from 13·5 million in 1933 to 20·8 million in 1939), the number of accidents and illnesses connected with work increased by one and a half (from 929,000 to 2,253,000). The incidence of occupational diseases more than trebled (from 7,000 to nearly 23,000), and fatality increased two and a half times (from 217 to 525).[20]

This negative overall trend was hardly surprising in view of the lengthening of the working day by 25 per cent among lead- and zinc-ore miners, for instance. But the bleak picture suggested by these figures requires qualification. The 1932–3 work-force represented an élite of the fittest and most dexterous, whereas full employment subsequently reactivated the less fit and efficient. In 1929 – the last boom year – there had been sixty-one cases of accident and occupational disease per thousand insured workers.[21] By 1932, the peak year of depression, this had dropped to thirty-nine. In 1937, with employment somewhat higher and living standards somewhat lower than in 1929, there were sixty-six such cases. The true increase compared to the Weimar situation cannot be accurately gauged from these statistics, since in the Third Reich both plant physicians and *Krankenkasse* doctors were less ready to grant medical certificates and more insistent on an early return to work than previously; even so, the figures speak for themselves. In June 1938 the regime promulgated a duty-service law under which all workers could be 'industrially conscripted', i.e. transferred to fortification work on the Western Rampart or channelled into essential industries. While supplementing the 'war-industrial-labour force', this comb-out of workers from expendable trades – ranging from street-vending to textile manufacturing – naturally precipitated a rise in the industrial accident and sickness rate. And yet the duration of absence from work per individual case of sickness – 4·2 days in 1932 – averaged only 3·2 days in 1937, although the average fitness of the replenished labour-force was obviously lower than that of the pared-down force of 1932. Interruptions to work had to be reduced to an absolute minimum. 'Plant followers' with minor injuries were switched to work that the slightly handicapped could cope with. More serious cases were speedily reintegrated into the production process by being given light work during convalescence, and this was followed by a gradual intensification of their work-load. The National Hermann Goering Works, which pioneered this form of accelerated rehabilitation, claimed in 1940 that the average duration of sickness among their personnel was less than half of that in industry as a whole.[22]

The fact that, despite longer working-hours, industrial conscription and over-exertion, stimulated by high bonus payments,* the health of workers did not deteriorate even further was a function of the central role that 'fringe benefits' played in the Third Reich's industrial scheme. Since the widespread application of the wage freeze largely ruled out traditional forms of industrial incentive, substitute rewards assumed far greater importance.† Perks replaced fuller pay packets as work incentives and were trumpeted abroad as the 'socialism of deeds', a corollary of the Nazis' reconstructed definition of socialism, which posited an identity of interest between employers and employees, to be promoted by means of the factory community. The regime projected the specious notion of such a community into the vacuum it had created by semantically abolishing employers and physically abolishing trade unions. This community was built round the plant leader, acting jointly with a council of confidence representing the plant followers. These mutated shop stewards were essentially Labour Front nominees (though in the early years of the regime election procedures were actually set in motion), and their rights vis-à-vis the plant leader were so circumscribed that they would not infringe the industrial 'Führer principle'. Even when a majority of council members opposed a plant leader's directive, it remained in force pending a ruling from the labour trustees. The submission of complaints by the council of confidence to the labour trustees could even be actionable if the latter judged the complaints to be unjustified. The trustees could exercise

* The incidence of the novel '*Schipperkrankheit*' (a lesion of discs on the backbone) at *motorway* construction sites, for example, was traced back to attempts by piece-rate workers to earn maximum bonuses by working up to ten hours a day with only brief lunch breaks. (cf. Dr L. Debuch, '*Die Schipperkrankheit und ihre Bedeutung*', in *Deutsche Medizinische Wochenschrift*, 6 November 1936, p. 1837).

† In 1938–9, 164,000 enterprises participated in the N.S. model enterprise competition. Out of 50,000 firms statistically analysed, 2,500 engaged full- or part-time physicians; in 4,800, 600,000 workers received medical advice; in 4,000, first-aid rooms were available; 1,000 employed special welfare workers; 5,000 granted extended leave of absence to expectant mothers, established rest rooms for young mothers, and gave marriage and children's allowances; 1,700 paid the difference between wages and sickness insurance; 1,000 provided funds in addition to old-age benefits; 5,600 paid supplementary pensions to widows and orphans. (cf. Hilde Oppenheimer-Blum, *The Standard of Living of German Labour under Nazi Rule*, New School for Social Research New York, 1943, p. 66.)

powers of intervention in cases of dispute between plant leaders and followers or divergence between plant directives and government regulations. But in spite of this form of control, an employer still substantially remained the master during the Third Reich. If – in the usual military parlance of Labour Front leader Robert Ley – workers were 'soldiers of labour', it followed that the ideal relationship of plant leaders to their followers was that of officers and men.

But what of the relationship of employers to the Labour Front? This was an important consideration, since there was no lack among the labour-force of men who looked upon the Front as their trade union *manqué*. The answer is simple: size. The smaller a firm, the more it was exposed to interference from the Labour Front. Conversely, the larger the firm, the greater the immunity it enjoyed. Within the intricate, yet basically simple, structure of a Nazi hierarchy, a large industrialist inevitably had closer access to the levers of power than a subordinate of Dr Ley's. The tendency of workers to look upon the Labour Front in trade-union terms was linked with the predilection of the Front's officials for enforcing their will upon smaller employers. The Nazi labour code made a great deal of play with a concept called 'social honour' – an attribute apparently common to both employers and employees – and special courts dealt with breaches of the social-honour code, such as 'misuse of a position of power within the plant, the malevolent exploitation of labour, injuring the honour of a plant member, committing a breach of industrial peace, incitement of the followers against the plant leader' and so on. The maximum punishment that the honour courts could impose for misdemeanours such as these was dismissal of an employee without notice, or the revocation of an employer's qualification as plant leader.

In fact, plant leaders were arraigned before the social-honour courts far more often than followers. Thus in 1935, out of a total of 223 cases, only eighteen dealt with violations of the honour code by employees. Among the employers, the owners of small firms naturally bore the brunt of the prosecutions. Even so, their punishment was hardly severe.* In 1935 nine out of over 200 employers prosecuted lost the right to run their businesses outright.[23]

The social-honour court functioned alongside the labour courts which had traditionally arbitrated in litigation concerning wrongful dismissal,

* For instance, during the war a textile-mill foreman was fined 100 marks for hitting female mill operatives who had switched off their machines some minutes before the end of the shift and not cleaned them properly (cf. *Hamburger Fremdenblatt*, 8 May 1942).

e.g. in cases of workers being dismissed without due notice. In 1929 they had dealt with over 400,000 such cases. After 1933, the Labour Front monopolized access to the labour courts, and since it aimed at reducing wasteful litigation, labour-court cases had dwindled to a fifth of their pre-slump figure by 1940.[24]

The length of notice for industrial workers (after one year's employment and over) ranged from a week to a fortnight before the middle or the end of the month. White-collar workers, on the other hand, were entitled to six weeks before the end of each quarter year; this token of differentiation persisted despite a great deal of verbiage about folk and plant community. White-collar workers – known as the 'butterfly-collar proletariat' – had been neurotically apprehensive of being reduced to true proletarian status at the time of the Depression. This had not in fact occurred, either in terms of joblessness or in wage reductions. Whereas the slump put roughly every third industrial worker on the scrap heap, 'only' one white collar worker in every ten swelled the dole queues. Effective weekly earnings of the former dropped 33 per cent between 1929 and 1933; those of the latter declined by 17 to 20 per cent.[25]

The rise of the Third Reich none the less saw brown shirts rival butterfly collars as sartorial status symbols in offices, since the Nazification of the salaried staff (as of other self-styled 'Mittelstand' groups) was as much a function of autosuggestion as of actual social change. By the end of 1933, salaried staff formed nearly a fifth and industrial workers under a third of total Nazi party membership, which meant that compared to their distribution throughout the country, white-collar workers were 65 per cent over-represented and blue-collar ones 30 per cent under-represented.[26] (In Berlin for instance, just under half of all leading officials in the Party organization were salaried staff.)

Their economic destiny under the Third Reich hinged less on the regime's debt of gratitude to a social group strongly committed to its service, than on objective factors of economic development. During the mid-thirties a new wave of rationalization and modernization boosted the white-collar population both in absolute size and relative importance within industry as a whole.* By 1938 the blue-collar work-force showed

---

* This development was also in some way connected with the absorption of many people who had formerly been self-employed among the white-collar population. In 1938, 7½ per cent of this group earned more than 50 marks a month, as against 5 per cent in 1929. No comparable upgrading was discernible among industrial workers, of whom 38 per cent in 1929, but only 33½ per cent in 1938, averaged more than 36 marks per week. (cf. Hilde Oppenheimer-Blum, *op. cit.*, p. 43).

a 10 per cent increase over 1929, and the white-collar one of 25 per cent: 4 million as compared to 3,200,000. This meant that the proportion of white-collar to other workers, which had been 1:13 in 1895, 1:9 in 1907 and 1:5 in 1933, approached 1:4 in 1939. At the latter date the real disposable income of white-collar workers had also climbed 10 per cent beyond its 1928 average, whereas blue-collar income had barely been restored to its pre-Depression level.

Boom industries, piece-work and overtime notwithstanding, the earnings of the two-groups followed a divergent trend. Average blue-collar pay amounted to 53 per cent of white-collar income in 1929, but to only 50 per cent in 1936.*

From the point of view of folk community, social distinctions between salaried staff and workers were probably even more anomalous than financial ones. Reforms giving blue-collar workers of a certain seniority the same job security as office staffs were never implemented, and distinctions concerning status, pension schemes, insurance benefits and even forms of address – '*Sie*' for white-collar workers and the less respectful '*Du*' for blue-collar ones – persisted.[27]

In order to remove another form of distinction – the blue-collar worker's obligation to clock in – the infinitely resourceful Dr Ley suggested plant reveilles (industrial variations of morning assembly in schools) as a joint plant ceremony preceding the start of work in office and shop floor alike.

The idea was not widely taken up; nor was Ley's 'plant family scheme', under which industrial threesomes consisting of plant leader plus one white-collar and one blue-collar plant-followers each shared a week's accommodation and leisure-time pursuits at Labour Front holiday homes; a photograph of one such end-of-the-week celebration† showed employer and employees standing at either side of a ditch and shaking hands across the symbolic chasm while a swastika flag fluttered overhead.[28]

Under another, equally short-lived, scheme heads of firms arranged beer-and-sausage evenings at which all participants addressed each other as '*Du*'. But in spite of the absurdity of such schemes the regime's efforts to bridge the gulf between the two sides in industry were quite successful.

* At that date the actual average amounts were 1,373 marks and 2,727 marks p.a. respectively (cf. *Wirtschaft und Statistik* Nr. 23/1938). By comparison the average annual salary of dentists was 7,300 marks, of lawyers 10,850 marks, of doctors 12,500 marks and of top-ranking civil servants (e.g. secretaries of state) 26,500 marks (cf. Jack Schiefer, *Tagebuch eines Wehrunwürdigen*, Grenzland, Aachen, 1947, p. 233).

† Published in the German Labour Front publication *Arbeitertum*.

Though labour was denied the full benefit of its own scarcity it prospered – albeit modestly – in relation to the early thirties. Fringe benefits, though only a substitute for higher wages, had their undoubted attractions: thus nearly 60,000 new housing units for workers were constructed by firms competing in the National Socialist Model-Enterprise Competition.[29]

Holidays were another fringe benefit that occasioned widespread satisfaction among the working-class. Firstly, there was a virtual doubling of holidays with pay from the average of three to eight days under Weimar (depending on length of employment) to between six and fifteen days.[30] Secondly, large sections of the labour-force were for the first time ever given the opportunity of holidaying away from home. Strength-through-Joy, the Labour Front's super-agency for programmed leisure, indefatigably promoting evening classes, amateur cultural activities, recitals, travelling art exhibitions, block-bookings in theatres and so on, as well as truly massive sports and gymnastics programmes, was first and foremost the regime's mammoth, non-commercial, travel bureau.

Unorganized leisure would have constituted a vacuum* in the structure of Nazi day-to-day existence, and it is the nature of totalitarianism to abhor a vacuum. 'Much of physical, mental and nervous activity such as music, sports celebration, housework, etc., is never paid for at all,' Ingenieur Arnhold, an early Strength-through-Joy ideologist, wrote in the twenties.[31] 'The problem of modern human efficiency is to make this tremendous spiritual and emotional energy available for the production of goods.'

Though this was the objective motivation behind Strength-through-Joy, it gave many German workers a great deal of enjoyment, especially on holiday. The organization's tourist ships, gleaming symbols of folk community, provided identical accommodation for crew and passengers. They were the cynosure of all eyes (including friendly foreign ones).[32] 'The worker sees that we are serious about raising his social position,' Dr Ley proclaimed. 'It is not the so-called educated classes that we send out as representatives of the new Germany, but himself' [sic].[33]

Passengers on the pleasure cruises, to Madeira, for instance, or Norwegian fjords, did in fact form a social composite in which workers, though not predominant, were strongly represented. It was part of the

---

* Methodical as always, the Nazis actually quantified the size of this potential vacuum as 3,740 hours per annum (a figure arrived at by subtracting 24 per cent work time and 33⅓ per cent sleep time from the yearly total of 8,760 hours) (cf. Franz Neumann, *Behemoth*, New York, 1942, p. 429).

cruise ritual that all passengers from the most exalted managing director – one of that rare species was usually thrown in for good measure – to the lowliest had to draw lots for the allocation of cabins.[34]

One hundred and eighty thousand Germans went on cruises in 1938 and 10 million – three-fifths of them workers – participated in Strength-through-Joy vacation trips of all types.[35] With a labour-force of 20 million this meant that one worker in 200 took a sea trip abroad, and that one worker in every three* spent some time away from his home environment. The operative word in the last statement is *some* time: the statistics of the Mannheim Strength-through-Joy bureau, for instance, showed 100,000 participating in trips of a few days, 11,000 in two-week trips, and barely 1,000 on foreign cruises.[36]

The holidays ranged in price from a week in the Harz Mountains (28 marks) or one week at the North Sea coast (35 marks), through a fortnight at Lake Constance (65 marks), to a tour of Italy (155 marks).[37] The Mannheim statistics become comprehensible if we consider that the average weekly industrial wage was equivalent to the cost of a week in the Harz (although the picture was modified by many employers either wholly or partly subsidizing their employees' trips). At any rate, between 1932 and 1938 the volume of tourism doubled,† not least because Strength-through-Joy channelled low-income visitors to previously unfrequented backwaters such as the Bavarian forests, the Rhône and Eiffel areas and the Masurian Lakes. Many of the workers who, except in wartime, had probably never been beyond the outskirts of their home town, were among the most obvious beneficiaries of the 'Socialism of Deeds' that posters ubiquitously conjured up on the hoardings. 'Socialism', a term invariably pressed into service to describe industrial innovations sponsored by the regime, was also applied to the 'self-inspector' and 'self-calculator' schemes that were pioneered at the Kloeckner-Humboldt-Deutz motor works. 'Self-inspectors' were particularly reliable workers, whose work was exempted from the scrutiny of inspectors. This was a purely moral honour – the men's reward consisted of a plaque on their work-benches. 'Self-calculators' were particularly fast workers, who were empowered to fix their own piece-rates. Self-calculators gained a small margin of

* Of a representative sample of 350 workers' families investigated by the German Labour Front in 1937, 130 could not afford to spend any money whatever on holiday excursions. (cf. Theodor Bühler *Deutsche Sozialwirtschaft*, Kohlhammer, 1943, p. 47.)

† The 1932 figures of 3·5 million individual registrations amounting to 46·5 million nights spent in hotels, pensions, guest houses compared with 27·5 and 109·5 million respectively in 1938. (cf. *Statistisches Jahrbuch für Deutschland 1939–40*, pp. 76–77.)

independence as well as a chance of improving their earnings, but at the expense of their colleagues, since the management soon adjusted overall piece-work rates to the productivity of the self-calculators. Press photographs showed Kloeckner workers' families in their Sunday best, solemnly gathered round the 'I inspect myself' plaque on daddy's work-bench.

'Socialism' here meant either that the firm saved on supervisory personnel, or that some workers profited at the expense of others.[38]

Against this dubious use of the term 'Socialism' where 'Social Darwinism' would have been more appropriate, must be set some instances of the solidarity of German labour after the seizure of power. The smashing of the German labour movement in 1933 was followed by the arraignment of former and current (i.e. underground) trade-union activists at a series of 'monster trials' (so called because they involved hundreds of accused). 1936 and 1937, years of incipient full employment, were marked by subterranean industrial unrest in which – according to a plaintive memo from Schacht to Hitler[39] – certain local Labour Front officials played a rather equivocal role. Lightning strikes, which, for instances spasmodically irrupted in the motor industry, could be highly variable in their effect.

Thus a seventeen-minute stoppage at the Rüsselheim Opel Works in June 1936, at which 262 workers protested against a wage cut brought about by short-time and raw-material shortages, led to the immediate arrest of seven 'ringleaders', and Opel's permanent blacklisting of another thirty-six,[40] while a six-hour strike at the Alte Union plant at Berlin–Spandau some months later successfully averted a threatened pay reduction.[41]

As time went on the regime's usual savage reaction to manifestations of discontent were to some extent mitigated by the shrinking of the labour market (which, as we have seen, even led to labour exchanges being under-staffed). A further slackening of industrial discipline was checked by the outbreak of war; there were, however, isolated instances of strike action even in wartime (for instance, among Ruhr miners, Hamburg dockers and Dortmund port workers).[42]

Although working-class opposition during the war was in fact significantly smaller than the Gestapo had anticipated, Ley was moved to expostulate: 'A soldier is not a member of a solidarity but rather a comrade engaged in noble competition based on performance. German workmen, lay aside your outmoded and distasteful solidarity and be good comrades in achievement – then you will be good socialists.'[43]

One of the chief impediments to solidarity was the progressive wartime dilution of the work-force by foreign labour (bond as well as free); the regime had, of course, already fashioned an iron broom for sweeping malcontents out of the factories – industrial conscription. Thus under the industrial service law, 400,000* workers from all over Germany had been literally dragged out of their beds in June 1938 to build the West Wall fortifications. An additional deterrent to shop-floor rebelliousness that came into play when war broke out was the power of plant leaders either to grant exemptions from military service to key workers or to withhold them.

September 1939 also saw the abrogation of such peacetime safeguards against exploitation as limitations on working hours, and the requirement to pay higher rates for overtime and nightwork, but this proved to be temporary because of grass-roots resistance and, more important, because of the regime's policy of popularizing the war by mitigating its effect on the home front. Until the 1941 attack on Russia certain grades of skilled labour were, even after conscription into the Wehrmacht, liable to be sent back to their factories on extended work-leave.[44]

After the initial wartime vacillation concerning hours the working day lengthened, gradually but inexorably; by 1944 the average working week was sixty hours, and seventy-two hours in priority arms industries.[45]

Air-raids affected industry in a number of ways apart from the damage and dislocation they caused: the dispersal of urban factories into country areas of lower average pay† naturally affected the living standards of evacuated workers. Overall living standards were also – though more diversely – affected by the wage reforms that Manpower Mobilization Commissar Sauckel initiated in 1942 in order to boost output. The Sauckel scheme aimed at higher output for the same outlay by paying proportionally more to workers with high productivity. This further application of Social Darwinism to industrial affairs meant that after the Sauckel reforms a worker had to produce 115 screws for the same wages as 100 had earned him before.[46]

---

* It should not be thought, however, that all – or even necessarily the majority – of that number were industrial troublemakers. The bulk of the West Wall labour force were men attracted by relatively high pay and opportunities for additional overtime earnings; the Labour Front moreover, entertained the huge migrant work population lavishly by putting on as many as 300 entertainments, such as film shows and concert parties, per night. (Interview with Tim Mason, London, January 1967.)

† Thus at the height of the war the flat hourly rate for labourers in Pomerania was 50 pfennigs – compared to 90 pfennigs in Hamburg.

However, the war placed the German worker in a context not only of heavier exertion but also of greater solicitude. Firms offset vitamin deficiencies by distributing pills to their employees and counteracted fatigue by interspersing work with PT drill (thereby, in fact, lengthening the working day). Plants with canteen facilities managed to provide additions to rationed and scarce food; others provided makeshift accommodation for workers unable to commute from home because of dislocation produced by air-raids.

But on the whole labour discipline remained high,* so high, in fact, that the output of armaments increased 230 per cent between 1941 and 1944 (during which time the work-force involved expanded a mere 28 per cent)[47] Albert Speer, who masterminded this wartime economic miracle, has reason to claim he helped to stave off Nazi Germany's defeat by two years.

In other words, the working class that Karl Marx had seen as being in the van of the international proletariat (and Lenin as the fulcrum of the revolutionary post-war transformation of Europe) significantly extended the life span of the Third Reich by exertions which came very close to giving it victory.

What motivated the attitude of the German workers? Feelings of intense nationalism and vengefulness against the Allies on the one hand, and gratification at material advance – both real and imaginary – on the other. The Nazi exorcism of the slump meant more than everyone getting their job back; the initial 50 per cent expansion of the peacetime labour force (from 13·5 to 20 million), followed by its simultaneous inflation and dilution during the war, elevated thousands of workers to supervisory positions. (In wartime, for instance, it was not unusual for a checkweighman from the Aachen area to go to the Donbas as a colliery inspector, or for a Krupp maintenance electrician to be plant manager at Krivoi Rog.)[48]

During the last years of the Third Reich the workers displayed closer affinity with the rest of German society than they had done in the final stages either of the Empire or the Weimar Republic. The explanation for this phenomenon could be expressed as a co-efficient of nationalism and *embourgeoisement*, both of which are highly effective devices for encouraging social integration.

---

* This was also partly a function of stringent legislation. Workers faced three months' jail for desultory lateness, a year for refusing overtime, two years for playing truant twice (cf. Max Seydewitz, *Civil Life in Wartime Germany*, New York 1945, p. 182).

Nazi nationalism, focusing on the 'ex-worker' Hitler, transmuted the lowliest German into a member of Europe's 'Master Race'; *embourgeoisement* meant that by purchasing wireless sets, theatre-tickets, Strength-through-Joy holidays and (undeliverable) People's Cars, the workers could slough off their proletarian skins.

14

CONSUMPTION

Between 1932, the last year of Weimar, and 1938 – Nazism's last full peacetime year – the turnover of food in Germany increased by one sixth, that of clothing and textiles by over a quarter, and that of furniture and household goods by a good half.[1]

These figures are impressive, even when adjusted to a population growth of 4½ per cent, but the picture changes dramatically if they are compared with the consumption statistics for 1928, the last year in the Weimar Republic, when the economic situation was still normal. If we compare 1938 with ten years earlier, we find that out of the three key branches of consumption listed only furniture and household goods showed an increase; and it is arguable that this was less a function of rising standards than of the regime's provision of cash inducements for newly-weds. The total domestic supply in 1938 actually exceeded that of 1928 by nearly 10 per cent, but an increase in the population plus changes in the consumption pattern induced by the slump (Nazi *per capita* consumption of high-quality items being lower than Weimar's while the consumption of low-quality items was greater) combined to reduce the overall level for 1938.[2]

The average citizen of the Third Reich, however, was hardly in a mood to make retrospective statistical comparisons. By 1938 most people not only knew themselves to be far more affluent than in 1932, but also – turning upside-down Marx's celebrated dictum about Being (*Sein*) determining Consciousness (*Bewusstsein*) – thought themselves better off than before the Depression.

One of the most remarkable things about the Third Reich was in fact its success in inverting Marx: in the sphere of consumption psychologic affluence did not so much reflect material prosperity as precede it. Put crudely, this meant that the grounds for satisfaction at the prevailing state of affairs felt by the average German in, say, 1937 had probably more to do with his expectations for 1939 than his actual standard at the time. These expectations were so palpable that thousands of Germans enthusiastically responded to the *Volkswagen* scheme, which involved taking delivery of the car at the end of the repayment period and not, as was done everywhere else, at the beginning.

Even in a field as tangible and earthbound as consumption the regime managed to generate an atmosphere in which propaganda and auto-suggestion transformed people's appraisal of their own concrete situation. Four years after the seizure of power a newspaper commented on the 'intensive impression of popular enjoyment making itself felt in restaurants, beer-gardens and open-air cafés, where customers often could not afford to purchase more than a cup of coffee or a glass of beer.'[3] During this period of growing labour shortage and incontrovertibly rising living standards cafeterias dotted round the environs of Berlin still permitted customers to boil water for their own coffee.

In the assessment of living standards food is the most important single item. The higher the proportion of income spent on it, the lower the standard of living. In the later thirties consumer spending on food by the average German accounted for about 45 per cent of total expenditure (compared to 41 per cent in the United Kingdom).[4]

Bread was a key item in the German diet and the regime could take credit both for increasing consumption – in 1938 the consumption of wheat flour was a sixth higher than in 1932[5] – and a fractional reduction in price. At the same time the quality of bread deteriorated; under new regulations flour was ground 5 per cent more intensively and as the rye and wheat content of bread gradually diminished, it was compensated for by an increased mixture of maize and potato flour.[6] Depending on the consumer's income, bread served as a 'budget regulator', making up for the shortage of more expensive foods. It clearly fulfilled this function in Germany, where *per capita* consumption of rye bread was four times greater than in the United States, although the consumption of wheaten bread amounted to only three-fifths of the American average.[7]

During the war, when bread remained freely available in the UK and the USA, it was rationed in Germany. The 'normal consumer's' allocation fluctuated between 2 and $2\frac{1}{2}$ kg. per week, but the élite of 'extra-heavy workers' received twice as much; Ruhr miners, for instance, consumed a third more bread in 1942 than in 1936.[8] The admixture of substitute materials, increased in wartime, of course, when it also became standard practice to sell bread when it was a day old (since it required more chewing and thus went further). Wartime bran-bread caused widespread flatulence, which became an unpleasantly noticeable phenomenon in public places. Throughout the war the bread supply remained relatively plentiful, but downward adjustments (from 2½ to 2 kg. in 1942), for instance, invariably lowered morale.

By 1938 the Germans were eating only one-eighth more meat than during the Depression, and their annual *per capita* consumption was 48·6 kg. (cf. 64 kg. in the UK and 57 kg. in the US).[9] Pork accounted for over half the German meat diet, with veal and beef consumption as much as a third below the American level.[10]

Discharging their officially prescribed duty 'to develop a political stomach', consumers increasingly turned to fish as a substitute for meat, and fish consumption accordingly increased by 40 per cent between 1932 and 1938.[11] Wartime meat rationing was initially not very stringent – with 500 g. per week (somewhat less than in the UK) during 1940.[12] In 1942 the normal consumer's ration was cut sharply to 300 g., i.e. to just a third of the peacetime average; even so, 16 kg. per annum still compared favourably with the 1917 allocation of 12½ kg.

The normal consumer was not, however, an entirely representative figure, since the Wehrmacht – which was invariably better provisioned than the home front – plus seven million 'heavy workers' pushed up the average. Those Ruhr miners who were 'extra-heavy workers' had an allocation two and a half times that of normal consumers, though even then their meat intake in 1942 was 40 per cent lower than before the war. In the autumn of 1942 there was a morale-boosting increase to 350 g. per week, but the following spring saw a drastic reduction to 250 g.; this level was, none the less, still more than twice that of France (120 g.) or Poland (100 g.).[13] Late 1944 saw a vast upswing in German meat consumption because in its retreat the Wehrmacht drove large herds of cattle back into the Reich for slaughter, and thus left countries like Holland in the grip of famine.

It is difficult to judge the figures for butter and margarine consumption; whereas normally margarine is the butter of the poor, the Nazis' self-sufficiency drive was as liable to inhibit the consumption of (imported) margarine as economic stringency did that of butter elsewhere. The increase of one sixth in the *per capita* consumption of butter, and the concurrent drop of one quarter in that of margarine, between 1932 and 1938 should therefore not be regarded as evidence of greater affluence. In 1938 German *per capita* butter consumption – 8·8 kg. per annum – was a quarter below Britain's, though it somewhat exceeded America's.[14]

Volume alone, however, is hardly a foolproof standard of comparison:

one also has to take into account the gradual adulteration of dairy produce and fats throughout the Nazi era.

Shortages made themselves unpleasantly felt as early as the mid-thirties – *pace* Goering's celebrated motto, 'Guns before Butter'. By the winter of 1936–7 a rudimentary form of rationing began to operate: shopkeepers sold butter only to their regular customers[15] and the new allocations were a fifth below the previous average, although the water content seemed to be correspondingly increased.

Butter was one of the commodities that was affected little by the war from the point of view of availability and quality (except for a 10 per cent increase in price). The average war allocation of 9 kg. per annum represented absolute continuity with peacetime. (During the period of great victories in 1940–1 the ration was even increased by 10 per cent.)

The – reduced – *per capita* consumption of margarine in peacetime had also been about 9 kg.[16] For most of the first half of the war, however, the ration stood at about 3½ kg., after which it was reduced to less than 3 kg.

Peacetime consumption of fats remained fairly constant, but the use of inferior vegetable fats in the concoction of new compounds led to a marked deterioration in quality. In 1938 *per capita* consumption of fat (excluding butter and margarine) was 7 kg.[17] The early wartime ration was three-quarters of that, with the normal consumer somewhat better provided for than in the UK; but 1941–2 saw reductions. A yearly allocation of only 2¾ kg. turned the last war years into a period of bitter deprivation.

The peacetime scarcity of fats also affected the availability of eggs; though normally in adequate supply, eggs tended to be at a discount whenever the public fell back on them as a fat substitute. Between 1932 and 1938 *per capita* consumption declined by 10 per cent, with Germans eating half as many eggs as Americans or Britons.[18] German peacetime consumption averaged 2½ eggs per week and the wartime ration was fixed at 1½ (compared to Britain's one per week), but this was reduced later on.

Sugar consumption increased by 10 per cent between 1932 and 1938, when it stood at 24 kg. per annum (approximately half of the British and American average).[19] In 1941 the normal consumer ration for sugar and jam was nearly 18 kg. (cf. Britain's 13 kg.) and was two-fifths higher than in 1917.[20] During the last year of war this ration was discontinued altogether.

Milk consumption increased by only 6 per cent between 1932 and 1938 – at 112 litres per annum it equalled Britain's – but import restrictions on cattle fodder adversely affected quality. The regime's peacetime austerity measures created a pent-up demand for 'luxury' dairy produce; after the *Anschluss* with Austria locust-like swarms of German tourists in Austrian coffee-houses and *patisseries* caused the *Schwarzes Korps* to expostulate: 'Anybody would think Greater Germany was only created so that this raving Philistine rabble can wolf whipped cream.'[21] Under the wartime rationing scheme German adults were entitled to no milk at all, whereas children were rather lavishly provided for (in Britain and the US there was no wartime rationing of milk).

Cheese was another item which deteriorated markedly in quality in the late thirties, by which time its consumption had increased by 7 per cent over 1932, at 5½ kg. per annum in 1938 it was on a par with the British average. The normal consumer ration of 2.6 kg. in 1941 was two-fifths larger than the British one.

The consumption of imported fruits declined by an eighth between 1932 and 1938.* The consumption of indigenous fruit decreased even more, although a grand total of 4½ million allotments was a mitigating factor in the situation (thus 100 out of the representative sample of 350 working-class families investigated by the Labour Front in 1937 were partly self-sufficient in fruit and vegetables).[22] In 1938 the adult fruit consumption averaged 31 kg., equalling the British intake of only three types of fruit: apples, oranges and bananas. During the war the relative shortage of fruit containing vitamins was to some extent counteracted by official distribution of pills. In 1942 a reduction in the fruit and vegetable allocation was compensated for by increases in the meat and bread rations.

Peacetime *per capita* vegetable consumption declined by 10 per cent to 47 kg. in 1938, which was somewhat below the British average. Within the German total, white cabbage was the most important single item; the average intake of cabbage was nearly double that of the Americans, for instance.[23] Rationing initially halved the average vegetable consumption of 2·3 kg. in 1938, but during the middle years of the war the allocation gradually increased to three-quarters of the peacetime average.[24]

Potatoes could almost be described as the consumer's staff of life in the Third Reich, although the consumption declined by about 5 per cent between 1932 and 1938. At the latter date – with *per capita* consumption running at 3½ kg. per week – the German intake of potatoes was roughly

---

* Nazi Press reaction to the intermittent shortages of lemons was couched in the following terms: 'Only through the German soil are the finest vibrations transmitted to the blood . . . therefore, fare thee well, lemon, we need thee not. German rhubarb will replace thee altogether.' (cf. *Fränkische Tageszeitung*, quoted by Wallace R. Deuel, *op. cit.*, p. 194.)

double that of the British and Americans. Rationing allocations fluctuated between 2 and 5 kg. per week, the medium amount representing absolute continuity with the pre-war average.[25] Despite intermittent local shortages, potatoes were one of the most dependable items in the wartime provisioning of Germany, and helped the authorities to meet the consumer's minimum requirements with impressive regularity – impressive by comparison with 1917–18 anyway.

Coffee consumption increased by about a fifth during the thirties, when with an average of under 3 kg. per annum the German coffee intake was less than half the American (but of course vastly exceeded the British). In the later thirties the public demand for coffee notoriously exceeded supply. The police prevented the purchase of coffee by other than regular customers, while Goebbels fulminated, 'In times when coffee is scarce a decent person simply drinks less or stops drinking it altogether.'[26] During the war coffee substitutes, euphemistically called 'German coffee', predominated; the 1941 ration of real coffee was 2½ kg. per annum and illicit trading flourished almost from the very start. After the occupation of Western Europe (with its large stores of produce) black-market coffee changed hands at 40 marks per kg. in the Reich.[27] The 'black' coffee price kept rising dizzily. During the last winter of the war a pound of coffee had the same value on the black market as 20 litres of petrol (at 40 marks per litre).[28]

Throughout the thirties there was an overall disparate increase in alcohol consumption. Beer consumption increased by a third and would undoubtedly have gone up more but for a restriction on the acreage under hops; with 68 litres per annum in 1938 it was comparable to the British beer intake and exceeded the American one by a third. By 1938 average German wine consumption had risen 50 per cent to 6 litres per annum (three times that of Britain and the US), while that of brandy had virtually doubled; at 1·2 litres it was far in excess of the British and roughly half of the American consumption.[29] The wartime situation was characterized by the gradual adulteration of beer – nicknamed 'bladder irrigation à la Conti'* – and by alcohol rationing. A black market tapping sources all over occupied Europe and ubiquitous illicit practices (Berlin cafés purveyed alcohol in coffee cups) rule out statistical evaluation.

Compared to 1932, cigar and cigarette consumption had gone up by nearly 50 per cent in 1938, and in spite of increased taxation, the war further accelerated this upward trend, so that 1941 actually saw a doubling

* Dr Conti was the head of the Nazi Doctors' Association.

of the output of tobacco products before the Third Reich. Figures alone do not reflect the wartime importance of tobacco. The growing addiction of women to smoking sparked renewed controversies[30] and tobacco gradually assumed the function of a reserve currency. The wartime dearth of consumer goods – especially in the countryside – robbed money of its attraction as an exchange medium, and farmers traded eggs for cigarettes (at the rate of one for one), pounds of butter for packets of pipe tobacco, and pounds of meat for ten cigarettes.[31]

A number of conclusions emerge from a survey of the German public's supplies with food and drink during the Third Reich: after the severe impact of the slump the Nazi regime engendered an overall – but rather uneven – improvement in living standards, with increases in the consumption of meat, fish, dairy produce, coffee, alcohol and tobacco, offset by reductions in the consumption of such items as fruit, certain fats, eggs, poultry, vegetables and rice. (Reductions in quantity were, moreover, compounded by deterioration in the quality of a whole range of foodstuffs.) It should be borne in mind, however, that deterioration in quality did not inevitably reduce nutritional value. The more intensive grinding of flour for bread did not, for one thing. By comparison with the USA and the UK the peacetime diet of Nazi Germany was far from attractive. The Anglo-Saxons – especially the Americans – consumed more meat, white bread, sugar and eggs, and the Germans more cabbage, rye bread, potatoes and margarine. Even so, it was the palate and not the health of the average German that suffered as a result of this form of deprivation. This also held good for most of the war; it was not until 1943 that shortages of fats and proteins proved more than merely vexatious to the German consumer.

Statistics of the type quoted must present the situation in blanket terms and fail to sketch in the important sociological aspects of consumption. Some indication of the consumption pattern shaped by mass unemployment came from an NSV (Nazi People's Welfare) cookery-book poster displayed at the Berlin Agricultural Exhibition in 1933. The poster, captioned 'What we want is the 10-pfennig meal!' explained how 50 g. of buckwheat (costing 3½ pfennig) could, with an admixture of some fat and onions, be stirred into a gruel constituting a nourishing meal. The restoration of employment removed the need for 10-pfennig meals, and yet in 1938 – a year of full employment when brandy consumption doubled – it was observed that in firms with factory canteens many workers preferred sandwiches of bread and sausage, or even bread soaked in beetroot-juice or linseed oil (total cost: 20 pfennigs) to the consumption of a hot meal costing 45 pfennigs.[32]*

Autarchy reinforced financial stringency as a limiting factor in consumption, and the Nazi League of Women undertook the important task of instructing housewives in how to husband their resources by adjusting diets to the seasonal availability of homegrown foodstuffs. Their monthly list of recommended foodstuffs for October 1937, for instance, featured fish, cabbage, marmalade, cottage cheese, skimmed milk, grapes and porridge oats.[33] As we have seen, party propagandists exhorted the public to develop a 'political stomach'[34], a secular extension of the 'One-Pot Meal', which was known as the 'Lenten Sacrifice' of the whole nation.

The nation's 'political stomach', however, occasionally showed itself to be less highly developed than the dietitians demanded: the applause that greeted Goering's announcement (made at the 1938 Nuremberg Rally) of the renewed availability of wheaten rolls prompted acrid editorial invective against 'those who pretend starvation stares them in the face unless they have their regular supply of vol-au-vent and whipped cream'.[35]

Grocers – invidiously placed between 'dietitians' and housewives – were another target for censure. The newspaper of the National Food Estate castigated them as 'grumblers and alarmists behind the counter who, instead of re-educating the 17 million housewives with whom they were in daily contact, spent their time bemoaning unavoidable shortages'.[36] But Germany's grocers were not really as irremediably sunk in querulousness as all that. In 1935, when the first shortages made themselves felt, they showed sufficient resourcefulness to deflect the resultant disadvantages on to others; this they did by means of 'coupling transactions', i.e. by compelling customers who asked for foodstuffs in short supply to purchase additional items. Attempts to scotch this practice were not altogether successful, and the public's acceptance of the obligation to purchase articles of no immediate use was reflected in the popular catch-phrase 'Der deutsche Gruss ist Pflaumenmuss' (the German form of greeting – i.e. 'Heil Hitler', the first thing a customer had to say on entering a shop – is plum jam).

Such dislocations of the distributive apparatus resulting from the autarchy and arms drives were, however, not the only features of the

* A little earlier the *Frankfurter Zeitung* had commented on the 'solidarity of calculation' that existed between shop assistants and purchasers working out the correct change down to the last pfennig (cf. *Frankfurter Zeitung*, 3 January 1937).

consumption scene. The demand for, as well as the supply of, some consumer goods was visibly rising, and during the last pre-war years department stores and shops exhibited all the symptoms associated with boom conditions, from lavish displays of goods and throngs of avid purchasers to indifferent (if not downright rude) sales assistants. But this boom was as lopsided as the expansion of food consumption referred to above. Alongside impeccable glassware, porcelain, cutlery, electrical goods and watches (their prices partly reduced by government decree)[37] were ranged textile products and toiletry items (e.g. *Ersatz* soap) suffering from a carefully camouflaged deterioration in quality.

Since the slump the consumption of clothes had increased by over a quarter and their cost by about the same.[38] A lot of them were made of *Zellwolle*, a substitute wool material that was normally serviceable, but was rather ineffective in keeping out the cold in winter. Dress materials, table cloths, even handkerchiefs were made of artificial silk; purchasers were warned against laundering them in hot water.[39] Sheets were scarce, curtaining limited and expensive, and carpets prohibitive in price.[40]

The public were admonished to practise strict economy in their consumption of textiles. Noting with disapproval that the dead were being laid out in expensive clothes, the mayor of Pirmasens passed a local ordinance against sumptuaries depriving posterity of essential textiles.[41]

Restaurateurs received guide-lines on the re-utilization of left-overs: 'Left-overs which would induce nausea in a normal person are unfit for use – but no account need be taken of the requirements of hypersensitive palates.'[42]

The immediate pre-war consumption scene was a highly complex one, with instalment-buying on an unprecedented scale as much a feature as shortages and economic stringency. When the fairly adequate ration scales of September 1939 were put into operation – to popularize the war the regime narrowed the gap between normal and war provisioning – it was calculated that two-fifths of the population were actually entitled to more than their peacetime living standards.[43] In one important area of food consumption – butter and fats – where virtual rationing had of course been in operation before the war, the government came to the assistance of the least affluent by a system of cards guaranteeing 22 million people minimum quantities of margarine, butter, fats, sausage, bacon and cheese at between 25 and 50 per cent below the market price.[44]

It was a measure of Germany's tight textile supply that she was the first of the warring countries to ration table and bed linen, curtains and rugs.[45]

Textile rationing operated by means of ration cards and purchase chits. The universal Reich Clothing Card obtained an annual fluctuating allocation of points – 150 in 1940, 80 in 1942 – negotiable for a wide, but not comprehensive, range of clothing articles.* The supplementary purchase chits were issued selectively to applicants able to prove either that they did not have certain articles, such as men's coats and women's winter coats, or that they were threadbare. Four sheets, one pillowslip, one blanket or eiderdown, one mattress and three towels were considered sufficient. If a purchase chit was granted because an article was threadbare it had to be surrendered.[46]

Women's fur coats (not in the rationing scheme) were greatly in demand, and this demand was met to a large extent after the occupation of Scandinavia. There and elsewhere the occupying forces proved so (skilfully) acquisitive that an official ruling eventually made soldiers' loot deductible on their next-of-kin's ration card.[47]

In 1942 the clothing ration was slashed and simultaneously extended to cover such items of daily use as braces and sewing thread. After mid-1943 the manufacture of new civilian clothing ceased altogether, and certain consumer groups, such as children, air-raid victims or eastern evacuees, which were the object of a visual solicitude, received priority for whatever scanty stocks were still available.[48]†

Although a considerable lower social stratum continued to exist during the war (in 1940 factory workers in Hamburg were selling clothing coupons they could not afford to redeem),[49] the wartime tightening of the commodity market gradually created a 'money overhang', i.e. a situation where free purchasing power was channelled into evasion goods and services; savings which could have earthed this free-floating energy lost their attraction as the war progressed. The pre-war annual increase of deposits and interest credits (6 to 10 per cent) had more than trebled by 1940,[50] yet the post-1941 'iron savings scheme', under which industrial

* Men's allocation: 5 points for socks, 20 for a pair of trousers, 15 for a vest, 20 for a shirt, 30 for a pair of pyjamas, 32 for a jacket, 60 for a whole suit, 25 for a raincoat, 12 for a pair of shorts, and 7 for a scarf.

Women's allocation: 4 points for a pair of stockings (two additional pairs were obtainable for 8 points each), 5 for a scarf, 25 for a pullover, 16 for woollen knickers, 15 for a petticoat, 10 for a vest, 12 for an apron, 25 for a pair of overalls, 25 for a dressing-gown, 18 for a night-dress, 40 for a brassière, 8 for corsets, 40 for a woollen dress, 30 for a non-woollen dress, 15 for a blouse, 20 for a skirt, 25 for a jacket, 45 for a suit and 35 for a summer coat. (cf. Max Seydewitz, *op. cit.*, p. 119.)

† Soldiers – another favoured consumer category – were often the last refuge of civilians standing in dire need of a new pair of braces or having a watch repaired.

savings were tax-free but could not be withdrawn during the war, attracted only one worker in every five.[51]

Entertainment ranked high among these evasion goods and services: cinema attendance, which had been steadily rising throughout the thirties, virtually doubled between 1939 and 1940.[52] During the early part of the war other forms of non-essential consumption, such as holiday-making, winter sports or beauty care for women, were maintained at the same levels as in peacetime. These pre-war survivals co-existed with manifestations of scarcity: private transport laid up for lack of petrol, a shortage of leather, prompting recourse to wooden clogs, shop-windows ordered by the authorities to display goods for show, but not for sale.[53] Artificial shortages arose as a result of surplus money being invested in available commodities of every description, so that young couples had difficulty in obtaining furniture, linen and even baby cots.[54] The more affluent could also take advantage of a loophole in the rationing system by eating out in restaurants, where expensive non-rationed items, such as game, poultry and fish, formed part of the bill of fare. They accumulated surplus coupons (e.g. for bread) which they could barter or sell on the black market.

The power of the purse was only one of the factors determining the food intake of the ordinary citizen during the war. Because of rationing the daily calorie consumption by civilians – 3,116 in peacetime[55] – was reduced by about a third for normal consumers, while 'heavy workers' (who numbered 7 million, i.e. one in every five gainfully employed Germans) received somewhat more than their peacetime average. A section of labour enjoying a slighter advantage over their fellows were employees of plants equipped with their own bulk-supplied works canteens; to an extent, of course, this group overlapped with the heavy workers. 1,800 calories represents minimum subsistence. For most of the war normal consumers lived at levels 7 to 15 per cent above minimum;[56] in 1944 their quota actually dropped to below 1,800.

The ability of the normal consumer to supplement these tight – though not starvation – rations hinged on contacts in the countryside or among the occupation forces, and on having the money (as well as the opportunity) for black-market purchases.

The black market became, in fact, an integral aspect of wartime consumption. Though on most counts (as the regime not unwarrantably kept proclaiming from the rooftops) the home front was better administered than in the First World War, racketeers dogged the heels of Armageddon more closely in 1939 than they had done in 1914. From a minority pursuit in the early stages of the war, when Party officials were the group principally involved, the black market mushroomed into a countrywide practice. An SD evaluation compiled in the fifth winter of the war illuminates both the facts of the situation and the rationalizations commonly put forward in mitigation:

In the early stages of the war black marketeering was rejected as a form of sabotage, but since then there has grown up a practice of evading rationing regulations without any consciousness of wrong-doing.

Catchphrases like 'He who has one thing has everything', or 'Everybody swops with everyone else' are in circulation, and folk comrades who do not join in these practices are considered stupid. Farmers profiteer, shopkeepers barter (butchers and drapers interchange meat and cloth) craftsmen carry out repairs where they are offered scarce goods, 'contacts' are needed to redeem purchase chits, and officials dealing with the public receive gift parcels. The black market is considered essential to correct deficiencies in the official distribution system. The former sharp condemnation of profit-motivated black-market deals is on the wane. There is a feeling that the powers that be turn a blind eye to them.[57]

The last statement was a half-truth; on the one hand many Party and state (not excluding Wehrmacht) officials were involved in black-market practices, while on the other the police and the judiciary prosecuted transgressions of war-economy measures most rigorously, if somewhat selectively. Popular cynicism about their effectiveness was reflected in the joke about 15,000 Lilliputians being directed into the Berlin grocery shops – for under-the-counter work.

The group most directly involved in under-the-counter work, or, to use the current phrase, 'stoop transactions', the shopkeepers, adapted themselves to the situation by evolving a dialectical view of right and wrong. At the funeral of a Berlin butcher who committed suicide while under investigation on charges of slaughtering animals illegally, officials of the butcher's guild eulogized him as a model of probity and honest business dealings. The SD report instanced these obsequies as an example of the prevailing view of shopkeepers that breaches of the law by traders arose from the incomprehensibility of bureaucratic regulations rather than personal dishonesty.[58]

The extreme bureaucratization of wartime life in turn stimulated a black-market fringe industry: the production – hazardous but lucrative – of faked documents. During the last winter of the war it was possible to purchase for 80,000 marks the complete range of papers legitimizing a person's existence in the Third Reich: passport, army pass, work book, ration card and *Volkssturm Z* card.[59]

Like any non-regulated market* the black market was capable of registering impending changes in the supply and demand position with seismographic accuracy: among the more exotic items obtainable on the Berlin black market in the spring of 1945 were hammer-and-sickle badges and even six-pointed Stars of David.[60]

In a chapter on the details of consumption it may not be altogether inappropriate to touch on the more general question of how closely – or distantly – the Third Reich approximated to a consumer society. The United States at the time presented a model of such a society that at first sight could serve as a basis for comparison, since, although victorious in 1918 and richer in resources,† they were industrially and technologically similar to Germany and had been affected by the slump in a comparable way. The motor-car constituted the badge of the consumer society; the fact that Henry Ford personified the 'industrial programme' of America and Krupp von Bohlen that of Germany was symptomatic of the divergence between the two economic cultures. The different traditions which led each country in a different industrial and economic direction resulted in a dramatic imbalance between their respective bases for the establishment of a consumer society. In 1930, when the American/German population ratio was two to one, the US had 23 million motor cars on the road, compared to Germany's half a million.[61] The gap between the UK and Germany in the same year was far narrower: approximately 1 million as against half a million; the population ratio was just under two Britons to every three Germans, with a corresponding disparity in industrial potential. During the thirties total car ownership trebled in Germany and doubled in Britain, but even so the pre-war proportion of German car ownership was still 50 per cent below the British level of four years earlier.[62]

Thus Germany was not moving appreciably closer to a consumer society. In 1936 the former cabinet minister Eltz von Ruebenach had calculated[63] that, given prevailing cost and incomes, 1,600,000 Germans at

* A type of market with an official licence for selling second-hand goods should be mentioned in this connection: in the winter of 1943–4 the authorities set up exchange centres where members of the public could swop items such as furniture, household utensils or old clothes (cf. *St Galler Tagblatt*, 6 March 1944).

† These factors applied even more after 1945 without militating against the unmistakable emergence of a highly consumer-orientated pseudo-American society in the Federal Republic.

most could become car owners in the foreseeable future. The optimum extent of this car-owning élite had been virtually reached by 1939, but of course a year earlier the Volkswagen project had presaged the breakthrough to a genuinely popular form of car ownership. Yet this project, too, aroused rather greater expectations than it was capable of fulfilling. Priced at below 1,000 marks (repayable over four years) the VW would have involved buyers in weekly instalment payments (plus insurance) of 6 marks, exclusive of running charges. In other words: the total weekly expenditure on a car would have accounted for between a third and a quarter of the take-home pay of most wage-earners. The likelihood of the People's Car becoming most people's car was therefore highly conjectural, even before the war intervened to kill the project at birth.

Germany had had to contend with a housing problem ever since the First World War. In 1914 there had been only 100,000 fewer dwellings than households, but subsequently, despite the Weimar Republic's considerable building record, this gap between housing target and achievement had widened, to reach 900,000 by 1932. Between that date and the outbreak of the war the Nazi regime was responsible for creating 1,800,000 new dwelling units, a percentage of which, however, was not newly built.*

Compared to Weimar's total of 2,650,000 new dwellings in thirteen years (i.e. 200,000 a year) the Nazis' average annual output of 300,000 units was certainly impressive,† but, since the Nazi peacetime increase in population of 3,250,000 almost equalled that of a far longer Weimar period, the pressure on accommodation actually increased. The gap between the number of households and the existing dwellings widened to 1½ million by 1938,[64] a result of the rising birth-rate as well as of internal migration. Between 1934 and 1939 1½ million people left the land, partly because of wretched rural housing. Entirely new industrial settlements, such as the Hermann Goering Works' town of Salzgitter and the Volkswagen site of Fallersleben, came into existence; the chemical centres of central Germany (Halle, Magdeburg, Halberstadt and Dessau) doubled their population. Magdeburg grew from over 100,000 to nearly a quarter of a million[65] and in 1938 it had an absolute deficiency of 25,000 dwellings,

* By 1935 300,000 new dwelling units – or a quarter of the total – had resulted from a scheme for modernizing and splitting up existing dwellings, under which the government paid a fifth of the cost and lent landlords the remainder at 4 per cent (cf. William Sheridan Allen, *The Nazi Seizure of Power*, Chicago, 1965, p. 230).

† As were such slum clearance operations as those undertaken in Leipzig's Seeberg quarter or Cologne's Buttermarket.

while 44,000 inhabited ones were either condemned, sub-standard or overcrowded.[66]

These Magdeburg statistics were issued at the end of the regime's peak construction year: in 1937, 320,000 new housing units had been put up at a cost 30 per cent below Weimar's expenditure on less than half that number in 1932.[67] This saving reflected a lowering of standards; indeed one of the types of dwelling favoured by the regime was the 'people's flat' (*Volkswohnung*). The standard size of a *Volkswohnung* for a childless couple was 26 sq. m. (34 sq. m. for a family of four). The Weimar average, by comparison, had been 40 sq. m. and Britain's 1936 housing act laid down 50 sq. m. as a standard area of accommodation.

The housing situation was further aggravated by the conjunction of a relatively inadequate building programme with the construction of the wrong type of accommodation. In Berlin for instance, small flats of up to three rooms had accounted for almost two-thirds of all new constructions in 1932, but this proportion had been reduced to just over one-third by 1935. Overall during the Nazi peacetime years, medium-sized flats of four to six rooms accounted for over half of all new constructions,[68] with the result that financial considerations prevented poorer families (those in greatest need of re-housing) from moving into new accommodation. An internal German Labour Front survey on the housing situation disingenuously concluded that the main problem was one of internally balanced imbalance – a minus factor of 1,750,000 medium-size flats and an excess of the same number of small ones – without once touching on the financial factors involved.[69] The rent for old (i.e. pre-1914) medium-sized apartments as well as for new flats of two and a half rooms and upwards was about 38 marks per month; this put either type of accommodation beyond the reach of most workers, who would have had to earmark between a quarter and a third of their take-home pay for rent. (It must be remembered that expenditure on food accounted for just under half the average working-class income.) The Labour Front survey was less disingenuous in criticizing the yardstick whereby flats were termed overcrowded if the number of occupants was double that of the rooms (including kitchen). Thus six people living in two rooms and a kitchen were overcrowded, but five were not.[70] According to the official criterion less than a million dwellings were listed as overcrowded, whereas out of a national total of 17·8 million flats only 11·3 million provided their occupants with genuinely adequate accommodation. In other words 37 per cent – more than one out of every three German dwellings – were in fact, if not in law, sub-standard.[71]

While agrarian workers' dwellings represented the blackest spot in the housing situation, the accommodation of industrial labour also left a great deal to be desired. Investigating a representative sample of 2,000 working-class homes in 1937, the Labour Front found that 96 per cent of them lacked bathrooms or showers, 22 per cent had no direct access to a water supply and 14 per cent depended on means other than electricity for illumination.[72]

One must, however, beware of viewing the housing situation, and indeed the whole consumption scene of the Third Reich, in purely statistical terms. Even looked at statistically, two out of every three Germans were spared the discomforts of overcrowding or sub-standard accommodation. As for the remaining third, they tended to let the regime's summer of glory blind them to their present discontent. When Hitler envisaged Berlin turning into the 10 million capital of an ever more powerful Reich, with public buildings and highways to match its importance and entire built-up areas were being ripped apart to accommodate Speer's great new North/South and East/West axis, the average Berliner with his 35 sq. m. of accommodation could not help but feel less cramped emotionally than he did physically.[73]

In addition the regime had another device for making not a few of its subjects feel less hemmed in, both in the material and the psychological sense of the term: the twin process of expulsion and massacre that eventually rendered Germany entirely 'judenrein' (clear of Jews) put as much dwelling space on the housing market as one year of somewhat below-average building activity. In Vienna, for instance, within four years of the Anschluss one out of every ten inhabitants availed himself of the re-housing opportunities that followed in the train of genocide.

By this time, of course, the regime's general housing programme had virtually come to a standstill. The number of wartime dwellings constructed dwindled from 115,000 in 1940 to 28,000 in 1944.[74] The crowding of German as well as foreign labour into the Reich's industrial growth areas reached such proportions that in the Styrian iron-mining centre of Eisenerz men on night shift rented their beds to day workers.[75] In 1941, before the onset of the really heavy air attacks, it was officially estimated that there was a shortage of 5 to 6 million flats.[76] In the middle of 1943 the government started to build emergency accommodation for air-raid victims. By 1944 the estimated shortage of dwellings approached 11 million, and 4 million flats had been put out of commission by Allied bombs.[77] At this point, according to the folklore of humour, many Germans – looking around with smarting eyes – recalled housing commissioner Robert Ley's promise* of airy, sunlit homes and concluded wryly: 'Well, now we have really got houses with plenty of light, air, and sunshine.'[78]

* Hitler had in October 1942 promoted the leader of the Labour Front to overlord of the Reich's housing programme (cf. *Bundesarchiv Koblenz*, Bestand R 41, Reichsgesetzblatt I, p. 623).

15

HEALTH

In any modern state health is a function of many interconnected factors: standards of hygiene, diet and housing, working conditions, quality of medical services, the psychological climate. The Third Reich hardly permitted a *status quo* in any of these spheres, but the changes it wrought did not follow a clear-cut pattern; advances in some areas were compounded with deteriorations elsewhere, and an increase in quantity occurred alongside a decline in quality.

This dichotomy was exemplified by fluctuations in the supply of doctors. In the Republic there had been complaints of overcrowding in the medical profession, and some claimed that there were 5,000 more doctors (a tenth of the total) than were needed. But suggestions for regulating entry into faculties of medicine by means of a *numerus clausus* were never acted upon.

Soon after the seizure of power the regime reduced the overall student population; a subsequent upswing in university enrolment, however, accompanied by a two-year reduction in the length of medical studies, eventually resulted in 19,000 more doctors being put on the register during the first ten years of Nazi rule than during the last decade under Weimar.[1] A preoccupation with the need for adequate medical reserves led the regime to waive its own one-tenth quota for women students (by 1944 every eighth doctor was a female, compared to Weimar's one in twenty) and to grant long-term Wehrmacht exemptions to male medical students. The Nazis also increased the nursing force, so that between 1932 and 1939 the proportion of nurses to every 10,000 of the population went up from eighteen to twenty.[2]

The ostensibly greater number of trained personnel did not, however, improve the overall quality of medical care. The debit side of the accounts included a decrease of 40 per cent in the number of specialists (from 16,500 in 1938 to less than 10,000 in 1944), the elimination of 5,500 Jewish doctors, and lower standards resulting from the two-year speed-up in medical training. In addition – and this is why the wider availability of medical care suggested by the above figures existed only on paper – the functions assigned to Nazi medicine actually left the general public less well provided for than before. The majority of newly trained doctors no longer took up private practice but entered government health services or the medical branch of various party formations. The Wehrmacht, which literally expanded a hundredfold within a decade, pre-empted a large segment of medical skill; so, to a varying extent, did the SA, the Hitler Youth, the National Labour Service, and the SS. The SS, of course, also deployed many doctors in concentration and death camps, where their professional duties ranged from 'hospital work' to medical experiments which defy description and to selection for the gas chambers.

Additional 'selection procedures' engaging a great deal of medical interest and energy were the sterilization programme initiated by the 1933 Act for the Prevention of Hereditarily Diseased Offspring, and the war-time mercy-killing of the mentally and physically handicapped.

Another, more innocuous, new channel into which medical activity was deflected was industry, which eventually retained over 4,000 – mainly part-time – factory physicians (to whom must be added the medical personnel exercising wartime epidemiological control over millions of foreign workers).[3]

All this meant that as far as access to doctors was concerned the ordinary *Krankenkasse* patient (protected under the health-insurance scheme) found himself pushed to the end of a queue – a situation which in effect corresponded to a deliberate Nazi design. The transformed economic situation whereby mass unemployment had yielded to over-employment blunted the incentive for regular work attendance, and the fully reactivated working population naturally showed itself more accident- and illness-prone than the pared-down labour force of the Depression. The regime calculated that if doctors were relatively inaccessible the effort involved in obtaining certificates would inhibit malingering and industrial absenteeism. For this reason – and because of rising employment – the number of insured patients per doctor had by 1936 increased to 600 from 450 during the Depression.[4] At the same time the health-insurance outlay on medicines prescribed per average case of illness dropped by a seventh, from 3·45 to 3·00 marks.[5]

Taking the population as a whole (i.e. insured as well as uninsured) the ratio of available doctors to patients dropped by 6 per cent – from 1:1351 to 1:1432 – during the Nazis' peace-time years.[6] Nor did the 10 per cent expansion of the nursing force really produce a commensurately intensified coverage of the public-health sector. This expansion accrued partly from the founding of a 'brown sisterhood' of nurses steeped in the Nazis' eugenic ideology and taking their oath on 'the gospel of the indivisible folk community'.[7] These 'brown sisters' were less of an addition than a replacement for the nursing establishment, which was partly denominationally organized; for instance, they undertook duties in connection with the sterilization programme that Catholic nursing nuns found unacceptable.

The regime did none the less achieve certain improvements in the health situation; for instance it promoted more intensive detection of disease in its early stages by medical fitness tests, which were mandatory for all newly-weds and applicants for marriage loans and family allowances.

Possibly more important was the availability of certain Party organizations as an auxiliary health apparatus that could be activated when the occasion arose. Having taken over a well-functioning public health service, the regime thus disposed of additional resources to remedy deficiencies in the working of that service. If, for instance, a local health office found the establishment of welfare centres for babies too expensive in a thinly populated area, the local National Socialist People's Welfare branch might step into the breach and set up a mother-and-child voluntary centre, and the latter would officially order all mothers and children in the area to attend compulsory examinations for rickets.[8]

Specialized Party organizations were also in a position to carry out mass X-rays (in Pomerania, a province with a population of under 2 million, the special SS Roentgen-unit claimed to have compiled an X-ray register of 800,000 inhabitants during 1938).[9] During the war, when louse-borne typhus was spreading across the Reich, no public announcement about quarantine measures appeared in the Press – this might have lowered morale – but the Party network relayed directives by word of mouth concerning preventive measures.[10]

In addition, the Nazis' preoccupation with sport and physical fitness could not but have a beneficial effect on health, though standards prevailing in this sphere had in fact been quite high before, and the typical Nazi tendency towards over-exertion created its own health hazards. Thus the journal of public health service, quoting the case of a middle-aged winner of a sports medal who shortly afterwards applied for sick leave to his insurance fund, wrote:

The call to sports for the over-forty-fives is of dubious value. One recent sports call involved men of up to fifty-five throwing a 3-kilo medicine ball a distance of $6\frac{1}{2}$ metres, doing a 2·8-metre long jump, and running 1,000 metres in six minutes. Most men are reluctant to appear sick or weak in the eyes of their comrades and thus to become targets of derision, and they force themselves to a physical performance which can have unfortunate results.[11]

Similarly, in order to prevent 'ill-treatment and over-exertion' the Wehrmacht prohibited such contests as boxing bouts unless they took place under the supervision of officers.[12]

Such negative by-products of the officially promoted fitness mania were only part of the picture, however. The fact that at the height of the war (with many men away at the front) there were over 5 million holders of the Strength-through-Joy sports certificate[13] obviously owed a great deal to the officially promoted provision of sports facilities at industrial enterprises and compulsory PT during the working day, and similar attitudes such as that of the railways, which made a permanent appointment dependent on possession of the national sports medal.[14]

Sport was allotted five periods per week on the time-table of schools, and school-leavers frequently found their apprentice training programme interlarded with physical drill.[15] Between 1935 and 1938 the number of individual nights spent annually at Youth Hostels increased by over a fifth (from 7 to $8\frac{1}{2}$ million),[16] and a Bavarian investigation established that for every one youngster who suffered loss of appetite at Hitler Youth summer camps, two put on weight.[17]

On the other hand, the orthopaedic health of Hitler Youths was adversely affected (37 per cent of the 1936 call-up group had flat feet),[18] and so was their mental health. Signs of increased nervousness were not diagnosed only among the young, but also among women who combined domestic responsibilities with wage-earning, and among men, particularly piece-rate workers.

As far as overall nervous strain was concerned, the impact of the Third Reich on the national psyche was rather ambivalent. There can be little doubt that the seizure of power engendered a wide-spread improvement in emotional health;[19] this was not only a result of the economic upswing, but of many Germans' heightened sense of identification with the national purpose; this effect was similar to the one that wars normally have on the incidence of suicide and depression (in fact Nazi Germany recorded this phenomenon twice over: in 1933 and 1939). But at the same time the sense of living more intensively that resulted from the constant stimulation of mass emotions also led to greater indulgence in drinking, smoking and entertainment. During the relative boom years of the late thirties most Germans 'worked hard and played hard' – and over-exertion as well as overstimulation are hardly conducive to a balanced state of mental health. The actual incidence of mental derangement under the Nazi regime is difficult to establish: although the number of people in asylums increased quite markedly – by over a third in Bavaria, for instance[20] – some of this increase may have been due to more stringent hospitalization measures arising from the regime's eugenic priorities.

The suicide rate, as reflected in official statistics, showed an upward trend somewhat in excess of the population increase (1932: 18,934, 1939: 22,288),[21] but this was only marginal. The German suicide incidence, which was double that of England (28·6 as against 12·4 per 100,000 of the population in 1936), did not change appreciably. On the other hand, the incidence of fatal accidents was a form of death that increased by over a half (1932: 24,870, 1939: 39,767).[22] It was the result of greater economic activity and deliberately fostered attitudes of self-assertiveness and disregard for the sanctity of life – one's own as well as that of others.*

Almost every weekly issue of the *Schwarzes Korps* carried half a dozen obituary notices of young SS men killed in training, while railway mishaps (which in Bavaria, for instance, doubled during this time)[23] were no doubt partly caused by worn-out rolling stock.

The increase in road accidents conformed to the general pattern of fatal accidents. In the mid-thirties the German fatality rate averaged 8,000 per annum; this compared with 6,000 for the UK, where car ownership was three times as widespread as in Germany. The German road-accident rate was variously ascribed to increased alcoholism, official encouragement of the motor car, and the ambience of brutal self-assertion. (Though this was probably true, the interpretation leaves out of account one residual factor: the elusive entity called national character. The post-war road-accident rate in Germany is still markedly higher than in Britain.)†

The general mortality rate showed an increase during the Nazi era, but it was so gradual that it cannot be traced to the regime. At the beginning of the Third Reich the death rate per 1,000 was about eleven; by the

* Prosecutions for homicide through negligence before the courts increased by nearly 50 per cent between 1934 and 1938, for bodily injury through negligence by nearly a third (cf. *Statistisches Handbuch für Deutschland 1928–1944*, p. 634).

† The relevant American figures are not included here, since the incidence of car ownership in the United States was so much higher than either in Britain or in Germany that any comparison would be meaningless.

outbreak of war this had gone up to just over twelve. The British peace-time death rate averaged twelve per 1,000 and America's (both in peace and war) between 10½ and eleven. It was really only during the war that the German civilian death rate showed a marked increase, so that by 1944 (excluding war casualties) it stood 1½ points above that of Britain and 4½ points above that of the USA.

Another set of statistics – at the other end of the scale, as it were – deserves close attention: the infant mortality rate. Heavily preoccupied with population increase, the Nazi health authorities placed great emphasis on reducing infant mortality and notched up some definite advances in this field. Starting from an average mortality of seventy-seven per 1,000 new-born babies, they managed to reduce this to sixty just before the outbreak of the war; but it rose again to seventy-two by 1943. Throughout the whole of this period the English figure (fifty-three in 1939 and forty-eight in 1944) was rather lower than the German one and the American (fifty-one in 1938 and forty in 1944) even more so. Developments in the sphere of mortality among new-born infants were rather analogous; the Germans, though fairly successful in reducing its incidence at all times, were somewhat behind the British and the Americans in their results.

Ideologically linked to the 'battle for births' was the sterilization campaign against possible begetters of 'hereditarily diseased offspring'. By the outbreak of war 375,000 people (including 200,000 feeble-minded, 73,000 schizophrenics, 57,000 epileptics and nearly 30,000 alcoholics)[24] had been sterilized, the vast majority of them involuntarily, i.e. under official duress. Occasionally forcible sterilization was extended to cases right outside the sphere of eugenics legislation: thus a workman in Saxony who had lost a leg in an industrial accident was sterilized on the grounds that his diminished earning capacity precluded him from raising a family. He committed suicide.[25] Incidentally, one group which welcomed sterilization were feeble-minded females with a low threshold of sexual inhibition (in other words, part-time prostitutes).

Other peacetime Nazi innovations in the health sphere that deserve mention relate to changes in nutrition and to new forms of medical regimen. In pursuance of the autarchy programme the authorities set up a dietetic laboratory under the National Health Office for the purpose of investigating new foods, such as whale-meat, new fish preserves, milk-protein bread, 'German cocoa' and new apple juices. The new apple juices were bad for the teeth, but most of the other innovations proved quite success-ful.[26] Rather more crucial for overall health standards, however, was the deficiency of fruit and vegetables, and the change in the dietetic pattern resulting from the officially decreed substitution of wholemeal bread for its wheat-germ predecessor. During the war especially the new type of black bread was considered to be responsible for the wide prevalence of stomach disorders, and the campaign for setting up factory canteens was prompted by the authorities' concern at the incidence of gastric disorders among the labour force. 12 million working days were lost in 1940 be-cause of gastric disorders, and some time later a leading medical journal admitted, 'The army of sufferers from stomach diseases has greatly in-creased in this war.'[27] Nervous tension obviously contributed to this, as did such symptoms of dental ill-health as caries; its prevalence among school-children prompted marked increases in the number of personnel in school dental clinics.[28]

In 1937 a Labour Front investigation into a representative sample of 350 workers' families established that over a quarter of them used no tooth-paste,[29] and another survey revealed that only 30 per cent of a wider local sample (8,000 Cologne health-service patients) enjoyed perfect dental health.[30]

Good examples of the Nazi regimen introduced into some areas of medical prophylaxis were prison-type hospitals for 'anti-social elements' suffering from venereal disease or tuberculosis. At Stadtroda in Thüringia recalcitrant or careless tubercular patients were kept under guard and left to their fate without any medical attention whatever if they resisted the severe hygienic rules governing life in the 'ordinary wards' of the health prison.[31] At tuberculosis hospitals rigorous discipline was enjoined upon nurses too: one was summarily dismissed after having twice given a patient extra helpings of food.[32]

Certain Nazi innovations in the health sphere naturally served more positive aims than deterrence pure and simple. The best-known symbol of positive departures in Nazi medicine was the institute at Hohenlychen, which (to quote an English commentator), specialized in producing 'yes-men for this life'.[33] At Hohenlychen patients were never allowed to feel lonely or useless; thus a man who had lost his right arm worked jointly at carpentry with another who had lost his left one; an air mechanic without hands had someone else doing manual work for him, and after release they were both (on official instruction) given employment at the same factory. The institute exemplified Nazi medical science in two ways: most of the disabilities catered for were created by the regime (the result of over-exertion at sport, motorway construction or other work accidents); in addition the institute clothed the Nazi shibboleth of the triumph of the will over adversity with a vestige of scientific credibility.

Linked to the 'triumph-of-the-will' theme was the demotion of death; since, in the context of medicine, the phenomena of death and pain could not be minimized as plausibly as in the surreal world of Nazi ritual or documentary war films, they were invested with an aura of pseudo-spirituality. In 1938 Dr Conti, the Nazi doctors' leader, condemned the growing habit among general practitioners of sending patients in a terminal condition to hospital, and managed to cloak a concern for conserving limited hospital resources with the phrase 'Death, like birth, constitutes a natural event which belongs among the most significant in family life.'[34] The advocacy of death *en famille* as a spiritually enriching experience dovetailed easily with received notions about the role of pain in the universal scheme of things.

Already in the pre-Nazi era the British ambassador to Berlin, Lord d'Abernon, had been struck by a widespread tolerance of pain: 'Not only do the Germans bear pain stoically but they apparently feel it less than men of other races.'[35] Addressing the German Philosophical Association in 1935, the eminent surgeon Sauerbruch said: 'Nothing great in life is created without the shock of pain; pain transforms and purifies man for his higher task.'[36]

The practical results of the fusion of such attitudes with the heroic ethos of Nazism were apparent in a number of ways. German surgeons resorted to anaesthetics less than their Anglo-Saxon colleagues, and pregnant mothers eschewed analgesia during labour, since it would have been unfitting for German women to undergo the supreme experience of their existence with their consciousness dimmed.

Despite such manifestations of stoicism, the citizens of the Third Reich were not notably more healthy than either their predecessors or their contemporaries in other countries. On the contrary, both the sickness rate and the accident rate of Germany under Nazi rule showed an increase. Thus the annual incidence of hospitalization rose from nearly 4 million in 1932 to 5,800,000 in 1938,[37] an increase which was not wholly explicable in terms of population growth (which was 4 per cent) nor of more thoroughgoing prophylaxis. From 1935 to 1937 industrial accidents rose by one third (from 1,354,000 to 1,789,000),[38] while the labour force grew by roughly half that amount.[39]

A description in terms of a health graph showing a consistently downward curve cannot be substantiated, but some of the evidence available does point in that direction. One such indication was a drop of 2 per cent in the number of men passed as fit for military service between 1936 and 1942. It is unlikely that Wehrmacht doctors would apply stricter criteria in war than in peace, and the figure of 2 per cent is not all that small when applied to a sample approaching two-thirds of a million (the respective percentages for 1936 and 1942 were eighty-three and eighty-one.[40] Other indications can be gleaned from an alphabetical survey of the German health situation in terms of some major diseases.

Alcoholism increased gradually throughout the thirties and even more so in the course of the war (one noteworthy aspect of this was the increased addiction of women).[41] The death-rate from alcohol poisoning was five times as high as in England, but considerably below that of the United States. Estimates put the number of habitual drunkards in the country at 300,000, another figure that compared unfavourably with the British one, though favourably with the American.[42]

Cancer: Throughout the thirties the German death-rate was slowly rising, but it still remained somewhat below the British one, while exceeding that of the United States appreciably. The war saw a more marked increase, which medical officials partly attributed to 'inappropriate feeding'.[43]

Cerebrospinal Meningitis: The German peacetime incidence was somewhat lower than in Britain and much lower than in the USA. During the war the Germans did considerably better than the British and rather worse than the Americans.

Diphtheria: The incidence more than doubled between 1932 and 1938, when it stood at nearly 150,000. It subsequently increased to almost 250,000 at the height of the war, when the mortality rate was twice the peacetime average. This was in marked contrast to Britain and even more to the United States, where the period saw a virtual halving of the number of cases and of the mortality rate. In the late thirties the death-rate from diphtheria was four times as great in Germany as in the United States.

Dysentery: In the thirties the situation compared favourably with Britain and unfavourably with the United States. Early in the war the incidence was double the peacetime one (but – as Dr Conti pointed out – still only one-eighth of that obtaining during the First World War). Wartime mortality overall was appreciably higher than in Britain and lower than in the United States.[44]

Heart diseases: In the thirties German mortality figures rose gradually but still remained substantially below British and American ones. The war-time incidence of rheumatism, which can be a contributory cause of heart disease, was sufficiently heavy to cause official concern (in addition to which it accounted for one-eighth of all absences from work).

Influenza: The German death-rate showed a certain decline both in peace and in war. It was rather lower than in Britain and markedly higher than in the USA.

Measles: The German mortality rate was consistently lower than the British, but somewhat above that obtaining in the United States.

Pneumonia: In peacetime the mortality rate of the Germans somewhat exceeded the British one. During the whole period the American mortality rate gradually declined from its relatively high level so that it was eventually lower than in Germany.

Polio: In peace and war alike, both the incidence and the mortality rate were considerably higher than in Britain (some of this was blamed on the Hitler Youth, who constructed open-air swimming-pools lacking adequate safeguards against the spread of infection). A comparison with trends in the United States is difficult because of the great fluctuations that occurred in that country.

Puerperal septicaemia: There was a gradual reduction both of sickness and of mortality in the thirties, but the figures still somewhat exceeded the simultaneously declining British ones, though remaining much lower than those of the Americans.

Scarlet fever: The incidence more than doubled between 1932 and 1938. The sickness rate compared quite favourably with Britain, though not with America, while mortality was higher in both Anglo-Saxon countries. During the war, the rate of infection as well as of fatality roughly trebled in Germany – involving almost a million patients between 1941 and 1943 – while Britain and America showed a steady decline under both headings. By 1943 twenty times more Germans than Britons – and six times more than Americans – were dying of scarlet fever.

Tuberculosis: The mortality rate, which had been declining steeply since

1900 (when it stood at 225 per 100,000 of the population), had settled below the British level and only slightly above the American level by the late thirties, with seventy per 100,000. Recognition was given to German advances in this sphere by the convening of the 1939 International Tuberculosis Congress in Berlin. War saw a notable expansion of radiography, and in 1942 the state extended financial support to uninsured patients and their dependants.[45] By this time the German mortality rate exceeded the British rate slightly and the American rate quite markedly. The prolongation of the war increased the urban incidence of tuberculosis. By 1944–5 the death-rate from tuberculosis among Berliners was 252 per 100,000 (cf. 1918:282 per 100,000).[46]

Typhoid: There was a rather heavier peacetime incidence and mortality rate than in Britain, though it was not higher than in the United States. At the height of the war both mortality and incidence increased markedly in Germany, while the opposite trend operated in the Anglo-Saxon countries. Even so, the Germans could point out that the increase had only reached a fifth of its Great War level.[47]

Whooping-cough: Both the incidence and the mortality rate was lower than in Britain and in the United States – during the war, at any rate.

The war of necessity modified the health pattern quite fundamentally. Of an available stock of half a million hospital beds, 185,000 were diverted to military use,[48] but the resultant shortage was partly made good by means of the Euthanasia Programme, which exterminated an estimated 100,000 inmates of institutions. Another – far more innocuous – wartime campaign centred on the dental health of boys aged fourteen to eighteen because tooth decay among that age-group (especially in the countryside) was adversely affecting the intake into the armed forces.

While special priority was accorded to the young – this also applied in the sphere of rationing – the highest age-groups found themselves rather out in the cold. The almost annually increasing toll taken by cancer, cerebral apoplexy, paralysis and heart failure was officially linked with senescence,[49] and the *Schwarzes Korps* blandly stated in 1944, 'The over-sixties are in poor health because they are ill-cared-for medically.'[50]

The old were the most vulnerable segment of the wartime civilian population which as a whole was deprived of medical services by comparison with the army. In 1937 a metropolitan centre like Berlin had fifteen doctors per 10,000 of the population while, at the opposite end of the scale,

East Prussia deployed five for the same number.[51] By 1941 the ratio throughout the country was one doctor for between 10,000 and 20,000 inhabitants,[52] and sixty to eighty patients waiting in surgeries were a normal feature. The Press kept appealing to the public to call their GPs only in cases of genuine emergency; health-insurance patients found that it took doctors so long to visit them and issue medical certificates that they forfeited part of their sickness benefit in the interim.[53]

To solve this problem the *Schwarzes Korps* ingeniously suggested that doctors who found that the patients they visited were fit enough to come to surgery should charge them the fees paid by private patients.[54] After a while arms workers were denied a free choice of panel doctors and officially assigned to ward-doctors '*Revierärzte*' in their area of employment.[55]

By 1944 the medical needs of the home front had become so pressing that a number of army doctors were redirected into civilian practice, and certain military hospitals started treating civilians.[56] The health of medical personnel themselves was affected by this pressure. During the third winter of the war newspapers were referring to the incidence of nervous breakdowns among chemists;[57] this phenomenon was associated with the public's increasing dependence on pills. There were plants which – with official approval – included sedatives in their employees' pay packets, though at the same time the authorities tried, without much success, to curb over consumption of medicines and pills, which some people used as substitutes for food in the later stages of the war.[58]

Reference has already been made to the relative neglect of the old, but the country population found itself in a similar position when it came to the distribution of scarce resources. Rural health standards were further depressed by the need for women and young people to perform heavy manual labour that had formerly been done by men. Adolescent health was impaired so much that in certain country areas 40 per cent of the lads called up for the Wehrmacht were found to be medically unfit.[59] War also took its toll of the health of girls in the countryside. The strain of separation from home and unaccustomed work caused disturbances in the menstrual cycle of over half the members of the female labour service;[60] this phenomenon was bound to cause apprehension among the strategists of the 'battle of births'.

By and large the population planners had little cause for concern at first, though the war engendered a crop of still births and 'criminal abortions'.[61] The birth-rate remained rather high, dropping slowly from the inter-war peak of 20·4 per 1,000 in 1939 to between 15 and 16 at the height of the war. The Anglo-Saxon countries, paradoxically, showed a contrary trend. From under 15 per thousand in the mid-thirties the British birth-rate climbed to 17·6 in 1944, thus overtaking Germany for the first time since 1933, the year of the seizure of power, while America registered a continuous rise from 18·7 in 1935 to 21·2 in 1944.

A year later the war ended and it became possible for Allied experts to evaluate the quality of the Third Reich's medical services. There could be no gainsaying the effectiveness of the Nazi authorities in preventing major health breakdowns – let alone epidemics – among 100 million resident Germans, evacuees, resettled 'ethnic Germans', foreign workers, slave workers, and prisoners of war, concentrated into the area of the Reich and subsisting – towards the end, at any rate – on limited resources, that were subject to disruption by Allied air attacks. Against this must be set the relative backwardness of Nazi medicine. This backwardness, compounded by the army medical corps' predilection for amputations, resulted in the Reich having the largest percentage of limbless people in Europe. The Germans had no penicillin and practised direct blood transfusion which might have fatal consequences for the donor. There were few radiological facilities in their hospitals, and many operating theatres even lacked emergency lighting.[62] This was not the only form of illumination lacking in the medical sphere. The number of medical men (including university professors and lecturers) involved in concentration camp 'experiments' was 350 – that is one out of every 300 members of the German medical profession. At Weimar, in early May 1945, when a Red Cross sister was asked to tend a liberated Buchenwald survivor, she replied indignantly, 'Why should I have to nurse tubercular criminals?'[63]

16

THE FAMILY

In calling the family the 'germ-cell of the nation' the Nazis, for once, did not simply indulge their penchant for pompous verbiage: the phrase actually meant what it said. The regime set out to make the automatic activity of cells – self-multiplication – the conscious motive force behind family life and looked to success in the battle of births as a prerequisite for victory on all other fronts.

Looking back, it attributed Germany's centuries of weakness before unification largely to the decimation wrought by the Thirty Years' War; looking forward, Hitler, in a secret address to his top brass in 1937,[1] extrapolated a steadily increasing population lead of the Slav countries over the Reich – and resolved to meet this threat by 'pre-emptive' war at the earliest practicable moment.

The gradual levelling out of Germany's demographic growth curve had in fact been comparatively recent. At the turn of the century the annual average of births per thousand of the population had been a spanking thirty-three, but this figure was more than halved during the next three decades.

There were various reasons for this decline. Even before the Great War – itself a major check to population growth – the notion of limiting one's family had percolated downwards to the middle strata of society, unionization was spreading awareness of birth-control techniques among the workers, and even country folk were becoming acquainted with it. The war familiarized all classes with the use of contraceptives. After the war there was no potential husband for one out of every four women aged twenty-five to thirty, and inflation further aggravated this shortage. It became accepted, moreover, that smaller families enjoyed higher living standards and could give their children a better start in life. But contraception did not operate uniformly throughout the country: it was actively opposed in Catholic areas and had to contend with ingrained traditions in country districts.

The average birth-rate in the twenties had been 20·3 per 1,000. This relative decrease – which was to be intensified by the Depression – provoked dire forebodings among nationalists, who simultaneously (and paradoxically) adopted the title of Hans Grimm's novel *People Without Space* (*Volk ohne Raum*) as a summary of the country's post-war ills.

It was this tradition that led the Nazis, while clamouring for *Lebensraum*, to give absolute priority to a growing birth-rate. Their concern for the family was motivated by power politics, but dovetailed with wider popular aspirations. 'Restoring the family to its rightful place' seemed to be a non-political battle-cry round which the yearnings of those in retreat from the complexities of the present could crystallize.

In reality of course, this slogan, was anything but non-political: the pre-1914 family pattern had been male-centred and authoritarian. Those who profited from it saw the post-war liberalization of family relationships and sexual mores as an attack on the foundations of the social order; those who disliked the Republic attributed the increase of juvenile prostitution bred by the Depression to the same cause.

But they saw the concurrent decline in the birth-rate as far more crucial. The slump had affected it for two reasons: married couples practised far stricter family limitation, and job-discrimination in favour of family men, kept bachelors out of work – and wedlock. As a result the birth-rate dropped by well over a quarter – from 20·3 in the twenties to 14·7 in 1933.* (Marriage was less drastically affected, declining by an eighth from 9·1 per 1,000 to 7·9 in 1932.)

The new regime proved its claim to be better protectors of family life by imposing harsh curbs on equality for women, abortion, homosexuality and (conspicuous) prostitution. Beggars – who had proliferated during the slump – were cleared from the streets so that anxious matrons need no longer go in fear of assault. Above all, by a combination of revived economic activity and special eugenic measures it produced a spectacular upswing in the demographic curve; fertility increased and the incidence of marriage grew in the proportion of 2:1.[2]

The baby boom that followed constituted a biological vote of confidence in the regime. Already during its second year the birth-rate climbed by over a fifth to 18 per 1,000; with 20·4 (or 1,413,000 live births) by 1939 it both relatively and absolutely exceeded the twenties

---

* According to the *Statistische Handbuch für Deutschland 1928–44*, Franz Ehrenwirt, Munich, 1949, p. 47, the annual marriage average for the decade 1920–9 had been 575,183, compared with 516,793 in 1932; the annual average of live births was 1,285,902, as against 993,126 in 1932.

average. Inevitably there was a falling-off after 1940, but the figure for 1943 (1,124,000) still compared favourably with the all-time low of 1933 (971,000).

The regime's eugenic measures – apart from the negative one of sterilization (to be dealt with subsequently) – were chiefly of a monetary or propagandist nature. Financial inducements to fecundity were basically threefold: marriage loans, child subsidies and family allowances.

Under the terms of the marriage-loans programme newly-weds initially received loans of up to 1,000 marks and the birth of each of the first four children converted one-quarter of that loan into an outright gift.[3] The loan – minus deductions resulting from births – was repayable at 3 per cent per month if both parents went to work, and at 1 per cent if only the father did so.

Child subsidies were grants of lump sums to parents of large families with limited incomes, to be spent on furniture, implements and clothes. These subsidies were limited to a maximum of 100 marks per child and 1,000 marks per family. To be eligible, the families had to have at least four children under sixteen, but this stipulation did not apply to widows, divorcees and unmarried mothers.[4]

The actual child allowances amounted to 10 marks per month for the third as well as the fourth child, and 20 marks a month for the fifth child.

The figures show a remarkable correlation between the Nazi exchequer's bounty and the upswing in Germany's birth-rate. By the end of 1938 a grand total of 1,121,000 marriage loans had been advanced since 1933, compared with 980,000 cancellations due to births; this represented an almost 90 per cent human yield on the fiscal investment made. In addition, the availability of this public money provided a strong inducement for legitimizing marriage after conception had already taken place.

Propaganda inculcated a philoprogenitive mood by the manipulation of language, rituals and social pressures, as well as by a blueprint for domestic revolution. Exhibitions were staged showing that the world's greatest men had a dozen siblings (or children, e.g. Johann Sebastian Bach)[5] and the term 'family' was given aristocratic rarity-value by being officially reserved for parents with four children and over. The highly emotive phrase *Kindersegen* (blessed with children) was used constantly, while the desire for a life unencumbered by children – or even for strict family limitation – was called – a 'by-product of the asphalt civilization', as reprehensible as desertion in battle.

A veritable motherhood cult was set in motion. Annually on 12 August (the birthday of Hitler's mother), fertile mothers were awarded the Honour Cross of the German Mother (in three classes: bronze for more than four children, silver for more than six, gold for more than eight).[6] The medals, which had the motto 'The mother ennobles the child' engraved on the obverse, were presented at ceremonies conducted by the local Party ward leaders. The prolific German mother was 'to occupy the same honoured place in the folk community as the front-line soldier, since the risks to health and life she incurs for *Volk* and Fatherland are the same as equal those of the soldier in the thunder of battle'.[7] The *Völkische Beobachter* announced: 'In August 1939 three million German mothers will be honoured; in future all members of the Party's youth organizations will be duty-bound to salute wearers of the Mother's Honour Cross, and thus the young generation will be paying homage to them.'[8]

The homage reflex spread beyond the Party ranks. On trams, buses and tubes men would jump up and offer their seats to pregnant women or mothers with small children. Mothers-to-be also received preferential rations and safer air-raid shelter accommodation in the war, when Nazi mother-worship reached its climax in the slogan, 'I have donated a child to the Führer.'

But what of the wives who had given the Führer no children? They were a sizeable group: one married woman in five; one in three in Berlin.* By the mid-thirties a eugenic lobby of Party spokesmen and lawyers was stressing the genetic wastefulness of allowing such marriages to continue, since currently barren partners might successfully cross-fertilize in other combinations.† This concern with procreation had all sorts of ludicrous repercussions. Public (and private) employees were liable to be reminded that their duty to the state – or the firm – did not end when they left the office. At one point even the *Schwarzes Korps* registered dismay at the manner in which certain supporting actions for the birth-battle were being fought:

It is inadmissible for a superior to admonish his subordinate publicly to be blessed with children (*zum Kindersegen*) and when the latter objects that the marriage is not barren through any fault of his, to state: 'In that case, you must get a divorce or adopt somebody else's child.'[9]

* At the end of 1938, 22·6 per cent of Germany's sixteen million married women were childless (cf. *Frankfurter Zeitung*, 24 May 1939). In Berlin, 34·6 per cent of 1,126,000 married women had no children. (cf. Kurt Pritzkoleit, *Berlin*, Karl Rauch, Düsseldorf 1962, p. 15.)

† Dr Kleeman stated in the *Schwarzes Korps* on 24 December 1936: 'There is nothing absolutely sacrosanct about a childless marriage. This is obviously so where the childlessness is intended, but even involuntary childlessness harms the nation. It is possible that both partners might prove fertile in other marriages.'

But such unusual delicacy was short lived. When the Dresdner Bank – Germany's largest – published its annual balance sheet (which, characteristically, included data about the incidence of marriage and fertility among its staff) the S S organ expostulated 'The figures are alarming! One half of the bank's married employees are childless.'[10]

In its preoccupation with the birth-battle the *Schwarzes Korps* produced a blue-print for a revolution in the German home. Since the increased work-burden that large families imposed on women militated against an all-out population growth, the paper, in addition to advocating nappy services, launched a campaign for intra-marital equality, backed up by photographs of exemplary (and therefore quite un-German) husbands pushing prams and carrying shopping bags.

Though the wielding of shopping bags or dish-cloths by German males remained largely in the realms of fantasy, concrete domestic assistance was made available to mothers by means of the duty-year for girls, by such Party institutions as 'Mother and Child', and the *NS-Frauenschaft* (see p. 258), as well as through the wartime conscription of 'maids' from occupied Europe.[11] A special association – the National League of the German Family (*Reichsbund Deutscher Familie*) – was set up to deal with general family problems; it was a clear reflection of the fragmentation of German social life during the Third Reich that the association established a network of marriage bureaux for eugenically eligible candidates (who, by the way, had to pledge themselves to the principle of massive procreation).

In the matter of arranging marriages many Germans still had recourse to newspaper advertisements. The emphasis on money in this type of advertising had often aroused foreign comment. With the advent of the Third Reich the content of marriage advertisements began to reflect a subtle change of values; though money remained a consideration, eugenic qualifications now loomed even larger: thus a widowed schoolmaster, in the *Neueste Nachrichten*,[12] who stated no cash requirements, unblushingly described himself as an idealist; and one characteristic advertisement read: 'fifty-two-year-old pure Aryan doctor, veteran of the battle of Tannenberg, who intends to settle on the land, desires male progeny through a registry-office marriage with a healthy Aryan, virginal, young, unassuming, economy-minded woman, adapted to hard work, broad-hipped, flat-heeled and earring-less – if possible also property-less',[13] while another stated, 'Widower aged sixty once again wishes to have a Nordic mate who is prepared to present him with children, so that the old family shall not die out in the male line.'[14] (These two advertisements, incidentally, though steeped in the official breeding dogma, shocked that self-appointed moral tutor to the Nazi public, the *Schwarzes Korps*, which commented testily on the fifty-two-year-old doctor, 'He's left it rather late before remembering his eugenic obligations'.[15] Of the sixty-year-old widower it wrote, 'If he has not yet been presented with a male heir, he will have to forgo one at his age, unless he wants to be guilty of irresponsibility towards a young woman who ought to be more than simply a guinea-pig on whom an old man carries out experiments. Since this advertisement has already been inserted a few times, he must be someone who derives furtive gratification from the sort of replies he obtains.'[16]

As these censorious outbursts showed, the implementation of the population policy was beset by problems of its own, particularly those of large families. Eugenic experts stressed the fact that parents practising no family limitation at all were often of racially inferior stock (cf. the 'improvident poor' of Victorian terminology) and that official encouragement of their offspring would contradict the sacrosanct Nazi principle of racial selection. Therefore the authorities awarding marriage loans contacted local health offices, school medical services, welfare agencies for the mentally ill, and so on, before making their grants, in order to ascertain whether applicants were racially valuable; among those whose applications were turned down, half were adjudged either physically or mentally 'below par', and one-third consisted of unskilled workers.[17]

The Race Policy Office of the Nazi Party also initiated a national eugenic register, in which 'decent' large families were listed separately from the anti-social ones living at public expense.[18]

Next to the anti-Semitic Race Defilement legislation, the regime's chief device for improving racial stock was the law for the prevention of hereditarily diseased offspring.[19] Under its terms, Germans suffering from physical malformation, mental retardation, epilepsy, imbecility, deafness or blindness were compulsorily sterilized. Sterilized persons were not allowed to marry and if they were discovered to have done so, their marriages were judicially annulled.[20] The offspring of 'hereditarily diseased persons' who had slipped through the sterilization net could also be legally aborted* (as could embryos reputed to be half-Jewish)[21] although abortion *per se* was one of the most heinous crimes in the Nazi statute book.

Immediately after the seizure of power, the advertisement and display of contraceptives was banned (their manufacture and sale, on the other

* This required the approval of a commission of three doctors as well as the mother's consent (cf. Wallace R. Deuel, *People under Hitler*, Harcourt Brace, New York, 1942, p. 248).

hand, were not limited) and all birth-control clinics were closed down. Abortions were termed 'acts of sabotage against Germany's racial future', involving commensurately heavy punishment. Whereas in Republican Berlin fines on abortionists sometimes did not exceed 40 marks, Nazi courts imposed jail terms of six to fifteen years on doctors found guilty of abortionist practices.* Before 1933 the annual average of abortions was estimated at between 600,000 and 800,000, as against between a million and 1¼ million births per year: a ratio of almost two to three. For the Third Reich, even approximate figures are hard to come by. In 1938 every eighth in 1½ million pregnancies was officially listed as a miscarriage;[22] the preceding four years had seen an increase of 50 per cent in prosecutions against abortionists (1934; 4,539 and 1938; 6,983).[23] Positing a 1:100 ratio of detected and indicted abortions as against ones which had actually been committed,† we infer that the decline after 1933 was not so much absolute as relative to an increased total of pregnancies.

Another highly publicized method of boosting the birth-rate was the official campaign to reduce infant mortality. This achieved a reduction of several tenths of 1 per cent during each peacetime year of the regime. (Thus in 1936, 6·6 per cent of all babies born died during their first year; in 1938, only 6·0 per cent.)[24] The war, however, reversed this trend so that by 1943 the incidence of infant mortality in Germany was 7·2 per cent as against a British one of 4·8 per cent and an American one of 4·0 per cent. (In peacetime, too, the Anglo-Saxon record had been rather better than that of the Germans.)

One of the reasons for this comparatively unimpressive performance was the reluctance of German employers and female workers to heed the provisions of the 1927 'law for the protection of mothers' which prohibited their working for six weeks before and after confinement. Pregnant employees frequently preferred to work right up to the onset of labour pains rather than incur a pay reduction of 25 per cent. For the same reason they nursed their babies for only a few days and then handed them over to somebody else's care. To combat this practice the 'Mother and Child' organization set up post-natal convalescent homes and village crêches.[25]

---

* At Nordhausen a doctor received six years in a penitentiary for four completed abortions and a number of attempted ones (cf. *Frankfurter Zeitung*, 2 September 1937). At Göttingen, a colleague of his was jailed for fifteen years for fifteen completed abortions (*Frankfurter Zeitung*, 16 June 1939).

† This is the concept of the so-called *Dunkelziffer* (literally 'dark figure') with which German sociologists – e.g. Wolf Middendorff in *Soziologie des Verbrechens*, Dusseldorf, 1959 – operate.

Another aspect of the country's overall demographic situation was the increase of the average expectancy of life by over twenty years, between the Franco-Prussian War and the outbreak of the Second World War. This meant that whereas before 1914 one-third of the population had been under sixteen, during the nineteen-thirties only one-quarter were.[26]

Changes in the relative number of young and old were, however, more than a matter of shifting proportions. Right up to 1933 the Nazis had successfully – and not unjustifiably – presented themselves as the Party of Youth versus Age; upon seizing power they had authoritatively declared the struggle of the generations to be at an end: no divisive issue was to be allowed to mar the internal harmony of the family and the Reich. Actually the regime successfully rejuvenated the heads of both institutions: the average age of members of the Reich Cabinet was about ten years below that of their Republican predecessors (or their Western counterparts), while the average age at which young couples married was reduced by two to three years as a result of the economic revival and the measures to promote population growth.[27]

Undercurrents of conflict between the generations nevertheless continued to affect family life, though in more covert form. Being more susceptible – and, in school and the Hitler Youth, more exposed – to indoctrination, the young tended towards greater conformity (not to say fanaticism) than their elders.

With parents fearful of being denounced by their children or having family talk innocently regurgitated in public, dialogue between the generations dwindled further.

Mother and son relationships were particularly affected. Ten-year-old lads who were awarded daggers not surprisingly entertained vastly inflated notions of their self-importance, and many a mother's patience was sorely tried by a pre-adolescent 'Master in the House' for whom the thought of having to defer to the authority of mere women seemed unnatural.

Another group of women found themselves reduced to a state jocularly described as political widowhood: although their husbands were alive, Party involvement prevented them from using the home for more than bed and board. In certain cases the clash of loyalties between political commitment and domesticity was so great that it constituted a new category of divorce. A Berlin paper wrote in 1937: 'It is a husband's duty to participate in National Socialist activities and a wife who makes trouble on this score gives grounds for divorce. She must not complain if her husband devotes two evenings per week to political activity, nor do Sunday mornings always exclusively belong to the family.'

Though this sounded reasonable, it was belied by a subsequent court decision: 'The accused cannot excuse her refusal to participate in political activity on the grounds that she has been unable to lead the sort of family life she had anticipated when marrying, because the plaintiff had been kept away from home almost every night by Party work. At times of political high tension, German women must make the same sacrifices as the wives of soldiers in the present world war.'[28]

Although 'political widows' completely outnumbered 'widowers', there were occasional instances of the latter phenomenon. A Halberstadt court granted a woman a divorce because her husband had said that membership of the National Socialist Association of Women (*NS-Frauenschaft*) was like belonging to a ladies' coffee circle.[29]

But the explicitly political encroachment on family life (as depicted in the joke about the SA* father, *NS-Frauenschaft* mother, Hitler Youth son and BDM† daughter who met each year at the Nuremberg Party Rally) was only one aspect of a wider process of erosion. The regime engendered a whole range of additional pressures inimical to family cohesion: the removal of young people for long periods (for military and labour service, Hitler Youth camps or the girls' duty year), the widespread industrial employment of women,‡ the increasing incidence of overtime and shift work, the creation of work places from which employees could only come home at week-ends (or even less frequently), and so on.

Juvenile delinquency figures soon showed the effect of these developments on family life: within the overall context of a decreasing crime rate (the total number of court convictions dropped from almost half a million in 1933 to just under 300,000 in 1939) juvenile criminality showed an increase from just under 16,000 in 1933 to over 21,000 in 1940.

The war, of course, accentuated this trend, and further undermined family relations. The casualty figures made the regime accord even greater precedence to their 'population policy' at the expense of conventional morality. The Nazi poet laureate, Hanns Johst, writing of his impressions in a transit camp for 'ethnic Germans', mentioned a *ménage à trois*

* *Sturmabteilung.*
† Bund Deutchen Mädchen (German Girls' League).
‡ The female labour force increased by nearly 50 per cent between 1937 and 1939: by 1942, it was almost twice as large as it had been before the seizure of power.

consisting of a farmer, his barren wife and his pregnant maid with every sign of approval. The *Schwarzes Korps* publicized a similar situation under the heading, 'A private matter – craftsman in childless marriage has child by wife's sister'.[30]

The vindication of the eugenic principle at the expense of social taboo was typified by litigation initiated by the forty-two-year-old wife of a grammar-school teacher to prove that she was not the legitimate offspring of her deceased mother's marriage to a Jew.[31] Fortunately for the plaintiff two aged witnesses were on hand to testify that her mother had been of very vivacious disposition and had spent much time in the company of army officers.

Compared to this form of posthumous exoneration, other instances of officially promoted bad taste seemed almost to be innocuous *jeux d'esprit*, one example being the autobiographical details inserted by the playwright Hans Erich Forel in the programme of the Dessauer Theatre when his play *Frauendiplomatie (Female Diplomacy)* was performed there.[32] 'As the last male scion of my line, I would dearly love to have a son and heir, but all my attempts to date have been fruitless. I have attempted it with two wives, but the result was four daughters. If my wish for a son and heir is not fulfilled, I shall have to give up the race.'

If the degradation of family life in the Third Reich thus had its aspect of sick humour – wittily illustrated by such neologisms as *Rekrutenmachen* (producing recruits) for sexual intercourse, *Gebärmaschinen* (childbearing machines) for procreative women and *bevölkerungspolitische Blindgänger* (eugenic duds) for barren women – it could also lead to unmitigated tragedy. Apart from the cast-off wives, whom we shall return to later on in this chapter, there were quite a few cast-off parents, i.e. fathers and mothers whose political or religious convictions led the authorities to take their children away from them. The official procedure was quite simple: if the local Youth Office discovered a child being reared in a nonconformist family atmosphere, it applied to the guardianship court for an order of removal to a 'politically reliable' home.[33] Among parental offences punishable by judicial kidnapping were friendship with Jews,[34] refusal to enrol children in the Hitler Youth,[35] and membership of the Jehovah's Witnesses.[36]

Nazi courts were kept very busy with actions involving family legislation. Maternity proceedings were a case in point. Premarital sexual intercourse was very widespread in the Third Reich (the estimated frequency varying from 51 per cent in Saxony to over 90 per cent in Munich).[37] In its racially motivated concern to establish the pedigree of every newborn child, the government empowered the authorities in 1938 to require both the mother and all putative fathers to submit to blood tests, after which the child could be removed from its home. Whereas previously a father was only able to start paternity proceedings within twelve months of the child's birth, such a probe could now be undertaken throughout the child's life and even after its death. If a husband tried to cover up his wife's adultery, the state intervened to establish the correct paternity. Since a growing proportion of the Third Reich's biological fathers were below the permitted age for marriage, the authorities instituted a special procedure by which minors were legally declared to have obtained their majority, so that their marriage could be solemnized. A special application form for the award of majority status to men under twenty-one bore this wording:

I ask to be declared of full age. I have been engaged since ... to ..., who has borne a child on the ..., whose father I am. I want to marry my bride, who is an orderly, industrious and thrifty girl, as soon as possible, so that I can care for her and my child better than I am able to do at the moment. My weekly income is ..., which means that I can take care of a family. We have/are going to get a flat. I know what marriage means.[38]

When members of the legal profession had to adjudicate on matters of sexual morality, they frequently discovered that the foundations of their own code rested on quicksand. Thus in one and the same year two separate judicial bodies treated cases of adultery in diametrically opposite ways. The Thüringian Disciplinary Chamber (*Dienststrafkammer*) dismissed from his post a forty-five-year-old primary-school teacher who had committed adultery, whereas the Hereditary Estate Court (*Landerhofgericht*) at Celle refused to declare a farmer accused of the same offence as ineligible for a hereditary estate and quoted village opinion in support of its decision.[39]*

In the case of the Reich Labour Court, it was one and the same tribunal that handed down mutually contradictory decisions. The court upheld the

---

* It was the latter judgement that came increasingly to typify the attitude of the courts, often arrived at in deference to an opinion expressed by the *Schwarzes Korps*. One court actually quoted a *Schwarzes Korps* diatribe in justifying the reversal of a previous decision in which it had defined tolerance by the future parents-in-law of sexual intercourse between an engaged couple as 'procuring' (cf. *Juristische Wochenschrift*, 1937, p. 2, 387). A Berlin court ruled that living in sin constituted valid grounds for terminating a tenancy only if the couple concerned aroused their neighbours' indignation by unseemly conduct (cf. *Frankfurter Zeitung*, 23 August 1939).

dismissal of an unmarried shop assistant since 'the visibility of her condition might offend customers' susceptibilities',[40] but arrived at an opposite conclusion concerning an industrial employee dismissed on analogous grounds. 'Such pregnancy need no longer be regarded as *ipso facto* immoral and reproachable.'[41]

Nothing exemplified the internal inconsistency of the Nazi moral code as clearly as the position of women under the terms of the race-defilement legislation of 1935 and the 1938 divorce reform respectively. The race-defilement law reflected Hitler's characteristically banal and outdated view of sex as a subject/object relationship with the male cast in a relentlessly active role *vis-à-vis* the helpless playthings of his desires. This resulted in obvious discrimination against male offenders. Race-defilement cases provided the absurd spectacle of Nazi courts favouring Jewish accused at the expense of Gentile ones, but only where Aryans had been male partners in an act of 'mixed' coitus. (Incidentally, even the *Schwarzes Korps* was moved to criticize the bias built into race-defilement legislation [cf. *Schwarzes Korps*, 8 December 1938].)

In the sphere of divorce legislation the law tended to be biased in the opposite direction. As far as comparative incidence was concerned, the divorce rate climbed more steeply during the peacetime years of the Third Reich than either the marriage-rate or the birth-rate. While the total of marriages in 1939 exceeded that of 1932 by a fifth and births had increased 45 per cent, there were half as many more divorces;[42] from just over 42,000 divorces in 1932, the number mounted to over 50,000 in 1935 and 1936, dropped slightly in 1937 and 1938, and in 1939 shot up to well over 61,000. It was axiomatic from the very start that certain categories of marriage were ripe for dissolution, i.e. mixed marriages between Aryans and non-Aryans and marriages in which one of the partners was politically obstreperous. With the passage of time, the notion that infertility in marriage was not all that dissimilar from political opposition to the regime gained ground. The official concern with fertility also found expression in a campaign to transform separation into actual divorce, so that separated marriage partners might be enabled to start new families.

These various considerations eventually prompted the promulgation of the 1938 divorce-reform law by the Minister of Justice, Dr Gürtner.* Divorce reform, incidentally, was also connected with the incorporation

* It was the operation of this law that accounted for the sharp increase in divorce figures between 1938 and 1939.

of Austria, where the Catholic laws that had previously been in operation had condemned thousands of separated individuals to live in sin with their new partners.*

The following constituted grounds for divorce under the terms of Gürtner's law: adultery, refusal to procreate, dishonourable and immoral conduct, a diseased mentality, serious contagious infection, three years' separation of marriage partners, and infertility (unless a child had previously been conceived or adopted – even so, the infertility clause was only to be applied in accordance with what Nazi legislators defined as the healthy instinct of the people).

The *Frankfurter Zeitung* welcomed the reform for facilitating the *de jure* dissolution of *de facto* broken marriages and forging new marriage bonds.[43] But within three months it announced the supreme court's first decision interpreting paragraph 55 of the new law: 'After a three-year separation divorce shall also be granted if the husband has left the wife for the sake of another woman and the wife's conduct has been entirely blameless.'[44] Within two years, Gürtner's reform in fact produced 30,000 instances of marriage partners being cast off; 80 per cent of such proceedings were initiated by husbands whose wives were completely innocent of the loosening of the marriage bonds. Three out of every five of the cast-off wives were women over forty-five years of age and had been married for twenty years and more.[45]†

While the divorce rate climbed steadily during the peacetime years of the Third Reich, the incidence of illegitimate births declined. In the nineteen-twenties the annual average of children born out of wedlock had been about 150,000; this decreased by almost half during the Depression, to level out at just above 100,000 per annum in the mid-thirties. As a fairly constant segment of the Third Reich's expanding overall birth-rate, illegitimate births in fact showed a relative decrease from 10·5 per cent in 1932 to 8 per cent in 1939. The absolute illegitimacy figures, however, started to climb from about 1937 onwards,‡ and during the war there was an

* But the 1939 divorce statistics we have quoted exclude the Austrian figures; in Austria the introduction of the new law led to such a flood of divorce applications that new forms had to be printed to ease the strain on the officials concerned (cf. *Frankfurter Zeitung*, 14 August 1938).

† Under the 1938 law, ex-wives who had been innocent parties in divorce proceedings had to forgo any claim to alimony or maintenance, unless they were old, infirm or had children who were minors.

‡ From 101,094 in 1937 to 112,339 in 1939 (cf. *Statistisches Handbuch von Deutschland 1928–44*, already referred to, p. 47).

obvious further increase (which cannot, however, be thoroughly documented* because of the dearth of statistical information).

Long before this, the regime had launched a drive – partly administrative,† partly propagandist – designed to confer parity of status as well as of public esteem on unmarried mothers and their offspring. This campaign found its institutionalized expression in *Lebensborn* (Spring of Life), Himmler's very own foundation for unwed mothers of progeny sired by S S men and other racially valuable Germans. In the founder's words, '*Lebensborn* started from the premise that there was a great need to give racially satisfactory women bearing illegitimate children the opportunity for doing so free of charge and for spending the last weeks of pregnancy in harmonious surroundings.'[46] In addition to ante-natal and post-natal residence in its homes, *Lebensborn* arranged nominal legitimizations, defined the financial obligations of fathers, and acted as an adoption service to interested Party members. (Not all *Lebensborn* children were eligible for adoption, however, since a fair number of their parents eventually married.)

The population at large got to know of the existence and purpose of the homes, which sported a white flag with a red dot in the middle and were better appointed and more lavishly supplied (especially in wartime) than maternity homes for married mothers.[47]‡

What people were not sure about and what naturally roused their prurient curiosity was the stud-bull question. Rumour had it that *Lebensborn* employed permanent 'procreation helpers' (*Zeugungshelfer*) around whom all sorts of myths clustered. Himmler himself stated, 'I fostered rumours to the effect that every single woman desiring a child could turn to *Lebensborn* in the strictest confidence ... We only recommended genuinely valuable, racially pure men as *Zeugungshelfer*.'[48]

For *Lebensborn* mothers, the procedure was something like this:

At the Tegernsee hostel, I waited until the tenth day after the beginning of my period and was medically examined; then I slept with an S S man who had also

* In Cologne, for instance, out of every thousand live births there had been eighty-six illegitimate ones in 1937 and 103 in 1940 (the figure for 1933 had been ninety-six).

† The Minister of the Interior issued the ruling that mothers of illegitimate children were to be referred to as '*Frau*'. If birth had occurred outside the usual residential district of the mother, the local registration authority no longer had to be informed (cf. *Frankfurter Zeitung*, 28 October 1938).

‡ Within the health service as such, the encouragement of illegitimacy was connected with the staffing of hospitals by the Brown Sisterhood of Nazi nurses, holding diametrically opposed views to their colleagues drawn from the religious orders.

to perform his duty with another girl. When pregnancy was diagnosed, I had the choice of returning home or going straight into a maternity home . . . The birth was not easy, but no good German woman would think of having artificial injections to deaden the pain.[49]

Good German maidens resolved to make the Führer the gift of a child did not hide their light under a bushel: in the autumn of 1937, people travelling on a local Bavarian train were taken aback when a girl passenger suddenly announced with blazing eyes, 'I am going to the SS Ordensburg Sonthofen to have myself impregnated.'[50] As was the case with large families, the illegitimacy issue raised problems of racial evaluation, and 'conservative' elements within the Party employed eugenic arguments to curtail the enthusiasm of the advocates of unrestricted procreation. In 1934 the official Party newspaper had ruled authoritatively: 'Non-marital liaisons are, as a rule, liaisons of frivolity or of the selfish exploitation of one partner by the other. Because of this, the illegitimate child is generally racially below par.'[51] Even after the outbreak of war, restraining voices made themselves heard. The Race Policy Office of the Nazi Party published a letter from a mother to her soldier son in its journal *Neues Volk*: 'There is a limit which a girl must not transgress, unless she wants to lose her self-respect. Once this transgression has been committed, it is very difficult for a girl to remain decent.'[52] But it was also at this time that Himmler issued his notorious procreation order to the entire SS.

Only he who leaves a child behind can die with equanimity . . . Beyond the bounds of perhaps otherwise necessary bourgeois law and usage, and outside the sphere of marriage, it will be the sublime task of German women and girls of good blood acting not frivolously but from a profound moral seriousness to become mothers to children of soldiers setting off to battle, of whom destiny alone knows if they will return or die for Germany.[53]

When one such mother lost the father of her child in action at the front, Rudolf Hess, Hitler's deputy, addressed the following widely publicized open letter to her.

I declare my readiness to act as your child's godfather. As far as state support is concerned, you and your child will be treated in exactly the same way as if the marriage had already been concluded. When the names of children such as yours are to be entered on the register of births, the term 'war father' will be put in the space provided for the father's name. The mother will retain her maiden name, but will be addressed as '*Frau*'. If the mother so desires, the Party will appoint a guardian for the child.[54]

Although it is impossible to assess statistically how successful these campaigns for the promotion of illegitimacy were, one can deduce from a number of sources that they gathered pace throughout the war. At a late stage of the war, Himmler told his private physician, Kerstern,

Only a few years ago illegitimate children were considered a shameful matter. In defiance of the existing laws I have systematically influenced the SS to consider children, irrespective of illegality or otherwise, the most beautiful and best thing there is. The results – today my men tell me with shining eyes that an illegitimate son has been born to them. Their girls consider it an honour, not a source of shame, in spite of existing legal circumstances. You can read announcements to that effect at all times in the *Schwarzes Korps*.[55]

And indeed, advertisements in all newspapers had displayed unwonted frankness since about 1940. 'Teacher's daughter, twenty-seven years old, with child, seeks gentleman of up to thirty-three with a view to marriage. Dowry available.'[56] '*Fräulein* with child, twenty-nine years of age, is looking for sympathetic, ambitious life-comrade with the final object of marriage.'[57]

Obituary notices were couched in a similar language:

My bridegroom and dearest father, Sepp Schauerhuber, lance-corporal in a panzer unit, died for the Führer and Greater Germany on 16.8.41. He lives on for us in his son Gerhardt. In proud mourning, Anna Maria Koch, bride, with her little son Gerhardt and the Koch family.[58]

Extracting grist for its own mill of eugenic propaganda from situations of wartime bereavement and pathos, the *Schwarzes Korps* published this letter from the mother of an SS man killed in action:

I went to the last place at which he was stationed. Knowing he had a little friend there, I nursed the secret hope that the girl might be expecting a child by him. Unfortunately this hope was not fulfilled.[59]

During their own 'period of struggle', the Nazis had elicited a great deal of female support by promising every German woman a husband; now, at a point when the whole country's *Kampfzeit* took an almost daily toll of thousands of men, they came close to promising every girl a baby. A report to the Ministry of Justice in the summer of 1944, stated that

The parents of girls enrolled in the German Girls' League have filed a complaint with the wardship court at Habel-Brandenburg concerning leaders of the League who have intimated to their daughters that they should bear illegitimate children; these leaders have pointed out that in view of the prevailing shortage of men, not every girl could expect to get a husband in future, and that the girls should at least fulfil their task as German women and donate a child to the Führer.[60]

The president of the Berlin Cameral Court reporting to the Ministry of Justice in the same year deplored the fact that judges were taking too little account of marriage as a foundation of the racial and moral life:

In the consciousness of folk-comrades, divorce proceedings are being reduced to a mere formality, in which the guilty party admits his own transgressions without any compunction – quite often in exchange for such financial advantages as the renunciation of maintenance claims by the other party.[61]

It was at this time, too, that the leaders of the Protestant Church were expressing alarm at their own clergy's acceptance of public indifference to the sanctity of marriage.* A high official of the Ministry of Education had already observed two years earlier,

The general run of young boys and girls experience the pleasure of sex soon after puberty. It appears that most men count girls among the conventional pleasurable items of consumption such as beer and cigarettes . . . German girls in turn are nowadays credited with particularly little inhibition in sexual matters.[62]

It is estimated that by the end of the war 23 per cent of all young Germans were infected with venereal disease and that the peacetime incidence of prostitution had quadrupled.[63] While, in view of the Allied occupation, these figures cannot be ascribed to internal causes alone, they nevertheless provide an eloquent commentary on the erosion of family life in the widest sense during the Third Reich. (Had German arms triumphed, this process, incidentally, would have been carried even further. During the later stages of the war, Himmler and Bormann – the two most powerful Nazi potentates next to Hitler – were in all seriousness mooting a social engineering project of considerable originality: this was the post-war institution of double marriage among large deserving groups of German men, e.g. Party officials or soldiers decorated for bravery. Selective polygamy could still redress the drop in the birth-rate and correct the imbalance in the marriage market resulting from the war; beyond that, it was to serve as an official mark of distinction between the estate-owning élite and the urban commonalty of a reconstituted society, half industrial, half tribal.)[64]

Oddly enough, when it came to the actual reconstruction of German post-war society, the family's regenerative potential proved stronger than

* See the chapter on religion, page 435.

developments during the Third Reich would have led one to anticipate. Though the war had had the effect of further exacerbating disturbed family relationships, in general it tended to knit integrated families, as well as indifferently coexisting ones, closer together. Possibly this was not so surprising; after all, in the zero situation of 1945, the family must have seemed the only viable social institution left in the country, just as family names were the only badges of identity by which people no longer Nazi, and unsure whether they were even still German, recognized each other.

17

WOMEN

Just as eternal vigilance is the price of liberty, so the price of progress is eternal change. This price often seems prohibitive enough to cloud the realization that the consequences of non-payment are worse than paying it.

In Germany these stark alternatives have often prompted fraudulent compromise: acceptance of material and technical change went hand-in-hand with rejection of its social corollaries. A case in point was the persistence of the 'Gretchen image' of womanhood: while more and more women lived physically in the shadow of sewing (and other) machines, they were mentally still regarded as plying the spinning wheel.

In fact formulations of women's role in society tended to become over-simplified in direct proportion to the increased diversification of their lives – to reach absolute intellectual bedrock in the slogan *'Kinder, Kirche, Küche'* (kids, kirk and kitchen). The cry 'Woman's place is in the home' found an ever-wider echo the more the logic of circumstances – economic necessity, wartime industrial mobilization, post-war demographic imbalance (the surplus of 1·8 million marriageable women) and inflation – forced female labour into factories and offices. Between 1907 and 1925 the female labour force increased by over one-third (8·5 million to 11·5 million), whereas the net population growth amounted to a mere seventh (54·5 million to 62·4 million).[1] But change was more than a matter of numbers; the Weimar constitution gave women the vote, and a feminist élite, ranging from Rosa Luxemburg and Clara Zetkin on the far left, through the Social Democrat Lily Braun and the Democrats Gertrud Baumer and Maria Luders to some Nationalist Reichstag deputies on the right, had helped shape the political post-war scene. Interposed between these national figures and the army of working women was the professional vanguard of the second sex: nearly 100,000 women teachers, 13,000 women musicians and 3,000 women doctors. The last figure indicated a male/female ratio in medicine of fourteen to one, the same, incidentally, as among Reichstag deputies.[2]

Women formed a tenth of the membership of local elected bodies, and – with 18,678 out of 97,500 in 1932[3] – a fifth of the student population. Yet they constituted barely 1 per cent of university teachers,[4] though it must be remembered that German universities had ceased to be all-male preserves only in 1900,* twenty years later than their Anglo-Saxon counterparts.

Student corporations had remained all-male, as had a powerful body in the commercial sphere: the Shop Assistants' League (*Nationale Handlungsgehilfenverband*). The Depression naturally intensified the sex war in the labour market as employers held on to cheaper female labour while laying off expendable men.

The drastic economic deterioration made the three K's *Kinder, Kirche, Küche* sound equally attractive to dole-receivers and to middle-class conservatives. As mass unemployment reinforced the after-effects of war and inflation as an impediment to marriage, the average woman began to look upon the three K's in a much more favourable light.

It was in this situation that Hitler – with a unique blend of cynicism and psychological insight – assured a delegation who had come to discuss women's rights with him that in the Third Reich every woman would have a husband.[5]

Nor must it be thought that women's organizations themselves were necessarily opposed to the three K's. Some of the most powerful feminist lobbies† were closely linked to the National Party and the Lutheran Church, and wanted women's voices to be raised in defence of the *status quo ante*; their particular opposition to the modernizing tendencies of the Weimar era only differed in degree from that of the Nazis. Except for blunt outspokenness, National Socialism contributed nothing new to the discussion of woman's role in German society. Whereas on other issues the Nazis managed to refurbish outworn slogans with a pseudo-revolutionary or socialist patina, the 'women's question' only elicited a rehash of ultra-conservative ideas from them.

The kernel of Nazi thinking on the women's question was a dogma of inequality between the sexes as immutable as that between the races. While this did not exactly degrade women to the status of Jews in the sex war, it did signify their irremediable confinement within the domestic round. The visible badge of feminine unworthiness was debarment from the political kingdom: one of the earliest Nazi Party ordinances (of

* In 1908 at the University of Berlin.
† The *Königin Louisa Bund*, the *Evangelische Hilfswerk* and the *Deutsche Frauenschaft*.

January 1921) excluded women for ever from all leading positions in the Party.[6]

Anti-feminism served as a non-lethal variant of anti-Semitism. Just as the latter fused divergent resentments into a single hate syndrome, anti-feminism provided men with the opportunity for abreacting a whole complex of feelings: paterfamilias authoritarianism, anti-permissiveness, Philistine outrage at sophistication, white-collar workers' job insecurity, virility fears and just plain misogyny.

Hitler called the emancipation of women a symptom of depravity on a par with parliamentary democracy and Krenek's jazz opera *Johnny spiel auf*.[7] Walter Darré, the pig-husbandry theorist turned Nazi Minister for Agriculture, attributed the desire for feminine emancipation to frustrations set up by malfunctioning sex glands.[8] Goebbels actually turned to animal life for corroborating the role assigned to women in the Nazi scheme of things. 'Woman has the task of being beautiful and bringing children into the world, and this is by no means as coarse and old-fashioned as one might think. The female bird preens herself for her mate and hatches her eggs for him.'[9] Nor did the feathery metaphor necessarily imply disparagement; the birds' habitat is the sky – the same word as 'heaven' in German – and Schiller had apostrophized women as weaving heavenly roses into life on earth. Schiller's peer Goethe had called political song a nasty song and Goebbels cynically seized on this age-old German distaste for politics to turn the Nazi derogation of women into its fake opposite. 'Our displacement of women from public life occurs solely to restore their essential dignity to them.'[10] 'It is not because we did not respect women enough but because we respected them too much that we kept them out of the miasma of parliamentary democracy.'[11]

Goebbels's cabinet colleague, Frick (Minister of the Interior), talked of grading women according to their child output,* a point which Hitler put less succinctly: 'Equal rights for women means that they receive the esteem they deserve in the sphere nature has assigned to them.' To underline the genuineness of this equality, Hitler invested parturition with epic significance: 'Woman has her battlefield too; with each child that she brings into the world for the nation she is fighting her fight on behalf of the nation.'[12]†

* Wilhelm Frick, quoted in *Dokumente der Deutschen Politik*, vol. I, p. 17: '*Die Frau wird nach Gebärleistung eingestuft.*'

† cf. Edgar Jung, in *Die Herrschaft der Minderwertigen*, 1934, p. 100: 'The deployment of woman does not take place in the social sphere, but in the erotic one. The fulfilments of love, conception and birth are the heroic climacterics of feminine existence.'

Other propagandists, while similarly addicted to pompous verbiage, tended to see women as dreamily ruminating domestic creatures rather than as Amazons of the labour ward. 'Can woman,' asked Dr Kurt Rosten, 'conceive of anything more beautiful than to sit with her beloved husband in her cosy home and to listen inwardly to the loom of time weaving the weft and warp of motherhood through centuries and millennia?'[13]

There was no gainsaying the appeal of Rosten's matrimonial Gretchen idyll to the collective feminine subconscious, and indeed the economic revival and Nazi measures to promote marriage lent substance to this vision of domestic bliss in the eyes of millions who had despaired of ever attaining married status because of the slump.

Rosten's idyll glossed over a number of contradictions, however: the intra-masculine Nazi ethos was so inimical to domesticity that though a jackbooted 'combatant' might mellow into a slippered bourgeois on his hearthstone, he would hardly become a considerate husband; many women, moreover, found it hard to attune their inner ear to the loom of time for the din of power-looms or the clatter of typewriters.

Though there was much talk of forcing married women back into their home to provide jobs for men, this mainly affected the professions, and fluctuations in the female labour force were only marginal. The truth was that female labour was cheaper: skilled women earned 66 per cent of men's wages, unskilled ones 70 per cent, which explains why during the Depression nearly one man in three (29 per cent) was dismissed but only one woman in every ten (11 per cent).[14]* Furthermore women workers were indispensable. In 1933 women formed 37 per cent of the total employed labour force in Germany. Every second agricultural worker was female; in addition, 75 per cent of female labour on the land was not hired but consisted of members of the family.[15]†

Since the absorption of men into the resurgent economy proceeded at a much faster rate than that of women – between 1933 and 1937 800,000 newly married women received loans on condition of not seeking re-employment – the female proportion of the total labour force declined to 31 per cent in 1937, although the total numbers actually increased. By 1939, women again constituted exactly a third of the employed labour force, comprising nearly 7 million white-collar and blue-collar workers.

* Unskilled men earned more than skilled women.

† In farming, women worked $10\frac{3}{4}$ hours a day, every day of the year. Their annual total of 3,933 working hours exceeded the average of 3,554 hours worked by men quite considerably (cf. Joseph Müller, *Deutsches Frauentum zwischen Gestern und Morgen*, Wirtsburg, 1940, p. 14).

In industry as a whole they represented almost a quarter (23 per cent) of the personnel, but in certain branches, such as clothing and textiles, they constituted two-thirds and just over half of the total respectively. Even in the metalworking industries every eighth employee was a woman. In the distributive trades and in food production two out of every five workers were female, and the same applied to office work, where, incidentally, women were generally confined to subordinate positions. In catering their role was similar to that in agriculture. Nearly three-fifths of all workers were women, but four out of every five of those were not employees in the strict sense of the term.[16] It was also found that women provided useful semi-skilled and unskilled labour in the relatively new industries linked with the arms drive and the self-sufficiency programme, the manufacture of rubber, chemical and electrical goods. With this ever-growing demand for female labour, the government rescinded in 1937 its stipulation that women qualified for marriage loans only if they undertook not to enter the labour market.

Since there was now a strong tendency for female labour to seek better-paid jobs in the commercial sector and in the towns, the government instituted a compulsory 'duty year' for all unmarried girls or women under twenty-five entering the labour market as office workers or employees of the clothing, textile or tobacco industries; during this duty year they had to do either agricultural or domestic work (or alternatively two years as auxiliary nurses or social-welfare workers). This decree was passed early in 1938. By the end of that year it was extended to cover entry into all private or public undertakings. Within two years, as the result of this measure, the female section of the labour service totalled 200,000.[17] Before the outbreak of war women were also being taken on as tram conductresses and postal workers in various parts of the country, and later on some worked on the railways. This demand for female labour improved their bargaining position, although women in agriculture, catering, and so on, whose work was a function of their family membership, derived no benefit from their relative scarcity.

Women's wages showed a slightly faster rate of increase than men's: 18 per cent as against 16·5 per cent between 1935 and 1938.[18] The women's department of the German Labour Front was continually pressing for greater parity of wage-scales as well as for other improvements, but to no avail; any benefit above the norm accruing to labour was largely due to its scarcity. A case in point was Germany's $1\frac{1}{4}$ million domestics, whose working conditions were so far removed from the Third Reich's much-vaunted socialism of deeds that the German Labour Front had to address a direct appeal to employers to give their maidservants some time off for a holiday.[19] The *Schwarzes Korps* shamefacedly explained that trustees of labour lacked legal powers of intervention between domestics and their employers; eventually, however, when unfilled domestic vacancies outnumbered job-seekers by four to one,[20] the SS paper was to complain that maids were selfishly exploiting the sellers' market by taking up employment in childless households while mothers of large families teetered on the verge of breakdowns.[21] In the early part of the war, domestics did even better; May 1941, however, saw an official redirection of labour[22]* from such sectors as domestic service, catering and retail distribution into more essential industries; but even so it was not a thorough comb-out. Thus it was still permissible for *Hausschneiderinnen* (tailoresses catering for private customers) to ply their trade. Finally, on 27 January 1943, under the impact of Stalingrad, there was an attempt at total mobilization of female labour. Gauleiter Sauckel, the Reich's plenipotentiary for labour conscription, called up 3 million women aged seventeen to forty-five.[23] Only mothers with one child under six, or two children under fourteen, and women in poor health were to be exempt. Yet, of the 3 million potential additional workers, only just over 900,000 were actually inducted into the economy.† One million had been found unfit, over half a million were doubtful cases, and of the rest just under half could be employed only part-time. (The method of calculation used was that two part-timers equalled one full-time worker.)[24]

Attempts to evade labour conscription‡ were widespread: feigned illness, taking up honorary Party work or fake employment in a friend's firm, volunteering to foster children, or actually having them.[25] The resultant boost to the birth-rate, incidentally,§ was accompanied by a harvest of miscarriages, which was hardly surprising in the year of Stalingrad and the Hamburg 'fire storm'.[26]

Feminine labour conscription also raised class issues; since the women already in the factories had gone there out of economic necessity, the

* The government's first stage in the mobilization of female labour was complemented by a not very effective drive to recruit non-working women into the factories. At Dresden, for instance, 1,250 women were invited to a recruiting meeting; 600 turned up and 120 volunteered for work.

† The *Schlesische Tagezeitung* talked of 'fear of the factory' as a new disease. 'Most women desire outdoor work or sedentary employment.' *Schlesische Tagezeitung*, 23 September 1944.

‡ Among those who were inducted, nine out of every ten asked for office jobs, but discovered that these had been cornered by the wives of Nazi functionaries.

§ See reference to war-time births in the chapter on the family, p. 235.

Sauckel decrees bore disproportionately on the middle classes. There were persistent complaints that women belonging to the so-called better circles were shirking their duties[27] or that plant managers were conferring privileges on the new women workers they had denied to their older and socially inferior colleagues.[28]

By 1944, when there were 14½ million of them, women workers were liable to work up to fifty-six hours a week, despite the fact that the office for the implementation of the Four-Year plan had, soon after the outbreak of war stated that environmental factors (long hours, transport difficulties, shift switches and the blackout) had a greater adverse effect on female labour productivity than on male, and that ten-hour shifts for women sometimes produced the same output as eight-hour ones.[29]

There were, none the less, certain alleviations of women's work burden, including one in the psychological sphere: anti-feminism on the shop floor prompted a Labour Front drive against masculine prejudice in industry,[30] though hardly elsewhere. In a display of practical solicitude for female labour, the Labour Front – on behalf of footsore postwomen – asked house-owners to fit collective ground-floor letter-boxes for all their tenants.[31]

The authorities passed legislation dispensing women workers from having to lift objects heavier than 15 kilogrammes in weight;[32] some accommodating plant-leaders gave married women – a category forming 40 per cent of the female labour force in 1942 – a choice of shifts and others allowed them to work five-day instead of six-day weeks.[33]

None of this could obscure the basic contradiction that those whom Nazi rhetoric had destined for the kitchen and the nursery eventually formed three-fifths of Germany's wartime labour force.

The Third Reich could be compared to a double-ended gun trained both on the twentieth century and the Treaty of Versailles, with nostalgia for a pre-industrial past speaking out of one barrel, and streamlined industrial preparation for war out of the other.

To gloss over the divergence between Nazi promise and fulfilment, propaganda scaled new heights of casuistry. 'It has always been our chief article of faith,' wrote an official in the Nazi Women's League, 'that woman's place is in the home – but since the whole of Germany is our home we must serve her wherever we can best do so.'[34]

The Nazi Women's League itself pointed to the paradoxical situation of women in the Third Reich – mobilizing creatures officially designated as sub-political for political ends and inculcating domestic expertise among increasingly part-time housewives.

The Nazi Women's League leader, Scholz-Klink, made the ringing declaration at the 1937 Party Rally, 'Even though our weapon is only the soup ladle its impact should be as great as that of other weapons,'[35] and this encapsulated all the ingredients of a situation in which supine deference to male supremacy and non-recognition of the facts of economic life were tricked out in mock-heroic verbiage. Nevertheless, within the domestic and ancillary spheres the Party's huge distaff side managed to generate a considerable volume of activity: inculcating cookery techniques and eating schedules geared to the self-sufficiency programme, providing consumer guidance in the use of left-overs, propagating the substitution of domestic butter and animal fats for imported oils, of home-produced substitutes for imported woollens and linen, of rayon for cotton and silk. In addition, the members of the League dispensed pre-natal instruction, ran mothercraft classes for brides and domestic economy courses for schoolgirls and others. During the war the scope widened:[36] they served refreshments at railway stations to servicemen and evacuees, did auxiliary Red Cross work, helped in the collection and sifting of scrap metal and other materials, produced stewed fruit for military hospitals and comforts for the troops, ran cookery courses and sewing circles, and allocated domestics, i.e. deportees from occupied Europe, to mothers of large families.

This wide-ranging programme combined with the vastness of potential membership to make the Nazi Women's League one of the mammoth organizations of the Third Reich, with a full-time establishment smaller only than that of the German Labour Front and the League of Civil Servants.[37]

The fact that a large proportion – 70 per cent, in fact – of these officials were not Party members[38] indicates how many women were prepared to undertake organizational, administrative and educational tasks for non-political reasons, either as a means of self-expression or of acquiring social esteem.

The anti-feminist Nazi regime thus paradoxically succeeded in eliciting the participation of larger numbers of women than the Weimar state, which had first enfranchised them. Within this large contradiction there operated a smaller contrary one: although the Nazi Women's League was no more than a tame adjunct of the male-centred Nazi Party, it comprised elements of suffragettism; this huge organization, with political ambitions inversely proportional to its size, gave a few women scope for challenging received truths about the second-rate sex.

A volume published in 1934 called *German Women to Adolf Hitler* actually articulated complaints about some of the most glaring deficiencies of the Nazi system, from a woman's point of view. 'Today, man is being educated not for, but against, marriage. Men are grouped together in *Vereine* (clubs) and *Kameradschaftheime* (hostels).* Married people now have less in common and decreasing influence over their children. Woman stays back further and further in the shadow of loneliness.'[39] 'We see our daughters growing up in stupid aimlessness, living only in the vague hope of perhaps getting a man and having children. If they do not succeed, their lives will be thwarted.'[40] 'A son, even the youngest, today laughs in his mother's face. He regards her as his natural servant, and women in general as merely willing tools of his aims and wishes.'[41]

The suffragettes-on-sufferance also took up cudgels on behalf of working women. 'One cannot expect people to do their utmost at work all the time,' stated the publication of the German Labour Front's Women's Department, *Frau am Werk*, 'if they are simultaneously being made to feel that their activity, nay, their very presence, is undesirable.'[42] A major area of contention was the professions. The head of the women's section of the Nazi Teachers' Organization pleaded for parity of intellectual training between men and women: 'It is a regrettable fact that a war of the sexes is raging inside the teaching profession. Not only have women teachers a right to their own existence, but bringing up children requires the best possible training of mothers.'[43]

In 1937 a leading Nazi feminist, Sophie Rogge-Berne, was officially silenced.[44] Other advocates of emancipation took care to argue the case against the denial of educational opportunities for women from within the Nazi-prescribed context of sex-conditioned spheres of activity.

Women doctors could give aid and comfort to fatigued mothers and provide spiritual support to girls in puberty. Women teachers would be most suited to instruct adolescent girls in such delicate subjects as biology and heredity. Women jurists would be most qualified for dealing with cases involving children, marital difficulties, divorces, etc. Women scientists and economists could be employed in the planning of consumption and domestic matters, as well as in town planning and housing policy.[45]

This attempt to present title-deeds to a modest nature reserve in areas until then designated as masculine preserves illustrates the erosion of the position of professional and academic women.

* Residential hostels designed to foster a particular *esprit de corps*.

Married women doctors and civil servants were dismissed immediately after the seizure of power. The number of women teachers at girls' secondary schools had decreased by 15 per cent by 1935. In the following academic year the entry of girls to training departments for university teachers was completely suspended.[46] By this time the number of women academics had declined from fifty-nine to thirty-seven (out of a total academic teaching body of over 7,000).[47] A change in the syllabus of girls' grammar schools, gearing them more specifically towards domestic science training, prompted this comment in the *Frankfurter Zeitung*: 'After the educational reform, women will once again be confronted with difficulties in preparing for academic careers, although we have been officially assured of late that there are still uses for academically trained women.'[48]

From June 1936 onwards women could no longer act as judges or public prosecutors, and female *Assessoren* (assistant judges, assistant teachers, and so on) were gradually dismissed.[49] Women were declared ineligible for jury service on the grounds that 'they cannot think logically or reason objectively, since they are ruled only by emotion'.[50] (Even so, certain branches of the legal profession were still kept open to them.)

The Evangelical Church, too, joined in the process of eliminating women from leading positions. In 1935 the Bishop of Hamburg rescinded an ecclesiastical reform of the Weimar period, under which women were admitted to certain functions inside the Church.[51]

The situation of female students underwent two drastic (and contrary) reversals during the Third Reich, one soon after the seizure of power and the other during the war. In 1933 women had constituted about a fifth of the entire student body[52] and the regime early on devised measures to reduce feminine representation at institutes of higher learning to a one-in-ten ratio of the undergraduate total. Out of 10,000 girls who had passed the *Abitur* examinations in the following year, no more than 1,500 were granted university admission.* By stringent regulation of faculty entry (e.g. seventy-five women into medicine each year)[53], the *numerus clausus* of one in ten was made operative across the whole range of studies, although a number of marginal disciplines, such as journalism,

---

* At the same time the regime introduced the 'domestic year', which meant that girls of eighteen had to spend twelve months as domestic servants, either of farmers or of large families. They were provided with bed and board, but received no pay. Their employers had to pay health insurance, but could claim tax benefits. The girls of this year and the subsequent years up to the war were among the principal victims of Nazi discrimination.

pharmacy and physical education, in fact showed a growth in female enrolment.*

By 1938–9 there were again a little over 2,000 female freshers out of a total of 9,000 girl students; at the outbreak of war the *numerus clausus* was dropped and the total number of girl students doubled in two years, to reach an all-time high of 25,000 by 1943–4.

The war also saw a partial return of previously retired female lecturers,[54] but even so, not a single university chair was occupied by a woman during the Third Reich. The employment figures for women teachers showed fluctuations similar to those for student enrolment. After the initial reduction there was a levelling off (in 1938, every fourth primary-school teacher was female) and the war witnessed a feminine counter-movement at both ends, with more girls entering the profession and more retired women returning to it.

Nor were women ever entirely displaced from the civil service; although there was a rather thorough purge early on, the regime at all times maintained administrative posts in the social services as a special feminine preserve: in 1938 every tenth civil servant was a woman. (It must also be borne in mind that large numbers of women gravitated into the Party's own civil service, the apparatus of the Nazi Women's League, the National Socialist People's Welfare, the women's section of the German Labour Front, the Mother and Child organization, and so on.)

The women's section of the established civil service also provided the authorities with pace-setting opportunities for the moral reconstruction of German society. In 1939 Reichsminister Lammers issued a ruling that extra-marital motherhood was not a reason for initiating disciplinary measures against members of the service.[55] Although these and similar measures still fell short of changing the image of illegitimate motherhood into a socially esteemed one, the Third Reich did manage to inculcate new notions about the sexual role of women in society. Most previous arrangements of society had been characterized by the advantage men enjoyed over women in the sexual sphere, an advantage exemplified by what is known as the double standard of morality. The Third Reich replaced the conventional double standard of bourgeois society by immorality pure and simple, and the sexual role of women by their biological one.[56]

The average marriage age had been creeping upwards ever since the

* They increased respectively from 21 to 28 per cent, from 28 to 30 per cent and from 23 to 52 per cent. (cf. Charlotte Lorenz, *Zehn-Jahresstatistik des Hochschulbesuchs und der Abitursprüfung*, Berlin, 1943, p. 48.)

Great War, but the seizure of power immediately reversed that trend. The Third Reich furthermore made a woman's child-bearing period the apogee of her life-cycle. Women basked in Nazi public esteem between marriage and the menopause, after which they imperceptibly declined into a twilight condition of eugenic superfluity. But under the strain of war and separation from their menfolk, many women reacted against the officially prescribed biological *raison d'être* of their existence and craved the satisfaction of their erotic impulses. Even before 1939 the practice of herding young men together in barracks or camps for long periods at a time had led to a stultifying of contacts between the sexes before marriage. As a result young women tended to have affairs with older men; this was a sufficiently widespread phenomenon to provide the theme of two contemporary novels.* After 1939 proscribed sexual contact with prisoners of war and foreign workers reached significant proportions, and during the final stages of the war the erosion of sexual taboos among women became a pervasive feature of the social scene.

Closely related to women's sexual role in society was the question of their dress and demeanour. The seizure of power betokened a drastic reversal of the role women's appearance had played before 1933, when it had helped to inject an air of elegance and lightness into German life. Party militants, predominantly lower middle class and provincial, poured forth an unstaunched flood of polemics, exhortations and threats to make German womanhood return to its alleged primordial virtues. The *Völkische Beobachter* castigated make-up as blatantly un-German, defining it as suitable for the sensual faces and thick lips of Levantines:'The most unnatural thing we can encounter in the streets is a German woman, who, disregarding all laws of beauty, has painted her face with Oriental war-paint.'[57] Such strictures were enough to earn heavily made-up girls travelling on Berlin buses epithets ranging from 'whore' to 'traitress'.[58]

Where popular feeling was devoid of that quality of spontaneity, the authorities supplied administrative guidance. Thus the inhabitants of Erfurt were told by their chief of police to stop women who smoked in public and to remind them of their duties as German women and mothers.[59] The provincial factory-cell organization of the NSBO (forerunner of the German Labour Front) in Lower Franconia excluded all women wearing powder and lipstick from its meetings; those seen smoking in public automatically forfeited their membership.[60] This campaign was motivated by something more than Comstockian provincialism and prudery:

* *The Angel of Love* by Kasimir Edschmid and *The Secret of the Right Life* by Hans Carossa.

biological preoccupations also loomed large. Since slimness was held to be incompatible with bearing many children,* women were to be persuaded not to trouble about their figures. An additional aspect of the anti-modernist and anti-glamour movement was the pseudo-socialist tinsel of the Nazi revolution. Because the Hitler Youth decked itself out with the anti-bourgeois ideology of the Youth Movement, some young women considered it an affirmation of principle not to be interested in smart clothes and cosmetics. Compounding these various considerations, the regime produced an ideal type of feminity, for which the leaders of the women's section of the Reich Labour Service were groomed as prototypes. They were trained in Spartan severity, taught to do without cosmetics, to dress in the simplest manner, to display no individual vanity, to sleep on hard beds, and to forgo all culinary delicacies; the ideal image of those broad-hipped figures, unencumbered by corsets, was one of radiant blondeness, crowned by hair arranged in a bun or braided into a coronet of plaits.[61] As a negative counter-image Nazi propaganda projected the combative, man-hating suffragettes of other countries.[62]

Although this campaign met with a certain response – above all among members of the German Girls' League – elsewhere it stirred a fashion-conscious reaction which eventually attracted support from such highly placed Nazi personalities as Magda Goebbels, who agreed to become the patron of a badly needed German Institute of Fashion.† Her husband (arguably the Third Reich's chief connoisseur of feminine charm) felt impelled to speak out repeatedly in defence of grace and beauty:

It is a sad state of affairs that actresses, dancers and singers have to be exempted from the Reich Labour Service by a special decree from the Führer, so that at least the artistic sphere provides a nature reserve, where feminine beauty and grace can lead a modest but secure existence safe from the officially demanded coarsening and masculinization of German womanhood.[63]

Goebbels also entered the lists during the wartime controversy that raged around the 'trouser-women':‡

* Smoking was also held to have a negative effect on fertility; see p. 264.

† How badly needed it was is borne out by the comment of two Americans. 'I was struck by the ugliness of German women. They walked badly, they dress worse than English-women used to do' (cf. William Shirer, *Berlin Diary*, Hamish Hamilton, London, 1941, p. 141). 'The married women mostly looked dumpy, they all wore dark colours. Nobody wore gay clothes' (cf. Pat Z. Siemer, *Two thousand and Ten Days of Hitler*, Harper, New York, 1940, p. 124).

‡ In the Alpine regions 'trouser-wenches with Indian warpaint' was a favourite epithet applied to evacuees from the Rhenish industrial towns.

Whether women wear slacks is no concern of the public. During the colder season women can safely wear trousers, even if the Party mutinies against this in one place or another. The bigotry bug should be wiped out. Long live the Metropole and the Scala.[64]*

The campaign of the anti-slacks brigade none the less gathered pace. In Stuttgart women were forbidden to wear riding breeches unless they were participating in equestrian events,[65] and the Wehrmacht General-Officer-Commanding at Garmisch-Partenkirchen ordered his men not to let themselves be seen in public in the company of 'trouser-women'.[66]

As more and more women took up jobs for which skirts were hardly the most suitable apparel, the Press, too, was torn by the trouser controversy. Thus the *Hamburger Fremdenblatt* eschewed value-judgements in reporting the fact that trousered train conductresses worked complete nightshifts,[67] while the *Bodensee Rundschau* loosed a flood of invective on women wearing trousers on voluntary air-raid duty.[68]

The war, with its heavy incidence of mental strain and nervous fatigue, also led to an increase in women smoking, and a medical expert attacked this practice in an article postulating a positive correlation between excessive nicotine indulgence and infertility.[69] (Smoking allegedly harmed the ovaries: a marriage between heavy smokers only produced 0·66 children on average compared to the normal average of three.) Thus the battle over women's rights to dress and to smoke continued throughout the war, but, like many other controversial issues, it never elicited a definite ruling from the highest arbitrator. Hitler more than once actually echoed Goebbels's concern with feminine appearance. 'Above all, we must not wage war on womanhood in the course of total war. Women represent a huge force and as soon as one encroaches on their beauty care one turns them into enemies.'[70]

The aesthetics *versus* ideology tussle about women's appearance had, in fact, dragged on unresolved ever since the seizure of power, with the *Schwarzes Korps* (on behalf of the sartorial self-sufficiency lobby) alleging that bourgeois fashion editors promoted styles evocative of 'Jewish *cocottes*' while the fashion trade itself tried to reassure the public of Germany's continued participation in the international *beau monde*.† The

---

* Berlin variety theatres, roughly comparable to London's Windmill as it used to be.

† cf. *Frankfurter Zeitung*, 24 February 1937. Two months later the *Deutsche Frauenwerk* stated officially: 'Rumours concerning the official institution of something called German fashion are completely unfounded' (cf. *Frankfurter Zeitung*, 23 April 1937).

Hitler Youth leadership had the perspicacity to let 'Faith and Beauty' (the continuation section of the German Girls' League, for those aged from eighteen to twenty-one) run special courses and even schools of fashion design. A major counter-impulse to sartorial primitivism was represented by the wartime importation – by means of purchase or pillage – of huge stocks of dresses, stockings, furs and perfumes from occupied Europe.

The austerity programme necessitated by a total war effort was in fact not put into operation until a year before the end of the war. Two months after Stalingrad, Goebbels still noticed that some regional administrations, though by no means all, were operating a ban on hair-dyeing and perming, a situation that led members of the so-called better circles to indulge in commuting from one Gau to another to go to the hairdresser.[71]

Muddles of this sort, however, did not drastically impair the authorities' ability to supply the civilian population with the essentials of life throughout most of the war. Peacetime standards of consumption obtained up to 1941, and it was not until the last phase of the war that debilitating shortages were making themselves felt.

Shortening dole-queues early on, crowded nurseries half-way, and honoured rations near the end – it was in terms such as these that feminine eyes largely viewed the Third Reich. German women were possibly even readier than Germans in general to trade theoretical birth-rights for a practical mess of pottage. Some remained blissfully unconscious of the fact that the Gretchen-cum-birth-machine function to which they were assigned affronted their human dignity. Most others found that on balance economic security and the motherhood cult more than compensated for sex discrimination and political widowhood.

Nor, one suspects, was sex discrimination really a major issue in the minds of many women below the academic and professional levels.* Even the purge of women in public life was partly compensated for by the outlet that work in the Women's League and the People's Welfare provided for their displaced energies. In addition the regime catered for the psychological needs of women who craved vicarious identification by constantly keeping a number of exemplary female personalities in the

* When the periodical *Die Frau* wrote, early in the war, 'It is necessary to do away with a patriarchic concept of marriage as the only possible vocation for women, it is necessary to give them a better training in the professions, not merely a quick and superficial training for office work, which has hitherto only been considered a waiting-room for marriage', one suspects that these remarks were not addressed only to the powers-that-be, but also to some extent to the journal's readers (cf. *Die Frau*, August 1940).

public eye, such as the screen-idol-turned-film-producer, Leni Riefenstahl, who earned a place in the national pantheon with her documentaries of the 1934 Nuremberg Rally and the 1936 Olympic Games in Berlin. She was subsequently joined by Hannah Reitsch, the first German woman to be awarded the glider pilot's badge, the certificate of an aircraft captain and the Iron Cross (Second Class).[72] Another feminine exemplar was Gertrude Scholz-Klink, the *soignée* housewife who managed to combine leadership of the Nazi Women's League with running a home and bringing up a real family (in the Nazi sense of the word, i.e. consisting of four children). In addition there were the wives of the two men ranking immediately below Hitler in the Nazi hierarchy: Emmy Goering, an ex-actress of Wagnerian proportions and demeanour, and the fashion-conscious Magda Goebbels. (The latter, however, though a mother of six children, hardly qualified as an object of vicarious identification, in view of her husband's extra-marital proclivities.)

But though this sort of projection was a factor in the fantasy life of women, it paled into insignificance beside the Führer-cult. Since the Weimar Republic had been even less effective among women than among men in inculcating a linked sense of personal autonomy and public commitment, the collective feminine psyche remained apolitical and littered with a residue of dynastic loyalty and unfocused religiosity, dormant impulses which Hitler activated to a pitch of unprecedented intensity. Already in January 1932, during the meeting at the Düsseldorf Industrial Club between Hitler and the Ruhr tycoons, the assembled ladies paid the cloakroom attendant a mark apiece for the privilege of sniffing the bouquet that had been presented to the Führer on entering.[73]

On public occasions in the Third Reich the female section of the crowd often exhibited a form of mass hysteria known as *Kontaktsucht* or 'contact-seeking', an uncontrollable urge to touch him physically; at mass meetings Rauschnigg noted the eyes of women listeners 'filming over and glazed with a religious sort of exultation'.[74]

At the end of the war, too, more women than men preferred self-immolation to living in a world devoid of the Führer's presence; their suicides ironically corroborated the received Nazi truth about the congenital difference between reason-motivated man and emotion-guided woman.

18

YOUTH

In the young generation the regime found the population group that was the most malleable to its own purpose and one that returned the highest yield of self-sacrificing allegiance for the blandishment invested. The Nazis in opposition had been the party of Youth *versus* Age less by championing youthful causes than by uninhibited assault upon the staid Republic; when in power they instantly called off the age-war and managed to make their subsequent manipulation of the young serve two ends that were not readily reconcilable: liberating the full potential of juvenile aggressiveness, while at the same time impressing the adult public with the degree of discipline to which youth could be subjected.

Thus liberation and regimentation can be said to have formed the poles of the magnetic field in which German youth moved after 1933, a paradox that was finally exemplified by fifteen-year-old Hitler Youth soldiers, who were debarred from evening visits to the cinema on age grounds, barring the Red Army's advance into the Reich.

Nazi liberation of youth took various forms: interposing the Hitler Youth amid family and school as a rival court of appeal, bestowing uniforms (and daggers) on all the young (but only on selected grown-ups), making children guide ill-adapted parents into the new age, and arousing expectations of an inheritance no previous generation had been promised.

Yet each of these glittering newly minted coins had its obverse: emancipation through the Hitler Youth meant a harsher form of tutelage; the ubiquity of uniforms spelt total uniformity; the child that had to guide its elders forsook child's estate, and many hopeful inheritors eventually had a lifespan far briefer than their parents.

The Third Reich's young people should not only be looked at under the aspect of family, school or Hitler Youth; work, too, was a predominant factor in their lives. Its predominance was borne out by the educational statistics for 1938–9, which list 877,849 fourteen-year-old school leavers, 88,492 sixteen-year-old junior matriculators, and 45,150 candidates for the *Abitur* certificate;[1] this meant that on average seventeen out of every twenty youngsters were educationally predestined for work as distinct from professional, civil service or academic careers. (For some of the fourteen-year-old school leavers, work was not a complete novelty, either, since child labour formed an integral part of agricultural production and of the cottage industries – such as garment-making, weaving or toymaking – which provided subsistence for up to a million people in economic backwaters.)*

In industry itself, child labour was banned (but factory inspectors could sanction the employment of youngsters of over ten years of age for up to four hours per week).[2] Normal working-time for young persons (between fourteen and eighteen) amounted to forty-eight hours a week. It was obligatory to grant young employees one free afternoon per week, a measure which aroused a certain degree of opposition from employers. In the course of intensified industrial mobilization, young people were inevitably exploited more. A government decree on shift work in December 1938 stipulated that lads under sixteen could work until ten o'clock at night in engineering factories and docks, while those aged sixteen and upwards could be put on night shifts. When war broke out, various safeguards against sweated juvenile labour were waived, but this had such adverse effects on health that in December the ceiling for youngsters below sixteen was fixed at fifty-four hours and for those over sixteen at fifty-six hours per week. If, however, their work was deemed essential to the war effort it was within the factory inspector's discretion to extend the permissible working time.[3]

From 1938 onwards school-leavers had to register with labour exchanges and were directed into priority occupations. 'The foremost goal is not the enrichment of individual existence but the increasing prosperity of the nation . . . Individual wishes can be respected only to the extent that they do not run counter to the general interest.'[4] But although the element of choice was reduced, actual career opportunities for working-class youngsters certainly improved during the Third Reich compared to earlier on. Though, after the seizure of power, young workers had been discriminated against in favour of fathers of families, by the mid-thirties all school-leavers were automatically assured of places in industry, and the authorities paid close attention to their vocational training. German industrial training had always been of a high standard; what the Nazis did was to make it more widely available by easing formal entrance requirements

* The September 1938 census listed 675,233 home-workers in the old Reich territory; to these must be added Austrians as well as Sudeten Germans.

for training schemes and granting skilled workers parity with master craftsmen as instructors of apprentices.[5]

The number of craft apprentices increased by over one-half during the peacetime years of the Third Reich (from 420,000 to 660,000).[6] The German Labour Front had originally mooted a scheme whereby every single boy was to serve an artisan apprenticeship; it was not until 1936 that they could be undeceived of this romantically medieval notion and made to accept industrial training as preferable to craft apprenticeship. It then became official policy to guide apprentices away from artisan workshops and into the better-equipped training shops of large plants, where there was also less likelihood of their being exploited as cheap labour.[7] The authorities boosted the ratio of apprentices to total labour force to such effect that by 1937 there was one apprentice to every three workers in the metallurgical industries and one to every five in building.[8]

An annual competition for workers, known as the National Vocational Competition (*Reichsberufwettkampf*) attracted a vast number of entrants (4 million in 1939)[9] and provided a great incentive throughout the ranks of juvenile labour in the whole Reich. Winning competitors received rewards attractive both in terms of prestige and material advantage: photographs in the Press, radio interviews, invitations to tea and a harangue by Hitler at the Reich Chancellery, as well as shorter apprenticeships, additional training, technical-school places or promotion within their firm. Post Office messengers, for instance, who came top in their particular competition, were upgraded to civil-service rank.

The Vocational Competition was one of the few Nazi innovations to make a genuine – if partial – contribution to the proclaimed aim of folk community: 80 per cent of the winning competitors had failed as children to reach secondary-school standard; beyond this, in a number of outstanding cases, lads awarded scholarships at technical schools went on to the technological faculties of universities.[10]

To prevent the abuse of apprentice labour by employers, apprentices were issued with books in which details of the work were to be entered day by day. These books were to be submitted to the local chamber of industry for inspection at regular intervals, though some of the entries were none the less obviously faked.[11]* Another government regulation at which many employers jibbed was payment to apprentices for time lost while

* Some masters – incorrectly – believed themselves entitled to inflict corporal punishment on apprentices (cf. *Frankfurter Zeitung*, 1 September 1937).

attending trade schools.* Shortly before the outbreak of war, however, the authorities themselves shortened periods of apprenticeship and reduced the time during which apprentices attended trade schools as part of day-release schemes.[12]

Although, on the surface, industrial training programmes looked impressively efficient, a number of deficiencies became ever more apparent as time went on. Thus the annual report of the Halle Chamber of Industry and Trade for 1938[13] stated that fewer candidates than ever before managed to satisfy the examiners in shorthand and typing; as far as industrial work proficiency was concerned the results were much better, but this was counterbalanced by widespread failures in the academic part of the examination, in German, mathematics, drawing, and so on.

With the coming of war, sellers' labour market conditions became more pronounced and there were many complaints about the deteriorating standards among apprentices and industrial trainees.† Employers complained that Hitler Youth and Labour Front officials always emphasized young workers' rights but omitted to acquaint them with their corresponding duties. They also alleged that undue leniency on the part of school and trade-school examiners was adversely affecting the quality of the current intake into industry.[14]

Early in 1941 the German juvenile labour force totalled 5 million, for whose benefit the Youth Department of the Labour Front arranged special youth factory meetings, leisure-time activities, vocational guidance and health supervision, as well as the construction of special apprentice hostels. (The ever-growing attraction of industrial employment for young people in country districts meant that more and more of them were billeted in hostels attached to such large industrial complexes as the Volkswagen works at Wolfsburg.)

The tendency of young people to emigrate from the countryside, which the regime counteracted by channelling urban youth into agrarian work *via* the Reich Labour Service, the Hitler Youth or the Girls' Duty Year,

* Nor were employers very happy about holiday entitlements of apprentices, which involved fifteen days for fifteen-year-olds, twelve days for sixteen-year-olds and ten for seventeen- and eighteen-year-olds. Moreover, if young workers applied for attendance at Hitler Youth courses, employers had no redress against their exceeding the statutory periods (cf. *Frankfurter Zeitung*, 29 July 1937, quoting the Trustee of Labour for Central Germany).

† In 1940, Chambers of Trade and Industry took exception to the fact that the authorities insisted on employers paying monthly subsidies for apprentices' and trainees' education, from which deductions could not be made for occasions on which the latter played truant. (cf. Bundesarchiv, Coblenz, R II/234 B.)

was prompted by low pay, lack of amenities and amusements, and conditions of work that could be positively debilitating.

Thus in 1937, of 17,000 rural applicants medically examined for an intensive physical-training course initiated by Food Estate Leader Darré, only 4 per cent satisfied the – admittedly exacting – entrance requirements.[15] Some were discovered to be suffering from foot defects and distortions of the spinal column due to overwork. Most showed evidence of the toll the shortage of labour in agriculture was taking among youth in the countryside.

As for the health of young people in general, the first years of the Nazi era were marked by an increase in children's diseases rather greater than that of births (which rose by 25 per cent as between 1931–3 and 1934–6). Thus the incidence of scarlet fever rose by roughly half between 1933 and 1937 (79,830 to 117,544); that of diphtheria nearly doubled (77,340 to 146,733); infantile paralysis showed the same amount of increase (1,318 to 2,723); dysentery nearly trebled (2,685 to 7,545) and meningitis increased one and a half times (617 to 1,574).[16] Two to four per cent of all young people were estimated as prone to organic heart disease and similar figures applied to nervous disturbances.[17]

The increased nervousness of young people in the Nazi era was a matter of widespread comment, both in Germany[18] and abroad.[19] Investigating youngsters aged ten to eighteen who had attended Hitler Youth camps, doctors diagnosed fifty cases of disturbance of the alimentary process, presumably due to nervous tension, although the overall ratio of lads who had gained weight in camp to those who had not was two to one.[20]

Another area of obvious deterioration was orthopaedic health. In 1937 a medical journal stated that symptoms formerly found among apprentices and during the years of adolescence were now often appearing among school-children.[21] 'Too much is demanded of the feet of these boys and girls, who have to march on hard roads, carry heavy burdens . . .'

Shortly afterwards it was reported that over one in three of the conscripts examined in 1936 had been diagnosed as suffering from flat feet.[22] In a significant move the regional Youth Leader for Hanover ordered the reduction of Hitler Youth duties to the absolute minimum during the winter of 1937–8, and he appealed to school authorities to do likewise, since 'youngsters, especially leaders, were so preoccupied with their youth service that health defects and fatigue symptoms had become unavoidable.'[23] Within two years a new wave of nervous unsettlement spread through the adolescent population. When the outbreak of war inaugurated

a succession of lightning victories, many who were too young to participate in the fighting experienced feelings of acute frustration. At the height
of the war neutral observers noticed that even children were affected by
the general mood of tension and expectancy; expectancy in their case took
the form of grandiose post-war dreams, in which they saw themselves as
Gauleiters in such remote parts of the globe as Africa, India or South
America, whilst others had their imagination fired by Himmler's project*
for dotting vast spaces of the Slavic East with the fortified farms of German
overlords.[24]

Cumulatively the war also had adverse physical effects on young people.
This was borne out by the setting-up (in 1944) of special pre-military
training camps (*Wehrertüchtigungslager*) at which newly inducted conscripts
were brought up to the required standard of fitness – through a combination of toughening-up exercises and nourishing meals – before being transferred to their basic training camp.[25]

There are also estimates that by the end of the war more than one in
every three young Germans were suffering from neurosis[26] but the
evidence for this is somewhat inconclusive. By contrast the graph of social
health among young people can be more accurately plotted. The incidence of juvenile delinquency had been very marked at the end of the
Great War (with almost 100,000 cases coming before the courts in 1918),
but after the inflation it had declined by three-quarters, a decline which
continued even during the Depression. Then, from 21,529 in 1932, the
figure dropped spectacularly to 15,958 in 1933 – proof of the Third Reich's
ability both to absorb and to intimidate criminal energy. Although a series
of amnesties confuses the subsequent picture, the general upward trend
during the Third Reich is unmistakable. In 1937, a year without criminal
amnesty (and of full employment), there were 24,562 cases, more than at
the height of the slump. Within the next five years of increasing family
dislocation, the juvenile share of total criminality trebled (6 per cent in
1937 to 17·5 per cent in 1943 – though even then it still compared favourably with the 27 per cent of 1917).[27] A breakdown for those five years
showed juvenile crimes against property up by 100 per cent, sexual offences
somewhat more, and forgeries up by 250 per cent.[28]

Forgeries frequently consisted of faking identity documents stating the
bearer's age, an offence motivated by young people's craving for the adult

* According to the *Hakenkreuz Banner* of 22 January 1942, Hitler Youth volunteers for
the *Wehrbauern* scheme were plentiful. Doubts and refusals came chiefly from the parents.
'But it is surely tempting to be a master of a fine farm at twenty-eight.'

pleasures from which a censorious government debarred them by law. The same regime which presented ten-year-old boys with lethal weapons took extraordinary pains to enforce decorous conduct among the young, by exhortation and deterrent alike.

The purification drive among the teenage population proceeded in a piecemeal fashion. The police chief at Mecklenburg had issued an ordinance forbidding boys and girls under eighteen to smoke in public on penalty of two weeks' jail or a fine of 150 marks.[29] His colleague at Breslau decreed that girls under eighteen who were found in dance-halls unaccompanied by either parents or responsible adults were liable to be sent to remand homes,[30] but after the outbreak of war the authorities clamped down on the young by means of the comprehensive Law for the Protection of Youth (promulgated on 9 March 1940),[31] which banned young people under eighteen from the streets after dark, as well as from frequenting restaurants, cinemas or other places of entertainment after 9 p.m. (if unaccompanied by an adult), and young people under sixteen from being served with spirits or smoking in public.* This wartime curtailment† of young people's leisure activities accorded ill with the duties they were expected to perform. It was illogical to ban youngsters from smoking in public, if seventeen-year-old messengers attached to the Air Raid Service received a cigarette ration as part of their emoluments.[32] Similarly, the prohibition on juvenile alcohol consumption made little sense if these Air Raid messengers were attached to patrols of older men, who whiled away their off-duty hours in public houses. A rather piquant moral danger to adolescents arose out of their having to work alongside prostitutes conscripted to work in armaments factories. The contradiction between officious solicitude for youth and the realities of the situation was highlighted by this complaint by Hitler Youths that was frequently heard in 1944: 'We are

* Public prohibition was complemented by a propaganda campaign to have the ban extended into homes and places of work (cf. *Deutsche Bodensee Zeitung*, 1 May 1940). As far as the incidence of smoking among the young was concerned, a survey of 200 fourteen-year-old boys in Hanover established that nine out of ten were familiar with smoking and that one in ten was a regular smoker (cf. W. Hermannson and H. Lüpke, *Erzieher und Erzieherinnen: Ein Wort an Euch*, Reichsgesundheitsverlag, Berlin-Dahlem, 1940, p. 13).

† The increasing incidence of juvenile misdemeanours led the authorities to introduce a new form of punishment for young offenders: the 'youth arrest'. Introduced in October 1940, this was a term of imprisonment awarded in the courts, the details of which were not entered on the reports of children at school and not allowed to affect the professional chances of young people in employment. Two-thirds of all offences punished by youth arrest involved crimes against property. Youth arrest, incidentally, was awarded in over half of all cases in which young people appeared before the courts in 1941 (cf. Werner Klose, *Generation im Gleichschritt*, Stalling, Oldenburg, 1964, p. 218).

good enough to become soldiers at fifteen or sixteen and get ourselves killed, but we're not allowed into cinemas to see "adult" films until we are eighteen.'[33]*

Remand homes to which chiefs of police threatened to commit un-chaperoned dancers were a deterrent constantly evoked by Nazi educationists. Their importance within the Nazi scheme of things was above all attested by the increase in the number of inmates: within three years of the accession to power, the number of Prussian children 'taken in care' more than doubled (forty-two out of 100,000 in 1932, eighty-six in 1935).[34] This steep increase was officially attributed to the rigorousness with which the 'co-ordinated' welfare agencies, supplemented by the People's Welfare and the Hitler Youth, were discharging their functions, but an authoritative statement added significantly, 'Youngsters are found to be in need of care and protection, not only because of parental dereliction of duty, but also because the ideological upheaval is undermining family relationships.'[35]†

Children in correctional institutions were subjected to a regimen in which whipping traditionally formed an integral part. They were, however, theoretically entitled to appeal against maltreatment, but all appeals had to be addressed to the head of the institution, who was thus judge and jury in his own case. The vocational training given to inmates in remand homes tended mainly towards agriculture.[36] If an inmate, upon reaching the age of eighteen, was held not to have benefited from his correctional training, he was liable to be sent to a workhouse (such as the notorious one at Rummelsburg near Berlin).[37] Correctional institutions also served eugenic functions. 'Biologically inferior' children were committed to them and the directors of the institutions could order their sterilization.[38] The homes also accommodated malendowed children, since guardianship courts, as a matter of eugenic policy, refused to hand over the children of criminals, prostitutes and habitual drunkards for adoption by foster-parents.[39] (Considering the basically punitive purpose to which the regime put remand homes, the *Schwarzes Korps* was being more than usually disingenuous when it plaintively stated in 1937, 'The public today looks

* Although the authorities in Berlin realized the illogicality of this situation and eventually lowered the age of universal cinema admission to fourteen, theirs was an isolated decision. Under a general ruling issued in 1944, young people were not allowed even to see films passed as suitable for children at evening performances unless they were accompanied by adults (cf. *Völkischer Beobachter*, 22 July 1944). This policy had already been put into operation in various parts of the Reich earlier on (cf. *Deutsche Bodensee Zeitung*, 1 May 1940).

† For references to the removal of children from parental care on religious grounds, see the chapter on the family, p. 242.

upon pupils in correctional institutions as it did twenty years ago – as youngsters of minor value and of criminal tendency.'[40]

In addition to all the adult-staffed agencies so far listed the authorities also deployed a specially created adolescent variant of the military police – the Hitler Youth Patrol Service – to combat juvenile delinquency and deviant behaviour. This employment of the young to police the young was a corollary of the 'Youth leads youth' ethos, in which the Hitler Youth gloried. Their claim to a monopoly of juvenile autonomy was a fake one, but though the Hitler Youth was not the only youth movement free of adult leaders, it was certainly the largest and the most important one in German history. In fact, it was the largest organization for young people ever to exist in the Western world. It underwent an unprecedented growth from small beginnings in a very short time: at the end of 1932, i.e. at a time when 13 million adults voted for the Nazi Party, the strength of Hitler Youth membership throughout Germany was just over 100,000 yet within two years of the seizure of power, membership increased thirty-five times.[41]

The numbers kept on growing at a slower rate beyond that date; by the outbreak of the Second World War virtually every young German between ten and eighteen was a member of the Hitler Youth. In fact, the movement never achieved 100 per cent enrolment, although figures of 90 per cent and above (claimed by its leader, Baldur von Schirach, as early as 1937) were no doubt correct.[42] Until December 1936 the Hitler Youth paraded the fiction of a voluntary organization; after that date it called itself State Youth, and membership became obligatory. (Even so, it took another two years before various executive decrees of the Hitler Youth Law actually plugged the last loopholes for evasion.)[43]

In a manner comparable to the way the Nazi Party acted as a parasite upon conservative, *Mittelstand* and socialist ideologies, the Hitler Youth purloined its ethos from other youth movements, such as the *Jugendbewegung*; in addition, it cannibalized their leaders. Suppressing the *Bündische Jugend*, the Scouts and the Protestant youth groups within eighteen months of the seizure of power (the Catholics lingered on until 1939), Schirach adroitly incorporated many of their leaders into his own apparatus. The resultant organizational machine, backed by vast state support and invested with the 'Youth leads youth' mystique, proved capable of generating a great charge of energy and of eliciting a sacrificial response from millions of young people.

Youth's latent potential for idealism was skilfully aroused by strong emphasis on the collective taking precedence over individuals. Thus, although the Hitler Youth placed an enormous premium on sporting prowess and endurance, it disparaged athletes who were only concerned with breaking records and unwilling to subordinate themselves to a team. Another competitive sphere in which the emphasis was deflected away from the individual was that of the Winter Relief collections. Results, as communicated to the branches of the Hitler Youth and the German Girls' League, never stated the amount credited to individual members, only the total achieved by the branch as a whole. Similarly, on excursions, participants were made to place their sandwiches or cakes in a common pool, from which each was given an equal share. The aim was not the fostering of self-regard, but of a readiness to sacrifice, and was related to attempts made in the wider sphere of German society to breathe life into the high-sounding notion of the folk community.

Early on in the Third Reich, as we have seen, grammar-school boys ceremoniously burnt their multi-coloured caps, in token of the disappearance of class distinctions.[44] A scarcely unhoped-for expression of the spirit of the folk community inside the Hitler Youth was the baiting of 'posh-spoken' grammar-school boys by working-class Hitler Youth leaders;[45] but this, too, was a feature of the earlier period: before membership became compulsory (and thereby universal) in 1936, the leadership had largely consisted of apprentices and shop clerks. After this date about 50 per cent of the higher ranks were drawn from the respectable bourgeoisie; of the rest half were students and graduates.[46]

In fact, within the Hitler Youth the concept of the folk community quite often fell short of realization. Planned outings might not be carried out because the parents of poorer members were unable to raise the fare money; in the summer middle-class children would holiday *en famille* in comfortable hotels while the underprivileged camped under canvas.[47] Up to the mid-thirties, at any rate, the quasi-compulsory Hitler Youth membership of their children embarrassed poorer parents, who had difficulties in paying for the obligatory uniform and in keeping up the monthly subscriptions.

An additional factor militating against the homogeneity of the Hitler Youth was young people's tendency to strike up friendships among school mates and neighbourhood children rather than with fellow group members. Though the Hitler Youth thus failed to fuse sociologically disparate elements, it did obviate class differences to the extent of letting underprivileged youngsters compensate via athletic proficiency or advancement within the command structure.

By a process of analogy adolescent attachment as such to the Hitler Youth was motivated by compensation for dependence feelings in an adult-dominated world. The whole panoply of uniforms, drill and officiousness was bound to heighten young people's self-esteem. The resultant dramatization of their self-image was so much a part of the climate of the Third Reich that it inspired an outcrop of jokes. The continuously reiterated slogan, 'Youth leads youth' was neatly parodied in the story of a policeman who encountered a helplessly sobbing small boy in the street: the mite was crying because he had lost his way; the policeman asked him what he was doing so far away from home, to be answered, in between sobs, 'I've just been to a leadership conference.'

When plans for organizing children below the age of ten in the Hitler Youth were publicized, popular wags suggested 'A-A men' as the appropriate abbreviation for the projected units ('*A-A*' is German baby-talk for excrement and the whole was a play on the words: 'S A men', i.e. Storm Troopers). Occasionally reality could be more rib-tickling than invention. The mother of a ten-year-old Hitler Youth, who had asked her son to play with the little girl from next door, was given this answer: 'It's out of the question. I'm in uniform.'[48]

Equally comic, though less spontaneous, was this official definition of the difference between a child and a *Pimpf* (a member of the *Jungvolk*, the ten- to fourteen-year-old group of the Hitler Youth): 'The term "child" describes the non-uniformed creature who has never participated in a group meeting or a route march.'[49] A *Pimpf*'s initiation test, after which he received his first dagger, consisted of the reiteration of highly compressed synopses of Nazi dogma ('*Schwertworte*') and of all the verses of the 'Horst Wessel Song', a map-reading exercise, participation in pseudo-war games (*Geländeübungen*) and collection drives for waste paper, scrap metals, and so on, as well as the following sporting achievements: running 60 metres in twelve seconds, a long jump of 2·75 metres, putting the shot and participating in a cross-country route march that lasted a day and a half.[50] After staying in the *Jungvolk* until fourteen, during which period he learnt semaphore reading, bicycle repairs, the laying of telephone wires and small arms drill (including practice with dummy hand grenades, air guns and small-bore rifles) the *Pimpf* joined the Hitler Youth proper.

The *Kern* or nucleus of the Hitler Youth catering for the bulk of the fourteen-to-eighteen-year-olds was not, by any stretch of the imagination, an élite formation. Most of its members had left school and were thus no longer subject to the writ of the education authorities. All of them were

Jungvolk veterans, and four years of strenuous attendance, drill and fairly monotonous activities had eroded their early enthusiasm, so that the prevailing tone was coarse and reminiscent of a non-commissioned officers' mess.[51] Morale certainly compared unfavourably with that of such crack formations as the motorized Hitler Youth, the marine Hitler Youth, the Hitler Youth Gliding Corps and the wartime Hitler Youth Patrol Service; during the war, 700,000 Hitler Youths were trained in fire-fighting and formed auxiliary fire brigades in areas under Allied air attack.[52]

The BdM (*Bund deutscher Mädchen* – German Girls' League) was the female counterpart of the Hitler Youth. Up to the age of fourteen girls were known as Young Girls (*Jungmädel*) and from seventeen to twenty-one, as we have seen, they formed a special voluntary organization called Faith and Beauty (*Glaube und Schönheit*). The duties demanded of *Jungmädel* were regular attendance at club premises and sports meetings, participation in journeys and camp life, memorizing data about the Führer and his henchmen during the 'period of struggle', learning all verses of the Deutschland and 'Horst Wessel Song', the high holy days of the Nazi Party, the names of Hitler Youth martyrs, an outline map of Germany, the significance and details of the Treaty of Versailles, facts about German minorities scattered throughout the world, as well as local history, customs and sagas. Added physical requirements were running 60 metres in twelve seconds, a 2½-metre long jump, throwing a ball over a distance of 20 metres, somersaulting, tightrope walking, two hours' route-marching, or swimming 100 metres.[53] The League attached special importance to achievements connected with 'journeys'. Each *Jungmädel* had to have participated in Youth Hostel week-ends, had to have a knowledge of bed-making and of packing standard equipment, and to have taken part in fatigues and chores at the hostel.

After the age of fourteen, the attachment of girls to the League tended to grow somewhat tenuous; school-leavers' interests were increasingly engaged by their jobs, as well as by the opposite sex, and since girls mature more quickly, they did not find the company of boys of their own age in parallel Hitler Youth formations very stimulating. But Faith and Beauty managed to elicit a rather keener response from girls between seventeen and twenty-one by a programme of physical culture, eurhythmics, health instruction and domestic science. Faith and Beauty also paid particular attention to fashion consciousness and feminine aesthetics in general, although – as we have seen – scope in these spheres was rather circumscribed. The ideal League type exemplified early nineteenth-century

notions of what constituted the essence of maidenhood. Girls who in-
fringed the code by perming their hair instead of wearing plaits or the
'Gretchen' wreath of braids had it ceremoniously shaved off as a punishment. The general pre-Raphaelite aura was enhanced by white blouses,
dark scarves, virtually ankle-length skirts and sturdy shoes. (Every so often,
however, fashion claimed its own: in 1936 the sudden vogue of the Olympia roll took a toll of thousands of plaits, and just before the war calf-
length boots were becoming popular.)[54]

The image of the Hitler Youth and the Girls' League in the public mind
tended to waver. Early on there was a widespread impression that lack of
supervision and meaningful activities produced general unruliness. In 1933
Hitler Youth units resembled armed bands waging furious internecine
warfare with air guns, and youngsters would limp home to distraught
parents, with sprained limbs and other scars of battle. Numerous Hitler
Youth evenings degenerated into free-for-alls or a quite meaningless killing of time.[55] The official preoccupation with physical fitness encouraged
lads to indulge in reckless endurance tests and to overtax their physical
resources, eventually forcing the Hitler Youth leadership to take energetic
counter-measures.[56]

The leadership also tightened up discipline, instituted a 'schooling campaign' to correct glaring educational deficiencies* in 1934, and early in the
war launched a special politeness drive (during which members we
exhorted to perform boy-scout type good deeds).

All these measures helped to transform the image of the Hitler Youth
into a rather positive one – after all, the lads in it were being subjected to
discipline, were trained in hardihood and made to perform useful chores.
Even so, the Hitler Youth cannot be said to have enjoyed an esteem
comparable to the Wehrmacht – the time-honoured 'school of the
nation'.

The image of the German Girls' League tended to be the object of a
tug-of-war between published opinion and public opinion. A typical
League Press photograph[57] featured a circle of blonde maidens holding
hands in a meadow, intoning a secular blessing over food they were about
to share. The accompanying shot showed the same group resting amidst
flowers in positions of idyllic repose while one of their number played the
flute. Sections of the public tended to see the League in quite a different
light, however, and invested its very initials with obscene meanings (see
p. 335).

* This is dealt with more fully in the chapter on education, p. 292.

It is hard to establish to what degree popular opinion was justified in ascribing a general aura of sexual laxity to the League. The degree of parental supervision naturally diminished as young people went to camp and hostels for long periods of time. In 1936, when approximately 100,000 members of the Hitler Youth and the Girls' League attended the Nuremberg Rally, 900 girls between fifteen and eighteen returned home pregnant.[58] (It was an ironic comment on the mammoth structure of the organization that the subsequent investigations by the authorities failed to establish paternity in 400 of these cases.) The League's reputation could not but be affected by such rumours, and every so often discipline was tightened up to the extent of enforcing a rigid separation of the sexes. But the sexual apartheid nurtured a sense of estrangement and the leadership found itself throwing out the baby – i.e. the socializing influence of the interplay between boys and girls – with the bathwater. In places it learned its lesson. Thus in 1938 the Ulm district of the Hitler Youth congratulated itself upon the organization of mixed social evenings with dancing which, according to a Press statement, 'had a more beneficial effect on the relationship between boys and girls than any number of exhortations and lectures'.[59]

Yet it was precisely by means of exhortation that – especially in war-time – League girls were persuaded to avail themselves of the services offered by *Lebensborn* so that they might 'donate a child to the Führer'. Quite apart from this officially (though clandestinely) sponsored form of immorality, sexual misdemeanours constituted a dynamic segment of the Third Reich's rising juvenile delinquency problem.

Offences dealt with by the courts after the seizure of power increased 300 per cent in three years (from 779 in 1934 to 2,374 in 1937)[60] and reached seven times their 1934 level by 1942. One of the inescapable reasons for this increase was alluded to by the Nazi Women's League's monthly journal in 1938.

It must be seriously considered whether the character of our youth is not profoundly affected by pornography and illustrated sex crimes displayed at every street corner. Youngsters cluster round, and one hears the most obscene comments and perverse questions.[61]

Although the allusion was to the display boxes of *Der Stürmer*, for obvious reasons the journal had to belie its grandiose title – *Die Deutsche Kämpferin* (The German Woman Fighter) and refrain from actually dotting the i's and crossing the t's of its pronouncement.

A comparable form of mealy-mouthedness afflicted the SD in reporting the wartime behaviour of girls in the League age-range.

The moral deterioration among young girls is especially evident in areas where units of the Wehrmacht or of the Reich Labour Service are stationed. The undignified sexual importuning by girls who, in many instances, are still of school age is an expression of the admiration they feel for the soldierly estate.[62]

As far as the Hitler Youth was concerned, the sexual problem did not loom unduly large for the simple reason that its activities were so orientated towards unleashing the libido in a competitive, aggressive direction that erotic impulses tended to be sublimated.

Side by side with aggression, the Hitler Youth cultivated a romantically macabre form of cosiness, as evidenced by this description of some *Jungvolk* premises:[63]

The inscription in huge letters on the wall reads 'Be fighters'. The leader picks up a guitar and the group sing songs of defiance (Trotzlieder). From the works of the heath poet, Herman Löns, a lad reads a chapter dealing with the blood bath on the river Auer. Then another distributes stencilled texts from a folder – a piece for choral speaking which the group have composed themselves. The chief items in the room are a bookshelf with volumes of prescribed literature open at the pages where passages relevant to the weekly theme set by the Reich Youth Leader are to be found, and the People's Radio Receiver (*Volksempfänger*) on which broadcasts of important speeches and Party ceremonies are listened to collectively. A curtain separates the special sanctum from the rest of the premises. In that consecrated area, the wall space is draped in black and the '*Siegrune*' (the runic flash of lightning which was the Hitler Youth emblem) stands out white against a stark surface. Flags are suspended from chains, there is a wreath, a dented steel helmet, a photograph of a Hitler Youth killed in battle, guttering candles, and the text of the 'Horst Wessel Song' is emblazoned on a large poster surmounted by a votive slogan.

Even though a *Jungvolk* lair of this sort closely approximated to the ideal Nazi youth environment, it still fell short of the total *ambience* that could be created in the setting of a camp. Hitler Youth camps were characterized* by an extreme attention to military forms and procedures, which

---

* Two other characteristics were Spartanism and a Big Brother atmosphere. Thus a reporter from the *Liverpool Echo* in 1936 described dinner in the officers' quarters in a Hitler Youth camp as consisting of soup and bread, adding, 'The big brother atmosphere was made palpably real by such devices as forcing boys to post letters to their parents unsealed through a slot in the officers' tent so that they could be duly inspected and censored.' cf. *Liverpool Echo*, 5 September 1936.

ranged all the way from the perfect linear arrangement of tents to a pre-occupation with sentry duties, reveille, watchwords and so on, which on occasion could have lethal consequences. A sentry at Grimma in Saxony, shot a ten-year-old *Pimpf* who had failed to memorize the password.[64] Questioned by the police, the fourteen-year-old murderer stated that he had felt compelled to use his revolver when confronted with a spy who had infiltrated into the camp.

In fact, the Hitler Youth acquainted children with lethal weapons on a scale unprecedented in history. Nearly a million Hitler Youths participated in shooting competitions in 1938,[65] and early in the war lads of ten were instructed in the use of dummy hand grenades at children's homes.[66] Ideally the *Pimpf* was to experience the whole genesis of modern weapons from blowpipes and clubs through swords and pikes right up to small-bore rifles by graduating from simpler to more complex ones as time went on.[67] This form of conditioning reached its climax when – in the words of the official manual – 'during military manœuvres, youngsters stand with yearning eyes behind blazing machine-guns'.[68]

During the concluding stages of the war this phrase achieved an un-dreamt-of actuality alongside such *obiter dicta* of Hitler Youth philosophers as 'Towards the ultimate truth, there leads but a small gate inscribed with the old Samurai saying, "Through the door of death we enter the door of true life"'; and 'He who does not risk his life to gain it ever anew is already dead, though he still breathes, eats and drinks. Death is only a departure for the sake of a higher life.'[69]

The pithiest summing-up of the Hitler Youth ethos, however, was a slogan simply stating, 'We are born to die for Germany'.[70] Even so, death did not obtrude unduly on the fantasy life of German youngsters, for although preparation for death was the ultimate purpose of Hitler Youth training, it was constantly overlaid by life-affirming activities such as sport and music, collecting charity contributions or waste materials, helping to bring in the harvest, or gathering berries, mushrooms and wild fruit. Another significant aspect of all Hitler Youth activities was their sheer, stupefying size. To take a purely administrative example, the centrally published fortnightly 'club night' folders, providing guidelines and material for group meetings, increased in circulation from 100,000 in 1934 to 620,000 in 1939.[71]*

---

* In that year the Hitler Youth leadership corps consisted of 8,000 full-time officers and 765,000 part-time officers and NCOs. (Full-time leaders started on an initially quite austere salary of 80 marks a month) (cf. Werner Klose, *op. cit.,* pp. 79 and 187).

It was this very mammoth structure that increasingly alienated young-sters, as the enthusiasm and personal contact that had characterized the early Hitler Youth turned into the depersonalized routine of a giant apparatus. Those alienated adolescents hardly formed a political under-ground; they were young people in a state of non-political rebellion against such mandatory Hitler Youth activities as drill, PT, open-air games and political indoctrination. They formed cliques to pursue such perfectly natural youthful hobbies as dancing, listening to records and frequenting cafés. In wartime Hamburg the 400-strong illicit 'swing club' was broken up by the police, who arrested more than sixty – mainly middle-class – members. They had committed a triple offence: forming a clique, indulging in dancing (which was banned whenever a military campaign was in progress) and identifying with the enemy by affecting shag pipes and long cigarette holders, wearing slit jackets with check patterns, and listening to decadent swing music.[72] Others would go on hikes wearing motley clothes that the irate Hitler Youth leadership re-ferred to as 'robber's mufti' (*Räuberzivil*). They formed coteries sporting romantic names redolent of the Middle Ages or the Wild West and chose the edelweiss (probably because of its association with the idea of purity and aloofness*) as their emblem; although lacking a positive political ideology, some of their members risked sentences of imprisonment by painting it on walls and hoardings.

Lastly, there were delinquent cliques whose conduct, though overtly entirely criminal, did not lack a certain flavour of opposition. The '*Stäu-ber*' of Danzig, for instance, whom Günther Grass describes in *The Tin Drum*, waylaid soldiers on leave to rob them of their small-arms, paybooks and medals, stole petrol canisters from ack-ack emplacements, and assaulted leaders of the Girls' League in the blackout. One of the by-products of the spread of wartime delinquency, incidentally, was the regime's redefinition of the term 'youth'. Under a decree of 4 October 1939[73] young offenders of sixteen and upwards were moved from the jurisdiction of juvenile courts to the full rigour of the adult penal code, should 'their mental or moral development put them on a par with adults'.

* As an opposition motif, the edelweiss was far better known in the Third Reich than the white rose of Hans and Sophie Scholl, despite the latter's far more clearcut resistance pro-gramme. The Scholls, incidentally, had been strongly influenced by the pre-1933 Youth Movement, as had such outstanding Resistance figures as Stauffenberg, Trott zu Solz, Hau-bach and Reichwein (cf. H. G. Adlow, *Die Erfahrung der Ohnmacht*, Europäische Verlagsan-stalt, Frankfurt, 1964, p. 128).

Though passed for purely deterrent purposes, this law exemplified the distortion of the whole life-cycle of youth under the Nazi regime.* For girls this meant earlier marriage and initiation into sex in general; for boys, progressively earlier mobilization and acquaintance with death. Yet, even though of all Germans the young were most deeply influenced and affected by Nazism, they did not display any marked long-term effect of this experience. Such is the resilience of youth that the *Werwolf* spectre of last-ditch fanatics conjured up by the Hitler Youth leadership in defeat remained a myth, and that, when the Allies initiated their (occasionally maladroit) post-war education schemes it was found that the Hitler Youth generation did not differ significantly from any other sub-group of German society in the intensity of its attachment to the deposed National Socialist deity.

* In 1937 delegates of the British Board of Education had reported that 'young people of Germany are being subjected to intense nervous strain – we were impressed by the tenseness and seriousness of expression among young people at school and in the Hitler Youth' (cf. *The Times*, 2 July 1937).

19

EDUCATION

The influence of Germany's educational system on her national fortunes invites comparison with that of the playing-fields of Eton on the Battle of Waterloo. It was in the classrooms that the foundations were laid for Bismarck's victories over Danes, Austrians and French abroad and over German parliamentarians at home. It could be said of the teachers that they had *travaillé pour le roi de Prusse* both in the metaphorical and the purely literal sense of the phrase: they earned meagre salaries and inculcated an ethos of Prusso-German patriotism.

This they largely contrived to do even when the Empire had followed the Kingdom of Prussia into the limbo of history. Though after 1918 some (mainly elementary) teachers supported the Social Democrats or middle-of-the-road political parties, the schools in general acted as incubators of nationalism under the Weimar Republic. The choice of Hans Grimm's *Volk ohne Raum (People without Space)* as a standard matriculation text reflected a virtually nation-wide consensus among teachers of German language and literature, while schoolboys would inject new topicality and *frisson* into the game of Cowboys and Indians by calling it 'Aryans and Jews'; by 1931 Jewish communal newspapers were publishing lists of schools where children suffered less exposure to anti-Semitism so that parents could arrange transfers.

Given this overall educational atmosphere, the Nazi rulers saw little need for radical innovation after the seizure of power; apparent continuity had the dual advantage of conserving resources and reassuring conservative opinion. Thus there was little surface disturbance of the routine of education. Few teachers were dismissed (among those who were, some of the non-Jews were reinstated during the subsequent shortage) and a sizeable proportion of old textbooks remained in use for the time being. One drastic new departure, which, however, only affected the top strata of the school population, stemmed from the regime's law against the overcrowding of German schools and universities, which in January 1934 froze the female share of diminishing university places at 10 per cent.[1] At the academic level the resultant contraction was quite drastic. By the outbreak of war, university enrolment as such had declined by almost three-fifths* and the number of grammar-school pupils had been reduced by under one-fifth.†

Within the grammar-school population, the proportion of girls was reduced from 35 per cent to 30 per cent.† In 1934 only 1,500 out of 10,000 girls who had taken the *Abitur* were allowed to proceed to university, and up to the outbreak of war the number of girls taking the school-leaving examination remained well below the pre-1933 average.[2] When new boarding-schools for rearing a Nazi élite (the *Nationalpolitische Erziehungs-anstalten* or National Political Educational Establishments – 'Napolas' for short) were set up, the allocation of places for girls was given such low priority that only two out of thirty-nine Napolas constructed before the outbreak of war catered for them.[3]

Girls staying on at higher schools were shunted into either domestic-science or language streams,‡ the former leading up to an examination that became derisively known as 'Pudding Matric', and represented an academic dead-end. The inadequacy of these arrangements occasioned widespread discontent. In 1941 girls who had obtained the 'Pudding Matric' at last became eligible for university studies in the same way as their colleagues who had gone through the language stream.[4] So keen was the competition for the limited academic career opportunities available that sixth-formers on occasion even resorted to denouncing classmates to the Gestapo.

Denunciation also constituted an ever-present occupational hazard for teachers, since low marks or adverse comments on essays lifted verbatim from articles in the Nazi Press could be construed as evidence of political opposition. In actual fact, however, the teaching profession represented one of the most politically reliable sections of the population. Ninety-seven per cent of all teachers were enrolled in the Nazi Teachers' Association (the *Nationalsozialistische Lehrerbund* or NSLB), and as early as 1936 (i.e. before the moratorium on Party recruitment after the seizure of power

* Fifty-seven per cent between 1933 and 1939 (cf. David Schoenbaum, *Germany's Social Revolution*, Weidenfeld and Nicolson, London, 1967, p. 274).

† In 1931 there had been 494,950 boys and 255,234 girls at grammar schools. In 1940 the number was 441,390 boys and 187,809 girls (cf. *Statistisches Handbuch für Deutschland 1949*, pp. 619–21).

‡ Girls in the language streams were obliged to take qualifying examinations in domestic science (cf. Rolf Eilers, *Die Nationalsozialistische Schulpolitik*, Westdeutscher, Verlag, Cologne/Opladen, 1963, p. 20).

was lifted) 32 per cent of all NSLB members belonged to the Nazi Party; this incidence of Party membership was nearly twice as high as that found among the Nazi Civil Servants' Association.[5]

Fourteen per cent of teachers compared to 6 per cent of civil servants belonged to the Party's political leadership corps. This remarkable commitment to the regime was exemplified in the highest ranks of the Party hierarchy by seventy-eight District Leaders and seven Gauleiter (and deputy Gauleiter) who had graduated from the teaching profession. It also found expression in the schoolmasterly, moralizing tone which – as we have noted elsewhere – informed so many Nazi utterances. The Party image also benefited from the presence of many teachers at the grass-roots level of its organization, where they acted as 'notabilities' (*Respektspersonen*), masking the more disreputable elements entrenched in the local apparatus. (The alacrity with which teachers – many of them, incidentally, former Social Democrats – accepted Party posts inspired the following quip: 'What is the shortest measurable unit of time? The time it takes a grade-school teacher to change his political allegiance.')

Even so, not all teachers were absolute conformists, and the regime forbore to exercise overt surveillance over lessons, since even the views of non-Nazis in the teaching profession often overlapped sufficiently with official dogma to render this unnecessary. For instance, a monarchist history master at a Munich Grammar School who could not bring himself to expatiate on the glories of the 'days of struggle', was never taken to task for glossing over the Munich Putsch and Horst Wessel: it sufficed that his lessons were laced with personal recollections of the First World War and the suppression of the Bavarian Soviet in 1919, as well as with fulminations against Weimar.[6]

In addition, although there was no surveillance of class-room lessons, indoctrination was virtually inescapable. By 1938 two-thirds of the country's entire teaching force had been to camp, attending compulsory one-month training courses where the unaccustomed surroundings, the drill and the lectures all tended towards the depersonalization of participants.[7] The style of living at these camps was one of enforced youthfulness, the intention being that participants should feel closer to their youthful charges after returning to school.[8] The mental efforts they had to make in this direction were supplemented by physical ones: all members of the teaching profession below the age of fifty were pressed into compulsory PT courses.[9]

By analogy, sport also achieved unprecedented importance in school curricula. The normal timetable allocation of PT periods was increased from two to three in 1936 and – at the expense of religious instruction – to five in 1938. As a discipline PT was enlarged both in scope and academic standing: cross-country running, football and boxing (which was made compulsory in upper schools)[10] were incorporated in it, and it became an examination subject for grammar-school entry as well as for the school-leaving certificate. Persistently unsatisfactory performance at PT constituted grounds for expulsion from school and for debarment from further studies.[11] Games masters advanced from the periphery of the teaching body almost to the very centre; it was their comment on a report that informed the parent of his child's character development, and the suggestion was seriously put forward that the PT instructor at each school should be automatically appointed deputy headmaster.[12]

Other subjects to be upgraded were history, biology and German (whose subject specialists had long been professionally disposed towards Teutomania). The Nazi approach to the teaching of German involved a preoccupation with Nordic sagas and the Germanization of loan-words; essays required the regurgitation of propaganda hand-outs, as exemplified by the theme of an essay set for school-leavers, 'The educational value of the Reich Labour Service'.[13]

Another innovation in this subject was the devising of new reading matter for various age-groups. The youngest, between nine and twelve (the 'Robinson Crusoe' group), were no longer to be regaled with fairy stories, animal tales and the like, but to make the acquaintance of World War and Hitler Youth epics. 'The monstrosity oozes forward with stinking breath, roaring, greedy, possessed. Impudent and unsoldierly, timid and cowardly, unconcerned and arrogant, the mutineers ascend. They spit at the officers who stand there with iron faces.'[14] So ran an excerpt from a book called *The Mutiny of the Fleets in 1918*, designed for the ten- to twelve-year-olds. A book entitled *The Battle of Tannenberg* and aimed at fourteen-year-olds included this cameo: 'A Russian soldier tried to bar the infiltrator's way, but Otto's bayonet slid gratingly between the Russian's ribs, so that he collapsed groaning. There it lay before him, simple and distinguished, his dream's desire, the Iron Cross.'[15]

As if to compensate for the diminished importance of religious instruction in the curriculum, history offered a variation on the catechism in a special course on the Nazi Party's *Kampfzeit* which was grafted on to the normal syllabus.

The importance of biology was derived from the special emphasis the regime placed on race and heredity. Pupils were trained to measure their skulls and to classify each other's racial types. One incongruous aspect of Nazi biology teaching was the taboo on sexual instruction that accompanied the fetish made of the Mendelian law. Sex instruction was, in fact, declared to be outside the province both of school and the Hitler Youth. The educational authorities limited their concern to influencing parents in the right direction* and the Hitler Youth similarly defined the parental home as 'centre of gravity of moral education'.† But, as if to repair this omission, fourteen-year-old boys and girls leaving school were handed a ten-point eugenic *vade mecum*, which bade them marry only for love and offered this advice on the choice of a spouse: 'Health is a precondition of external beauty – choose not a playmate but a comrade for marriage – wish for as many children as possible.'[16]

While mathematics teaching remained much as before, Nazi ideologists adroitly seized on the opportunity for subliminal conditioning presented by the wording of problems, so that a head for figures was now developed by questions about artillery trajectories, fighter-to-bomber ratios and budget deficits accruing from the democratic pampering of hereditarily diseased families.

The erosion of religious instruction occurred after the regime's deceptive initial solicitude for religion. In 1933, *Sammelschulen* (i.e. elementary schools without religious instruction in their curriculum) were dissolved and enrolment of their children in religious instruction courses was made mandatory upon all parents,[17] but in 1935 religious instruction ceased to be a subject for the school-leaving examination and attendance at school prayers was made optional.[18] Two years later, priests were debarred from taking religious classes at school and shortly afterwards timetables were re-arranged in such a manner that religious instruction lessons occurred either at the beginning or the end of morning sessions – an obvious inducement to truancy. At the same time the option to drop the subject was placed partly within the child's own prerogative.‡ Religious instruction

* Education Minister Rust in the *Frankfurter Zeitung*, 19 August 1938: 'The school's task lies in the sphere of influencing parents at meetings and lectures, but should they fail to do the right thing, the teacher or school doctor will have to step in.'

† Hitler Youth Judge Tetzlaff, as quoted in the *Frankfurter Zeitung*, 20 November 1938: 'The centre of gravity of moral education is the parental home. The Hitler Youth eschews any mass enlightenment programme but its leaders are instructed about the dreadful consequences of homosexuality at special courses.'

‡ This was accompanied by a campaign inside the Hitler Youth to influence members into dropping the subject of religion, while the Nazi Teachers' Association appealed to its members to stop taking religious instruction (cf. Rolf Eilers, *op. cit.*, p. 25).

lessons were reduced to one per week for the twelve-plus group, and during the war the over-fourteens stopped having these altogether. Before that the subject disappeared from school reports; weekly morning assemblies were drained of all religious significance and turned into straightforward Party ceremonies. During the mid-thirties an important change in the pattern of religious education occurred in largely Catholic Bavaria, where the Party managed through propaganda* backed by intimidation to shift parents from their attachment to Church schools; out of ninety-three Munich elementary schools, seventy-six were converted into inter-denominational community schools within two years.[19]

While clerical influence was being diminished, 'brainworkers' as a whole – including teachers – were similarly affected. The profession's gradual loss of public esteem after 1933 was related to the anti-intellectual mood engendered by the Nazis' transformation of all traditional values. Teachers and priests tended to be the only members of village communities with educational qualifications above elementary or trade-school level – i.e. the only ones accustomed to conceptual thinking. Nazi egalitarianism – 'we think with our blood' – encompassed a pseudo-revolution across a wide segment of rural society by inflating the self-esteem of villagers, while simultaneously lowering that of teachers.[20]

In an analogous manner the Third Reich inflated the self-esteem of pupils *vis-à-vis* their teachers (or parents come to that); the younger generation had to be axiomatically in the right because the future belonged to them.[21] Baldur von Schirach drew a contrast between glowingly inspired youth marching forward to the new dawn and pedantically stupid schoolmasters. Even so, over 11,000 of the latter acted as part-time Hitler Youth officials, though it would still be true to say that the majority of teachers tended to view the Hitler Youth with a certain amount of reserve. The 11,000 worked mainly in the country, where pressure could be most easily exerted; or else they were reluctant to let the Hitler Youth take complete charge of their pupils' leisure-time activities. Additional part-time chores demanded of teachers in rural areas† were librarianship – in connection with the Ministry of Education project for a network of volunteer-staffed

* Part of the propaganda material against Roman Catholic schools was derived from the current show-trials of members of monastic houses on charges such as homosexuality or embezzlement.

† In parishes too small to have their own priest, teachers often acted as preachers and delivered the sermon on alternate Sundays (cf. Milton Mayer, *They Thought They Were Free*, Chicago University Press, 1955, p. 107).

People's Libraries* – and clerical work for the local administration (during the war the call-up of teachers was to deprive many rural communities of their town clerks).[22]

It was not merely that teachers' energies were overtaxed by extra-curricular duties and an increase in the pupil/teacher ratio (the average number of elementary-school pupils went up from thirty-nine to a class to forty-five between 1931 and 1939);[23] the very *raison d'être* of teaching was insidiously undermined by the existence of the Hitler Youth. The programme of the Hitler Youth was such that it appealed to the childish psyche in a much more immediate manner than the learning process, with its dependence on steady and methodical maturation. Pupils were physically exhausted because of their involvement in Hitler Youth activities, and exhibited a sense of unrest and an inability to settle into the routine of school work after the excitement of a march, a competition or a collection drive.

The pupil/teacher situation was also the setting for abrasive contact between conflicting forms of hierarchy (which were to continue an uneasy coexistence throughout the Third Reich): one of these was based on academic standing, and the other on the intensity of political commitment. Extreme tact was therefore officially enjoined upon the teaching body in its treatment of Hitler Youth leaders, lest they damage their standing in the eyes of fellow-pupils (Hitler Youth leaders, naturally, had great difficulty in subordinating themselves to authority in school time, while exercising it themselves out of school). In Pomerania and elsewhere specially appointed teachers had to arrange crammer courses, so that educationally laggard Hitler Youth leaders could keep up with their classmates.[24]

By decreeing that any reference to political activity be omitted from school reports, Schirach prevented teachers from explaining – as well as remedying – the reasons for frequent unsatisfactory performance. One teacher trustee of the Hitler Youth in every staffroom was deputed to plead the cause of Hitler Youths whose scholarly records were unsatisfactory and to prevent their relegation to lower forms.[25] School authorities were instructed to grant pupils leave of absence to enable them to attend Hitler Youth courses.[26]

The cumulative effect of extra-mural distractions on education – at a Westphalian school of 870 pupils, 23,000 school days were lost through

* Under this scheme every parish of over 500 inhabitants was to have its own library. Full-time trained librarians were only to be appointed in places where the population exceeded 20,000 (cf. *Frankfurter Zeitung*, 30 October 1937).

avoidable disturbances during the 1937–8 session[27] – made the authorities initiate a series of none too effective counter-measures. To redress the imbalance between *mens sana* and *corpus sanum*, the Hitler Youth called 1934 its 'Year of Schooling' and tried to wean its members from their habitual – but self-defeating – anti-intellectualism by redefining an intellectual as 'someone imbued with a passion for investigation and thought'.[28] Rather more helpfully, the executive decree to the Hitler Youth Law, promulgated in the spring of 1939, empowered grammar schools to apply for a pupil's exemption from Hitler Youth duties if his scholastic performance ruled out additional burdens.[29] Notwithstanding these palliatives, the gap in pupils' knowledge yawned ever wider and official rationalizations did little but paper them over perfunctorily. One such bromide stated:

The range of examinees has been greatly extended, so that a larger proportion of less-endowed candidates submit themselves for examination; at the same time, the type of question set reveals a concept of general knowledge which has become highly problematical, since it bears no relation to the concrete life of people nowadays. The amount of crammed knowledge has been reduced, but not the thoroughness of its assimilation. Methods of education are more natural, the relationship between teachers and pupils is more comradely and, in assessing a pupil, note is taken not only of achievements in individual subjects but of his general maturity.[30]

While the Nazi Teachers' Association thus made much of advances in the direction of the folk community, the Wehrmacht put another gloss on the low standard of recruits. 'Our youth starts off with perfectly correct principles in the physical sphere of education, but frequently refuses to extend this to the mental sphere.' Having said which, the army proceeded to state with military forthrightness: 'Many of the candidates applying for commissions display a simply inconceivable lack of elementary knowledge.'[31]

In 1940, the SD reported an all-round decline in pupils' performance which was most marked at elementary and vocational schools; although the war was partly to blame, the SD postulated a steady downward trend, dating back two to three years.[32] During the war it became customary for universities to submit new undergraduates to sixth-form refresher courses; university lecturers bore out the SD's report about steady deterioration of scholarly standards by stating that men on study leave after years at the front showed fewer gaps in their knowledge than freshmen newly arrived from grammar schools.

The vocational and technical schools similarly complained they were unable to cover the prescribed curriculum because of the need to make good deficiencies dating back to elementary school. A Hamburg newspaper asked plaintively, 'Is our youth getting more stupid?' It announced that, at a local apprentice examination, out of a total of 179 entrants, ninety-four had spelt proper names without capital letters and eighty-one had been unable to spell the name of Goethe, Germany's foremost poet.[33] These manifestations of semi-illiteracy become more explicable in the light of the dilution of the teaching profession. At one vocational school, for instance, no more than thirty out of 166 timetable periods were taken by qualified teachers in 1942.[34]

The gradually increasing teacher shortage in the Third Reich was a function of two complementary processes: the migration of teachers into better-paid branches of the educational service, into the Party apparatus or the Wehrmacht officer corps (vide the saying, 'The war won't be over until the last elementary schoolmaster has got his commission') and the drop (in quality and in quantity) in recruitment, due to the profession's loss of status. None of these factors applied absolutely, however. Grammar-school teaching, for instance, continued to be highly regarded as well as over-subscribed. Grammar-school masters (Studienassessoren) were the exclusive top stratum of the teaching profession; graduates to a man, they looked upon compulsory membership of the Nazi Teachers' Association, which was led by elementary teachers, as the cross they had to bear under the swastika. The Assessoren were subdivided in turn into permanent and temporary ones, and the unconscionably long time it took probationers to become established – on average, not until just before they turned forty – produced a situation in which three out of five grammar-school masters were still single at the age of thirty-three (as compared to only one in five among the general population).[35] In a memorandum which aimed to make the career of Assessoren less hazardous, the Teachers' Association suggested that pensionable age in the grammar-school service should be reduced to sixty-two in order to create more vacancies, that the size of classes should be reduced, and that if an established teacher was off work sick for any length of time a Studienassessor should be engaged at full pay to replace him.[36]

These suggestions fell on stony ground: in 1938, the authorities reduced the age of university admission from nineteen to eighteen, and the resultant shortening of grammar-school courses by one year obviously militated against any improvement* in the position of temporary

* It also militated against maintaining educational standards that had previously been attained.

Assessoren* The temporary employment of *Studienassessoren* as supernumerary teachers meant that they could be dismissed at a moment's notice, even if they had been at a school for a number of years. The war further exacerbated their feelings of insecurity, since the widows of temporary teachers killed on active service were not entitled to pensions.[37]

Whilst the upper branches of the profession suffered from overcrowding,† elementary and vocational teachers were at a premium. By 1938–9 the elementary teaching force was 17,000 down on its full Weimar complement;[38] in outlying areas like East Prussia, one teaching post in twelve was unfilled.[39] The army, private enterprise and the expanding bureaucracies of Party and state were deflecting entrants from a profession which at the elementary level offered a starting salary of no more than 2,000 marks per annum.[40] After deductions, this worked out at approximately 140 marks per month, or twenty marks more than was earned by the average lower-paid worker.‡

Two years before the outbreak of war Berlin's municipal director of education warned that in the urban centres where lower and middle forms accommodated fifty to sixty pupils, teachers were approaching the limit of their potential. 'This is proved by higher sickness figures, which cannot be traced back to malingering because of the rigorous medical checks involved ... Young people are in danger of losing every incentive for entering the profession.'[41]

Of about 30,000 children taking the *Abitur* who expressed career preferences at the end of that academic year, only 2,300 (7·5 per cent, or half the proportion of would-be officers) chose teaching; this was barely a third of the intake needed to maintain the service at full strength. To offset this diminished recruitment from traditional sources, the authorities

---

* Their female colleagues were, if anything, even worse off, since the partial elimination of girls from higher studies further lengthened the odds against the probationer's establishment; in 1937, out of a total of nearly 4,000 assistant-teachers, a mere 1,600 enjoyed security of tenure – the rest were either temporary or redundant (cf. *Frankfurter Zeitung*, 12 October 1937).

† Though even at this level certain shortages made themselves felt, e.g. the supply of laboratory assistants dried up in 1937 (cf. *Frankfurter Zeitung*, 16 September 1937).

‡ An elementary teacher with an academic training (married but without children) with six years' service earned 269 marks a month, of which he spent 76 marks on rent (for a modern flat), 20 on social insurance and subscriptions, 80 on food, 15 on gas, light and newspapers, 30 on cleaning and laundry – which left him with 35 marks to be spent on clothing, consumer durables, and so on. Realizing the inadequacy of this remuneration, the educational authorities permitted teachers to earn money by spare-time coaching, but if the monthly income from these pursuits exceeded 40 marks, they had to obtain the permission of their superiors.

henceforth tapped the lower educational strata. In 1938 they lowered the entrance requirement for training as an elementary teacher from the *Abitur* to the *Mittlere Reife* (which was at the age of sixteen and was roughly comparable to O-level GCE).[42] In 1940 a 'preparatory course' (*Aufbaulehrgang*) was instituted, by which suitable elementary pupils were selected at fourteen and prepared for teacher's training after the age of eighteen.[43] This meant that whereas previously nobody without a grammar-school education could qualify as a teacher, now an entirely new social segment (especially in the countryside) was made eligible for the teaching profession and the achievement of middle-class status. Emergency measures prompted by the threat of an acute shortage could thus be decked out as equalization of opportunity and the belated fulfilment of the twentieth point of the Nazi Party programme (which was, of course, fundamentally contradicted by the regime's retention of school fees at all levels of education).

The selection of these potential future teachers was in the hands of Party officials and Hitler Youth leaders. Classes on the preparatory courses were grouped together as Hitler Youth units and teachers as well as pupils wore Hitler Youth uniforms.[44] Another and more direct device for overcoming the shortage of teachers, which was exacerbated by the wartime call-up, was the institution of school helpers. Drawn from walks of life that had a purely nominal link with education (for instance, the full-time staff of the German Girls' League or the female Reich Labour Service), school helpers underwent three months' preliminary training, two years' teaching practice, and – if found suitable – a year's instruction leading up to a qualifying examination.[45]

The introduction of unqualified auxiliaries into the schools aroused much adverse comment. In the eyes of parents, school helpers were ne'er-do-wells who, having failed at everything else, were now being let loose upon their children. Elementary teachers saw them as diluted labour further undermining their already tarnished professional status.[46] It was not only in the sphere of teacher-training that the educational authorities carried out wartime experiments. Non-fee-paying High Schools (*Hauptschulen*) were instituted on the assumption that some children, whom financial rather than educational considerations had kept out of grammar schools, constituted a potential reserve for the lower ranks of the professions and the administration. Reactions to the project were mixed: welcomed as a state-subsidized boon for the more gifted section of the elementary-school population, it also aroused fears that the drawing off of the talented top stratum would virtually reduce elementary education to the level of educationally subnormal schools, and would accelerate the drift of young people from the country into the towns. The scheme was discontinued, not least because the Wehrmacht lent its powerful voice to the opposition lobby.[47]

Instability and experiment were also characteristic of other aspects of the educational situation. The large-scale pulping of Weimar textbooks in 1933, for instance, created a partial vacuum that was not adequately filled until the publication of new ones early in the war; in the interim teachers depended on pamphlet substitutes, with such revealing titles as *History in Sub-Headings*. The general lack of resolution clinging to Nazi educational policy was reflected in the quip about Herr Rust, the Reich Minister for Science, Education and Popular Instruction: 'A Rust is the standard unit of measurement for the minimum time elapsing between the passing of a decree and its cancellation.' These oscillations of educational policy were, however, no more than one facet of the regime's general ambivalence. Alongside its unprecedented dynamism, the Third Reich, with Party ranged against state and rival bigwigs locked in near-mortal combat, manifested a staggering degree of procrastination.

The duality of Party and state also coloured the development of the Nazi élite schools, with the Napolas serving as incubators for top-ranking government and army personnel, while the Adolf Hitler Schools were to nurture future political leaders. Conceived as successors to the Prussian cadet academies* and despite a fixed allocation of places for officers' sons and close all-round liaison with the Wehrmacht, the Napolas, which passed under SS control in 1936, developed a completely Nazified ethos. The syllabus was that of ordinary grammar schools with political inculcation in place of religious instruction and a tremendous emphasis on such sports as boxing, war games, rowing, sailing, gliding, shooting, driving motor-boats and riding motor-cycles (as well as motor cars).[48] Lessons were taken in the open as far as possible, and discussions on editorials in the *Völkische Beobachter* formed part of the daily routine.[49] The curriculum was complemented by journeys to various parts of Germany and abroad; in his sixth year every Napola scholar spent six to eight weeks helping a farmer, in the seventh year, the same period working either in a factory or a coalmine. Classes were called 'platoons' and the routine of school life was

* In token of this ancestry the Napola curriculum for top forms included dance evenings with young middle-class ladies in white ball gowns, who carried posies of flowers and wore their hair in plaits, ringlets or braided coronets.

based on that of a military camp, with 'camp fatigues', 'reveille', a communal style of living, and PT drill before breakfast.[50] Under these circumstances it is not surprising that the intellectual level reached was – in the words of the SS Napola administrator Heissmeyer – 'not above but rather below that of the average German grammar school'.[51] An additional drawback was the dearth of textbooks, for which the *Hilf Mit* series published by the Teachers' Association provided only a perfunctory substitute.[52]

The basis of admission to a Napola was quite simple: Hitler Youth membership, good health, high standard of proficiency at PT, incontrovertibly Aryan origin, and sponsorship by the Party district chief. Selection took place after a week's trial, during which all candidates had to submit to tests of physical prowess and endurance and were under constant observation by Napola selectors. In addition, heads of schools ascertained the reliability of parents by personal interviews. The nominal fees were 1,200 marks per annum, but since many deserving old Party members as well as serving officers secured free places for their offspring and a special fund subsidized poorer entrants, the fee paid was in fact as little as 50 marks per year.[53] This helps to explain why, as time went on, Napola recruitment was increasingly drawn from the poorer sections of the population, especially in Catholic areas, where the schools absorbed an intake that might previously have gone into priests' seminaries. The highlight of the Napola year was manoeuvres placing great demands on the physical endurance of the participants.* The war games lasted two days at a stretch and were played out over an area measuring 140 kilometres in diameter. (In them each participant had to tear off his opponent's 'life thread' [*Lebensfaden*].)[54]

To prepare their pupils for these battles, more enterprising heads of schools devised toughening-up exercises, which involved pupils grappling with infuriated Alsatian dogs.[55] Since teachers also participated in these exercises, they were forced to maintain a very high standard of physical fitness to shore up their moral authority.

The Napola system was continuously being expanded. Even during the war, while ordinary school building stagnated, new Napola schools were established, into which the SS drafted the best teachers from the civilian

---

* Addressing 2,500 Napola pupils at Ahrenshoop camp, Minister Rust told them, 'In ancient Persia three things were demanded of the young – riding, archery and truthfulness – and yet Mesopotamia was a paradise with architects, engineers, savants, etc.' (cf. *Frankfurter Zeitung*, 6 July 1938).

sector.[56] In 1942, when there were over two score of them dotted all over the Reich, they were renamed *Deutsche Heimschulen* (German Boarding Schools) and given the additional task of accommodating the children of soldiers killed on active service, government officials and scientists on distant tours of duty.[57]

Although the Napolas came under the aegis of the SS, the Ministry of Education maintained control over academic programmes; the Adolf Hitler Schools broke with this convention entirely. The two branches of the Nazi-created school system also differed in methods of recruitment; whereas it was the parents who initiated Napola applications, the intake into Adolf Hitler schools was a matter of the schools applying for certain pupils pre-selected in the Hitler Youth. The parents were merely involved to the extent of underwriting the *fait accompli*, unless they had the courage or resourcefulness needed to do otherwise. Since Nazi ideology leaned heavily on Darwinist notions, the Party's educational pioneers – like Baldur von Schirach or Robert Ley – liked to talk of the Adolf Hitler Schools institutionalizing the principle of continuous selection.

Having been pre-selected during their second year in the *Jungvolk*, potential Adolf Hitler pupils were racially examined and sent to a fortnight's youth camp for a final sifting. A main criterion of selection was physical appearance; after acceptance, Adolf Hitler scholars were largely evaluated according to qualities of leadership. The Adolf Hitler schools dispensed with many of the ingredients of normal German school routine, such as individual examinations with numerical marks, conduct books, impositions, relegation to lower forms in case of failure, and even reports. In addition, pupils addressed their teachers with the familiar '*Du*' instead of the polite '*Sie*'. Forms were known as 'squads' and each squad was commanded by NCOs drawn from the upper school who exercised the minutest surveillance over pupils' standards of bedmaking, dressing, deportment and personal hygiene. Squads competed with each other and were collectively judged during achievement week, which took the place of examinations.[58] The extreme anti-intellectual bias of the schools was, however, gradually rectified, especially as Heissmeyer had stated publicly in 1939 that 'National Socialism sets insufficient store by knowledge. The knowledge pupils can acquire at Adolf Hitler schools is in every respect inferior to that provided by the best upper schools.'[59]

Whereas the original daily work-load had consisted of five periods of physical training and one and a half periods of intellectual pursuits, which included the study of newspapers, the weekly timetable during the war comprised twenty-two academic and fifteen physical lessons; by 1941 more than half the pupils of the Adolf Hitler schools had passed Common Entrance examinations, and from 1945 onwards intellectual criteria would have weighed as heavily as physical ones. Furthermore, in 1942 Adolf Hitler schools were empowered to award diplomas to their eighteen-year-old graduates, which entitled them to proceed to university.[60]

Not that universities were necessarily the institutions for which Adolf Hitler scholars were destined. The ultimate destination for the élite of Adolf Hitler alumnae were the *Ordensburgen* (castles of the order), finishing schools for the future leadership, endowed with the mystique – and the trappings – of medieval orders of chivalry. The four *Ordensburgen* of Sonthofen, Crössinsee, Vogelsang and Marienburg were established in remote and romantic settings. Both their romanticism and their remoteness were further accentuated by their chilling architectural style. Each *Ordensburg* accommodated a thousand students called 'Junkers' plus 500 instructors, administrative staff and grooms (who waited on the Junkers in white, gold-braided uniforms). Riding was accorded a dominant role in the curriculum – not, in the words of Robert Ley, 'to perpetuate a social prejudice, but because it gives the Junkers the feeling of being able to dominate a living creature entirely'. Ley, who, as organizational chief of the Nazi Party, was the prime mover in the *Ordensburg* programme, struck the note of folk community again and again. 'The *Ordensburg* opens the door to political leadership to the man in the street,' he claimed in a statement which bore the characteristic heading 'The Marshal's baton in one's knapsack';[61] 'We don't ask a candidate "Are you a graduate lawyer?" but "What sort of a *Kerl* (full-blooded man) are you?"' By implication, classlessness in this context also meant eschewing intellectual criteria for selection, and indeed admission to the *Ordensburgen* did not depend on examinations but on a candidate's sponsorship by his local district or Gauleader.

The *Ordensburgen* were impressively equipped. Vogelsang boasted the world's largest gymnasium, in which all the apparatus could rise out of the floor and disappear into it again. At Sonthofen the dining-hall (630 ft long, seating capacity 1,500) had its walls and floors finished in German marble – as did the *Ordenssaal* (hall of the order) – the venue of special celebrations and neo-pagan services.[62]

Ordensburg entrants were in their mid-twenties, having spent six years – from twelve to eighteen – at the Adolf Hitler schools, two and a half years in the Labour Service and the Wehrmacht, and another four acquiring professional qualifications, which in most cases meant that they had been full-time Party officials. Their course of study was peripatetic, taking them to each of the four *Ordensburgen* for a year at a time. At Crössinsee the accent was on athletics, sailing, riding and gliding; at Sonthofen, on skiing and mountaineering; at Vogelsang, on P T; and in the concluding year at Marienburg the Junkers underwent their final physical and spiritual maturation. Discipline was rigorously enforced. The punishment for slight infringements of the rules consisted of compulsory fasting, a deterrent of maximum impact on bodies strained to the limit of physical endurance. At Vogelsang, for instance, Junkers were tested by diving from a thirty-foot springboard, and they had to wash in an icy stream one and a half miles away from their quarters. In winter they were roused in the middle of the night to do open-air P T exercises. War games involved the use of live ammunition and trench-digging in the path of advancing tanks, both of them exercises that were bound to claim fatal casualties.[63]*

Intellectually standards at the *Ordensburgen* were far less rigorous. It was estimated that at Vogelsang about one in every ten Junkers had taken the *Abitur* and only one in a hundred was a university graduate; the average mental calibre was such that a talk on Anglo-German relations went above the heads of 90 per cent of the listeners.[64] But despite the obvious ease with which candidates were admitted, despite the financial inducements, the *Ordensburgen* failed to attract their full complement and frequently operated at no more than two-thirds capacity. Similarly, although *Ordensburg* graduates were intended to provide the Third Reich's upper echelons, the wartime deployment of some of them belied the élitist expectations they doubtless entertained. Many of those who went into the army were casualties, and a significant proportion failed even to receive Wehrmacht commissions. Others, with gaze firmly fixed on the political kingdom, became administrators of the occupied eastern territories – in other words, 'golden pheasants' – the corrupt, contemptible base-wallahs and bogymen of Germany's soldierly folklore during the Second World War.[65]

It was the war, too, that presented the regime with an opportunity for making the traditional sector of education approximate rather more closely to specifically Nazi-sponsored schools. As part of the overall scheme for evacuating the population of bombed towns, the authorities set up children's evacuation camps, i.e. they moved day schools into reception areas,

* The Junkers were educated at public expense, their dependants received a monthly allowance of 100–300 marks, and the Party assumed responsibility for their outstanding debts.

where they continued as boarding institutions. Denied parental visits on emotional grounds and to economize on transport, evacuation-camp children were entirely caught up in their new atmosphere – a climate of para-militarism created by the Hitler Youth functionaries (many of them Wehrmacht veterans) who shared supervisory duties with the teachers. At the camps far more importance was attached to military than to academic discipline: test exercises were written collectively, with examinees freely copying from each other, while a trace of dust discovered in the course of a room inspection occasioned the most rigorous punishment.[66] Inevitably, academic subjects failed to arouse the pupils' interest to anything like the same extent as war games, route marches and weapon training.

The decline of educational standards in wartime was a country-wide phenomenon. Though transfer to evacuation camps affected only pupils in areas threatened by air-raids – actually children whose parents refused to have them evacuated often received no schooling at all – education elsewhere was similarly disturbed by the conscription of senior grammar-school forms for anti-aircraft duties. 'Flak helpers', i.e. sixteen- to eighteen-year-old grammar-school pupils, lived in military barracks and received eighteen hours of teaching instruction per week. Under these circumstances it was not surprising that examination criteria were also relaxed, a process that at times reached the heights of absurdity. Under the heading of 'Wartime Matric without Examination Fear', for instance, the *Völkische Beobachter* reported a ceremony in Vienna at which members of the German Girls' League were welcomed back after having spent ten weeks on agricultural work in the Warthegau (the German-incorporated part of Poland) and in doing so had earned their school certificates.[67]

A close connection between work on the land and schooling had been initiated earlier on in the Third Reich. What was known as Agricultural Auxiliary Service consisted of classes of schoolchildren over fourteen who went into the countryside as a body to help with the harvest during the holidays as well as in term-time. (The actual number of weeks spent away from school during term-time was graded accorded to age-group – the matriculation year itself was exempt.) As a supplement to the Agricultural Auxiliary Service, the authorities instituted the 'land-year', a device for extending the education of fourteen-year-old elementary pupils by an additional year, which was spent in agricultural camps. As a rule land-year participants worked for farmers during the morning and received instruction in Nazi history, race and current affairs in the afternoon; at the height of the farming season, however, this timetable was abandoned and work from sunrise to sundown became the order of the day. The fourteen-year-olds were given no holidays for nine months on end, and were not allowed to receive visits from their parents.[68] Although some parents opposed the land-year on religious grounds – at the farming camps (as at the subsequent evacuation camps), pupils were denied clergymen's pastoral care – others, especially among the poor, approved of an institution that absolved them of the necessity to provide their offspring with food and shelter for a whole year.

In subsidizing the education of socially underprivileged groups, the Nazi regime's record was one-sided. When it was a question of replenishing the depleted teaching force, educational opportunities were extended to social strata which had earlier been excluded; in the training of the second-generation Party leadership, the financial – and even the intellectual – qualifications that had long made education a middle-class preserve were similarly dispensed with (thus in 1940 the Napolas had a 13 per cent working-class enrolment – roughly double that of the ordinary grammar schools),[69] but within the broad structure of grammar-school education reforms implementing the concept of the folk community were conspicuous by their absence. Little was done about school fees, although Education Minister Rust declared in the spring of 1939 that the time was ripe for abolishing them;[70] he justified this statement by invoking the shortage of teachers and engineers. Having been increased by a third in 1935, Prussian school fees amounted to 240 marks per annum.[71] Bavarian fees were 200 marks per annum.[72]

The regime's eugenic orientation expressed itself in a steeply decreasing fee-scale for large families; in Prussia, for instance, the second child secured a reduction of 25 per cent, the third child, a 50 per cent reduction, and all subsequent ones had no fees whatever to pay. Elsewhere the reductions worked out differently, but a general policy of assisting large families to attend secondary and technical schools was operated.[73] Highly priced school textbooks were an additional factor militating against equal educational opportunity in the Third Reich. The authorities subserved the vested interest of the publishers to the extent of actually banning the sale of secondhand textbooks,[74] although they did stipulate that 5 per cent of any consignment must be made available to schools free of charge for distribution among impecunious pupils.[75] If one adds the gradual reduction of grammar-school places (for an expanding population) to fee-paying and the purchase of textbooks, one realizes why the revolution carried out by the National Socialist German Workers' Party left the sociological pattern of German education virtually undisturbed: after 1933 the workers, who formed 45 per cent of the population, continued to furnish the same minute segment of the university student body – 3½ per cent – as they had done in the days of Weimar. The fact that the revolutionary powers-that-be were not even aware of the irony of this situation was exemplified by their practice of continuing to publish lists of parental occupation for all grammar-school pupils.[76] This tendency towards continuity operated through the whole spectrum of education, and although a fair amount of space has been devoted to the Party-sponsored school system, with its rejection of conventional intellectual and social criteria, this should not be taken to indicate the inevitable superseding of grammar schools by Adolf Hitler schools or of universities by *Ordensburgen*. The Nazi view of education (as of so much else) was bifocal: they made the opposites of folk community and continuous selection, the regime's self-cancelling needs of popularity and of expertise, part of one and the same fractured pattern. Continuity also characterized that key figure in the educational field of force – the teacher or '*Herr Professor*', whose profession the youth-orientated Nazi revolution was feared to have undermined. By imperceptible degrees of farce blending with tragedy, this exemplar of German society (*vide* Palmerston's 'Germany – that country of damned professors') refurbished his old aura during the Third Reich: in 1935, the Nazi Teachers' Association managed to procure a ban on radio performances of the song, *The Poor Village Dominie* – on the grounds that it was defamatory of the teaching profession.[77] In 1936 even staff at some Berlin grammar schools managed to have *Stürmer* display boxes removed from the school buildings; but they scored a strictly circumscribed victory, since their pupils were still assailed by displays of Streicher's pornography at every other street corner.

In 1938, a *Jugendschutzkammer* (an official body adjudicating on the rights of young people) dismissed a charge against a teacher who had hit a girl and caused her to bleed from the nose on the grounds that corporal punishment could be applied without distinction of the sexes;[78] 1941 saw an official vindication of face-slapping as a disciplinary measure, provided pupils were of an age at which this was unlikely to result in impairment of their vision or hearing.[79]

20

THE UNIVERSITIES

By 1933, despite towering achievements in many disciplines, the German universities had for many decades failed to resolve their central problem: that of the interrelationship between *Geist und Macht* (spirit and power). Viewed from an academic vantage-point – i.e. with an astigmatism inducing a corporate squint to the right – spirit and power appeared irreconcilably opposed. This created a dilemma that appeared to be susceptible to only two, equally dangerous, resolutions: subservience to the state or mole-like burrowing beneath the groves of Academe.

The final point of bifurcation had been 1848. The imbalance between intellectual stature and political effectiveness revealed by the Revolution polarized subsequent academic attitudes into chauvinist power worship on the one hand and, on the other, a preoccupation with *Geist* so total as to merit the appellation 'idiotic' (in the Greek sense).

Nothing illustrated the interrelationship of *Geist* and *Macht* under the Kaiser as clearly (if as cruelly) as the anecdote about the emeritus professor of philosophy whom Wilhelm II received in audience and promised the grant of any request – whereupon the venerable savant fixed his rheumy gaze imploringly upon his interlocutor and said 'Could your Majesty have me promoted from Second to First Lieutenant of the Reserve?'

One anecdote will have to do duty here for many professorial pronouncements during the Imperial sunset – except for one: the philosopher Max Scheler's gloss on the German artillery bombardment of Rheims cathedral during the Great War: 'If the cathedral had been capable of thinking and feeling it would have realized that the force firing the cannons was part of the same force that had once created this heaven-storming Gothic masterpiece.'[1]

Throughout the First World War the German academic community took patriotism not only to intellectual extremes – in 1915 the war aims controversy elicited 450 professorial signatures endorsing German self-aggrandizement, as against 120 against it – but also to physical ones: at Langemarck (a place-name that was to become a programme) wave after wave of raw student recruits walked into enemy machine-gun fire, to be mown down still singing the *Deutschland Lied*.

After defeat, retrospective academic dedication to the triumph of German arms became, if anything, even more intense. In the twenties inaugurations of new rectors tended to turn into heroes' remembrance days, laced with classically formulated denunciations of the Versailles settlement. The refusal of the universities to acknowledge Germany's military defeat and the complex of socio-political changes arising out of it injected unassimilable toxins into Weimar's body politic. Eduard Spranger, not a very reactionary pedagogue, expressed the opinion of most academics when, as we have seen, he dubbed the German Republic a 'shadow state'.[2] This consensus about Weimar was so widespread among the collegiate fraternity that – to quote Walter Jens's pithy observation[3] – a single expulsion list could have accommodated the names of all the professors loyal to the Republic.

The bulk of academics, though, did not necessarily work for the overthrow of democracy; they were simply hostile – or at best indifferent – to its survival.

Flanked by a straggling file of democrats on one side and a formidable authoritarian phalanx on the other, there were congeries of pure academics, whose horizons converged with the demarcation line of their discipline, and who, if asked about a man's first duty when his neighbour's house was on fire, would have answered: 'It is to notify the fire brigade, i.e. the officially accredited body with the requisite specialist training for mishaps of a conflagrationary nature.'

Some specialists, such as historians or constitutional lawyers, were, of course, drawn into politics by the very nature of their disciplines, but the academic *Zeitgeist* militated against their doing so in a spirit of democracy and humanism. The late Weimar years were the period of *Voraussetzungslose Wissenschaft* (science stripped of all preconceived notions, i.e. of all moral values). In history, historicism was in vogue, claiming validity only for what was currently applicable, i.e. opportune, while in philosophy, existentialism vaulted over the wall of metaphysics on the pole of irrational affirmation.

Sociologically the university population remained essentially unchanged by the war: upper and middle class, with a preponderance of entry from academic and civil-service families. Although workers constituted half the country's inhabitants, they supplied no more than 3 per cent of its students. The fact that 29 per cent of Weimar's parliamentarians were of proletarian origin further reinforced academic antipathy to the Republic. After the war, the student population expanded by about 10 per cent annually (1914, 69,000; 1932, 118,000),[4] but since the number of openings for graduates at first remained static and then diminished sharply during the slump, an intellectual proletariat of degree-holders and academic drop-outs emerged. The contrast between undergraduate expectations and their fulfilment triggered the further radicalization of a group that was already élitist and anti-democratic.* Oddly enough, this radicalization was clearly right-wing in direction: in 1927, i.e. at a time when there was still relative prosperity, 77 per cent of all Prussian students demanded the insertion of an 'Aryan paragraph' (the exclusion of Jews) into the instrument of university self-government.[5] With the onset of the Depression student opinion showed itself twice as susceptible to the appeal of Nazism as public opinion in general. Early in 1931 about 60 per cent of all undergraduates supported the Nazi Student Organization, while Nazi support among the electorate stood at approximately half that level. In that year anti-Semitic riots erupted at the universities of Berlin, Cologne, Greifswald, Halle, Hamburg, Breslau, Kiel, Königsberg, Munich and Vienna.[6] (Austrian universities were, incidentally, the pacemakers of Jew-baiting throughout the German-speaking student world.) In 1932 the Königsberg conference of the German National Students' Organization abolished its own democratic constitution in favour of the *Führerprinzip* (leadership principle). Appropriately enough, the venue of this conference was a military barracks.[7] The national wave sweeping the country encountered no academic breakwaters. Although in the twenties many professors had been right-wing, the number of actual Nazis among them had been relatively small (this explains why Professors Lenard, Krieck and Baeumber, who were early Nazi converts, played such a disproportionate role in the Third Reich). Shortly before and during the seizure of power, however, a professorial lurch to the far right occurred. A prestigious bloc of 300 occupants of professorial chairs addressed a manifesto to the electorate, asking them to vote for Hitler in March 1933.[8] Many academics who were by no means committed Nazis welcomed the national wave as regenerative and healthy in essence, despite such regrettable side-effects as Jew-baiting and storm-troop brutality. The philosopher and pedagogue, Eduard Spranger (who later resigned his chair in protest against the regime), had in 1932 opposed a joint statement by vice-chancellors against right-wing

* The most obvious manifestation of student élitism had always been the membership of exclusive student corporations.

extremism, because he considered Nazism a suitable device for over-coming Marxism and psycho-analysis.[9]

As Spranger's reference to psycho-analysis shows, interdisciplinary attitudes and jealousies played a significant part in determining academic attitudes to the regime. An eminent psychologist* looked to the Third Reich to restore the honour of his subject, which Weimar education ministers had allegedly trodden underfoot. Natural scientists hoped that the new dispensation would free them from the tutelage of metaphysics, while classicists anticipated a renaissance of Hellenic studies. Researchers in the entire complex of Germanic studies – prehistory, literature, linguistics, folklore – expected and received preferential official treatment. The Nazis' suppression of sociology elicited the approval of many economists, lawyers and anthropologists, who considered it an upstart discipline intruding on their own academic domain. Legal studies, too, were, in fact, doomed to relegation in the Third Reich – as was theology – but this was not imme-diately apparent to the subject specialists concerned.

The academic community as a whole was prone to this form of myopia, and often gave unsolicited support to Nazi measures that tended to destroy not merely the ethos but the very *raison d'être* of the universities. The pace at which the 'co-ordination' (*Gleichschaltung*) of academic life proceeded after the seizure of power was made possible only by the voluntary self co-ordination of many faculties. The speed of this process aroused the suspicion and ridicule of many Nazi leaders. Hitler warned the Party against those who 'suddenly changed their colours and moved into the new state as though nothing had happened'.[10] Walter Frank, the Maverick historian who entertained an excessive hatred of academics (whom he called 'little Greeks'), alongside notions of himself as architect of a new Nazified form of intellectual life, wrote:

The National Socialist movement enjoyed the unlimited scorn of the *Graeculi* domiciled in Germany throughout its years of hardship. The movement was too unspiritual for them. But everything changed as soon as National Socialism was victorious, as if victory itself was endowed with spiritualizing attributes. The *Graeculi* now came from everywhere, clever and educated and without charac-ter. They loyally greeted *Heil Hitler* and offered their services in spiritually underpinning the Nazi victory.[11]

Spiritual underpinning assumed many forms. In May 1933, ceremonial burnings of defamed books took place all over Germany in the presence of

* Professor Jänsch of Marburg.

suitably capped and gowned academic senates. Appropriately, the orations inaugurating these university quadrangle *autos-da-fé* were delivered by luminaries of German literary studies, such as Professor Bertram of Cologne and Professor Naumann at Bonn. The rector of Göttingen expressed himself 'proud of the new appellation – barbarians';[12] to his theological colleague, Professor Hirsch, Hitler was 'an instrument of the Creator of all things'. Professor Petersen, dean of German studies at Berlin, detected archetypal National Socialists in Schiller and Goethe.[13] The existentialist philosopher Heidegger assumed the rectorship of Freiburg University with a speech in which he drew analogies between the soldier's army service, the worker's labour service and the scholar's knowledge service.[14] The occupant of another chair of philosophy raised the Nazi notion of folk community to the status of an 'axiomatic scientific concept'[15] The physicist Professor Jordan – co-founder of quantum mechanics with Heisenberg and Born – saw the leadership principle corroborated in nature, i.e. in the organization of molecular structure. In the eyes of the eminent historian Ritter von Srbik, Hitler was comparable to Freiherr von Stein,* in those of Professor of Journalism Dovifat, to Demosthenes.[16] Würzburg's rector Seifert demonstrated 'science stripped of all preconceived notions' in action by personally supervising his students' attacks on Jewish homes and shops during the Crystal Night of 1938.[17] Five years earlier the resignation of his chair by James Frank, the Jewish Nobel prizewinner, in protest against official anti-Semitism, had elicited a rejoinder from thirty-three Göttingen professors and lectures condemning his gesture as an act of sabotage against the new Germany. Their statement concluded, 'We hope that the government will speed up the requisite cleansing measures.'[18]

The actual sabotage of Germany's intellectual life (and with it, of her economic and even military potential) had, of course, been effectively initiated by the Nazi purge of the universities. Although, numerically, the turnover of academic personnel after the seizure of power had not been drastic – the 1,200 dons dismissed (Jews, Social Democrats, liberals, and so on) constituted little over a tenth of the university teaching force,† its repercussions were disproportionately grave. When Reich Education Minister Rust asked the eminent Göttingen mathematician, David Hilbert,

* During the Napoleonic wars, von Stein had modernized Prussia by a series of great reforms and thus prepared her for her subsequent role in the unification of Germany.

† Post-war de-Nazification procedures, by contrast, affected 4,300 academics, i.e. one out of every three (cf. *Bilanz des Zweiten Weltkriegs*, Gerhard Stalling, Oldenbourg, 1958, p. 262).

if his institute had suffered as a result of the departure of the Jews and their friends, the professor replied, 'Suffered? No, it hasn't suffered, Herr Minister, it just doesn't exist any more.'[19]

The famous Göttingen circle of quantum physicists was dispersed, an event causally connected with the subsequent development of the atom bomb in the United States. Broadly speaking, Germany lost the world leadership in natural science that she had previously enjoyed, with the long-term result that to this day her universities have an uphill task in recovering lost ground and German industry is handicapped by the possession of patents by other countries.

But to academic minds consideration of these long-term possibilities – nay, probabilities, since Jews had accounted for 12 per cent of all German professors and a quarter of her Nobel Prize winners – was shrouded by the euphoria of the great Nazi transformation. Feelings of patriotic resurgence and social reconciliation were compounded by the basest motives; the creation of vacancies amounting to a tenth of all academic posts opened up unprecedented possibilities of advancement, as well as of financial gain, since the 'audience money' (*Hörgeld*) system meant that an academic's income fluctuated according to the number of students attending his lectures. The readiness of academics to benefit from this situation was strikingly exemplified by C. G. Jung, who assumed the editorship of the prestigious *Zentralblatt für Psychotherapie* in December 1933 after his Jewish predecessor had been dismissed.[20] Similarly, the award of the Third Reich's 'National Prize' to Sauerbruch made that eminent surgeon suppress his early misgivings about the regime's substitution of mysticism and speculation for natural science.[21]

But despite a massive demonstration of loyalty to the new regime – at Tübingen, for instance, only two out of thirty professors maintained an attitude of reserve in 1933[22] – the academic estate as such, by and large, had a bad press in the Third Reich. Anti-intellectualism and social demagoguery remained constant factors in the Nazis' manipulation of public opinion, and academics were castigated for having only been concerned with *Wissensbereicherung* (the selfish acquisition of knowledge) while the Party's 'old fighters' had poured out blood and treasure for the national cause. Gauleiter Grohe wrote, 'Their caste-consciousness – despite all academic erudition – arose out of unlimited stupidity and unsurpassable irresponsibility.'[23] On a somewhat different tack, Robert Ley, as we have seen, dissected the learned professions' contribution to the good of society with the scalpel of comparative analysis: 'A roadsweeper sweeps a thousand microbes into the gutter with one brush-stroke; a scientist preens himself on discovering a single microbe in the whole of his life.'[24] Whereas Ley had revealed this insight to a captive audience of munition workers, Gauleiter Streicher delighted in casting his pearls before academics themselves. In the course of an address before students and the academic senate of Berlin University he drew a tilted pair of scales on the blackboard. Pointing to the lower scale, he informed his audience that it contained the Führer's brain, while the light one was filled with the composite *Dreck* (rubbish) of their professors' brains.[25] On another occasion he told educationists assembled at Munich,

I am accustomed to using the whip in order to educate, but here, among you academic men, I suppose the word would have an even stronger effect. You old men with beards and gold-rimmed glasses and scientific faces are really worth next to nothing. Your hearts are not right, and you can't understand the people as we can. We are not separated from them by so-called higher education.[26]

In addition to this blanket denigration of intellectuals, specific attacks were launched against particular university disciplines at different times. Reference is made to the denigration of theology and of legal studies in the relevant chapters of this book. What concerns us here is the vicissitudes of physics during the Third Reich. This ostensibly apolitical subject became enmeshed in a surrealist controversy, in the course of which the *Schwarzes Korps* labelled such scientific luminaries as Heisenberg, Sommerfeld and Max Planck as 'white Jews in the sphere of science'[27] because they disagreed with the root-and-branch rejection of Einsteinian physics pioneered by the anti-Semitic Nobel Prizewinner Lenart. Lenart postulated the existence of a mystical entity called 'German physics' and, abetted by his fellow Nobel Prizewinner Professor Stark and various Party ideologists, made life vexatious for scientific colleagues upholding the 'Jewish spirit' at the university.

While this eccentric aberration did not entirely impede physical studies, it nevertheless took its toll – not least in the form of a brain drain. During the war, for instance, Professor Joos exchanged his Göttingen chair for the directorship of Zeiss-Jena, 'because' – in the words of the SD report – 'he had been attacked in such a hateful way in the course of the polemics against theoretical physics'.[28]

One branch of learning that was half choked by the miasma of Nazi ideology was *Germanistik* (German literary and linguistic studies). Since there was a traditional affinity between *Germanistik* and Teutomania at all academic levels – down to elementary schoolteachers – departments of German effortlessly adjusted their researches to the requirements of the regime. Their endeavours bore manifold fruits, from the discovery that the word-order in Heine's poetry reflected the structure of the Jewish palate, to the coining of German substitutes for words of foreign derivation (e.g. *Zeitunger* for journalist and *Zieh* for locomotive). These products of linguistic autarchy failed to gain acceptance, incidentally; in this connection, the antipathy of some *Germanisten* to the word '*Konzentrationslager*' (concentration camp) deserves mention: they objected to the Latin derivation of the term, and suggested *Sammellager* (collection camps) as an indigenous substitute.

Historical studies were similarly predestined for ideological adaptation. Although the concept of Germany as a nation wronged by history had become axiomatic among most historians after the war, the 'National Liberal' right-of-centre orientation prevalent in this discipline failed to meet the exigencies of the new situation. The straitjacketing of the historical muse produced a famous early casualty: Hermann Oncken, who, despite his previous disdain for Weimar democracy, became an object of scandal by publishing *L'Incorruptible*, a study of Robespierre with unmistakable anti-demagogic undertones. As self-appointed custodian of Nazi historiography, Walter Frank indicted him on a charge of *lèse-majesté*, and Oncken was relieved of his professorship.

Other 'National Liberal' historians fared marginally better. Gerhard Ritter retained his chair even when he was rumoured to be hiding Goerdeler after the failure of the 20 July conspiracy. Meinecke, the doyen of German historians, also continued to teach, but was relieved of the editorship of the history journal *Historische Zeitschrift* in 1936.[29] The *Historische Zeitschrift* itself was an interesting phenomenon. Since academic periodicals catered for a small, erudite clientele and met an acute need for quality reading matter, they were permitted a minimal degree of latitude. Thus it was possible for the *Historische Zeitschrift* to publish learned contributions casting doubt on such peripheral aspects of Nazi dogma as the historical foundation of *Blubo* and the image of Charlemagne as a Saxon-slayer projected by Rosenberg. Statistically, of 337 articles published by the *Historische Zeitschrift* between 1933 and 1943, 101 were pro-Nazi, 195 neutral and forty-one 'anti-Nazi'.[30]

The authors of the last-named forty-one items of nonconformist scholarship contributed to a groundswell of academic opinion which reacted against the politicization of scholarship rather than the overall politics of the regime as such. In so far as university people were actively engaged in opposing official policy, they did so as academics rather than as citizens; in other words, they opposed the perversion of their own subjects to Nazi ends and not the perversity at the very core of Nazism. There were, in fact, multiple gradations of conduct and attitude among the academics. At one end of the spectrum was the self-inflated figure of Walter Frank, in whom obsessive hatred of all academic conventions – above all, of objective scholarship – mingled with a quixotic ambition to graft an intellectual skin on to the dead tissue of Nazi thought. Next came a professorial straggle of 'old fighters' – Lenart, Krieck, Baeumber, and others – who loomed so large in the post-1933 firmament precisely because of their small number. They were flanked by a block of former National and German People's Party supporters, *völkische* sectarians, time-servers and pure scholars whose loyalty to the regime was derived from motives of interlinked national and personal self-interest. In their threatening shadow existed a far smaller body of genuine pure scholars, who in lectures and articles tried to insulate academic truth against the contagion of politics. Lastly, the most perceptive or courageous among them formed the minuscule academic resistance.

This resistance, though small in scale, was widely scattered: Heisenberg, Sauerbruch and Carl Bosch fought rearguard actions against the disruption of the physical sciences by Nazi metaphysics; in the theology faculties Bultmann and Soden more circumspectly echoed the expelled Karl Barth; among educationists, Spranger resigned his chair, and Litt publicly challenged Rosenberg's concept of the immutable race soul; under Hartmann's editorship the philosophy journal *Philosophische Blätter* presented a microscopic neutral enclave within the co-ordinated intellectual sphere; the personal influence of law-professors Kohlrausch and Mitheiss was exerted against Nazi radicalization of the student body – their colleague Jessen (together with Goerdeler's confidant, Popitz) belonged to the exclusive Berlin *Mittwochgesellschaft* (Wednesday Circle) of academics, industrialists and civil servants, which acted as a theoretical forum of conservative resistance. Lastly, an academic resistance figure of unique stature: Professor Huber of Munich, who was executed for his part in the White Rose conspiracy alongside the Scholl siblings. The absurd aspect of Huber's university career lay in the fact of his having professionally benefited from the Third Reich, since additional money was allocated for his researches into German folk songs; the tragic aspect of his death was compounded by the conduct of the Munich University Senate, who stripped him of all academic honours prior to his trial and execution. In an analogous display of abject subservience to the regime, the Bonn academic senate had, in 1936, stripped Thomas Mann of his honorary doctorate. At the time of the Crystal Night pogrom the Bonn academic establishment was involved in another ignominious episode. After the wife of the eminent Orientalist, Professor Kahle, had been discovered helping a Jewish friend to sweep up her ransacked shop, he suffered such harassment that he emigrated to England with his family as soon as circumstances permitted. The intervening months were a period of quarantine during which a total of three people – out of the Professor's entire social and professional circle – called on him under cover of darkness. He received one other communication from the outside world: a letter from a group of colleagues expressing regret that he had forfeited an honourable exit from the university through his wife's lack of instinct.[31]

In preparation for the euthanasia campaign the Nazi authorities summoned leading members of university medical faculties to secret recruiting sessions for *Assessoren*, i.e. selectors of feeble-minded and incurably ill inmates of institutions for mercy killing. At one such session a medical luminary (Professor Ewald*) walked out in protest – but none of his eight fellow-professors present followed suit.[32]

The participation of medical men in concentration-camp 'experiments' is too well known to require additional documentation, though the role of German savants in another and related sphere of research deserves mention. A branch establishment of Walter Frank's Institute for Research into the Jewish Question – situated at Litzmannstadt (formerly Lodz) in close proximity to the ghetto and the gas-chambers – was headed by the theologian Adolf Wendel, lecturer in Old Testament studies at the University of Breslau.[33]

Phenomena like these resulted less from the impressment of academics than from the reinforcing interaction of their own volition with outside pressures. The seizure of power had set off a stampede towards the feeding troughs of academic patronage: in 1933-4 it was not unusual for career-minded dons to appear at lectures caparisoned in uniforms of Party organizations they had not yet had time to join. Later on, as the value of Party membership decreased because it became so widespread, ambitious

---

* Ewald, incidentally, had the 'courage of his convictions' (*Zivilcourage*) to send letters of protest against the projected measures to Goering, the Reich doctors' leader Conti, and the Dean of the Göttingen medical faculty.

academics increasingly engaged in compiling secret dossiers on their colleagues.

Thus when the Gestapo, after 20 July, demanded the names of suspects at Göttingen, Rector Drechsler was able to oblige with a list of twenty faculty members on which his immediate predecessor had pride of place; but ex-Rector Blischke seems to have been able to pull strings in Berlin and to ward off arrest by a hurried visit to Gestapo headquarters.[34]

It would be wrong to deduce from this that snooping became an absolute preoccupation in the faculties; nor did the nonconformist few necessarily stand in perpetual fear of the majority. Like their 'lay' Party comrades, collegiate Nazis divided fairly clearly into 'good' and 'bad' ones, a good Nazi being someone who identified with a regime that publicly perpetrated misdeeds he would not have entertained in private.

Despite a corporate leaning towards authoritarianism, the academic fraternity had over the decades evolved an ambience of its own that necessarily included vestiges of *laissez-faire*. This lingered on fitfully after 'co-ordination' and made universities still relatively freer than other areas of Nazi life; even so, the passage of time brought ever tighter restrictions.

Rector Krüger of Berlin (whose stepping-stone to the chair of veterinary surgery had been the directorship of the municipal *abattoir*) decreed that all faculty members must obtain his consent before contributing to learned periodicals.[35]

Minute surveillance was perhaps preferable to the sense of apprehension that made a South-German law faculty overprint the cover of a doctoral dissertation with the legend, 'The department has been permitted not to express its attitude on the views herein represented.' If the academic board concerned congratulated itself on its dexterity it did so prematurely: the journal of the Nazi lawyers' association got wind of this piece of legal 'sharp practice' and published a philippic against academics lacking an ideological sense of responsibility.[36]

One method open to adroit academics for deflecting intolerable political pressure was to embroil the educational civil service in in-fighting with the Party apparatus by emphasizing the damage that such activities as witch-hunts of staff were inflicting on their departments. Some awareness of this prompted Education Minister Rust's warning to students in 1936 against subjecting their professors to political tests, a warning that the *Berliner Tageblatt* hoped would – three and a half years after the seizure of power – at long last put an end to the purge of lecturers.[37] During the war Rector Süss of Freiburg, with almost as much courage as persistence, triggered off a paper war between the Reich Ministry of Education and the Party Chancellery over the admission of ex-service *Mischlinge* (half- or quarter-Jews) to university studies.[38]

But whatever local advantage an academic politician might wrest from the Party/state duality in the Third Reich, this could hardly affect the twilight situation of higher studies – indeed, of all intellectual pursuits as such. Although the nimbus surrounding academic life never quite wore off – and conditions of pay and work at universities by and large compared favourably with those outside – academics inevitably suffered a loss of self-esteem. When, during the war, Goebbels delivered himself of some platitudes about the value of *geistige Berufe* (professions involving brain work) to the community, the brain-workers' response was symptomatic:

> We are grateful for the distinction drawn between intelligence and intellectualism on this, the first occasion that the cause of intellectual labour has been championed. It is to be hoped that the cheap denigration of brain-workers will stop and folk comrades will no longer be attacked simply because they have studied.[39]

A confidential wartime SD report summarized the reasons for intensified self-doubt and increased turnover among academics:

> They are commonly held to contribute so little to political development and the strengthening of the Reich that they have to be grateful not to be dismissed out of hand as intellectuals and *Weltfremde* (other-worldly beings) – people in public life and large firms enjoy quite different esteem.
>
> Industry offers not only greater research opportunities but also higher salaries; assistant lecturers transferring to industry sometimes earn more than their former professors.[40]*

The 1943 conference of German vice-chancellors heard Rector Süss of Freiburg attribute the decline of university standards to the emigration of many important scholars and the precedence that ideology was taking over academic achievement.[41]†

* The other-worldliness of German academics was also demonstrated – though not in the sense implied above – during an interview that the ex-chemistry graduate Primo Levi had with Dr Pannwitz of the Auschwitz-Bunawitz *Polimerisationsbüro* late in the war, when skilled labour was selected from among surviving inmates. Looking at the malodorous skeleton in zebra-striped rags standing before him 'as if across the glass window of an aquarium' Dr Pannwitz asked his interviewee the title of his degree thesis and Levi reflected, 'The measurements of dielectrical constants are of particular interest to this blond Aryan who lives so carefully' (Primo Levi, *If This Is a Man*, London, 1959, pp. 122–4).

† One's surprise at this officially condoned expression of criticism in wartime must be tempered by the realization that Rector Süss was addressing a closed forum where everyone must have been fully aware of the truth he alone had the candour to articulate.

Early on in the Nazi era the *Völkische Beobachter* had suggested a new approach to intellectual training. 'The very best thoughts are those inculcated by marching; in them reverberates the secret German spirit, the spirit of centuries.'[42] This unique teaching method was in fact incorporated into study programmes: in 1937 the Reich Ministry of Education informed Munich's university authorities, 'Students who have missed lectures through attendance at training camps, etc., should not therefore do worse in examinations.'[43]

Other innovations were of a more crucial nature. The rate of professorial appointment was accelerated and the length of a lecturer's term of service reduced in the faculties of medicine, science, law and theology. The number of people who attained the qualification for university teaching (*Habilitation*) decreased from 2,333 between 1920 and 1933 to 1,534 between 1933 and 1944, a drop of one-third.[44] Teaching and research potential was further impaired by the part-time employment of dons as officials of the powerful Nazi Lecturers' Association (*NS-Dozentenbund*).* Membership was obligatory and the leading officials wielded considerable powers of denunciation as well as of patronage. Sometimes patronage turned into blatant self-advancement: when the Frankfurt association's leader was asked to recommend someone for the chair made vacant by the dismissal of the eminent philosopher Paul Tillich, he blandly put forward his own name – to the utter consternation of his colleagues.[45]

No one could take up an academic post without having undergone a six weeks' training course of the Lecturers' Association camp, where political indoctrination was interspersed with military drill, PT and endurance tests. The offices of university rector and leader of the Association were not necessarily held by the same person. There were instances where the rector was actually confronted by an anti-rector in the person of the lecturers' leader, and in this way the traditional animosity between the *Ordinarien* (regular professors) and *Nichtordinarien* (academics enjoying professorial status without actually holding a chair) was perpetuated inside the Lecturers' Association.

One of the Association's prime functions was the selection and training of university personnel; in 1937 Professor Krieck caused wild flutterings in academic dovecotes by publicizing his grave concern about the future

* The wartime Rector of Hanover Technical University, for instance, combined this onerous function with the regional leadership of the Lecturers' Association, while his deputy was the leader for all the academic staff at Hanover itself.

supply of professors, in terms both of quantity and of quality.* The rectors tried to exculpate themselves by emphasizing a decline of standards among students; the Nazi Students' Association denied this, and quoted a certain amount of evidence to the contrary, whereupon the rectors issued a heretical but irrefutable rejoinder to the effect that the achievements of which the students' association boasted rested on foundations laid before 1933.[46]

In prudent response to deteriorating standards academic staffs lowered their sights and reduced the stringency of examinations. Besides this negative reinsurance against the charge of denying the state the required number of future graduates, they took, as we have seen, the positive step of instituting crammer courses for first-year students in subjects in which their grammar-school instruction had been below par.[47]†

During the war it was found that soldiers on study leave, who had been in the Wehrmacht for up to five years, were academically ahead of recent university intake.[48] Among explanations offered for this phenomenon were the reduction in the period of grammar-school studies, lack of leisure time, the diversion of both pupils' and teachers' energies into non-scholastic duties, a long-term shortage of textbooks, the conscription of schoolteachers, and the general denigration of education.[49]‡

Students' preferences fluctuated during the Third Reich in accordance with the exigencies of the economic situation and the gradations of esteem attaching to various professions. The percentage of students enrolling for technological courses actually declined from 1933 to 1937, but there was a definite upswing thereafter, when the technocratic ideal seemed to exercise a permanent attraction. Undergraduates' choice of career was also influenced markedly by the re-introduction of conscription, which entailed a sudden inflation of the officer establishment (between 1934 and the outbreak of war, this increased five-fold from the level of 4,000 fixed by the Treaty of Versailles). The choice of a military career

* Krieck's statement appeared under the heading 'A Burning Problem' in *Der Angriff*, Berlin, 31 January 1937.

† The trade journal *Chemische Industrie* wrote: 'It is no secret that examination results have declined compared with previously,' and added, 'The leadership in chemical research has passed to foreign countries,' (cf. *Neue Weltbühne*, 3 August 1939).

‡ The SD report listing these points added: 'Greater publicity is given to industrial or harvest service undertaken by students than to their actual academic studies.' It also mentions the fact that foreign undergraduates (French ones at Strasbourg or Yugoslavs at Graz) were doing rather better than their German colleagues; occasionally the shortage of lecturers had to be made good by the recruitment of foreigners (cf. Bundesarchiv Coblenz, File R 58-323, 5 October 1942).

conferred enormous social prestige; the consideration that this was the only calling in which the two and a half years a student spent in military and labour service training before going up to university constituted a useful investment of time was undoubtedly not lost on applicants either.

The relevant figures were these: the enrolment for technical studies – one out of every eight pupils with the *Abitur* in 1935 – had doubled by 1939; for the officer corps – one in six in 1935 – it rose to nearly one in three (!) immediately afterwards, but then levelled off at over one in five. Medicine also increased its attraction – 12 per cent in 1935 and 17 per cent in 1939 – whereas teaching dropped from 16 per cent to 6 per cent during the same time span and the law held its own at 13 per cent throughout.[50]

During the war, however, legal studies so declined in public esteem that although the number of students did not significantly decrease, the majority shifted their vocational choice from the civil service or the legal profession *per se* to commercial pursuits.[51] Law students had always had an élitist picture of themselves, sustained by career expectations centring on the Bench or the senior civil service; this shift therefore indicated their distancing from the whole political process, but since in wartime patriotism swamped political reservations this hardly affected the regime's standing.

The student body, to whom the seizure of power had heralded both Germany's providential destiny and the victory of Youth over Age, never in fact withdrew its allegiance to the regime.

Their sense of identification with the Third Reich did not, however, preclude the recurrence of strain; this was unavoidable in the relationship between a totalitarian apparatus and an intelligent section of youth that it was bent on subjecting to even more stringent regimentation than any other.

An early attempt to enrol all male students in the SA and to subject them to a barrack-like existence failed, partly because of the diminished role the Storm Troopers played after the Roehm purge of June 1934. There followed the experiment of one year of obligatory residence in 'comradeship houses' (*Kameradschafthäusern*), where freshmen were drilled both militarily and politically. These efforts coincided with a drive to suppress and entirely supplant the previously very active and multiform student corporations (see below, p. 320). The corporations were officially disbanded but never entirely broken up. It was due to their resilience that the project for compulsory residence for second-year students in comradeship houses was eventually dropped and replaced by a voluntary scheme.

Once the comradeship houses (which were largely sequestered corporation 'dens') were put on a voluntary basis, it proved to be not difficult for their (illegally continuing) former owners to recapture them, so that at many universities the houses, staffed with out-and-out Nazi students, coexisted with others in which the old corporation traditions were perpetuated. This did not, however, mean that the students significantly resisted the Nazi organizational octopus. Only one student out of every four attending university during the Third Reich managed to shirk the many additional duties incumbent upon members of the National Socialist Students' Association; not that such membership altogether lacked its positive aspect: 'comradeship' leaders could exert considerable powers of patronage on behalf of a favoured student.[52] Evasion was in fact possible by enrolling in another Nazi organization at one's home address and then omitting to ask for a transfer to the organizational branch in the university town. On the other hand, it was impossible to evade membership of a *Fachschaft* (i.e. a group comprising all students studying the same subject). Faculty groups met twice a week for political or organizational lectures, in addition to which they ran comprehensive training programmes. During the first term physical-fitness exercises included gymnastics, boxing and cross-country running; during the second, light athletics and small-calibre shooting; and during the third, swimming and combative sports such as rugby. A student required 150 points before being awarded the university's sports-achievement badge, without which he was debarred from further studies unless he could produce a medical certificate.[53]

This interlocking system of coercion could not fail to engender rebelliousness. In the autumn of 1935 250 students in Berlin protested against compulsory faculty group lectures on the programme of the Nazi Party. In the same year there were protest demonstrations at Munich, where students demonstrated their loyalty to the anti-Nazi law professor Mitheiss and punctuated a speech by Deputy Gauleiter Nippold with sardonic interjections.[54] At Freiburg, philosophy students countered the official denigration of Professor Jaspers by boycotting the lectures of Heidegger, which in consequence were transferred from the *auditorium maximum* they had filled in 1933 to a much smaller hall.[55] When war broke out universities as far apart geographically as Göttingen, Breslau and Marburg reported that a third of their new intake were reluctant to participate in Party activities and woefully immature in their attitude to studies.[56]

The Nazi student leaders energetically countered these outbursts of 'rowdyism'. They had some recalcitrants transferred to the Reich Labour

Service, drafted others into the fatigue parties that loaded goods trains and cleared snow from the streets, and threatened the rest with rustication. When, in 1943, Gauleiter Geisler charged Munich students face-to-face with lack of patriotism and went on to allege that girls came up to university in search of husbands rather than knowledge – or simply to evade industrial war service – his speech was drowned by jeers, and police had to clear the hall.[57]

Yet none of these displays of student discontent constituted a challenge to the political nature of the regime.* Even the most successful instance of student nonconformity, the attenuated survival of the corporations, hardly involved political or moral disapprobation of the Third Reich. The Nazi view of corporations was somewhat bifocal; while their élitist fighting ethos earned vague approval – official equivocation on the duelling issue notwithstanding – corporate separateness was seen both as an obstacle to co-ordination, and as an affront to the spirit of folk community.

Some student fraternities were of course exclusive – not to say semi-feudal – and as such provided the *Schwarzes Korps*, which was determinedly cornering the market in social demagoguery, with excellent copy. Things reached breaking-point in 1935 when members of the Corps *Saxo-Borussia* gathered at a Heidelberg tavern questioned Hitler's acquaintance with the etiquette governing the eating of asparagus.[58]

Such *outré* conduct elicited swift retribution. The regime, which had already previously deprived the corporations of new recruits by appropriate Hitler Youth ordinances, now ordered them to be dissolved and their premises to be converted into student comradeship houses.

One of the Third Reich's disagreements with the corporations concerned the time-honoured student institution of duelling. In theory, the Nazis, with their emphasis on soldierly character-building, should have considered duelling essential to a student's education, but a widely publicized fatal *affaire d'honneur* – known as the Strunk Affair – precipitated a ban on duels. It was officially stated that since the Third Reich had a shortage of personalities suitable for leadership the national interest precluded their exposure to the hazards of duelling; furthermore, in the new Germany, a man's honour was no longer his own affair but that of the whole community.[59]

The ban on the corporations, allegedly amounting to a total transformation of the social – and visual – scene at the universities, was in effect

*Characteristically, in 1943 Munich students both jeered Gauleiter Geissler and cheered the Student Association leader's call for the execution of Sophie and Hans Scholl.

never fully put into practice. The Associations of Old Boys (*Altherren Verbände*) sponsoring the corporations were not dissolved, but merged into a National Socialist League of Old Boys, and continued as such to act as discreet caretakers for confiscated corporation property. Even duelling continued, albeit in a rather modified form, and the war years witnessed a partial restoration of the ritualistic corporate practices that had coloured the whole existence of the fraternities. This tendency was strengthened by soldiers returning to the universities on study leave, who brought with them something of the spirit of corporate independence prevalent among the Wehrmacht's officer corps. The effect of this counter-movement was not spread evenly throughout the country. Some universities, such as those of Berlin, Königsberg and Breslau, were hardly affected by it, while in Göttingen and Heidelberg it was very marked.

In the summer of 1939, at a time when the National Socialist Students' Association seemed to be in total control of the entire university population – its leader, Dr Scheel, could blandly announce, 'I am ordering 25,000 students into harvest work'[60] – fraternity practices had been revived to a remarkable extent. At Heidelberg the traditional annual pilgrimage to Maria Spring was resumed, the customary ritual drinking bouts took place again, and duels were being fought – though with rapiers instead of the outlawed sabres.[61] Göttingen had restored the fag system and old boys attended the ritual drinking sessions wearing their sashes and later on their coloured caps. In view of the official ban on *Bestimmungsmensuren* (pre-arranged duels in which combatants represented their respective corporations), the old boys shrank from awarding sashes to younger members; on the other hand the *Bierzipfel* (a ribbon attached to one's watch) had largely replaced the badge of the Students' Association, whose uniform disappeared.[62]

Yet none of these steps were aimed at anything other than preserving certain areas of private and group activity against the encroachment of the state. The underlying concordance of Nazism with the ethos of the student population emerges from a declaration drawn up in Göttingen in the middle of the war.

We base ourselves on the principle of unconditional satisfaction with unsheathed weapons ... We furthermore demand permission to hold *Bestimmungsmensuren* as the most important means of inculcating courage and chivalry, as well as a criterion of selection. We are under no illusion about the fact that the practical realization of these demands will only become possible after the war.'[63]

The criterion of selection emphasized in this statement was, of course, an axiom of the Nazis, and they put it into practice most rigorously in regulating the numbers of student admissions: 1932 had seen 118,000 students at German universities, roughly a fifth of them girls. By 1938 the Nazi policy of throttling admission had more than halved the university population; there were now 51,000 students, including 6,300 girls – a figure somewhat in excess of the 10 per cent female quota fixed by the government. The subsequent relaxation of the *numerus clausus* resulted in an increase of up to nearly 80,000 by 1943.[64]

Although absolute numbers thus alternately contracted and expanded, the social composition of the student body remained fairly constant throughout. Under Weimar, 34 per cent had been upper class, nearly 60 per cent middle class, and just over 3 per cent working class. After six years of folk community, in 1939, $3\frac{1}{2}$ per cent of pupils newly qualified for university admission were workers; the proportion of farmers had dropped from 7 per cent in 1932 to 5 per cent; that of students with a white-collar and professional family background, on the other hand, had increased from 7 to roughly 11 per cent each.[65]

One needs to bear in mind that the total cost to parents of sending their child to university varied from about 5,500 marks to roughly 8,000 marks, depending on the length of the course of study; medicine, the longest course, was naturally also the most expensive.[66] On average only one out of every ten students in the Third Reich was completely supported by grants, although about half of them were subsidized to the extent of having college fees and textbooks paid for them.[67] In 1938 the cost of overheads for the average student per term – for board, lodging, fees and books – amounted to almost 500 marks.* On the whole the living standards of German students compared unfavourably with British ones; at one university every third undergraduate had to subsist on a monthly allowance of 80 marks.[68]

From about 1937 onwards, when Germany's need for more technologists was acknowledged, a number of additional schemes to subsidize science and engineering students were introduced. Various large industrial firms endowed university scholarships, and winners of the National Vocational Contest were prepared for academic careers through the Langemarck scheme – a reactivation of the Weimar machinery for enabling talented youngsters without grammar-school education to achieve

* In wartime this sum was increased to just over 600 marks (cf. *Deutsche Allgemeine Zeitung*, 19 June 1943).

university admission. Despite a great deal of publicity, sponsored students of this type amounted to under 1 per cent of the 1939 intake at universities, and to 2 per cent at technical colleges.[69]

Candidates applying for such awards had to appear before a selection board and answer questions about their background, interests and hobbies. From one such interview, one can gather a great deal about how eager-to-please young men thought they might advance themselves in the Third Reich. Asked how he would spend his leisure time after a hard day's studying, a Langemarck candidate instantly replied, 'Reading *Mein Kampf*' – 'As a form of relaxation?' – 'Well, in that case I would read Goethe's *Faust*.'[70]

21

NAZI SPEECH

In the process of repeating itself history is supposed to occur first as tragedy and then as farce. This sequence was oddly reversed in the realm of language: when Karl Kraus wrote his huge pacifist satire *The Last Days of Mankind* during the Great War he loaded its every rift with the pinchbeck ore of Nazi speech nearly two decades before the *lingua Tertii Imperii** or language of the Third Reich was to gain currency.

When it did so in 1933 Kraus lapsed into silence – capitulating before the linguistic corollary of Gresham's Law with the remark 'Nothing occurs to me apropos of Hitler'.

The Nazis despoiled and corrupted the German language with the same unrelenting thoroughness that they applied to human and material resources, draining it of all grace, subtlety and multiformity.

They deployed words not as bridges extended to the listener's mind, but as harpoons to be embedded in the soft flesh of their subconscious. The varied usages of speech – as communication, argument, *plaidoyer*, monologue, prayer or incantation – were reduced to one single incantatory one.

Incantation lent itself with equal facility to incitement – '*Deutsch-land erwache! Ju-da ver-reck!*' (Germany awake! Perish Judah!) – or to moralizing. This was significant in view of the key function of moralizing in the Nazi manipulation of the German mind. A sledgehammer of preachment beat in the cadence of slogans like 'You are nothing – your nation is everything!' and infinite variations on the same theme.

An additional effect was produced by the use of imperative verb forms such as '*Räder müssen rollen für den Sieg!*' (Wheels must turn for victory!) which set up associations with the idea of the categorical imperative, so beloved of German idealist philosophy. Next to moral imperatives, Nazi speech abounded in superlatives, which in fact become the common form

---

* cf. Victor Klemperer, *Lingua Tertii Imperii*, Aufbau Verlag, Berlin, 1949, a fascinating study of the Nazis' misuse of language, which Professor Klemperer undertook as a Jewish victim of the regime from the inside, as it were; dismissed from the university, he was conscripted for slave labour and only survived by going underground.

of adjectival expression. Certain emotionally coloured adjectives such as 'historic' or 'eternal', which, though not superlative themselves, carried a similar connotation, were pressed into service on every occasion. Other adjectives underwent a complete revaluation. 'Blind' – in phrases such as 'in blind faith' or 'to follow blindly' – which previously had a negative connotation, now acquired a positive one, indicating total commitment. Even the word 'total', with its fairly neutral emotional origin, was given a radically new meaning: *Das Reich*, for instance, talked of 'the total educational situation existing at a National Socialist girls' school'[1] and a toyshop advertised a new type of 'total game' for children.[2]

'Fanatical' – originally a pejorative term indicating bigotry beyond the reach of reason – underwent a similar metamorphosis by a process Klemperer described thus: 'If someone says "fanatical" instead of "heroic" and "virtuous" for long enough, he will eventually really believe that a fanatic is a virtuous hero and that heroism is impossible without fanaticism.'[3]

The tendency towards superlatives and heightened speech in Nazi language produced tautologies; we have only to think of Goebbels's wartime *cri de cœur*, 'The situation can only be retrieved by wild fanaticism'[4] (as though a gentle form of fanaticism were conceivable), and newspaper headlines like 'Youth experiences *Wilhelm Tell*',[5] which was meant to convey the deep impression that a performance of Schiller's classic had made on a Hitler Youth audience.

The same tendency towards more intensified forms of language expressed itself in the transitive use of normally intransitive verbs. '*Wir fliegen Proviant*' (we are flying supplies), or '*Wir frieren Gemüse*' (we are freezing, i.e. refrigerating, vegetables).[6] Another device for making speech more emotional was constant recourse to nouns with hallowed associations; these alternated between the primordial (womb, earth, runes, giant, barrow) and the medieval (altar, cathedral, chorale and grail).*

Constant propagandist usage reduced such grand concepts as God, eternity, providence, life and death to the small change of linguistic currency. 'No death is grander than one which brings life, no life nobler than that which issues from death' was the title of a radio feature.[7] Goebbels described Germany during a speech by Hitler as 'transformed into a single place of worship, in which her advocate stepped before the high throne of the Almighty',[8] and the obituary notice for a show-jumper read 'Another saddle is empty. Axel Holst has followed his peers to Valhalla. Germania's

---

* For an exploration of this technique see Erns Loewy, *Literatur unterm Hakenkreuz*, Europäische Verlagsanstalt, Frankfurt am Main, 1966.

riders mourn a man of supreme mastery.'[9] In the words of Hans Schemm,* artists were 'organs of the nation which reach up into the sky to bring down eternal values and feed spiritual bread to the organism of the people'.[10] When the chairman of an East Berlin social club announced the end of the business half of the annual meeting he used the following words: 'If we now go over to dancing, we do so in the knowledge that we are not indulging in alien lustfulness. Our dance is a struggle for Germany's rebirth.'[11]

As an art form such use of language clearly afforded as much scope to enthusiastic amateurs as to professionals, although the latter could still out-distance lay competitors; a portrait in a literary magazine discussing the top Nazi authors' physiognomies, ran

Hans Grimm's eye shows that the self-enclosed taciturnity of Nordic man has been broken up by hard experience and transformed into manly, bitter fellow-suffering. In Hermann Stehr's case, the spiritualized flesh predominates. In the case of Grimm, the bone structure, in that of Frank Thiess, the forehead. A soft-ness and semi-darkness lies in the physiognomy of Hanns Johst. The solid and choleric mobility of his peasant flesh is dissected. The rock-like quality of his rustic bone structure has been loosened and transformed into something re-sembling tufaceous limestone. Refinement is shown with special clarity in his ears. Their intensive convolutions, tending towards filigree, betray Johst's sensi-tive receptivity to the musicality of speech. In Johst's case the ear is warm and specifically developed downwards; in that of Thiess, it is colder and specifically developed upwards.[12]

We could find enough effusions of this type to fill the rest of this volume, but we shall content ourselves with one final lay contribution – that of a guide who told a coach party of Strength-through-Joy excur-sionists, 'Alight now for co-ordination (*Gleichschaltung*) with mother nature'.[13]

Although weighed down by rhetoric, Nazi speech could be an effective vehicle of one-way communication, at times even managing to convey meanings extraneous to its literal content. A good example of the latter was this radio 'trailer' for a speech by the Führer to be relayed from the Berlin Siemens plant: 'There will be a festive hour from 1300 to 1400 o'clock. At the thirteenth hour, Adolf Hitler comes to the workers.'[14] This announcement combined programme information with the notion of a saviour coming to the poor and underprivileged. The phrase, 'the thirteenth hour', suggested an arrival occurring after the twelfth or final

† Bavarian Minister of Education and leader of the Nazi Teachers' Association.

hour; in other words, an arrival that might have been delayed for too long, but since it is that of a saviour, the laws of time cannot affect it.

One sphere in which the *Lingua Tertii Imperii* was particularly effective was in coining new words, which were speedily absorbed into current usage. Nazi neologisms were of varied provenance: some were technical terms given political significance (e.g. the term *'Gleichschaltung'*, which was borrowed from electrical engineering); others were new compounds denoting Nazi innovations (e.g. *'Ahnennachweis'*, literally 'evidence of ancestry', meaning authenticated proof of Aryan ancestry); others artificially resuscitated archaisms (e.g. *'Thingstätte'** for 'amphitheatre', or *'Dietwart'* for 'sports warden'). A neologism with instant appeal was *'Kohlenklau'* (coal thief), a bogyman featured on the posters issued for the wartime fuel economy drive; leaving doors of heated rooms ajar provoked the reaction *'Kohlenklau kommt'* (the coal thief is coming).

Not every attempt at introducing linguistic usage was successful. The phrase *'Euer Deutschgeboren'*[15] (Your German-born honour) failed to replace *'Euer Hochwohlgeboren'* (Your wellborn honour) as the correct formula for starting letters, despite ideological attractiveness. An innovation which did catch on to an extraordinary degree was the use of abbreviations. NSDAP, SA, SS, KdF, OKW, Ge-Sta-Po – there was no institution of Party or state whose initials did not quickly pass into general usage. The Nazis' abbreviation mania was motivated by various factors: (*a*) since words *per se* convey man's ability to describe, categorize and thereby master things, initials indicate a more organized form of mastery; (*b*) to the 'oath-bound band of brothers' abbreviations were Masonic-like symbols of togetherness; and (*c*) there is something unmistakably martial about the speed and explosive force with which abbreviations trip off the tongue (some Nazi military shorthand words, in fact, achieved currency far outside Germany: Stuka, flak, strafe).

Shorthand speech-patterns spread far and wide. Private motor-cars were called PKW's (the initials of *Personenkraftwagen*, 'passenger motor-vehicle'), lorries, LKW's (the initials of *Lastkraftwagen*, 'freight motor-vehicle'); and social workers defined non-professional prostitutes as 'persons with HWG' (*häufig wechselndem Geschlechtsverkehr* or 'varied sexual relationships'). From 1939 onwards, when the militarization of life accelerated the drift towards abbreviations, a sub-culture of shorthand words developed: Berliners emerging from air-raid shelters in the early hours of the morning would wish each other *'Popo'*[16] (*Penne ohne Pause*

* *Thingstätte* was actually withdrawn from linguistic circulation in 1935.

oben – may you sleep upstairs undisturbed). It also became common usage to express a decidedly negative reply by the acronym *Kakfif* (*Kommt auf keinen Fall in Frage*, 'it is completely out of the question').

Linguistic folklore was similarly enriched in other countries too (cf. the contemporary vogue for abbreviations like TTFN in England), but these German neoplasms were uniquely anal in their inspiration: *'Popo'* means 'posterior' in infantile speech and the first syllable of *'Kakfif'* literally means 'faeces'.

From folklore catchwords of obscene absurdity we turn to the absurd misuse of language to camouflage obscenity. After the seizure of power, the phrase 'Shot while trying to escape' instantly became a popularly understood euphemism for 'deliberately done to death in a concentration camp'. 'Protective custody', which meant the very opposite of protection, and 'Winter Relief', a compulsory tax dressed up as a voluntary charity, were equally transparent linguistic subterfuges. Within the Nazi apparatus double-think became so ingrained that Goebbels could in all seriousness talk about 'simple pomp' and the SD could conclude its report on the 1937 carnival issue of the *Münchner Neueste Nachrichten*, unique in being uncensored, with, 'This has led to a widely expressed desire for the liberalization of the freedom of the Press'.[17]

War necessitated the heavy use of camouflage in the verbal sphere as elsewhere. Retreats were presented as a 'straightening of the front', and grave difficulties were transmuted into 'bottle-necks'. Goebbels presented the battle of Stalingrad as a boxing contest:

We wipe the blood from our eyes, so that we can see clearly, and in the next round we shall be standing firmly on our feet again, a people which has hitherto only boxed with the left hand is now in the process of bandaging its right hand, so that it can make unmerciful use of it in the next round.[18]

But it was in the sphere of the Final Solution, itself the smoke-screen phrase of the century, that the Nazi usage of euphemism reached its apogee. The notice, 'The Jew X.Y. lived here', on a door meant that the occupant of the flat was now deported, i.e. dead, and the overprint 'Addressee has moved away' on returned mail had the same meaning. 'Resettlement' meant 'deportation', 'work-camp' 'incinerator', 'action' 'massacre', and 'selection' 'gassing'.

The holocaust also yielded other semantic side-effects: the Hertz, as a unit of physical measurement, was abolished at the universities; Handel's *Judas Maccabaeus* could only survive under the title of *Hero of a People*, and

Howard Spring's novel *O Absalom* appeared in translation as *Beloved Sons.*[19]

The verbal purification stakes attracted a strong field of entrants. One semantic Savonarola publicly commended a journalist colleague for drawing attention to the continued toleration of words of Yiddish derivation in the German language, but disputed the inclusion of 'Mamma' among these, contending that the suspect expression derived from the Latin word for the female breast and not from the Yiddish for 'mother tongue', *Mamme loschen.*[20] Actually even words of Latin – or Greek – derivation were strong candidates for elimination. As we have seen, purists objected to concentration camps on grounds of linguistic self-sufficiency, suggesting the homegrown substitute *Sammellager* (collection camps). Geographers with a flair for linguistics wanted to replace *Geologie* (geology) by *Flözkunde* (stratum science) and *Oase* (oasis) by *Grünfleck* (patch of green).[21] In the realm of gastronomy, the last effects of the Treaty of Versailles were removed when *Sole bonne femme* and *consommé* appeared as *Seezunge zur guten Frau* and *dürre Suppe.*

The French were also charged with having deliberately given a pejorative connotation to the Vandals – a Germanic tribe coeval with the Visigoths and the Ostrogoths – and the term 'vandalism' was officially excluded from the German language on grounds of racial piety.[22] Veneration for the world of the Teutonic tribes also found expression in the popularity of Christian names derived from the Germanic sagas, a trend dating back to the Wagner cult and the romantic Youth Movement, which the Nazis continued and fostered. As late as 1944 six out of every nine children[23] were christened Sieglinde or Edeltraud, Günther or Ekkehard – and occasionally the authorities had to prevent overenthusiastic parents from choosing names so Nordic (i.e. Scandinavian) that they ceased to be German.[24] One interesting development was the fascination for hyphenated Christian names, *à la* Horst-Dieter; in the case of girls this produced ludicrous hybrids, part diminutive, part heroic, like Klein-Karen.

Another naming innovation which – though hardly widespread – exemplified both Nazi pedantry and Nazi symbol-hunting, was the trick practised by those who left the Church had of spelling the names of daughters who had been baptized Christa as Krista.[25]* While there is no physical proof that in the language of the Third Reich Antichrist was ever

* The Teutomaniacs rejected the spelling of Christ's name with 'ch' as Greek, and therefore un-German.

spelt Antikrist, there is abundant semantic evidence of his existence. Thus the Nazi Press *expressis verbis* described a commemorative ceremony for the *Fehme* murderers of Foreign Minister Rathenau as a 'festive act at the graves of the Rathenau-removers'.[26] The standard phrase used by SS record clerks for new arrivals at Dachau was 'Which Jew-whore shit you out?' – a question designed to elicit the name of the inmate's mother. At Belsen the female warders talked of handling so and so many new 'pieces of prisoner per day' and the correspondence between IG-Farben's drug research section and the Auschwitz camp authorities referred to 'loads' or 'consignments' of human guinea-pigs.[27]

Auschwitz guards would facetiously ask their colleagues detailed to drop the Cyclone-B crystals through the grille into the gas chamber 'Have you given them their grub yet?'

The *lingua Tertii Imperii* lent itself with equal facility to dehumanization and to sentimentalizing and euphemism. The same loom of language which produced the warp of 'Rathenau removers' and 'pieces of prisoner' produced the weft of *Konzertlager* instead of *Kazettlager* (KZ-Lager or concentration camp) and *Pour le Sémite* (a punning of *Pour le Mérite*) description of the yellow star. The same SS guards who coined the monstrous oxymoron 'Cyclon B grub' would address each other in such self-deprecating (not to say self-pitying) terms as 'KZ rabbits' and 'old barbed-wire fighters' (a pun on the 'old fighter' appellation given to Party veterans of pre-1933 vintage).

22

HUMOUR

When totalitarianism blights every manifestation of thought except humour it causes political jokes to flower like long-rooted weeds tapping springs of imagination and wit that are denied their natural outlets. Such 'flowers' proliferated in the sealed hothouse of Nazi Germany, which was awash with steam-bath vapours of rhetoric and national self-intoxication.

If exhalations from these flowering weeds wafted a spurious scent of freedom to susceptible nostrils, the regime did benefit marginally, though this consideration did not deter rulers whose chief attribute was *viehischer Ernst* (bestial seriousness) from reigning in their subjects' irreverent impulses with savage thoroughness. The penalty for anti-Hitler jokes was death.*

Anti-Nazi humour was both a low-keyed expression of resistance (or at least disapproval) and a form of therapy. None the less, for many Germans the circulation of political jokes represented a comfortable (or even socially admired) substitute for thinking – let alone acting – about evils which existed on a plane extraneous to word-play and punch-lines. Defeatist jokes could occasionally cancel out the regime's efforts at morale-boosting, but the average joker prefacing his *sotto voce* delivery with 'Preamble – this one carries three years' hard labour' was actuated less by political awareness (let alone anger) than by the raconteur's perennial craving for an audience.

In addition, a great many political jokes conveyed little hostility to the regime. This frequently applied to Hitler jokes; jokes about Goebbels, on the other hand, were almost invariably derogatory.

The jokes of the Third Reich thus tended to reflect the state of public opinion, since Hitler was an object of general veneration whereas Goebbels – though respected for sharpness of brain and tongue – failed to scale the barrier dividing respect from popularity. There was naturally also a host of

---

* In July 1967, the West Berlin Assize Court established that former People's Court Judge Hans Joachim Rehse had collaborated in passing the death sentence on a priest who had told an anti-Nazi joke to an electrician working at his parsonage. (cf. *Guardian*, 3 July 1967.)

quite savage anti-Hitler jokes; as for their 'positive' counterparts, these often articulated the most widespread myth in the whole body of the Third Reich's folklore and contrasted the exemplary Führer with his corrupt or hypocritical underlings, the 'little Hitlers'. Here are two examples:

Goebbels's children, invited in turn to tea at the houses of Goering, Ribbentrop and Robert Ley, return successively happier after each visit to rave about ever huger cream cakes and other good things. Then, after a visit to Hitler, they come back quite dejected – having only been given malt coffee to drink and little cakes to eat. They ask, 'Daddy, isn't the Führer in the Party?'

Hitler goes into a small village inn. The innkeeper notifies the mayor and all the village notables sit down at table with him. The waiter comes and Hitler orders mineral water. All the others do the same, except for an absent-minded, inconspicuous man at the far end of the table who orders a glass of beer. His neighbours nudge him and look scandalized. Hitler calls across to him, 'You and I seem to be the only two honest men in the village.'

The Führer's name also figured prominently in word combinations satirizing innovations brought about by the Third Reich: the fat shortage gave rise to 'Hitler-butter' as a euphemism for margarine, and the regime's eugenic measures produced the term 'Hitler-cut' (*Hitlerschnitt*, a word play on *Kaiserschnitt* or 'Caesarian operation') as a grimly jocular code word for sterilization. The allegedly – and often factually – abnormal sex life of the Nazi leaders provided inexhaustible raw material for political jokes. At the time when the campaign for full employment dominated official publicity, it was asked why Hitler always pressed his peaked cap against his abdomen when reviewing march-pasts. Answer: 'He's protecting Germany's last unemployed.' Another version contained the answer, *'Ihm ist keiner gewachsen'* (a *double entendre* signifying 'No one can match up to him' or 'He has not sprouted a penis').When Hitler retrospectively justified the murder of Roehm by professing himself to be deeply shocked at the sudden discovery of the SA chief's homosexuality, the jokers inquired: 'What will he do when he finally finds out about Goebbels's club foot?' The Night of the Long Knives, during which Hitler supervised the massacre of Roehm and his *entourage* at Weissensee, also gave rise to a mock addendum to the Reich constitution: 'The Chancellor both appoints and shoots his ministers in person.'

Of all the Hitler jokes, the one that most aptly conveyed the flavour of his personality dealt with a fishing session in the company of Chamberlain and Mussolini. The British Premier patiently pays out his line, lights his pipe and within two hours has hauled in a large catch, after which the *Duce* hurls himself headlong into the pond and grabs a fat pike. When it is Hitler's turn, he orders all the water to be drained out of the pond. Seeing the fish thrash about helplessly on the dry bed, Chamberlain asks, 'Why don't you scoop them up?' Hitler replies, 'They have to beg me first.'

Goering's role in the mythology of political humour resembled Hitler's in that Goering jokes were by no means straightforwardly negative; revolving in the main about the Reichsmarshall's outsize clothes-horse act, they focused on all too human weaknesses that the average German found endearing in a slightly ridiculous way: 'A military encampment of timbered huts was pulled down to make way for brick barracks. A carpenter ordered to fashion all the surplus wood into a wardrobe for Goering was unable to complete the order. Goering had insisted that he first make the coat-hangers.'

Or: 'Turning up for a naval inspection ahead of Hitler and Goebbels, Goering boarded a flagship and went below deck to gaze out of a porthole. Catching sight of him from ashore, Goebbels says to Hitler, "Look at Goering. He's draped a whole battleship round his neck."'

Sent to Rome for delicate negotiations with the Holy See, Goering wires Hitler, 'Mission accomplished. Pope unfrocked. Tiara and pontifical vestments are perfect fit.'

A watermain bursts in the Air Ministry cellar. Informed of the mishap in his upstairs office, Air Minister Goering raps out the order, 'Fetch me my admiral's uniform.'

Having come across the ex-Kaiser's splendid collection of uniforms, Goering has himself rushed to the nearest hospital to have his left arm shortened surgically.

It is announced in Berlin that no petrol will be available to motorists for a week – Goering has sent his uniform to the cleaners.

Sex jokes about Goering were in marked contrast to these innocuous fabrications. Arising at the time of his marriage, they derived additional piquancy from the fact that a year elapsed before his wife, the actress Emmy Sommermann (who was herself rumoured to have shunted her progeny from a previous illicit liaison abroad) became pregnant.

On his wedding-day, Goering splits his trousers – through strength at the back or through joy in front?

Seeing Goering attired in full evening dress on his wedding-day, Goebbels asks him, 'Why all this flummery? You're not going to a first night.'

After the honeymoon, Emmy Goering relinquished her membership of the Church – she had lost faith in the resurrection of the flesh.

At night, Emmy Goering wakes up and sees her naked husband with his back turned to her perform a weird ritual with his marshal's baton. Challenged by her, he explains, 'I am promoting my underpants to overpants.'

Similarly *déshabillé*, Goering also figured in wartime jokes. In 1944, he was to be seen padding along Unter den Linden with nothing on, wearing a cellophane mac when it rained, to remind Berliners of what two sides of ham looked like.

A whole cluster of wartime jokes about Goering hinged on his boast that he would change his name to Meyer if the enemy should ever penetrate German air space. Hence air raid sirens became popularly known as Meyer's Buglehorn. Finally, according to the standard unit game played with abbreviations or short names, a 'Goer' was the maximum amount of tin a man could carry on his chest without falling flat on his face. A 'Ley' was the maximum time during which a man could speak without saying a single sensible thing. A 'Rust' was the minimum time span between the promulgation of a decree and its cancellation. A 'Goeb' was the minimum unit of energy required to switch off 100,000 radio receivers simultaneously. Alternatively, a 'Goeb' was the maximum extent to which a person could pull his mouth open without actually splitting his face. Variations on this theme told of the oldest and tallest tree in the Black Forest being cut down, an event causing vast indignation among nature-lovers. The authorities hastened to explain that, on his birthday, Goebbels had asked Hitler for the present of a mouth-organ. Similarly, the Minister of Propaganda was likened to a tadpole – consisting of nothing but mouth and tail (the German word for tail, *Schwanz*, is also a slang word for penis).

The latter point was reiterated by the wartime story about the angel atop the victory column in Berlin being the only virgin left in the capital for the simple reason that the diminutive Goebbels could not climb that high.

Ribald tales of Goebbels's sexual peccadilloes were legion, but translation difficulties – exemplified by the joke about the film actress Lida Barova setting out for the studio one rainy morning and sending her maid back for the *Knirps* (mini-umbrella or mannikin) she had left lying on her bed – preclude elaboration of this theme.

The fact that he was the least manly and Nordic-looking of the Nazi leaders also earned Goebbels a number of soubriquets such as 'poison dwarf', 'Mahatma Propagandhi', 'unbleached shrinkage Teuton', 'Wotan's Mickey Mouse'.

The coining of the last of these epithets was actually attributed to Goebbels's bitter enemy, Captain Roehm, who had been executed in June 1934. But, dead or alive, the homosexual SA chief provided an obvious target for jokes arising out of the interplay of political and sexual perversion. A joke current shortly after his death ran: 'It is only now that we can realize the full significance of Roehm's recent address to Nazi youth, Out of every Hitler Youth a Storm Trooper will emerge.'

According to another joke, Roehm had a pokerwork motto above the desk in his office, which proclaimed, 'At work I wait for night to come and look forward to the evening's bum.'

Similarly, Hitler Youth premises were supposed to sport the slogan 'Arse to the wall, Roehm is over all.'

A basic undertone of obscenity also pervaded the countless jokes that hinged on the Nazi mania for abbreviations. The abbreviation KdF (*Kraft durch Freude* or 'Strength through Joy') was represented as standing for *Kind durch Freund* (child by a friend) or *Kotz durchs Fenster* (vomit through the window). The letters BdM stood for *Bund deutscher Mädchen* (German Girls' League) or alternatively represented *Bund deutscher Matratzen* (German Mattresses League), *Bund deutscher Milchkühe* (German Milchcows' League), *Baldur, drück mich* (Baldur, squeeze me)* or *Bedarfsartikel deutscher Männer* (commodities for German men).

Hitler Youth jokes revolved either around sex or – as befitted an organization in which 'youth was led by youth' – around precocity.

A class is set the essay 'Would young Werther have committed suicide if he had been in the Hitler Youth?' and the top boy is allowed to suggest the next essay topic; he chooses 'Would the Maid of Orleans have kept her maidenhead if she had been a member of the German Girls' League?'

A schoolboy expresses his chagrin at low marks by carving 'It was not

* Baldur von Schirach was the leader of the Hitler Youth.

for this that we waged a fourteen-year struggle' (a famous Hitler dictum) across the top of his desk with a Hitler Youth dagger.

The drive for economic self-sufficiency gave rise to many jokes about poor quality substitute materials.

A man who had ordered a suit from his tailor is charged in the courts with wilful destruction of timber reserves.

A would-be suicide buys a length of rope with which to hang himself, but the rope snaps. He jumps into the river, but is kept floating on the surface by the wood in his clothes. Thereupon, he decides to live, only to starve to death after four weeks on normal consumer rations.

The poor quality of wartime beer which, as we have already seen, was defined as 'bladder irrigation à la Conti' after the head of the Nazi Doctors' Association, occasioned the story of the dissatisfied drinker who sends a sample of the beer he had been offered to a laboratory for testing; after a few days, he receives the diagnosis, 'Your horse suffers from diabetes.'

Corruption among officials figured in the anecdote about two full-time Party officials going for a walk, in the course of which one of them finds a 50-mark note in the gutter. The other asks him what he intends to do with it. 'Donate it to the Winter Relief,' to which the other replies, 'Why do it the long way round?' Nest-feathering also inspired some 'definitions'. The replacement of an incompetent official by someone actually qualified to do it was called 'sabotage', and a 'reactionary' was the occupant of a lucrative post coveted by a Nazi.

The bewildering impact of the self-sufficiency programme on agriculture inspired the tale of the Reich Food Estate leader Darré asking some farmers about their methods of feeding chickens. The first answers, 'I give them grain', only to be upbraided for depleting the country's economic reserves. The second replies, 'I feed them potatoes', and is censured for diverting food essential for human consumption, whereupon the third says, 'I just throw one Reichsmark into the chicken coop and tell them to buy their own grub.'

The heavy deductions in industry – amounting to up to 20 per cent of total wages – were an obvious target.

A large factory went en fête because the wages clerk had inadvertently paid out the deductions instead of the wages.

In the course of a factory inspection Goering has a meritorious armament worker presented to him and notices his limp. 'Is this a war
injury?' he asks, full of concern. 'No, last Friday I accidentally dropped a
wage packet on my foot.' 'Was it that heavy?' 'Quite heavy enough.
Luckily, the deductions hadn't been put in, otherwise I would have had to
have the whole leg amputated.'

Another industrial joke featured a chronically constipated patient prescribed ever stronger laxatives by his panel doctor, but to no avail. Puzzled,
the doctor inquires as to his occupation. 'Motorway construction worker.'
Heaving a sigh of relief, the doctor hands him a 2-mark piece. 'You'll see
how effective the laxative is once you've got some food inside you.'

The financial hardships of the lower middle classes inspired the story of
the brutal murderer sentenced to death by hanging. Reading of the
court's decision Hitler irately turns to Goering: 'A swift death is too good
for a criminal like that. He ought to be made to starve to death slowly and
agonizingly', whereupon Goering replies, 'How about opening a small
shop for him?'

From the economic victims of the new dispensation folk humour
inevitably turned to jokes about groups who were the beneficiaries.

Members of which choral society earn individually more than Caruso?
Reichstag deputies – they perform once a year, sing two songs (the *Deutschland
Lied* and the 'Horst Wessel Song') and receive twelve thousand marks each.

A stranger passing through a village notices a weathervane being dis-
mantled from the church steeple. He asks the workmen, 'Are you going to
put a new one up?' 'Oh no, we're replacing it with a civil servant. A civil
servant knows better than any weathervane which way the wind is blowing and which way he has got to turn.'

As we have seen, the Party members who joined as part of the general
stampede when the Nazis officially took office in March 1933 were nicknamed 'March violets'. The Party badge was known as *Angstbrosche* (the
brooch of fear).

The ubiquity of uniforms in the Third Reich – the Party seemed to be
constantly spawning new units with a distinctive 'battle-dress' – gave rise
to the suggestion that the army should wear mufti to distinguish it from
the rest of the population. Within a Party given over to the myth of

masculinity, women affiliates were naturally not held in high esteem. The Nazi Women's Association was dubbed 'the varicose-vein squad'.

The '*Heil Hitler*' salute, officially known as the 'German greeting' inspired the expression 'the German glance' (*der deutsche Blick*) which consisted of someone standing stock still and furtively rotating his head through the widest possible arc to ascertain that no one was listening before he started a *sotto voce* conversation. Such conversations would end with the phrase, 'You have said a few things, too', to which the appropriate reply was, 'I deny having spoken to you at all.'

The Big Brother theme was another obvious source of humour.

The Germans represent a medical miracle. They are able to walk about upright in spite of having a broken backbone.

A man with an aching tooth visits the dentist. The dentist tells him to open his mouth. 'I'll take good care to do no such thing in front of a perfect stranger.' 'Then how am I to pull out your tooth?' 'Through the back of course.'

In winter, two silent men riding on a train make barely noticeable gestures with their hands beneath the blankets draped across their laps. They are deaf mutes telling each other political jokes.

Jokes coined during the immediate pre-war period reflected the successes of the regime's foreign policy.

What is the difference between Chamberlain and Hitler? One takes a week-end in the country while the other takes a country in a week-end.

On the occasion of his fiftieth birthday, the National Socialist motor-cycle corps are making Hitler a present of movable frontier posts.

From 1940 onwards Mussolini's forces became the butt of many derisory jokes, exemplified by the one about the Italian army order which stated that all decorations were to be worn at the back – they had been awarded for valour displayed in advancing backwards.

Gradually, however, as the war expanded, the Reich's own military situation became the subject of similar barbed comment.

Can Germany lose the war? Unfortunately not; now we've got it, we'll never get rid of it.

The state of the anti-aircraft defences (on whose effectiveness Goering had staked his reputation) gave rise to the story of the criminal condemned to a novel form of execution. He was placed on top of a high pillar encircled by flak batteries which subjected him to concentrated bombardment. Six weeks later, a low-flying aircraft accidentally discovered that he had died of starvation.

The official Wehrmacht accounts of the battle of Stalingrad gave rise to mock communiqués:

'Our troops captured a two-roomed flat with kitchen, toilet and bathroom, and managed to retain two thirds of it despite hard-fought counter-attacks by the enemy.'

During this phase of the war there was an increase in derogatory Hitler jokes:

Churchill inspects Longworth House on St Helena and comments, 'It will do; the occupant can do his own decorating.'

A Berliner and a Viennese exchange air-raid reminiscences. The former says, 'The raid was so heavy that for hours after the all-clear window panes were hurtling down into the street.' 'That's nothing. In Vienna, portraits of the Führer were raining down into the street for days after the raid.'

It will be peace when Franco's widow stands before the open grave of Mussolini and asks, 'Who has shot Hitler?'

After the end of the war, Hitler's corpse is discovered with a note pinned to it, 'I plead not guilty in the sense of the indictment. I was in the Party to protect myself against Kaltenbrunner's vendetta.'

The SS itself projected such a chilling image that there was a dearth of jokes about it, yet any account of humour in the Third Reich would be incomplete without instances of the wit that flourished within the ranks of the death's-head formations – the gallows-humour of men who combined the conscience of troglodytes with science.

At Dachau, the guards called the party of prisoners who had to remove sewage from the open latrine 'squad 4-7-11' after the eau de Cologne.

At Mauthausen, Jews about to be pushed over the edge of the quarry precipice were called 'paratroopers'.

At Auschwitz prisoners employed in the extraction of tooth fillings from the mouths of gassed corpses were referred to as 'the gold-diggers of Alaska'.

Lastly, what of the Jews themselves? With persecution since time out of mind a living scar across their psyche, the Jews had long been conditioned to assuage pain with the balm of humour. Though impaired, this faculty did not desert them even in the Third Reich.

Meeting the worried and abstracted Goldstein, Kohn tells him that Davidsohn has died. Goldstein shrugs his shoulders. 'Well, if he got a chance to better himself . . .'

Levi tells Singer about the funny dream he had last night. 'I was sitting in Dobriner's coffee house on the Kurfürstendamm and saw a familiar figure walk past outside, so I turned to my wife and said, "That man out there, wasn't that Hitler, *nebbich*. . .?"'

A concentration camp guard informs a Jewish prisoner that he has a glass eye, which is completely indistinguishable from his good one. If the Jew can guess which one is the glass eye, his life will be spared – if he can't, he will be killed. The Jew makes the correct guess, and when the astounded SS man asks him how he managed it, the Jew answers, 'The glass eye has a kindly gleam in it.'

In camp, too, at Treblinka, where the prisoners were employed to carry gassed corpses of inmates to the crematorium, prisoners who ate too much would be told by their fellows, 'Hey, Moishe, don't overeat! Think of us who will have to carry you', and slackers were known as 'child specialists'. At Treblinka, too, the sad consolation to friends whom one had to leave was, 'Come on, cheer up, old man. We'll meet again some day in a better world – in a shop window as soap.' The appropriate reply to this last remark was, 'Yes, but while they'll make toilet soap from my fat, you'll be a bar of cheap laundry soap.'[1]

23

LITERATURE

Literature was the branch of the arts on which the seizure of power had the most immediately visible effect: an estimated 2,500 writers, including Nobel Prizewinners and writers of world bestsellers, left the country voluntarily or under duress to constitute a diaspora unique in history.

Their departure was precipitated by the mid-February purge of the Prussian Academy of Poetry, the presidency of which Heinrich Mann (author of the *Blue Angel* novel *Professor Unrat*) had to yield to Hanns Johst, an erstwhile expressionist poet long changed into the portrayer of solitary hero figures *à la* Leo Schlageter.* The purge also removed the Nobel Prizewinner Thomas Mann, Alfred Döblin, Leonhard Frank, Georg Kaiser, Jakob Wassermann, Franz Werfel and others; the place of these 'degenerates and racial undesirables'† was taken by a group of writers none of whom enjoyed their predecessors' international renown:‡ Werner Beumelburg, Hans Friedrich Blunck, Hans Grimm, Erwin Guido Kolbenheyer, Agnes Miegel, Börries von Münchhausen, Hermann Stehr and Emil Strauss.

Beumelburg, an ex-officer, represented the 'War as a Spiritual Experience' (*Fronterlebnis*) school of writing. In his tough, sentimental, best-selling *Gruppe Bosemüller* he alternated brutal descriptions of fighting with bathos-dripping 'comradeship', evocations of which were much in demand among post-war readers§ painfully conscious of its absence from everyday civilian existence.

* Schlageter was a notorious *Frei Korps* terrorist executed by the French during their 1923 occupation of the Ruhr.

† Some of the non-Jews among them, such as Kellermann and Paquet, actually continued to live and publish within Germany in spite of this.

‡ The *völkisch* literary critic Wilhelm Stapel provided his own rationalization of this phenomenon: 'The German–Jewish novels of a Wassermann, a Feuchtwanger or of the Jewish-assimilated Heinrich Mann . . . are not linked to the German language at source. They might as well have originally been written in English, French or Swedish . . . Language is merely the fortuitous garb of these works.' (*Die literarische Vorherrschaft der Juden in Deutschland, Forschungen zur Judenfrage*, Hamburg, 1937, vol. I, p. 188.)

§ cf. Ernst Loewy in his *Literatur unterm Hakenkreuz*, Frankfurt am Main, 1966 – from which a great deal of the facts and value judgements in this chapter have been culled.

Blunck was a Low German drawing on local folk-tales, Nordic Promethean myths and Viking sagas for his subject matter. In what might be described as an attempt to establish a 'race-time continuum' he espoused, in his prehistoric *Urvätersaga* the trilogy form that was *de rigueur* among *völkische* writers, with their obsession with eternity.

Hans Grimm, who had lived in South Africa before the war, published in 1926 the instantly best-selling 1,200 page epic *People without Space*, which made the point that: 'The cleanest, most decent, most honest, most efficient and most industrious[1] . . . white nation on earth lives within too narrow frontiers.'[2] The sales exceeded half a million by the mid-thirties[3] and the very title constituted one of the most potent weapons in the arsenal of Nazi propaganda. . .

Erwin Guido Kolbenheyer, a *Volksdeutscher* from Hungary, was a rather talented historical novelist. His *Paracelsus* trilogy had won acclaim in the twenties, but in his fiction and non-fiction alike Kolbenheyer was given to metaphysical pontificating which, stripped of its pretentious phraseology, amounted to little more than a vindication of German self-aggrandizement.

The novelist and poetess Agnes Miegel had a literary horizon that was virtually co-terminous with the boundaries of East Prussia, her home province. As a ballad-writer she was an outstanding exponent of the genre of *Heimatdichtung* (regional writing) which held a strong appeal for a reading public craving an escape from modernity and mass existence.

Börries von Münchhausen, a descendant of the immortal lying Baron and an ex-cavalry officer turned gentleman-farmer, shared Frau Miegel's habitat as well as her preference for the ballad form. His work appealed especially to the *Bündische Jugend* because it was full of the ethos of chivalry. This romanticism so clouded his judgement that he fell an easy prey to lies beside which his illustrious ancestor's paled into insignificance; when the moment of truth dawned in 1945, he took his own life.

Hermann Stehr was a former elementary schoolteacher from Silesia, a province in which both religion and literature were tinged with mysticism. He exemplified this tendency in his works: physical blindness was equated with spiritual vision and the sexually induced recovery of sight [*sic!*] spelt severance from God and therefore from the source of life. This type of profundity made Stehr a favourite among the petit-bourgeois Philistines, known in Germany as *Spiesser*, to whom an author's degree of 'inwardness' was the touchstone of his literary excellence.

Emil Strauss, a bourgeois Swabian, was another regional writer in whose work life on the land assumed spiritual significance. He juxtaposed an idyll of rustic serenity and isolation to the 'asphalt' of the big cities and preached a cult of hardihood. Thus the impecunious hero of *Der Spiegel* dissolved a happy marriage because his wife's acceptance of a legacy would have deprived him of the whetstone of drudgery on which to hone his character.

These were the writers whose elevation to the praesidium of the Academy was the literary symbol of Germany's national rebirth. Though it may have been true that a number of them received the accolade for what they wrote rather than for how they wrote, there was no gainsaying the merit of others. Emil Strauss, for instance (whom Hermann Hesse credited with the gift of writing classical, peerless prose), had already been an academician once before, as had Guido Kolbenheyer.*

Yet whatever their literary merit, neither informed German opinion before 1933 nor the universal republic of letters would have placed them at the peak of Germany's Parnassus. In the estimation of the world such expatriate authors as Thomas and Heinrich Mann, Erich Maria Remarque, Jakob Wassermann, Emil Ludwig, Vicki Baum, Leon Feuchtwanger, Leonhard Frank, Bruno Frank, Arnold Zweig, Stefan Zweig,† Franz Werfel,‡ and the dramatists Georg Kaiser, Ernst Toller, Carl Zuckmayer and Bertolt Brecht remained the accepted exemplars of German literature and drama.

But what the world thought became increasingly irrelevant to a country dedicating itself to self-sufficiency in cultural matters no less than in economics.

Moreover, though Germany's cultural isolationism and self-absorption was government-decreed it did not altogether contradict the freely expressed preferences of the reading public. A breakdown of the twelve best-selling authors[4] during the last year of Weimar shows that seven of them – Beumelburg, Grimm, Stehr, Hans Carossa, Ina Seidel, Edwin Erich Dwinger and Heinz Steguweit – were subsequently sponsored by the Nazis, three – Hans Fallada, Manfred Hausmann and Ernst Wiechert – were tolerated, and only two – Werfel and Stefan Zweig – were proscribed.

* Both had resigned in 1931, partly in protest against the cultural 'ascendancy' of Berlin, and partly out of hostility to Weimar democracy; they had been joined by Wilhelm Schäfer, the author of *Thirteen Books of the German Soul*.

† An Austrian, who had the prescience, however, to leave before the *Anschluss*.

‡ Another Austrian who stayed on till 1938.

Of the sponsored authors the most interesting was the ex-doctor Hans Carossa, an urbane exponent of Goethean serenity who suited the regime perfectly by remaining apolitical. His novels soothed the lurking apprehensions of a devoted readership about the Third Reich by enabling them to indulge in the antiseptic luxury of abstract humanitarian ideals.

Frau Seidel was a gushing advocate of the irrational with an obsession about nature, part-Lutheran, part-theosophist; her best-seller *Das Wunschkind* featured a mother wresting her son from the reluctant grasp of fate, only to lose him stoically in the War of Liberation.

Heinz Steguweit's and Edwin Erich Dwinger's respective muses were closely related. Steguweit, alternately sentimental and humorous, kept ringing the changes on the *Fronterlebnis* theme; Dwinger specialized in prisoner-of-war or volunteer-corps epics in which Germans were heroes and Communists fiends, while life was excessively raw.

Far more important, as well as complex, was Ernst Wiechert, a writer whom the regime just about tolerated (and temporarily imprisoned), while simultaneously using him. Religious and humane, Wiechert could not but impugn the new system; the dénouement of his novels, however, smacked of back-to-nature therapy and trailed vague echoes of 'Blood and Soil': his heroes tended to be tormented men finding solace in humble, solitary, non-urban pursuits. Moreover, by staking out a zone of 'inner freedom' in the imagination of his readers he helped to blunt their sense of the loss of actual freedom.

Manfred Hausmann's forte was the evocation of romantic pictures of vagabond life, and Hans Fallada's* a latter-day naturalism, which, however, eschewed the depressing aspect of his precursors' work; somewhat suspect in Nazi eyes because of a tendency towards decadence, Fallada subsequently adapted his work to the 'exigencies of the situation'.

Although the new incumbents of power could arguably claim to represent a consensus of readers as solid as that of voters, they were not insensible to the damage the mass-flight of intellectuals was inflicting on Germany's standing in the world. Even the celebrated poet Stefan George – high-priest of the cult of classical aestheticism – whom the Nazis had (not unjustifiably) claimed as a partisan,† emigrated to Switzerland, where he

---

* Fallada's widely translated *Little Man, What Now?* was one of the most successful – and symptomatic – novels of the Depression.

† Stefan George's 1928 poem '*Das Neue Reich*' was a dithyramb to a charismatic Führer.

Models of what was initially called the Strength-through-Joy car on display at the laying of the foundation stone of the Volkswagen works in 1938. (INSTITUTE OF CONTEMPORARY HISTORY AND WIENER LIBRARY)

Hitler was the object of hysterical adulation among many Germans. The photograph shows girls in national costume face to face with the Fuehrer in the Breslau sports stadium, 1938. (INSTITUTE OF CONTEMPORARY HISTORY AND WIENER LIBRARY)

A view of the Hitler Youth camp—complete with public address system—at the Nuremberg Party Rally of 1934. (ULLSTEIN BILDERDIENST)

Boys of an Adolf Hitler school during an exercise. The purpose of the Adolf Hitler Schools was the training of future generations of Nazi leaders. Pupils were selected according to their Nordic appearance, 'leadership potential' and physical prowess. (SÜDDEUTSCHER VERLAG)

Hitler Youth marching through the streets of Breslau during the 1938 Sports Festival.

The open-air theatre and memorial at Annaberg, Silesia. (INSTITUTE OF CONTEMPORARY HISTORY AND WIENER LIBRARY)

A still from the film *Jud Süss*—a cinematic curtain-raiser for the Final Solution—showing Ferdinand Marian, who played the title-role (right), and Werner Kraus.

Relaying the sound of the goose-step to the listening millions. Hitler called the wireless a precondition of his victory and contrived to give Germany the densest radio coverage in the world. (INSTITUTE OF CONTEMPORARY HISTORY AND WIENER LIBRARY)

Works concert at a Hamburg tram depot under the auspices of the Strength-through-Joy organization. (INSTITUTE OF CONTEMPORARY HISTORY AND WIENER LIBRARY)

View of a housing estate on the outskirts of Stettin. Note the school building (with clock tower) in the background. (INSTITUTE OF CONTEMPORARY HISTORY AND WIENER LIBRARY)

Model of the Königsplatz at Munich—venue of some of the chief ritual occasions in the Nazi calendar—designed by Hitler's first court architect Professor Troost. (INSTITUTE OF CONTEMPORARY HISTORY AND WIENER LIBRARY)

Motorway construction served the threefold purpose of providing work, of military preparation, and of speedier traffic flow. View of the Kaiserberg access point on the edge of the Ruhr industrial complex. (INSTITUTE OF CONTEMPORARY HISTORY AND WIENER LIBRARY)

Professor Thorak at work on the model of his Autobahn monument. The final version—three times the size of the model—was to be placed alongside the Munich-Salzburg Autobahn. (INSTITUTE OF CONTEMPORARY HISTORY AND WIENER LIBRARY)

The Hitler Youth's Hans Mallon memorial on the Island of Rügen. The quasi-runic inscription reads 'The fame of the dead lives forever'. (INSTITUTE OF CONTEMPORARY HISTORY AND WIENER LIBRARY)

Nazi post-war plans included the construction of *Totenourgen* (Castles of the Dead) through-out Europe. This is Wilhelm Kreis's design for the victory-monument-cum-military-cemetery at Kutno, Poland. (INSTITUTE OF CONTEMPORARY HISTORY AND WIENER LIBRARY)

When US troops liberated the concentration camp at Landsberg near Munich in 1945 they ordered the townspeople to help inter the remains of the Jewish camp inmates. (ULLSTEIN BILDERDIENST)

died soon afterwards. The Berlin government tried to redress the balance by making behind-the-scenes approaches to Thomas Mann, designed to make the tutelary genius of the literary emigration return to Germany,* but these negotiations proved abortive.

In their somewhat perilous situation, Nazi book-burners, whom the émigré writer Heinrich Mann, seconded by Romain Rolland and other spokesmen of the international republic of letters, subjected to a withering indictment, received covering fire from two quarters – one expected, the other less so. The expected quarter consisted of a 'patrician' group of neo-romantics and neo-classicists (Börries von Münchhausen, Rudolf Binding† and Wilhelm von Scholz‡) who clothed the staleness of their apologies ('One can't make an omelette without breaking eggs') in appropriately poetic diction. Münchhausen, for instance, transfigured the Nazi purge with a stilted and specious metaphor of the threshing-floor: 'What matters if, in sweeping away the chaff, a handful of golden grains are lost? Germany, the heart of the nations, is wasteful and prodigal, like all genuine hearts.'[5]

The unexpected advocate was Gottfried Benn, arguably the most important literary personality to lend his name to the embalming of German culture. Endowed with a gift of 'making visible the transience of being and of conjuring up the iridescence of the world',[6] Benn had expounded a highly individual form of aesthetic nihilism within the Expressionist movement. A preoccupation with the isolation of the human ego made him hanker after the primitive, a longing for which the atavism implicit in Nazi ideology signally catered.

Benn professed to see 'National Socialism pouring floods of ancestral vitality through the eroded spaces of Europe', elevated the seizure of power into a 'mutation of history' and embellished the suppression of freedom with aesthetic analogies: 'How do you imagine that during the twelfth century the transformation from Romanesque to Gothic consciousness took place? Do you think it was discussed, do you think people cast votes as to whether arches should be pointed or round?'§ Though

---

* The same course of action was urged upon Thomas Mann by his Jewish publisher, Samuel Fischer of Frankfurt, who himself emigrated to Sweden as late as 1936.

† Rudolf Binding enjoyed a wide reputation as an exponent of chivalry and the manly virtues.

‡ Wilhelm von Scholz was a novelist and dramatist in whose work veneration for classical models mingles with German patriotism.

§ Gottfried Benn's rejoinder to Klaus Mann's polemical open letter from France in 1933, quoted in Franz Roh's *Entartete Kunst*, Hanover, 1962, p. 109.

himself under attack on the grounds of suspect lineage,* he gave full approbation to the new cult of the archaic and of pedigree-hunting: 'We have entered the epoch of genealogy. One sees the picture of a near ancestor and it bears the features of the primordial huntsman, the pattern of the brachycephalic solitary hunter . . .'[7]

Though Benn's *volte-face* in 1933 was the most spectacular, it was by no means the only instance of adaptability among German authors. Thus Frank Thiess, the urbane exponent of a preoccupation with Eros and Psyche far removed from *völkische* precepts,† grafted an anti-Weimar preface on to a re-issue of his twenties novel, *Der Leibhaftige*, which was not warranted by anything in the body of the book. Rudolf Herzog, whose sagas of industrial dynasties were a staple middle-class literary diet, carried fulfilment of the newly prescribed literary norms to lengths which would have made one suspect satiric intent in any setting other than that of the 'bestially serious' Third Reich.

Herzog's *Uber das Meer verweht* was studded with gems of Teutomaniac hyperbole: 'She wants to keep troth with her lover unto death, but this is a very long time, since he is of German blood, and German blood is immortal' – or 'We think we are already undertaking a heroic labour when we suckle a child with mother's milk. Great children, however, demand our heart's blood.'[8]

But even though many a literary '*Selbstgleichschalter*' (self-co-ordinator) attempted to pass off his individual Pegasus as a brown shaft-horse, the regime was not disposed to award good marks merely for trying. The *Schwarzes Korps* found fault with Herzog's novel[9] and – not unexpectedly – started a witch-hunt against Gottfried Benn. It denounced him as congenitally obscene (under the headline '*Der Selbsterreger*' – the self-agitator or masturbator!), and illustrated this charge with a stanza from his poem *Synthese*, with the last line left blank on the grounds of propriety.‡

* Börries von Münchhausen has publicly alluded in 1934 to the suspicious similarity between the poet's family name and the Hebrew prefix Ben, denoting son, whereupon Benn had gone to inordinate lengths to establish his racial authenticity. By dint of diligent research he established that (a) Benn was the name of a type of wine from Dürkheim featured on the wine list of Kempinski, the famous Berlin restaurateur; (b) at Dürkheim the term Benn denoted wine produced at vineyards situated at a certain altitude; and (c) the Benns domiciled in England were pure Nordics. He published these proofs of his origin in *Lebensweg eines Intellektualisten*, Berlin, 1934 (cf. Loewy, *op. cit.*, p. 335).

† Thiess's *Der Weg zu Isabelle* had incestuous overtones, and his *Frauenraub* had a lesbian protagonist.

‡ *Das Schwarzes Korps*, 7 May 1936. The editorial comment next to the blank line read, 'Cannot be reproduced'.

Benn, an ex-officer of the medical corps, now exchanged the perils of civilian existence for the security of army life, opting for (to use his own rather specious phrase) the 'aristocratic form of emigration'. This way out of the impasse of the creative mind under totalitarianism was also chosen by Ernst Jünger, whose relationship with Nazism in some ways resembled Gottfried Benn's. A co-founder of the *Fronterlebnis* school and panegyrist of mechanized Armageddon, Jünger had probably undermined the Weimar Republic's foundations more effectively than any other author, yet he remained fastidiously aloof from the beneficiaries of his demolition work. Thus he rejected such Nazi honours* as a seat in the Reichstag, or in the Prussian Academy of Poetry, and a column in the *Völkischer Beobachter*, but he allowed the large reprints of his works that were officially sponsored after 1933 to produce financial dividends for himself and ideological ones for the regime. His eventual choice of an officers' mess as a haven of refuge from Nazi reality followed the same pattern of ambiguity.

In the interim the Third Reich extracted every possible advantage from the popularity of a writer who brought high stylistic accomplishment to the officially prescribed apotheosis of war. War was the most important of the four pillars constituting the edifice of Nazi literature, alongside 'Race', 'Soil' and 'The Movement' (or 'Leader-and-Followers').

While Jünger evinced many of the stock attitudes of the *Fronterlebnis* school of writing – such as the substitution of male comradeship for love – he outdistanced his colleagues as the metaphysician of total mobilization. He held that in the First World War Germany had been ill-equipped spiritually for total mobilization but would not fail a second time. The war-dead had passed from a state of incomplete reality to one of complete reality – from the 'ephemeral' to the 'eternal' Germany – and thus set a norm which their successors could reach by total spiritual exertion. These metaphysics were shot through with affirmations of the delirium of fighting and dying.

Now man is like the storming tempest, the raging ocean and the roaring thunder. Now he is fused with the cosmos, hurtling towards the gates of death like a projectile towards its target.[10]

Or this:

It is the lust of the blood lowering over war like a red sail above a black galley, in its boundless ardour related only to love. It claws at the nerves already in the

---

* Hitler's offer to place Jünger on the Nazi Reichstag list in 1927 – a time when the Party's electoral prospects were none too bright – was, strictly speaking, not an honour in the sense in which the other two (made after the seizure of power) were.

womb of agitated cities when the columns march to the stations through a rain of glowing roses, the *Morituri* song on their lips.[11]

The last quotation firmly anchors Jünger in the emotional climate of Germany during the First World War, and in fact few examples of *Fronterlebnis*, or even common-or-garden patriotic literature worthy of note, came out of the Second World War – or the Third Reich as a whole, for that matter. But this did not worry the cultural stage-managers of National Socialism, since they had a hoard of treasure laid up by earlier writers to draw on. Had not Rudolf G. Binding written: 'Thrice sacred war has leapt out of the hearts of the nations',[12] and did not Ernst Bertram's poem 'Only graves create a homeland'[13] and Hans Carossa's

> Whether he kills or dies, he knows
> All this is merely seed of future love
> Much blood, much blood must sink into the earth
> Else she will never be the home of men[14]

give suitably elevated expression to the government-decreed mood? And beyond the circle of these accomplished practitioners there were countless others from whom the rising seller's market in *Fronterlebnis* commodities drew work whose bulk was inversely proportional to its merit.

The following is a representative excerpt from Beumelburg's *Gruppe Bosemüller*, which in 1936 ranked fourth on the German booksellers' lists.[15] The scene is a German trench on the Western Front. Corporal Wammsch has informed Private Siewers – whose nerve had given way during a recent action – that he can go on leave.

'But I don't want to go away . . . I have to make up for something . . . give me time, why won't you give me some time? I don't want to go home, I don't want my leave . . . I don't want it . . . I want to go back to Fleury and the Souville ravine . . . that's all I want.'

He is sobbing and shaking as if in a fever.

Wammsch is terribly afraid. He hadn't expected this.

'I don't want to go home . . . I'll go down on my knees before the captain . . . he will listen to me . . . I don't want to go home to my mother . . . I want to go to the Souville ravine and Fleury again.'

Now he is exhausted at last. He is still sobbing and his whole body heaves. But he no longer resists. He calmly lets himself be taken into Wammsch's embrace, lets himself be caressed by Wammsch's hard hands, and there is something wonderfully dissolving in this feeling.

'There . . .' says Wammsch, deeply moved, 'I'll go straight to the captain and talk to him. Of course you'll stay with us. The first one to give you an old-fashioned look is going to get my fist in his face . . .'

This excerpt is typical not only in its maudlin mixture of fatherliness and homo-eroticism but also because it conforms, albeit obliquely, to the pre-vailing pattern of war literature. By consensus, more than by overt direc-tion, the key theme of the whole *genre* concerned the alchemy whereby life at the front transmuted a motley of self-centred atoms into an 'oath-bound band of brothers'.[16] The trenches, where iron hoops of interdepen-dence grappled men together and all dross was purged away in the fire of war constituted the passing-out examination of a community of national renaissance; but since, alas, the civilian population had not been poured into the crucible of the *Fronterlebnis*, the new Germany prefigured in the trenches remained stillborn. (It mattered little to the authors and their vast readership that it was precisely the much-derided 'home front' and the even more execrated *Etappe* – base or rear HQ – that alone made it possible for the front line to function.)

Another illuminating paradox common to much *Fronterlebnis* writing concerned the enemy. As soldiers they elicited a perfunctory meed of sympathy, but this was immediately negated in the context of their enmity. Thus the hero of Heinz Steguweit's Christmas play *Petermann Makes Peace* (or *The Parable of German Sacrifice*), fired by a seasonal impulse to halt the carnage, rushed out of his trench to plant a lighted Christmas tree in no-man's-land. He performed this quixotic act against a back-ground of pealing bells, Yuletide hymns and distant machine-gun fire. Suddenly a shot rang out near by, Petermann collapsed, and when his sobbing platoon-mates recovered his body, they found to their bitter dismay that enemy sharpshooters had picked off all the lights on the Christmas tree.[17]

The second major category of Nazi letters, the *genre* included under the heading of 'the Movement' or 'Leader-and-followers', was an extension of the *Fronterlebnis* – both in its themes and chronologically – with *Freikorps* literature serving as a connecting link. In view of their sameness, relatively little need be said about either. In fact, *Freikorps* literature in the Third Reich was less interesting than the fate of some of its leading practitioners.

Ernst von Salomon, himself a veteran of *Freikorps* affrays in the Baltic and Upper Silesia, as well as of a notorious *Fehme* murder (complicity in the 1922 assassination of Foreign Minister Walter Rathenau brought him a five-year jail term)* took fastidious care not to be too closely associated with the regime, while benefiting from the popularity that his largely autobiographical novels enjoyed under it. Salomon's particular form of 'inner emigration' – script writing instead of creative authorship – was also that chosen by that Maverick of Weimar letters, Arnolt Bronnen. Bronnen's ability to come down on both sides of the fence was attested by his authorship of exalted Expressionist dramas – one of them entitled *Parricide* – as well as of the best-selling *Freikorps* novel *Rossbach*, which glorified Hitler's abortive Munich Putsch of 1923.

Whereas every man can be said to be reborn within seven years, the time the human body takes to renew all its cells, Bronnen managed to transform himself from an intimate of Brecht's into the anchor-man of Goebbels's literary entourage in far less time; but he could not defy the laws of biology for ever. It transpired that Bronnen senior had been Jewish, and although the author of *Parricide* produced his mother's sworn admission of marital infidelity in open court, a genetic blemish clung to him throughout the Third Reich.†

'The Movement' *genre* was eminently unremarkable, and since – with one solitary exception‡ – only party hacks engaged in the compilation of hagiography, the fertility of invention by which a Berlin pimp named Horst Wessel and assorted riff-raff of that ilk got themselves embalmed in Valhalla, and won mass-readership appeal, shall go unremarked. (But see p. 380.)

The 'leader-and-followers' variations on the same theme are equally devoid of interest, although Heinrich Zillich's ode to the Führer[18] perhaps deserves mention as a unique blend of rhetoric and mendacity:

> Benign blue eye and iron sword-hand
> Husky voice, thou and the children's most loyal father
> Behold across the continents banded together
> Stand man and wife in the flames of the soul
> Sacredly joined, an endless chain

* This episode had a bizarre sequel in the Federal Republic, when a German film company commissioned Ernst von Salomon to do a shooting script for a film based on Rathenau's life and death.

† In 1937 he was forbidden to publish in Germany. Bronnen's political *perpetuum mobile* achieved completion when, at the end of the Second World War, he re-emerged into the limelight as a member of the Austrian Communist underground.

‡ Hans Heinz Ewers, a noted pornographer, had pre-empted the Horst Wessel biographical market.

Wave-encircled before the morn
Which your shoulders alone
Have raised across the mountain-ridges out of the chasms of distress.

On the same theme of leadership, Josef Weinheber's *Imperial Crypt* is sadly juxtaposed with Zillich's concoction. Weinheber,* a highly talented Austrian poet reared in an orphanage and denied recognition for years, had fallen easy prey to Nazi blandishments.

> Sombre coffin to coffins: and yet you stiff
> Skull still wear the crown? Yes, dust he will be
> Dust. Yet prince stays prince. Only beggars die
> Wholly with the flesh.

> Would beggars depart if the kings remained?
> Therefore princes must go down, because those
> Weaklings succeeded at nothing but their flesh, this rank growth
> Between two darknesses.

Although Weinheber's poetry – as shown in these stanzas – reflected a baroque sensibility and nostalgia for the Imperial past, the Nazi literary manipulators succeeded in making it serve the modern pseudo-revolutionary cult of Caesarism.

They were even more successful with the practitioners of the *Heimatroman* (or regional novel). This *genre*, which overlapped with the *Schollenroman* (novel of the soil – also known as *Blubo*, after *Blut-und-Boden*, blood-and-soil), owed its perennial vogue to various factors: a persistent, strong, regional identification in a country that had been unified relatively recently, a national mystique that equated German-ness with the natural and foreign-ness (especially *Welsch*-ness†) with the artificial; and – more crucially – the anti-modern, anti-urban mood of a tradition-craving middle class ill at ease in a dynamic industrial society.

A special attraction of the regional novel was its tenuous link with time. Although frequently set in the present, such novels exuded an aura of eternity by the device of linking the life and work of their characters to the immemorial cycle of the seasons. The resulting loss of realism‡ was

---

* The Third Reich's sponsorship of Weinheber was the only instance of it showing literary discernment. The poet expiated his lack of political discernment by committing suicide in April 1945.

† *Welsch* in German connotes both membership of the nations speaking Romance languages, and underhandedness.

‡ There were notable exceptions, however, such as Oskar Maria Graf, whose writing was steeped in rustic realism. Although the Nazis wanted to appropriate him, Graf went into

over-compensated for by lavish infusions of spirituality or escapism, as exemplified by the specious magnification of the 'eternal' at the expense of the temporal and contingent.

Christian, especially Roman Catholic, writers (and readers) divined – and treasured – another sort of spiritual merit in this literary *genre*: the assertion that religion is a rich strand in the local fabric of peasant life. (This did not necessarily always apply, however; we shall give examples of pagan regional writing later.)

In fact, the spiritual – or ideological – *karma* engendered by the work of the regional novelists resists classification. In Ernst Wiechert's *Die Majorin* the emphasis was on therapy: humble duties performed within the rural cycle restored health to a diseased mind. Emil Strauss's *Das Riesenspielzeug* had a male hero who forsook urban civilization for an experiment in communal rural living. The attempt at an 'inorganic' (i.e. cerebral) return to nature having failed, he was finally integrated into life on the land with the aid of a genuine daughter of the soil. In H. Kunkel's *Ein Arzt sucht seinen Weg* a restless college-weary undergraduate leaves medical school and home to go to earth in the heathland hideout of his shepherd grand-father, whom he eventually reincarnates as a herbalist capable of effecting miraculous cures.

Kunkel's brand of mysticism, however exalted, seemed rational beside Herbert Böhme's account of a Nordic village wooing.[19] In this scene, the suitor is called '*Sandwegbauer*' after the name of his farmstead – *Bäuerin* means 'farmer's wife':

Around two beating hearts a circle closed, stronger than the rock out of which cathedrals and minsters were hewn . . . *Sandwegbäuerin* . . . the farmstead trembled secretly to hear its own name. It took it up and swung it through stables and barns so that the field still quivered under its impact. But the name of the farmstead sounded more beautifully out of the full pealing of the ears of corn than the call to prayer from towers of churches and cathedrals had ever done. And the *Sandwegbauer* realized that the name was inscribed with sweat and blood upon the furrows of the field, that it was more adamantine than the text of the Holy Writ, and that he himself was the priest who had to preserve this name under the heart of his wife.

From this type of effusion it was but a short step to the openly avowed equation of the fertile soil with the fecund womb, the pagan apotheosis of seed-grain and spermatozoa as agents of the world spirit. Friedrich Ludwig

exile, whence he publicly protested at the omission of his work from the book-burning cere-monies in May 1933.

Barthel sang of maternity and the soil's submission to the plough in *Von Männern und Müttern*[20]

> Mothers are ever the same
> And lie in the fields
> Spaciously suffering the plough, they sleep
> So you think; but they take
> Up their joy unto themselves and become.

Paradoxically, one of the factors boosting the appeal of Nazi 'eugenic' writing was that some of it marginally overlapped with the Church's emphasis on procreation as the purpose of marriage and the justification of sex.

Thus, when a Nazi critic wrote apropos of the eugenic novel *Die Kindlmutter* by Maria Grengg,[21] 'A childless marriage is not a marriage, but a tame form of prostitution and a woman who weds without wanting children is morally not much better than a whore', the sentiment – though hardly the form of expression – may well have elicited clerical approval. When eugenic writing, extolled motherhood as every woman's manifest destiny (*Der Sommergast*, for instance, features an unmarried pregnant heroine who, after vast soul-searching, decides not to go to confession 'since love could never be a sin')[22] this consensus naturally broke down. Broadly speaking, the whole eugenic *genre* – novels of illegitimate, widowed, difficult and doomed motherhood – was presented as an exposition of Mussolini's, 'What war is to man, childbirth is to woman'.

Thus the farmer's maid in Carossa's *Der Arzt Gion* and the mother in Ina Seidel's *Das Wunschkind* earned Nazi acclamation, the former for desiring a child in spite of being incurably ill and the latter for incarnating woman as 'lover and mother, guardian of biological law, social virtue and eternal morality'.[23]

Nor did the *genre* lack the support of scholarship. Josef Prestel interpreted the traditional role of the princess in fairy-tales thus: 'The King's daughter as the hero's reward is the symbol of eugenic improvement, of racial thinking and the continuity of the clan.'[24]

'Race' was another stereotyped literary *genre*, depicting the uniquely endowed Germans ('whose princes almost all European nations had put on their own thrones' not out of any 'love for the German people')[25] as 'more childlike than any other nation',[26] while the French were 'biologically virtually defective, the representatives of Africa in Europe',[27] and the Russians, 'a malevolently squinting, debilitated racial mish-mash'.[28]

A secondary theme of the racial *genre* – *Germania sub specie aeternetatis* – merits closer attention, if for no other reason than its rootedness in a popular ideology that had existed before the Nazis. This was the literature of 'Germany's mission', stretching back beyond the Teutons' entry into recorded history (cf. Felix Dahn's perennially popular *Struggle for Rome*)[29] to the dawn of time (Blunck's archaic *Urvätersaga*). It presented all subsequent vicissitudes of the race – a dizzy pattern of well-nigh irremediable disaster alternating with peaks of unconsummated triumph – as phases in a millennial pilgrimage towards the Holy Grail of German world power.

The Holy German Empire is as infinite as the world itself, established by God and conferred upon the Germans as the eternal task to create order and law in the visible world against the spirit of age and matter, of fear and intellect.[30]

As for the 'leader-and-followers' *genre*, its essence was distilled in one sentence by a leading practitioner: 'Order can exist only where not opinions but forces manifest themselves.'[31] It put forward a view of the world as governed by laws beyond rational comprehension and a view of destiny as unfolding in a dimension accessible only to a visionary leader. Though the mysterious forces revealing themselves to the leader made him their instrument, he was also – thanks to a post-Christian doctrine of transubstantiation – their master:

> Into eternity arises the cathedral
> Which towers darkly over all Germans
> A restless sepulchre to the world;
> For he commands what none has ever dared.[32]

But it is time to turn from the four pillars supporting the Nazi temple of the muses to the spaces between them in which the regime permitted 'non-sponsored literature' to eke out a shadowy existence.

'Non-sponsored literature' is a generic term that needs to be redefined: thus 'entertainment literature' (*Unterhaltungsliteratur*, light, inconsequential reading-matter) which had been deprecated as inappropriate to the greatness of the age after the seizure of power, later received official approbation – and preferential paper allocation – as a wartime morale booster.

Definitely frowned upon was the literature of 'inner emigration', though the actual significance of this *genre* inside the Third Reich ought not to be gauged by the degree of acrimony surrounding it since the war.* The very term 'inner emigration' has been used loosely ever since its inception and any attempt at concise definition involves pitfalls. The dilemma confronting a writer of integrity who had stayed on (unless, like Erich Kästner, he was proscribed, though still resident†) was this: whereas continued appearance in print sustained a fraudulent charade of normality and thereby bolstered the regime, abstention meant abandoning the field to inferior and harmful types of writing. Certain writers thought they saw a way out of this impasse: secure in the resourcefulness of their literary invention, they took up a stance within the nature reserve that the regime had – for reasons of its own – apportioned to a domesticated species of humanist and religiously inspired *belles-lettres*.

All this resulted in a situation of considerable complexity. Ernst Wiechert, who had been sent to a concentration camp after subversive remarks at a public lecture‡ and castigated because his novel *Die Majorin* failed to reflect 'the positive experience of war, the victorious force of man's soul and the glowing resurrective power of the nation',[33] none the less collaborated indirectly with the regime.§

On the other hand Ernst Jünger, the enthusiastic advocate of *Total Mobilization*,¶ from whose work humanist values had been conspicuously absent, published *The Marble Cliffs* in 1939; this veiled attack on dictatorship was, however, so esoteric that some critics have classified it as 'hermetic literature'.

After his earlier vacillating,‖ Frank Thiess, too, made a coded anti-totalitarian statement in his novel *The Realm of the Demons*, which was banned after the first edition had rapidly sold out in 1941. So did the uncompromisingly Christian novelist and poet, Werner Bergengruen, in

---

* After the war Thomas Mann was involved in exchanges with such 'inner emigrants' as Walter von Molo and Frank Thiess; the latter managed to introduce a particularly contentious and resentment-charged note into the debate.

† Erich Kästner had been in the unique situation of seeing his own novels consigned to the flames as part of the great *auto-da-fé* in Berlin in May 1933; he stayed on in Germany although forbidden to publish. The only works of his still allowed to circulate were his children's books (such as *Emil and the Detectives*).

‡ Before students at Munich University in 1936.

§ cf. Loewy, *op. cit.*, p. 29: 'By commending escape into edification, inwardness and sterile traditionalism, they (Wiechert and Carossa) contributed to their readers' acquiescence in evil.'

¶ A book in which Jünger likened the deployment of all resources – including human ones – in war to industrial development.

‖ See page 346; besides which Thiess had called 1933 the year of 'Germany's breakthrough into new historic space' (cf. *Der Spiegel*, 29 April 1968).

Der Grosstyrann und das Gericht. (To these should be added Hermann Oncken's *Cromwell*, Rhoden's *Robespierre*, Oertzen's *Pilsudski*, all interpretations by historians of totalitarian regimes at other times and places from which perceptive readers might have deduced a relevance to the present).

In 1934 Friedrich Georg Jünger – younger brother of Ernst and a militant chauvinist under the Weimar Republic – published a volume of poetry of which 20,000 copies were sold before it was banned. The offending item in it was called *Mohn (Poppy)*:[34]

> Poppy juice soothes out pain. Who grants us oblivion from baseness
> More keenly than fire and steel can that which is base inflict pain
> When it struts in the purple and rules – the muses take flight
> Oh, the lovely ones hastened to flee to far lands
> When she came to the frontier Clio turned back
> And leave-taking uttered a sharp valediction:
> 'Fools are cured with blows and scorn. Soon shall I return with scourges
> Which a judge has twined for you; I shall with nine-tails return.'
> Tribunes have oftentimes reigned. Coriolanus, too, fled
> Into exile unloved. He – the nobler man – left
> And the braggart remained, wildly cheered by the crowd.
> Histrionically stretching to reach buskin height
> He besots you with glory, with ancestral bequests; procures for himself
> Whilst speaking of gold, copious coins in a flash
> He paints superbly with ore. Were iron a colour
> He'd resemble a dragon of steel. His mouth belches fire
> Singing praises he thinks himself worthy of praise. He copies
> The voice of the lion with skill and deception,
> Every utterance is battle. He rouses you daily to battle
> Till all that is hostile drowns in floodtides of words
> Phantom armies sink down. So shout triumph aloud!
> Celebrate phantom victories, burst with cannons the air.
> 'I cannot tolerate laxness.' Silence borders on treason
> Evermore shall your brow drip with sweat of applause!

The core of the inner emigration was formed by such committed Christian writers as Werner Bergengruen, Gertrud Le Fort, Reinhold Schneider and Jochen Klepper (who committed suicide in 1942 alongside his Jewish wife and step-daughter after receiving deportation orders). Their (mainly historical)* work was instinct with religious values and they

---

* Exemplified by Reinhold Schneider's *Las Casas vor Karl V*, which dealt with the confrontation of Church and state in sixteenth-century Spain.

spoke with a still, small voice into the teeth of a gale. Klepper's suicide was paralleled by the death of the poet Oskar Loerke, who simply lost the will to live; by the judicial execution of the anti-Hitler conspirator Albrecht Haushofer (author of the renowned prison poems *Moabiter Sonnette*), and death in a concentration camp of Friedrich von Reck-Malleczewen, whose clandestine *Diary of a Despairing Man*[35] reflected an aristocrat's outrage at being overwhelmed by the plebeian tide.

(To these could be added the deaths in concentration or death camps of Erich Mühsam and Jura Soyfer, of the Nobel Prize winner Carl von Ossietzky and the nun Edith Stein, as well as the suicides of Kurt Tucholsky, Ernst Toller, Josef Roth, Walter Hasenclever, Walter Benjamin and Stefan Zweig; but they form part of the story of the outer emigration which is beyond the scope of our study.)

The means whereby the regime regulated the output and resonance of non-sponsored literature effectively combined elements of mock-freedom with rigid coercion. Although there was no precensorship as such, publishers knew full well what was expected of them, especially as the Gestapo frequently impounded whole editions. For potentially nonconformist writers, however, the intervention of the state's terror machine was a relatively remote contingency compared to the threat of a *Schreibverbot* (the official prohibition to publish).

Then there was the massive panoply of state and Party sponsorship (publicity, prizes, personal appearances, preferential paper allocation in wartime) denied to non-approved authors; they also had to run the gauntlet of criticism by inquisitorial '110-per-centers' and time-serving hacks.

Literary criticism as such was a Pandora's box to leaders uncomfortably aware of the poverty of much sponsored writing, as Goebbels's ideologically suspect rationalization 'Genius cannot be bred'[36] indicated. His Gauleiter colleague, Streicher, provided a characteristic illustration of his own view of the critic's role by forcing a Nuremberg journalist who had panned a juggling act at the local music-hall to go on stage the following night and do better. Not surprisingly the censorious ink-slinger was hoist with his own petard – and so cerebral activity and life stood revealed in stark opposition.

In 1936 literary criticism as hitherto understood was abolished; henceforth reviews followed a pattern: a synopsis of content studded with quotations, marginal comments on style, a calculation of the degree of concurrence with Nazi doctrine and a conclusion indicating approval or otherwise.

On the other hand, even critics securely ensconced in the editorial chairs of Party publications had little room for manœuvre when confronted with the *Unbedenklichkeitsvermerk* (the certificate of unexceptionability issued by the Party literary office) on a book, since criticism of a work endowed with the official *imprimatur* amounted to a breach of inner-Party discipline.* (The *Unbedenklichkeitsvermerk* represented the minimum degree of official sponsorship. Beyond that, the Party office for *Schrifttumspflege*, the sponsorship of literature, could recommend certain books to all affiliated organizations – or, best of all, include them among the 'six books of the month', which meant the possibility of best-seller status.)

Yet none of these inducements sufficed to redress a marked imbalance in literary output: the dearth of writing on the urban scene, which, after all, was the context in which the majority of Germans were spending their lives. This was typical of a literature conceived on the Procrustean bed of dogma, and moved a critic to conjecture that foreigners deriving their knowledge of Germany solely from books would think her 'a country of few cities and no industry . . . whose people try to render great forests and moors habitable.'[37] Goebbels similarly found 'such important literary themes as those of "the town" and "the worker" treated in an extraordinarily cursory manner.'[38]

This native avoidance of the contemporary social scene partly accounted for the vogue of foreign authors in the Third Reich. In its quite untypical toleration of alien bookish influences the regime was guided by two considerations: for one, translations of C. S. Forester, Harvey Allen, Charles Morgan and Thomas Wolfe†, provided German readers with a badly needed enrichment of their native literary gruel; for another, the socially critical work of Galsworthy, Cronin, Steinbeck or Erskine Caldwell corroborated the Nazis' description of Western society as Mammon-ridden and corrupt.

A. J. Cronin's *The Citadel*, for instance, was recommended to German readers as demonstrating the connection between medical malpractices and Jewish influence among doctors in Britain.[39]

Pride of place among translated works was accorded to the products of 'Nordic' Scandinavia, particularly to those of Knut Hamsun, the elderly,

* cf. Hans Langbuch in *Völkischer Beobachter*, Nr. 244, 1 September 1934: 'In addition, the book carries the *Unbedenklichkeitsvermerk*, so that an attack on it is to be interpreted as an attack on an agency of the Party leadership.'

† Other foreign favourites of the German reading public were Robert Graves, Liddell Hart, T. E. Lawrence and Esther Meynell (cf. Dieter Strothmann, *Nationalsozialistische Literaturpolitik*, Bonn, 1960, p. 201).

tetchy Germanophile whose earthbound, race-conscious, anti-urban novels approximated quite closely to the ideal categories of the Nazi literary ethos.

The sickliness of the Nazi muse necessitated transfusions of writing that was distant in time as well as in space. The lack of quality reading matter after the burning of books in 1933 made long-dead authors popular again; characteristically presenting a deficiency as its opposite, the regime paraded the resultant vogue for the classics as proof of its own reverence for the national heritage. From 1939 onwards it also used the classics as ammunition in its psychological warfare. National Dramatist Schlösser wrote of 'the thunder of cannons at Sedan and Mozart's *Kleine Nachtmusik* as products of the same artistic endowment of the German people.'[*] The value of *Wilhelm Tell* to the nation was placed on a par with the military potential of three army corps,[40] and 'Goethe, Schiller and the Romantic Movement' were credited with having made possible the victory at Leipzig.[41]

On the subject of Goethe's share in the victory over Napoleon, however, Party comment was not all of one piece. Rosenberg[42] found it severely remiss of the 'prince of poets' that he had refused to recognize 'the dictatorship of thought without which a nation cannot remain a nation nor ever create a true commonwealth. Just as Goethe forbade his son to take part in the German War of Liberation . . . so, were he alive today, he would not be a leader in the struggle for the freedom of our century.'

Schiller escaped similar strictures, and the regime's only sanction against the poet of freedom was the omission (ordered by Hitler) of *Wilhelm Tell* from schoolbooks published after 1941.[43] Another wartime change in literary policy concerned the renewed emphasis for morale-boosting purposes – on writing with erotic content. The first reactions against the prudery that accompanied the original Nazi revolution had actually set in much earlier. 'Are we not all awaiting the resurrection of that genuine German eroticism that distinguished Goethe, Kleist, Storm and Mörike?'[44] inquired Rainer Schlosser rhetorically, before he came to the sanguine conclusion, 'How tempted must our writers feel to oppose the symphony of the earth-rooted Germans' glowing blood to the alien sexual ravings of now happily repulsed Asiatic-ness'.[45] Hanns Johst expressed a similar concern more succinctly: 'What is healthy is our heroic

---

[*] Rainer Schlösser, *Die Notwendigkeit des Schönen in 'Wille und Macht'*, Vol. II, seventh series, 1939, p. 2. cf. Werner Sombart's 'Militarism is . . . Potsdam and Weimar in supreme union. It is Faust and Zarathustra and a Beethoven score in the trenches,' quoted by Hermann Glaser in *Spiesser Ideologie*, Freiburg, 1964, p. 24.

command'[46] and Goebbels – echoing his colleague Robert Ley's eugenic slogan 'Live joyfully' – welcomed 'strong and healthy sensual joy which gratefully affirms life in the here and now'.[47]

Although many Germans did in fact experience a revival of sensual joy during the Nazi period (particularly in wartime), latterday eroticists on a par with Goethe or Mörike failed to materialize, either in peace or in war. The war itself produced a number of interesting literary changes. In addition to extending official sponsorship to 'light reading' and writings with a healthy erotic content, the authorities also sponsored the output of 'literature of consolation and edification'. With titles such as *Mothers and Men, A Book of the Courageous Heart, Maternal Countenance, Courageous Grief, Consolation Letters, Lancers Laugh, Bunker Tales, With a Merry Pen, Turn Away Gloom, A Book of German Drolleries,* and *Laughing Field-Grey,*[48] this literature of emotional shock absorbers of the maudlin or rib-tickling variety was designed for a key market that was liable to expand, and that the regime had little intention of sharing with the Churches. After September 1939 the demand for religious literature had in fact increased quite noticeably, until in 1941, by the brutally simple device of depriving religious publishing houses of paper supplies, the state effectively denied the Churches any means of reaching the reading public.

One type of writing that apparently proved its two-fold merit in wartime comprised the redskin sagas of Karl May. Not only did those traditionally popular adventure yarns continue to entertain youngsters of all ages, but large numbers of Wehrmacht soldiers expressed their gratitude to the publishers for having provided them with 'the best manuals for anti-partisan warfare available'.[49]

Whatever the truth of this assertion, there can be no doubt that literary support of the fighting front as such left little to be desired. By 1941 no less than 45,000 'front-line libraries' were supplying soldiers with reading matter. In the course of five great wartime collection drives a staggering total of over 43 million books had been donated by civilians for Wehrmacht use.[50] At the same time, stories of the fighting service were of course favourite reading matter on the home front: Kohl's *We Fly Against England* and *Sea-Hero Prien,* for instance, headed the list of borrowings from Hamburg libraries in 1940–1.[51] (But although there was a sellers' market in this type of literature, the authors of war stories did not necessarily lead an untroubled existence. The air-force novel *Men Fall from the Skies* was faulted for its 'panicky', 'suicide-minded' pilots,[52] and Bernd von Heiseler was said to have 'devalued the unconditional concept of manly death' by letting the soldier hero of his novel *Appollonia* seek death in action after discovering his fiancée's unfaithfulness.)[53]

The wartime mobilization of literary resources was only the culmination of thorough-going measures put in hand soon after the seizure of power. State-run libraries increased from 6,000 in 1933 to 25,000 at the height of the war[54] – even though the projected aim of establishing one such library in every parish with over 500 inhabitants was never realized. Fifty-five thousand school libraries were set up between 1937 and 1941, and by the end of 1938 4,000 individual industrial plants had stocked their libraries with 3 million books; employees could borrow them either free of charge or for 10 pfennigs apiece.[55] (At private circulating libraries the charges varied from 20 to 90 pfennigs – a fairly prohibitive amount.) There were in addition ships' libraries, hotel libraries, Labour Service camp libraries – as well as prison and concentration-camp libraries!

This impressive deployment of literary resources was regulated by Department VIII of Goebbels's Ministry of Propaganda and Popular Enlightenment. At the beginning of the war this department supervised no less than 2,500 publishing houses, 23,000 bookshops, 3,000 authors, 50 national literary prizes, 20,000 new books issued annually, and a total of 1 million titles constituting the available book market.[56]

If the Hegelian law that quantity turns into quality upon reaching a certain point applies to literature, the Third Reich should have been well on the way to becoming a latter-day Athens. Instead, the most widely-read – or displayed – book of the period was Hitler's *Mein Kampf*, a collection (according to Leon Feuchtwanger) of 164,000 offences against German grammar and syntax; by 1940, it was, with 6 million copies sold,[57] the solitary front-runner in the German best-seller list, some 5 million copies ahead of Rainer Maria Rilke and others.

24

THE THEATRE

By some mysterious law of compensation the politically infertile Weimar era had been prodigal of new life in the arts. In the theatre (and cinema) the first post-war decade constituted nothing less than a golden age; the stage, throbbing with ideas of political, psycho-analytical, religious and technological origin, exploded into great diversity: it became pulpit, tribunal, fairground, confessional, operating-theatre, peepshow or chamber of horrors.

Talent abounded. Among the directors three great innovators dominated the scene: the baroque magician, Max Reinhardt, the cerebral Leopold Jessner, and Erwin Piscator, who admitted no dividing line between the revolution in the theatre and that in the streets. Among the playwrights, although the *Zeitgeist* spoke in the Expressionist accents of Georg Kaiser, Ernst Toller, Ernst Barlach, Fritz von Unruh and Franz Werfel, different accents – both older and newer – gained a hearing too: Gerhart Hauptmann, Hugo von Hoffmansthal, Artur Schnitzler, Bruno Frank, Karl Zuckmayer, Walter Hasenclever, Karl Sternheim and Bertolt Brecht.

The array of acting talents on which these directors and playwrights could draw was equally impressive: Albert Bassermann, Alexander Moissi, Paul Wegener, Emil Jannings, Fritz Kortner, Heinrich George, Werner Kraus, Ernst Deutsch, Max Pallenberg, Gustav Gründgens, Käthe Dorsch, Käthe Gold, Fritzi Massary and Elizabeth Bergner.

This teeming and variegated theatrical scene was drastically impoverished by the Nazis' seizure of power. All the directors listed above were proscribed and nearly all the playwrights, except Hanns Johst, who was made the poet laureate of the new regime, and the venerable Gerhart Hauptmann, whom Goebbels alternately cast into the limbo of obscurity or embalmed in specious veneration. Of the leading actors listed, exactly half (Bassermann, Bergner, Deutsch, Kortner, Massary, Moissi and Pallenberg) were defamed as Jews and forced into retirement or exile.*

* Albert Bassermann, wearer of the Ifland Ring (the highest award of the German acting profession), was not a Jew himself but refused to divorce his Jewish wife Elsa and went into exile with her.

At the time more sanguine foreign observers – including many *émigrés*–doubted whether the land of poets and thinkers would permanently reconcile itself to the rule of Philistine bullies. Such illusions stemmed from a misconception: the poet-and-thinker image created by Madame de Staël over a century earlier had never entered the self-awareness of the German people, only that of an educated minority.

To the majority the arts were a closed book, and even the minority had become inured to the summary dismissal of artists by the Depression, which had closed nearly half of Berlin's forty-five theatres by early 1933.[1]

More relevant to post-1933 attitudes, though, was the verve and skill with which the non-purged artists stepped into the breach to cozen the public into mistaking the haemorrhage inflicted on the theatre for a blood-transfusion. They helped turn the stage into a gilded figleaf concealing Nazi nakedness – and the regime in return loosed a cornucopia of subsidies, contracts, state councillorships, Goethe Prizes and managerial posts upon appreciatively bowed Thespian heads.*

Economic recovery and the efficiency of Nazi audience mobilization did the rest, so that by 1942 the number of visitors to Germany's 197 municipal theatres (i.e. those subsidized by the rates) was exactly double that of ten years earlier.[2]

Immediately after 1933 the theatre's rising popularity owed something to the emergence of the *Thingspiel* – the Nazis' solitary contribution to theatrical art form. The *Thing* had been a Teutonic tribal assembly (cf. the *Storting* – the Swedish parliament) and *Thingspiele* were open-air medleys of Nazi 'agit-prop', military tattoo, pagan oratorio and circus performance.

The construction of the special *Thingspielstätten* (rudimentary amphitheatres incorporating hilly slopes and ancient ruins) exemplified Nazi gigantomania: the one near Koblenz – population 90,000 – could accommodate half the town's inhabitants; but the logistics involved in mass-transport never baffled Party organizers.

Size was also the hallmark of the performance: entire SA or Hitler Youth battalions participated in battle scenes, processions or choric declamations, and these epic elements, reinforced by sword play, horsemanship or fanfares, helped give the *genre* considerable (if short-lived) audience appeal.

The leading *Thingspiel* author was Richard Euringer, from whose

* At the same time, it must be remembered that some of the artists so honoured actually used their influence to help persecuted colleagues.

Deutsche Passion we quote an exchange between the spirit of the war dead and the evil spirit mocking their sacrifice:

THE EVIL SPIRIT: Heads into the slime, ye skeletons! Haven't you bedded down snugly, aren't you the saviours of Germany? Kindly take care of your compost.

THE SPIRIT OF THE DEAD WAR VOLUNTEERS:
What use is it to live on and to mature? Those who survived will never grasp it, those who survived will never know it. Bliss was it to burn to death.

Euringer doubled as both leading practitioner and chief theorist of the new art form. As the latter he formulated a set of *Thingspiel* theses:

From theatre art, the *Thingspiel* leads away to the abode of judgment. Fire, water, earth and air are evoked. Stones, stars and solar orbits are the *Thingspiel* elements. Mermaids, fairies, nymphs and fauns escape to the theatre of nature. On the *Thingplatz*, the people act the blood-oath and exorcism. Without outlawry and banishment, there is no *Thing*. Silence receives the oath-bound host of the boundary and they enter the place of judgment mutely, for this is holy ground. The people's actions become an act of creation and sacrifice. The people beholds its martyrs, honours them and adores them. The cult of the dead is attained fact, the fallen arise and out of stones screams the spirit.[3]

But despite a flair for bluster, Euringer produced nothing else comparable to *Deutsche Passion*; his colleagues' effusions were even more substandard, and this, plus the public's aversion to dampness and insects, persuaded the authorities to let the *Thingspiel* die a natural death a few short years after its highly publicized beginnings. A theatrical weekly deplored the 'lack of congenial balance between the idea and its realization' and ended this obituary with the consoling reflection that the Reich Party Rally was 'the *Thing* idea become flesh and blood'.[4]

In the wider sense of the word, the regime was anything but barren of theatrical invention. It politicized the stage as effectively as it stage-managed politics, and Nazi 'spectaculars', mixing theatre with propaganda, speedily established themselves as a part of the German entertainment scene.

Typical examples of this hybrid form of entertainment were the 1936 Olympic Festival of Youth – with a cast of 10,000! – and the revue *Struggle Has Been the Germans' Eternal Destiny* at the huge Deutschland Halle in Berlin. This show featured jousting knights, wimpled chatelaines, viola-playing pageboys, morris-dancing peasants, bewigged courtiers and marching Prussian grenadiers. Then followed a 'one-pot meal' sequence symbolic of the present: nutritious vegetables performed a ballet, while real farmyard animals cavorted among the gyrating greenery. A heavily satirical grumblers' sequence led into a martial finale struck up by massed bands of the Wehrmacht and the police.[5]

This *Eintopf* ballet had its barnyard parallels on the legitimate stage. *Row over Iolanthe*, which featured a live sow being fought over by two litigious smallholders, was the hit of the 1934–5 Berlin season (achieving 500 performances at the Lessing Theater).[6] Almost as popular was the *Whitsun Organ*, whose cast, according to the *Frankfurter Zeitung*, won *rapport* with the audience by becoming coarse and folksily obvious – often in defiance of stage directions. The paper commented plaintively, 'Berlin has gone over to farce almost 100 per cent.'[7] Though the figure was somewhat inflated, comedy was undoubtedly king on the stage of the Third Reich. In 1936 twenty-three Berlin theatres carried out the following division of labour: eight performed musical comedies, seven modern comedies, four heroic Nazi drama, two opera and ballet, and two classics plus some modern drama.[8]

Over the country as a whole the greatest hits of the year were: *The Base Wallah*, a comedy of army life, and *Uproar in the Tenement*, a domestic farce; other successful titles were *Hilda and the Four Horsepowers*, *A Leap out of the Workaday World,* and *Tovarich*, the White Russian émigré confection.[9] The classics were not completely eclipsed, however. At the 175 theatres listed in the 1936 statistics, Schiller's dramas were given 1,182 separate performances, achieving just half of *The Base Wallah*'s total.[10]

A somewhat less powerful box-office magnet was *Petermann Sails to Madeira*, a comedy actually set in the Third Reich. Its hero was a crabbed fault-finder, whose moroseness melted in the communal gaiety of a Strength-through-Joy trip. Though fairly successful, *Petermann Sails to Madeira* was doubly unrepresentative of Nazi-sponsored plays, both because of its lightness of touch and its contemporaneity. Nazi drama was, almost by definition, heroic and historic; the closest it approached to contemporary reality was in the *Kampfzeit* epics centred on the venerated Party martyr Horst Wessel or Heinz Norkus, his Hitler Youth counterpart.

Since 'struggle had been the Germans' eternal destiny' the whole of national history could be treated as a *Kampfzeit*; moreover it was capable of infinite extension backwards in time. On this eternal time scale the primordial mist-shrouded *Thor's Guest* made the Fall-of-Rome epic *Totila* or the Charlemagne drama *Wittukind* almost appear modern. The last-named play gained topicality (and gave offence to Catholics) by presenting the Saxon chieftain Wittukind as a pagan martyr of Charlemagne's Christianizing crusade.

Medievalists and Nazi ideologists failed throughout Hitler's reign to pull the two divergent Charlemagne images – Architect of Empire or Romanizing Perverter of Germandom – into one, Party-approved focus. In consequence, historical playwrights gave Charlemagne a wide berth and concentrated on some of his less equivocal successors, such as Frederick Barbarossa and Henry IV. Even though fledgeling playwrights found much of this particular ground staked out by their elders and betters – to wit Joseph Wentner and Guido Kolbenheyer – a truly assiduous prospector could dredge up gold from every stratum of the racial past.

One of the richest veins was the war of liberation against Napoleon – the setting of the box-office hit *Hockewanzel*. Its hero, a Catholic archdeacon in the Austrian Empire, is offered a bishopric in a Slav-inhabited area – but, shunning pastoral miscegenation, he exchanges the proffered crozier for a flintlock gun to fight in the Tyrolean uprising against French rule. The play owed its audience-appeal to the mixture of priestly cunning and peasant horse-sense in Hockewanzel's character.

Journey to Ophir – a totally humourless play in contrast – exemplified the 'eternal struggle' theme in a naval-warfare setting. An old German captain, taken prisoner on the high seas by his English son-in-law, does not tell his captors that they are steaming into a German minefield until it is too late. 'Wouldn't you have done the same if you had been in my place?' he asks his son-in-law. During their last minutes on earth, before the explosion, each of the protagonists is vouchsafed an intimation of bliss: the captain sets out on an imaginary South Sea cruise, the cabin boy paces the captain's bridge, and the English son-in-law has a vision of his wife heavy with child.

The drama *Einsiedel*, too, had a 1914–18 background. It concerned a shell-shocked ex-serviceman and amnesia victim, who has found post-war employment as a cemetery gardener. A tattoo, played during an officer's funeral, springs the trap of his memory. Remembering Germany's past greatness, he screams out a plea for her resurrection and dies of a stroke.

Another dramatic *genre* made much of during the Third Reich was the peasant play, or *Heimatstück*, which, in fact, had reputable antecedents, both in German and Austrian literature. The Nazis fostered a particular variation called *Blubo* plays; this *genre*, which we have already referred to when discussing the novel, celebrated the German farmer's rootedness in the soil (*Blubo* is short for *Blut* and *Boden*, 'blood and soil') and placed human procreation on a par with soil fertility as manifestations of God immanent in nature. Pursuing the rootedness theme, 'blood and soil' dramatists produced soliloquies like this:

I am a man, you see, who is made of earth, out of a clod of earth, as the Scripture puts it. I can't make myself be anything else. If you were to push earth down my throat, I would chew it and I would find it tasted good.[11]

One of the best-known *Blubo* plays was *Vroni Mareiner*, in which a peasant lad carelessly makes love to a dairymaid while planning to marry a rich farmer's daughter for her dowry. Fatally hurt in a mountaineering accident, he marries the pregnant dairymaid on his deathbed and she moves into his neglected home – his legatee in both the legal and the biological sense.

The eugenic theme was also to the fore in the play *The Giant* by Richard Billinger, in which an old farmer demonstrates his obstinate attachment to the soil by turning down a profitable drainage project put to him by an industrial firm. His daughter falls in love with an engineer and deserts the ancestral farm for the big city, where she comes to a bad end, but her indomitable father creates new life by bedding down with his house-keeper.

In the *Blubo* plays the chain of the generations had to be continued at all costs, even if this conflicted with traditional morality. A sympathetic reviewer had written about an earlier Billinger play, *Rauhnacht*:

While throughout the world everyone prepares for the feast of Christ, primordial feelings stir in remote hamlets. Dark and powerful instincts, which almost two millennia of Church-imposed discipline could not repress, are coming into their own again.[12]

In another widely performed 'blood and soil' play, *Schwarzmann and the Maid*, Schwarzmann, a rich farmer's son, seduces a peasant maid with a bogus offer of marriage and then tries to persuade her to have an abortion. Rather than abandon his child, she prepares to bear the stigma of illegitimate motherhood. Her final death in childbirth was likened by the critics to that of a soldier on the field of honour.[13]

There were endless permutations of the eugenic motif, as can be seen in this newspaper summary of *Peter Rothman's Maid*:

The farmer Peter Rothman's marriage was originally harmonious, but after ten years the lack of an heir causes it to go to pieces. The farmer is drawn to the young and strikingly healthy peasant maid, who presents him with the long-hoped-for son, and herself becomes mistress of the farm after the wife's suicide.[14]

But not all plays of a rustic *genre* aimed at dramatic effect. There were a number – by no means the least popular – which struck a lighter note. The most successful of them was *The Frogs of Büschebul*, which features a village mayor pursuing two pet schemes from motives of personal gain. One involves draining the local swamp, so that hotels providing mud-bath facilities can be built; the other hinges on a profitable marriage for his ward, from which the mayor also hopes to derive profit. He gets his comic deserts when both projects fall through simultaneously. *The Frogs of Büschebul* thus ran the triumph of romantic love in double harness with the romanticizing of tradition, however unprofitable and unhygienic.

Elsewhere in the repertoire of Nazi-sponsored plays, attitudes so remote from the twentieth century were less evident. The staple light-comedy fare that the Third Reich offered to an appreciative public hardly differed from examples of the same *genre* in pre-Nazi Germany or in other countries.

Excursion into the Big World has a chambermaid heroine who borrows both the name and the jewellery of her mistress to good effect. *Das Mädchen Till* repeats *The Taming of the Shrew* motif; a young paediatrician manages to bludgeon a self-willed girl into marriage and to convert her father's castle into a sanatorium. The highly popular *Sparrows in the Hand of God* features a savings-bank clerk who spreads false rumours about a large inheritance and enjoys unlimited credit in consequence. Unmerited promotion to a directorship enables him to cover the debts incurred by his cheeky confidence-trickery.

Yet even among the light comedies, 'blood and soil' reared its ugly head. In *Christa, I await you*, the heroine, who has completed medical school, gives up her medical career as well as her bookish fiancé to marry an estate owner. The whole play is a frothy concoction into which grains of received Nazi truth – the irrelevance of university studies to women's lives, the soil-bound man's superiority over the bookworm, the triumph of instinct over reason – have been expertly stirred. The play seems to have been rather atypical, however, an impression confirmed by the statement of the Kassel municipal theatre's literary manager: 'The playwrights of our new era seem to lack humour.' The perceptive *Dramaturg* drew equally scant comfort from other aspects of the theatrical scene:

Because society, in the traditional meaning of the term, no longer exists in the Third Reich, and our dramatists cannot write about something non-existent, many theatres unfortunately make do with Oscar Wilde revivals. In its spoilt way, the public clings to antiquated attitudes and displays a continually growing antipathy towards *Tendenzstücke* i.e. plays with a message.[15]

Goebbels, for his part, was not unduly perturbed by tepid audience reaction to political plays; having assigned a primarily escapist function to the arts, he was content for theatre-goers to receive a certain minimum dosage of Nazi drama. Thus in Berlin, only one theatre out of every six was completely politicized – although a purely statistical analysis may be misleading. 'Blood and soil' and other Nazi concepts also crept into super-ficially escapist entertainment, such as *Christa, I Await you*. In addition, Nazi drama reached the public through channels other than the legitimate stage; Hanns Johst's play *Schlageter* (which contains the celebrated phrase, 'Every time I hear the word "culture", I release the safety-catch of my revolver')* was staged not only professionally but by schools, student groups, and amateur societies. True to its avowal of folk traditions, the regime placed special emphasis on *Laienspiele* (amateur dramatics), and one of the officially sponsored playwrights, Heinz Steguweit, carved out a special niche for himself as a *Laienspielautor* of plays for amateurs.

Overall, the Nazis assigned a more crucial role to the classics than to political drama. Schiller, Goethe, Kleist, Shakespeare and Hebbel were given performances of as high a standard as munificent authorities and dedicated thespians could contrive. The avid participation of the more sensitive actors and directors in this undertaking stemmed from an uneasy conscience; rationalizing their servility to the regime, they persuaded themselves that classical revivals preserved an oasis of culture in the Third Reich's Philistine atmosphere and thus shored up the crumbling ramparts of civilization. Nazi addiction to the classics was motivated by various factors. The classically biased repertoires of the state theatres camouflaged the paucity of new serious plays and substantiated the regime's claim to dedicated stewardship of German culture. Above all, a penumbra of eleva-tion and decorousness – two qualities much beloved by the educated middle class – hovered around the classics; their ubiquitous and incessant performance obscured a barren landscape behind a ribbon development of Potemkin villages.

Such political considerations notwithstanding, the Nazi-sponsored

---

* *Schlageter* was a jingoist passion play about a *Freikorps* hero whom the French executed during their occupation of the Ruhr.

renaissance of the classics produced some notable artistic achievements. Certain open-air performances – Goethe's *Götz von Berlichingen* at Heidelberg Castle or his *Faust* in front of the *Römer* in Frankfurt – achieved undeniable distinction, as did a whole range of productions in the capital. Despite the exodus of 1933, Berlin still boasted an impressive array of theatrical talent (actor-managers such as the legendary Gustav Gründgens and Heinrich George, actors like Werner Kraus and Käthe Dorsch, and producers like Heinz Hilpert, Jürgen Fehling and Erich Engel).

Classical productions involving these glittering names invariably drew crowded houses; this – for the reasons previously stated – served the regime's aims perfectly, though the presentation of Schiller and Shakespeare was not without its ambiguous aspects. Even if the classics (contrary to some actors' hopes) lacked the power of inducing catharsis – and no audience ever needed purging through terror and above all through pity more than theirs did – they were not so devoid of pith as to supply the required pabulum for theatre-goers. The curtain-line from Schiller's *The Parasite*, 'Justice exists only on the stage', often triggered off frenetic applause, as did the climax of the Marquis de Posa's plea to King Philip in *Don Carlos*, 'Sire, grant us freedom of thought.' Official reaction to the *Don Carlos* incidents varied; certain theatres switched on the house-lights during Posa's speech to inhibit applause. In 1937 the Berlin Stadtstheater dropped the play from its repertoire after eight weeks, and the Party's ideological journal pontificated, 'It was men like the Marquis de Posa who caused the French Revolution. Freedom linked to obedience such as Schiller knew it in later life was unknown to Posa.'[16] Four years later – presumably again distinguishing between the younger and the more mature Schiller – Hitler banned the use of *Wilhelm Tell* as a school-text; this was poetic justice indeed, since the Swiss patriot's 'Rütli oath' had been ceremoniously recited by the Nazis in the Munich beer-cellar before they set out on their abortive November 1923 *putsch*.

In 1944 Gründgens produced Schiller's apprentice work, *The Robbers*, as an evocation of nihilism, and cast himself as the villainous Franz Moor with a maniacal mien and a hairstyle reminiscent of Hitler's. Physical resemblance was also central to Jurgen Fehling's production of Shakespeare's *Richard III*. In the leading part, Werner Kraus dragged himself across the stage with a clubfoot suggestive of Goebbels's; when his murderous henchmen removed their cloaks, they revealed brown and black shirts, belts and cross-straps underneath.[17] The chancery clerk's musing on the indictment against Hastings, 'Who is so gross that cannot see this palpable device? Yet who so bold but says he sees it not?' provoked applause in mid-scene.[18]

By contrast, Lothar Müthel's version of another Shakespeare classic revealed that well-known producer as an aesthetic accessory after the fact of genocide. Commanded by the Viennese Gauleiter, Baldur von Schirach, to put on *The Merchant of Venice* at the Burgtheater in 1942 – the time of the mass-deportations to Auschwitz – Müthel accepted, because (in his own words) he 'found the theatrical problems involved absorbing'. He commissioned the well-known critic, H. Ihering, to adapt Shakespeare's text to the exigencies of the Nazis' race laws, so that Jessica emerged as a product of the adultery of Shylock's wife with a non-Jew, and this – under the terms of the Nuremberg laws – qualified her as a marriage partner for the Aryan Lorenzo. In the role of Shylock, Werner Kraus, who had previously insisted on portraying all the Jewish characters in the film version of *Jud Süss* lest (in his own words) 'half a dozen actors should vie with each other in anti-Jewish caricature', gave a performance of unsurpassable anti-Semitism.

But there were men on the German stage who took a different stand on these matters. In 1942 the young actor Joachim Gottschalk chose death alongside his Jewish wife, just as the venerable Albert Bassermann had preferred exile to separation from his own Jewish wife eight years earlier.

In 1934, too, a more trivial – but none the less noteworthy – form of philo-Semitism had been displayed by the cabaret artist Werner Finck. Once when he reeled off a string of politically ambiguous gags at Berlin's minuscule *Katakombe*, Finck was called 'lousy Yid' by an irate listener, to which he retorted in a flash: 'I only happen to look intelligent.' Finck's *pièce de resistance* was a cabaret sketch, in which he got his tailor to measure him for a suit.

TAILOR: What sort of jacket should it be? With chevrons and stripes?
FINCK: You mean a straitjacket?
TAILOR: How would you like your pockets?
FINCK: Wide open – in the current fashion.

As Finck kept his right arm extended in a gesture resembling the Nazi salute, the tailor took sleeve measurements, mumbling, 'Nineteen – thirty-three – suspended rights', and that was how it went on until Goebbels closed the *Katakombe* and dispatched Finck to a concentration camp. Released after Käthe Dorsch (a *protégée* of Goebbels's rival Goering) had interceded on his behalf, Finck meekly resumed his gadfly role until expelled from the Reich Chamber of Culture and thereby entirely debarred from the acting profession. He eventually went to earth in the Wehrmacht's *Truppenbetreuung* ('troops' welfare', the German equivalent of ENSA).

The seating capacity of the *Katakombe* had been only 300, but Finck's gags (like those of his Bavarian counterpart, Weiss Ferdl) gained virtually nationwide currency via the grapevine of political jokes. The regime's attitude to this tended to be equivocal. While treating some political jokes as quite literally a hanging matter, it turned a blind eye to the discreet dissemination of others – judging them, correctly, to be a form of therapy and not of resistance. Even so, anti-regime humour ranked as an expression of dissatisfaction, and Goebbels had – in a memorable phrase – described grumbling as 'defecation of the soul.' The headline under which the *Schwarzes Korps* reported the closure of the *Katakombe* had incidentally been equally *recherché*: HOUSE OF JOY (i.e. brothel) CLOSED DOWN'.[19]

Not wishing to deprive the public of all professional political humour, the authorities sponsored a number of tame cabaret substitutes. A popular revue in the spring of 1936, for instance, featured foreign political *aperçus* – a photographer telling the British Foreign Secretary, Eden, to hold his olive branch a little higher, and admonishing the French Premier, Flandin, not to look too much to the left – as well as home policy ones; jokes about pedigrees[20] and a station-master announcing Berlin as the capital of North Bavaria and Munich as that of South Prussia.

Other essays in the same field were more sophisticated: a cabaret on the Kurfürstendamm showed a factory owner who, with tears streaming down his face, tried to force a pay rise on his resisting employees; or, more purposeful, a Strength-through-Joy mobile cabaret brought to a climax a programme castigating grumblers, pessimists, astrology addicts and other backsliders, with an agit-prop type of ditty: 'I want you all to understand that there can be no greater blessing than living in a fatherland that gives you work and is progressing.'[21]

The co-ordination of cabaret art was part of the same process as the decree issued by Goebbels in the autumn of 1936 to reduce reviewers to eunuchs dispensing guide-book information. Criticism was replaced by so-called 'consideration of a work of art', with results for the theatre which Werner Kraus described after the war: 'Previously, we had trembled with fear before every first night, but from now on we no longer trembled because nobody would dare say that we were no good; but that became boring and, above all, we no longer learnt anything. In the end, we our-selves no longer knew whether we were good or bad.'[22] However damaging Goebbels's decree may have been to acting standards, it proved prophy-lactic for critics, who had previously incurred considerable occupational hazards. A poor review of Rehberg's *Johann Keppler* in the *Wuppertaler Zeitung*, for instance, caused the local Party boss to write to the paper's proprietor:

> The saddest and bitterest aspect of the situation is the fact that Rehberg has been a Party comrade since 1930 (membership No. 360,000). Perhaps your critic is not even a Party member, or maybe a very young one, without any inkling of the depths of National Socialist culture. I am no longer prepared to tolerate sabotage by such malcontents at Wuppertal. At the very next opportunity I shall denounce these characters to Minister Goebbels and Minister-President Goering and shall demand that they be sent to a concentration camp. As for yourself, I must ask you most cordially, as an old Party fighter, to remove this critic at once.[23]

Goering, who showed the proprietory interest of a territorial prince in the Prussian state theatres, had the critic Alfred Muhr of the *Deutsche Zeitung* placed under Gestapo surveillance as a 'saboteur of National Socialist construction', because of the tone of his reviews.[24]

But the personal involvement of the Nazi potentates in the theatre went beyond a simple straitjacketing of critics. Some of the armed Bohemians forming the Nazi élite kept yellowing manuscripts next to the revolvers in their drawers. One such dilettante was Gauleiter Kube, who had written a play about the early Germanic king, Totila (one of the tragic heroes in Felix Dahn's nineteenth-century best-seller *The Struggle for Rome*). When theatrical managements in Berlin failed to show any interest in *Totila*, the Prussian Ministry of Culture issued the following missive:

> The old National Socialist fighter, the current *Oberpräsident* Kube, has written a play which has already been successfully produced in other towns. In Berlin it has not so far been possible to put it on. I ask you to take all necessary steps immediately so that Kube's drama can also be put on in Berlin. Time limit: three days.[25]

The other towns referred to were, of course, in Kube's own Gau of Kur-mark, where a local Nazi paper had commented on the play: 'Wilhelm Kube's *Totila* cannot be put under the dissecting knife of antiquated aesthetic criticism. One can only experience *Totila* as German.'[26]

If Kube saw himself as a latter-day Kleist, other Gauleiters liked acting the part of Maecenas. Sauckel of Thüringia, for instance, ordered the Weimar National Theatre – famed for its past associations with Goethe and Schiller – to perform Otto Erler's play *Thor's Guest* on 21 March (day of the vernal equinox), in perpetuity.[27] This 'Maecenas' move placed theatrical stars in a rising sellers' market as Gauleiters vied with each other to entice them – with gifts that ranged from titles and Mercedes cars to country estates – to take up permanent residence in their particular fief.

Taken overall, however, actors were not the most important social group to derive specious benefit from the Nazis' manipulation of the theatre. Though workers had been recruited as theatre-goers before 1933 (notably by the trade-union-supported *Volksbühne* [People's Stage] organization), the Third Reich mobilized mass audiences on a scale amounting to a cultural revolution – not so much to expose them to propagandist theatre, as to turn their very presence in the theatre into propaganda. What better proof of folk community than the sight of the uneducated and property-less in places of entertainment associated with the bourgeoisie of education and property!

'Places of entertainment', incidentally, is something of a misnomer, since the middle-class citizen traditionally went to the theatre for elevation and self-improvement. It was the avowed object of Nazi social engineering to inculcate the masses with this 'middle-class' ethos. The debit side of the operation, i.e. the lowering of standards of dress and decorum in the larger theatres* (epitomized by the expression *Stullenoper* – 'bread-and-dripping opera house'), dwindled into insignificance beside the success in promoting the *embourgeoisement* of the working class. Cheap theatre tickets, along with cheap wireless sets and the (eagerly expected) cheap motor-car, were all means to this end.

How did the Third Reich accomplish this pseudo-cultural pseudo-revolution? Having poached the entire assets of the People's Stage, the Nazi 'Cultural Association' (annual subscription: 1 mark!) enabled its members to see ten plays per season at half-price; subscribers could, however, choose neither the play, the date, nor the theatre. The Strength-through-Joy organization recruited an entirely new type of audience for the theatre by making tickets available at the sort of bargain rate – between 75 pfennigs and 1·50 marks – that was only conceivable in a mammoth organization with its own distribution network.[28] Via Strength-through-Joy and the Labour Front, the German theatre had at its disposal a potentially captive audience running into tens of millions. The term 'captive

* The smaller houses largely remained the preserve of subscription holders.

audience' is used advisedly, because Strength-through-Joy theatre outings involved an element of compulsion: if the proffered tickets were not taken up voluntarily in a particular factory or office, the expense was charged to the members.[29]

Theatre-booking organizations also functioned within the Hitler Youth (with 250,000 subscribers in 1941) and the Reich Food Estate. Twenty-five touring companies served the farming communities in 1936, in addition to the mobile groups performing at Reich Labour Service camps. During the war the mobilization of entertainers by the Wehrmacht Troops' Welfare was so well organized and lavish – during the peak months of 1942, a total of 14,000 artists was involved[30] – that it made a considerable contribution to military morale. Nor was the civilian sector overlooked. Berlin's 1941-2 theatre season showed almost the same range as six years earlier. The proportion of classics within the whole repertoire had remained steady, the 'blood and soil' *genre* had lost ground, whereas more plays than before exuded the ambience of high society. Unmitigated National Socialist drama was notable by its absence, but even more notable was the fact that at the height of the war – the season coincided with unprecedented battle in the east – Berliners were given the choice of no less than one hundred different plays.

If one bears in mind that the Covent Garden opera house in London served as a dance hall at that time, one cannot but be impressed by the priority the German authorities accorded to the provision of culture. No segment of the population was left out. This unprecedented cultural diffusion (and the deference to artists that accompanied it) was illustrated by the following reminiscence from Dieter Borsche:

> In the winter of 1943 I was a member of a company which performed before the SS guards at the extermination camp of Auschwitz. We actors received prodigal hospitality and were waited on by prisoners – long columns of whom we saw with our own eyes. We were greatly astonished at their wearing only striped prison smocks in mid-winter.[31]

25

THE CINEMA

The German cinema had entered a golden age with the appearance of *The Cabinet of Dr Caligari* (1919). Caligari's successors – *The Golem, Siegfried, Metropolis, The Student of Prague, Destiny, Vaudeville, The Last Laugh* each made a distinct contribution to the art of the cinema. After *Faust* (1926) the lustre of the Weimar screen dimmed somewhat, though few contemporaries thought *Kameradschaft* and such early talkies as *Dreigroschenoper, Dr Mabuse, M* and *The Blue Angel* less than brilliant.

These classics were, however, hardly typical standard cinematic fare during the last phase of Weimar; indeed, in no other art form did 1933 – at least on cursory inspection – constitute as little of a break as in film-making. Had a cinema-going Rip van Winkel dozed off in the Depression and woken in the Third Reich he would have found the screen filled with the self-same images: spike-helmeted, hollow-eyed soldiers 'going over the top', bewigged courtiers posturing before rococo backdrops, poachers and milkmaids tangling among ears of golden corn, and ganglia-flexing mountaineers scaling cloud-wreathed pinnacles.

This continuity was partly due to the coincidence that the ultra-conservative pro-Hitler leader and press baron Hugenberg also controlled the UFA (*Universum-Film-Aktiergesellschaft*) film company – Germany's largest.

More crucial though – as well as less easy to explain – was the uncanny way in which the Weimar cinemas reflected the deformities resulting from Germany's aborted post-war revolution. German democracy in spastic motion threw shadows on the screen to people the no-man's-land between *Dr Caligari* and Hitler: homunculi evolving out of a retort, Philistines escaping from plush interiors to 'joyless streets', God-seekers forsaking the megalopolis for mountain peaks, and adolescent rebels graduating in submission or suicide.

This uncanny correspondence of screen and society was again underlined when the Depression revolutionized society – at the same time as sound revolutionized the screen. Both developments boosted cinema attendances: the general public were as riveted by the talkies as the unemployed were by glimpses of Eldorado (and heated cinema interiors). The slump led film-makers and Nazis alike to exploit a curious reflex of the German psyche: the propensity of men denied work to compensate for this affront to their manhood with fantasies and rituals connected with war. During the slump the UFA complemented Hollywood's drilled chorus lines and high-stepping drum majorettes with marching columns of Frederick the Great's redcoats or Great War battle-greys. One single chapter of German military history alone – the 'War of Liberation' against Napoleon – inspired no less than eight films between 1930 and 1933.

Cinema attendances – already growing during the slump – continued to rise throughout the Third Reich, though for different economic reasons. Restored employment led to modest affluence; the war produced a hankering for escapist entertainment as well as an excess of purchasing power over commodity supply. The annual number of movie-goers quadrupled within nine years (1933: 250 million; 1942: 1,000 million)[1] – which means that throughout the Third Reich the average German more than trebled the frequency of his cinema visits.

Besides tracing parallel popularity curves, Nazism and the cinema were both heavily dependent on dream projections, monumental effects. Steam baths of sentiment and the reduction of language to cliché.

Film personalities thus inhabited a world made doubly bogus by the overlap of showbiz artificiality and political deceit. Some screen idols considered the Third Reich to be a country-wide extension of their own pocket empires of tinsel and incense; it was probably the atmosphere rather than the actual ideology of Nazism that inspired Emil Jannings, Werner Kraus and Heinrich George to Stakhanovite exertions in Goebbels's dream factory.

Not that they were therefore entirely indifferent to ideology: Werner Kraus's insistence on playing half a dozen Jewish parts in *Jud Süss* – the cinematic curtain-raiser for the Final Solution – must have been motivated as much by anti-Semitism as by vanity. During the filming Kraus, steeped himself in a Jewish ambience, and with macabre dedication, walked about his villa in a greasy gaberdine and a stocking pulled over his head, while the objects of his mimicry were being killed in the ghettoes of the East.

Heinrich George, the Nazi-appointed manager of a Berlin theatre, was equally prone to histrionic displays. Once, when addressing his 'plant followers', he stopped short in mid-sentence after the mention of Hitler's name, to bellow at the assembled stage-hands and usherettes, 'I'm talking about the Führer, do you hear? Get down on your knees, everybody!'

A similarly megalomaniac but less overtly political self-conceit characterized Emil Jannings, who boasted publicly about the number of extras killed during the shooting of the anti-British Boer War epic *Ohm Kruger* (in which he had the name part).

These celluloid idols not only served the regime in a professional capacity; by participating in what passed for the Third Reich's 'court life', they and their female counterparts (Leni Riefenstahl, Olga Tschechowa and Zara Leander) cast a sheen of glamour over an élite deficient in the social graces.

The new power-holders, in turn, were acutely movie-conscious. Hitler credited the cinema – alongside radio and the motor-car – with having made the Nazi victory possible. He was sufficiently alive to the importance of the medium to intervene personally in details of casting; thus he decreed that Otto Gebuhr, the Weimar screen's perennial Frederick the Great, should appear again in the first Nazi Fredericus film instead of the projected star – Werner Kraus – who would have broken the continuity of the image in the minds of cinema-goers.

In 1933 there was a mass flight of screen talent, including directors like Josef von Sternberg, Fritz Lang, Erich Pommer, G. W. Pabst, Robert Ziodmak, and such stars as Elizabeth Bergner, Marlene Dietrich, Peter Lorre, Oskar Homolka and Conrad Veidt. Goebbels, himself an inveterate movie addict, showed considerable ingenuity in papering over the cracks left by this exodus. Moreover, he had the elasticity of mind to discard his own blueprint for politicizing the German screen, once he grasped the fact that conveyor-belt brownshirt epics were box-office poison – not because of the public's political antipathies, but because of its craving for experiences in the cinema which were different from those outside it.

Government and governed thus arrived at a consensus about the prime function of the cinema: to facilitate escapism or *Wirklichkeitsflucht*. Though, broadly speaking, films in other countries served a similar function, *La Grande Illusion, Modern Times, Fury* and *Love on the Dole* prove that the contemporary French, American and English cinema was less completely escapist.

In 1930, at the onset of the Depression, Germany's annual film output had stood at an all-time high level of 140. Averaging roughly 100 films per year from 1933 to 1944, the Third Reich produced about 1,100 films in all. Of that total, virtually half were either love stories or comedies, and a quarter adventure stories, crime thrillers or musicals; the rest consisted of historical, military, youth and political films in almost equal proportions.

This breakdown reflects both the diversification of Nazi screen fare and its underlying escapism, although in fact the German screen was more heavily 'ideologized' than the statistics suggest. While only about one feature film in every twenty was overtly political, this usually had a disproportionate amount of money, artistry and publicity expended on it; thus political films like *Ohm Kruger* or *Jud Süss* left a deeper imprint on the minds of cinema-goers than a score of romances or comedies. In addition, since all programmes had to be seen from beginning to end in a country which did not have continuous admission, newsreels and documentaries could ensure the regular dose of indoctrination. Last but not least, many an 'entertainment' carried a heavy charge of Nazi ideology.

The 1848-Revolution romance *Der Weg ins Freie*, for instance, was both a tear-jerker (stage-struck, estranged wife feigns suicide to stave off blackmail, husband remarries unawares and is blackmailed over 'bigamy', whereupon she commits 'genuine' suicide to ensure his newly found child-blessed happiness) and a subliminal essay in Nazi historiography: Metternich acts as a frontman for the Rothschild interest, Polish migrant labour carries the revolutionary virus into patriarchal Prussian villages, and mongrelized Vienna is much more prone to infection than racially undiluted Berlin.

An interesting hybrid of human-interest story and inferred political message was the 'Führer-type' biography. These did not necessarily deal with leaders as such, but could centre on any historical figure whose life provided analogies to Hitler's career. Thus the life-stories of the alchemist Paracelsus, the poet Schiller or the inventor Diesel were presented as exemplifying the triumph of untutored genius over formal learning and of intuition over pedantic myopia.

Nor did Nazi film-makers have much difficulty in milking the Fredericus theme for parallels with Hitler: movie-goers unaware of Eva Braun's existence could not but draw the intended inference when Frederick the Great displayed a rock-hard public persona while suffering tragic solitude as a man.

'The solitary-leader-versus-the-mass' theme had many permutations. *Der Höhere Befehl* (The Higher Order) featured a Prussian garrison commander who, during the War of Liberation, most insultingly flouts the opinions and wishes of his townsfolk: clairvoyantly assured of the rightness of his course, he proceeds to discover and root out a French espionage network.* In *Der Tunnel* (based on Bernard Kellermann's best-selling novel), after a disaster involving the death of 200 construction workers, the rest of the labour force clamours for greater safety precautions, and is answered by the engineer in charge, who screams at them, 'Safety?? Faith!! Faith is what I demand of you!' Another variation on the leadership theme occurred in Leni Riefenstahl's 1934 documentary of the Nuremberg Party Rally called *Triumph of the Will*, which opened with shots of steeply banked cloud formations underscored by the drone of Hitler's invisible aircraft. Here the pagan myth of All-Father Odin and his host raging in the skies was fused with the mountain cult of the Weimar cinema, whose priestess Leni Riefenstahl had herself been.

While the High Mass celebrated at Nuremberg translated effectively to the screen, fictionalized essays in hagiography proved embarrassing in their ineptness. The celluloid chronicles of the Nazi martyrs engendered little reverence among audiences. The film canonization of Horst Wessel was adjudged to be so devoid of the Nazi patron saint's *afflatus* that it was coyly rechristened *Hans Westmar*. *Hitlerjunge Quex*, a screen apotheosis of the Hitler Youth martyr Heinz Norkus, *S A Mann Brandt* and similar attempts at creating cinema out of the cliché-encrusted *Kampfzeit* legends proved equally undistinguished. Goebbels, ever a pragmatist – despite his ludicrous forecast that 'one day the Nazi cinema will produce its own *Battleship Potemkin*' – thereupon liquidated the *genre* with the adroit rationalization 'The SA's proper place is in the streets and not on the cinema screen.'[2]

Even so, the flawed Horst Wessel epic *Hans Westmar*, for one, repays scrutiny. It transmuted its hero – who, incidentally, had actually been a ponce – into an ascetic with burning eyes and jutting jaw, utterly indifferent to such mundane emotions as family feeling, personal friendship or sexual desire. Such unfocused identity – neither son, friend nor lover – made him simultaneously totally unbelievable and an ideal object of audience wish-projection.

To turn from an export reject of Goebbels's factory to a *de luxe* product: *Ohm Kruger*. This Boer War epic underscored the anti-British theme in a variety of effective ways. One of these was the film's projection of gold: object of desire to the denatured British; symbol of barrenness and evil to the crop-raising, flock-tending, God-fearing Boers. Anti-Mammonism was reinforced by prurience: news of Queen Victoria's death (at the height

* This links with Hitler's emphasis on intuition in political decision-making, as reflected in his statement, 'I go the way Providence has decreed with the assurance of a sleepwalker.'

380

of the war) reaches the Prince (later Edward VII) while he watches uniformed and kilted *Folies Bergères* show-girls performing travesties of military ceremonial. A third – and superficially apolitical – ingredient of *Ohm Kruger* was the generation conflict, in this case between the Boer leader and his son Jan, ending in the latter's submission. (An analogous filial submission – that of the cadet who later became Frederick the Great – belonged to German history as well as cinematic folklore. Foiled in an escape bid, the young prince had been forced to witness the execution of his best friend and accomplice, a traumatic experience causing the erstwhile rebel by and by to be transformed into an exemplary Prussian.) The trauma responsible for Jan Kruger's submission is equally violent: his wife is raped by some British soldiers.

Jud Süss, too, reached its climax with a rape sequence, counterpointed for good measure by a torture scene; having besotted Württemberg's duke with gold, the Jew wreaks Old Testament vengeance by forcing the daughter of his chief political adversary to endure ravishment on pain of having her fiancé broken on the wheel. After the rape the heroine commits suicide, true to the Nazi screen code by which all dishonoured women had to expiate their own defilement through death.·

Sado-masochism thus became the standard substitute for erotic titillation on the Nazi screen. German women were *virgines intactae* before marriage and chastely monogamous ever after; sensuality was the generic trait of non-Germans.

Thus concessions to the filmgoer's libido involved foreigners – bra-less, though bolero-clad, senoritas in *Pedro Must Hang*, a bare-breasted Russian tavern dancer in Pushkin's *Der Postmeister*. As a special bonus, however, 'native' films sometimes provided water-refracted glimpses of the nude Christina Soderbaum, or close-ups of Zara Leander's dizzily plunging neckline.

Zara Leander was the Nazi cinema's flesh-and-blood monument to feminine allure – surplus flesh fuelled by calculatedly thin blood. She projected a screen-filling *décolletage* beneath which, with chaste and steady rhythm, beat a woman's heart.

If Zara Leander appeared as the chastity-belted *Ewige Weib* (feminity incarnate) of the Nazi screen, Christina Söderbaum was its perpetual child bride. A snub-nosed Nordic naiad cocooned in little-girlish feminity, she packed cinemas with a series of marrow-withering characterizations which mingled treacle with hymeneal blood.

Her fate in *Jud Süss* was ravishment and suicide. In *The Eternal Heart*, which opens with a visually stunning shipwreck sequence, she is wedded to an ailing master craftsman frantically keeping one step ahead of death to complete an invention that would prevent further disasters at sea. In a nocturnal scene of unique bathos, she tries to recall the inventor, slumped wearily over his workbench, to his conjugal duties by stealing up on him and pressing her bare body against his back – a gesture not prompted by sexual desire, but by the hope that coitus may wean him away from his fatal *idée fixe* and make him advance the date of the operation that alone offers an outside chance of his survival.

In the film of Billinger's novel *Gigant* (*Giant*), Christina Söderbaum is cast as a Sudeten German farmer's daughter so bewitched by the spell of the big city that she deserts the ancestral farmstead for Prague's doubly alien – urban as well as Czech – ambience. Seduced, pregnant and abandoned, she returns home; at this point in the novel the old farmer, broken by his daughter's shame, walks into a watery grave. The film version, however, culminates in Fräulein Söderbaum's Ophelia-style suicide, because the Propaganda Ministry had insisted on the soiled daughter, and not the guiltless father, paying the price of transgression.*

For similar moral reasons the transfer of Binding's *Opfergang* (*The Sacrificial Rite*) to the screen entailed surgery that amounted to death by a thousand cuts. Binding's male protagonist has dissolved an amorous liaison in order to marry another woman – entirely breaking with his mistress save for sentimental early-morning rides past her window. After his sudden death the widow, who has known of those rides, puts on male riding attire and continues the equestrian ritual to spare the mistress the pain of discovering the truth. During the filming the Reich Chancellery intervened and ruled that the mistress had to die instead of the husband. The resultant ending, though nonsense in terms of plot and completely destroying Binding's lyrical concept, demonstrated the indestructability of marriage and served warning notice on any would-be violators of the sixth commandment.

The difficulty of infusing glosses on the sixth commandment with riveting drama – or even titillation – led to the (strictly rationed) provision of extra-marital sex on the screen. Such laxness did not meet with universal approval, least of all in wartime. An SD report of 1940 reflecting

---

* The screen convention whereby the last reel of a Christina Söderbaum film invariably showed her floating in the waters of Lethe – irrespective of whether earlier ones had involved her in rape, seduction or desertion – earned the actress the soubriquet *Reichswasserleiche* (national floating corpse).

public dismay at the drift of a number of recent films declared: 'It is inopportune to extenuate adulterous conduct at times when numerous families are separated because of the call-up of their menfolk.'[3]

One of the films complained of was *Leidenschaft* (*Passion*), which featured a Lady Chatterley situation – old husband, young wife and virile forester – in a setting of stately homes and hunting lodges. The elderly count's death while hunting prompts rumours which lead to court proceedings against the forester; but the latter manages to escape the noose in a cliff-hanger trial scene and the cause of true – because potentially reproductive – love triumphs in the end.

The eugenic theme also gave rise to humorous variations. *The King of the Wet-Nurses* – a box-office hit – was a Ruritanian *jeu d'esprit* about a young guardsman whose off-duty conduct results in the eagerly awaited arrival of an heir to the throne.

At times audiences were taken aback by the directness with which the eugenic message was articulated. In *Urlaub auf Ehrenwort* (*Leave on Parole*) a lieutenant allows the men on a troop train bound for the front six unscheduled hours' home-leave – in return for their promise not to desert. What startled the public was the officer's emphatic order to one of the men setting out from the station, 'Make sure you give your wife a child during these few hours!'

Yet elsewhere the approach was ridiculously mealy-mouthed. Tarzan and his mate were censored in 1934 because they were too scantily dressed.[4] A Marlene Dietrich film called *Das Hohe Lied* (*The Sublime Song*), tracing the rise of a simple country girl to the status of kept woman and her subsequent descent into the gutter, was banned outright.[5] Similarly, the French film *Nana*, based on Zola's novel, was banned because of a brothel scene between a soldier and a prostitute; it was said that, since the army was the foundation of any state, to depict a soldier cohabiting with a prostitute undermined the authority of the state.[6] In a German film, Zara Leander played a famous singer who let an air-force officer spend the night with her. The army high command objected to the screening of this episode because such behaviour was contrary to an officer's code of conduct; but Goering intervened and adjudicated in his blunt manner, 'The man would not be an officer if he did not take advantage of such an opportunity.'[7] Admiral Doenitz, the naval commander-in-chief, was more straitlaced, and had *Die grosse Freiheit* (*The Great Freedom*) banned because it depicted a sailor (played by the famous screen hero, Hans Albers) in a state of frequent drunkenness. (Symmetry – rather than Nazi sex equality –

demanded that a screen without promiscuous German women should be equally devoid of drunken German men.)

While such comparatively harmless derelictions were excised from the screen, producers such as Max Kümmich came close to cornering the market in sado-masochism with films featuring torture sequences. Kümmich's *A Life for Ireland* showed the son of an Irish freedom fighter being forced to undergo revolting – and minutely recorded – 'initiation tests' by his fellow inmates at a British prison boarding-school. In *Friesennot* (set among 'ethnic Germans' in Russia) a German girl who has fallen in love with a Russian is violently drowned in the village pond by her neighbours; this punishment for race pollution was declared to accord with ancient Germanic usage. *Germanin* – which traces the discovery of the sleeping-sickness vaccine – features a close-up sequence of the discoverer's assistant allowing himself to be bitten by disease-carrying mosquitoes. The interlinking of sadism and masochism was particularly characteristic of films set in all-male environments – boarding-schools, training camps, soldiers' barracks – whose heroes had to undergo endurance tests to prove themselves worthy of their colleagues' comradeship.

The homosexually tinged ethos of the all-male collective permeated a whole group of films: *Hitlerjunge Quex, Cadets, D3 88, Stukas, Crew Dora,* and so on. In the Air Force film *D3 88* the squadron leader and the chief maintenance engineer act out the respective roles of father and mother to the young pilots; one scene depicts them in a typical family situation, with the female parent trying to wrest concessions for the more difficult children from the unbending father. The jealous rivalries among some of the younger airmen[8] point in the same direction – as in the Hitler Youth leaders' *cri-de-cœur* in *Hitlerjunge Quex*: 'Lads are something wonderful, after all.' In *Crew Dora*, a joint feat of courage lets the two main protagonists forget their conflict over a girl. It seems superficially paradoxical that a regime inflicting savage punishments on homosexuals should sponsor such evocations of their ethos; but the Nazi movement itself was of course essentially an all-male collective, and the cult of comradeship fostered in its formations represented a pervasive, though naturally unacknowledged, form of homosexuality. To that extent the last-mentioned group of films can be said to have reflected an aspect of the Third Reich's reality.

There were further intimations of reality in films purporting to highlight the existence of certain problems currently in the process of being solved. Thus the preliminary stages of the Final Solution overlapped with the showing of *Jud Süss*, and the secret implementation of the mercy-killing programme coincided with the screening of *Ich Klage An* (I *Accuse*), in which a doctor kills his wife, who is afflicted with sclerosis, and convincingly restates all the arguments for euthanasia from the dock.

An SD intelligence report quoted one cinema-goer's Delphic comment on *Ich Klage An*: 'Quite interesting, but, in this film, the same thing happens as in the asylums where they are finishing off all the lunatics right now. What guarantee have we got that no abuses creep in?'[9] This sort of boomerang effect was not isolated. The SD reported apprehension among Germans in the ethnically mixed eastern provinces that Polish viewers of colonial liberation epics – e.g. *A Life for Ireland* or *Song of the Desert* (which showed Arabs rebelling against their British overlords) – might be stimulated into identifying themselves with the rebels on the screen.[10]

On one unique occasion a film made during the Third Reich was sufficiently controversial to spark off public polemic. In *Der Herrscher* (*The Ruler*), an aged industrial magnate, embittered by selfish children, writes them out of his will and bequeaths his factory to the nation.

A newspaper published by the Reich Food Estate (which had 'freed agriculture from the operation of market forces') detected officially sanctioned antipathy towards private enterprise in the ending of the film. For this it had been severely taken to task by the pro-business *Deutsche Allgemeine Zeitung*. When the film went on release it carried a postscript signed by Reichsminister Dr Goebbels which emphatically repudiated any anti-capitalist intentions.[11]

Explanations had to be given on other occasions too. The makers of the innocuous Old Heidelberg frolic *Die Blonde Katrein* (*Fair Catherine*) felt constrained to preface their concoction with a portentous preamble: 'Our film parodies a type of student life as it has always been shown to the public from motives of false romanticism. In reality, student existence today is work and service for the nation.'[12]

The lack of correspondence between screen and reality was so palpable that Party newspapers singled out films recognizably set in the Third Reich for special praise. Thus, the *Schwarzes Korps* eulogized the director Karl Ritter in 1938:

In *Pour le Mérite*, you have shown men wearing the Party badge and greeting each other with '*Heil Hitler*', because in the cinema there is no one who would expect anything else from you. On the day of restoration of defence sovereignty, (i.e. the re-introduction of conscription) you had Goebbels's voice ringing out of loudspeakers and you showed waving flags. You can take this so-called risk because you depict people as they really are, even with their weaknesses.[13]

A few months later the *Völkische Beobachter* stated, *à propos* of a forthcoming film on motorway construction workers,

We are not really topical in our film-making if all we can do is to show the date on the calendar or display the Reich eagle on the wall. We do not have to make do without the German form of greeting. One cannot omit the Reich Labour Service or the storm troopers without being guilty of a cowardly evasion of contemporary reality.[14]

There are numerous examples of the evasion of reality – contemporary or otherwise. A typical one was *Die Degenhards*, a gerontophile weepie featuring an old crotchety civil servant who, instead of achieving well-earned promotion, finds himself pensioned off as the result of a misunderstanding; but he chokes back his sense of personal humiliation once war addresses its categorical imperative to the whole community. At the end his son's death in action shocks him into a change of attitude towards the daughter-in-law and grandchild he has previously shunned.

Scripts were often so uniformly sentimental that the mere recitation of titles – *Motherlove, The Second Mother, The Sin Against Life, The Charitable Lie* – could do service for a summary of the plot. In *The Première of Butterfly*, for instance, the opera-singer heroine faces the selfsame problem in real life that she has depicted on the stage.

Karl Ritter's war-film *Stukas* featured therapy-through-music: a shell-shocked flier whose only hope of a cure – according to medical opinion – lies in undergoing a profound experience, actually recovers during the performance (at Bayreuth) of the Great March from Wagner's *Siegfried*.

In *Katzensteg* (set in the Wars of Liberation) the hero is the patriot son of a collaborationist mayor who nevertheless insists on his father's burial in consecrated ground; the heroine is a village outcast who collaborated under a threat from the mayor to hang her poacher father. The film ends with the star-crossed lovers – despite their outstanding joint record of filial piety – dying at the hands of the demented old poacher.

Proof positive that concoctions of this particular degree of speciousness could be placed just as effortlessly in contemporary settings as in period costume was provided by *Hohe Schule* (*Haute Ecole*) whose ex-officer-turned-show-jumper hero loves a woman to whom he has been unable to reveal his name – let alone propose – because he has killed her brother in a duel before the war. He finally finds happiness, however, through the heroine's discovery that the duel was prompted by a selfless concern for the honour of her brother, whom gambling debts had exposed to black-mail by foreign spies.

Every so often the film industry's predilection for convoluted tear-jerkers embarrassed the authorities into banning a particularly egregious specimen – such as *Die Ewige Maske* (*The Eternal Mask*) whose doctor hero, despite prohibition from above, has injected a serum he has himself discovered into a patient, with fatal results. Unaware of the actual cause of death (a weak heart) the distraught doctor destroys the serum – only to lapse into madness upon learning the true facts of the case; but the eventual restoration of his sanity enables him to rediscover the serum.

The rules about preliminary inspections of film-plots became so strict that no film could go into production until its outline had been submitted to Goebbels in standardized form (thirty-four nineteen-syllable lines per page of typescript). This type of centralization sometimes created its own problems, however: once, hurrying from the preview of a medical drama to another appointment, Goebbels remarked to his adjutant in passing, 'Now we've got enough *Ärztefilme* (doctor films) to last us for a long time.' But the adjutant thought he heard the Minister refer to *Ernste Film* (serious films), with the result that production schedules everywhere were re-arranged and the Propaganda Ministry found itself inundated with comedy synopses at a rather critical juncture of the war.

It was during the war, incidentally, that the two greatest box-office hits of the Third Reich were screened. Nearly 28 million people saw *Die Grosse Liebe* (*The Great Love*) which focused on the solidarity in suffering of women separated from their menfolk at the front. Characteristically omitting any reference to the events or the background of the war, it made wartime separation seem to be a form of alchemy whereby the gold of marital love could be purged of all dross.

In the same vein of sympathetic magic the film gave married soldiers a more favourable statistical rating than single ones by implying that a wife's loving concern for her husband at the front could – like some incorporeal bullet-proof vest – shield him from harm.

The second most successful of the 1,100 films made during the Third Reich was *Wunschkonzert* (*Request Concert*), which was also the name of a weekly radio programme linking soldiers and their families via musical requests. *Wunschkonzert* was a portmanteau film, featuring the Reich Broadcasting Service as the central switchboard of a continent-wide network of emotional ties. One of its scenes flouted Nazi wartime screen conventions to the extent of actually showing a soldier dying in a church under enemy bombardment, but this concession to reality was more apparent than real. By depicting death in a heavily stylized form – i.e. as occurring in a cathedral (cf. the Nibelungs' holocaust in Attila's palace) and affecting a single organ-playing soldier – the film simultaneously glamorized death and drained it of its significance.

An identical approach (concerning the death of Germans, at any rate) governed the making of Nazi documentaries and newsreels. Thus, in *Victory in the West*, death was vicariously represented by the visual metaphor of a flower-decked grave. *Baptism of Fire* contained a single reference to fatal casualties: the shot of a badly wounded soldier in hospital, his face transfigured by elated anticipation of a visit by the Führer. None of this, however, means that war reporting on the German screen was equivocal. The horrors of war were there for everyone to see, but they were invariably shown as being visited upon the enemy. The Propaganda Ministry in fact stated that the demand for newsreels also showing German soldiers being wounded and killed deserved to be denounced as a form of sensation-mongering.[15]

During the war, cinema-going became more widespread and popular than ever, a trend the authorities catered for by dispatching mobile film vans to remote villages and even establishing some open-air cinemas in bombed areas. During the closing stages of the war, Berlin cinemas were usually besieged by long queues in the early afternoon. The heavy pressure on reduced seating capacity created a black market in tickets; as the distance between the capital and the front grew shorter, priority for soldiers in cinema queues was revoked.

At this critical juncture Goebbels starved the front of 10,000 infantrymen, 1,000 cavalry and 250 gun carriages so that they might be deployed in Frederician battle scenes before the cameras of Veit Harlan. *Kolberg*, a film named after the town that refused to surrender in the Seven Years' War, was intended to stir a Dunkirk response in the collective psyche; but although it was premièred before the beleaguered Königsberg garrison it could no longer go on general release.

Kolberg was thus the last of the thousand-plus films produced during the 1,000-Year Reich. Did any of that vast number deserve to last? Hardly: the majority were utterly expendable,* a minority downright pernicious. The rest fall under two headings: films making a valid comment on Nazi

---

* It was significant that even screen representations of country life – a hallowed task in Nazi eyes – provoked constant complaints from the co-ordinated farming community.

reality* and those with intrinsic artistic merit. To the first of these minus-cule groups belonged *Kleider machen Leute* (*Clothes Make the Man*), a satire on the glamour attaching to uniforms, and *Der Maulkorb* (*The Dog's Muzzle*), a small-town period farce, in which an attorney charged with investigating a case of *lèse-majesté* discovers that he is the culprit. Reinhold Schünzel's *Das Land der Liebe* (*The Land of Love*) contained more obviously pointed satire and achieved topicality with such snippets of dialogue as 'In this country we do not read books. We swim, we wrestle and we lift weights', or 'Why, this jail is half-empty. What on earth is the use of an empty jail?' These three films would, of course, have gone unremarked in any setting other than that of the Third Reich.

The three belonging to the second category, and rating an honourable mention in any context, were Helmut Käutner's *Unter den Brücken* (*Under the Bridges*), Hans Steinhoff's *Rembrandt* and Josef von Baky's extra-terrestrial colour extravaganza, *Münchhausen*. The last-named was scripted by Erich Kästner, who had been officially prohibited from any form of writing by the authorities. But UFA wanted a scenario worthy of the festive twenty-fifth anniversary production and managed to procure a temporary lifting of the ban on Kästner. The fact that, despite its vast resources, and the wealth of talent clamouring to exploit the celluloid sellers' market, UFA had to fall back on a proscribed 'degenerate' provides as fitting an epitaph on the Nazi cinema as any.

* Leni Riefenstahl's propagandistic documentaries – *Triumph of the Will* and *Olympiade* – were in a hybrid category of their own: though technically highly accomplished, they were a tainted comment on aspects of Nazi reality.

26

PRESS AND RADIO

Unlike its British counterpart, the German Press has never had a group of mass-circulation dailies published in the capital. This lack of a 'national Press' had two root causes: greater geographical distance between towns, and a much slower and less thorough development of the nation-state. In Germany, the pull of regional loyalties and cultural particularism remained so strong that even after half a century of unification Berlin had failed to make the transition from being the hub of an administrative network to becoming the focal point of national life. (Prussian, Protestant Berlin had always aroused southern and Catholic antipathies; after 1918, the additional stigma of liberalism – moral as well as political – attached to it in the eyes of many provincials.)

In Weimar days the circulation of some Berlin quality papers, such as the *Vossische Zeitung* or the *Berliner Tageblatt*, certainly extended beyond the capital; even so, these constituted a supra-regional rather than a national Press, and differed in no essential respects from the *Kölnischer Zeitung* or the *Frankfurter Zeitung*. The latter, with its highly esteemed business section, was probably more of a national institution than the Berlin papers. As if to compensate for the absence of a national Press, Germany had an extremely varied regional and local one. Before the Nazi takeover the country boasted a grand total of no fewer than 4,700 dailies of varying size. Smallest among them were the 'district papers' (*Kreisblätter*), which depended for the bulk of their reading on material syndicated by Press trusts (such as Hugenberg's Scherl Verlag) to which they added items of parochial interest.

Local news, as seen from a higher vantage-point, was also purveyed by the various apolitical newspapers (*Generalanzeiger*) that offered news rather than views and were to be found in almost all towns of any size. In 1932 this group accounted for 24 per cent of the national daily newspaper consumption, the Catholics for 10 per cent, the political Right for 38 per cent and the Left (further subdivided into Liberal, Social Democrat and Communist) for 28 per cent.[1]

The structure of the German Press was so varied that a middle-sized provincial centre like Stuttgart (population 400,000) was served by nine separate dailies, while the 25,000 inhabitants of the Franconian backwater of Coburg had three local papers to choose from.[2]

A newspaper's status was frequently at variance with its circulation figures. Thus Germany's leading Liberal daily, the *Berliner Tageblatt*, edited by the incomparable stylist, Theodor Wolff, and carrying Alfred Kerr's drama reviews and Alfred Einstein's music criticism, sold on average only 130,000 copies in 1932.[3] Although it had in fact never reached a very wide audience its circulation figures at that date reflected – apart from the general tightness of money at the worst moment of the Depression – both the *Tageblatt's* long-term high standards and its recently diminished influence.

The very opposite applied on both counts to the *Völkische Beobachter*, whose daily printing at the time of the Nazi takeover roughly equalled that of the *Berliner Tageblatt*.[4] This central organ of the National Socialist Party, owned by Hitler's First World War sergeant, Max Amann, and nursed from obscure beginnings by the drunken, drug-addicted poet Dietrich Eckart and the Party ideologist Alfred Rosenberg, had 127,000 readers early in 1933, an absurdly small figure compared to the 17 million or 43 per cent of the electorate, who voted Nazi on 5 March of that year. Until 1933 the impact of the *Völkische Beobachter*, which was published in Munich, had been confined to southern Germany; but even the country-wide circulation of all Nazi dailies – 800,000 – shows that no more than one out of every twenty Nazi voters had been primarily influenced by the printed word.

This discrepancy between voting and reading patterns stemmed from the essential nature of the Nazi appeal. Shunning ideas, the Nazis addressed themselves to layers of the sub-conscious mind. Such emotional manipulation worked best at meetings where the single participant, incontinently moved by rhetoric and crowd feeling, underwent a metamorphosis – in Goebbels's characteristic phrase – from 'a little worm into part of a large dragon'.

It was as a rhetorician that Hitler had first broken through the confines of the sectarian fringe eventually to gain the ear of almost half the nation through his and his followers' gift of tongues.

In the Nazi beginning was the word – print reinforced it, but in an ancillary capacity. One of Goebbels's key directives to journalists succinctly laid down: 'The reader should get the impression that the writer is in reality a speaker standing beside him.'[5] As a result the pages of the Nazi Press exuded the aura of their mass meetings, an aura of sweat, leather and bloodlust, and the *Völkische Beobachter* was little more than a poster tricked out as a newspaper. Its style was exemplified by such front-page headlines as BROTHEL-KEEPER'S PARAMOUR APPOINTED AS UNIVERSITY PROFESSOR[6] and epithets like 'World champion belly-crawlers' (for the Weimar government) and 'Parliamentary *cloaca*' (for the Reichstag).[7]

These factors contributed to the peculiar inversion of the allegiance of right-wing readers and voters before the seizure of power: while the Nazis outvoted their allies in the National Party by more than four to one during the 1932 elections, Hitler's share of the nation-wide right-wing Press readership (38 per cent) was less than a quarter. Hugenberg's position was typical; though he was Germany's greatest communications tycoon (as head of the Scherl publishing house and the UFA film company), he was very much Hitler's junior partner in the Nazi/National Party alliance. After 1933 he was to be entirely eclipsed on the first count, too, while Max Amann inexorably turned himself into Germany's (if not the world's) greatest newspaper magnate, to control 82 per cent of the country's Press by 1942.[8]

The *Völkische Beobachter* represented the spearhead of the growth of the Amann Press empire. It became the first national newspaper in the history of German journalism by being published simultaneously in Munich, Berlin (from 1933 onwards) and Vienna (after 1938). In addition it became the first German daily ever to top the million mark in circulation and registered a tenfold increase in as many years (1932: 116,000; 1941: 1,192,500).[9] A contributory reason for this staggering advance was that its editor, Wilhelm Weiss, marginally transformed the erstwhile 'combat paper' into a vehicle of information. He improved the news service and extended its range of coverage, but most of Weiss's other plans for editorial reform came to grief on the rock of Amann's stony rigidity.

It was obduracy, on the part of the owner, for instance, that prevented the leading newspaper of Europe's foremost power from having a single full-time correspondent in any foreign capital.[10] Nor, of course, did the *Völkische Beobachter* employ after 1933 a different vocabulary to match its new status as Germany's equivalent to *The Times* or *Le Temps*. In triumph, as in obscurity, the paper's style was a combination of staccato incitement, bathos and perfidious mendacity, *pace* this 1934 report of a former Reichstag deputy's suicide in a concentration camp: 'Although treated with the same tolerance as all other people in protective custody, he acted in an unfriendly and provocative manner towards the supervisory personnel.'[11]

The real reason for the paper's steady arithmetical progression (circulation increased by 100,000 annually) is simply this: subscription to the *Völkische Beobachter* was both a corollary of Party membership and proof of political fealty on the part of civil servants and others. Schoolmasters, Hitler Youth leaders, Wehrmacht instructors and university lecturers alike used it as a basic educational aid, and, as we have seen, non-Nazi teachers needed to read it as a safeguard against unwittingly marking down essays pupils had lifted verbatim from its editorial columns; adverse comments on such essays were sometimes expiated in concentration camps.

Although a large segment of the bourgeoisie of education were thus subscribers to the Nazi Press, Goebbels hesitated to prescribe it for the entire class. The Social Democrat and Communist Press disappeared entirely after the seizure of power, soon to be followed by the Catholic dailies, but some liberal papers of high repute (such as the *Frankfurter Zeitung* and the *Berliner Tageblatt*), suitably divested of their former Jewish associations, though still employing non-Nazi staff, were surprisingly permitted to continue. At home these simulacra of a great journalistic past were spurious evidence of diversity in a hermetically closed system. Abroad, they served as finely tuned propagandist mouthpieces, engaging in a dialogue with foreign newspapers for which avowed Nazi papers, with their sledgehammer approach, would have been quite unsuited. In this way sensitive German readers who baulked at the crude style and arguments of the *Völkische Beobachter* had essentially the same arguments served up to them in the *Berliner Tageblatt*, though there they were clothed in the refined prose of Paul Scheffer – himself trained in the great school of Theodor Wolff. Scheffer, who became editor in the autumn of 1933, sought to make the paper, which was by then almost moribund, into a focus of conservative intellectual opposition, and his staff of largely young academics concurred in this aim. Subsequent increases in circulation seemed to confirm such sanguine expectations, but they had of necessity to write in code, which made it difficult for any but the most perceptive readers to supply their own 'key'. Very occasionally, there was no mistaking the *Berliner Tageblatt*'s tone of subdued nonconformity: to define what he meant by 'the private sphere', the sculptor Gerhard Marcks (subsequently defamed) wrote at Christmas 1935,

I should like to substitute the term 'secret' for 'private', in other words: the source flows secretly – the stream publicly. The source can dispense with the stream if need be – but the latter can never do without the source.[12]

Rather more gnostic was a leader on the Roehm purge, which opened with a philippic against forcible collectivization in the USSR. Some readers may have been perceptive enough to realize that subtle analogy, i.e. damning Hitler by implied comparison with Stalin, was a favourite editorial device of Scheffer's. Few, however, could have divined that Scheffer's publication of an article about Jung and depth psychology on the occasion of Freud's eightieth birthday (no reference to which was allowed to be made in Germany) was intended as an arcane act of homage to the defamed founder of psycho-analysis.

In the mid-thirties Scheffer recruited Werner Finck as a contributor to the paper's special Saturday edition,* which in consequence sold 25 per cent more copies than the mid-week average. In his column Finck purveyed a characteristic blend of politically tinged humour relying heavily on *doubles entendres*, e.g.:

Ladies and gentlemen, the window is open and we are talking very loudly. Maybe we had better shut it. 'If I may be quite open', the window wanted to say at this moment as if to intervene in the conversation, but it only creaked. Walls can join in more readily, at least they have ears.[13]

The manner in which the *Berliner Tageblatt* implemented its opposition thus bordered either on the obscure or on the humorously *risqué*. The paper's most tangible resistance function probably consisted of acting as a linguistic nature reserve, in which a dying species of uncorrupted German was saved from extinction.

The formerly apolitical *Generalanzeiger* Press stood midway between the *Völkische Beobachter* and such officially tolerated bourgeois newspapers as the *Berliner Tageblatt* that were still tolerated. Although Amann's publishing octopus eventually achieved preponderant control over the German Press, the regime was for some years content to control newspapers through outward regimentation rather than internal change of ownership and staff.

* Toleration of Finck as a satirist in Berlin had a unique counterpart in Bavaria. On the occasion of the 1937 carnival, Goebbels licensed a special humorous pre-Ash Wednesday issue of the *Münchner Neueste Nachrichten*. This contained such unvarnished intimations of Nazi reality as, 'Last night, someone entered the tavern under the guise of a respectable gentleman. A spirit of conviviality was engendered, in the course of which two guests were instantly removed to Dachau.' Hitler categorically banned any repetition of this venture.

The lynchpin of its whole apparatus of regimentation and pre-censorship were what were known as *Sprachregelungen* (language rulings); these were directives issued in the course of daily briefings at the Propaganda Ministry and transmitted to all editorial desks in the country. As soon as the editors concerned had assimilated their instructions they were duty bound to destroy every trace of them and sign affidavits to that effect. The directives themselves were so minutely detailed and so destroyed all journalistic initiative that Goebbels, in a moment of candour, admitted, 'Any person with the slightest spark of honour left in him will take good care in future not to become a journalist.'[14] Quite a few practising journalists, actually, far from resenting the fact that their columns had become official notice-boards, welcomed Goebbels's scheme because it freed them from the burden of responsibility.

The Press directives were staggeringly comprehensive; headlines like COMMANDER-IN-CHIEF OF THE NAVY RECEIVES THE FÜHRER were declared inadmissible, for the reason that a subordinate could not receive his supreme commander. Thomas Mann was never to be mentioned, even critically, because his name was to be expunged from the consciousness of all Germans. Charlie Chaplin was to be treated in the same way. Greta Garbo, on the contrary, had to be handled in a friendly manner. Even more positive – in fact, *sympathisch* – was the obligatory press reaction to the Duke of Windsor's wedding. There were to be no press photographs showing cabinet ministers attending banquets, nor any reports on them. Other censored news included outbreaks of cattle-poisoning resulting from the effect of German potassium on cattle fodder, a car accident involving von Ribbentrop in which his eldest daughter had been badly hurt, and the participation of Fräulein Hess in the Berlin dog show. The question of whether Jesus had been Jewish was not to be broached, for the reason that it could no longer be decided after two thousand years. Cases of race defilement before the courts were to be reported with the utmost care, omitting details such as 'the Jew X.Y. had frequented the German brothel at Z.', and lastly,

The carrying out of executions is subject to standardized procedure throughout the Reich. All criminals will in future be executed with a guillotine, and executions will be centralized in a few towns; lest too frequent mention of these towns' names harm their reputation, newspaper reports will in future only state in which town the court has pronounced sentence, not where it is to be carried out.[15]

Yet despite the comprehensiveness of these directives the occupational hazards of journalists in the Third Reich remained considerable. A tiny local 'district paper' – the *Schweinitzer Zeitung* – had to suspend publication temporarily because its issue to celebrate the Führer's birthday in 1935 featured a large photograph of Hitler which blotted out the first seven letters (i.e. *Schwein* – pig) of the paper's masthead. Similarly, two lines of print inadvertently transposed by the compositor, so that the eulogy on a retiring local Party official concluded with the pejorative ending of the obituary of a French cabinet minister, triggered off Gestapo investigations of a regional paper published in Brunswick.[16]

A journalist on the *Berliner Tageblatt* was fined 200 marks for compiling the facetious headline HAPPY IN SPITE OF BEING MARRIED. A colleague of his, who had written a *reportage* on the Hitler Youth, was summoned to the local Hitler Youth headquarters, where von Schirach's adjutant called him a snotty-nose and resoundingly slapped his face. Despite these mishaps, it was the '*feuilletons*', or cultural sections of newspapers, that presented the greatest hazards. One contributor to the *Frankfurter Zeitung* was briefly jailed for a note on Van Gogh, another for an obituary of Virginia Woolf after her suicide in 1941.[17] As we shall see, a journalist was dismissed from *Das Reich* for disparaging a painting which Hitler had given to the Gauleiter of Munich as a wedding present. A member of the *Berliner Tageblatt*'s *feuilleton* staff who had omitted Arno Breker from a feature on young sculptors lost the right to practise journalism. (The instigator of this ban had been the offended sculptor himself.)*

Yet, as if in compensation for such drawbacks, the *feuilleton* did initially also offer a limited scope for the exercise of critical ingenuity in the political sense as well as in the cultural one. The *Frankfurter Zeitung*'s theatre critic, commenting on Moeller's play *Rothschild Wins at Waterloo*, managed to impugn its credibility with such ambiguous phrases as 'The author is less concerned with historic authenticity than with moral inferences.'[18]

This review appeared two years before Goebbels's notorious decree of November 1936, by which criticism had to be replaced by 'art consideration', but even after Goebbels's decree certain things were still possible. Thus Gert Teunissen, the art critic of the *Kölnischer Zeitung*, managed to inject an ironic note into his reviews of the annual Munich exhibitions by using terms like 'dead exact' and 'fireproof', or phrases like 'plaster of Paris permits a mirror-like smoothing out of the surface'.[19] Literary criticism could similarly be adapted to genuinely critical purpose, with reviews of

* cf. Chapter on art, p. 431.

books on Caesar, Cromwell or Napoleon providing obvious opportunities for implied parallels with the totalitarian present.

Although writers on the staff of the *Berliner Tageblatt*, the *Kölnischer Zeitung* and the *Frankfurter Zeitung*, or of periodicals like the *Deutsche Rundschau* occasionally availed themselves of these opportunities, the Third Reich's journalists on the whole found their privileges in quite different spheres. The orthodox among them felt corporately ennobled, because Hitler had, ever since *Mein Kampf*, been wont to describe his professional status as 'Writer'. A characteristic effusion by a Party scribe stated,

A journalist is born just like the leader to whom he is closely related – only in the journalistic estate the leader's prophetic vision turns rather to poetic intuition ... just as the poet walks alongside the king, the journalist must march with the leader. The leader divines the essence of the folk soul by intuitive vision, the journalist by listening to language.[20]

A more prosaic privilege bestowed on journalists was connected with the fact that the secret 'Language Rulings' gave them an insight into political and diplomatic realities denied to the population at large. Journalists were the only citizens of the Third Reich ever to be officially informed that the central organ of the Nazi Party was publishing falsehoods. They were told on 9 January 1940 that 'Today's *Völkische Beobachter* report on the Jewish origins of British statesmen is regretted. The statements made therein are largely incorrect.'[21]

Another – and undoubtedly more highly appreciated – privilege enjoyed by selected journalists in wartime was access, through the good offices of the Propaganda Ministry, to foreign newspapers and captured Allied feature films. (Before 1939 people who lived in large towns had been able to acquaint themselves with the contents of such organs of 'moderate' foreign opinion as *The Times, Le Temps* and the *Neue Zürcher Zeitung* by buying them at kiosks or perusing them at coffee-houses, though to be seen purchasing foreign newspapers was not likely to endear one to the Party or to the Gestapo.)

The fact that journalists had closer access to information than ordinary mortals did not necessarily give them deeper insight into things. Rudolf Kircher, the editor of the *Frankfurter Zeitung*, was caught so unawares by events that he had a nervous breakdown in the middle of an editorial conference when news of the German attack on Poland came through. When Margaret Bovery was due to be sent to New York in the summer of 1940 to cover further war developments from a neutral vantage-point, fellow journalists thought her journey quite pointless – the war would be over before she had even reached the shores of America.[22] But indubitably the greatest single benefit – from a purely material point of view – that the regime bestowed upon the journalistic profession consisted of wiping out the effects of the Depression which had made so many of them jobless.

Although the purge and 'co-ordination' measures removed certain areas of journalistic employment, there was no dearth of vacancies for suitable applicants in the expanding Party Press, the proliferating propaganda sections of the Party apparatus, and the public-relations sector of a booming industry. The storm-troop weekly, *Der SA-Mann*, for instance, sold 750,000 copies – a figure reflecting not so much the quality of its reading matter as the thoroughness of SA subscription drives.

Techniques for promoting Nazis newspapers are best illustrated by Julius Streicher's own local daily, the *Fränkische Tageszeitung*, which sent this circular to all readers reluctant to renew their subscriptions:

> Your intention expresses a very peculiar attitude towards our paper, which is an official organ of the National Socialist German Workers' Party, and we hope that you realize this. Our paper certainly deserves the support of every German. We shall continue to forward copies of it to you, and hope that you will not want to expose yourself to unfortunate consequences in the case of cancellation.[23]

Streicher's other and far better known journalistic venture, *Der Stürmer*, achieved a phenomenal increase, rocketing from an average of 65,000 copies in 1934 to close on 500,000 in 1937.[24] The mendacity of this paper, each issue of which Hitler read avidly from cover to cover, was so extraordinary that the Nazi authorities themselves were occasionally obliged to withdraw it from circulation.* Yet perverting the truth was only one facet of the all-encompassing perversion that made the *Stürmer* a model of Nazi journalism. A representative *Stürmer* headline in 1933 was worded, THE DEAD JEW: FRITZ ROSENFELDER SEES REASON AND HANGS HIMSELF; a typical 'open letter' contained this reminder from an SS official to a purged government official: 'Do you recall the memorable night when I put a permanent wave into your crooked backbone with a horsewhip?'[25]

---

* 'The deputy police president of Breslau announces the confiscation of Issue 32 of the weekly *Der Stürmer*, published at Nuremberg. Under the heading "Ritual Murder in Breslau", *Der Stürmer* carried an extensive report concerning a sexual murder committed on the children of the family Fäse in 1926, a report which in its essentials is entirely untrue and is calculated to undermine public esteem for the police force to a considerable degree' (cf. *Beobachter am Main*, published in Aschaffenburg, 21 August 1934).

However, it would be wrong to deduce from the examples quoted that sadism and obscenity dominated the press columns of the Third Reich, for although the *Stürmer* printed up to half a million copies and had an even wider resonance – its public-display boxes provided cursory reading matter for millions – many a paterfamilias (even if he was a political conformist) banished the paper from his household on grounds of respectability, and women tended to find it embarrassing to be seen reading it. The taste of this segment of the reading public was partly catered for by the illustrated press, a feature of the Nazi publishing scene that must not be overlooked. Hugely popular in peace and war alike, the illustrated magazines overlaid reality with a patina compounded of glamour and elevation. Typical of such qualities were the full-page monochrome reproductions in the *Berliner Illustrierten Zeitung* series, 'Pictures of the German Soul' – evocations of contemplative serenity, with names like 'In the magic spell of the muse', 'Maria's passage through the mountains', 'The fairy tale' and 'In the forest'.* The popularity of illustrated magazines was to some extent a by-product of the public's declining interest in newspapers *per se* after 'co-ordination' had drastically levelled the journalistic landscape.

The national total of newspaper copies printed daily declined – while employment figures rose – from 20·25 million early in 1934 to 18·75 million by mid-1935.[26] The year 1936 therefore saw a campaign against public indifference to the Press; ubiquitous posters proclaimed 'Without newspapers one lives on the moon' and coaxed or challenged non-readers with such slogans as 'Newspaper readers get ahead faster' and 'My name is *Hase* (Rabbit) and I know nothing'. A contributory factor to the overall decline in circulation was the reaction of some former readers of the proscribed Marxist Press (i.e. the Communist, socialist and trade-union papers), who stopped reading newspapers altogether, while others had switched over to the Catholic Press. In 1934, Catholic newspapers in Rhein-Westphalia actually showed an increase of readership, but they were subsequently eliminated from the publishing scene, and an overall reduction in the number of newspapers took place. Out of a grand total of 4,700 dailies at the time of the Nazi takeover, a third had ceased publication by the end of 1934; ten years later fewer than 1,000 dailies were appearing in the Reich. Between 1933 and 1938 a national total of 10,000 diverse periodicals and learned journals had been reduced to 5,000, a figure attesting to the

* The painters were respectively Max Klinge, Josef von Furich, Hans Thomas and Moritz von Schwind – an array of names which in itself constituted an artistic programme.

decline of intellectual life under the Nazis, though the continued appearance of some learned periodicals still insulated an educated minority against a full realization of this.

The war, during which the public's attention was riveted on current events, produced a rise in total daily newspaper circulation from 20·5 to 26·5 million; the circulation of weeklies and illustrateds, on the other hand, almost doubled, from 11·9 to 20·8 million. Thus in the sphere of the Press as in related spheres, the Nazi public tended to prefer illusion to reality.[27] The war also produced important shifts in press ownership. As late as 1939 the total daily circulation of Party newspapers amounted to only half that of the non-Party Press, but by 1944 the Party controlled four-fifths of all the then remaining dailies. Proportionate to the growth of Himmler's own empire within the Nazi state, the *Schwarzes Korps* grew increasingly influential – and censorious; a self-appointed guardian of the rest of the Press, keeping its charges under constant surveillance and savaging them intermittently for such innocuous instances of dereliction as the publication of horoscopes, of Edgar Wallace-like thriller serials and of 'Lonely Hearts' columns.

In 1940 the increased interest in news and newspapers prompted Goebbels to launch the weekly *Das Reich*, a psychological-warfare weapon rendered formidable by the literary expertise which went into its production. *Das Reich* employed an impressive array of bourgeois journalists and writers of the inner emigration (Oskar Loerke, Luise Rinser, Gertrud von Lefort, Albrecht Goes), while Goebbels's frequent contribution compensated for lack of style with the weightiness of political content. Topicality, framed by literary excellence, made *Das Reich* a uniquely successful example of Nazi newspaper promotion: by 1943, its printing was 1·5 million.[28]

The same year witnessed the final demise of the *Frankfurter Zeitung*, a newspaper so reviled before 1933 as a mouthpiece of Judeo-Liberalism that its continued appearance had struck gullible readers as an exercise of unwonted tolerance. Even though the paper had purchased its continued survival by furthering the regime's aims in its own patrician manner, it never ceased to present an inviting target for sharp-shooting Nazi fundamentalists. Isolated but recurring instances of its nonconformity to the general pattern of Third Reich journalism, such as criticizing the dismissal of Professor Oncken,[29] calling the première of Alban Berg's opera *Lulu* a great day for Zürich, mentioning the canonized Party bard Dietrich Eckhart's alcoholism and drug addiction,[30] had long scandalized Party circles. In the summer of 1943 a climax was reached when the paper printed a less than laudatory appreciation of the work of Professor Troost. The widowed Frau Professor had little difficulty in kindling Hitler's Olympian wrath against those who dared to criticize his first court architect. The *Frankfurter Zeitung* instantly ceased publication.

Soon afterwards its deputy editor, Erich Welter, was summoned by Max Amann, who blandly told him, 'Perhaps it would be simplest if we lined you all up against a wall, but we want to give you another chance. We want to cross-breed the political reliability of the *Völkische Beobachter* with the journalistic expertise of the *Frankfurter Zeitung*.'[31]

There could have been no more fitting epitaph on the Nazi Press than that shortly before the Party's central organ was put to bed for the last time its proprietor should actually have toyed with the idea of turning it into a newspaper.

The crucial role of radio in the Nazi scheme of things was reflected in Hitler's dictum, 'Without motor-cars, sound films and wireless, no victory of National Socialism.' In the same way in which the sudden upswing in Nazi Party fortunes overlapped with the advent of the talkies, so did the Nazi era coincide with the rapid growth of radio ownership in almost all social strata. At the time of the seizure of power 4·5 million out of a possible 20 million households had access to broadcasting; by 1942, the former figure had almost quadrupled, accounting for 16 million out of a total of 23 million (Greater German) households.[32] In other words, 70 per cent of all Germans (in the towns, the proportion was 80 per cent) were receiving radio programmes; the wireless had thus been converted from a minority medium to an all-embracing form of mass communication. This expansion, which was part of a world-wide process, had been hastened in Germany by the regime's success in providing radio sets that even the poorest could afford. Shortly after the Nazi takeover the VE (*Volksempfänger* or 'People's receiver') 3·31 – selling price 76 marks or £6 – went into mass production. Some time later the cheapest radio set in the world – the DKE (*Deutscher Kleinempfänger* or 'German mini-receiver') came on to the German market at 35 marks, i.e. little more than the weekly wage of an average industrial worker.

The extreme radio-consciousness of the regime manifested itself in many other ways: during his first year in office, Hitler made no fewer than fifty broadcasts, and to obviate the problems posed by the relative dearth of sets, communal listening was instituted. Collective listening to important transmissions became a typical feature of public life in Nazi Germany;

many broadcasts were arranged during working hours, and factories and offices had to suspend work for the occasion so that the country's entire labour force could be reached. All restaurants and cafés had to be equipped with wireless sets for such public occasions, and loudspeaker pillars were erected in the streets.[33] Although the war interrupted a comprehensive scheme for the construction of 6,000 loudspeaker pillars, there can be no doubt that the Third Reich achieved a denser radio coverage than any other country in the world.[34] The human links in this tight network were Nazi Party 'radio wardens', whose duty it was to coax people living in their particular block into listening to Party-prescribed programmes, to snoop on listeners to foreign broadcasts, and to forward reports on such factors as audience reactions, listeners' preferences and requests to a central co-ordinating agency.[35]

This activity was not to be underestimated, since the Nazis were nothing if not democratic in their approach to programme planning. Chief radio commentator Hans Fritsche outlined their policy for the medium in one succinct phrase, 'Radio must reach all or it will reach none.'[36] Whereas programme planning during the first months after the seizure of power had largely focused on elevated aspects of culture, the next year saw an abrupt change in programme concepts. In order to keep listeners tuned in to propaganda broadcasts, the new radio-station managers substituted a diet of light music for the Beethoven recitals with which they had briefly filled the ether.

The increasing percentage of broadcasting time given over to music, especially light music, was indicative of a long-term trend in Nazi programme planning. Between 1932 and 1937 the proportion of total broadcasting time set aside for music increased by almost a fifth; from 58 per cent to 69 per cent[37], seven eighths of which was for light music.[38] The war years saw a further accentuation of this trend – particularly after 1942, when the radio wardens reported that listeners fatigued by work, air-raid alarms and queueing craved a lighter diet on the air.[39]

The music broadcast was mainly of the 'entertainment' brand, comprising light operas by such nineteenth-century masters as Weber, Lortzing, Cornelius and Nicolai, and operettas. Johann Strauss tended to be so over-performed that one radio manager remarked: 'Surely we are not so poverty-stricken that *Die Fledermaus* or the *Gypsy Baron* overture has to be performed once every day!'[40] But since the exclusion of un-Aryan composers had narrowed the field considerably, Strauss, Lehar, Paul Lincke and minor figures like Eduard Kunecke and Emil Reznicek were continuously pressed into service. In addition there was some dance music – its degree of syncopation fluctuating in accordance with the intensity of the drive against the pernicious influence of the saxophone and the 'hot' style – as well as folk music and military marches. An interesting aspect of broadcast march music was the German radio's predilection for relaying the thud of goose-stepping columns on every possible public occasion.

Public occasions, as well as military ones, began to acquire a musical choreography of their own. Thus the *Badenweiler March* signalled Hitler's imminent arrival to the listener's trained ear, and as time went on he also learnt which military formation was associated with which particular march tune.

The purveyance of humour on the Nazi radio was a somewhat perilous undertaking because of the taboos with which so many potentially humorous topics and situations were hedged round. This difficulty was exemplified by the reaction of Nazi officialdom to attempts at satirizing the regime's preoccupation with fecundity and heredity. Although it was possible for a humorous weekly like *Die Brennessel* to feature this exchange between two lovers. 'How about us two doing something for the perpetuation of the race, Roswitha?' – 'Not so hasty, darling. Remember Grandpa had diabetes', similar 'obscenities' on the air elicited a sharp official rejoinder: 'If the Party is about to rouse the will to marriage and procreation in our young people, then no compère must in future dare to make fun of these matters in more or less ambiguous form.'[41]

A typical example of officially approved radio fare – politically impeccable, rooted in the soil, and suitably elevated – was the 1935 radio series, 'German Nation on German Soil',

designed to give town-dwellers an awareness of the forces of organic growth as they manifest themselves in the eternal recurrence of the seasons.[42]

The series serves the aim of at least reintegrating urban man's soul in the life of the land. We project a cyclical presentation of the rural year in four transmissions: 'A Rustic Day in Winter' (Leipzig), 'Song and Spring Sowing' (Munich), 'Swabian Summer' (Stuttgart) and 'Autumn Festival' (Frankfurt). Added to this there will be broadcasts concerned with the relationship between the rustic character and other professional estates: farm servants and maids, seamen and artisans (Cologne), wherein a humorous, droll note should not be omitted – 'Farmer and Miner' (Breslau), 'The Green Tent' – a symphony of the German forests – (Königsberg), 'Sun, Sea and Sand' (Hamburg) and 'Soldiers and farmers on *Märkische* soil' (Berlin). The series will be terminated by 'The Ages of Man' –

divided into three phases, which are exemplified in the farmer's experience of birth, marriage and death. The farmer's death is not an end; blood and soil are eternal.[43]

The local stations had a dual function – providing programmes for their particular region or for a nation-wide hook-up. Except for transmissions of a political and ritualistic nature, listeners had a choice between their regional station's programme and the national programme of the *Deutschlandsender*. During the war, at peak listening times on Sunday evenings, for instance, they could either hear light music on their local wavelength or tune in to the classical symphony concerts relayed by the *Deutschlandsender* from Berlin or Vienna. The orchestras were either the Berlin or the Vienna Philharmonic, conducted respectively by Wilhelm Furtwängler or Clemens Krauss.

These transmissions had nothing Third-Programmish about them – as a rule the symphony concerts were restricted to an hour's broadcasting time, which ruled out the performance of lengthy or more difficult pieces. There were some exceptions, such as Bruckner's seventh symphony, which held a special place in the affections of the Nazi leadership.[44] The *Mastersingers* overture and the *Eroica* were given ritual performances on great occasions: the former preceded Goebbels's annual panegyric about Hitler on the Führer's birthday, and the latter introduced Hitler's own peroration on Heroes' Remembrance Day.

In wartime, Sundays were peak radio days, and two items were special favourites of the listening public. The discerning minority looked forward all week to *Das Schatzkästchen* (*Treasure Trove*), a morning feature in which good music was interspersed with suitable poetic and dramatic excerpts culled from the German classics; public interest as a whole was focused on the two-and-a-half-hour 'Request Concerts' in the afternoon. 'Concert', in this context, meant a medley of hit tunes, soldiers' songs, operatic arias, famous concert pieces, and comedians' patter. This programme was of nation-wide interest, since each item was requested by serving soldiers (mentioned by name) for their next-of-kin, or vice versa. The importance attached to these concerts by public and government alike was reflected, as we have seen, by the popularity of the film *Wunschkonzert* (Request concert). (Cf. p. 387.) Large firms procured free advertising time by impressive donations to regimental benefit funds, and the programmes usually came to a climax with the arrival of a surprise visitor – a soldier on unscheduled leave from some exposed sector of the front. 'Request Concert' was always broadcast from Berlin; the fighting services, with the exception of the surprise guest, did not participate in the actual transmission, except vicariously; the situation was quite different in the 'front theatres' series; these were broadcasts from base camps behind the front line, at which artists entertained the troops.[45]*

During the war Allied monitors of Nazi radio programmes noted that the civilian population – despite their exertions in industry and civil defence – received incomparably less flattering attention from the programme planners than did the services. Another interesting feature of the wartime broadcasting scene was the ban on the transmission of church services; as a substitute the public were offered features with a vague religious connotation, such as a programme about the nature of German piety.

A wartime theme of rather wider concern than prayer – namely revenge – was demonstrated by a broadcast in 1944 from a V-weapon launching ramp beside the English Channel. At this time the special victory communiqués, with their blast of fanfares, followed by a march appropriate to the theatre of operations (*Wir Fahren gegen England* for Britain, *Watch on the Rhine* for France, the *Balkanlied* for Greece, and so on) – or the sound of the Lutine Bell for announcements of U-boat sinkings – were being heard ever more infrequently, and audience response to the transmission of the rocket-launching was such that it had to be repeated by public demand. But the Third Reich would not have been the place it was if at the end of each day's broadcasting listeners had not also been treated to a farcical juxtaposition of reality and sentimentality. The late night Wehrmacht communiqué, which usually terminated in the phrase, 'The population sustained losses', was invariably followed by a record of Maria von Schmedes singing 'Another beautiful day draws to its close'.

Right up to the very end of the war the radio maintained a key-role in transmitting orders and impulses from the centre to a shrinking periphery. Hitler's broadcast a few hours after his rumoured death on 20 July 1944 was a major factor in strengthening public morale on that crucial date in German history; conversely, Flensburg station, on 2 May 1945, announced Hitler's death and the end of the Third Reich to an audience which – metaphorically speaking – had already switched off.

* The *Truppenbetreuung*, arranged jointly by the Wehrmacht and the Strength-through-Joy organizations, was popularly given credit for the attempt it made to live up to its boast that the German soldier had the best leadership, training, arms and entertainment in the world.

27

MUSIC

Thomas Mann's choice of a composer Leverkuhn as the pivotal figure of *Dr Faustus*, his unique attempt at a novel defining the German soul, was not fortuitous. Music has long had a special significance for Germans – a circumstance which Teutomaniacs saw as proof of the sublimity of the German soul, while it has caused sceptics to correlate the excellence of certain nations in non-verbal art with their acquiescence in tyranny.

Nazism, that tainted progeny of German Romanticism, inherited the romantic view of music as the soul's magical access to Infinity. It also added contributions of its very own: music as a metronome for marching, as accompaniment to collective dreaming, and as an aural stimulant in charnel houses.

From the seizure of power onwards the regime bathed the country in music as in a foetal fluid. At Bayreuth Frau Winifred Wagner's annual welcome to the Führer symbolized the laying on of hands by the immortal presence (Wagner's *Rienzi* had first roused the demons in Hitler's adolescent psyche); at Nuremberg the roar of the Party Rally trailed echoes of *The Mastersingers*; barrack-squares, Labour Corps hutments and Hitler Youth clubrooms all over the Reich resounded to the command '*Ein Lied-zwei-drei!*' as did the assembly area of every concentration camp.

Through the sacrament of song the Nazis celebrated their martyred saint, Horst Wessel, and commemorated the heroic *Kampfzeit*; Liszt's *Preludes* introduced the wartime *Sondermeldungen*, the special victory communiqués, over the air, and the Third Reich finally expired to the strains of a slow movement from Bruckner's Seventh Symphony, played after the announcement of Hitler's suicide by Radio Berlin.

By common consent the Weimar period was a golden age of music. Germany was the birthplace of atonal music, and composers of traditional music, such as Richard Strauss and Hans Pfitzner, were gradually joined by the spokesmen of modernity – Schoenberg, Alban Berg, Hindemith – in orchestral and operatic repertoires, as well as in the teaching academies. There were music festivals celebrating the illustrious dead (Wagner at

Bayreuth and Mozart at Salzburg), while Baden-Baden and Donaueschingen served as sounding-boards for living composers. Leo Kestenberg wrought a transformation in education by bringing instrumental music into the school curriculum and linking music with culture in general. In the sphere of conducting, five stars shone with brighter lustre than others in the Weimar firmament: Felix Weingartner, Wilhelm Furtwängler, Otto Klemperer, Bruno Walter and Erich Kleiber. All in all, the German musical scene was alive with richness and experiment, and centres like Berlin became post-war Meccas for students, opera-lovers and concert-goers from all over the world.

The seizure of power disastrously interrupted the flow of musical life, and a stream hitherto enriched from new sources was frozen in a state of late Classical and Romantic immobility. Everything modern was condemned: atonality – the later work of Stravinsky, a great deal of Hindemith, jazz-influenced works such as Krenek's *Johnny spielt auf* and Kurt Weill's *Threepenny Opera* and *Mahagonny*. The exodus of musical talent involved the composers Schoenberg, Berg, Krenek, Schreker, Weill, Eisler, Toch, Hindemith and Webern; as well as Carl Ebert, Adolf and Fritz Busch, Arthur Schnabel, Alfred Einstein, Alexander Goehr, Leo Blech, Lotte Lehmann and Elisabeth Schumann; of the five top conductors listed above, three – Walter, Klemperer and Kleiber – emigrated as non-Aryans, while Weingartner returned to his native Austria.

Last – but by no means least – Furtwängler; despite initial gestures of defiance such as championing Hindemith, he arrived at a mutually beneficial *modus vivendi* with the regime. This earned him a slap in the face from Toscanini, but also maximum wartime security: SS squad cars were on permanent stand-by to rush him away from towns threatened by air attack.

Richard Strauss's readiness to become first president of the Reich Chamber of Music was probably even more advantageous to the new government. The great composer subsequently resigned 'because of his age' (in August 1935); this was attributed to official displeasure at his collaboration with the Jewish librettist Stefan Zweig,* but by this time the regime was solidly established and Strauss's gesture aroused little comment.

The great Strauss interpreter (and sometime librettist) Clemens Krauss even gave the maestro's continued presence in Germany as his own

---

* They worked jointly on the opera *Die schweigsame Frau* (*The Silent Woman*) based on Ben Jonson's play.

reason for taking up residence there; he stated after the war that if need be he would have gone to Stalin's Russia to conduct the première of *Arabella*.

At the opposite end of the spectrum Karl Amadeus Hartmann forbade the performance of all his works in Germany, except for his string quartet, which was based on Jewish themes.

Jewish themes were of course entirely expunged from the country's musical repertoire, and a number of reputable German composers actually assisted the regime in this 'cleansing process': both Carl Orff and Wagner-Regeny accepted commissions for scores to replace Mendelssohn's incidental music to *A Midsummer Night's Dream*.

The Jewish theme also impinged on the private lives of many musical personalities: Richard Strauss had a Jewish daughter-in-law, whom he protected; the famous Wagnerian soprano Frieda Leider remained married to a Jew who emigrated; and Hitler's favourite operetta composer, Franz Lehar, had a Jewish wife – a handicap which he used to rationalize his reluctance to save his librettist Beda Löhner from the gas chamber.

A composer who was not tainted by Jewish sympathies or connections of any sort was Hans Pfitzner; although this irascible octogenarian essentially subscribed to the Nazi creed – one of his compositions was entitled *Von Deutscher Seele* (Of the German soul) – he dared to address the new rulers in uncommonly outspoken terms. When Goering had peremptorily dismissed his application for a state pension as 'scrounging' (*Schnorrerei*) Pfitzner replied, 'I shall preserve your letter as a "cultural document" of inestimable value and a companion piece to the kick the Bishop of Salzburg could administer to Mozart with impunity. *Heil Hitler!*'[1]

Not that Mozart was posthumously spared the kicks of other theologians. Brown zealots stigmatized *The Marriage of Figaro*, *Don Giovanni* and *Cosi Fan Tutti* because the libretti were by Lorenzo da Ponte, a baptized Jew. *The Magic Flute*, though racially unsullied, did not escape censure either: it was called a vehicle of masonic ideas, a charge that stung Hitler into a highly untypical advocacy of moderation at the Party Rally in 1938: 'Only a man lacking in national respect would condemn Mozart's *Magic Flute* because it may sometimes come into conflict with his own ideas.'[2]

Wherever the regime deemed it advisable pieces of music were reinterpreted. Thus, in *Fidelio*, the emphasis was placed on Leonora's marital loyalty to Florestan and attention was deflected away from the prison scenes so relevant to the contemporary situation. Hermann Burte, an eminent

Teutomaniac, was commissioned to refurbish Handel's *Judas Maccabeus* with a new Nordic text. In its Aryanized form the oratorio became known as *Wilhelm von Nassau,* and *Israel in Egypt* was transmogrified into *Mongol Fury.* This remoulding of musical classics was not concerned merely with externals. At a Schumann concert, sponsored by the Nazi Cultural Community, the *Völkische Beobachter* professed to detect a new interpretation in Wilhelm Backhaus's rendering of the piano concerto. 'Schumann has become heroic. Although this master is frequently performed in a soft, effeminate manner, out of Backhaus's conception a new image of Schumann can be crystallized – a German Schumann image.'[3]

Related to this new image was the question of the respective values of the major and minor key, which agitated certain Nazi musicologists. One of them thought 'to be able to create something enduring in a major key, one has to be possessed of greater gifts and more inner strength than would seem necessary for a composition in the minor key. He who creates a work in a major key has come to understand and take upon himself the contradiction and paradox of life.'[4] Another made the alarming discovery that a large number of the songs of the movement were not written in a major key. He found it disturbing that 'in these very days of our racial awakening, part of the new songs show a marked affinity with an alien system of sound.'[5]

Another problem occupying Nazi aesthetes concerned the nature of artistic inspiration. On this matter opinions varied enormously, from Hitler's élitism to the aesthetic egalitarianism of Hadamovsky, the head of Nazi radio.* Hitler was wont to speak of artists as mysteriously endowed with superhuman talent from on high, whereas his broadcasting chief held that 'the lowliest apprentice at his lathe who whistles a gay song in essence does the same as the artist. In the work of a composer, man's greatest gifts are expressed in the same way as in a neatly trimmed garden or a freshly painted wooden beam.'[6]

There was no end to theorizing about what was expressed in various art forms and why – and it was all listened to and discussed with great solemnity.

> In the dance we relive the great primal laws of nature. As far as the male partner is concerned, the basic movement attuned to the thrust and the blow, inevitably tends towards the soldierly. In the case of the female the instinctive vibration is of a circular character – a circular character connected with the swastika, the rune of life with its eternally circular motion.

* Hadamovsky had in fact been a revolutionary sailor in 1918–19.

So wrote a disciple of Rudolf Bode, the Nazi's chief mystagogue of dancing.[7]

Nazi dogmatists looked on dancing as a very problematical pursuit, both musically and socially. Musically it was an accretion of alien influences: Jewish confections of meretricious trash crossed with jungle emanations of Negro jazz. Socially the then popular tea-dance represented bourgeois exclusiveness inimical to the spirit of folk community, and ballroom dancing a form of selfishness at war with the folk spirit of the community dance. An additional social danger present in every type of unreformed dancing was its incitement to sexual depravity. The *Schwarzes Korps* detected 'a type of music to which one can only dance with the upper body bent back and the abdomen pressed forward against someone else's, while wiggling one's hips like a lustful homosexual.'[8]

Similar moral disgust throbbed in Goebbels's rejoinder to Furtwängler's plea, 'In view of the world-wide paucity of truly productive musicians we cannot forgo a man like Hindemith.' Referring expressly to the latter's *Neues vom Tage* Goebbels railed: 'Opportunity creates not only thieves but also atonal musicians who out of sheer sensationalism stage scenes involving nude women in their bath-tub in the most disgusting and obscene situations, and further befoul these scenes with the most atrocious dissonance of musical impotence.'[9] Dissonance was, of course, the key attribute of modern music to arouse Nazi ire. Severus Ziegler, the manager of the Weimar theatre, ambitious to play a role in music analogous to that of his brother in art, mounted a 'degenerate music' exhibition, in which such composers as Mahler, Schoenberg, Kestenberg, Stravinsky, Milhaud, Hindemith and Weill were held up to public obloquy. He had this to say on the subject: 'We do not reject dissonance *per se*, or the enrichment of rhythm, but dissonance as a principle, and the irruption of alien rhythm.'[10] Ziegler's rather nebulous definition of the line of demarcation between proscribed and permissible innovations in music reflected a situation in which nobody knew exactly where the official Party line ran. Certain works were easy to define negatively. Boris Blacher's *Geigenmusik* could be dismissed with impunity as cats miaowing, and Richard Mohaupt's almost bitonal *Wirtin von Pinsk* was taken off after one performance at the Dresden Opera; but in the case of Carl Orff's *Carmina Burana* (the first part of a triptych of pagan cantatas with the bucolic bounce of the Munich October Festival) there was some critical hedging of bets:

This is a significant expression of our times, even if one feels impelled towards a negative attitude. It represents a new form of theatre . . . Orff can be accused of

Brechtian and Stravinskyan tendencies ... At the very foundation of *Carmina Burana* lies the medieval symbolism of the wheel of fortune. Such fatalism does not correspond to the world picture of today's Germany.[11]

Yet – partly thanks to *Carmina Burana* – Orff was to become one of the two most successful younger composers of the Third Reich. His peer and fellow-Bavarian, Werner Egk, himself experienced a startling turn of the wheel of fortune when his *Peer Gynt*, a modernistic opera with varied rhythms and bold harmonic effects, was produced in Berlin in November 1938. At the final curtain the audience did not know whether to boo or cheer. The critics spoke darkly of '*Threepenny Opera* plagiarism', but Hitler, who attended a subsequent performance, indicated approval by inviting the composer to his box. Egk received a commission worth 10,000 marks and *Peer Gynt* was placed in the repertoire of opera houses all over the Reich.

Although the pseudo-egalitarian character of Nazism also spilled over into the arts, with the Strength-through-Joy organization marshalling a new and totally unsophisticated mass audience, in other aspects the Third Reich revived the 'electoral' framework out of which German cultural institutions had historically evolved. The armed Bohemians who had become Nazi potentates indulged their vanity and compensated for earlier artistic frustrations by acting as latter-day electors dispensing princely patronage to the arts. As with all Nazi institutions, there was a great deal of rivalry and overlapping, but basically Goebbels's cultural fief comprised all radio and film studios, Goering's and Schirach's the opera houses and major theatres of Berlin and Vienna respectively, while Hitler was patron of Munich, Weimar, Bayreuth and Linz. He singled out Linz – which was to house the world's greatest art collection – as his posthumous shrine, and endowed it with a large orchestra (known as the Bruckner orchestra), under the baton of Jochum Jr. In Munich, it was the visual arts that most engaged Hitler's attention, while his solicitude for Weimar found expression in an annual allowance of 60,000 marks (out of his personal Endowment Fund), in giving advice on problems of staging and casting and in convivial intercourse with the artists.

But it was Bayreuth that ranked supreme in the Führer's affections. Already an honoured guest at *Haus Wahnfried* in the twenties, he subsequently returned there year after year for prolonged stays during the festival season. The first German head of state since Ludwig of Bavaria to take a personal interest in the Bayreuth Festival, Hitler endowed it with an annual subsidy similar to Weimar's, in addition to granting it complete tax exemption. Heinz Tietjen, the festival director, who, according to Friedelind Wagner, was not satisfied unless he had 800 people and a dozen horses milling round on stage, found Hitler such an indulgent sponsor that he could – for instance – expand the chorus of the Gibichungs with its sixty-four members to over a hundred. The festival became an annual highlight in the calendar of the Third Reich and a useful adjunct to the Party propaganda machine. An article entitled 'Richard Wagner and the German Conductor Today' in the festival handbook for 1938 stated,

> Wagner's work teaches us hardness in the figure of Lohengrin . . . through Hans Sachs, it teaches us . . . to honour all things German . . . In *The Ring of the Nibelungs* it brings to our consciousness with unexampled clarity the terrible seriousness of the racial problem . . . in *Parsifal*, it shows us that the only religion Germans can embrace is that of struggle towards a life made divine.[12]

It is, of course, true that these interpretations did little violence to the spirit of Wagner's work. Developments during the Third Reich actually produced a closer approximation to Wagner's original Bayreuth concept. With the steady reduction of foreign visitors, the festival was becoming a predominantly German musical event. There were not only changes in the composition of the audience. In 1933 the Jewish artists List and Kipnis no longer sang there, and Toscanini stayed away, despite a letter from Hitler inviting him to conduct. Kirsten Flagstad, mindful of her standing in America, ceased to appear at Bayreuth shortly afterwards, and so did Herbert Janssen and Frieda Leider, who were both married to Jews, some time later. Though the loss of these musical personalities made itself felt, it was to some extent counteracted by Tietjen, who, as former director of the Prussian State theatres, managed to procure the finest talents available in the capital. Nor must we leave out of account the penumbra of patronage by the All-Highest, which lent Bayreuth an air of enchantment in which critical disbelief was suspended.

When war broke out the festival – in contrast with 1914–18 – continued though on a different, pseudo-socialist basis: it became the Führer's gift to audiences of convalescent soldiers, deserving munitions workers, nurses and others. Another wartime change was the dropping of *Parsifal* from the repertoire, presumably because its Christian overtones antagonized the neo-paganists round Rosenberg. A wartime film none the less transposed Bayreuth into a musical Lourdes where a shell-shocked officer might regain his mental health during a performance of *Siegfried*.*

* See chapter on the Cinema, p. 386.

A contemporary SD report bore out some of the film's basic premises. After recording the resentment of the local population at the luxury surrounding the festival (artists were much better fed and housed than the soldiers for whose benefit they were allegedly appearing), it described a *Meistersinger* audience as so overwhelmed with gratitude to the Führer and appreciation of Wagner's patriotic sentiments that tears glistened in their eyes during Hans Sachs's aria 'None would know what German is and true unless he lived in German masters' honour'.

Wagner's influence made itself felt elsewhere, too; for instance, in the music of Paul von Klenau. After combining the twelve-tone scale and folksong in *Michael Kohlhaas* (1933), Klenau employed a near-Wagnerian idiom in *Rembrandt van Rijn* (1936), his best-known work. Traces of Wagner also suffuse Richard Strauss's *Liebe der Danae* (1940), which boasted a Jupiter who would have been more at home in Valhalla than on Olympus.

Among his younger and lesser colleagues Strauss in his turn continued to inspire the highest form of musical flattery: imitation. Kurt von Wolfurt conceived *Dame Kobold* (1940) in a *Rosenkavalier* manner, and there were many who detected Straussian accents in Werner Egk's eclectic idiom. Be that as it may, with *The Magic Violin*, full of appealing folk-tunes, robust humour, *opera-bouffe* touches, slow waltz and polka rhythms, Egk came close to creating a new type of German folk-opera. In addition, he maintained his commanding position in the contemporary musical scene with a stream of compositions which included other operas, orchestral pieces, ballet-pantomimes and radio cantatas. Carl Orff provided a fitting sequel to his *Carmina Burana*, based on a medieval minstrel text, with *Carmina Catulli* (1943), in which dancers mimed the action while the chorus sang of the Roman poet Catullus's unrequited love for Lesbia. With *Die Kluge* (*The Clever Woman*) of that same year, an opera suffused with rhythmic *élan* and truly melodic passages, Orff was considered to have reached his peak. Attentive listeners also had an ear for such lines as 'Whoever has the might also has the right (*Recht*, which in German also means "law") and whoever has the law, bends the law', as well as 'When loyalty was born, she crept into a huntsman's horn; the huntsman blew her into the wind: that's why loyalty cannot be found'.* Other successful

---

* A special significance attached to this cynical couplet on loyalty, because of the enormous play the Nazis had made with the concept of loyalty, as in the SS watchword, 'Our honour is loyalty'.

works by Orff were *Antigone* and *The Moon* (1939), a part-farcical, part-fairy tale opera based on Grimm.

An opera with religious and fairy tale elements which achieved considerable success was *Tobias Wunderlich*, by Max Reger's pupil, the liturgical composer Josef Haas. *Tobias Wunderlich* had a Pygmalion theme involving a woodcarver and the statue of a female saint, as well as a climax in the form of a pilgrimage scene inspired by Bruckner – none of which endeared it to the Party's pagan lobby.

Boris Blacher was another composer not altogether *persona grata* to the regime: his music was thought to be not sufficiently German. Blacher's wide range extended especially to oriental influences; a composer of ballets, operas, and dramatic oratorios, he was also an important teacher, numbering von Einem among his pupils.

The prolific late romantic Paul Graener continued along conventional paths during the Nazi era, reaching his hundredth opus with *The Prince of Homburg* (1935). In the same year the neo-classicist Wagner-Regeny gained a sizeable success with *The Favourite* (based on Victor Hugo's *Mary Tudor*); he did not quite repeat this success with *The Burghers of Calais* (1939).*

Richard Strauss – to turn from lesser-known names to the most illustrious one – continued to compose throughout the Third Reich. His *Arabella* was first performed at Dresden, shortly after the Nazi take-over. *The Silent Woman*, first performed there two years later, had a very brief run because its libretto had been written by the 'full Jew' Stefan Zweig. (Hoffmansthal, Strauss's librettist for *Arabella, Der Rosenkavalier* and *Electra* had, by contrast, been only a quarter-Jew.)

In 1938 there followed two one-act operas, often performed together, the mythological *Daphne* and *Friedenstag* (Day of Peace) which was set at the end of the Thirty Years' War. The latter concluded with a paean to peace – which perhaps accounted for Hitler's absence from the Munich première.

First performed at Munich in 1942, *Capriccio*, an unduly extended one-act disquisition on the nature of opera (with a libretto by Clemens Kraus), played to audiences restricted by wartime dislocation. *The Love of Danae*, a three-act opera with Wagnerian echoes, was completed in 1940 and scheduled for Salzburg in 1944, but only heard at one dress rehearsal before Goebbels's totalitarian edict came into force. Strauss, who ten years earlier

---

* Other operas deserving mention were Ottmar Gerster's *Enoch Arden* (1936), Robert Heger's *Prodigal Son* (1936) and Mark Lothar's tragi-comic *Schneider Wibbel*.

had congratulated Goebbels on freeing Germany from such men as Hindemith and Kleiber, now inveighed against the regime for depriving him of a fortune in royalties by banning concert and opera performances.

Hans Pfitzner also continued to be productive. A 'cello concerto appeared in 1934, and in 1939 Furtwängler conducted the first performance of his *Kleine Symphonie*. Pfitzner's personal rancour against Goering and other Nazi leaders did not prevent him from participating in Nazi schemes for bringing art to the people. In 1937 he conducted a concert of his own symphonies in the unconventional setting of a railway repair shop, standing on an up-ended cable spool while the orchestra was arranged along an elevated engine turntable.[13] This concert was only one of two hundred similar events staged during that year, and although the popularization of art was hardly an invention of the Nazis (invaluable pioneering work in this sphere had been done by the *Volkshochschulen*, the trade unions and the *Volksbühne* organization long before 1933) the regime's mass mobilization exceeded in scope anything previously attempted. Not surprisingly, the Nazi cultural revolution did have its difficulties:

Last Easter, through the arrangements of a Strength-through-Joy organization, a great number of workers were taken to a performance of the Bach St Matthew Passion . . . During the second part of the performance they unwrapped their sandwiches, unscrewed potato-salad containers and enjoyed the last part of the Passion as a musical accompaniment to their supper.[14]

Even so, attendances at concert and opera performances rose impressively during the Third Reich. A number of factors going beyond the merely technical one of efficient audience mobilization accounted for this increase: the economic revival, the slowly widening gap between purchasing power and the supply of consumer goods, and the conservatism of Nazi music policy (since conventional fare obviously possessed wider mass appeal than innovation). Official disapproval of new departures eventually created a situation of diminishing returns. Having exhausted its stock repertoire, the Deutsche Oper in Berlin, for instance, was reduced to resurrecting from well-deserved obscurity such minor nineteenth-century pieces as *Der Postillon von Logimeau*, Weber's *Euryanthe*, Thomas's *Mignon*, Humperdinck's *Königskinder* and Kienzl's *Evangelimann*. The war created further confusion among programme planners when enemy composers like Ravel, Debussy, Chopin, Bizet and Tchaikovsky had to be expunged from the repertoire. (The ban, however, was not total; *Prince Igor*, for instance, was performed at Hamburg during the Russian campaign.)

There was similar inconsistency in the regime's approach to modern music. Though Honegger could be performed, most of Bartok could not, and Stravinsky's *Fire Bird* enjoyed official approval, while his *Sacre du Printemps* was placed on the Nazi Index. In fact in 1937 Stravinsky was at one and the same time pilloried at Ziegler's Exhibition of Degenerate Music and performed in Brunswick (*Persephone*). As they officiously inserted their scalpels into the body of modern music, the regime's Musical Officers of Health claimed that they differentiated between 'malignant growths of orgiastic dissonance' (*sic*) and less noxious phenomena. Even so the operation of taboos confining German musicians inside a straitjacket had repercussions too obvious to be overlooked. The *Völkische Beobachter* noted plaintively, 'it is not easy to find the way back to good German music',[15] and State Councillor Severus Ziegler disingenuously disclaimed any intention 'to make it difficult for German musicians to earn their daily bread'.[16]*

One group of musicians encountering little difficulty in this connection was made up of those who worked on official commissions. For the 1936 Olympics, for instance, the regime pulled out all the stops in the creative register of Nazi music and commissioned Richard Strauss, Carl Orff and Werner Egk – i.e. *the* German maestro and his most promising juniors – to provide aural *chiaroscuro* for the mammoth athletic junket with which it so effectively dazzled foreign opinion.

These three composers were at least chosen on merit; lower down the scale it was usually a musician's close contacts with the Reich Music Chamber or some other Party institution that determined his inclusion. Having put the *Gebrauchsmusik* (consumer music) of the late twenties on the index, the Nazis commissioned a large volume of their own, since their calendar of public life was studded with anniversaries and ritual dates requiring suitable musical ornamentation. A fairly typical example of the work to which such sponsored composers as Cesar Bresgen and Heinrich Spitha turned their hands was the Horst Wessel commemoration cantata of 1938. Entitled *The SA Lives For Ever*, it consisted of three movements: 'His song kept time with our marching', 'The world belongs to leaders', 'Soldiers are always soldiers'. The *German Prayer*, first performed in the great hall of Munich University, contained these three motifs: 'Revelation

---

* At the same time, the regime's chief musical whipper-in offered cold comfort to reviewers, whom Goebbels had already reduced in November 1936 from critics to 'considerers' of works of art: 'If German art critics are in a difficult position today, let them blame it on the decadent *literati* who formerly held sway as satellites of the degenerate musicians.'

out of the experience of war', 'Achievement of grace through battle', 'The triumph of obedience'.[17]

Whatever the quality of such works, they certainly added up to a considerable total of musical activity. In addition, the Party units with their fife-and-drum or brass bands and incessant marching songs generated a volume of music which – in terms of decibels at any rate – eclipsed anything heard before.

Yet at the same time Dr Rave, the sometime President of the Reich Chamber of Music, noted:

> Adults involuntarily leave all musical activities because the duty imposed upon them by their organizations compels them to do so. . . . Private musical instruction has declined to an alarming extent. . . . Children are so much in demand by their organizations that they have no more time for practising . . . A paralysing phenomenon is to be observed throughout the whole sphere of German music.[18]

These strictures were passed in 1934 and the institutions responsible did subsequently do something to rectify the situation. The Hitler Youth, for instance, which was notorious for spoiling children's voices by encouraging them to bellow rather than chant their marching songs and slogans, eventually showed sufficient concern for its members' vocal chords to organize its own professionally directed choirs and orchestras. It was to discover, however, that the trained personnel required by its mass-membership was in short supply, and in 1939 it described the lack of young music teachers as 'the most urgent of our problems'.[19]

A year earlier the Reich had – according to Goebbels – boasted 25,000 male-voice choirs, a mixed choir membership of 125,000, 8,000 amateur bands (comprising 120,000 musicians) and a threefold increase in the sale of pianos over 1933.[20] À propos of pianos: the slump had cut Germany's annual output from 40,500 to 6,000, so that the 1933 figure still amounted to less than half the total for 1930, a year with an overall production index comparable to 1938. String instruments proved a similar drug on the market – though not wind instruments, the demand for which was stimulated by the proliferation of brass bands attached to military and Party units.

Other sets of statistics, which Goebbels wisely did not quote, referred to the small circulation of musical journals (50,000 throughout the whole of the Reich) and the absurdly small percentage of children receiving musical education at school; at Wuppertal in 1936–7, for instance, only 790 out of 37,246 pupils (or 2 per cent) did so.[21]

In addition, the very system of co-ordination which enabled Goebbels to indulge in statistical gigantomania spelt artistic decay, because it turned every single amateur society into a fief to be disputed by Party officials and empire-builders. The whole sphere of amateur music was thrown into turmoil, with old-established choirs and ensembles being dissolved and re-merged in accordance with the pronouncement of Mannheim's cultural leader: 'Today the problem is not whether we sing with one voice or many, but whether we are artistically and ideologically above all criticism. Let us do away with *Vereinsmeierei;* * the small clubs must be amalgamated.'[22]

Co-ordination proceeded remorselessly, however much Dr Rave warned against the artistic drawbacks inherent in organizational streamlining.[23]†

The economic aspects of amateur music also came under close official scrutiny. To obviate the dangers of dilettantism the Reich Chamber of Music instituted stiff examinations for works bands; failure disqualified them from competing with professional bands for hire at such functions as dances and socials.[24]

The authorities' concern for the interests of professional musicians had bizarre results. A wartime SD report, warning of the strangulation of village culture, spoke of the government-licensed 'Society for the Utilization of Musical Copyright' enforcing contracts on all places of entertainment and demanding royalties from publicans at whose taverns music was performed, with the result that non-contributing tavern-keepers even forbade their clients the use of the pub piano.[25]

On the other hand, the regime managed to maintain an impressive façade of musical activity in the main centres of population. Thus during the 1941-2 season, which coincided with heavy fighting on the eastern front, no less than eighty separate operas, operettas and ballets were produced in the capital. Such surface manifestations of a rich cultural life endured right up to the last year of the war, when totalization measures led to the closing down of all places of entertainment.

From August 1944 onwards the Reich radio became the sole purveyor of musical entertainment to the public – quite a hazardous assignment. Thus six months later, with Allied troops deep inside the Reich, its music programme committee still had to deal with complaints about the amount

* A sectarian exclusive absorption in the life of one's own club.
† In addition the Gestapo dissolved some well-known choirs on the suspicion that they were being used to camouflage resistance groups.

of non-German dance music being broadcast.[26] Protests of this sort had been uttered with unfailing regularity ever since 1933, when the earliest forms in this sphere dealt with sexually suspect practices: professional male dancers were completely abolished[27] and the conduct of female 'hostesses' was closely regulated.[28]★

'Perverse jazz music', seemingly eliminated in 1933, showed astonishing powers of resilience: in 1937 the official S A paper discerned 'impudent swamp flowers of Negroid pandemonium in German dance-halls regrettably abetted by so-called German dance bands'.[29]

To obviate this danger, a dehydrated form of syncopated music called 'German Jazz' was pioneered by Peter Kreuder, Theo Mackeben and Barnabas von Geczay. Other innovations included programmes stringing together purely German items of ballroom dancing; one such programme included the following: a *polonaise* as a greeting dance, a marching dance, an *ersatz* tango (which involved changing one step in 4/4 time), a slow waltz, a 'Rhinelander', a type of polka in which the female partners were exchanged, the 'German *Achte*' (a dance involving four couples) and a galop as the concluding item.[30]

The Hitler Youth wanted ballroom dancing to be gradually replaced by folk-dancing, and proclaimed weightily 'Individual couples should be drawn out of their isolation into the great circle of all dancers expressive of the community. This, however, could not be done by means of formation dancing in which isolated couples were only arranged in symmetrical figures, but no actual exchange of partners occurred.'[31] New forms of dancing required new styles of performance, and these in turn necessitated the re-arrangement of instruments in dance bands. The saxophone was purged as a symbol of Negroid lewdness, and percussion instruments existed only on sufferance. A marked divergence between Nazi dogma and public taste manifested itself during the final heat of the 'Unknown German Dance Band' contest at Berlin in 1936. Although a Hamburg band's rendering of *I'm in Heaven* with a great deal of percussion received most applause, the first and second prizes were awarded to bands using percussion much more sparingly. A Press report on the event carried the headline ON THIS NIGHT OF TRUE FOLK COMMUNITY, NEGRO JAZZ WAS BURIED AMIDST GENERAL DERISION.[32] Publicity of this type was

★ But in the capital, at any rate, the clean-up campaign did not produce a complete change of atmosphere – no doubt for reasons connected with the tourist trade. The Femina nightclub, for instance, continued to feature table telephones by which male clients could communicate with female partners of their choice, and provided pneumatic tubes for transmitting cigarettes or chocolates as tokens of a client's desire for the next dance.

reinforced by a barrage of admonitions and prohibitions, with local Party functionaries quite often acting in advance of officialdom to prohibit the 'Negroid excrescence' of such decadent dance-forms as swing, the Lambeth Walk and the 'Hot Dance'.

Very occasionally visiting foreign bands relieved the bleakness of the musical scene. In 1935 Jack Hylton earned acclaim at Berlin's Philharmonic Hall and drew this comment from a Nazi newspaper: 'Every German with some feeling must have left the hall embittered and saddened to see the public reveal such lack of judgment.'[33] Yet, two years later, when Hylton's band returned for the Berlin Press ball – playing 'The Organgrinder's Song' and 'Dinah', among other items – both Goering and Goebbels danced to it.[34]

The war severed Germany's last tenuous links with Western dance music, although even then isolated oases (like Berlin's Café Holländisches Eck, which featured bands from the Low Countries) survived. It was the teenage urge to dance unconfined by the swaddling clothes of the Nazi aesthetic that prompted the formation of youth groups whose unorthodox wartime conduct was regarded as an expression of opposition – or delinquency.*

* See chapter on Youth, p. 283.

28

ART

Some of the loudest premonitory rumbles to disturb the smug tranquillity of life under the Kaiser had emanated from the sphere of visual art. The most noteworthy successors to the *fin-de-siècle* painters were iconoclasts and innovators whose forays into modernity aroused shrill hostility from establishment and public alike. '*Meschuggismus*' – 'fostering a cult of insanity' – was the accusation flung at the Dresden *Die Brücke* group of Schmidt-Rottluff, Kirchner, Pechstein, Haeckel and Muller and a Munich newspaper called in all seriousness for the arrest of the *Blaue Reiter* painters, Kandinsky, Klee, Marc and Macke.[1]

Earlier Kaiser Wilhelm had dismissed Dr Tschudi from the directorship of Berlin's *Nationalgalerie* for aesthetic *lèse-majesté* in purchasing Impressionists, while the Austrian heir-presumptive, Franz Ferdinand, wanted his batman to give Kokoschka the thrashing of his life.

But the royal Canutes could not bid the waves recede. The years 1910–11 saw Kandinsky produce the first-ever abstract painting in Munich, while Gropius designed the Fagus Works, almost an equally significant departure in the realm of architecture. War and its aftermath enriched the Expressionist art of Nolde and Barlach with new religious and humanitarian impulses; and Hans Arp and Max Ernst reacted to an absurdly changed world with Dada and Surrealism. In the early twenties as singular a concourse of artist-teachers as any in history gathered under the flat roof of the *Bauhaus*: Klee, Gropius, Kandinsky, Feininger, Schlemmer, Moholy-Nagy, Marcel Breuer.

This post-war impression of artistic richness made Fernand Léger actually envy Germany her wartime defeat. The French painter's thinking implied a causal connection between a country's receptivity to *avant-garde* impulses and her power-political eclipse, a view shared – for diametrically opposite reasons – by German conservatives in politics and art.

'Combat Leagues of German Culture', pronounced modern art to be aesthetically repellent and politically subversive, and discharged their wrath impartially upon the pacifist expressionists such as Ernst Barlach,

Otto Dix and Georg Grosz, exponents of the *Neue Sachlichkeit* and the architects Gropius, Mies van der Rohe and Mendelsohn. They stigmatized a settlement designed by Gropius as 'an enemy fortress in the midst of the Fatherland' and called Le Corbusier 'the Lenin of architecture, hurling Moscow's blazing torch into an unsuspectingly tranquil Europe'.[2]

The Dresden exhibition of modern German painting in 1926, a token of Germany's post-war advance into the front rank of international art, prompted half a dozen patriotic associations to protest to President Hindenburg about the 'slap in the face of Germany, its heroic army and the leader of this army, Your Excellency'.[3]

A year earlier the *Bauhaus* had been compelled to move from Weimar to Dessau, partly because its changes in the design of housing, furniture and domestic utensils had antagonized the Association of Thüringian Craftsmen. Opposition to modern art was a cause common to many segments of the population: traditionalists, dizzied by the yawning chasm between *avant-garde* and public taste, artisans wedded to old techniques, architects hostile to glass and concrete, chauvinists outraged by pacifist war memorials, and the inhabitants of plush parlours looking to art as a substitute for reality. The impact of these rabid anti-modernists closely reflected the political fortunes of the far right. 1930 – the year of the Nazi electoral breakthrough – witnessed the dismissal of Dr Gurlitt, director of the Dresden Museum, for 'pursuing an artistic policy affronting the healthy folk feeling of Germans'.[4] Scenting blood, the National Socialist Combat League prophesied an imminent 'picture tornado'[5] and threatened brazenly: 'We shall turn Munich into the cultural centre not merely of Germany but of the world.'[6]

The prospective global metropolis of art was, of course, already the 'capital of the Movement' and the headquarters of the Nazi Combat League, Alfred Rosenberg, Combat League Leader and Party ideologist, devised the Third Reich's official aesthetic with the aid of the anthropologist Professor Günther and the architect Schulze-Naumburg. This aesthetic centred on *Auslesevorbilder* (exemplars of selection), which Günther and Schulze-Naumburg culled from Greek classicism and such manifestations of the German Romanesque style as the cathedrals of Bamberg and Naumburg. The particular contribution of Rosenberg, a former architectural student who turned out insipid drawings, lay in the valuation of artistic trends.

The nineteenth century lacked a generally valid image of beauty and culminated in a state of Impressionist and Expressionist impotence. German post-war art is that of *mestizos* laying claim to the licence of depicting bastard excrescences, the products of syphilitic minds and painterly infantilism as expressions of the soul.[7]

Typical of the Nazi aesthetic was Goering's comment on Leistikow's painting, *Grunewald Lake* (Kaiser Wilhelm II had already opposed the idea of the National Gallery buying it): 'As a huntsman, I know that the Grunewald does not look like that.'[8] The self-appointed *Praeceptor Germaniae* in all artistic matters, Adolf Hitler, in a speech inaugurating the House of German Art in Munich in 1937, expressly forbade any painter to use colours different from those perceived in Nature by the 'normal' eye. (By coincidence Max Beckmann left Germany the very morning after Hitler's speech.)

The new art canon enjoined the banishment of all evocations of human anguish, distress and pain – in other words all ugliness from people's consciousness. (In the Nazi's own subconscious the aesthetic defeat of ugliness by beauty dovetailed with the extermination of the Jews – ugliness incarnate – by the Nordics.)

Oddly enough, co-ordination proceeded less hurriedly in the sphere of the visual arts than in some other spheres. Basically it was only the concurrent exhibitions in Munich of Nazi-sponsored art and Degenerate Art in the summer of 1937 that signified the completion of the purging and whipping-in process. The delay was in part due to the overlapping activities of Rosenberg's Combat League and Goebbels's Reich Chamber of Art (which had squeezed Germany's 42,000 Nazi-approved painters, sculptors, architects, graphic artists and art publishers into one organizational straitjacket). In addition, some ministerial heads of department and gallery directors blunted the impact of the purge measures by Fabian tactics; they were abetted in this by a moderate Nazi lobby comprising Party officials such as Otto Andreas Schreiber and journalists on the art periodicals *Kunst der Nation* and *Kunstkammer*. Moderate is, in fact, a misnomer. Objectively speaking they were a radical coterie within the Party, who wanted to fuse German Expressionism with National Socialism in the way that Futurism had been linked with Italian fascism. Their spiritual godfather was the writer Gottfried Benn, whose collection of essays *Art and Power*, published in 1934, included a vindication of Expressionism and a homage to Marinetti, chief exponent of Futurism. By stressing the native German elements in Barlach's and Nolde's work, the Schreiber group tried to procure their admission to the Nazi pantheon. In 1934 *Kunst der Nation* used a Barlach sculpture as a cover design for its Winter Relief issue and featured articles on Beckmann, Rohlfs and Nolde. Emil Nolde, a crusty recluse living in a fisherman's cabin in Schleswig-Holstein, and, incidentally, a Party member, was even championed by the Berlin Nazi paper, *Der Angriff*, which Goebbels had founded, and it was known that Noldes and Barlachs actually graced Goebbels's own home. The hopes of the Schreiber group were accordingly centred on Goebbels, who initially veiled the Nazi arts purge behind a façade of relative moderation because he feared that total artistic 'co-ordination' would discredit Germany in the eyes of the world. This twilight situation was of short duration; arbitrating in the aesthetic demarcation dispute between Rosenberg and Goebbels, Hitler at last promulgated his irrevocable late-Victorian art canon. In direct consequence of this Barlach and Nolde vanished from the walls of Goebbels's mansion, Schreiber was shunted into the mobile exhibitions department of the Strength-through-Joy organization, and in 1936 moderate art periodicals were supplanted by Rosenberg's ultra-orthodox publication, *Die Kunst im Dritten Reich*. For a little longer it somehow still remained possible to mount exhibitions of condemned artists in Berlin: Schlemmer in January 1937 and Nolde in April. Then, in June, a Barlach-Marcks exhibition was peremptorily closed down on the orders of Schweitzer-Mjölnir, 'Reich Plenipotentiary for Artistic Formulation', and all the exhibits were confiscated.[9]

The opening shot in what later developed into a wholesale campaign of confiscation had been the closure in October 1936 of the modern section of the *Nationalgalerie* in Berlin's former Kronprinzen-Palais, the last official sanctuary of genuine art left in the Reich. A four-man purge tribunal (Professor Ziegler, Schweitzer-Mjölnir, Count Baudissin and Wolf Willrich) toured galleries and museums all over the Reich and ordered the removal of paintings, drawings and sculptures that were regarded as 'degenerate'. Ziegler was the Third Reich's aesthetic Torquemada; rumour had it that an eccentric old Schwabing★ painter had become so enamoured of the meticulous young copier of Dutch flower-pieces that he had revealed the secret of grinding colours to him, and that this esoteric lore had impressed Hitler sufficiently to promote Ziegler to the presidency of the Reich Chamber of Art. Under his pseudonym Mjölnir (the ancient Germanic name for Thor's hammer), Schweitzer published in *Der Angriff* cartoons peopled by iron-jawed Storm Troopers and prehensile-nosed Jews. Count Baudissin had unleashed the 'picture tornado' at the famous Volkswang Museum in Essen, of which the Nazis had made him director;

★ The Bohemian quarter of Munich.

424

his contribution to the new aesthetic was: 'The most perfect shape, the sublimest image that has recently been created in Germany has not come out of any artist's studio, it is the steel helmet.'[10] (Baudissin's demand in 1938 that all degenerate work be removed from private as well as public collections prompted Rudolf Kirchner's suicide in Switzerland.) Wolf Willrich, a bigot given to denouncing Party comrades to the Gestapo if they considered Barlach or Nolde suitable for public exhibition, had couched his contribution to the Nazi aesthetic in book form: his *Cleansing the Art Temple* characteristically sported his own painting, *Guardian of the Race*, as its cover design. (After 1939 coloured post-card reproductions of his portraits of war heroes sold in prodigious quantities, and he amassed a personal fortune.)

The swathe these four apocalyptic Norsemen cut through Germany's stored-up artistic treasure has been estimated at upwards of 16,000 paintings, drawings, etchings and sculptures: 1,000 pieces by Nolde, 700 by Haeckel, 600 each by Schmidt-Rottluff and Kirchner, 500 by Beckmann, 400 by Kokoschka, 300–400 each by Hofer, Pechstein, Barlach, Feininger and Otto Müller, 200–300 each by Dix, Grosz and Corinth, 100 by Lehmbrück, as well as much smaller numbers of Cézannes, Picassos, Matisses, Gauguins, Van Goghs, Braques, Pisarros, Dufys, Chiricos and Max Ernsts.[11] Of that total, 4,000 were actually burned in the courtyard of the headquarters of the Berlin fire-brigade in 1939. In addition to burning canvases, the regime also used them as fuel for stoking the fires of Philistinism. The first exhibition of degenerate art, entitled 'Government Art 1918–1933', was mounted within months of the seizure of power at Karlsruhe. Its organizers had adroitly seized on two preoccupations of the human psyche – money and sex – by listing inflation prices – naturally without their stabilized currency equivalents – and roping off a special 'for adults only' section given over to the display of nudes.

The organizers of the huge Exhibition of Degenerate Art at Munich in 1937 were guided by similar considerations, and there can be little doubt that this three-ring circus of obscenity repaid the care lavished on its preparation. We have only to consider the spontaneous reaction of one visitor: 'The artists ought to be tied up next to their pictures, so that every German can spit in their faces – but not only the artists, also the museum directors who, at a time of mass unemployment, poured vast sums into the ever-open jaws of the perpetrators of these atrocities.'[12] The Degenerates, in fact, constituted the most popular display ever staged in the Third Reich, attracting 2 million visitors, five times as many as came to the concurrent first exhibition of German art. Pictures were displayed in a mad jumble, without frames, as if arranged by fools or children without any sense or reason, high and low, just as they came, furnished with inciting titles, explanations or filthy jokes. In sections with headings such as 'Jewish desert-longing finds expression' or 'Thus did sick minds view Nature' or 'German peasants looked at in the Yiddish manner', 112 eminent artists were publicly pilloried.* How many of the spectators jamming the exhibition's turnstiles (on Sundays, the attendance reached football cup-tie proportions) were drawn by prurient curiosity and how many came to take a last look at art earmarked for oblivion is a question defying statistical analysis.

While the regime celebrated the funeral obsequies of degeneracy in one building, the newly resurrected phoenix of German art was cradled in a specially constructed edifice near by. Designed by Hitler's favourite architect, Professor Troost, the House of German Art was a monotonous, outsize pastiche in the classical manner with an unaccented pillared façade, which quickly inspired popular epithets such as 'Munich Art Terminal' and 'Palazzo Kitschi'. This nest of stone was representative of its brood. Shortly before the ceremonial opening, a furious Hitler discovered that the hand-picked jury, which included Professor Troost's widow, had rejected some unbearably *Kitsch* items, and ordered his court photographer, Hoffman, to countermand the jury's decision.

On the opening day of the First Exhibition of German Art, Munich hung out its flags. In the streets perspiring Teuton warriors manhandled a giant sun and carried the tinfoil-covered cosmic ash-tree Yggdrasil (of Germanic legend), in solemn procession. 'Nornen' on stilts dexterously sidestepped overhead tram cables as they continued weaving the loom of fate, and columns of wimpled châtelaines and medieval burgesses evoked the age of Albrecht Dürer and Lucas Cranach.

Regaled with these evocations of the past, the crowds entered the exhibition hall and found themselves – back in the past. In the words of the semi-official *Berliner Illustrierte Zeitung*:

Adolf Wissel's 'Peasant Group' told intimately of the secrets of the German countenance; Karl Leipold's 'Sailor' experienced the sea as creative world-fluidum; Adolf Ziegler's 'Terpsichore' combined a grasp of modern painting with the purity of classical antiquity in its conception of the human body; Elk-

* These included Nolde, Schmidt-Rottluffe, Kirchner, Otto Müller, Rohlfs, Beckmann, Kokoschka, Corinth, Dix, Franz Marc (represented by his renowned 'Tower of the Blue Horses') and the non-Germans Chagall, Feininger, Kandinsky and Mondrian.

Eber's 'The Last Hand-Grenade' showed movingly how the artist had experienced the Great War and given sublime expression to this vision.[13]

Every single painting on display projected either soulful elevation or challenging heroism. Cast-iron dignity alternated with idyllic pastoralism. The many rustic family scenes invariably showed entire kinship groups, Spartan, hard, robust, barefoot and fecund. All the work exhibited transmitted the impression of an intact life from which the stresses and problems of modern existence were entirely absent – and there was one glaringly obvious omission: not a single canvas depicted urban and industrial life. The 1938 exhibition did actually include two industrial scenes, a bridge over a motorway with a monumental wooden scaffolding, and an equally monumental tar-distillation plant. The most representative companion pieces of these two were 'Clear the Streets' (stern-visaged Storm Troopers displaying flexed muscles and swastika banners), an Arcadian fruit-harvesting idyll, an enormous, bare-breasted Amazon, and a peasant family with children in the cradle, in their mother's arms, and on her lap. An exhibit richly suggestive in its overtones was Udo Wendel's 'The Art Magazine', depicting an incomplete family group: pensioner-father, mother and unmarried painter-son. Both parents were looking at different copies of *Kunst im Dritten Reich* with the mother's copy open at a reproduction of Fritz Klimsch's sculpture 'Die Schauende' (The Gazing Woman). The effect of Wendel's painting operated on two levels. Superficially it showed a German family – oozing probity from every pore – taking its Sunday afternoon culture in accordance with the Führer's commands; more subliminally it could be taken to feature a mother selecting a model bride for her bachelor son from an aesthetic mail-order catalogue.[14]

In the more obvious sphere of '*Fleischbeschau*' (the examination of female flesh), Rothang's 'Amazon after Battle' was eclipsed by 'The Goddess of Art' by Adolf Ziegler, whose painstakingly executed confections of lifeless nudity earned him the soubriquet of 'Reich Master of Pubic Hair'. Besides Ziegler, the star of the 1938 exhibition was the sculptor Professor Thorak (popularly nicknamed 'Professor Thorax', because of his preoccupation with Herculean masculinity). Thorak's *penchant* found its clearest expression in the design for a huge motorway monument consisting of three contorted, muscular nude figures pushing boulders up an incline in a paroxysm of effort; his gigantomania inspired the story of the visitor who had asked the studio assistant about the sculptor's whereabouts, only to be told, 'The Herr Professor is up in the left ear of the horse.'

Open-air sculptures like 'The Gazing Woman' were seen by tens of thousands annually; attendance at the Munich exhibitions rose year by year, from 480,000 in 1937 to 720,000 in 1943,[15] but the chief means of informing millions about developments in Nazi art remained the Press. In November 1936, Goebbels had, as we have seen, banned criticism as hitherto known, and had limited the critic's scope to drawing up inventories of exhibitions.* Yet even 'cataloguing' could amount to an exercise in opposition in the hands of a subtle journalist. Gert Teunissen of the *Kölnische Zeitung*, for instance, managed to deflate the two stars of the 1938 exhibition:

This time it is not Terpsichore but a life-sized Goddess of Art which expresses Ziegler's praise of beautiful nudity. Once again reality has been hit off so accurately that one would think this *soignée*, pink-cheeked female had only a second ago shed the light burden of her clothes. Her nudity, whose careful artistic execution breathes the air of warm life, conceals manifold charms in its opalescent flesh tints.

Thorak's giant bronze figure of a muscular man holding a bunch of grapes in his left hand has now received an equally muscular, heavy-hipped, taut figure of a woman as its counterpart, a figure which the artist has called *Hospitality*. Another figure – *Enthronement* – is that of a very massive naked woman holding a wreath in her raised hands and pressing her feet backwards against a pedestal. The sculptor is thereby trying to convey the impression that the massive figure is in a state of suspension.[16]

The *Deutsche Allgemeine Zeitung*, another bourgeois paper continuing on sufferance, sold every copy of a special edition featuring the 1937 Munich exhibition. The editorial staff attributed this success to the full-page pictorial supplement in which the worst excesses displayed at Munich were reproduced.[17]

In a dispatch entitled 'Everyday routine in the House of German Art', purporting to show how National Socialism had purged the art world of pretentiousness and involved ordinary people in culture, the *Frankfurter Zeitung* wrote:

A Viennese stands in front of a painting by a famous Viennese artist. Berliners

* Critics exceeding these bounds – and it required considerable acumen to divine exactly where the line was drawn – were liable to dismissal. Karl Korn, for instance, lost his wartime job on *Das Reich* for adverse comment on Truppe's painting *Being and Passing Away*, which the Bavarian Gauleiter Wagner had received as a wedding gift from Hitler. By juxtaposing a nude maiden and a fully dressed old crone, Truppe had hit on a variation of the skull-beneath-the-head theme, profitably combining eroticism and mock-profundity. Hitler and Gauleiter Wagner, incidentally, did not share the same taste in erotic art. Wagner was shocked at his Führer's predilection for Padua's near-pornographic *Leda and the Swan*.

discuss the work of one of theirs. Two members of the German Girls' League show each other a painting and one informs the other that the painter comes from Danzig. An inhabitant of Munich assures a visitor from elsewhere, 'I know this painter. He lives in our street. He is a nice man.'[18]

Even more equivocal was an opinion expressed in the (once renowned) satirical periodical *Simplicissimus*: 'There were times when one went to exhibitions and discussed whether the pictures were rubbish, whether the painter knew his job, etc. Now there are no more discussions – everything on the walls is art, and that is that.'[19]

But the regime was not popularly regarded as hostile to culture. On the contrary, an aura of Graeco-Germanic renaissance seemed to suffuse its peacetime and early war years. This aura owed something to the sheer numerical scale of officially sponsored art events: 170 competitions for painters, graphic artists, sculptors and architects, with prizes totalling $1\frac{1}{2}$ million marks in 1938, and over a thousand art exhibitions throughout the Reich in 1941;[20] nor must the Third Reich's building frenzy be left out of account. This was not merely a matter of state and municipal construction programmes: the general economic upswing had prompted massive building activity on the part of industrial firms, investors, large farmers and others. As far as the aesthetic merit of these new constructions was concerned, it has been noted that the corruptive influence of Nazi ideology was inversely proportional to the degree to which buildings served a practical purpose.[21] The buildings commissioned by industry were the finest put up in the Third Reich. Their architecture was untouched by Nazi influences and continued a tradition of industrial design that had started after the turn of the century and reached its apogee during the Weimar Republic. Quite a few of the bridges across the motorways tended to be impressive, both technically and aesthetically. The same is true of social buildings for workers (even when constructed by such government institutions as the National Postal Service and the railways) and of administrative offices, youth hostels, hospitals and churches put up during the Nazi peacetime years.

Werner March's Olympia Stadium in Berlin was a unique example of officially commissioned architecture that cannot be faulted aesthetically. This is not true of public housing, which was accorded exaggerated folkloristic treatment, especially in suburban and rural areas. Here the backward-looking sentimentality central to the Nazi aesthetic burgeoned forth in a profusion of thatched roofs, wooden balconies, hand-hewn oak beams and wood panelling which prompted Baldur von Schirach, the self-appointed arbiter of Nazi taste, to comment, 'The suburban Berlin-type villa in a peasant village is no doubt nonsense. No less of a nonsense, however, is the whitewashed Tyrolean peasant house transplanted to a Berlin suburb.'[22]

Elsewhere the erection of endless high-gabled, tight little houses, each in its separate courtyard, completely reversed the enlightened town-planning trends initiated under Weimar.

One town-planning idea produced by the Weimar Republic that the Nazis corrupted for their own ends was that of the 'city crown' (*Stadtkrone*), the civic centre envisaged by Bruno Haupt as focusing the life of an urban community in the way that cathedrals had done during the Middle Ages. Looming large – in every sense of the word – on the Nazis' architectural blueprints, these buildings were placed round a representative plaza geometrically aligned to an enormous avenue of approach along a central dominating axis and decorated with sculptures and ornamental plants.[23]

Although war and defeat prevented these projects from coming to fruition, a few were partly realized, such as Berlin's North/South and East/West axes, which were part of Speer's scheme for reconstructing the capital in a manner befitting the metropolis of the Nazi empire. Speer's main architectural contributions to the visual flavour of the Third Reich were his Party buildings in Nuremberg and Hitler's Chancellery; the latter, a compound of ancient Hellas and severe Prussian classicism, was adorned with the gaudy and lavish encrustation of Nazi symbolism. The effect was dull, oppressive and sinister: Speer's designs and Breker's sculptures evoked the pervasive scent of the Minotaur, in which all Nazi architecture was sheathed.[24]

There were further intimations of barbaric rites in such classical structures as the Party Headquarters complex around the Königsplatz in Munich, where massive administrative buildings flanked the square-columned open porticoes that housed the stone sarcophagi of the SA martyrs; and in the romantic architecture of the *Ordensburgen* – medieval edifices which exuded a brooding aura of asceticism and remoteness both in space and in time.

Finally, there were the *Totenburgen* (castles of the dead), monumental soldiers' memorials, planned to fulfil the role of pagan ossuaries and symbols of conquest:

On the rocky coast of the Atlantic there will grow up grandiose structures facing west, eternal monuments of the liberation of the Continent from British dependence ... Massive towers stretching high in the eastern plains will grow into symbols of the subduing of the chaotic forces of the eastern steppes through the disciplined might of the Germanic forces of order.[25]

The architect-designate of this network of sepulchres across a whole continent was Wilhelm Kreis, whose aesthetic, surprisingly, excluded gigantomania: 'A building can also appear monumental without outsize dimensions.' On the other hand, Kreis was not exactly a stranger to Hubris; by his own admission the Halle Museum of Prehistory, which he had designed, always reminded him 'of a Bach fugue'.[26]

Kreis's monumental masonry staked out the area of Hitler's aesthetic blueprint for post-war Europe; at its centre was the Führer's Linz Project, a scheme to convert Hitler's stuffy provincial birthplace into the world's greatest treasure house of (looted) art. Though the project itself did not get beyond the drawing-board stage, Hitler's art-collecting activities proceeded sufficiently for the value of his collection to reach an estimated £100 million. Against the backdrop of a war-ravaged continent he and his heir-presumptive, Goering (the value of whose collection was estimated at £60 million), virtually fought a collector's war, each trying to outdo the other in his looting exploits.

Hitler's taste reflected his late-Victorian small-town origins: in *Mein Kampf* he extols the facile romantics Moritz von Schwind and Arnold Boecklin; convinced that the stock of the Austro-Bavarian *genre* would rise in future, he wanted pride of place at his Linz museum to be accorded to Defregger, Waldmüller and Grutzner, whose paintings of bibulous monks and rustics at work or play were saccharine fantasies of a serenely intact world.

Goering's aesthetic tastes were somewhat less stunted. He both eulogized the florid Victorian titillator Makart* in public and clandestinely confiscated fourteen 'degenerate' masterpieces (by Van Gogh, Gauguin, Munch, Marc and others), which were auctioned off at Lucerne in June 1939 to obtain foreign currency for the Reich.

Compliant artists could, if competent, grow exceedingly prosperous under this patronage; there was a non-stop flow of titles, prizes, commissions and popular acclaim. The sculptor Arno Breker, whose reliefs depicting paroxysms of rage and aggression (the well-known 'comradeship' group, for instance) tapped a main-spring in the Nazi mind, earned nearly 100,000 marks in 1938.[27]

* On the centenary of Makart's birth Goering stated at Salzburg: 'Makart will for ever occupy an honoured place in German art.' (cf. Hermann Glaser, *Spiesser-Ideologie*, Rohmbach, Freiburg, 1964, p. 212).

His colleague Georg Kolbe was the only outstanding German artist to adapt to the regime; compare the introverted diffidence of his *'Der Einsame'* ('The Lonely One', 1927) and the extroversion of *'Der junge Streiter'* ('The Young Warrior', 1934). He turned his studio into a venue for guided tours of Strength-through-Joy rubbernecks. Fritz Klimsch had his 'Gazing Woman' placed at a vantage-point along the slopes of the Bavarian Alps.

It must not be thought that such rewards were lightly earned. The painstaking effort expended on items of officially approved art in the Third Reich was often prodigious. It was precisely the meticulous attention to technical detail evident in Werner Peiner's pseudo-Breughel landscapes, Adolf Ziegler's Dutch flower-pieces and Sepp Hilz's near-obscene Venuses that seemed to lend those paintings an aura of authenticity. The two prerequisites for artistic success in the Third Reich were meticulousness and receptiveness to official guidance.

The manner in which guide-lines were transmitted could be astonishingly uncomplicated: while preparing their entries for the annual Munich exhibition, artists received lightning visits* from 'aesthetic officials' who were full of helpful advice: 'Much too gloomy; let's have a little more joy in your composition. People in Germany no longer have such careworn faces', or 'Why aren't the faces of the people in the background recognizable? The Führer insists on everything being represented clearly and distinctly.'[28] Unfortunately the advice reaching artists from on high was not always consistent; for instance Baldur von Schirach said: 'Pictures which can be confused with colour photographs may at best be miracles of technique, but are not miracles of art, since art has another truth than that of reality.'[29] But Schirach's periodic airing of latitudinarian sentiments was really quite irrelevant to the state of the arts in the Third Reich – more to the point was a statement by the chief Nazi official of culture in Westphalia, who quite unconsciously provided the pithiest commentary on the Third Reich's policy: 'It may well be that many an artist will no longer have the courage to create anything new after the opening of the House of German Art at Munich.'[30]

Lastly, what about those artists who did not lack the courage to create anything new, either after or before the opening of Hitler's late-Victorian art emporium? Their number has been estimated at 15,000. Among the painters, especially, there seems to have been an almost total refusal to

* In Düsseldorf two such officials, one of whom was himself an animal painter, 'attended' to no less than forty painters and sculptors in three days.

capitulate before a regime armed with formidable sanctions. These sanctions ranged from *Lehrverbot* (deprivation of the right to teach) through *Ausstellungsverbot* (deprivation of the right to exhibit) to the most crippling of all, *Malverbot* (deprivation of the right to paint). Lest the *Malverbot* should be circumvented in the privacy of an artist's home, the Gestapo would carry out lightning raids of inspection, checking up – as in Carl Hofer's case – on whether the paint brushes were still wet. They also placed lists of proscribed artists in the paint shops, so as to cut off their supply of materials at source. Even more effective in enforcing the *Malverbot* was the penury of the artists, who dismissed from their posts and prohibited from selling their work, were too poor to buy materials.

Under the circumstances it is remarkable how few defamed artists actually went into exile. Apart from the non-Germans among them who returned to their native countries (Klee to Switzerland or Feininger to the United States),* Kokoschka went to England, Beckmann to Holland, Kirchner to Switzerland, and Grosz to the United States, as did leading *Bauhaus* personalities like Moholy-Nagy and architects such as Gropius, Mies van der Rohe and Mendelsohn. Of the defamed artists two outstanding ones died relatively early on: the doyen of the Impressionists, Max Liebermann, and the Expressionist Ernst Barlach, a painter, sculptor and dramatist of great distinction. Liebermann, a Jew renowned for his Berlin salon and his ready wit ('Madam, this portrait resembles you more closely than you do yourself'), said shortly before his death, 'I cannot eat as much as I would like to throw up.' Barlach, already virulently abused in Weimar times for his pacifist war memorials, had been badly shaken by SA vandalism in 1933 and spent his last years as a timid recluse. The indomitable Käthe Kollwitz – one of the handful of individuals sufficiently courageous to attend both Liebermann's and Barlach's funerals – said of the latter's death: 'He turned his head sideways as if he wanted to hide.'

A year after Barlach's death, Kirchner committed suicide in exile in Switzerland. Oscar Schlemmer died in 1943, essentially from grief at not being allowed to paint. He had been forced to earn a meagre living by putting camouflage paint on Stuttgart's municipal gasometer before finally finding work alongside the abstract painter Baumeister in Dr Herbert's paint and varnish factory at Wuppertal. Other industrialists sympathetic to defamed artists were the Hamburg cigar manufacturer Reemstma, who helped Barlach, and Paul Beck of Stuttgart, a benefactor of Käthe Kollwitz. There were also some art dealers, notably Günther Francke and

* Kandinsky went to France.

Ferdinand Moller, who did their best to succour the proscribed painters, sometimes by putting on clandestine exhibitions of their work. Occasionally one painter would buy another's work to boost his morale – as Schmidt-Rottluff did for E. W. Nay; a few courageous members of the public did the same.

The artists reacted to this situation in different ways. Otto Pankok, Hans Grundig and Otto Dix produced anti-Nazi paintings in secret. Emil Nolde, aged, crotchety, eccentric, who failed to comprehend why he – a Party member – had been proscribed, feared detection, but nervously painted water-colours in his North Sea cottage, hoping to expand them into big paintings after the war. A circumstance that somewhat mitigated Beckmann's difficult wartime exile in Holland was the ingenuity of his son, an officer in the medical corps, who smuggled his father's pictures across the frontier in army lorries.

To the abstract sculptor Hartung life under the Nazis was an existence in the catacombs with hardly anyone ever knocking at his door. Baumeister managed, thanks to a wealthy mother-in-law, to continue painting secretly throughout the whole period; indifferent to official proscription, he nevertheless felt his social ostracism very keenly, and was quite overwrought by Schlemmer's death. But the certainty that better times would return never deserted him. He had SS billeted in his flat and guarded himself against discovery by referring to his abstract paintings as experiments in camouflage techniques. When Stuttgart was bombed he and his family were evacuated. They occupied one room in a farmhouse, and it was in that room in 1943 that he began to write *Das Unbekannte in der Kunst* (*The Unknown in Art*).[31] At the end of the war he returned to his Stuttgart home to find that all his belongings had been looted. The only items the looters had not bothered with were his abstract paintings, stacked away in the cellar – what better proof that the regime's notions of what constituted art commanded the support of the broad mass of the people![32]

29

RELIGION

Germany is both the cradle of the Reformation and the only major European country to be left irremediably divided by it. By its failure to carry the Rhineland, Bavaria and, most importantly, Austria, Luther's reformation in fact added to the division of Germany. Yet, at the same time, it aroused stirrings of German self-awareness that were never to be entirely absent from the national conscience until, more than three centuries later, Bismarck expanded Prussia into an empire from which Catholic Austria was excluded. Based on the alliance of Hohenzollern crown and Lutheran altar, this empire was essentially Protestant, even though Catholics constituted roughly a third of its population. The confrontation of this compact minority and a non-pluralistic state gave rise to the *Zentrum Partei* – a party with the single aim of defending the Catholic interest.

While the Centre Party was allegedly debasing Catholicism by politicizing it, Christianity as a whole came under attack from various quarters. The intellectual trend in late nineteenth-century Germany was in many ways inimical to established Christianity: materialism and rationalism on the left, and on the right pseudo-scientific racism linked to an atavistic penchant for Germandom. Richard Wagner, the novelist Felix Dahn* and *völkische* philosophers such as Langbehn, Lagarde and Frenssen strove to redirect the psychic energies of a public disoriented by the rise of industry and a mass-society towards the racial past, tribal duty and primeval customs.

In the purely religious sphere the 'ethnic' ideology spawned two divergent trends. One tended towards a purely German i.e. de-Romanized, and de-Judaicized form of Christianity; the other towards 'New Heathenism' (*Neuheidentum*). German Christianity focused on the Aryan saviour Jesus, transfigured physically into a Nordic and psychologically into a bearer of the sword rather than the crown of thorns. The new heathenism dethroned him entirely and substituted either Wotan-worship or a cult of

* Author of the perennially best-selling *Struggle for Rome*, a paean to the heroic Goths' combat against decadent Rome.

nature centred on the sun. Neo-pagan sun worship eventually overlapped with tendencies towards nudism, hiking and bathing, all of which gained ground among young people in the inter-war period.

The end of the First World War produced significant changes in the two great religious establishments. To the extent that Protestantism had been the state religion of the *Kaiserreich*, defeat and the collapse of the Empire necessarily undermined its standing. But whether *triumphans* or no, the Church held fast to a vision of itself as *ecclesia militans*. In 1913 the journal *Protestantenblatt* had stated unequivocally: 'Pacifism is blasphemy against God.'[1] In 1917, when five Berlin pastors issued a plea for peace by negotiation, 160 of their colleagues signed a victory-or-destruction counterblast.[2] As late as 1928 a Protestant divine could become embroiled in a drawn-out controversy by questioning the claim that a soldier's death for his country was equivalent to martyrdom on behalf of the Christian faith.

At the universities it was often theological rectors (such as Seeberg at Berlin or Procksch at Greifenwald) who called most clamorously for the rejection of Versailles and – *mutatis mutandis* – of the Weimar State.

This growth of revanchist sentiment was accompanied by an upsurge of German Christianity and neo-paganism on the fringes of the Protestant establishment. 'Theological' studies appeared under such titles as 'Wotan and Jesus', 'Baldur and the Bible', and 'The German Saviour'; the last-named, incidentally, blandly unravelled the paradox of the German Saviour's Israelite origin by posing the counter-question 'Why can't a beautiful flower grow on a dung heap?'[3]

The official Protestant attitude to the 'Jewish problem' – a touchstone for the survival of Weimar democracy – was best summed up by a scholarly theologian from the faculty at Erlangen at the 1927 Evangelical Congress. While warning against rabid anti-Semitism he asserted: 'The Church must have eyes and words for the threat that Jewry poses to German folkdom. Service to the Fatherland is divine service.'[4] To the Protestant Church the Great War had meant a crusade of the divinely ordained *Kaiserreich* against blasphemous Republican France. When a German Republic was set up it seemed both un-German and ungodly – a charge for which Weimar's separation of church and state provided ostensible justification.

The Catholics, for their part, castigated Weimar's religious policy for granting the same rights to truth and error; Cardinal Faulhaber impugned the very legality of the Republic by describing its origin in the November 1918 upheaval as characterized by perjury and high treason.[5] (This was the same Republic that gave the Catholics unprecedented freedom of action and made possible the creation of new bishoprics, abbeys, and over a thousand new religious settlements.)[6]

Although others in the hierarchy undoubtedly agreed with Faulhaber, the overall Catholic relationship with the new state was rather more complex than this. As a socio-political group which (like the Social Democrat workers and middle-class liberals) had been denied a commensurate share of political power in the *Kaiserreich* the Catholics – not entirely fortuitously – sustained the shifting coalitions that provided governmental continuity of a sort during most of the Weimar era. The leading Centre politician, Erzberger, who had signed the Treaty of Versailles for Germany was one of the first victims of *Fehme* assassins; *völkische* denigrations of the Republic's red-gold-black flag hinged, *inter alia*, on the association of its three colours with three internationals allegedly dedicated to the ruin of Germany: the red international of Marxism, the yellow international of Jewish mammon, and the black international of Catholicism.

It was partly because of its vulnerability to chauvinistic attack that the Church went out of its way to stress its patriotism; the *Völkische*, on the other hand, hesitated to condemn Catholicism *per se*; Hitler, for one, was only too conscious of the affection in which millions of Germans, in Bavaria and elsewhere, held the Church. Bavaria, in fact, illustrated a marked convergence of Catholic prejudice and Nazi hatred of the Left, Weimar democracy and the Jews, as seen in the violent regional swing to the right after the collapse of the short-lived Munich Soviet of 1919. Religious anti-Semitism was a living tradition in Bavaria, exemplified by such phenomena as the Oberammergau Passion Play, with its stress on Jewish deicide, the pilgrimages to Deggendorf commemorating a medieval ritual murder, and the *Miesbacher Anzeiger*, a notoriously anti-Semitic local paper edited by a priest.

Catholic anti-Semitism was, moreover, not just a regional aberration. In 1930 the Vicar-General of Mainz stated that although it was un-Christian to hate other races, he concurred with Hitler's evaluation of Jewish influence in the Press, theatre and literature;[7] in this respect he held a similar viewpoint to that of the Lutheran Bishop of Kurmark, Dibelius, who had written: 'One cannot fail to appreciate that Jewry plays a leading role among all the disruptive phenomena of modern civilization.[8]

But despite an overlap in some spheres, there was no such thing as a political consensus between the two denominations. Protestants who found their political home mainly in the DNVP (German National People's Party) and the DVP (German People's Party) sniped at the Centre

Party for its readiness to form a coalition with the Marxists, i.e. the Social Democrats. Dibelius explained a fine point of Protestant political theology before the 1932 Presidential election:

Seven years ago we openly expressed our incomprehension of the readiness of certain Protestants to vote for the (Catholic) candidate of the Centre Party. This time we have done nothing of the sort, although among the candidates there is once again a Catholic, namely Hitler. But he is not a candidate of the Roman Catholic Church, rather the leader of a great national movement, to which millions of Protestants belong.[9]

The seizure of power by this 'great national movement' placed both Christian denominations in a uniquely complex situation. Although certain basic aspects of the Third Reich, such as the quasi-Messianic nature of the political upheaval and the State's unjustified claim to unlimited power, were of relevance to both Churches, they each found themselves in quite different situations. The Protestants, with their synodal organization and division into variously oriented regional churches (*Landeskirchen*) (cf. the strength of the German Christians in Thüringia and Schleswig-Holstein) were wider open to Nazi permeation than the more autonomous and compactly structured Catholics, who were in any case part of a universal church under a supranational head. In the Third Reich the universalism of the Catholics could, of course, be made to seem a particularly heinous attribute, though events were to show that Germany's Romanists, clergy as well as laity, were not one whit less nationally minded than the followers of Luther and Calvin. Then there was also the consideration that some sort of compromise leading to the establishment of a German Christian State Church might be arrived at between the Nazis and a section of Protestantism, whereas the very nature of Roman Catholicism ruled this out. Hence the Catholic leadership, both lay and religious,[10]* decided during the early stages of the Nazi consolidation of power to establish a *modus vivendi* with Berlin by means of the Concordat in June 1933; they thus retained narrowly circumscribed control over education and communal institutions in exchange for the Vatican's diplomatic recognition of the regime, and the German hierarchy's political submission to it. To reassure apprehensive conservatives in both religious camps, the Nazis resorted to

* Monsignor Kaas, a key figure in the Concordat negotiations, successively combined both functions; as last floor leader of the Centre Party in the Reichstag he helped to procure the necessary two-thirds majority for the Nazis' 'constitutional' abrogation of the constitution; he subsequently became a high Vatican official with special responsibility for German affairs.

large-scale juggling during their early months in office; for instance, they recognized seven Roman Catholic feast days as legal holidays. The Prussian government gradually abolished interdenominational schools, made religious instruction obligatory, and re-introduced it into vocational schools where it had previously been omitted. The unusual mass attendance of Storm Troopers at Sunday services turned them into veritable SA church parades, and church weddings *en bloc* became the fashion among the Storm Troop officer corps. Party comrades who were lapsed church members rejoined on superior orders and – wondrous to relate – during 1933 the number of baptisms in Berlin actually exceeded that of births.[11] The scent of these incense-flavoured smokescreens elicited an avid response in church circles. Ecclesiastical spokesmen vied with the leaders of the non-Marxist political parties, of some of the trade unions, of industry, the professional bodies and the universities in their expressions of support for this regime of national resurrection. 'The aims of the Reich government have long been those of the Catholic Church,' claimed the Roman Catholic Bishop Bürger, and much was made of Catholic concurrence in the Nazi anathema on Communism, Liberalism, Atheism, Relativism and Permissiveness. Bürger's brother in Christ, Bishop Gröber of Freiburg,[12] invoked venerable Catholic traditions in support of Nazi racism by referring to the Jesuit Order's stringent exclusion of applicants of Jewish ancestry. Other theologians became quite lyrical in their apotheosis of Hitler.

Now he stands before us (wrote Professor Adam of Tübingen) he whom the voices of our poets and sages have summoned, the liberator of the German genius. He has removed the blindfold from our eyes, and through all political, economic, social and confessional covers has enabled us to see and love again the one essential thing – our unity of blood, our German self, the *homo germanus*.[13]

When Nazi Germany startled the world by a countrywide boycott of Jewish shops in April 1933, *Generalsuperintendant* Dibelius lent the moral support of a leading Protestant dignitary to the boycott as a means of reducing 'Jewish over-representation in business life, medicine, law and culture.'[14] German Protestants concurrently reduced Jewish over-representation in the Holy Scriptures and the liturgy: Abraham's sacrifice of Isaac was excised from the syllabus in Schleswig-Holstein, and the Evangelical Church of Saxony replaced the Hebrew terms 'Amen' and 'Hallelujah' by 'May God grant it' and 'Praised be the Lord'.[15]

The German Christians, however, did not merely envisage piecemeal alterations in teaching and liturgy, but the restructuring of the whole of German Protestantism – both in its theology and in its organization. During the Church elections of 1933 the German Christians – with overt support from such outside bodies as the Storm Troopers – managed to poll three-quarters of the votes and to gain majorities in most provinces, whereupon they moved to reshape the Church in the image of the Nazi state, i.e. to subject it to the operation of the leadership principle.

This attempt was spearheaded by Pastor Hössenfelder, Dr Krause and regimental chaplain Müller (a confidant of General von Reichenau's). Müller was duly elected National Bishop, an honour he was not to enjoy for very long; the other two met with even briefer success; their career as Church reformers reached both its climax and its end at a mass meeting at the Berlin Sports Palace in November 1933, where 20,000 participants agreed to the introduction of the Aryan paragraph into the Church, for laity and clergy alike. But Dr Krause's clarion call for cleansing the Gospels of all un-German traces, such as 'the scapegoat and inferiority theology of Rabbi Paul', was so extreme that it produced a reaction that forced him and Hössenfelder off the religious stage.[16] Hitler was adroit enough not to let the reaction to the 'Sports Palace Scandal' run its full course. He met the chief Protestant dignitaries and cajoled them into collaborating with the chief Nazi ecclesiastical whipper-in, National Bishop Müller. This agreement did not, however, commit the entire Church. The opposition to collaboration crystallized around a dissident group that became known as the *Bekenntniskirche* (or Confessional Church). The *Bekenntniskirche*, however, derived its *raison d'être* not from opposition to National Socialism as such, but from a determination to defend the integrity of the Church against state interference.[17] At its 1934 Synod it declared itself to be the only legitimate church, and thus unambiguously challenged the authority of the German Church leadership and of National Bishop Müller. Though it eventually gained the adherence of over 5,000 members of the Protestant clergy, the Confessional Church was itself split between moderates, such as the provincial bishops of Bavaria (Meiser) Hanover (Mahrens), and Württemberg (Wurm), and a less conciliatory group around Niemöller; however, not even Niemöller displayed the root-and-branch-antagonism to the regime of the eminent Swiss theologian Karl Barth, who was deprived of his chair and expelled from Germany in 1935. Just how split the non-collaborationist Protestants were may be gathered from Bishop Mahrarens's description of Karl Barth as 'Germany's greatest misfortune'.[18]

But in spite of discord, the very fact of the Confessional Church's existence undermined the credibility of Bishop Müller, and in 1935 the regime created a new Department of State for Church Affairs under *Reichsminister* Kerrl. Kerrl assumed many of the functions originally intended for the National Bishop, and Müller, who refused to resign, was left by the authorities to rot away in full regalia (as the contemporary phrase had it).[19]

Müller's replacement by Kerrl signalled a new departure. Though chagrined at their failure to bring about Evangelical 'co-ordination', the Nazis subtly switched from a policy of intervention to one of exploiting the divergences within the Protestant camp from the outside. The German Christians controlled such regions as Thüringia, Saxony, Mecklenburgh, Hesse-Nassau and Schleswig-Holstein; the Confessional Church controlled Hanover, Bavaria, Württemberg and Hamburg. In the key area of Prussia Dr Werner was made head of the provincial Church, holding this office concurrently with the Presidency of the National Church. He was assisted by a 'Council of Spiritual Confidants' which included the German Christian Bishop Schulz and the Hanoverian Bishop Mahraren, who, despite his confessional allegiance, studiously eschewed confrontation with the Nazi regime. The main spokesman for Church interests *vis-à-vis* the authorities was Mahraren's colleague in Württemberg, Wurm. Unlike the more outspoken members of the Confessional Church, Wurm did not believe in public protest either: most of the tug-of-war between him and the authorities was waged on paper and in private.

While Hitler looked upon the German Christians as the sect most amenable to his purpose, it was Rosenberg's total opposition to Christianity in any form that articulated the Party's basic attitude to religion. Rosenberg's pseudo-philosophical *Myth of the Twentieth Century* calumnified Christianity and the churches with such acrimony that the Catholic Bishop of Münster, Count Galen, felt moved to issue a closely reasoned refutation of it in 1934, entitled *Studies on the Myth of the Twentieth Century*. Galen's refutation appeared both as a pamphlet and as a supplement to the diocesan gazette in Cologne and Münster, and in this way reached hundreds of thousands of Catholic readers. During the same year the circulation of the diocesan weekly of the See of Aachen went up from 38,000 to 90,000; this increase was to some extent the result of

'Marxist' readers, whose press had been entirely eliminated, switching over to Catholic publications in preference to Nazi ones.[20] This type of politically significant yet basically tepid opposition (Hitler had assured Bishop Berning of Osnabrück that Rosenberg's *Myth* was merely a private publication)[21] occurred in a zone of indeterminate legality; thus the joint pastoral letter of the Catholic Bishops' Conference at Fulda, which stated: 'Religion cannot be based on blood, race or other dogmas of human creation, but only on divine revelation', was widely disseminated despite the Gestapo's ban on its publication,[22] and a pastoral letter impugning neo-paganism was actually allowed to be freely read from the pulpits.[23]

Edmund Kiss's drama *Wittukind* which, to the annoyance of Catholic audiences, attacked Charlemagne and (by overt inference) Christianity itself, elicited the following reply from the *Kirchenblatt*, the Catholic journal: 'Without consideration for the historical truth in the Christian faith of millions of German folk comrades this play impugns the Church in the most brutal and nauseating manner.'[24] The *Kirchenblatt*'s complaint could not, of course, affect the run of *Wittukind*, which was itself a subsidiary part of the elaborate campaign against political Catholicism. At the 1934 Nuremberg Party rally the Hitler Youth sang:

No evil priest can prevent us from feeling that we are the children of Hitler. We follow not Christ, but Horst Wessel. Away with incense and holy water. The Church can go hang for all we care. The Swastika brings salvation on earth. I want to follow it step by step. Baldur von Schirach, take me along![25]

and a perennial favourite of the SA had this refrain: 'Storm Trooper comrades, hang the Jews and put the priests against the wall.'

In Bavaria the Nazis initiated a drive against religious separateness in the school system, and managed, within a few terms, to pressurize most parents into transferring their children to interdenominational schools. Cardinal Faulhaber's retaliatory pastoral letter, *Mit brennender Sorge* (1937), stated unequivocally: 'The enrolment of Catholic pupils in these schools has taken place in circumstances of notorious coercion, is the effect of violence, and devoid of all legality.'[26] Although this statement was read out from all pulpits the Church was helpless to prevent the inexorable erosion of its influence on youth. In 1936 Hitler Youth membership became obligatory for all boys and girls between the ages of ten and eighteen, and the Episcopate had to be content with warning Catholic parents against entrusting their children to Hitler Youth leaders known to be actively hostile to the Church.[27] The years 1936 and 1937, moreover, saw a key area of institutional Catholicism – the monasteries and the convents – subjected to a sustained official campaign of vilification. Hundreds of monks and nuns were arraigned in the courts* on charges ranging from illegal currency transactions to sexual malpractices. (Thus monks whose nursing duties included holding the penises of sclerotic patients when they urinated were accused of homosexuality.)[28]† Goebbels, who had, ironically, been destined for the priesthood by his parents, compelled all German newspapers to publish accounts of the trials issued by the government news agency unabridged, thus turning dailies into pornographic special editions.[29] 'Two worlds wrestle for our souls,' orated Dr Ley, the Third Reich's self-appointed advocate of the Dionysian life, in the midst of all the muck-raking. 'These men's denial of life has led them into the monastic orders. Our affirmation of life leads us into the ranks of our laughing youth.'[30]

The currency and immorality trials failed to achieve the effect intended – the Upper Bavarian District President reported, 'Priests still enjoy the greatest respect, especially in country districts'[31] – but the Episcopate had the gravest apprehensions about the impact of National Socialism on the minds and hearts of the laity. In the tense summer of 1935 Bishop Buchberger of Regensburg warned Cardinal Bertram that in the event of a rupture between Church and state 'the fidelity of many Catholics towards the Church might fail the test'.[32]

The Catholic Church's official relationship with the regime was largely governed by that apprehension, with individual members of the Episcopate varying to a certain extent in their attitudes. Bishop Preysing of Berlin was uncompromisingly anti-Nazi, while Berning of Osnabrück preached obedience and loyalty towards the state when visiting concentration camps in his diocese.[33] Bishop Gröber of Freiburg published a *Manual of Contemporary Religious Questions* (for the enlightenment of the laity). It contained definitions that were distinguishable from the corresponding sections of *Mein Kampf* merely by their more elegant style; for instance Bolshevism was described as 'an Asiatic state despotism in the service of a group of terrorists led by Jews'.[34]

Anti-Semitism provided a tempting point of convergence for Nazi

---

* One monster trial at Koblenz involved 267 members of the Franciscan order (out of a national total of 500); the charges related to offences against the frequently imbecilic youngsters under the brothers' care.

† This is not meant to imply that there was absolutely no substance in the official charges (cf. visits by Thomas Cromwell's commissioners to the monasteries before their dissolution by Henry VIII).

dogma and a deep-seated Catholic animosity. In his advent sermons in 1933 Cardinal Faulhaber expressed incredulity that the Old Testament with its 'condemnations of usurious land grabbing and of the farmer's oppression by debt' should be a 'product of the spirit of Israel',[35] and the official Catholic *Klerusblatt* justified the Nuremberg Laws in 1936 as 'indispensable safeguards for the qualitative make-up of the German people'.[36]

(There were, however, exceptions such as the Westphalian village priest who rhetorically asked his congregation 'Why do some people adore the Mother of God?' and answered 'Perhaps because she is not of Aryan descent.')

German patriotism represented another – and less contentious – area of agreement between Church and state. When Wehrmacht units re-entered the demilitarized Rhineland in 1936, they were met at the Rhine bridges by censer-swinging Catholic priests who conferred blessings on them. Bishop Count Galen thanked the Führer for all he had done for the honour of the German People and asked Almighty God to bless his further endeavours. Bishop Gröber, too, avowed his enthusiasm but expressed himself unable to vote 'Yes' in the plebiscite on the remilitarization of the Rhineland because it was linked to an election of Reichstag deputies, many of whom – as members of the German Faith Movement (*Deutsche Glaubensbewegung*) – were sworn enemies of the Church.

The Movement, whose adherents were simply called 'God-believers' (*Gottgläubige*), constituted the neo-pagan Church of the Third Reich – although the term 'Church' is in fact too definite a description for this improvised adjunct of Nazism in the spiritual sphere. The Movement, being a rather amorphous construct, could best be defined by its negative articles of faith of which the chief was enmity to Christianity and the established churches. Planning to use neo-pagan 'conversion' to complement its own more general anti-Church measures (such as hamstringing communal and youth organizations, or attenuating religious instruction at schools), the Party therefore launched a drive to make individual parishioners withdraw from Church membership. The 'Church Secession Campaign' was particularly effective among professions materially dependent on the regime: civil servants, municipal employees, teachers, full-time Party workers; and by 1939 the Reich Statistical Yearbook listed 3,481,000 Germans – 5 per cent of the population – as '*gottgläubig*'.[37]

The 'positive' activities of the Faith Movement – which in a memorable phrase called Christianity 'Germany's religious Versailles'[38] – centred mainly on de-Christianizing the rituals surrounding birth, marriage and death, and on reconverting Christmas into a pagan solstice festival. Since the practices of the Faith Movement remained uncodified throughout the Third Reich, it did not evolve a definitive version of its own rituals but merely tried a number of experiments. The following description of a marriage ceremony in Tübingen at which Professor Hauer, the Faith Movement's leader, acted as *Weihwart* (votive warden), should therefore be taken as an illustration, but not necessarily a representative one, of neo-pagan usages.

The betrothal took place in the open under a lime tree.

The ceremony had begun with the bridal pair's arrival.

There were songs by Mozart, and a recitation of poems by Hebbel and Hölderlin. The *Weihwart*'s sermon revolved round passages from the *Edda* (the old Icelandic saga), and concluded with a quotation from Zarathustra. 'Marriage I will call the will of two to create one which is more than they who created it.' After the bridal couple's exchange of rings, the *Weihwart* pronounced the blessing: 'Mother Earth, which lovingly bears us all, and Father Sky, who blesses us with his light and his weather, and all the beneficent powers of the air, may they rule over you until your destiny is fulfilled.' The ceremony concluded with a rendering of Johann Sebastian Bach's 'Wedding Cantata' by string quartet and solo soprano.[39]

A different type of marriage ceremonial was followed by the SS, which, as a closed order led by the mystagogue Himmler, practised neo-paganism in its purest form. Under the SS dispensation the role of the *Weihwart* was minimal – Himmler had no intention of creating a specific priestly caste – and heads of clans conducted family ceremonials. SS betrothals took place in oak-panelled rooms decorated with carved runes of life, sunflowers (symbol of the sun wheel), and fir twigs. The bridal pair stood facing a short column crowned by a basin in which an eternal flame was lit to symbolize the fire of the hearth. They then exchanged rings, as well as bread and salt, the emblems of the soil's fruitfulness and of purity; lastly, the husband gave the wife his dagger in token of her *Wehrhaftigkeit* (capability of bearing arms), and received another one from his superior SS officer in replacement.[40]

At SS 'christenings' the rune of life constituted the main motif in the décor. The child was carried in by its father on a Teutonic shield, wrapped in a blanket of undyed wool, which was embroidered with oak leaves, runes and swastikas. The child's name and date of birth were inscribed on the first page of its 'book of life', and both parents placed their hands on the child and pronounced its name.[41]

SS Christmas celebrations as practised by aristocratic members of Himmler's entourage occurred on the twenty-first instead of the twenty-fifth of December in homes decorated in the Bavarian rustic style, with runic formulas carved into the woodwork. A fashionable Christmas present for high-ranking SS officers' wives was a modern replica of a newly excavated Germanic fibula.

Carols and nativity plays were banned from schools in 1938, and the very expression 'Christmas' was officially proscribed during the war, to be replaced by the term 'Yuletide', semantic manipulation being an essential feature of dechristianization. In keeping with Teutomanic tradition, German archaisms were substituted for the names of the months derived from Latin: for instance March became *Lenzing* (*Lenz* = spring). A typical neo-pagan wedding announcement in a local newspaper was phrased thus: 'In the belief in the Divine Revelation of our nation through Adolf Hitler, Werner Liefet and Selma Liefet, née Kunzer, have today on the 9th Nebelung,* 1935, concluded their union for life.'[42] Even where the nomenclature of festivals was retained, their significance was modified. Starting with the *Busstag* (day of repentance) of 1937, the so-called serious Church holidays ceased to be 'government-protected', which meant that on these days theatres and cinemas could put on any programme of their choosing, and dance music could be played in public. Reference is made elsewhere to the transformation of Heroes' Remembrance Day into the day of – restored – Military Sovereignty, i.e. from an elegiac occasion into one of sanguine self-assertion. This particular change exemplifies how the concept of death itself underwent radical alteration. In an existence permanently suffused with struggle, the death of the individual, whom the chain of the generations linked inextricably with his ancestors as well as with his descendants, was a minuscule event. Struggle was held to be a constant, its very permanence being a guarantee of resurrection.

The racial continuum drained death of its finality and the individual of his metaphysical significance. Thus wartime obituary notices for military personnel frequently opened with the stereotyped phrase 'In proud sorrow'; this complemented the 'In proud joy' cliché which abounded in birth announcements: 'A brother was born to our Torsten in Germany's greatest period.' Signed 'In proud joy by Martin and Helge Ritter . . .' was a typical example in the *Dresdner Anzeiger* on 8 November 1942. For

* *Nebelung*, derived from *Nebel*: fog (cf. *Brumaire* in the French Revolutionary Calendar), was November.

some time a practice seemed to be gaining ground whereby birth announcements featured the runic symbol for life, and obituary notices featured the death rune, but to the authorities' chagrin the runes did not succeed in replacing their Christian counterparts (the star and the cross) in the public consciousness.

The displacement of the cross was also attempted in other ways. In 1937 a regional directive banishing crucifixes from classrooms created such a furore in the region of Oldenburg that the edict was rescinded. But the war saw the gradual removal of this key Christian symbol from many hospitals and schools.[43] In 1937 the Faith Movement's journal *Sigrune* had the following words to say about Him who had died on the cross:

Jesus was a cowardly Jewish lout who had certain adventures during his years of indiscretion. He uprooted his disciples from blood and soil and, at the wedding at Cana, loutishly flared up at his own mother. At the very end he insulted the majesty of death in an obscene manner.[44]

Despite this extraordinary statement, the figure of Jesus resolutely defied Nazi pigeon-holing; *Der Stürmer*'s view of him, for instance, diverged dramatically from that of its neo-pagan competitor: in the gospel according to Julius Streicher the crucifixion figured as the first instance of Jewish ritual murder.

In 1935 prayers ceased to be obligatory in schools. In March of that year the Gestapo arrested 700 Protestant priests throughout Prussia for issuing condemnations of neo-paganism from the pulpit.[45]* Some time later the authorities deprived a similar number of clergy in Württemberg of the right to give religious instruction in schools – for disobeying the *Land* government's edict against 'violating the moral instincts of the German race' by references to Abraham, Joseph and David in the course of their teaching.[46]

Religious instruction in schools was either given by priests or by lay teachers, both of whom had to be licensed by the education authorities. The regime utilized the possibilities of blackmail inherent in its licensing powers to prevent priests from advising parents against letting their children participate in the Hitler Youth's rural-year scheme, where – just as in the Reich Labour Service – youngsters were exposed to a totally irreligious environment. Some of the teachers newly licensed by the

* If priests received jail terms exceeding one year they automatically forfeited the right to hold a benefice.

authorities were German Faith Movement activists who inculcated neo-paganism into their pupils during periods of religious instruction. In addition the Nazi Teachers' Association appealed to its members to stop taking religious knowledge lessons so that the subject should ultimately fall into disuse for lack of teaching personnel. On school reports, where religion had always ranked first, it was not merely relegated to bottom position but given the new name of 'denominational instruction'. Subsequently it disappeared from the school reports altogether, and marks for 'denominational instruction' were entered on separate reports. The number of religious instruction periods was reduced to only one a week. Trade schools dropped religion from their syllabus altogether; and elsewhere headmasters were made to re-arrange their timetables in such a way that religious instruction occupied either the first or the last lesson of the session, an obvious inducement for lessons to be cut. In addition, personal applications for exemption from religious instruction by upper-school pupils were given legal validity; between the ages of twelve and fourteen the pupil decided jointly with his parents whether to ask for exemption.[47] From 1941 onwards, religious instruction was discontinued altogether for pupils above the age of fourteen. When the Churches arranged voluntary religion classes the authorities prohibited teachers employed by the state from participating in them. The scheme for evacuating schools from bombed areas provided the regime with an unprecedented opportunity for transplanting pupils into a totally de-Christianized environment. At the evacuated schools *'Weltanschauung'* lessons replaced religious instruction, and in the absence of confirmation classes Hitler Youth officials managed to popularize the pagan National Youth Dedication Ceremony (*Reichsjugendweihe*).[48] Even so, battle honours in the struggle for the hearts and minds of young people did not all go to the same side. A pastoral letter from Cardinal Galen, for instance, which stressed that pupils at evacuation camps were deprived of all religious care, could still, in the third winter of the war, noticeably influence parents against participating in the evacuation scheme.[49]

For reasons already stated (and despite the fact that a whole new manifestation of Protestantism – the Confessional Church – had evolved out of the Church's confrontation with the state) the Nazi Moloch found the compact and closely knit body* of German Catholicism the more difficult

* Whereas a Protestant priest catered on average for 2,500 parishioners, the Catholic ratio was one per 1,000. Günter Levy (*The Catholic Church in Nazi Germany*, New York, 1964, p. 4).

one to swallow. The regime's time-table for suppressing denominational youth organizations bears this out. Whereas the Protestant ones were outlawed during the first stages of the Third Reich, the Catholic Young Men's Association was not finally dissolved until 1939, after a campaign of piecemeal suppression.[50]

Yet during the early stages of the war, at a time when the Hitler Youth was somewhat dislocated by the call-up of many of its leaders, individual priests successfully re-instituted parish youth groups. In April 1940 the SD reported that the celebration of Whit Sunday quite overshadowed Hitler Youth oath-taking ceremonies organized by the Hitler Youth in many Catholic areas.[51] The Protestant organization *Jugendwerk*, too, managed to sustain the allegiance of some young people to the Church; in Bavaria, for example, 13,000 girls and 5,000 boys attended its youth circles and parochial courses during the second year of the war.[52] But, the gradual wartime lowering of the call-up age to sixteen and even earlier militated strongly against the success of missionary work among youth.

The Catholics' policy *vis-à-vis* the regime coupled indifference in matters of peripheral concern with a tenacious defence of essentials; while opposing the regime's sterilization measures, the Church concurred in certain aspects of Nazi eugenic policy, such as the promotion of fecundity and family life. German intervention in the Spanish Civil War on the side of Franco elicited full Catholic approval, though at the same time (1936–7 being the years of the anti-Catholic show trials) the episcopate drew subtle parallels between the regime's anti-religious policy and the anti-clericalism of the mutually execrated Spanish Republic. The episcopate looked upon the Austrian and Sudeten crises of 1938, which brought Europe to the edge of Armageddon, as occasions for a patriotic rejoicing; the fact that 10 million Austrians and Sudeten Germans 'returning to the Reich' increased the Catholic proportion of its total population to 43 per cent made Cardinal Bertram exult: 'Now we are truly a People's Church.'[53]

In September 1939, when Hitler loosed aggression against Europe's most Catholic nation and partitioned her with atheist Russia, the Church exhorted soldiers to be ready to sacrifice their whole persons in obedience to him.[54] Two months later Cardinal Faulhaber, who had refused Church mourning in 1919 after the assassination of the Bavarian Socialist Premier Eisner, celebrated Hitler's 'miraculous' escape from an attempt on his life with a solemn *Te Deum* Mass at Munich.[55] The clergy brought pressure to bear upon Catholics who refused to bear arms on grounds of conscience. For violating his alleged Christian duty by refusing to take the military oath of allegiance to Adolf Hitler, Franz Rheinisch was denied Holy Communion by a Roman Catholic prison chaplain, and the Bishop of Linz gave Franz Jagerstätter a similar answer when the latter asked for guidance in his own spiritual agony.[56]

The attack on the Soviet Union in 1941 drew fulsome clerical approval. Archbishop Jäger condemned the Russians, because of their hostility to God and hatred of Christ, as a 'people who had almost degenerated into animals'; this theologically reasoned conclusion was indistinguishable from Nazi racist dogmas about 'Slav sub-humanity'. (In the archbishop's eyes the Western Allies were almost as bad: they embodied the despicable principles of liberalism and individualism.)[57]

Yet withal the Church was apprehensive – and with good reason – of the regime's paganizing tendencies, on which the war was acting as a catalyst. The Russian campaign repeated the paradoxes of the Spanish Civil War situation – with the Nazis re-opening disused cathedrals in occupied Russia while at the same time removing crucifixes from schoolrooms and hospital wards in Bavaria. Despite clerical assurances that 'diocesan gazettes will continue to make their contributions to the victorious outcome of the world historical struggle,' almost the entire Catholic Press was silenced in 1941; the shortage of paper provided Goebbels with a transparent pretext for his action.[58]

Similarly, the war-time shortage of metal provided an excuse for melting down church bells. (The authorities, in their concern for tired munitions workers, had already forbidden the pealing of church bells on Sunday mornings after air-raids late on Saturday night.)[59]*

The clearest pointer to the regime's future plans concerning religion was provided by the moribund state of the Church in the Warthegau (the recently Germanized border region of pre-war Poland), where it was severed from the religious institutions of the Reich and just about maintained by the contributions of parishioners. (Just as the genocide programme provided for certain areas to be made 'free of Jews' before others, so the Warthegau was envisaged as the first region to be 'free of churches' in the Reich.) Another prong in the attack on Christianity was the denigration of the religious-minded as unsoldierly; this charge was linked, in the case of Catholics, with lingering imputations of internationalism. The

---

* The peal of church bells had long marked Nazi state occasions, such as the Nuremberg Party Rallies, the Munich Day of German Art, the plebiscites and the solstice festivals (despite their faintly pagan flavour). The early wartime victories led to veritable orgies of tintinnabulation, which lasted as long as a week on the occasion of the fall of France.

chance fact that Mölders and Galland, Germany's leading air aces during the Second World War, were both Catholics gave the Church an excellent opportunity for rebutting these allegations. Mölders, who was killed in action, had written letters in which he proudly referred to Roman Catholics being accepted as fully-fledged Germans because of their dedication. These letters, which the regime denounced as forgeries because the Luftwaffe hero had also expressed his horror at the Nazis' mercy killings in them, had such a wide resonance that Bormann offered a reward of 100,000 marks for the discovery of their 'authors' and distributors.[60]

It was, in fact, the extermination of the incurably ill and the mentally defective that prompted the most effective episcopal protest against the actions of the Nazi regime. In a sermon at the St Lamberti Church at Münster Cardinal Galen publicly revealed the facts of the top-secret euthanasia programme, and cried out: 'Woe unto the German people when not only can innocents be killed, but their slayers remain unpunished!'[61] Details of the mercy-killing of about 70,000 patients were thereafter disseminated by word of mouth and clandestine publication. The effect of this revelation was such that within a few weeks of Galen's sermon an order from the Führer put a halt to the euthanasia programme, temporarily at any rate. Mercy-killings were in fact spasmodically continued, but Church officials scotched the attempt to start the programme again on a mass scale by refusing to fill in questionnaires from the Ministry of the Interior on the health of asylum inmates.[62] Anxious not to make martyrs of well-known Church leaders, the regime took no action against Galen, but, significantly, executed three Catholic priests at Lübeck who had distributed the text of Galen's sermon among soldiers.

In pastoral letters Galen and Bishop Frings of Cologne condemned such typical expressions of the Nazi military ethos as the killing of hostages and unarmed prisoners-of-war, and warned their flocks not to give way to feelings of vindictiveness against the enemy.[63]

German Catholicism managed to maintain its cohesion and the allegiance of a substantial hard core of believers by a policy of resistance that alternated with remarkable acquiescence: participants in duels and cremation ceremonies were threatened with exclusion from its sacraments, but no spiritual sanctions were invoked against the Catholics who constituted a fifth of the SS; Bishop Berning's cryptic advice to an Auschwitz guard was 'One must not obey immoral orders, but nor must one endanger one's own life'.[64] That the Church retained its firm hold on the affections of the laity was shown by the ostracism that was often met with by people leaving the Church. The authorities' ruling that only the number of secessionists, rather than their actual names, should be announced from the pulpit proved quite ineffective against a form of social pressure communicated by rumour and innuendo. The war years actually produced a countertrend to secessionism, with the Churches smoothing the path of those who wished to return to the fold. All that was required of them was to apply to their parish offices, a procedure that entailed no publicity whatever. In this way quite a number of Party members were re-admitted to Church membership, while their Nazi superiors continued to look upon them as merely 'God-believers'.[65] To obviate such 'regressive' tendencies, the regime spawned an unending series of relatively minor, but cumulatively effective, anti-Church measures.

All religious activities not actually centred within the Churches were made dependent upon official permission. Lists of church-goers on active service were confiscated by the Gestapo on the pretext that they endangered military security. Wounded soldiers at military hospitals could be visited by priests only if they specifically asked for them. The authorities seized Catholic convents in the Rhineland and Protestant seminaries at Württemberg, and in 1943 they closed down theological publishing houses as a wartime economy measure.[66]

If one compares the Protestant and the Catholic reactions to developments under the Nazi regime, one is struck by the varied response that was due to the fragmentation of Protestantism. At the height of the Sudeten crisis the Confessing Church of the old Prussian Union devised a confession of penitence to be read out from the pulpits. This statement of Christian witness, which included the key phrase 'We confess the sins of our nation', would have stood out in stark contrast to the current national mood of overweening chauvinism, but it was revoked after consultations between its sponsors and the Confessional bishops of Württemberg and Bavaria. At any rate, after Munich where the West had, by accepting Hitler's demands, underwritten the justice of his claims, the confession of penitence would hardly have evoked much resonance.[67] An even more poignant indication of division within the Protestant Church that Wurm's and Meyser's cautious *Realpolitik* was the statement of their colleague, the German Christian Bishop Sasse of Thüringia: 'The permanent Christian feeling of sinfulness is a by-product of physical bastardization.'[68]

This division was equally evident on the Jewish question, the supreme moral issue confronting the Churches during the Third Reich. The German Christians washed their hands of Jews and Jewish converts to Christianity alike. The Catholics and the Confessional Church were solicitously concerned about the fate of their non-Aryan co-religionists (a solicitude given practical expression by the Catholic *Rafaelsverein* and the Protestant *Bureau Gruber*, which promoted the emigration of Jewish Christians), but the Confessional Church of Prussia was the only Christian body in the twelve-year history of the Third Reich to protest publicly against the unspeakable outrages inflicted upon the Jews.[69]

This protest, in the form of a declaration by the Consistory of the Confessing Church (*Bruderrat*) of the old Prussian Union, was read out from the pulpits in 1943 – at a point, alas, when lamentation had superseded protest as the appropriate reaction to events. Eight years earlier, at the synod of the Confessional Church in Berlin-Steglitz, Dieter Bonhoeffer had failed to obtain the support of the majority for a resolution protesting against the newly promulgated Nuremberg Laws.[70]

The overwhelming silence of the Churches in face of the Jewish tragedy had many causes, some of which have been touched on in the early parts of this chapter; in the Third Reich they were partly tactical – fear of inviting government retaliation or alienating public opinion – and partly doctrinal. Even a Christian witness of the stature of Pastor Niemöller was, in his own words, 'anything but a philo-Semite',[71] and according to Dieter Bonhoefer many Christians (their number at one time included the martyred Protestant thinker himself) saw in such Nazi atrocities as the Crystal Night pogrom proof of God's curse on the Jews.

30

THE JEWS

Germany had had continuous Jewish settlement for far longer than France or England, where centuries elapsed between the expulsion of the Jews in the Middle Ages and their readmission in more modern times. As a result of the fragmentation of the Holy Roman Empire there had always been some German territory in which Jews were permitted to reside at any given time. This continuity of residence was, however, hardly indicative of a markedly greater tolerance towards the Jews; on the contrary, the worst pogroms in pre-modern Europe – apart from the ones in the Ukraine during the seventeenth century – occurred in the Rhineland at the time of the Crusades. The German Reformation and the Peasants' Wars were also attended by anti-Jewish outrages; except for the activities of court Jews, like Jud Süss Oppenheimer of Württemberg, Jews did not become a factor in German affairs until Prussia's participation in the partition of Poland during the latter part of the eighteenth century.

In 1812 the emanations of an enlightened *Zeitgeist* and the consequences of the Napoleonic wars led the Prussian government to grant quasi-civic rights to the Jews. This set in motion a process of emancipation which, though piecemeal and erratic, proceeded with seeming inevitability until, on the eve of the Great War, Jews were debarred only from the Prussian officer corps, the higher echelons of the civil service, and the judiciary.

After the collapse of the boom that followed the Franco-Prussian war, this gradual upward process was temporarily threatened by a counter-movement aimed at purging Germany of Jewish influence. This wave of anti-Semitism was fed by two currents, one economic and the other intellectual. In its economic aspect, anti-Semitism in late nineteenth-century Germany was a defensive reaction by the lower middle classes, artisans, shopkeepers and farmers to the advent of full-blown capitalism. Jews were agents of change: promoting free trade, commercial publicity, instalment payments and the sale of ready-made goods, they intruded between producers and consumers and breached the monopoly of special-ized shops at levels ranging from second-hand stalls to department stores.

In fact, they prefigured the twentieth-century trend towards urbanization, commercialization and white-collar specialization, a trend the rest of Germany followed several decades later.

Intellectually the anti-Semitism of the period was again a reaction against such features of modernity as parliamentarism, rationalism and enlightened self-interest – 'alien' notions, to whose corrupting influence racist writers and academics like Lagarde and Langbehn opposed their primitive and yet sophisticated *völkische* ideology.

Large-scale middle-class interest in anti-Jewish campaigns slackened off in the eighteen-nineties when the economy, which had been stagnating since the 1873 crash, once again moved into a state of expansion, and anti-Semitism receded from the public stage; it continued, however, to figure prominently in the thinking of socially conservative lobbies such as the Farmers' League (*Bund der Landwirte*) or the German National Association of Shop Assistants (*Deutsch-nationale Handlungsgehilfenverband*) and of many academic groups.

The approach of the war completely overlaid the anti-Semitic issue, while apparently placing the coping-stone on the edifice of emancipation: Jews were made eligible for commissions in the Prussian army. But, during 1916 – significantly, the year in which the last chance of decisive victory eluded the Germans – allegations about Jewish evasion of military service became so widespread that the War Ministry had to institute an official inquiry. Stalemate and the subsequent German collapse affected the position of the Jews in two ways. While the general breakdown in morale rekindled widespread anti-Semitism, there occurred a transfer of political power to new leaders, who favoured total emancipation and who included a few – though prominently placed – Jews. Out of the tension between these two aspects of the Jewish situation was fabricated a 'Jewish problem' that was to lie like an incubus on the Weimar Republic from its very inception; furthermore, the solution, as advanced by its fabricators, involved the very destruction of Weimar. The Republic was branded as Jewish, and its introduction of isolated Jews to posts in the government and the higher civil service lent credence to the charge that it was a 'Jewish republic', by virtue of the fact that such an innovation constituted an unprecedented break with German tradition.

The departure from previous policy concerning ministerial personnel in the Republic partly reflected the traditional dependence of the German labour movement on the only section of the educated bourgeoisie that was sympathetic to its aims, Jewish middle-class intellectuals. 'Normal' products of German universities – above all law graduates, from among whom the higher civil service was recruited – traditionally tended to lean to the Right; the new ministers, therefore, sought to correct the bias of the bureaucratic machine by placing some of their own nominees in key posts. In addition, the availability of Jewish lawyers for administrative posts provided the Social Democrats with a shadowy warrant for office; it helped them, in the face of middle-class scepticism, substantiate the claim that they possessed the expertise necessary to government.[1]

As for other aspects of the 'Jewish republic', the situation was as follows. While Jews formed just under 1 per cent of the total population of Germany, in certain professions and occupations there was a markedly higher percentage of them. Thus 16 per cent of all lawyers practising in the Reich were Jews, and about 10 per cent of all doctors and dentists. Among university lecturers, writers, journalists and theatrical producers the Jewish proportion was about 5 per cent. Among bankers it was as high as 17 per cent – though if one compares this figure (for 1925) with that of 1895, a marked decrease becomes evident. (In 1895 37 per cent of all German bankers had been Jews.) A corresponding decline is attested by figures of students at Prussian universities, where the Jewish proportion had come down from nearly 10 per cent in 1886 to less than 6 per cent in 1930.

This decline had occurred despite the fact that, as a result of wartime displacements of population, over 100,000 Polish Jews had come into the Reich, thereby increasing Germany's total Jewish population by roughly one-fifth. Yet even this eastern influx could not counteract a typical characteristic of German Jewish demography: the fact that the Jews were failing to reproduce themselves.

The thirty-three live births per thousand of the population registered in 1910 indicated an overall German fertility rate exactly twice as high as that of the Jews. Between 1911 and 1925 the excess of deaths over births among the Jews of Prussia was 37,000. These negative vital statistics were compounded by an increase in the number of mixed marriages and conversions to Christianity.

Nor were the Jews as uniformly prosperous as was currently believed. Against their over-representation in certain areas of lucrative commercial activity – 11 per cent in real-estate brokerage, 25 per cent in retailing, 30 per cent in the clothing trade, and 79 per cent in department stores – must be set the fact that in 1933 one in three Jewish taxpayers had an annual income of less than 2,400 marks and one in four Berlin Jews (31,000 out of 170,000) was receiving charity.[2]

Such was the social, economic and demographic situation of German Jewry at the onset of catastrophe. Although the Nazis introduced drastic anti-Jewish measures as soon as they seized power, many German Jews were slow to adjust to a radically altered situation and remained inert in face of the need to tear up their roots. Two factors significantly influenced this attitude: the reluctance of foreign countries to accept immigrants, and the pathetic fallacy of patriotism to which German-born Jews were extraordinarily prone. They deluded themselves into not believing the evidence of their own senses and confidently expected the innate German love of order and decorum to reassert itself once the head of steam built up by the national revolution had dissipated itself in boycotts, inflammatory statements and individual assaults on left-wing Jews.

Despite their eventual addiction to the irrationality of genocide, the Nazi rulers were still sufficiently rational in peacetime to temper ideological rigours with economic calculation. Because of this the weeding-out of Jews from different sectors of the economy proceeded at a markedly disparate pace. Jewish academics, civil servants, lawyers and intellectuals were eliminated within weeks of the seizure of power, whereas doctors, economic journalists and technicians enjoyed a period of grace. Jewish entrepreneurs, on the other hand, were, on occasion, actually prevented from liquidating their businesses since this might harm the government's drive for full employment, while Jewish employees and white-collar workers suffered harassment and instant dismissal.[3] Paradoxically, there even existed a not insignificant segment of the Jewish population – mainly connected with the clothing and retail trades – who benefited from the Nazi-promoted recovery of the German economy and the restoration of public purchasing power. Despite boycotts, many Jewish shopkeepers managed to stay in business until 1938, a year in which some of them were actually beginning to experience boom conditions. If, in spite of Party disapproval, many customers remained loyal to the Jews, this was motivated less by a desire to demonstrate opposition to the regime (although this existed, too) than by an awareness that Jewish shopkeepers gave good value for money and were readier to extend credit than their Gentile competitors. But these somewhat contrary tendencies merely counterpointed the inexorable erosion of the rights of citizenship (see the chronology on p. 467) and other measures of a more superficial, though equally insidious nature.

Jewish pupils were excluded from the state-school system, and all Jews were debarred from public swimming-pools, sports grounds and parks.

457

Jews living in villages and small towns were subjected to window-smashing and physical assault, sometimes culminating in murder. This made them seek the anonymity and sense of communal comfort to be found in large centres like Frankfurt and Berlin. Alongside the overall pattern of official persecution, anti-Semitism was more intense in some regions than in others, with Hesse, Franconia, Pomerania, Thüringia and Silesia the areas of greatest virulence. Four out of those five regions lay in the east of the Reich; this correlates anti-Semitism with the particularly inflamed species of German nationalism that was rife in the areas adjacent to Poland, as well as with their distance from the large urban concentrations. Country areas generally tended to be more anti-Semitic than urban ones. In the cities anti-Jewish feeling was roughly inversely proportional to size. Berlin and Hamburg,* Germany's only towns with populations exceeding 1 million, were also the least anti-Semitic. As the national capital and chief port respectively, they were less turned in upon themselves than smaller centres, which did not have comparable segments of Western-minded bourgeois and Marxist-influenced workers.

Proof that size alone was not the sole determining factor was, however, provided by Nuremberg (1939 population: 423,000) which, together with surrounding Franconia, formed the personal fief of Gauleiter Julius Streicher. There the local heritage of anti-Semitism was partly the by-product of the existence of a Protestant area in Catholic Bavaria; despite Bavaria's reputation as the birthplace of the Nazi movement, Catholic areas were marginally less prone to anti-Semitism than Protestant ones. Here, too, the exceptions were almost as important as the rule: in Catholic Austria and the Sudetenland, i.e. in the German-speaking heartland of the Hapsburg Empire, anti-Semitism had already supplied two of the three main parties† with a *raison d'être* half a century before incorporation into greater Germany; within days of the *Anschluss* the Austrians proved themselves such past-masters at persecution that they earned the commendation of the *Schwarze Korps*. 'The Viennese have managed to do overnight what we have failed to achieve in the slow-moving, ponderous north up to this day. In Austria, a boycott of the Jews does not need organizing – the people themselves have instituted it with honest joy.'⁴ Then Himmler's weekly waxed ghoulishly facetious: 'Some Austrian Jews cannot bear to

---

* In 1939 Berlin had a population of 4,339,000 and Hamburg 1,712,000 (cf. *Statistisches Handbuch für Deutschland 1928–1944*, Franz Ehrenwirth, Munich, 1949, p. 19).

† Dr Lueger's Social Christians and Georg von Schönerer's Pan-Germans; the Social Democrats, by contrast, were partly Jewish-led.

be parted from their homeland, for which reason they purloin a few cubic metres of gas without prepayment.'

The suicide epidemic among Viennese Jewry was caused by the actions of local Austrian Nazis, but this updraught of anti-Semitic sentiment was speedily transmitted across the whole Reich to find its culmination in an event of universal significance – the pogrom of 9 and 10 November 1938, known as the National Crystal Night, which signified that Germany had passed the point of no return on the path of regression to barbarism. The very term 'crystal night', suggestive of the plate glass shattered in the course of the pogrom, was in its way symbolic, as stressing material damage to the exclusion of physical and spiritual barbarity.* 'Crystal Night' could almost be described as a euphemism, though it does not come under the heading of obscenely facetious euphemisms, such as *Konzertlager* ('Concert Camp') for *KZ-Lager*, the abbreviation for *Konzentrationslager* or 'concentration camp' or *Pour le Sémite* (a word-play on *Pour le Mérite*, the German V C of the 1914–18 war) for the yellow star which all Jews had to wear before their deportation.

The pogrom divided the German public into three groups: the shocked but silent† at one end, the looters‡ and vicarious sadists at the other – and a broad middle stratum of inert bystanders given to comments like, 'A piano can't help who it belongs to' in response to the sight of Storm Troopers throwing a Bechstein from a second-storey balcony.[5]

Ever since the early thirties there had been a national consensus of opinion favouring the elimination of Jewish influence from German life, which meant that – irrespective of how people might judge the actual means employed – the broad ends of Nazi policy were essentially approved.§ This confusion between ends and means was combined with a

* Twenty-six male Jews were taken to concentration camps, hundreds injured or killed; 7,500 shops were destroyed and 400 synagogues burnt down (cf. H. G. Adler, 'Pogrome und Konzentrationslager' in Karl Heinz Deschner, *Das Jahrhundert der Barbarei*, Kurt Desch, Munich, 1966, p. 284).

† Dispatches from British consuls in Cologne and other towns to the Foreign Office bear this out.

‡ 'Berlin's man in the street, at long last, had an opportunity of filling himself out again. Fur coats, carpets, valuable textiles, were all to be had for nothing. The people were enraptured,' wrote Dr Goebbels in his diary (cf. H. G. Adler, *loc. cit.*).

§ An academic at a North German university noted in his diary a few months after the seizure of power: 'Anti-Semitism is so widely diffused that one can hardly imagine that a reversal of attitudes will ever occur on this point. Even people who condemn the manner in which this question has begun to be solved reveal themselves as emotionally deeply committed anti-Semites.' (cf. 'Soziologie der Nationalsozialistichen Revolution, in *Vierteljahresshefte für Zeitgeschichte*, fourth serves, 1965, p. 439).

certain divergence between abstract and concrete anti-Semitism: traditional (i.e. pre-Nazi) anti-Semitism, which was part of a cultural tradition putting a premium on abstraction, had tended to demand the extermination of 'Jewry' (or the 'Jewish essence') rather than that of individual Jews; this ambiguity helps to explain how a remorselessly anti-Semitic government could enlist ever-wider public support without engendering an overt pogrom mood.

The fact that until 1938 Jews living in the main towns were largely spared physical assault also had something to do with the regime's reluctance to affront either foreign susceptibilities or the native penchant for order. The relative absence of violence directed at Jews before the November pogrom cannot, however, be construed as evidence of widespread immunity to anti-Semitism. Just as primitive man's concept of God presupposed the existence of the Devil, so the German's progressive self-deification during the Third Reich depended upon the demonization of the Jew. The white outline of the Germans' image of themselves – in terms of character no less than of colour – acquired definition only via the moral and physical darkness of its Jewish anti-type. Metaphysically as well as materially, the roots of the German heaven were deeply embedded in the Jewish hell.

Even so, it is doubtful whether the majority of Germans shared the obsessional anti-Semitism of their leaders; conversely, there can be little doubt that they accepted Jew-baiting without undue perturbation as an integral part of a system beneficial to themselves. This acceptance was not confined to such obvious beneficiaries as Aryanizers large and small, defaulting debtors, exploiters of slave labour, and wearers of dead men's shoes; anti-Semitism was so central to the Nazi programme that every German who – consciously or otherwise – identified the regime with the national interest thereby countenanced what was done to the Jews.

Between 1933 and the outbreak of war roughly half the Jewish population of Germany emigrated, about 250,000 people (largely to the United States, the United Kingdom and Palestine); of the remainder no more than a few thousand survived. In their recollections of the nightmare years the survivors described the general German attitude to themselves as neither overwhelmingly hostile nor notably sympathetic – merely indifferent.

Public indifference became a reinforcing strand in the noose inexorably tightening around hundreds of thousands of necks. Almost poetically symptomatic of the Jews' terminal condition was the practice of teachers at Jewish kindergartens in Berlin during the early part of the war of letting their charges spend their playtime among tombstones: the communal cemetery was the only patch of green from which wearers of the Yellow Star were not debarred.

A typical scene took place at a Berlin greengrocer's, when a four-year-old Jewish girl begged her mother for some cherries; when told that fruit was excluded from the Jewish ration she ran out of the shop crying. Since no one else was about it would have been quite easy for the shopkeeper to make the child happy, instead of which* he observed the incident with imperturbable indifference.[6]

The ailing, aged Frau Bendix of Berlin-Moabit was surrounded by her neighbours' indifference like a palpable presence as in midsummer 1941 she sweltered in her single ground-floor room behind shuttered windows, afraid that if she opened them children playing in the courtyard would deliberately break the panes. When offered bean coffee (another item excluded from the Jewish ration) by a rare visitor, the old lady refused as she was afraid that the aroma of coffee emanating from her room would make one of the neighbours denounce her to the police.[7] Frau Bendix's visitor was a Gentile whose Jewish husband was arrested soon afterwards in a sudden Gestapo round-up. When she attempted, unsuccessfully, to visit him in prison, the official who turned down her request felt that he could not let her go until he had expressed his own personal distress that she – a German woman – had crawled into bed with a Jew. Her husband was sent to Auschwitz, where he was killed. When she reported her changed circumstances to the local food office at the beginning of the next rationing period, the clerk informed her that she was entitled to full rations again and – in all sincerity – congratulated her on her re-Aryanization.[8]

This utter lack of empathy† took on a ghoulish aspect when self-interest was involved. Immediately after the mother of a nurse at the Berlin Jewish hospital had left on her last journey with the scant luggage permitted to deportees, the janitor's wife turned to the overwrought nurse and asked in

---

* Shopkeepers did not always honour even the already meagre Jewish ration cards, identifying denial of food to Jews with their patriotic duty. Women shopkeepers tended to be worse than men.

† The regime's anti-Jewish measures also produced bizarre group reactions. There were civil servants who wanted all Jews to leave Germany in the shortest possible time simply because their continued presence gave the Party a pretext to enter the civil service's sphere of competence; there were also a number of Christians who saw the Jews' fate in the Third Reich as a palpable sign of their divine reprobation.

matter-of-fact tones, 'Now that your mother'll no longer need them, how about letting me have her two fur coats?'[9]

In their irremediable agony even sympathy could avail the Jews nothing. A 'privileged Jewish slave worker', i.e., one whom mixed marriage exempted from deportation, had hardly a day without being either advised to go and hang himself as a Jewish swine or demonstratively pitied; he dreaded the pity nearly as much as the hate, since his only tenuous hope of getting through each day lay in complete anonymity. This frantic need to avoid all contacts for fear of attracting attention was one reason – though by no means the most important – for the widespread German ignorance of their fate.

A steeply growing number of Germans, who had mixed socially with Jews before 1933, subsequently ostracized them, though for a while some deliberately sought their company: Jews were the only people whom malcontents could confide in, since even close friends might denounce them, while Jews were simply receptive ears existing in the void of their own isolation. Yet even philo-Semites were prone to the new national reflex of cautious non-involvement, so that, when saying good-bye for ever to Jewish friends, they sometimes omitted to inquire where they were going.

To a correspondingly greater extent the population at large who had not previously mixed with Jews avoided the contagion not only of contact but also of knowledge, for to know about the Jews implied some link with those carriers of leprosy. A few milked such information about the Jewish catastrophe as filtered through for titillation and abstract horror, like a tale by Edgar Allan Poe, while others dismissed it as rumour-mongering and consciously or unconsciously – repressed it. In this they were abetted by a regime which invested genocide with the aura of being top-secret (*Geheime Reichssache*) and camouflaged it with stringent security precautions. But, however camouflaged the practice – and the very scale of the operations militated against 100-per-cent secrecy – the theory had been the common property of millions for ten years and more. Hitler had set out his ultimate objectives in *Mein Kampf*, a book more widely distributed throughout Germany than any since the Bible. Even though the ubiquitous volume served a ritual purpose rather than as a means of communication on most people's bookshelves, its import was sufficiently well known to preclude ambiguity about the author's intentions. In October 1935 the Berlin periodical *Der Judenkenner* threatened that any foreign army entering Germany would step across the corpses of dead Hebrews. On 30 January 1939

Hitler told the Reichstag and the world: 'A war instigated by world Jewry will lead to the destruction of the Jewish race in Europe.'[10] From the Storm Troopers' marching song, 'When Jewish blood spurts from the knife, then things go twice as well', to the Party's official rallying cry, 'Germany awake! Let Judah perish!', the theme that Jews deserved the same treatment as vermin was incessantly plugged in speeches, newspaper articles, posters, lectures, documentary films, jingles and even children's rhymes.

Could a regime full of uniquely brutal purposefulness that showed undeviating commitment to this dogma be credited with hesitancy about its execution? During the period of the 'cold' pogrom, up to 1938, the worst apprehensions had been stilled, but the Crystal Night and Hitler's threat of January 1939 brooked no misinterpretation. The last feeble rationalization, that these were shock tactics to stampede the Jews into accelerating their exodus, collapsed when the war and official government measures throttled all further emigration. Sporadic, but cumulative, persecution of the Jews had been an inescapable feature of the Third Reich since its very inception. Any Berliner unaware of the existence of Oranienburg Concentration Camp (or any Bavarian or Thüringian ignorant of Dachau or Buchenwald) within a year of the seizure of power was either an anchorite or obtuse to the point of cretinism.

By contrast, the existence of the wartime extermination camps was a closely guarded secret, and the great majority of the population lacked precise knowledge about how they were operated until Auschwitz and Belsen became universal household words in the final stages of the war. Even so, the fact that, with the war, the persecution of the Jews had become total hardly escaped general attention: three-quarters of the Germans questioned about it after 1945 remembered Jews wearing the Yellow Star, and the forced labour and subsequent deportation of hundreds of thousands could not pass unnoticed either. In the course of the Second World War approximately 10 million Germans saw military service, the majority of them in the east, where, from the Polish campaign onwards, anti-Jewish and other atrocities were literally the order of the day. Few of this number (which was swollen by civilian administrators, supervisors and settlers) can have failed to come across evidence – either direct or at second-hand – of massacres. Over and above this a substantial circle of persons within Germany itself – such as civil servants, Gestapo officials, Party officials and railway administrators – were directly involved in the Final Solution. Proof that the secrecy officially enjoined upon them was sometimes honoured more in the breach than in the observance occurs in a letter, dated 23 November 1942, from a minor Westphalian Party official to a local Gestapo official about the removal of park railings, which, *inter alia*, contained the observation, 'You are permanently occupied in the extermination of the Jews.'[11]

The fact that by 1943 the idiom 'going up the chimney' was gaining currency indicated some public awareness of the existence of the gas chambers. There can be no doubt that fragments of the ominous truth became available on the black market of rumours in which the mass of the people shopped around in order to supplement the sparse information provided by the official media. The B B C's German service, which was widely listened to, supplied fragmentary but cumulative details of the holocaust; but these were sometimes discounted as a re-hash of atrocity stories about German-occupied Belgium during the Great War. Similarly, Germans in the Reich were prone to dismiss the reports of soldiers and others returning from the occupied east with the rejoinder, 'You chaps out there drink too much.' Opponents of the regime who quoted rumours of atrocities to buttress their political arguments often encountered obtuse incomprehension, expressed in the query, 'Can you prove your allegations?'[12]

The full truth about the horror of the death camps could not, of course, have been known at the time; even the Jews destined to perish there had only vague premonitions of their fate. Compared to the average German, they were, of course, infinitely handicapped when it came to gathering information. They were not allowed wireless sets and had neither relatives serving in the Wehrmacht nor acquaintances with access to officialdom.

Goerdeler, the Chancellor designate of the Officers' Plot, was reputed to have believed that after the *coup d'état* his government need do no more than confront the German people with the crimes of the Nazi regime to win instantaneous allegiance. His optimistic expectations (though never put to the test) are open to the gravest doubt, based as they were on the assumption that Germans would have been as appalled by Jewish sufferings as by their own. Such evidence as is available tends to disprove this. The only public demonstration of sympathy for the Jews ever staged during the Third Reich involved Gentile wives of Jewish husbands rounded up for deportation from Berlin in March 1943.[13] In the entire history of the Third Reich no single body – civic, academic or even religious – ever made use of such opportunities as it had for publicly protesting against the regime's inhumanity. The feasibility of protests of this nature was demonstrated (as we have seen) by Cardinal Galen's denunciation of euthanasia from the pulpit, which evoked a sufficiently strong resonance to halt the regime's 'mercy-killing' programme. But the euthanasia victims were flesh of German flesh, and those affected by their deaths ranged through all classes of society. Some Jews, too, had self-sacrificing, devoted friends – otherwise, 5,000 of them would never have survived as 'U-boats' in Berlin – but the 'righteous among the Gentiles' were individuals, representative only of themselves; as far as the great majority were concerned, Jewish suffering affected beings in another galaxy rather than inhabitants of the same planet as themselves.

The otherness of the Jew was both a pre-condition and a corollary of the notion of German uniqueness. Evidence of this innate otherness was supplied by pre-Nazi stereotypes adapted to every level of sophistication: Jews in folklore were physically repellent, malodorous and parrot-nosed; in academic eyes they were bundles of un–German reflexes, as exemplified by their desire to outlaw war.* Building on such pre-existing stereotypes, the regime deployed its vast resources in inculcating the notion that Jews were devoid of human attributes. Many Germans, and not only the uncritical young, allowed themselves to be so convinced. The incessant official demonization of the Jew gradually modified the consciousness even of naturally humane people. In the factory where Professor Klemperer did slave labour, his emaciated appearance aroused some compassion, and a woman working beside him, who knew that Jewish rations excluded all fruit, placed a big, shiny apple on his machine one morning. As she watched him eat it, she asked incredulously, 'Tell me, is it really true that your wife is German?'[14] Living in the climate of the Third Reich, she could no longer conceive of the pariah in front of her, endowed with all normal attributes and employing German as his mother tongue, as actually related to a German woman.

To produce this kind of result in the minds of the educated and half-educated, Nazi propaganda selectively rifled the treasures stored up in the national Pantheon. The thoughts of such cultural heroes as Luther and Wagner provided ideal underpinning for the official anti-Semitic ideology; additional grist for the genocidal mill flowed from the curious circumstance that few exemplars of German thought – not even Kant and Goethe – had been entirely free from anti-Semitism. This consensus of opinion among the illustrious dead (which sheds less illumination on the

---

* In 1932 the *völkische* writer Dr Wilhelm Stapel, who was not a Nazi in the true sense of the word, accused the Jews in a broadcast of corroding the people's community by advocating that war should be outlawed, whereas national-minded Germans had always acknowledged war as the father of all things (cf. Werner Mosse, *Entscheidungsjahr 1932*, Mohr, Tübingen, 1965, p. 519).

Jewish character than on German culture) contributed marginally to the atrophy of the sympathetic faculties.

Without anti-Semitism, Nazism would have been inconceivable, both as an ideology and as a catalyst of the emotions. As for German society only two of its many sub-groups, the cultivated liberal minority among the bourgeoisie, and the politically educated segment of the working class, were relatively immune to anti-Semitism. Ranged in the opposite camp were the partly dispossessed military and land-owning élite, the educated and property-owning bourgeoisie, disorientated by defeat and social change, and the huge, economically vulnerable petit bourgeoisie of shop-keepers, craftsmen, farmers and white-collar employees, whose backward-looking anti-capitalist yearning predisposed them towards the 'socialism of fools', as August Bebel had described anti-Semitism.

Although the interplay of social anxiety and national frustration turned many Germans into Jew-haters, their anti-Semitism barely approximated to the millennial Nazi vision of a universe purged of every trace of Jewish existence. Popular sentiment did, however, match the Nazi purpose in its preoccupation with the national interest – i.e. a magnified personal interest; this was so total that imagination and conscience alike were anaesthetized.

Had German wartime indifference to the Jewish catastrophe merely been due to ignorance, post-war revelations would have stirred far greater shock waves. As we have seen, during the war, the majority of Germans accepted the Nazi treatment of Russian forced labourers because they were easily persuaded that they lived under similar conditions at home; by analogy, the physical removal of the Jews went largely unremarked, because the Germans had long since removed them from their hearts and minds.

No doubt, by 1941–2,* the stress of war partly accounted for public indifference to Jewish sufferings, but basically the holocaust was not a real event to most Germans, not because it occurred in wartime and under conditions of secrecy, but because Jews were astronomically remote and not real people.

* Somewhat later in the war, after most of the Jews in Europe had already been exterminated, Nazi propaganda had little difficulty in further inflaming German anti-Semitic feelings by projecting Ilya Ehrenburg and Henry Morgenthau as the Russian and American incarnations of the Elders of Zion conspiring to crush Germany.

Chronology

1933

1 April First official boycott of Jewish shops, lawyers and doctors. Demands for the removal of Jewish pupils and students from schools and universities.

1934 Aryan origin gradually becomes the prerequisite of professional life in many spheres; anti-Jewish propaganda and incitement increases.

1935

15 September Promulgation of the Nuremberg Laws for the protection of German blood and German honour.

14 November National Law of Citizenship. First decree of the National Law of Citizenship: definition of the term 'Jew' and of the *Mischling* (mixed-blood) status. The Aryan paragraph becomes a precondition of every official appointment. First decree of the law for the protection of German blood and honour. Marriages between Jews and second-generation *Mischlinge* prohibited.

1936

Summer A decline of the anti-Semitic campaign because the Olympic Games were taking place in Berlin.

1937

Spring Intensification of the Aryanization process, by which Jewish owners lose their businesses without any legal justification.

12 June Secret order from Heydrich concerning protective custody of 'sacral violators' (*Rassenschänder*) after they have served their prison sentence.

1938

13 March The *Anschluss* of Austria, where all anti-Jewish legislation in force in the Reich is applied immediately.

26 April Decree concerning the registration of all Jewish wealth exceeding 5,000 marks.

9 June Destruction of the Munich synagogue.

14 June Third decree of the Reich Citizenship Law: the registration and marking of all remaining Jewish enterprises.

10 August Destruction of the Nuremberg synagogue.

17 August Second decree of the law concerning change of first names and surnames: the introduction of the compulsory prefixes Sarah and Israel, to come into force on 1 January 1939.

5 October Passports for Jews are only valid if they have the red letter J stamped in them.

28 October Expulsion of 17,000 former Polish Jews domiciled in Germany.

7 November	Assassination of von Rath, chancellor of the embassy in Paris, by Herschel Grünspan.
9 and 10 November	'Crystal Night' pogrom takes place throughout Germany. Destruction of synagogues, shops and flats. More than 20,000 Jews imprisoned.
12 November	Decrees concerning elimination of German Jews from the economy. Jews have to pay a collective fine of 1·25 thousand million marks and in addition pay for all destruction caused by the Nazis in the course of the pogrom.
15 November	Expulsion of all Jewish pupils from schools.
3 December	Decree concerning compulsory Aryanization of all Jewish enterprises and shops.
1939	Confiscation of all Jewish valuables.
30 April	Law concerning Jewish tenancies. Legal preparation for the concentration of Jewish families in 'Jewish houses'.
1 September	Jews forbidden to be out of doors after 8.00 p.m. in winter and 9.00 p.m. in summer.
23 September	Confiscation of all wireless sets owned by Jews.
1940	
12 and 13 February	First deportations of Jews from Germany, mainly from the province of Pomerania.
22 October	Deportation of Jews from Baden, the Saar and Alsace-Lorraine.
1941	
7 March	Employment of German Jews as compulsory labour.
31 July	Heydrich charged by Goering with the evacuation of all European Jews in German-occupied territories.
1 September	Decree compelling Jews to wear the yellow star from 19 September. Further limitation of Jewish freedom of movement.
17 and 18 September	Beginning of the general deportation of German Jews.
1942	
20 January	The Wannsee conference, concerned with the 'final solution' of the Jewish question.
24 April	Ban on Jews using public transport.
June	Beginning of mass-gassing at Auschwitz.
18 September	Drastic reduction of food rations for Jews in the Reich.
30 September	Hitler declares publicly that the Second World War will result in the destruction of European Jewry.
1943	
27 February	Start of deportation of Jews employed in the Berlin armaments industry.

1944	Start of the death-marches, by which the SS drives back inmates of concentration camps threatened by the advance of the Red Army into the interior of Germany.
End of October	Last gassings at Auschwitz.
27 November	The Auschwitz crematoria are blown up.
1945	
26 January	Auschwitz liberated by Soviet troops.
15 April	British troops liberate Bergen-Belsen.

Since 1945 time has slowly done its healing work – though not for the Jews of Europe. Even Russia, which suffered an estimated 20 million casualties at the hands of the Nazis, today has a larger population than prewar.

But world Jewry will never again number 18 million. Nor will synagogues ever rise again in the old Jewish heartland between the Baltic and Black Sea on soil fertilized with ashes. This will be Hitler's permanent memorial – and he would hardly have wished for another. History will record that just as hatred of the Jews was the kernel of Nazi theory so their murder was the culmination of Nazi practice.

GLOSSARY

Abitur	University entrance examination.
Anschluss	Incorporation of Austria into the Reich in 1938.
Bund deutscher Mädchen (*BdM*)	German Girls' League.
Blubo (*Blut und Boden*)	Blood and Soil.
Crystal Night	Nation-wide pogrom of 9-10 November 1938.
Deutsche Arbeitsfront (*DAF*)	German Labour Front.
Erbhofbauer	Hereditary farmer.
Final Solution (of the Jewish Question)	Extermination of the Jews.
Gauleiter	Regional Party leader.
Gleischschaltung	Co-ordination with the Nazi regime.
Gymnasium	Grammar School.
Hitlerjugend (*IIJ*)	Hitler Youth.
Jungvolk	Junior section of Hitler Youth.
Konzentrationslager (*KZ*)	Concentration camp.
Kraft durch Freude (*KdF*)	Strength through Joy.
Kreisleiter	District Party leader.
Landflucht	Flight from the land.
Mittelstand	The middle class.
Napola	Training school for future Nazi leaders.
NS Frauenschaft	Women's auxiliary of the Nazi Party.
NS Lehrerbund (*NSLB*)	Nazi teachers' organization.
NS Volkswohlfahrt (*NSV*)	Nazi People's Welfare.
Oberpräsident	Regional head of civil service administration.
Ordensburg	Finishing school for future Nazi leaders.
Ortsgruppenleiter	Ward Party leader.
Ostarbeiter	Eastern (slave) worker.
Ostmark	Austria.

Reichsberufswettkampf	National vocational competition.
Reichsnährstand	Reich Food Estate.
Reichswehr	German army (the term was not used after 1935).
SA	Storm troopers.
Schwarzes Korps	Weekly newspaper of the SS.
SD	Security service of the SS.
SS Verfügungstruppe	Militarized SS.
Stürmer	Anti-Semitic weekly (edited by Julius Streicher).
Vergeltungswaffen	V-weapons (or revenge weapons), e.g. V 2.
Völkisch	Literally ethnic; used in connection with an authoritarian, racist ideology.
Völkischer Beobachter	Official Nazi daily newspaper.
Westwall	Fortifications along the French border (Siegfried Line).
Wehrmacht	German army.

SUGGESTED FURTHER
READING

Allen, William Sheridan, *The Nazi Seizure of Power*, London and Chicago, 1965.

Brady, Robert A., *Spirit and Structure of German Fascism*, London and New York, 1937.

Bruck, W. F., *Social and Economic History of Germany 1888–1938*, London and New York, 1938.

Deuel, Wallace R., *People under Hitler*, London and New York, 1942.

Fest, Joachim, *The Face of the Third Reich*, London and New York, 1969.

Guillebaud, C. W., *Social Policy of Nazi Germany*, London and New York, 1941.

Haffner, Sebastian, *Germany: Jekyll and Hyde*, London and New York, 1940.

Hale, Oron J., *The Captive Press in the Third Reich*, Princeton, 1964.

International Council for Philosophy and Humanistic Studies, *The Third Reich*, London and New York, 1955.

Kohn, Hans, *The Mind of Germany*, New York, 1960, and London, 1961.

Lehmann-Haupt, Hellmut, *Art under a Dictatorship*, London and New York, 1954.

Lewy, Guenter, *The Catholic Church and Nazi Germany*, London and New York, 1964.

Mayer, Milton, *They Thought They were Free*, London and Chicago, 1955.

Milward, Alan S., *The Germany Economy at War*, London and New York, 1965.

Neumann, Franz, *Behemoth*, London and New York, 1942.

Schoenbaum, David, *Hitler's Social Revolution*, New York, 1966, and London, 1967.

Schweitzer, Arthur, *Big Business in the Third Reich*, London and Indiana, 1964.

Seydewitz, Max, *Civil Life in Wartime Germany*, New York, 1945.

Shirer, William L., *Berlin Diary*, London and New York, 1941.

Vermeil, Edmond, *The German Scene*, London, 1956 (Published as *Germany in the Twentieth Century*, New York, 1956).

Wunderlich, Frieda, *Farm Labour in Germany 1810–1945*, London and Princeton, 1961.

REFERENCES

1 Weimar

1 Ferdinand Friedensburg, *Die Weimarer Republik*, Hanover/Frankfurt, 1957, p. 211.
2 *ibid.*
3 Robert A. Brady, *The Spirit and Structure of German Fascism*, New York, 1937, p. 13.
4 Ferdinand Friedensburg, *op. cit.*, p. 211.
5 Edmond Vermeil, *The German Scene*, London, 1956, pp. 82–4.
6 Louis R. Franck, *Economic and Social Diagnosis of National Socialism*, in the anthology *The Third Reich*, London, 1955, p. 540.
7 Ferdinand Friedensburg, *op. cit.*, p. 243.
8 *ibid.*
9 Fritz Krone, *Die Soziologie der Angestellten*, Cologne/Berlin, 1962, p. 196.
10 J. Nothens, 'Soziale Auf- und Abstieg im Deutschen Volk', *Kölner Vierteljahresheft für Soziologie*, Vol. 9, pp. 70–3.
11 Theodor Geiger, *Die Soziale Schichtung des Deutschen-Volkes*, Stuttgart, 1932, pp. 74, 75.
12 Heinrich Uhlig, *Die Warenhäuser im Dritten Reich*, Köln/Upladen, 1956, p. 25.
13 Theodor Geiger, *op. cit.*, p. 73.
14 C. W. Guillebaud, *Social Policy of Nazi Germany*, London, 1941, p. 9.
15 Ferdinand Friedensburg, *op. cit.*, p. 222.
16 Arthur Schweitzer, *Big Business in the Third Reich*, London, 1964, p. 89.
17 P. B. Wiener, *Die Parteien der Mitte*, in the anthology *Entscheidungsjahr 1932*, edited by Werner A. Mosse, Tübingen, 1965, p. 320.
18 Seymour Martin Lipset, *Political Man*, London, 1960, p. 148.
19 Theodor Geiger, *op. cit.*, p. 72.
20 Ferdinand Friedensburg, *op. cit.*, p. 218.
21 W. F. Brook, *The Social and Economic History of Germany from 1888 to 1938*, London, 1938, p. 259.
22 Axel Eggebrecht, *Volk ans Gewehr*, Stuttgart, 1959, p. 190.
23 Franz Neumann, *Behemoth*, New York, 1942, p. 392.
24 Ferdinand Friedensburg, *op. cit.*, p. 218.
25 *ibid.*
26 *ibid.*, p. 215.
27 Louis R. Franck, *op. cit.*, p. 550.
28 *ibid.*, p. 551.
29 C. W. Guillebaud, *op. cit.*, p. 10.
30 Ezra Ben-Natan, 'Demographische und wirtschaftliche Struktur', in the anthology *Entscheidungsjahr 1932* already referred to, p. 124.
31 C. W. Guillebaud, *op. cit.*, p. 14.
32 Friedrich Hussong, *Kurfürstendamm*, Berlin, 1933, p. 100.
33 Herman Hass, *Sitte und Kultur in Nachkriegsdeutschland*, Hamburg, 1932, p. 165.
34 Hans Kohn, *The Mind of Germany*, London, 1961, p. 309.

35 Andreas Flittner, *Deutsches Geistesleben und National-sozialismus*, Tübingen, 1965, p. 33.
36 Helmut Kuhn, *Die Deutsche Universität im Dritten Reich*, Munich, 1966, p. 32.
37 Andreas Flittner, *op. cit.*, p. 45.
38 Helmut Kuhn, *op. cit.*, p. 30.
39 Werner A. Mosse, *op. cit.*, p. 130.
40 Anthology *The Third Reich* already referred to, p. 588.
41 Arthur Schweitzer, *op. cit.*, pp. 114, 156.
42 Werner A. Mosse, *op. cit.*, p. 165.
43 Hermann Hass, *op. cit.*, p. 32.
44 *ibid.*, p. 132.
45 Friedrich Hussong, *op. cit.*, p. 50.
46 Werner A. Mosse, *op. cit.*, p. 50.
47 William Sheridan Allen, *The Nazis' Seizure of Power*, 1965, p. 79.
48 Werner A. Mosse, *op. cit.*, p. 48.
49 Ferdinand Friedensburg, *op. cit.*, p. 154.
50 Thilo Vogelsang, 'Neue Dokumente zur Geschichte der Reichswehr', in *Vierteljahreshefte für Zeitgeschichte*, Munich, second year, 1954, p. 417.
51 Ernst Nolte, *Der Faschismus in seiner Epoche*, Munich, 1963, p. 415.
52 Seymour Martin Lipset, *op. cit.*, p. 141.
53 Franz Neumann, *op. cit.*, p. 23.
54 Seymour Martin Lipset, *op. cit.*, p. 145.

2 The Third Reich

1   *Statistisches Handbuch für Deutschland 1928–1944*, Munich, 1949, p. 484.
2   Hans Kohn, *The Mind of Germany*, Macmillan, London, 1961, p. 264.
3   Rolf Michaelis, 'Das wandelbare politische Gesicht eines Dichters', *Der Tagesspiegel*, 15 November 1962.
4   'The Word World of Nazi Germany', *The Times Literary Supplement*, 30 September 1965 (a review of Cornelia Berning's *Vom Abstammungsnachweis zu Zuchtwart*, Walter de Gruyter Verlag, Berlin, 1965.)
5   Tami Oelfken *Das Logbuch*, Berlin, 1955, p. 35.
6   Georg K. Glaser, *Geheimnis und Gewalt*, Stuttgart, 1953, p. 511.
7   Erich Ebermayer, *Denn Heute gehört uns Deutschland*, Vienna, 1959, p. 264.
8   Ferenc Kermendy, 'Warum ich Deutschland nicht verlasse', *Die Welt*, 10 January 1962.
9   Horst Krüger, *Das Zerbrochene Haus*, Rütten and Loening, Munich, 1966, p. 51.
10 *ibid.*, p. 45.
11 Katherine Thomas, *Women in Nazi Germany*, Gollancz, London, 1943, p. 33.
12 Charlotte Beradt, *Das Dritte Reich des Traums*, Nymphenburger Verlagshandlung, Munich, 1966, pp. 49–52.
13 SD Reports.
14 *Statistisches Handbuch für Deutschland 1928–1944*, Franz Ehrenwirth Verlag, Munich, 1949, p. 53.
15 Paul Klüke, 'Hitler und das Volkswagenprojekt', *Vierteljahreshefte für Zeitgeschichte*, 1960, p. 365.
16 *Statistisches Handbuch für Deutschland*, cited above, p. 484.
17 Martin Gumpert, *Heil Hunger*, Alliance Book Corporation, Longmans, New York, 1940, p. 37.
18 *Statistisches Handbuch für Deutschland*, cited above, pp. 58–61.
19 *ibid.*, p. 663.

20 Sebastian Haffner, *Germany: Jekyll and Hyde*, Secker and Warburg, London, 1940, p. 114.
21 Hermann Baer, ed., *Kriegsbriefe gefallener Studenten*, Rainer Wunderlich Verlag, Hermann Leins, Tübingen and Stuttgart, 1952, pp. 241, 156.
22 Louis Hagen, *Follow My Leader*, Allen Wingate, London, 1951, p. 351.
23 Heinz Boberach, *Meldungen aus dem Reich*, Luchterhand Verlag, Neuwied/Berlin, 1965, SD Report No. 83, 29 April 1940.
24 Helmut Krausnick and Hildegard von Kotze, *Es spricht der Führer*, Gütersloh, 1966, p. 317.
25 SD Reports, Bundesarchiv, Coblenz, File R 58/186, Report of 15 July 1943.
26 *ibid.*, File R 58, entry for 7 February 1944.
27 William Shirer, *Berlin Diary*, Hamish Hamilton, London, 1940, p. 389, entry for 5 September 1940.
28 Gustav Brecht, *Erinnerungen*, privately printed, 1964, p. 70.
29 Heinz Boberach, *op. cit.*, entry for 18 November 1943.
30 SD Reports, Bundesarchiv Coblenz, File 58/186, entry for 15 July 1943.
31 *Arbeiterzeitung*, Schaffhausen, 31 December 1943.
32 Hans-Georg von Studnitz, *Als Berlin brannte*, Kohlhammer Verlag, Stuttgart, 1963, p. 80.
33 *Münchner Neueste Nachrichten*, 24 July 1943.
34 Max Seydewitz, *Civil Life in Wartime Germany*, Viking Press, New York, 1945, p. 187.
35 H. G. Adler, 'The Failure of German War Industry', *Wiener Library Bulletin*, vol. IX, September/December 1955, p. 40.
36 Sarah Mabel Collins, *The Alien Years*, Hodder and Stoughton, London, 1949, pp. 90–1.
37 *Westdeutscher Beobachter*, 4 September 1943.
38 Louis P. Lochner, *Die Goebbels Tagebücher 1942–1943*, Atlantis Verlag, Zurich, 1948, p. 157, entry for 11 April 1942.
39 Interview with Frau Rosa Chlupaty in Vienna, April 1965.
40 Heinz Boberach, *op. cit.*, SD Report No. 304, 30 July 1942.
41 Viktor Klemperer *Lingua Tertii Imperii*, Berlin 1949, p. 105.
42 *ibid.*, p. 296.
43 'Stimmungsbericht des Regierungs-Präsidenten von Regensburg, *Archiv des Instituts für Zeitgeschichte*, Munich, File MA 300, photo roll 2955/3098.
44 H. Trevor Roper, *The Last Days of Hitler*, London, 1950, pp. 90–1.
45 Arthur Geoffrey Dickins, *Lübeck Diary*, Gollancz, London, 1947, p. 58.
46 Viktor Klemperer, *op. cit.*, p. 270.
47 Richard Brett Smith, *Berlin 1945 – The Grey City*, Macmillan, London, 1966, p. 31.
48 Josef Wulf, *Presse und Funk im Dritten Reich*, Siegbert Mohn Verlag, Gütersloh, 1964, p. 353.
49 Interview with Frau Carola Stern in Cologne, April 1966.
50 Richard Brett Smith, *op. cit.*, p. 31.
51 Wolf Mittendorff, *Soziologie des Verbrechens*, Düsseldorf, 1959, p. 242.
52 William E. Daugherty and Morris Janowitz, *A Psychological Warfare Casebook*, Baltimore, 1958, p. 747.
53 Interview with Herr Ziock, Bonn, May 1966.
54 Erich Kuby, *Die Russen in Berlin, 1945*, Schersverlag, Munich, 1965, p. 118.
55 *Bericht des Statistischen Bundesamts*, 4 April 1962.
56 Theo Findal, *Letzter Akt Berlin 1939–1945*, Hammerich & Lesser Verlag, Hamburg 1946, p. 194, entry for 11 May 1945.
57 Erich Kuby, *op. cit.*, p. 179.

3 Folk Community

1 Horst Krüger, *Das zerbrochene Haus*, Rütten and Loening, Munich, 1966, p. 43.
2 *Völkischer Beobachter*, 2 October 1935.
3 *Schwarzes Korps*, 17 November 1938.
4 Walter Hagemann, *Publizistik im Dritten Reich*, Hansische Gilden, Hamburg, 1948, p. 141.
5 *Frankfurter Zeitung*, 12 February 1939.
6 *Schwarzes Korps*, 12 December 1935.
7 *Deutsche medizinische Wochenschrift*, 22 November 1933.
8 *Berliner Illustrierte Zeitung*, 9 January 1936.
9 Interview with Professor Zorn, Bonn, May 1966.
10 Eugen Kogon, *Der SS-Staat*, Europäische Verlagsanstalt, Frankfurt, 1959, p. 284.
11 *Süddeutsche Zeitung*, 17 March 1964.
12 *Völkischer Beobachter*, 21 November 1936.
13 *ibid.*, 1 September 1935.
14 Report on the execution of Anita von Berg and Renate von Nazmer in *Neues Tagebuch*, 23 February 1935, p. 171.
15 *Illustrierter Beobachter*, Berlin, 30 January 1934.
16 *Sonntag Morgen, Auslandsblatt der Kölnischen Zeitung*, 8 October 1935.
17 *Frankfurter Zeitung*, 20 January 1937.
18 Max Damarus, *Hitler: Reden und Proklamationen 1932–1938*, Wurzburg, 1962, p. 793.
19 *Völkischer Beobachter*, 3 and 9 January 1939.
20 Interview with Graf Schwerin von Krosigk, Essen, May 1966.
21 *Die Zone*, Paris, 1934.
22 Friedrich Christian Prinz zu Schaumburg-Lippe, *Dr Goebbels*, Limes, Wiesbaden, 1964, p. 79.
23 *ibid.*, p. 108.
24 Bundesarchiv Coblenz, File R 11/39a.
25 *ibid.*
26 *Frankfurter Zeitung*, 11 June 1939.
27 *Der Spiegel*, 23 January 1967, p. 62.
28 Interview with Terence Mason, St Anthony's College, Oxford, January 1967.
29 *Was wir jeden Tag erleben*, brochure on the National-Socialist Imperial Symphony Orchestra, Munich, 1937, p. 21.
30 Photograph in the *Berliner Illustrierte Zeitung*, 13 May 1934, p. 646.
31 Karl Demeter, *Das deutsche Offizierskorps in Gesellschaft und Staat 1650–1945*, Frankfurt 1964, p. 227.
32 *Völkischer Beobachter*, 12 February 1935.
33 Hermann Stresau, *Von Jahr zu Jahr*, Berlin 1948, p. 80.
34 Gerhard Ritter, *Goerdeler und die deutsche Widerstandsbewegung*, Stuttgart, 1945, p. 62.
35 *Schwarzes Korps*, 10 July 1935.
36 Hermann Stresau, *op. cit.*, p. 363, diary entry for 10 June 1944.
37 Ernst Niekisch, *Das Reich der niederen Dämone*, Hamburg, 1953, p. 138.
38 *Schwarzes Korps*, 10 July 1935.
39 *ibid.*
40 Heinz Boberach, *Meldungen aus dem Reich*, Neuwied/Berlin, 1965, p. 17.
41 Elizabeth Hoemberg, *Thy People, My People*, London 1950, p. 114.
42 Sarah Mabel Collins, *The Alien Years*, London, 1963, p. 43.
43 Wilhelm Prüller, *Diary of a German Soldier*, London, 1963, p. 43.

4 The Party

1 Franz Neumann, *Behemoth*, Oxford University Press, New York, 1942, p. 379.
2 *Schwarzes Korps*, 15 May 1935.
3 David Schoenbaum, *Hitler's Social Revolution*, Weidenfeld and Nicolson, London, 1967, p. 236.
4 *ibid.*, p. 221.
5 *Schwarzes Korps*, 12 September 1935.
6 *ibid.*, 14 November 1935.
7 David Schoenbaum, *op. cit.*, p. 236.
8 *ibid.*, p. 225.
9 *Frankfurter Zeitung*, 8 May 1938.
10 Interview with Herr Thiele, Munich, April 1967.
11 Daniel Lerner, Ithiel de Sola Pool and George K. Schüeller, 'The Nazi Élite', in *World Revolutionary Élites*, Massachusetts Institute of Technology, Cambridge, Mass., 1965, p. 313.
12 *ibid.*, p. 197.
13 *ibid.*, p. 294.
14 David Schoenbaum, *op. cit.*, p. 72.
15 Franz Neumann, *op. cit.*, pp. 378–9.
16 Dr Neusüss-Hunkel, *Die SS*, Norddeutsche, Hanover/Frankfurt, 1956, p. 16.
17 Wolfgang Zapf, *Wandlungen der deutsche Élite*, Piper, Munich, 1965, p. 181.
18 Bella Fromm, *Blood and Banquets*, Harper and Bros., New York, 1942, p. 86.
19 Interview with Count Schwerin von Krosigk, Essen-Werden, April 1966.
20 Interview with Herr Bausch, Berlin, April 1967.
21 Interview with Countess von Schulenburg, Munich, May 1966.
22 A letter from Count Schulenburg to his wife, October 1940.
23 Christian, Prinz zu Schaumburg-Lippe, *Dr Goebbels*, Limes Verlag, Wiesbaden, 1964, p. 326.
24 Interview with Count Schwerin von Krosigk, *loc. cit.*
25 Achim Besgen, *Der Stille Befehl*, Nymphenburger, Munich, 1960, p. 183.
26 Erich Ebermayer and Hans Roos, *Gefährtin des Teufels*, Hoffmann and Co. Hamburg, p. 211.
27 *ibid.*, p. 208.
28 *ibid.*, p. 206.
29 Interview with Prinz von Wittgenstein, Munich, April 1967.
30 Bella Fromm, *op. cit.*, p. 243.
31 Fritz Thyssen, *I Paid Hitler*, Hodder and Stoughton, London, 1941, p. 213.
32 Bella Fromm, *op. cit.*, p. 222.
33 Interview with Fräulein Erna Hanfstengl, Munich, April 1967.
34 Louis P. Lochner, *Die Goebbels Tagebücher 1942–3*, Atlantis, Zurich, 1948, p. 260.
35 Bernhard Vollmer, *Volksopposition im Polizeistaat*, Deutsche Verlagsanstalt, Stuttgart, 1957, p. 189.
36 *Frankfurter Zeitung*, 6 March 1939.
37 Joachim Fest, *Das Gesicht des Dritten Reiches*, Piper, Munich, 1963, p. 404.
38 Hermann Glaser, *Spiesser-Ideologie*, Rombart, Freiburg, 1964, p. 86.
39 Achim Besgen, *op. cit.*, p. 183.
40 Interview with Herr Schleif, Berlin, April 1967.
41 Interview with Mrs Woodger, Hemel Hempstead, February 1967.
42 Interview with Herr Thiele, *loc. cit.*
43 David Schoenbaum, *op. cit.*, p. 236.

44   *Frankfurter Zeitung*, 18 September 1937.
45   *ibid.*, 16 November 1937.
46   *ibid.*, 6 January 1938.
47   Institut für Zeitgeschichte, Munich, File M A 292, Photoroll 8100.
48   *Schwarzes Korps*, 3 February 1938.
49   Max Seydewitz, *Civil Life in Wartime Germany*, Viking Press, New York, 1945, p. 145.
50   *Die Körperkultur in Deutschland 1917–1945*, Sportverlag, Berlin, 1964, p. 200.
51   Henrietta von Schirach, *The Price of Glory*, Muller, London, 1960, p. 163.
52   Hans Severus Siegler, *Adolf Hitler aus dem Erleben dargestellt*, Verlag W. Schütz, Göttingen, 1964, p. 173.
53   *ibid.*, p. 122.
54   Kurt Riess, *Gustav Gründgens*, Hoffmann and Co., Hamburg, 1965, p. 144.
55   Interview with Herr Schleif, *loc. cit.*
56   *Essener Volkszeitung*, 28 June 1934.
57   Allen S. Milward, *The German Economy at War*, The Athlone Press, London, 1965, p. 154.

5 Ritual and Führer Worship

1   *Frankfurter Zeitung*, 19 February 1937.
2   Karl Heinz Schmeer, *Die Regie des öffentlichen Lebens im Dritten Reich*, Paul, Munich, 1956, p. 85.
3   *ibid.*, p. 72.
4   *ibid.*, p. 95.
5   *ibid.*, p. 97.
6   Hans Gert Schumann, *Nationalsozialismus und Gewerkschafts-bewegung*, Norddeutscher Verlag-Anstalt, Hamburg, 1958, p. 135.
7   Karl Heinz Schmeer, *op. cit.*, p. 92.
8   Hans Jochen Gamm, *Der braune Kult*, Rütten and Loening, Hamburg, p. 141.
9   William L. Shirer, *Berlin Diary*, London, 1941, p. 22. Diary entry for 2 September 1934.
10   A report from Bielefeld in the *Völkischer Beobachter*, 1 February 1935.
11   Karl Heinz Schmeer, *op. cit.*, p. 23.
12   Hans Jochen Gamm, *op. cit.*, p. 73.
13   William L. Shirer, *op. cit.*, p. 20. Diary entry for 27 February 1932.
14   Karl Heinz Schmeer, *op. cit.*, p. 20.
15   *Frankfurter Zeitung*, 1 December 1934.
16   *ibid.*, 10 September 1937.
17   *ibid.*, 7 June 1937.
18   Heinz Boberach, *Meldungen aus dem Reich*, Luchterhand Verlag, Neuwied, 1965. Despatch No. 39, for 12 January 1940.
19   Unpublished reports of the Intelligence Service of the S D, Bundesarchiv, Coblenz. File R 58/147, No. 44 (24 January 1940).
20   *Frankfurter Zeitung*, 19 December 1934.
21   *ibid.*, 16 July 1937.
22   *ibid.*, 25 December 1938.
23   Walther Hagemann, *Publizistik im Dritten Reich*, Hansische Gilden, Hamburg, 1948, p. 74.
24   *Frankfurter Zeitung*, 11 January 1937.
25   *Deutsche Allgemeine Zeitung*, 4 December 1938.
26   *Schwarzes Korps*, 9 December 1937.

27 *Frankfurter Zeitung*, 24 November 1934.
28 *Starkenburger Provinzialzeitung*, quoted in the *Frankfurter Zeitung*, 1 December 1934.
29 *Frankfurter Zeitung*, 21 December 1934.
30 *ibid.*, 21 November 1934.
31 *ibid.*
32 *Schwarzes Korps*, 15 July 1937.
33 *Neue Weltbühne*, 30 April 1936.
34 Madeleine Kent, *I Married a German*, London, 1938, p. 173.
35 Christopher Sidgwick, *German Journey*, London, 1936, p. 96.
36 *Neue Weltbühne*, 30 September 1935.
37 *Schwarzes Korps*, 17 July 1935.
38 Erich Ebermayer, *Denn heute ghört uns Deutschsland*, Vienna, 1959, p. 196.
39 E. Höflich *Wie benehm ich mich*, Stollfuss, Bonn, quoted by *Schwarzes Korps*, 5 September 1935.
40 *Frankfurter Zeitung*, 9 August 1936.
41 *Völkischer Beobachter*, 15 December 1933.
42 *Der Spiegel*, 20 June, 1966.
43 Hermann Stresau, *Von Jahr zu Jahr*, Minerva, 1948, p. 156.
44 John Heygate, *These Germans*, Hutchinson, London, 1940, p. 179.
45 Wiener Library, eyewitness accounts, Section P A, file on Elisabeth Freund.
46 Olga Tschechowa, *Ich verschweige nichts*, Simmer und Herzog, Berchtesgaden, 1952, p. 195.
47 Tami Oelfken, *Das Logbuch*, Verlag der Nation, 1955, p. 37.
48 Madeleine Kent, *op. cit.*, p. 261.
49 *Schwarzes Korps*, 31 July 1935.
50 *Westdeutscher Beobachter*, 26 March 1936.
51 Josef Wulf, *Literatur und Dichtung im Dritten Reich*, Mohn, Gütersloh, 1963, p. 352.
52 Dietrich Bronder, *Bevor Hitler kam*, Piper, Hanover, 1964, p. 188.
53 Dr Arthur Dix, 'Politik als Staatslehre, Staatskunst und Staatswille', in *Zeitschrift für Politik*, Berlin, 1934, volume 24, p. 539.
54 *Reden und Aufsätze anlässlich der Tagung der Gau- und Kreisschulungsleiter der NSDAP*, Munich, 1938, p. 21.
55 Hans Jochen Gamm, *op. cit.*, p. 160.
56 Walther Hagemann, *op. cit.*, p. 131.
57 Wilhelm Prüllen, *The Diary of a German Soldier*, Faber, London, 1963, p. 110.
58 Interview with Frau Heinemann of Munich, May 1966
59 Interview with General von Blumentritt, Munich, May 1966.
60 H. Trevor Roper, *The Last Days of Hitler*, London, 1956, p. 90 of the third edition.

6 Corruption

1 Interview with Albert Speer, *Der Spiegel*, 7 November 1966.
2 Willi Frischauer, *Hermann Goering*, London, p. 223.
3 Gerhard F. Krämer, *The Influence of National Socialism on the Courts of Justice and the Police in the Third Reich*, Weidenfeld and Nicolson, London, 1955, page 630.
4 Willi Frischauer, *op. cit.*, p. 28.
5 Fritz Thyssen, *I Paid Hitler*, Hodder and Stoughton, London, 1941, p. 200.
6 Robert M. Kempner, *SS im Kreuzverhör*, Rütten and Löhning, Hamburg, 1964, p. 209.
7 Interview with Herr Nebelung of Ludwigshafen, April 1967.
8 *Trial of Major War Criminals*, Nuremberg, Volume 28, 1759, p. 251.

9   Fritz Thyssen, *op. cit.*, p. 199.
10 Bundesarchiv Koblenz, File R 55/24, Report of 1 April 1934.
11 *Neuer Vorwärts*, 20 March 1938.
12 *Neue Weltbühne*, 18 November 1937.
13 *ibid.*
14 Interview with Herr Nebelung of Ludwigshafen, April 1967.
15 Rudolf Diehl, *Luzifer ante Portas*, Interverlag, Zurich, 1948, p. 95.
16 Gerald Reitlinger, *SS. Alibi of a Nation*, Heinemann, London, 1957, p. 133.
17 Document PS 1757, IMT, *Trial of Major War Criminals*, Nuremberg, Volume XXVIII, p. 154.
18 *ibid.*, pp. 150, 148.
19 *ibid.*, p. 150.
20 *ibid.*, p. 151.
21 *ibid.*, p. 129.
22 *ibid.*, p. 141.
23 Bundesarchiv Koblenz, file NG 670, 20 December 1935 to 10 February 1936. Dr Birkhahn, *Niederschlagungsantrage in Unterschlagungsstrafsäche Wilhelm Reper.*
24 Institut für Zeitgeschichte, Munich file MA 261, photo-roll 9493. *Stellvertrtender General Wehrkreiskommando 20 Danzig, 26 January 1940.*
25 Institut für Zeitgeschichte, Munich, file MA 319, photo-roll 4826–4910.
26 *Neues Tagebuch*, 15 January 1938.
27 Louis Hagen, *Follow My Leader*, Allan Wingate, London, 1951, p. 125.
28 Jack Schiefer, *Tagebuch eines Wehrunwürdigen*, Grenzlandverlag Aachen, 1947, p. 257.
29 *Kölnische Zeitung*, 29 December 1939.
30 *New York Herald Tribune*, 16 February 1942.
31 *News Chronicle*, 7 October 1944.
32 Bundesarchiv Koblenz, file R 58/151, SD report 13 December 1943.
33 Bundesarchiv Koblenz, file R 41/268, *Akten über Stimmungsberichte ausländischer Arbeiter im Reich*, Volume VIII, Heft 2, 1943, folio 1–275.
34 *Die Zeitung*, 17 November 1944.
35 Max Seydewitz, *Civil Life in War-time Germany*, Viking Press, New York, 1945, p. 48.
36 Vienna Library files P IIIa, No. 502.
37 Vienna Library files P IIIf, No. 6.
38 Eugen Kogon, *Der SS Staat*, Europäische Verlagsanstalt, Frankfurt, 1959, p. 235.
39 Bella Fromm, *Blood and Banquets*, Harper, New York, 1942, p. 274.
40 Bundesarchiv Koblenz, file R 41/155, 7 January 1939.
41 Document PS 1208 IMT, Volume XXVII, p. 69.
42 *Völkischer Beobachter*, Viennese edition, 4 March 1939.
43 *Frankfurter Zeitung*, 4 July 1938.
44 Vienna Library, file P IIIf, No. 535.
45 Vienna Library, file P IIIe, No. 1186.
46 Henriette von Schirach, *The Price of Glory*, Muller, London, 1960, p. 186.
47 Gerald Reitlinger, *op. cit.*, p. 173.
48 Roger Manvell and Heinrich Fraenkel, *The Incomparable Crime*, Heinemann, 1967, p. 84.
49 Eugen Kogon, *Der SS Staat*, Berman and Fischer, Stockholm, 1947, p. 315.
50 Eugen Kogon, *op. cit.*, p. 302.
51 *ibid.*, p. 317.
52 Eugen Kogon, *op. cit.*, p. 313.
53 *ibid.*, p. 307.
54 Interview with Count Schwerin von Krosigk, Essen–Bergen, April 1966.

55 *News Chronicle*, 7 October 1944.
56 Institut für Zeitgeschichte, Munich, file M A 341, photo-roll 7418–7432.
57 Institut für Zeitgeschichte, Munich, file M A 430/1. A report on public morale (*Stimmungsbericht*) by the Supreme Head of the Court of Appeal at Bamberg to Minister Tierack.

7 *Denunciation*

1   Dr Stolzenberg in *Deutsche Justiz*, cf. *Frankfurter Zeitung*, 21 June 1938.
2   Statement dated 18 April 1934, cf. *Kölnische Zeitung*, 24 July 1934.
3   *Kölnische Zeitung*, 24 July 1934.
4   *Der deutsche Verwaltungsbeamte*, 17 October 1937.
5   *Schuhhändler Zeitung*, 17 November 1938.
6   *Frankfurter Zeitung*, 26 October 1934.
7   *ibid.*, 6 July 1938.
8   *ibid.*, 15 May 1938.
9   *Neues Tagebuch*, 15 November 1933.
10 *Frankfurter Zeitung*, 14 July 1937.
11 *ibid.*, 16 March 1937.
12 *ibid.*, 18 August 1937.
13 *Hakenkreuzbanner*, Mannheim, 25 November 1934.
14 *Frankfurter Zeitung*, 9 September 1935.
15 *ibid.*, 27 November 1934.
16 *ibid.*, 16 March 1937.
17 Interview with Herr Nebelung, Ludwigshafen, April 1967.
18 Bernhard Vollmer, *Volksopposition im Polizeistaat*, Stuttgart, 1957, p. 41.
19 *Frankfurter Zeitung*, 23 May 1937.
20 Bernhard Vollmer, *op. cit.*, p. 320.
21 Joseph Wulf, *Theater und Film im Dritten Reich*, Gütersloh, 1964, pp. 295–7.
22 *ibid.*, p. 95.
23 *Berliner Tageblatt*, 14 June 1936.
24 Joseph Wulf, *Presse und Funk im Dritten Reich*, Gütersloh, 1964, p. 289.
25 *Hamburger Fremdenblatt*, 5 February 1942.
26 Bundesarchiv Koblenz File R 22/4002 (Richterbriefe p. 78).
27 *Hakenkreuzbanner*, Mannheim, 24 December 1937.
28 Bundesarchiv Koblenz, File R 22/4002 (Richterbriefe p. 201).
29 *ibid.*, p. 199.
30 Wiener Library; eyewitness accounts by survivors File P III d/192.
31 *ibid.*, File P III f/1149.
32 *Neues Tagebuch*, 12 October 1935, p. 966 (decision by Amstegericht Lörrach).
33 *ibid.* (decision by Amtsgericht Gera).
34 *Neues Tagebuch*, 25 April 1936, p. 407.
35 *Neue Volkszeitung*, 31 May 1941.
36 Bella Fromm, *Blood and Banquets*, New York 1942, p. 208.
37 Wiener Library; eyewitness accounts by survivors, File P III a/54.
38 *Guardian*, 4 July 1967 (retrial of the former judge of the People's Court, Hans Joachim Rehse).
39 Interview with Helene von Sachno, Munich, September 1965.
40 Elizabeth Hoemberg, *Thy people, My people*, Dent, London, 1950, p. 50.
41 Louis Hagen, *Follow my Leader*, Allen Wingate, London, 1951, p. 311.

42 *Zwölf-Uhr-Blatt*, Berlin, 26 August 1944.
43 Ursula von Kardorff, *Berliner Aufzeichnungen 1942–1945*, Biederstein Verlag, Munich 1962, p. 163.
44 Archives of the Institut für Zeitgeschichte, Munich. *Stimmungsberichte des Regierungspräsidenten von Regensburg*, File M A 300, Photoroll 2955/3098. Report for 10 March 1943.
45 *Bodensee Rundschau*, Konstanz, 23 November 1943.
46 Viennese edition of the *Völkische Beobachter*, 9 March 1945.
47 Tami Oelfken, *Das Logbuch*, Verlag der Nation, Berlin, 1955, pp. 302/3.

8 Justice

1 Rolf Dahrendorf, *Gesellschaft und Demokratie in Deutschland*, Piper Verlag, Munich, 1965, p. 275.
2 Axel Eggebrecht, *Volk ans Gewehr*, Stuttgart, 1959, p. 199.
3 Rolf Dahrendorf, *op. cit.*, p. 260.
4 *Der Spiegel*, 17 April 1967.
5 Gerhard F. Kramer, *The Influence of National Socialism on the Courts of Justice and the Police in the Third Reich*, Weidenfeld and Nicolson, London, 1955, p. 618.
6 Erich Ebermayer, *'Denn heute gehört uns Deutschland'*, Paul Zsolnay, Vienna, 1959, p. 75.
7 Ilse Staff, *Justiz im Dritten Reich*, Fischer, 1964, pp. 148 to 152.
8 Franz Neumann, *Behemoth*, Oxford University Press, New York, 1942, p. 454.
9 *Neues Tagebuch*, 19 January 1935.
10 Otto Kirchheimer, *Criminal Law in National Socialist Germany*, Studies in Philosophy and Social Science, New York, No. 3, vol. VIII, July 1940, p. 447.
11 *Nürnberger Akten*, No. 1565 of 20 May 1947.
12 Gerhard F. Kramer, *op. cit.*, p. 630.
13 Franz Neumann, *op. cit.*, p. 456.
14 Werner Johe, *Die gleichgeschaltete Justiz*, Europäische Verlagsanstalt, Stuttgart, 1967, p. 40.
15 Martin Broszat, 'Zur Perversion der Strafjustiz im Dritten Reich', *Vierteljahreshefte für Zeitgeschichte* 1958, 4. Heft, p. 422.
16 *Deutsche Justiz*, 1939, pp. 58, 59, 175–8.
17 *Schwarzes Korps*, 16 December 1937.
18 *Schwarzes Korps*, 13 April 1938.
19 *Schwarzes Korps*, 5 March 1942.
20 Werner Johe, *op. cit.*, p. 39.
21 *Juristische Wochenschrift*, Leipzig, 3 November 1934.
22 *Völkischer Beobachter*, 27 January 1934.
23 *Neue Weltbühne*, 27 June 1935.
24 *Frankfurter Zeitung*, 22 December 1934.
25 Wallace R. Deuel, *People Under Hitler*, Harcourt, Brace, New York 1942, p. 148.
26 Ursula von Kardorff, *Berliner Aufzeichnungen 1942–1945*, Biederstein, Munich, 1962, p. 76.
27 *Statistisches Handbuch von Deutschland, 1928–1944*, p. 633.
28 *Frankfurter Zeitung*, 21 June 1938.
29 *Statistisches Handbuch, loc. cit.*
30 Wolfgang Harthauser, *Die Verfolgung der Homosexuellen im Dritten Reich*, Sender Freies Berlin, 1 December 1966, p. 15.

31 *ibid.*
32 *Reichsgesetz über Massnahmen der Staatsnotwehr* 3 July 1934, *Reichsgesetzblatt* 1934, vol. 1, p. 529.
33 Professor Dahm, *'Verbrechen und Tatbestand'*, Berlin, 1936, p. 46.
34 *Frankfurter Zeitung*, 29 June 1938.
35 Franz Newmann, *op, cit.*, p. 457.
36 *Hamburger Fremdenblatt*, 6 June 1943.
37 *Frankfurter Zeitung*, 5 December 1937.
38 Andreas Frittner, *Deutsches Geistesleben und Nationalsozialismus*, Rainer Wunderlich, Tübingen, 1965, p. 166.
39 *Frankfurter Zeitung*, 11 February 1937.
40 *Frankfurter Zeitung*, 29 May 1937.
41 Ilse Staff, *op. cit.*, p. 207.
42 Poliakov and Wulf, *Das Dritte Reich und seine Diener*, Berlin, 1956, p. 255.
43 Martin Broszat, *op. cit.*, pp. 394–8.
44 *ibid.*, p. 394.
45 Ilse Staff, *op. cit.*, p. 115.
46 *ibid.*, p. 117.
47 *Guardian*, 4 July 1967.
48 *The Times*, 24 April 1945.
49 Ursula von Kardorf, *op. cit.*, p. 76.
50 William L. Shirer, *Berlin Diary*, Hamish Hamilton, 1941, p. 199.
51 *Sondergericht Rohstock Akten*, 3 KLS 135/42.
52 *Völkischer Beobachter*, 31 August 1944.
53 Bundesarchiv Koblenz, *Dr Thieracks Richterbriefe*, File R22/4002, No. 6, p. 49.
54 Bundesarchiv Koblenz, File R22/4003. *Informationsdienst des Reichsministers der Justiz, Beitrag* 55, p. 86.
55 *ibid., Beitrag* 37, p. 60.
56 *Der Spiegel*, 6 March 1967, p. 53.
57 Werner Johe, *op. cit.*, p. 192.
58 Bundesarchiv Koblenz, File R58/149, No. 69, 27 March 1940.
59 Isle Staff, *op. cit.*, p. 105.
60 Martin Broszat, *op. cit.*, p. 432.
61 Werner Johe, *op. cit.*, p. 183.
62 Werner Johe, *op. cit.*, p. 187.
63 *ibid.*
64 *Die Nürnberger Akten des Ministerialrates Werner von Haacke*, NG – 949, 18 December 1947.

9 The Civil Service

1 Bundesarchiv Coblenz, File R 43 II/450a.
2 David Schoenbaum, *Hitler's Social Revolution*, Weidenfeld and Nicolson, London, 1967.
3 Heinz Boberach, *Meldungen aus dem Reich*, Luchterhand, 1965, p. 158.
4 *Neues Tagebuch*, 30 September 1934, p. 935.
5 *Deutsche Mitteilungen* No. 48, 2 June 1938, relating to memorandum from the Ministry of the Interior II SB 6160/6193, Berlin, 14 December 1937.
6 *Frankfurter Zeitung*, 14 April 1937.
7 *Frankfurter Zeitung*, 2 September 1937.

8   *Deutsche Mitteilungen, loc. cit.*
9   *Frankfurter Zeitung,* 1 March 1936.
10   *ibid.,* 10 March 1937.
11   *ibid.,* 29 September 1935.
12   *ibid.,* 27 July 1937.
13   Bundesarchiv Koblenz, File r 43 II/432b.
14   *Schwarzes Korps,* 11 March 1937.
15   David Schoenbaum, *op. cit.,* p. 211.
16   Franz Neumann, *Behemoth,* New York, 1944, p. 377.
17   Ulrich von Hassell, *Vom andern Deutschland,* Frankfurt, 1946, p. 36.
18   Hans Georg von Studnitz, *Als Berlin brannte,* Stuttgart, 1963, p. 167.
19   Bundesarchiv Koblenz, File R 55/29, Vol. I.
20   David Schoenbaum, *op. cit.,* p. 221.
21   Interview with Tim Mason, London, January 1967.
22   David Schoenbaum, *op. cit.,* p. 237.
23   *ibid.,* p. 232.
24   *ibid.,* p. 230.
25   *ibid.,* p. 221.
26   Institut für Zeitgeschichte, Munich, File MA 430/I. Report of von Bamberg, President of the Court of Appeal, to Minister of Justice Thirach, 27 November 1943.
27   David Schoenbaum, *op. cit.,* p. 205.

10 The Army

1   Joachim Fest, *Das Gesicht des Dritten Reiches,* Piper, München, 1963, p. 329.
2   Elias Canetti, *Crowds and Power,* Gollancz, 1962, p. 181.
3   Wolfgang Drews, *Die klirrend Kette,* Keppler Verlag, Baden-Baden, 1947, p. 24.
4   Interview with General Schimpf, Düsseldorf, April 1966.
5   Bernard Vollmer, *Volksopposition im Polizeistaat,* Deutsche Verlagsanstalt, Stuttgart, 1957, p. 196.
6   *ibid.,* p. 241.
7   *ibid.,* p. 285.
8   Daniel Lerner and others, 'The Nazi Élite' in *World Revolutionary Élites,* Massachusetts Institute of Technology, 1965, p. 272.
9   Decrees of 3 July 1934 and 10 September 1935, cf. David Schoenbaum, *Hitler's Social Revolution,* Weidenfeld and Nicolson, London, 1967, p. 217.
10   Gert von Klaas, *Krupps – the Story of an Industrial Empire,* Sidgwick and Jackson, London, 1954, p. 383.
11   G. Stolper, K. Hauser and K. Borchardt, *Die deutsche Wirtschaft seit 1878,* J. C. B. Mohr (Paul Siebeck), Tübingen, 1966, p. 194.
12   Interview with General Blumentritt, Munich, May 1966.
13   David Schoenbaum, *op. cit.,* p. 254.
14   Karl Demeter, *Das deutsche Offizierkorps in Gesellschaft vom Staat 1650–1945,* Bernard and Graefe, Frankfurt-am-Main, 1964, p. 55.
15   *ibid.*
16   David Schoenbaum, *op. cit.,* p. 259–61.
17   Interview with Ewald von Kleist, Munich, April 1967.
18   Karl Demeter, *op. cit.,* p. 107.
19   Interview with Herr Löhrich, Cologne, April 1966.

20 Interview with General Blumentritt, *loc. cit.*
21 *Hamburger Fremdenblatt*, 24 July 1944.
22 Bundesarchiv Koblenz, File R7X/428.
23 Bundesarchiv Koblenz, File R22/4003, *Informationsdienst des Reichsministers der Justiz*, p. 39.
24 John Laffin, *Jackboot*, Cassel, London, 1965, p. 218.
25 Fabien von Schlabrendorff, *The Secret War against Hitler*, Hodder and Stoughton, London 1966, p. 164.
26 Ulrich von Hassel's diaries, New York, 1947, p. 31.
27 Louis P. Lochner, *Die Goebbels Tagebücher 1942–1943*, Atlantis, Zurich, 1948, p. 408.
28 Interview with Ewald von Kleist, *loc. cit.*
29 David Schoenbaum, *op. cit.*, p. 218.
30 Munich Institut für Zeitgeschichte, File M A 261, Baldur von Schirach's letter to Colonel von Stockhausen, Commander of the infantry regiment *Grossdeutschland*, dated 14 September 1940.
31 *Die Zeit*, 6 May 1966, p. 50.
32 Ilse Staff, *Justiz im Dritten Reich*, Fischer, Frankfurt, 1964, p. 244.
33 *Der Angriff*, 24 July 1944.
34 Erich Ebermayer and Hans Roos, *Gefährtin des Teufels*, Hoffmann and Kampe, Hamburg, 1952, p. 325.
35 Interview with Herr Jean Schlösser, Cologne, April 1966.
36 Olga Tschechowa, *Ich verschweige nichts*, Zimmer and Herzog, Berchtesgaden, 1952, p. 278.
37 *ibid.*, p. 280.
38 *ibid.*, p. 201.
39 Interview with Frau Stuck-Resniczek, Munich, May 1966.
40 Hermann Rauschnigg, *Die Revolution des Nihilismus*, Europa Verlag, Zurich, 1964, p. 152.
41 Bundesarchiv Koblenz, *Volksgerichtshofakte*, File 3L293/44 to 4J/332/44.
42 Interview with Herr Michels, Düsseldorf, April 1966.
43 Wolf Mittendorf, *Soziologie des Verbrechens*, Diederichs, Düsseldorf, 1959, p. 242.
44 Interview with Prince Wittgenstein, Munich, April 1967.
45 Interview with Herr Werner Koch, Düsseldorf, April 1966.
46 Klaus Granzow, *Tagebuch eines Hitler-Jugends 1943–1945*, Bremen, 1965, p. 82.
47 Alfred Cobban, *A History of Modern France, vol. III*, Jonathan Cape, London, 1965, p. 179.
48 Interview with Herr Stöber, Berlin, April 1967.
49 Interview with Herr Jean Schlösser, Cologne, May 1966.
50 Louis P. Lochner, *op. cit.*, p. 308.
51 Saul K. Padover, *Psychologist in Germany*, Phoenix House, London, 1946, p. 137.
52 Ernst Niekisch, *Das Reich der niedern Dämone*, Rowohlt, Hamburg, 1953, p. 304.
53 Interview with Herr Lindlar, Düsseldorf, April 1966.
54 Interview with Terence Prittie, London, March 1964.
55 Ilse Staff, *op. cit.*, p. 252.
56 Joachim Fest, *op. cit.*, p. 332.
57 *Der Spiegel*, 2 October 1967, p. 37.
58 Karl Demeter, *op. cit.*, p. 206.
59 *ibid.*
60 *Der Spiegel*, 13 July 1967.
61 Gustav Brecht, *Erinnerungen*, privately printed, 1964, p. 72.
62 *Die Zeit*, 6 May 1966, p. 50.

11 The Land

1 *Statistisches Handbuch für Deutschland 1928–1944*, Franz Ehrenwirth, Munich, 1949, p. 31.
2 Frieda Wunderlich, *Farm Labour in Germany 1810–1945*, Princeton University Press, 1961, p. 41.
3 *Kölnische Zeitung*, 11 April 1944.
4 Frieda Wunderlich, *op. cit.*, p. 184.
5 Hans von der Decken, 'Mechanisierung in der Landwirtschaft', *Vierteljahrsheft zur Konjunkturforschung*, Winter issue, 1938–9, p. 355.
6 *Neues Tagebuch*, 22 May 1937, p. 529.
7 *Berliner Illustrierte Zeitung*, 27 May 1934.
8 *ibid.*
9 Max Rumpf and Hans Behringer, *Bauerndorf am Grossstadtrand*, Stuttgart/Berlin, 1940, p. 390.
10 Harold Münzinger, 'Die Arbeitsbelastung der Bauernfamilie – Ein Beitrag zur Landfluchtfrage in Württemberg', in *Raumforschung und Raumordnung*, 1940, Nr. 10, p. 390.
11 Hans Müller, *Deutsches Bauerntum zwischen Gestern und Morgen*, Witzburg, 1940, p. 28.
12 Frieda Wunderlich, *op. cit.*, p. 192.
13 Arthur Schweizer, *Big Business in the Third Reich*, Eyre and Spottiswoode, London, 1964, p. 167.
14 Franz Neumann, *Behemoth*, Oxford University Press, New York, 1942, p. 394.
15 Wolfgang Schumann, 'Der faschistische Reichsnährstand', *Zeitschrift für Geschichtswissenschaft*, East Berlin, May 1962, p. 1046.
16 *Schwarzes Korps*, 23 February 1939.
17 *ibid.*, 19 December 1935.
18 *New York Times*, 14 March 1937.
19 Interview with Frau von Kiekebusche, Munich, 1967.
20 Interview with Count Schwerin von Krosigk, Essen-Werden, May 1966.
21 Interview with Fräulein von Miquel, Cologne, May 1966.
22 Franz Neumann, *op. cit.*, p. 394.
23 Hilde Oppenheimer Blum, *The Standard of Living of German Labor under Nazi Rule*, New School for Social Research, New York, 1943, p. 19.
24 Frieda Wunderlich, *op. cit.*, p. 216.
25 *Frankfurter Zeitung*, 17 November 1934.
26 *Schwarzes Korps*, 5 March 1936.
27 Bundesarchiv Coblenz, File R 43 II/528, *Treuhänderbericht*, February 1937.
28 *Der Deutsche Volkswirt*, 10 March 1939.
29 Interview with Terence Mason, St Anthony's College, Oxford, January 1967.
30 Walter Goerlitz, *Die Junker*, Starke, Limburg, 1964, p. 391.
31 *Frankfurter Zeitung*, 24 April 1937.
32 Elizabeth Steiner, *Agrarwirtschaft und Agrarpolitik*, Ph.D. thesis, Munich, 1939, p. 27.
32a *ibid.*
33 Hans Müller, *op. cit.*, p. 12.
34 *Kölnische Zeitung*, 11 April 1944.
35 University of Göttingen, Institute of Agricultural Management and Labour Questions.
36 Hauptarchiv Berlin–Dahlem, RMI File Repositorium 320, No. 582, p. 59.
37 Bundesarchiv Koblenz, File R 58/149, No. 70.
38 Institut für Zeitgeschichte, Munich, File MA 300, Photoroll 3437–3489 (*Nachgeborene Kinder auf Erbhöfen*).

39 Gustav Stolper, K. Hauser and K. Borchardt, *Die Wirtschaft seit 1870*, J. C. B. Mohr (Paul Siebeck), Tübingen, 1966, p. 162.
40 Frieda Wunderlich, *op. cit.*, p. 193.
41 David Schoenbaum, *Hitler's Social Revolution*, Weidenfeld and Nicolson, London, 1967, p. 171.
42 Frieda Wunderlich, *op. cit.*, p. 193.
43 Wilhelm Rapke, *International Economic Disintegration*, London, 1942, p. 147.
44 Hans Müller, *op. cit.*, p. 28.
45 Karl Hopp, *Erbhofrecht in Zahlen, Deutsche Justiz*, 1936, p. 1566.
46 *Berliner Börsenzeitung*, 25 October 1941.
47 Max Seydewitz, *Civil Life in Wartime Germany*, Viking Press, New York, 1945, p. 226.
48 *Deutsche Allgemeine Zeitung*, 29 April 1944.
49 Frieda Wunderlich, *op. cit.*, p. 194.
50 Institut für Zeitgeschichte, File MA 300, Photoroll 2955–3098 *Stimmungsbericht* of the *Regierungspräsident* of Regenburg, 11 November 1943.
51 Institut für Zeitgeschichte, Munich, File MA 300, Photocopy 2955/3098.
52 *ibid.*, Report on Public Morale of the President of the Local Council of Regensburg, 11 November 1943.

12 Business

1 Franz Neumann, *Ökonomie und Politik im 20. Jahrhundert*, p. 11.
2 David Schoenbaum, '*Hitler's Social Revolution*', Weidenfeld and Nicolson, London, 1967, p. 136.
3 David Schoenbaum, *op. cit.*, p. 146.
4 Arthur Schweitzer, *Big Business in the Third Reich*, Eyre and Spottiswoode, London 1964, p. 158.
5 Arthur Schweitzer, 'The Nazification of the Lower Middle Classes and Peasantry in the Third Reich', in *The Third Reich*, Weidenfeld & Nicolson, London, 1955, p. 580.
6 William Sheridan Allen, *The Nazi Seizure of Power*, Chicago, 1965, p. 262.
7 *Neue Weltbühne*, 6 August 1936.
8 *Frankfurter Zeitung*, 3 November 1936.
9 David Schoenbaum, *op. cit.*, p. 139.
10 Franz Neumann, *Behemoth*, New York 1942, p. 265.
11 Bernhard Vollmer, *Volksopposition im Polizeistaat*, Stuttgart, 1957, p. 164.
12 *Fachzeitung, der Schuhmachermeister*, 18 May 1934.
13 *Der Deutsche Volkswirt*, 17 May 1935.
14 Bundesarchiv Koblenz, File R7X/428.
15 *Frankfurter Zeitung*, 10 October 1937.
16 *Frankfurter Zeitung*, 16 June 1939.
17 Bundesarchiv Koblenz, File R7X/421.
18 *Berliner Illustrierte Zeitung*, 27 June 1935.
19 *Kartell Rundschau*, December 1936, p. 829.
20 *Schwarzes Korps*, 6 October 1938.
21 *Deutsche Volkswirtschaft*, 2. Augustheft, 1939.
22 *Frankfurter Zeitung*, 24 May 1939.
23 Kurt Pritzkoleit, *Berlin*, Karl-Rauch-Verlag, Düsseldorf 1962, p. 37.
24 Garland, Kirchheimer and Neumann *The Fate of Small Business in Nazi Germany*, Senate Committee Print No. 14, Washington 1943, p. 140.
25 Heinrich Uhlig, *Die Warenhäuser im Dritten Reich*, Cologne-Opladen, 1956, p. 159.

26   ibid., p. 167.
27   ibid., p. 177.
28   Fränkische Tageszeitung, 22 November 1934.
29   Helmut Genschel, Die Verdrängung der Juden aus der Wirtschaft im Dritten Reich, Göttingen, 1966, p. 211.
30   Werner Mosse, Entscheidungsjahr 1932, Tübingen, 1965, p. 134.
31   Der Hoheitsträger, July 1939, p. 15.
32   Frankfurter Zeitung, 8 May 1935.
33   Helmut Genschel, op. cit., p. 211.
34   Werner Sorgel, Metallindustrie und National-sozialismus, Europäische Verlagsanstalt, Stuttgart, p. 30.
35   Louis P. Lochner, Tycoons and Tyrant, Chicago, 1954, p. 213.
36   ibid., p. 175.
37   Klaus Drobisch, 'Der Freundeskreis Himmler', Zeitschrift für Geschichtswissenschaft, East Berlin, 2nd issue, 1960, p. 304.
38   Arthur Schweitzer, 'Organisierter Kapitalismus, und Parteidiktatur', Schmöllers Jahrbuch, 1959, p. 46.
39   Franz Neumann, Behemoth, New York, 1942, p. 265.
40   Neue Weltbühne, 3 August 1939.
41   Arthur Schweitzer, op. cit., p. 260.
42   Franz Neumann, op. cit., p. 392.
43   International Military Tribunal – 2PA, ADJ–L, vol. II, Part 1, pp. 69, 70.
44   Akten des I.G. Prozesses, vol. 37/38, p. 8.
45   David Schoenbaum, op. cit., p. 135.
46   Bundesarchiv Koblenz, File R7X/453.
47   Bundesarchiv Koblenz, File R7X/453.
48   Günter Reimann, The Vampire Economy, New York, 1939, p. 126.
49   W. F. Brook, 'Social and Economic History of Germany from 1888–1938', Oxford University Press, 1938, p. 226.
50   Frankfurter Zeitung, 24 October 1937.
51   David Schoenbaum, op. cit., p. 151.
52   David Schoenbaum, op. cit., p. 156.
53   Basil Davidson, Germany What Now?, London, 1949, p. 125.
54   Gerd von Klaus, Krupps, the Story of an Industrial Empire, Sidgwick and Jackson, London, 1954, p. 415.
55   Peter Batty, The House of Krupp, Secker and Warburg, London, 1966, p. 178.
56   Bundesarchiv Koblenz, File R7X/421.
57   Ursula von Kardorf, op. cit., p. 30.
58   Hamburger Fremdenblatt, 5 June 1943.
59   Fabian von Schlabrendorff, The Secret War Against Hitler, Hodder and Stoughton, London, 1966, p. 144.
60   Louis P. Lochner, Tycoons and Tyrant, Chicago, 1954, p. 242.
61   Louis P. Lochner, op. cit., p. 246.
62   Jack Schiefer, Tagebuch eines Wehr unwürdigen, Aachen, 1947, p. 187.
63   Bundesarchiv Koblenz, File R11/1243; Industrie- und Handelskammer to the Reichswirtschaftskammer, 12 December 1941.
64   Alan Winward, 'Fritz Todt als Minister für Bewaffnung und Munition', Vierteljahreshefte für Zeitgeschichte, 1st issue, 1966, p. 55.
65   Frankfurter Zeitung, 13 February 1942.
66   Der Spiegel, No. 40, 1966.
67   Jack Schiefer, op. cit., p. 97.

68 Norbert Mühlen, *op. cit.*, p. 177.
69 Louis P. Lochner, *op. cit.*, p. 254.

13 The Workers

1 Hilde Oppenheimer-Blum, *The Standard of Living of German Labour under Nazi Rule*, New School for Social Research, New York, 1943, p. 15.
2 David Schoenbaum, *Hitler's Social Revolution*, London, 1967, p. 97.
3 Hilde Oppenheimer-Blum, *op. cit.*, p. 16.
4 Hilde Oppenheimer-Blum, *op. cit.*, p 24.
5 David Schoenbaum, *Hitler's Social Revolution*, London, 1967, p. 98.
6 *Der Deutsche Volkswirt*, 22 July 1938.
7 *Frankfurter Zeitung*, 22 July 1938.
8 Tim Mason, 'Labour in the Third Reich', *Past and Present*, London, April 1966, p. 133.
9 *Neue Weltbühne*, 15 April 1939.
10 Jürgen Kuczynski, *Die Geschichte der Lage der Arbeiter in Deutschland von 1789 bis in die Gegenwart*, Vol. II, 1. Teil, Berlin, 1953, p. 390.
11 C. W. Guillebaud, *The Economic Recovery of Germany*, London, 1939, p. 111.
12 Interview with Tim Mason, January 1967.
13 Emil Lederer, *Who Pays for German Re-armament?*, Social Research, New York, February 1938.
14 Bundesarchiv Koblenz, File R41/67. RAM. Treuhänder der Arbeit (IIIB 14222/39), 26 July 1939.
15 Arthur Schweitzer, *Big Business in the Third Reich*, London, 1964, p. 314.
16 *Textilzeitung*, 4 January 1939.
17 C. W. Guillebaud, *Social Policy of Nazi Germany*, Cambridge University Press, London, 1941, p. 73.
18 Hilde Oppenheimer-Blum, *op. cit.*, p. 29.
19 *Völkischer Beobachter*, 15 September 1944.
20 Jürgen Kuczynski, *op. cit.*, p. 123.
21 *Statistik des Deutschen Reiches*, Vol. VII, p. 529.
22 Hilde Oppenheimer-Blum, *op. cit.*, p. 30.
23 W. Müller, *Das Soziale Leben im Neuen Deutschland*, Berlin 1938, pp. 125, 126.
24 *Hamburger Fremdenblatt*, 30 December 1941.
25 Hilde Oppenheimer-Blum, *op. cit.*, p. 15.
26 *Parteistatistik*, 1935, Vol. I, p. 53.
27 *Das Schwarze Korps* 22 April 1937.
28 *Neue Weltbühne* 11. July 1935.
29 David Schoenbaum, *op. cit.*, p. 108.
30 Interview with Herr Lindlar, Düsseldorf, April 1966.
31 In *Der Betriebsingenieur als Menschenführer*, Berlin 1927, cf. Robert A. Brady *The Spirit and Structure of German Fascism*, New York, 1937, p. 167.
32 Wallace R. Deuel, *People under Hitler*, New York, 1942, p. 319.
33 David Schoenbaum, *op. cit.*, p. 111.
34 Interview with Herr Pampuch of Munich, September 1965.
35 Hilde Oppenheimer-Blum, *op. cit.*, p. 65.
36 *Hakenkreuz-Banner*, Mannheim, 27 November 1937.
37 Hilde Oppenheimer-Blum, *op. cit.*, p. 165.
38 David Schoenbaum, *op. cit.*, p. 109.

39 Hans Gerd Schumann, Nationalsozialismus und Gewerkshaftsbewegung. Norddeutsche Verlagsanstalt, Gödel-Hannover, 1958, p. 151.
40 Archiv des Instituts für Zeitgeschichte, Munich, File MA 292, photo-roll 8693–8719.
41 *Neue Weltbühne*, 15 April 1937.
42 Alan S. Milward, *The Germany Economy at War*, London, 1965, p. 41.
43 *Der Angriff* 20 February 1942.
44 Alan S. Milward, *op. cit.*, p. 41.
45 Bundesarchiv Koblenz, file 58 126/22 8 June 1944.
46 *Deutsche Allgemeine Zeitung* 15 December 1943.
47 Stolper, Hauser and Borchardt, *Deutsche Wirtschaft seit 1870*, Tübingen, 1966, p. 194.
48 Bundesarchiv Koblenz, file R58/178 29 December 1942.

14 Consumption

1   Heinrich Uhlig, *Die Warenhäuser im 3. Reich*, Cologne, 1956, p. 218.
2   Arthur Schweitzer, *Big Business in the Third Reich*, London, 1964, p. 317.
3   *Frankfurter Zeitung*, 3 January 1937.
4   League of Nations, *World Economic Survey, 1939–1941*, Geneva, 1941, p. 70.
5   *Landwirtschaftliche Statistik, 1939–1940*, Verwaltungsamt des Reichsbauernführers, p. 167.
6   *Neues Tagebuch*, 5 March 1938, p. 222.
7   Wallace R. Deuel, *People under Hitler*, Harcourt, Brace & World, New York, 1942, p. 314.
8   Hilde Oppenheimer-Blum, *The Standard of Living of German Labour under Nazi Rule*, New School of Social Research, New York, 1943, p. 52.
9   *Statistisches Handbuch für Deutschland, 1928–1944*, p. 501.
10 Wallace R. Deuel, *op. cit.*, p. 314.
11 *Landwirtschaftliche Statistik*, p. 67.
12 League of Nations, *World Economic Survey, 1939–41*, Geneva, p. 62.
13 Jürgen Kuczinsky, *Die Geschichte der Arbeiter in Deutschland, 1933–46*, East Berlin, 1947, p. 103.
14 *Statistisches Handbuch für Deutschland, 1928–1944*, p. 501.
15 *Frankfurter Zeitung*, 21 January 1937.
16 *Landwirtschaftliche Statistik*, p. 167.
17 Jürgen Kuczinsky, *op. cit.*, p. 100.
18 Wallace R. Deuel, *op. cit.*, p. 314.
19 *Landwirtschaftliche Statistik*, p. 167 and *Statistisches Handbuch, 1928–1944*, p. 501.
20 Hilde Oppenheimer-Blum, *op. cit.*, p. 54.
21 *Schwarzes Korps*, 6 July 1939.
22 Theodor Bühler, *Deutsche Sozialwirtschaft*, Kohlhammervergag, Stuttgart, 1943, p. 47.
23 Wallace R. Deuel, *op. cit.*, p. 314.
24 Jürgen Kuczinsky, *op. cit.*, p. 100.
25 Max Seydewitz, *Civil Life in Wartime Germany*, New York, 1945, p. 223.
26 *Völkischer Beobachter*, 11 March 1939.
27 Wiener Library, Eye-witness accounts, File P, IIIa, 526.
28 Hans Georg von Studnitz, *Als Berlin brannte*, Stuttgart, 1963, p. 253.
29 *Landwirtschaftliche Statistik*, p. 167 and *Statistisches Handbuch, 1928–1944*, p. 501.
30 *Strassburger Neueste Nachrichten*, 28 September 1941
31 Bundesarchiv Koblenz, File R 58/192 20 January 1944.
32 *Frankfurter Zeitung*, 16 February 1938.

33 *Der Angriff*, Berlin, 6 October 1937.
34 Wallace R. Deuel, *op. cit.*, p. 150.
35 *Schwarzes Korps*, 22 September 1938.
36 *Frankfurter Zeitung*, 16 May 1937.
37 C. W. Guillebaud, *Germany's Economic Recovery*, p. 178.
38 *Wirtschaft und Statistik*, 1944, No. 7, p. 111.
39 *Neues Tagebuch*, 1 April 1938.
40 Sarah Mabel Collins, *The Alien Years*, London, 1949, p. 19.
41 Wallace R. Deuel, *op. cit.*, p. 150.
42 *Frankfurter Zeitung*, 1 January 1938.
43 Bundesarchiv Koblenz, File R 43 II/558 – 'Arbeitswissenschaftliches Institut der DAF, Beiträge zur Statistik der Lebenshaltung des deutschen Arbeiter'.
44 Wallace R. Deuel, *op. cit.*, p. 314.
45 League of Nations, *World Economic Survey, 1939–41*, Geneva, 1941, p. 67.
46 Elizabeth Hoeniberg, *Thy People, My People*, London, 1950, p. 20.
47 Max Seydewitz, *op. cit.*, p. 117.
48 Jürgen Kuczinsky, *op. cit.*, p. 250.
49 Wiener Library, Eye-witness account, File P IIIa 526.
50 Hilde Oppenheimer-Blum, *op. cit.*, p. 56.
51 Max Seydewitz, *op. cit.*, p. 187.
52 Hilde Oppenheimer-Blum, *op. cit.*, p. 56.
53 Wiener Library, Eye-witness account, File P IIIa 615.
54 Bundesarchiv Koblenz, File R 58, No. 77, 15 April 1940.
55 *Frankfurter Zeitung*, 26 February 1938.
56 *Bilanz des Zweiten Weltkrieges*, Gerhard Stallin Verlag, Oldenburg, 1958, p. 337.
57 Bundesarchiv Koblenz, File R 58/192 20 January 1944.
58 Bundesarchiv Koblenz, File R 58/172, No. 284.
59 Hans Georg von Studnitz, *op. cit.*, p. 253.
60 *ibid.*
61 League of Nations, *Statistical Year Book, 1938–9*, Geneva, 1939, p. 197.
62 *Sonderbeilage zum Wochenbericht des Institutes für Konjunkturorschung*, No. 19, 13 May 1936.
63 *ibid.*
64 Theodor Bühler, *op. cit.*, p. 135.
65 David Schoenbaum, *op. cit.*, p. 153.
66 *Frankfurter Zeitung*, 7 December 1937.
67 *Wochenbericht des Institutes für Konjunkturforschung*, 2 March 1938.
68 *Frankfurter Zeitung*, 28 June 1939.
69 Theodor Bühler, *op. cit.*, p. 138.
70 *ibid.*
71 Hilde Oppenheimer-Blum, *op. cit.*, p. 49.
72 Theodor Bühler, *op. cit.*, p. 144.
73 Bundesarchiv Koblenz, File R 43/II–558.
74 Jürgen Kuczinsky, *op. cit.*, p. 211.
75 Bundesarchiv Koblenz, R 58/184 23 May 1940.
76 Max Seydewitz, *op. cit.*, p. 120.
77 Max Seydewitz, *op. cit.*, p. 308.
78 Helmut Lehmann Haupt, *Art under Dictatorship*, Oxford University Press, London, 1954, p. 119.

1 Foreign Office and Ministry of Economic Warfare, *The Nazi System of Medicine and Public Health Organization*, London, 1944, Chapter X, p. 255 (henceforth Chapter X).
2 *ibid.*, p. 256.
3 *Klinische Wochenshcrift*, 7 August 1943.
4 *Deutsches Ärzeteblatt*, 24 October 1936.
5 *ibid.*
6 Chapter X, p. 249.
7 *Frankfurter Zeitung*, 18 March 1937.
8 Chapter X, p. 246.
9 *Schwarzes Korps*, 27 July 1939.
10 Chapter X, p. 246.
11 *Der Öffenliche Gesundheitsdienst*, vol. IV, issue 15, 1938, p. 435.
12 *Frankfurter Zeitung*, 16 July 1939.
13 *Hamburger Fremdenblatt*, 24 July 1944.
14 *Frankfurter Zeitung*, 30 July 1938.
15 *ibid.*, 24 July 1937.
16 *ibid.*, 6 May 1939.
17 *ibid.*, 5 July 1938.
18 *ibid.*, 27 May 1937.
19 Erich Kuby, *Das ist des Deutschen Vaterland*, Stuttgart, 1957, p. 457.
20 *Bericht über das Bayrische Gesundheitswesen, 1939*, Munich, 1941, pp. 55 and 86.
21 *Statistisches Handbuch für Deutschland, 1928–1944*, p. 61.
22 *ibid.*
23 *Das Bayrische Gesundheitswesen*, pp. 21 and 51.
24 Wallace R. Deuel, *People under Hitler*, New York, 1942, p. 220.
25 *Neue Weltbühne*, 30 April 1936.
26 Chapter X, p. 244.
27 *Klinische Wochenschrift*, Berlin, 24 October 1942.
28 *Chemnitzer Neue Nachrichten*, 25 November 1941.
29 Theodor Bühler, *Deutsche Sozialwirtschaft*, Kohlhammer, Stuttgart, 1943, p. 47.
30 *Frankfurter Zeitung*, 1 February 1938.
31 Chapter X, p. 233.
32 *Neues Tagebuch*, 4 July 1936.
33 *The Listener*, 10 November 1937.
34 *Ärzteblatt Berlin*, 12 February 1938.
35 Wallace Deuel, *op. cit.*, p. 21.
36 *Völkischer Beobachter*, 2 February 1935.
37 *Statisches Handbuch für Deutschland, 1928–1944*, p. 609.
38 *Amtliche Nachrichten für die Reichsversicherung*, 1937, Beilage 12.
39 *Statistisches Handbuch*, p. 474.
40 Bundesarchiv Koblenz, File R41/282.
41 *Kölner Verwaltungsberichte.*
42 *Öffentlicher Gesundheitsdienst*, vol. 4, part 15, 1938, p. 472.
43 *Bericht über das Bayrische Gesundheitswesen*, Munich, 1941, p. 18.
44 Dr Conti, *Der Stand der Volksgesundheit*, 1943, p. 4, 'Aus den Handakten des Ministerialrates Dr Fabian'.
45 Bundesarchiv Koblenz, File R22/4003, Beitrag 30.
46 *ibid.*
47 Dr Conti, *op. cit.*, p. 4.

48 Dr Conti, *op. cit.*, p. 20.
49 Dr W. Klein, *Der Amtsarzt*, Jena 1943, p. 13.
50 *Schwarzes Korps*, 30 March 1944.
51 *Frankfurter Zeitung*, 28 April 1937.
52 Bundesarchiv Koblenz, File R58/158, 25 March 1941.
53 *ibid.*
54 *Schwarzes Korps*, 9 January 1941.
55 Dr Conti, *op. cit.*, p. 19.
56 *Arbeiterzeitung*, Schaffhausen, 18 November 1944.
57 *Stuttgarter N.S. Kurier*, 28 October 1941.
58 *Das Reich*, 13 September 1942.
59 Institut für Zeitgeschichte, File MA300, photoroll 2955 to 3098.
60 Dr Conti, *op. cit.*, p. 14.
61 Bundesarchiv Koblenz, R58/146, 13 December 1939.
62 *Manchester Guardian*, 19 May 1945.
63 Eugen Kogon, *Der SS Staat*, Europäische Verlagsanstalt, Frankfurt, 1959, p. 399.

16 The Family

1   Hossbach Memorandum in *Documents on German Foreign Policy 1918–45, Series D, Vol. I: From Neurath to Ribbentrop*, Washington, 1949, pp. 29–39.
2   Dr W. Klein, *Der Amtsarzt*, Gustav Fischer, Jena, 1943, p. 16.
3   *Gesetz zur Förderung der Eheschliessungen*, 5 July 1933 (*Neufassung 21 February 1935*).
4   Wallace R. Deuel, *People under Hitler*, Harcourt Brace, New York, 1942, pp. 242–6.
5   Madeleine Kent, *I Married a German*, Allen and Unwin, London, 1938, p. 323.
6   *Satzungen des Ehrenkreuzes der deutschen Mutter*, 16 December 1938, published in the *Reichsgesetzblatt* on 24 December 1938.
7   *Dokumente der deutschen Politik*, Band 6/I, p. 71, quoted in Joachim Fest, *Das Gesicht des Dritten Reiches*, Piper, Munich, 1963, p. 364.
8   *Völkischer Beobachter*, 24 December 1938.
9   *Schwarzes Korps*, 15 April 1937.
10 *ibid.*, 4 May 1939.
11 *Informationsdienst des Reichsministers der Justiz*, Berlin, June 1944, Bundesarchiv Koblenz, File R 22/4003, p. 12.
12 *Münchner Neuste Nachrichten*, 25 July 1940.
13 *Münchner Neuste Nachrichten*, 14 June 1935.
14 *Hamburger Fremdenblatt*, 5 December 1935.
15 *Schwarzes Korps*, 10 July 1935.
16 *ibid.*, 3 October 1935.
17 Dr Folbert, *Klinische Wochenschrift*, 1938, p. 1,446.
18 *Frankfurter Zeitung*, 19 May 1937, quoting a report from Saxony.
19 *Gesetz für Verhinderung des erbkranken Nachwuchses* of 14 July 1933, quoted in Franz Neumann, *Behemoth*, Oxford University Press, New York, 1942, p. 111.
20 *Frankfurter Zeitung*, 30 January 1937.
21 *ibid.*, 13 November 1938.
22 Dr W. Klein, *Der Amtsarzt*, Jena, 1943, pp. 14–21.
23 *Statistisches Handbuch für Deutschland 1928–44*, Munich, 1949, p. 634.
24 *ibid.*, p. 62.
25 W. C. Guillebaud, *The Social Policy of Nazi Germany*, London, 1941, p. 100.

26 Hans Stahlinger, 'Germany's Population Miracle', in *Social Research*, New York, May 1938.
27 Peter Heinz Seraphim, *Deutsche Wirtschafts- und Sozialgeschichte*, Theodor Gabler, 1962, p. 238.
28 Ilse Staff, *Justiz im Dritten Reich*, Fischer, Frankfurt a/M., 1964, p. 183.
29 *Frankfurter Zeitung*, 16 March 1937.
30 *Schwarzes Korps*, 4 November 1943.
31 Ilse Staff, *op. cit.*, p. 85.
32 *Schwarzes Korps*, 15 December 1938.
33 *Erlass des Reichsministeriums des Innern* of 27 December 1938, *Unterbringung von Kindern aus politisch unzuverlassigen Familien, Frankfurter Zeitung*, 5 January 1939.
34 Decision of the Landesgericht Torgau, quoted by Ilse Staff, *op. cit.*, p. 188.
35 *Times Educational Supplement* of 26 April 1941, quoting a judgement by a court at Wilster, Schleswig-Holstein, in January 1940.
36 Decision of the *Oberlandesgericht*, Munich, 3 December 1937, see *Frankfurter Zeitung* of 2 March 1938.
37 *Deutsches Ärzteblatt*, 12 December 1936, p. 1,230.
38 *Umdruck FAM 397/21*. cf. *Neues Tagebuch*, 16 October 1937, p. 990.
39 *Frankfurter Zeitung*, 7 July and 10 September 1937.
40 *Schwarzes Korps*, 6 January 1938.
41 *Juristische Wochenschrift*, 1937, p. 3,057.
42 *Neue Volkszeitung*, New York, 6 September 1941.
43 *Frankfurter Zeitung*, 14 December 1938.
44 *ibid.*, 26 March 1939.
45 *Neue Volkszeitung*, New York, 6 September 1941.
46 Felix Kersten, *Totenkopf und Treue*, Hamburg, 1952, p. 229.
47 Judy Barden, 'Freundin und Candy', in Arthur Settle's anthology, *Dast ist Germany*, Wolfgang Metzner, Frankfurt a/M., p. 149.
48 Felix Kersten, *op. cit.*, p. 230.
49 Louis Hagen, *Follow My Leader*, Allen Wingate, London, 1951, p. 265.
50 Interview with Fraulein Erna Hanfstängel in Munich, April 1967.
51 *Völkischer Beobachter*, 24 November 1934.
52 *Neues Volk*, Heft 5, May 1940.
53 *Himmler-Erlass* of 28 October 1939, quoted in Hans Jochen Gamm, *Der Braune Kult*, Rütten and Loening, Hamburg, p. 145.
54 Institut für Zeitgeschichte, Munich, File MA 293/0546.
55 Felix Kersten, *op. cit.*, p. 226.
56 *Rote Erde*, Dortmund, 23 March 1940.
57 *Schlesiger Tageszeitung*, 7 April 1940.
58 *Münchner Neuste Nachrichten*, 12 September 1941.
59 *Schwarzes Korps*, 9 September 1943.
60 The President of the Supreme Court, Berlin, to the Reich Ministry of Justice. Dispatch of 3 July 1944. Archives of the Institut für Zeitgeschichte, Munich, File MA 430/1.
61 *ibid.*, dispatch of 1 April 1944.
62 Ministerialrat (Senior Civil Servant) Helmut Stellricht, *Neue Erziehung*, Wilhelm Limpert, Berlin, 1942, pp. 125-7.
63 Amos Elon, *Journey through a Haunted Land*, Holt Rinehart and Winston, New York, 1967, p. 201.
64 *Ausgewählte Dokumente zur Geschichte des Nationalsozialismus*, edited by Dr H. A. Jakobsen and Dr W. Jochmann, Neue Gesellschaft, Bielefeld, 1960, and Felix Kersten, *op. cit.*, pp. 226-31.

17 Women

1   *Statistisches Handbuch für Deutschland 1928–1944*, Franz Ehrenwirt, Munich, 1949, p. 31.
2   Friede Wunderlich in *The American Scholar*, Camden, N.J., vol. 7, No. 1, Winter 1938.
3   Herman Glaser, *Spiesser-Ideologie*, Rohmbach, Freiburg, 1954, p. 171.
4   *Frankfurter Zeitung*, 4 February 1938.
5   Henry M. Pachter, 'National Socialist and Fascist Propaganda for the Conquest of Power', in the anthology *The Third Reich*, Weidenfeld and Nicolson, London, 1955, p. 720.
6   Joachim Fest, *Das Gesicht des Dritten Reichs*, Piper, 1963, p. 356.
7   *Adolf Hitler's Zweites Buch*, Stuttgart, 1961, pp. 198–200.
8   Herman Glaser, *op. cit.*, p. 184.
9   Joseph Goebbels, *Michael: Ein Deutsches Schicksal in Tagebuchblättern*, Franz Eher, Munich, 1934, p. 41.
10 Clifford Kirkpatrick, *Nazi Germany, its Women and Family Life*, Indianapolis and New York, 1938, p. 117.
11 Joseph Goebbels, 'Das Frauentum', in *Signale der Neuen Zeit*, Berlin, 1934¹ p. 118.
12 Werner Klose, *Generation in Gleichschritt*, Stalling, Oldenbourg, 1964, p. 177.
13 Kurt Rosten, *Das ABC des Nationalsozialismus*, fifth edn, Berlin, 1933, p. 198.
14 Gerhard Bry, *Wages in Germany*, Princeton, 1960, p. 246.
15 David Schoenbaum, *Hitler's Social Revolution*, London, 1967, p. 197.
16 *Westdeutscher Beobachter*, 21 June 1938.
17 G. W. Guillebaud, *Social Policy of Nazi Germany*, Cambridge University Press, 1941, p. 57.
18 David Schoenbaum, *op. cit.*, p. 195.
19 *Frankfurter Zeitung*, 20 April 1937.
20 *Berliner Tageblatt*, 3 June 1938.
21 *Schwarzes Korps*, 11 May 1939.
22 SD Reports of 26 May 1941, in Heinz Boberach, *Meldungen aus dem Reich*, Luchterhand, Neuwied, 1965, p. 189.
23 *Reichsgesetzblatt* I, p. 67.
24 *Deutsche Allgemeine Zeitung*, 31 May 1943, quoted in Max Seidewitz, *Civil Life in Wartime Germany*, The Viking Press, New York, 1945, p. 244.
25 SD Report of 4 February 1943, quoted by Heinz Boberach, *op. cit.*, p. 356.
26 Sarah Mabel Collins, *The Alien Years*, Hodder and Stoughton, London, 1949, p. 141.
27 SD Report of 7 March 1944, Institut für Zeitgeschichte, Archive, Munich, MA 442/2 1848–1503.
28 Max Seydewitz, *op. cit.*, p. 246.
29 *Der Vier-Jahres-Plan* Nr 3, 5 February 1940.
30 *Der Angriff*, 1 April 1942.
31 *ibid.*, 7 February 1940.
32 *Kölnische Zeitung*, 14 July 1942.
33 *Münchner Zeitung*, 17 January 1941, and *Bodensee Rundschau*, 19 November 1941.
34 Ruth Kohle-Irrgang, *Die Sendung der Frau in der Deutschen Geschichte*, Leipzig, 1940, p. 235.
35 *1937 Reichsparteitagbericht*, Munich, 1938, p. 235.
36 *Stuttgarter N. S. Kurier*, 15 February 1941.
37 Robert A. Brady, *The Spirit and Structure of German Fascism*, Viking Press, New York, 1937, p. 218.
38 David Schoenbaum, *op. cit.*, p. 191.

39 *Deutsche Frauen an Adolf Hitler*, Leipzig, 1934, third ed., p. 28.
40 *ibid.*, p. 57.
41 *ibid.*, p. 40. The authoresses of the excerpts cited were Irmgard Reichenau, Jella Erdmann and Leonora Kühn.
42 Alice Rilka in 'Arbeitseinsatz der Frauen', in *Frau am Werk*, issue of January 1938.
43 August Reber-Gruber, *Weibliche Erziehung im National-socialistischen Lehrerbund*, Leipzig Berlin, 1934, pp. 1–6.
44 David Schoenbaum, *op. cit.*, p. 191.
45 *Danziger Vorposten*, 3 September 1938.
46 *Frankfurter Zeitung*, 16 April 1936.
47 Clifford Kirkpatrick, *op. cit.*, p. 249, and *Frankfurter Zeitung*, 4 February 1938.
48 *Frankfurter Zeitung*, 27 July 1937.
49 *ibid.*, 16 July 1936.
50 *Morning Post*, 24 February 1937.
51 *Frankfurter Zeitung*, 3 July 1935.
52 Hermann Glaser, *op. cit.*, p. 171.
53 *Bucharester Tagblatt*, 5 September 1941.
54 *Deutsche Allgemeine Zeitung*, 26 September 1943.
55 Bundesarchiv Koblenz, R 43 II/443, 14 July 1939.
56 M. T. Ferting, *Die Frau in unserer Zeit*, Themis, Darmstadt, 1952, p. 53.
57 Wallace R. Deuel, *People under Hitler*, Harcourt Brace, New York, 1942, p. 161.
58 Interview with Herr Friedrich Luft, Berlin, April 1967.
59 Clifford Kirkpatrick, *op. cit.*, p. 105.
60 *Frankfurter Zeitung*, 11 August 1943.
61 Joachim Fest, *op. cit.*, p. 365.
62 H. Bretzlaw, *Arbeitsmaiden am Werk*, Leipzig, 1940, p. 7.
63 Wilfred von Ofen, *Mit Goebbels bis zum Ende*, Buenos Aires, 1949, p. 40.
64 *Sprachregelung* of 7 October 1940, Nr 138, signed Dr Kausch.
65 *Stuttgarter NS-Courier*, 1 October 1941.
66 *ibid.*, 11 August 1941.
67 *Hamburger Fremdenblatt*, 1 December 1941.
68 *Bodensee Rundschau*, 19 November 1941.
69 G. Wenzmer, 'Should Women be Allowed to Smoke?', *Hamburger Fremdenblatt*, 22 March 1944.
70 Louis P. Lochner, *Die Goebbels Tagebücher 1942–1943*, entry of 10 May 1943, Atlantis, Zurich, 1948, p. 335.
71 *ibid.*, entry of 13 March 1943, p. 270.
72 *Strasburger Neuste Nachrichten*, 31 March 1941.
73 Robert Birley, *Spectator*, 10 October 1969.
74 Herman Rauschnigg, *Gespräche*, New York, 1940, p. 240.

18 Youth

1 *Statistisches Handbuch für Deutschland 1928–1944*, Franz Ehrenwert, Munich, 1949, p. 843.
2 C. W. Guillebaud, *Social Policy of Nazi Germany*, Cambridge University Press, 1941, p. 76.
3 *ibid.*
4 A. Bremhorst and W. Bachman, *Ordnung des Berufseinsatzes*, Berlin/Leipzig, 1937, p. 13.

REFERENCES

5 David Schoenbaum, *Hitler's Social Revolution*, London, 1967, p. 100.
6 *Hamburger Fremdenblatt*, 26 February 1945.
7 David Schoenbaum, *op. cit.*, p. 100.
8 W. C. Guillebaud, *The Economic Recovery of Germany*, London 1939, p. 109.
9 Werner Klose, *Generation im Gleichschritt*, Stalling, Oldenburg, 1964, p. 100.
10 Artur Axmann, *Der Reichsberufswettkampf*, Berlin, 1938, p. 313.
11 Interview with Herr Lindler at Düsseldorf, May 1966.
12 *Frankfurter Zeitung*, 14 June 1939.
13 *ibid.*, 3 April 1938.
14 Bundesarchiv Koblenz, R II/234 B.
15 *Frankfurter Zeitung*, 11 November 1937, quoting Dr Rechenbach in *Das Junge Deutschland*.
16 *Statistisches Handbuch für Deutschland*, 1938.
17 Dr Ewald Hebeltreit of the Nazi Party's main office for health in *Deutsches Ärzteblatt*, January 1937, quoted in *Frankfurter Zeitung*, 23 January 1937.
18 *Bericht über das Bayerische Gesundheitswesen 1939*, vol. 58, Munich, 1941, p. 18.
19 *Neue Volkszeitung*, New York, 31 May 1941.
20 *Frankfurter Zeitung*, 5 July 1938, quoting Dozent Dr Joppich in the *Münchner medizinische Wochenschrift*.
21 Professor A. Blenke, *Münchner medizinische Wochenschrift*, 2 April 1937.
22 *Frankfurter Zeitung*, 27 May 1937.
23 *ibid.*, 6 November 1937.
24 *Neue Volkszeitung*, New York, 31 May 1941.
25 Jack Schiefer, *Tagebuch eines Wehrunwürdigen*, Grenzland, Aachen, 1947, p. 285.
26 Amos Elon, *Journey Through a Haunted Land*, New York, 1967, p. 201.
27 *Informationsdienst des Reichministers der Justiz*, Berlin, June 1944, p. 88. Bundesarchiv Koblenz, File R 22/4003.
28 *ibid.*
29 *Daily Telegraph*, 1 June 1936.
30 *Frankfurter Zeitung*, 17 August 1939.
31 *Völkischer Beobachter*, 21 March 1940.
32 *Kriminalität und Gefährdung der Jugend,* Jugendführung des Dritten Reiches, Berlin, Lagebericht bis zum 1. Januar 1940, p. 204.
33 Klaus Granzow, *Tagebuch eines Hitlerjungen 1943–1945*, Karl Schoenemann Verlag, Bremen, p. 46.
34 *Kriminalität und Gefährdung der Jugend*, p. 183.
35 *ibid.*
36 Walter Friedlander and Earl Dewey Myers, *Child Welfare in Germany Before and After Nazism*, University of Chicago Press, 1940, p. 13.
37 *ibid.*, p. 130.
38 *ibid.*, p. 132.
39 *ibid.*, p. 96.
40 *Schwarzes Korps*, 13 May 1937.
41 Arno Klönne, *Die HJ Generation*, Politische Studien, Heft 116, Isar Verlag, Munich, February 1959, p. 125.
42 *Frankfurter Zeitung*, 28 March 1937.
43 Werner Klose, *op. cit.*, p. 75.
44 *The Times*, 4 May 1934.
45 Louis Hagen, *Follow My Leader*, Allen Wingate, London, 1951, p. 78.
46 Arno Klonne, *Die Hitler Jugend*, Hanover/Frankfurt, 1956, p. 42.
47 Werner Klose, *op. cit.*, p. 132.

48 Wolfgang Dreffs, *Die Klirrende Kette*, Keppler-Verlag, Baden-Baden, 1947, p. 125.
49 Werner Klose, *op. cit.*, p. 92.
50 *ibid.*, p. 93.
51 *ibid.*, p. 94.
52 *ibid.*, p. 217.
53 Hans Jochen Gamm, *Führung und Verführung*, List, Munich, 1964, p. 339.
54 Werner Klose, *op. cit.*, p. 179.
55 *ibid.*, p. 61.
56 Bernhard Vollmer, *Volksopposition in Polizeistaat*, Deutsche Verlagsanstalt, Stuttgart, 1957, p. 133.
57 *Berliner Illustrierte Zeitung*, 16 May 1935, p. 714.
58 Hans von Wyl, *Ein Schweizer erlebt Deutschland*, Europa Verlag, Zurich, p. 255.
59 *Frankfurter Zeitung*, 2 February 1938.
60 *Statistisches Jahrbuch für Deutschland 1928–1945*, already cited.
61 *Die Deutsche Kampferin*, October 1938.
62 *Kriminalität und Gefährdung der Jugend*, already cited, p. 163.
63 *Völkischer Beobachter*, 10 February 1935.
64 *Neues Tagebuch*, 4 September 1937, p. 849.
65 *Frankfurter Zeitung*, 13 December 1938.
66 *Der Bund*, Berne, 22 April 1940.
67 Thilo Scheller, 'Wehrerziehung im Spiel' in the anthology *Erziehung zum Wehrwillen*, Rat, Stuttgart, 1937, p. 321.
68 *ibid.*
69 Professor Karl Haushofer in *Erziehung zum Wehrwillen*, p. 31, and Harry Griersdorf, *Der Kampf als Lebensgesetz, Reichsschulungsthema 1942–3*, Ether, Munich, p. 7.
70 Report on the Hitler Youth camp at Murnau, *Völkischer Beobachter*, 2 August 1934.
71 Werner Klose, *op. cit.*, p. 152.
72 *ibid.*, p. 222.
73 *Reichsgesetzblatt, 1939, I*, p. 2,000.

19 Education

1 Rolf Eilers, *Die nationalsozialistische Schulpolitik*, Westdeutscher Verlag, Cologne/Opladen, 1963, p. 19.
2 *ibid.*
3 *ibid.*, p. 20.
4 *Frankfurter Zeitung*, 14 September 1939.
5 Rolf Eilers, *op. cit.*, p. 73.
6 Interview with Professor Zorn at Bonn University, May 1966.
7 *Frankfurter Zeitung*, 15 December 1937.
8 W. Friedlander and Earl Dewey Myers, *Child Welfare in Germany before and after Nazism*, University of Chicago Press, 1940, p. 227.
9 Rolf Eilers, *op. cit.*, p. 21.
10 Werner Klose, *Generation im Gleichschritt*, Stalling, Oldenburg, 1964, p. 113.
11 Ministry of Science, Education and Popular Instruction, *Erlass über Schülerauslese an den höheren Schulen*, 27 March 1935.
12 R. Benze, *Rasse und Schule*, Braunschweig, 1934, p. 17.
13 Louis Hagen, *Follow my Leader*, Allen Wingate, London, 1951, p. 261.
14 Dietrich Strothmann, *Nationalsozialistische Literaturpolitik*, H. Bouvier, Bonn, 1960, p. 153, and *Neue Weltbühne*, 14 December 1933, p. 1,571.

15 *Neue Weltbühne*, 14 December 1933, p. 1,571.
16 M. Staemler, *You and Your Life*, quoted by Werner Klose, *op. cit.*, p. 178.
17 Rolf Eilers, *op. cit.*, p. 23.
18 *ibid.*, p. 25.
19 *ibid.*, p. 86.
20 Milton Mayer, *They Thought They were Free*, Chicago University Press, 1955, p. 110.
21 Rolf Eilers, *op. cit.*, p. 122.
22 *Report on Public Morale* by District President of Regensburg, 11 November 1943. Archives of the Institut für Zeitgeschichte, Munich, File MA 300, Microcopies 2955/ 3098.
23 *Frankfurter Zeitung*, 28 February 1941.
24 *ibid.*, 27 October 1937.
25 *ibid.*, 23 March 1938.
26 Werner Klose, *op. cit.*, p. 194.
27 W. W. Schutz, *The German Home Front*, Gollancz, London, 1943, p. 186.
28 *Frankfurter Zeitung*, 26 September 1937.
29 *Reichsgesetzblatt I 1939*, p. 710, cf. Rolf Eilers, *op. cit.*, p. 123.
30 *Deutsche Volksschule*, publication of the NSLB, quoted in *Frankfurter Zeitung*, 25 July 1939.
31 Coln Hilpert, *Frankfurter Zeitung*, 16 January 1937.
32 *Meldungen aus dem Reich*, Bundesarchiv, Coblenz, File R 58, No. 73, 5 April 1940.
33 *Hamburger Fremdenblatt*, 11 February 1941.
34 *Meldungen aus dem Reich*, Bundesarchiv, Coblenz, File R58, No. 178, 29 December 1942.
35 *Schwarzes Korps*, 1 April 1937.
36 *Frankfurter Zeitung*, 20 June 1937.
37 *Meldungen aus dem Reich*, Bundesarchiv, Coblenz, File R 58/148, No. 55.
38 Frankfurter Zeitung, 10 May 1938.
39 *ibid.*, 28 July 1938.
40 *Schwarzes Korps*, 2 February 1939.
41 Stadtschulrat Dr Meinshausen, *Der NS Erzieher* (cf. *Frankfurter Zeitung*, 28 October 1937).
42 *Frankfurter Zeitung*, 10 May 1938.
43 Hans Jochen Gamm, *Führung und Verführung*, 1964, p. 204.
44 Rolf Eilers, *op. cit.*, p. 9.
45 *Meldungen aus dem Reich*, Bundesarchiv, Coblenz, R 58/I 84, 3 May 1940.
46 *ibid.*, R58/157, No. 161, 10 February 1941.
47 Rolf Dahrendorf, *Gesellschaft und Demokratie in Deutschland*, Piper, Munich, 1965, p. 20.
48 Rolf Eilers, *op. cit.*, pp. 43–46.
49 Hans Jochen Gamm, *op. cit.*, p. 405.
50 Werner Klose, *op. cit.*, p. 204.
51 Heissmeyer to Himmler, 6 July 1942. Berlin Document Centre, Adolf Hitler Schools 270.II.
52 Rolf Eilers, *op. cit.*, p. 32.
53 David Schoenbaum, *Hitler's Social Revolution*, Weidenfeld and Nicolson, London, 1967, p. 278.
54 *Schwarzes Korps*, 3 August 1939.
55 Karl Neumann, *Other Men's Graves*, Weidenfeld and Nicolson, London, 1958, p. 48.
56 Hans Jochen Gamm, *op. cit.*, p. 380.
57 Dr Neusüss Hunkel, *Die SS*, Norddeutsche Verlagsanstalt, Hanover and Frankfurt, 1956, p. 39.

58 Dietrich Orlor, 'Die Adolf Hitler Schulen', *Vierteljahreshefte für Zeitgeschichte*, 3rd issue, 1965, p. 272.
59 *Völkischer Beobachter*, 5 November 1939.
60 R. Benze, 'Deutsche Schulerziehung', *Jahrbuch des deutschen Zentralen Instituts für Erziehung und Unterricht*, Berlin, 1943, p. 131.
61 *Völkischer Beobachter*, 25 April 1936.
62 Ernest Hearst, 'Finishing Schools for Nazi Leaders', *Wiener Library Bulletin*, July 1965.
63 Karl Neumann, *op. cit.*, p. 64.
64 David Schoenbaum, *op. cit.*, p. 283.
65 *ibid.*, p. 283.
66 Interview with Herr Mohl in Cologne, June 1966.
67 *Wiener Beobachter*, 9 April 1942.
68 Rolf Eilers, *op. cit.*, p. 38, and Walter Friedlander and Earl Dewey Myers, *op. cit.*, p. 212.
69 *Statistische Monatshefte* of the SS Erfassungsamt for November, National Archives, Microcopy T 74, Roll 15, Frame 3868/28.
70 *Schwarzes Korps*, 18 May 1939, on the tenth anniversary of the foundation of the NSLB.
71 *Westdeutscher Beobachter*, 28 January 1938.
72 *Münchner Neueste Nachrichten*, 15 August 1938.
73 David Schoenbaum, *op. cit.*, p. 276.
74 *Meldungen aus dem Reich*, Bundesarchiv, Coblenz, File R 58/184, 23 May 1940.
75 *Frankfurter Zeitung*, 25 August 1938.
76 Interview with Professor Zorn, University of Bonn, May 1966.
77 *Frankfurter Zeitung*, 5 March 1935.
78 *ibid.*, 23 June 1938.
79 *Hamburger Fremdenblatt*, 26 June 1941.

20 The Universities

1   Hellmut Kuhn and others, *Die deutsche Universität im Dritten Reich*, Piper, Munich, 1966, p. 26.
2   *ibid.*, p. 29.
3   Amos Elon, *Journey Through a Haunted Land*, Holt Rinehart and Winston, New York, 1967, p. 217.
4   Ferdinand Friedensburg, *Die Weimarer Republik*, Norddeutsche Verlagsanstalt, Hanover, 1957, p. 346
5   Helmut Kuhn, *op. cit.*, p. 41.
6   George L. Mosse, *The Crisis o German Ideology*, Weidenfeld and Nicolson, London, 1966, p. 271.
7   Hellmut Kuhn, *op. cit.*, p. 77.
8   *ibid.*, p. 83.
9   *ibid.*, p. 30.
10 Joachim Fest, *Das Gesicht des Dritten Reiches*, Piper, Munich, 1963, p. 343.
11 Walter Frank, *Kampf um die Wissenschaft*, Hamburg, n.d., p. 31.
12 Amos Elon, *op. cit.*, p. 214.
13 Franz Schoenberner, *The Inside Story of an Outsider*, Macmillan, London, 1949, p. 18.
14 Herman Glaser, *Spiesser-Ideologie*, Rohmbach, Freiburg, 1964, p. 96.
15 Professor Reinhard Hoehn in 'Die Volksgemeinschaft als politisches Grundprinzip', *Süddeutsche Monatshefte*, 1934–5, p. 5.
16 Interview with Herr Ockhart, Bonn, May 1966.
17 Interview with Margaret Boveri, Berlin, April 1967.

18 *Frankfurter Zeitung*, 28 April 1933.
19 Amos Elon, *op. cit.*, p. 214.
20 Franz Schoenberner, *op. cit.*, p. 17.
21 cf. Sauerbruch's address to the Ninety-fourth Annual Congress of the Association of German Scientists and Doctors, Dresden, 21, September 1936, reported in *Neues Tagebuch*, 3 October 1936.
22 Interview with Klara Stumpf, Stuttgart-Degeloch, September 1965.
23 *Westdeutscher Beobachter*, 19 January 1934.
24 *Bilanz des Zweiten Weltkriegs*, already cited, p. 253.
25 Interview with Herr Ockhart, Bonn, May 1966.
26 Address at closing ceremony of First Tutorial Week of German Academy of Education, reported in *Morning Post* 30 July 1935.
27 *Schwarzes Korps*, 15 July 1937.
28 SD report, Bundesarchiv Koblenz, File R 58/177 No. 337, (23 November 1942).
29 Hans Rotfels, 'Geschichtswissenschaft in den dreissiger Jahren', in *Deutsches Geistesleben un Nationalsozialismus*, Tübingen, 1965, p. 100.
30 *ibid.*
31 *Die Zeit*, 4 December 1964.
32 *Vierteljahreshefte für Zeitgeschichte*, 2. Heft, 1967, p. 143.
33 Helmut Heiber, *Walter Frank*, Stuttgart, 1966, p. 1, 157.
34 'Universität im Dritten Reich', in *Politikon, Göttinger Studentenzeitung*, January 1965, p. 24.
35 *Neues Tagebuch*, 24 July 1937, p. 710, quoting E.Y. Hartshorne, *The German University and National Socialism*, Allen and Unwin, London, 1937.
36 *Berliner Tageblatt*, 26 February 1937, quoting an article in *Der junge Rechtswahrer*.
37 *ibid.*, 3 October 1936.
38 *Vierteljahreshefte für Zeitgeschichte*, April 1966, p. 199.
39 SD report on reaction of Goebbels's speech at the 1942 *Weimarer Dichtertreffung*, Bundesarchiv Koblenz, File R 58/327 (19 October 1942).
40 Bundesarchiv Koblenz, File R 58/177/337 (23 November 1942).
41 *Vierteljahreshefte für Zeitgeschichte*, April 1966, p. 199.
42 *Völkischer Beobachter*, 3 July 1934.
43 Hellmut Kuhn, *op. cit.*, p. 163.
44 David Schoenbaum, *op. cit.*, p. 263.
45 Hellmut Kuhn, *op. cit.*, p. 90.
46 Interview with Professor Raul, Munich, May 1966.
47 SD report, Bundesarchiv Koblenz, File R 58/173/300 (16 July 1942).
48 SD report Bundesarchiv Koblenz, File R 58/323 (5 October 1942).
49 *ibid.*
50 *Frankfurter Zeitung*, 25 March 1939.
51 SD report, Bundesarchiv Koblenz, File R 58/186 (1 July 1943).
52 *The Scotsman*, 13 October 1937.
53 *Sunday Times*, 27 March 1938.
54 Interview with Professor Raul, Munich, May 1966.
55 *Nationalzeitung*, Basle, 10 November 1937.
56 *Meldungen aus dem Reich*, Archive of the Institut für Zeitgeschichte, Munich, MA 261, Microroll 9522.
57 Ruth Andreas Friedrich, *Schauplatz Berlin*, Rheinsberg, 1962, p. 68.
58 Erich Ebermayer, *Denn Heute gehört uns Deutschland*, Paul Zsolnay, Vienna, 1959, p. 555.
59 Supreme Party Judge Buch in *Westdeutscher Beobachter*, 14 September 1938.

60 *Frankfurter Zeitung*, 20 June 1939.
61 *Politikon*, already cited, p. 15.
62 Horst Bernhardi, *Die Göttinger Burschenschaft 1933 bis 1945, Sonderdruck aus Darstellungen und Quellen zur Geschichte der deutschen Einheitsbewegung, in 19. und 20. Jahrhundert*, vol. I, p. 233.
63 *Grundsätze der Gemeinschaft Friesland*, quoted by Horst Bernhardi, *op. cit.*, p. 238.
64 SD report, Bundesarchiv Koblenz File R 58/188 (20 September 1943).
65 David Schoenbaum, *op. cit.*, p. 275.
66 *Frankfurter Zeitung*, 1 January 1937.
67 *ibid.*
68 *The Scotsman*, 13 October 1937.
69 David Schoenbaum, *op. cit.*, p. 274.
70 SD report, Bundesarchiv Koblenz, File R 58/158 No. 169 (10 March 1941).

21 Nazi Speech

1   Victor Klemperer, *Lingua Tertii Imperii*, Aufbau, Berlin, 1949, p. 216.
2   *ibid.*
3   *ibid.*, p. 21.
4   *Das Reich*, 13 November 1944.
5   Victor Klemperer, *op. cit.*, p. 242.
6   *ibid.*, p. 223.
7   *Frankfurter Zeitung*, 8 November 1937.
8   Hildegard von Kotze and Helmut Krausnick, *Es spricht der Führer*, Siegbert Mohn, Gütersloh, 1966, p. 43.
9   *Völkischer Beobachter*, 31 January 1935.
10 Herman Glaser, *Spiesser-Ideologie*, Rumbach, Freiburg, 1964, p. 86.
11 *Saar Volksstimme*, 10 October 1934.
12 *Neue Linie*, March, 1934.
13 Victor Klemperer, *op. cit.*, p. 165.
14 *ibid.*, p. 45.
15 *Neues Tagebuch*, 13 January 1934.
16 Victor Klemperer, *op. cit.*, p. 97.
17 Bernhard Volmer, *Volksopposition im Polizeistaat*, Deutsche Verlagsanstalt Stuttgart, 1957, p. 188.
18 Victor Klemperer, *op. cit.*, p. 230.
19 *ibid.*, p. 85.
20 *Die Deutsche Presse*, No. 21, 1940, quoted by Josef Wulf in *Literatur und Dichtung im Dritten Reich*, Siegbert Mohn, Gütersloh, 1963.
21 *Deutsche Freiheit*, 19 September 1934.
22 Walther Hagemann, *Publizistik im Dritten Reich*, Hansische Gilden, Hamburg, 1948, p. 78.
23 Victor Klemperer, *op. cit.*, p. 83.
24 Wallace R. Deuel, *People under Hitler*, Harcourt, Brace, New York, 1942, p. 14.
25 *Illustrierte Beobachter*, 5 February 1945.
26 Victor Klemperer, *op. cit.*, p. 37.
27 Bruno Bettelheim, *The Informed Heart*, London, 1961, p. 248.
28 Herman Langbein, *Wir haben es getan*, Europa, Vienna, 1964, p. 92.

22 Humour

1 Jean François Steiner, *Treblinka*, Weidenfeld and Nicolson, London, 1967, pp. 204 and 304.

23 Literature

1 Hans Grimm, *People without Space*, p. 1,110 of the unabridged Munich edition, 341st to 365th thousand.
2 *ibid.*, p. 1,073.
3 Francis L. Carson, 'A Note on Hans Grimm', in *Journal of Contemporary History*, London, 1967, vol. 2, No. 2, p. 221.
4 Dietrich Strothmann, *Nationalsozialistische Literaturpolitik*, Bonn, 1960, p. 377.
5 Borries von Münchhausen in *Die Neue Literatur*, 9 September 1934, p. 599.
6 Ernst Loewy, *Literature unterm Hakenkreuz*, Frankfurt am Main, 1966, p. 335.
7 *Kunst und Macht*, Deutsche Verlagsanstalt, 1934, p. 111.
8 Published by Paul Neff, 1934.
9 *Schwarzes Korps*, 26 September 1935.
10 Ernst Jünger, *Der Kampf als inneres Erlebnis*, Berlin, 1928, p. 53.
11 *ibid.*, p. 8.
12 Rudolf G. Binding, *Aufbruch* in *Stolz und Trauer*, Rutten and Loening, 1937, p. 12.
13 In Th. Echtermeyer, *Auswahl deutscher Gedichte*, Weidmann, Berlin, 1943, p. 576.
14 Hans Carossa, *Der Himmel dröhnt von Tod*. In Will Vesper's *Die Ernte der Gegenwart*, Ebenhausen bei München, 1943, p. 314.
15 Dietrich Strothmann, *op. cit.*, p. 148.
16 Ernst Loewy, *op. cit.*, p. 335.
17 Heinz Steguweit, *Petermann schliesst Frieden, oder das Gleichnis vom deutschen Opfer*, Hamburg, 1933, p. 15.
18 Heinrich Zillich, 'Den Deutschen von Gott gesandt', in A. F. Velmede, *Dem Führer*, p. 24. (*Tornisterschrift des O.K.W. 1941*, Heft 37).
19 Herbert Bohme, 'Die Ellwangerin', in *Der Kirchgang des Grosswendbauern*, Eher Verlag, 1936, p. 83.
20 *Die Neue Literatur*, Jahrgang 39, 1938, p. 379.
21 cf. Wilhelm Westecker in *Volksschicksal bestimmt den Wandel der Dichtung*, Berlin, 1941, p. 55.
22 Dietrich Strothmann, *op. cit.*, p. 348.
23 *ibid.*, p. 343.
24 J. Prestel, *Volkhafte Dichtung*, Leipzig, 1935, p. 10.
25 Bruno Brehm, *Im Grossdeutschen Reich*, Leipzig, 1940, p. 56.
26 Ludwig Friedrich Barthel, quoted by Ernst Loewy, *op. cit.*, p. 134.
27 Gottfried Benn, quoted by Ernst Loewy, *op. cit.*, p. 143.
28 Edwin Erich Dwinger, *Dichter und Krieger*, Hamburg, 1943, p. 13.
29 Felix Dahn's *Kampf um Rom*, published in the nineteenth century, had sold 615,000 copies by 1938 (Dietrich Strothmann, *op. cit.*, p. 398).
30 Josef Magnus Wehner, 'Vermachtnis von Langemarck', in Kurt Ziesel, *Krieg und Dichtung*, Leipzig, 1940, p. 339.
31 Wilhelm Schäfer, *Deutsche Reden*, Munich, 1933, p. 258.
32 Gerhard Schumann, *Ins Ungeheure steigt dio Kathedrole*, quoted by Ernst Loewp, *op. cit.*, p. 239.

33 Lydia Ganzer-Gottschwewsky, 'Ernst Wiechert und das Mutterrecht', in *Deutsches Volkstum*, 1. Halbjahr, Hamburg, 1936, p. 205.
34 Friedrich Georg Jünger, *Gedichte*, Berlin, 1934, pp. 60–63.
35 Friedrich Percival von Reck-Malleczewen, *Tagebuch eines Verzweifelten, Zeugnis einer inneren Emigration*, Stuttgart, 1966.
36 *Völkischer Beobachter*, Nr. 123, 3 April 1937.
37 Helmut Giese, *Das deutsche Wort*, January 1937
38 Joseph Goebbels, 'Rede zum Weimarer Dichtertreffen 1942', *Völkischer Beobachter*, Nr 285, 12 October 1942.
39 *Berliner Börsenblatt*, Nr 242, October 1938, p. 5,694.
40 E. Neugebauer, 'Schülerbücherei und Jugendschriftum im Dienst der Wehrerziehung', in *Jugendschriftwarte*, Heft 5/6, 1940, p. 45.
41 Hans Magnus Wehner, quoted in Dietrich Strothmann, *op. cit.*, p. 6.
42 Alfred Rosenberg, *Mythos des 20. Jahrhunderts*, Munich, 1938, p. 515.
43 Memorandum from the Reich Chancellery to the Ministry of Education, 12 December 1941 cf. Joseph Wulf, *Theater und Film im Dritten Reich*, Gütersloh, 1964, p. 188).
44 Dieter Strothmann, *op. cit.*, p. 407.
45 *ibid.*
46 *ibid.*
47 *ibid.*
48 *ibid.*, p. 410
49 *Berliner Illustrierte Nachtausgabe*, 26 June 1944.
50 *Neuer Tag*, 20 August 1944.
51 *Hamburger Fremdenblatt*, 14 June 1941.
52 *Bücher Korrespondent*, No. 3, tenth series, 1943.
53 *Weltliteratur*, No. 1, 1941, p. 25.
54 Dieter Strothmann, *op. cit.*, p. 140.
55 *Der Angriff*, 1 November 1938.
56 Dieter Strothmann, *op. cit.*, p. 26.
57 *ibid.*, p. 383.

24 *The Theatre*

1 David Thompson, 'Culture Under the National Socialists', in *Foreign Affairs*, vol. XIV, no. 3, April 1936.
2 *Krakauer Zeitung*, 20 November 1942.
3 *Völkischer Beobachter*, 20 June 1934.
4 Wolf Braumüller in *Deutsche Bühnenkorrespondenz*, 20 July 1935, quoted in Josef Wulf, *Theater und Film im Dritten Reich*, Siegbert Mohn, Gütersloh, 1964, p. 170.
5 *Frankfurter Zeitung*, 22 February 1937.
6 *Morning Post*, 30 January 1935.
7 *Frankfurter Zeitung*, 9 March 1935.
8 Mary Seton in *Drama*, first issue, 1937.
9 *Danziger Vorposten*, 6 May 1936.
10 *Hakenkreuz Banner*, 27 May 1937.

REFERENCES

11 Friedrich Griese, *Mensch aus Erde gemacht*, Theater-Verlag, Langen/Müller, 1933, p. 35.
12 *Der Angriff*, Berlin, 19 December 1931.
13 *Hakenkreuz Banner*, Mannheim, 9 October 1937.
14 *Deutsche Theaterzeitung*, 21 January 1941.
15 Kurt Längenbeck in *Völkischer Beobachter*, 31 December 1935.
16 *Wille und Macht*, quoted in *Frankfurter Zeitung*, 2 April 1937.
17 Interview with Friedrich Luft, Berlin, April 1967.
18 *Prager Presse*, 11 April 1937.
19 *Schwarzes Korps*, 15 March 1935.
20 *Morning Post*, reporting the revue *Freut Euch des Lebens* at the Theater des Volks, 4 May 1936.
21 *Frankfurter Zeitung*, reporting on *Die Streusandbüchse*, 19 January 1939.
22 Interview with Kurt Riess in *Sie und Er*, 19 April 1946.
23 Josef Wulf, *op. cit.*, p. 26.
24 Kurt Riess, *Gustav Gründgens*, Hoffmann, Hamburg, 1965, p. 138.
25 Memo from Dr Stuckart dated 12 January 1934, in Josef Wulf, *op. cit.*, p. 60.
26 *Der Märkische Adler*, 23 November 1934.
27 *Frankfurter Zeitung*, 21 February 1937.
28 *St Galler Tagblatt*, 24 March 1945.
29 Lilian T. Maurer, 'The Totalitarian Theatre', in *Drama*, January 1936.
30 *Hamburger Fremdenblatt*, 6 August 1942.
31 Josef Wulf, *op. cit.*, p. 192.

25 The Cinema

1 Erich Wollenberg, *Fifty Years of German Film*, London, 1948, p. 38.
2 *Neue Weltbühne*, 18 May 1939.
3 Bundesarchiv Koblenz, File R 58, No. 79. 19 April 1940.
4 *Daily Telegraph*, 25 June 1934.
5 *Völkischer Beobachter*, 16 March 1934.
6 *Frankfurter Zeitung*, 22 July 1934.
7 Louis P. Lochner, *Goebbels Tagebücher 1942–1943*, Zurich, 1948, p. 213.
8 *Film Kurier*, second issue, 1965, p. 647.
9 Bundesarchiv Koblenz, File R 58/69, 15 January 1942.
10 *Ibid.* File R 58/79, 19 April 1940.
11 *Deutsche Allgemeine Zeitung*, 5 August 1937.
12 *Neues Tagebuch*, 23 June 1934, p. 598.
13 *Schwarzes Korps*, 22 December 1938.
14 Reichsfilmdramaturg Deinandowsky in *Völkischer Beobachter*, quoted in *Frankfurter Zeitung*, 4 February 1939.
15 Hermann Stresau, *Von Jahr zu Jahr*, Minerva, Berlin, 1948, p. 278.

26 Press and Radio

1   *1932 Handbuch der deutschen Tagespresse.*
2   Oran J. Hale, *The Captive Press in the Third Reich*, Princeton University Press, 1964, p. 144.
3   *Deutsche Presse*, 17 February 1934, p. 74.
4   Oron J. Hale, *op. cit.*, p. 31.
5   Joseph Goebbels, *Kampf um Berlin*, Berlin, 1934, p. 18.
6   *Völkischer Beobachter*, 4 June 1926.
7   *Der Spiegel*, 3 April 1967, p. 54.
8   *ibid.*, p. 52.
9   Oron J. Hale, *op. cit.*, p. 31.
10   *Der Spiegel*, 3 April 1967, p. 58.
11   Report on the suicide of the Social Democrat parliamentarian Ludwig Marrun, in *Neues Tagebuch*, 6 April 1934, p. 319.
12   Margaret Boveri, *Wir Lügen Alle*, Walther, Olten, 1965, p. 265.
13   *Berliner Tageblatt*, 28 August 1937.
14   Entry in Goebbels's diary, 14 April 1943, quoted in *Der Spiegel*, 3 April 1967, p. 52.
15   Josef Wulf, *Presse und Film im Dritten Reich*, Siegbert Mohn, 1964, pp. 94–9.
16   Interview, Herr Wilhelm Lange, Bad Godesburg, May 1966.
17   Margaret Boveri, *op. cit.*, p. 558.
18   *Frankfurter Zeitung*, 13 October 1934.
19   Herman Glaser, *Spiesser-Ideologie*, Ruhmbach Verlag, Freiburg, 1964, p. 31.
20   *Die Zeitungssprache*, inaugural dissertation, Franz Kiener, Philosophische Fakultät, Munich, 1937, p. 119.
21   Sprachregelung, 9 January 1940.
22   Interview with Margaret Boveri, Berlin, April 1967.
23   *Neues Tagebuch*, 31 March 1934, p. 297.
24   Josef Wulf, *op. cit.*, p. 252.
25   *Der Stürmer*, no. 41, 1933.
26   Oron J. Hale, *op. cit.*, p. 146.
27   *ibid.*, p. 276.
28   *ibid.*, p. 278.
29   *Völkischer Beobachter*, 12 December 1935.
30   Margaret Boveri, *op. cit.*, p. 558.
31   *Der Spiegel*, 3 April 1967, p. 58.
32   *Hamburger Fremdenblatt*, 6 August 1942.
33   Ernest K. Bramstead, *Goebbels and National Socialist Propaganda 1925–1945*, Cresset Press, London, 1965, p. 74.
34   Z. A. B. Zeman, *Nazi Propaganda*, Oxford University Press, 1964, p. 86.
35   Ernest K. Branstead, *op. cit.*, p. 75.
36   Ernst Kris and Hans Speier, *German Radio Propaganda*, Oxford University Press, 1944, p. 58.
37   Hans Joachim Weinbrenner, *Handbuch des Deutschen Rundfunks*, Kurt Vowinckel Verlag, Neckargemünd, 1938, p. 292.
38   *ibid.*
39   Ernst Kris and Hans Speier, *op. cit.*, p. 52.
40   Hans Otto Fincke, Intendant at Frankfurt, quoted in Hans Joachim Weinbrenner, *op. cit.*, p. 49.
41   Josef Wulf, *op. cit.*, p. 346.
42   *ibid.*, p. 338.

43 *ibid.*
44 BBC, *Nazi Wireless at War; I: The German Home Service*, Monitoring Service, July 1941, p. 35.
45 *ibid.*, p. 39.

27 Music

1 Erwin Kroll, 'Verbotene Musik', *Vierteljahreshefte für Zeitgeschichte, III. Heft*, July 1959, p. 312.
2 *Frankische Tageszeitung*, 20 August 1938.
3 *Völkischer Beobachter*, 3 February 1935.
4 R. Zimmermann, 'Dur oder Moll', in *Die Sonne*, No. 10. 1937.
5 E. Josefsky, 'Musik', in *Rassenpolitische Unterrichtspraxis*, ed. Dobers Higelke, Julius Klinkhart, Leipzig, 1938, p. 308.
6 *Frankfurter Zeitung*, 17 July 1936.
7 *Die schöne Frau*, Bielefeld, quoted in *Neues Tagebuch*, 1934, p. 1,613.
8 *Schwarzes Korps*, 25 November 1937.
9 Erwin Kroll, *op. cit.*, p. 311.
10 *ibid.*
11 *National Zeitung*, Essen, 15 June 1937.
12 Geoffrey Skelton, *Wagner at Bayreuth*, Barrie and Rockcliff, London, 1965, p. 144.
13 *Morning Post*, 22 March 1937.
14 Peter Rave, *Die Musik im Dritten Reich*, Gustav Bosse, Regensburg, 1934, p. 12.
15 *Völkischer Beobachter*, 1 July 1937.
16 *Frankfurter Zeitung*, 25 May 1938.
17 *ibid.*, 25 February 1938.
18 Peter Rave, *op. cit.*, pp. 43, 45.
19 *Deutsche Allgemeine Zeitung*, 15 February 1939, reporting the fourth National Musical Gatherings of the Hitler Youth at Leipzig.
20 Goebbels's address to the Reich Music Festival at Düsseldorf, reported in the *Frankfurter Zeitung*, 30 May 1938.
21 *ibid.*
22 *Hakenkreuz Banner*, 6 July 1938.
23 *Frankfurter Zeitung*, 20 December 1938.
24 'Reichsmusikkammerrichtlinien für Werk- und Werkscharkapeller', *Frankfurter Zeitung*, 26 May 1935.
25 SD Report, Bundesarchiv Koblenz, File R 58/187 (19 August 1943).
26 Josef Wulf, *Presse und Funk im Dritten Reich*, Siegbert Mohn, Gütersloh, 1964, p. 379.
27 *Manchester Guardian*, 14 January 1935.
28 *ibid.*, 9 March 1935.
29 *Der SA-Mann*, 18 September 1937.
30 *Frankfurter Zeitung*, 26 October 1934, 'Richtlinien für den deutschen Gesellschaftsanz', worked out by the '*Reichsfachschaftstanzlehrer der NSDAP, Leipzig*'.
31 *Frankfurter Zeitung*, 22 October 1937, quoting Karl Heiding of the Cultural Office of the Hitler Youth Leadership.
32 *Neue Weltbühne*, 23 April 1936.
33 *Börsenzeitung*, 2 February 1935.
34 *Daily Mirror*, 13 March 1937.

28 Art

1   Franz Roh, *Entartete Kunst*, Fackelträger, Hanover, 1962, p. 5.
2   Hildegard Brenner, *Die Kunstpolitik des Nationalsożialismus*, Rowohlt, Hamburg, 1963, p. 12.
3   Paul Ortwin Rave, *Kunstdiktatur im Dritten Reich*, Gebrüder Mann, Hamburg, 1947, p. 14.
4   Hildegard Brenner, *op. cit.*, p. 17.
5   Rudolf Schroeder, *Modern Art in the Third Reich*, Dokumente, Offenburg, 1952, p. 40.
6   *ibid.*
7   Paul Ortwin Rave, *op. cit.*, p. 13.
8   *ibid.*, p. 23.
9   Hermann Glaser, *Spiesser-Ideologie*, Rohmbach, Freiburg, 1964, p. 38.
10 Paul Ortwin Rave, *op. cit.*, p. 50.
11 Helmut Lehmann Haupt, *Art under a Dictatorship*, Oxford University Press, 1954, p. 81.
12 Karl Heinz Schmeer, *Die Regie des öffentlichen Lebens im Dritten Reich*, Paul, München, 1956, p. 109.
13 *Berliner Illustrierte Zeitung*, 27 February 1937.
14 Helmut Lehmann Haupt, *op. cit.*, p. 104.
15 Georg Hellach, 'Architektur und bildende Kunst als Mittel der NS-Propaganda', in *Publizistik*, fifth series, 1960, p. 81.
16 *Kölnische Zeitung*, 17 July 1938.
17 *Die Welt*, 3 November 1962.
18 *Frankfurter Zeitung*, 23 July 1939.
19 *Simplicissimus*, 25 February 1940.
20 S D Reports, Bundesarchiv Koblenz, File R 58/153, No. 116 (19 August 1940).
21 Georg Hellach, *op. cit.*, p. 79.
22 Helmut Lehmann Haupt, *op. cit.*, p. 125.
23 *ibid.*, p. 122.
24 *ibid.*, p. 117.
25 *Das Bauen im neuen Reich*, vol. II, p. 7, quoted in Helmut Lehmann Haupt, *op. cit.*, p 112.
26 *Deutsche Allgemeine Zeitung*, 14 March 1943.
27 Helmut Lehmann Haupt, *op. cit.*, p. 100.
28 Wolfgang Drews, *Die klirrende Kette*, Keppler, Baden-Baden, 1947, p. 68.
29 Speech of 6 October 1941, quoted in Hermann Stresau, *Von Jahr zu Jahr*, Minerva, Berlin, 1948, p. 268.
30 Landeskulturwalt Brouwers, quoted in the *Frankfurter Zeitung*, 8 October 1937.
31 Interview with Frau Gutbrot-Baumeister, Cologne, April 1967.
32 *ibid.*

29 Religion

1   Max Geiger, *Der Deutsche Kirchenkampf, 1933–1945*, Zürich, 1965, p. 15.
2   Klaus Scholder, 'Die evangelische Kirche und das Jahr 1933' in *Geschichte in Wissenschaft und Unterricht*, p. 700, November 1965.
3   Werner Mosse, *Entscheidungsjahr 1932*, Tübingen, 1965, p. 255.
4   Klaus Scholder, *op. cit.*, p. 700.
5   Günter Levy, *The Catholic Church in Nazi Germany*, New York, 1964, p. 5.
6   Kurt F. Reinhardt, *Germany, 2000 Years*, New York, 1961, p. 706.

7   Günter Levy, *op. cit.*, p. 271.
8   Dietrich Bronder, *Bevor Hitler kam*, Hanover, 1964, p. 277.
9   Dietrich Bronder, *op. cit.*, p. 276.
10 Günter Levy, *op. cit.*, p. 43.
11 *ibid.*, p. 43.
12 *ibid.*, p. 45.
13 Karl Adam of Tübingen in 'Deutsches Volkstum und Katholisches Christentum', *Theologische Quartalschrift 1933*, p. 59, quoted by Günter Levy, *op. cit.*, p.108.
14 *Jewish Chronicle*, 3 February 1967.
15 Ernst Niekisch, *Das Reich der niedern Dämone*, Hamburg, 1953, p. 229.
16 Max Geiger. *op. cit.*, p. 23.
17 *ibid.*, p. 35.
18 *ibid.*, p. 38.
19 *ibid.*, p. 35.
20 Bernhard Vollmer, *Volksopposition im Polizeistaat*, Stuttgart, 1957, p. 144.
21 Günter Levy, *op. cit.*, p. 151.
22 *ibid.*, p. 153.
23 Bernhard Vollmer, *op. cit.*, p. 205.
24 Joseph Wolf, *Theater und Film im Dritten Reich*, Gütersloh, 1964, p. 176.
25 *ibid*, Dokument PS 3751.
26 Günter Levy, *op. cit.*, p. 157.
27 *ibid.*, p. 131.
28 Interview with Dr Maurer of the Bavarian Ministry of Social Welfare in Munich, May 1967.
29 Walter Hagemann, *Publizistik im Dritten Reich*, Hamburg, 1948, p. 344.
30 *ibid.*
31 Johann Neuhäusler, *Kreuz und Hakenkreuz*, Munich, 1946, Vol. II, pp. 104 9.
32 Günter Levy, *op cit.*, p 174.
33 *ibid.*, p. 172.
34 *ibid.*, p. 227.
35 *ibid.*, p. 276.
36 *ibid.*, p. 281
37 *Statistisches Jahrbuch für Deutschland, 1939*, p. 29.
38 Kurt F. Reinhardt, *op. cit.*, p. 702.
39 *Kölnische Zeitung*, 24 July 1934.
40 *Berliner Tageblatt*, 11 October 1935.
41 Louis Hagen, *Follow My Leader*, London, 1951, p. 272.
42 *Gothaer Beobachter*, 9 November 1935.
43 Günter Levy, *op. cit.*, p. 313.
44 *Salzburger Chronik*, 30 April 1937.
45 Heinrich Hermelink, *Kirche im Kampf*, Rainer Wunderlich, Tübingen, 1950, p. 348.
46 *ibid.*, p. 449.
47 *ibid.*, pp. 568/9.
48 *ibid.*, p. 628.
49 Heinz Boberach, *Meldungen aus dem Reich*, Luchterhandverlag, Neuwied–Berlin, 1965, No. 267, dated 12 March 1942.
50 Günter Levy, *op. cit.*, p. 131.
51 Bundesarchiv Koblenz, file R 58/78, 17 April 1940.
52 Heinrich Hermelink, *op, cit.*, p. 688.
53 Günter Levy, *op. cit.*, p. 292.
54 *Martinus Blatt*, Nr 38, 17 September 1939.

55 *ibid.*, p. 311.
56 *ibid.*, p. 234.
57 *ibid.*, p. 231.
58 *ibid.*, p. 146.
59 Heinrich Hermelink, *op. cit.*, p. 506.
60 *ibid.*, p. 225.
61 *ibid.*, p. 264.
62 *ibid.*, p. 266.
63 *ibid.*, p. 234.
64 Amos Elon, *Journey Through a Haunted Land*, New York, 1967, p. 11.
65 Bundesarchiv Koblenz, file R 58/182, 22 April 1943.
66 Heinrich Hermelink, *op. cit.*, p. 575.
67 *ibid.*, p. 59.
68 *ibid.*, p. 678.
69 *ibid.*, p. 649.
70 H. D. Leuner, *When Compassion was a Crime*, Oswald Wolf, London, 1966, p. 134.
71 Dietrich Bronder, *op. cit.*, p. 34.

30 The Jews

1 Walter Gross, '*Das politische Schicksal der deutschen Juden in der Weimarer Republik*,' in *Zwei Welten*, Bitaon, Tel Aviv, 1962, pp. 545–7.
2 Wallace R. Deuel, *People Under Hitler*, Harcourt Brace, New York, 1942, p. 189, and the chapter 'Die demographische und wirtschaftliche Struktur der Juden' by Ezra Ben Natan, in *Entscheidungsjahr 1932*, edited by Werner E. Mosse, Mohr, Tübingen, 1965, pp. 87–131.
3 Konrad Heiden, *Der Führer*, H. Pordes, London, 1967, p. 512.
4 *Schwarzes Korps*, 28 April 1938.
5 Interview with Dr Voss, Cologne, April 1967.
6 Wiener Library, Survivors' Eyewitness Accounts, File P III a 4.
7 *ibid.*, File P III a 54.
8 *ibid.*
9 *ibid.*
10 Victor Klemperer, *Lingua Tertii Imperii*, Aufbau, Berlin, 1949, pp. 94 and 183.
11 Wiener Library, File 9 III a.
12 Interview with Herr Lindlar in Düsseldorf, May 1966.
13 Ruth Andreas Friedrich, *Schauplatz Berlin*, Rheinsberg, Munich, 1962, p. 67. Diary entry 7 March 1943.
14 Victor Klemperer, *op. cit.*, p. 103.

ACKNOWLEDGEMENTS

A work of this scale involves the co-operation of individuals too numerous to mention; many of the German personalities – from ex-Nazi functionaries to former illegal trade unionists – involved as interviewees are listed in the index. Others deserving my particular thanks are Tom Wallace, Professor Walter Laqueur, Elizabeth Wiskemann, Terence Prittie, Heinrich Fraenkel, Dr David Schoenbaum, Tim Mason and – last but by no means least – Janet Langmaid. Institutions I am indebted to are the Deutsche Forschungsgemeinschaft (for a research grant), the Institut für Zeitgeschichte, Munich, and – above all – the Institute of Contemporary History and Wiener Library, London.

Richard Grunberger

INDEX

Communists: newspapers of, 393, 399; *Rote Frontkämpferbund* of, 135; votes for (1928, 1932), 16

comradeship houses, at universities, 318-19

concentration camps, 23, 392; corruption among officers of, 104-5; doctors involved in experiments in, 221, 232, 313; Germanization of name of, 311, 329; male Jews sent to, 102; prisoners transferred to, on completion of sentence, 123-4; token releases from, by Hitler, 47; *see also individual camps*

Confederate Youth (*Bündische Jugend*), 139

conscription: industrial, 192, 200; military, re-introduced (1935), 22, 73, 136, 317; of women (1943), 256

consumption, standard of, 203-19

Conti, Dr Leonardo, head of Nazi Doctors' Association, 208 n, 227

contraceptives, 233, 238-9

Co-operative Societies, Nazis and, 90, 100, 168

Corinth, Lovis, painter, 425, 426 n

corporal punishment: for apprentices, 269 n; in schools, 274, 303

corruption: in the army, 141; jokes about, 336; Krupp objects to criticisms of, 175; in Nazi Party, 90-107; in trade guilds, 171

cosmetics, 15, 262

Councils of Confidence, representing workers in factories, 193

Courts, Labour, 68, 194-5, 243

Courts of Honour: for industry, 194; for lawyers, 118; for trade and commerce, 49; for trade guilds, 168

Courts of Social Honour, 158

crafts: apprenticeships to, 269; compulsory examinations for, 168; kept subordinate to interests of industry, 169; in war, 180-1

crime: juvenile, 241, 272-3, 280, 283; phenomenological criteria of, 122-3; under Nazis, 26, 121, 241; during war, 30

Cross of Honour of the German Mother, 78

cruises, organized by Strength-through-Joy agency, 197-8

Crystal Night pogrom (1938), 30, 82, 85, 102, 313; mock trials after, 24; public attitude to, 453, 459, 463; university students in, 308

Cultural Association, Nazi, 374

Culture, Combat Leagues of: German, 421; Nazi, 422, 423

Czechoslovakia, annexation of rump of, 30, 73

Dachau concentration camp, 24 n, 81, 94, 96, 103, 330, 339, 463; industrialists' tour of (1937), 175

Dahn, Felix, novelist, 354, 373, 435

dancing, 283, 410, 419-20

Danes, German attitude to, 32

Darré, Walter, head of Reich Food Estate, 93, 155, 271; and black market, 102; and emancipation of women, 253; jokes about, 336

Darwinism, in Nazi ideology, 298

death: announcements of, 446; *en famille*, 227; on films, 338; Hitler Youth and, 282; as a non-event, 73 n, 446

Death's Head, Order of the, 145

death rates, 224-5

defamation of character, prosecutions for, 37, 83 n, 131

Degenerate Art, exhibitions of, 423, 425-6

democracy: Jews associated with, 15; 'synonymous with corruption' to Nazis, 90; and unity of nation, 44; universities and, 305; in Weimar Republic, 2, 3, 7

Democratic Party, 14, 117, 185

de-Nazification (post-war), of universities, 308 n

denunciation to Nazi authorities, 38, 43, 108-15; in the army, 145; post-war, 54; in schools, 286; threats of, 373

department stores: boycott of, 45, 129, 168, 173; Jews in, 456

depreciation of industrial assets, Nazis and, 179

Deutsch, Ernst, actor, 362

Dibelius, Otto, Lutheran Bishop, 437, 438

Diehl, Karl Ludwig, actor, 144

Dietrich, Marlene, actress, 378, 383

Dimitrov, Georgi, acquittal of, 120

Ding-Schuler, Dr, at Buchenwald, 105 n

diphtheria, death rate from, 228

diplomatic service, under Nazis, 22, 50, 130

Dirlewanger, Oskar, SS Colonel, 104

District Leaders, 56; from teaching profession, 287

dividends: Nazi limit on, 19, 45; shareholders and, 177

Grengg, Maria, novelist, 353
Grimm, Hans, author of *Volk ohne Raume*, 234, 285, 326, 341, 342, 343
Gröber, Conrad, R.C. Bishop of Freiburg, 439, 443, 444
Grohé, Joseph, Gauleiter, on intellectuals, 309
Gröner, Wilhelm, General, Minister of Defence, 16
Gropius, Walter, architect, 421, 422, 433
Grosz, Georg, painter, 12, 422, 425, 433
Gründgens, Gustav, actor, 362, 370
Grundig, Hans, painter, 434
guild ethos, survival of, 45
guilds, *see* trade guilds
Günther, Hans, Prof. and Nazi aesthetic, 422
Gurlitt, Dr Hildebrand, director of Dresden Museum, 422
Gürtner, Franz, Minister of Justice, 126, 244

Haas, Josef, composer, 414
Hadamovsky, Eugen, head of Nazi radio, 409
Haeckel, painter, 421, 425
Handel, G. F., refurbishing of, 328, 409
Haniel, large firm, 176
Hanke, Karl, Gauleiter of Silesia, 60, 61
Harlan, Veit, film producer, 388
Hartmann, K. A., composer, 408
Hartmann, philosopher, academic neutral, 312
Hartung, sculptor, 434
harvest commandos: from factories, 160; from universities, 321
harvest festivals in villages, Nazis and, 156
Harvest Thanksgiving Day, 72, 75
Hasenclever, Walter, playwright, 12, 357, 362
Haupt, Bruno, civic centres envisaged by, 430
Hauptmann, Gerhart, playwright, 23, 24, 69, 362
Haushofer, Albrecht, poet, 357
Hausmann, Manfred, writer, 343, 344
health, 220–32; in industry, 192–3; of young people, 268, 271–2
Health Office, National, dietic laboratory of, 225
Heidegger, Martin, existentialist philosopher, 308, 319
Heidelberg asparagus incident, 46

Heil Hitler! ('German greeting'), 27, 82–3, 108; between lawyers, 118; in civil service, 129; in Wehrmacht, 142
Heine, Heinrich, 43, 311
Heiseler, Bernd von, writer of war stories, 360–1
Heisenberg, Werner, physicist, 312
Heissmeyer, on Adolf Hitler schools, 298
Helldorf, Wolf von, Count, Chief of Police, Berlin, and passports of Jews, 102
Heppel, Dr, in Eastern-Aid scandal, 154 n
Hermann Goering Works, National, 92, 174, 177, 178; 'accelerated rehabilitation' at, 193; new town for, 216
Heroes Remembrance Day, 73, 446
Hertzog, Rudolf, Nazi novelist, 346
Hess, Rudolf, Hitler's deputy, 88, 108–9, 247
Hesse, Prince of, in Nazi Party, 59, 64
high schools, proposed non-fee-paying, 295–6
Hilbert, David, mathematician, 308–9
Hildebrandt, Friedrich, Gauleiter of Mecklenburgh, 60, 61, 155
Hilpert, Heinz, theatrical producer, 370
Hilz, Sepp, Nazi painter, 432
Himmler, Heinrich, head of police forces and SS, 96, 104, 109, 124, 143, 445; Circle of Friends of, link between industry and Nazis, 175; *Lebensborn* foundation of, 246, 248; post-war plans of, 272; 'procreation order' of, 41, 247; proposes selective polygamy, 249; wife of, 62, 64
Hindemith, Paul, composer, 406, 407, 410, 415
Hindenburg, Paul von, Field Marshal, President of Reich, 3, 18, 21, 83, 92
Hinkel, Hans, assistant to Goebbels, 111
historicism, 13, 305
Historische Zeitschrift, 311
history, under Nazis, 305, 311
Hitler, Adolf, 3, 17, 28, 31, 182 n; and aristocracy, 60; and army, 21, 141–2; and art, 411, 423, 424, 426, 428 n, 431; bans *Wilhelm Tell* from school-books, 359, 370; at Bayreuth Festival, 25, 48, 406, 411–12; broadcasts by, 85 n, 88, 326, 401, 405; and Catholic Church, 437, 438; celebration of birthday, 72, 73; and cinema, 378; death of, 42, 406; denunciation of detractors of, 110, 114, 124; and future of Berlin, 218; and Gestapo, 126;

sport and physical fitness—*cont*
  Hitler Youth, 276; in schools, 287–8, 296;
  at universities, 319
Spranger, Prof. Eduard, educationalist, 14,
  306–7, 312
Sprenger, Jakob, Gauleiter of Hesse, 101
Srbik, Heinrich Ritter von, 308
SS (*Schutz Staffel*), 16, 66, 81; aristocracy in,
  60; Catholics in, 451; corruption in, 104–
  6; doctors in, 221; executions by, 38, 40;
  marriage ritual of, 445; Napola schools
  under, 298; procreation order to, 41, 247;
  reserves for, 49; on war service, 69, 145,
  175; and Winter Relief, 80
Stahlhelm (Nationalist Association of Ex-
  Servicemen), 135
'stand-by' syndrome, 75, 77
Stapel, Wilhelm, *völkische* writer, 341 n,
  465 n
Stark, Johannes, Prof., Nazi Nobel prizewinner, 310
state, German attitude to, 22–3
Stauffenberg, Col. Claus Schenk, Count
  von, in Officers' Plot, 39, 111, 142, 143
steel industry, 4, 176, 177–8
steel trust, 176
Steguweit, Heinz, Nazi writer, 343, 344,
  349, 369
Stehr, Hermann, Nazi writer, 326, 341, 342,
  343
Stein, Edith, nun and writer, 357
Steinhoff, Hans, film producer, 142, 389
sterilization: of 'biologically inferior' child
  ren, 274; for hereditary disease, 120, 221,
  222, 225, 238; popular term for, 332
Sternberg, Josef von, film director, 378
Sternheim, Karl, playwright, 362
Storm Troopers, 16; anti-Jewish song of,
  81, 463; aristocracy in, 60; Hitler
  procures acquittal of members of, 17, 23;
  regimental bands of, 20; on war service,
  69
Strasser, Gregor, 60
Strauss, Emil, Nazi novelist, 341, 342, 343,
  352
Strauss, Johann, composer, 402
Strauss, Richard, composer, 69, 406, 413,
  414–15, 416
Stravinsky, Igor, composer, 407, 410, 416
Streicher, Julius, 58, 66, 142; assists in film
  production, 70; at Berlin University, 310;

and *Frankische Tageszeitung*, 398; Gauleiter of Franconia, 47, 96–7, 458; *see also
  Der Stürmer*
Strength-through-Joy organization, 197–8,
  405 n; funds of, 97; mass audiences
  provided by, 411; mobile art exhibitions
  of, 424; sports certificate of, 223; theatre
  outings of, 374–5
strikes, 199
Stuckhardt, Wilhelm, 118
student fraternities, 46, 252, 318, 320–1
Students' Association, Nazi, 306, 317, 319,
  321
Stürmer, Der, Streicher's anti-Semitic weekly,
  58, 280, 398–9, 447; read by Hitler, 96,
  398; in schools, 303
Sturmverlag Koenigsberg, Nazi publishing
  house, 95
Styria, Rhinelanders evacuated to, 33
Sudetenland, annexation of, 30; Catholic
  Church and, 449
sugar, consumption and rationing of, 206
suicides, 30, 223, 224, 225; after death of
  Hitler, 89; of Viennese Jews, 459
Summer Solstice, Day of, 72, 74
superstitions, wartime, 38
Süss, Wilhelm, Vice-Chancellor of Frieburg
  University, 314–15
swastika, 409

taxation: of agriculture, 157, 161; Bayreuth
  Festival exempted from, 411–12; facilitated by compulsory account-keeping, 170;
  of industry, 179; on wages, 188
teachers: denunciations of, 286; as Hitler
  Youth Officials, 290; and Nazis, 20, 22,
  286–7; over-represented in Nazi Party,
  59; ratio of pupils to, 291; shortage of,
  and lowering of qualifications for, 293–5;
  under Weimar Republic, 285; women as,
  251, 260, 261, 294 n
Teachers' Organization, Nazi, 259, 286–7,
  289 n, 292, 303; grammar-school teachers
  in, 293; and religious instruction, 448
technology, at universities, 317, 318, 322
Terboven, Joseph, Gauleiter, marriage of,
  at Essen (1934), 73
terror, Nazi citizens and, 40, 185
Teunissen, Gert, art critic, 428
theatre, 362–75; under Weimar Republic,
  12, 362

532